CAMBRIDGE GREEK AND LATIN CLASSICS

TACITUS

HISTORIES

BOOK II

EDITED BY

RHIANNON ASH

Fellow and Tutor in Classics, Merton College, Oxford

CAMBRIDGE
UNIVERSITY PRESS

CAMBRIDGE UNIVERSITY PRESS
Cambridge, New York, Melbourne, Madrid, Cape Town, Singapore, São Paulo

Cambridge University Press
The Edinburgh Building, Cambridge CB2 8RU, UK

Published in the United States of America by Cambridge University Press, New York

www.cambridge.org
Information on this title: www.cambridge.org/9780521891356

© Cambridge University Press 2007

First published 2007

Printed in the United Kingdom at the University Press, Cambridge

A catalogue record for this publication is available from the British Library

ISBN 978-0-521-81446-1 hardback
ISBN 978-0-521-89135-6 paperback

CONTENTS

PREFACE

At the start of Edgar Allan Poe's short career as a student at the University of Virginia in 1826, he wrote a letter home to his guardian, John Allan, asking him to send soap and a text of Tacitus' *Histories* (Hayes (2000) 8). Times have changed since then. For one thing, most undergraduates today are unlikely to encounter Tacitus in the original Latin in their first term. Yet a deferred pleasure can often be more enjoyable, and it is the aim of this commentary to enrich students' understanding of Tacitus *Histories* 2 at whatever point they encounter the text. The goal throughout has been to elucidate how Tacitus' style and arrangement of material impose meaning on complex historical events. This process is enhanced by the chance survival of three parallel accounts of the civil wars by Plutarch, Suetonius and Cassius Dio, as well as relevant sections in Josephus. Indeed, the sheer wealth of material available means that an already long commentary could have been even more extensive. I can only hope that the guidance for students offered in the body of the commentary manages to steer a safe path between the Scylla (lack of relevance) and Charybdis (lack of clarity) faced by all commentators.

It is a great pleasure to be able to thank a number of people who provided me with generous help and encouragement. Tony Woodman, Chris Kraus and David Levene have been supportive throughout. Cynthia Damon kindly supplied me with a pre-publication draft of her commentary on Tacitus *Histories* 1 in this same series, which offered me invaluable guidance at a time when my own commentary was in its earliest stages. Two colleagues at University College London have been especially kind. Simon Hornblower spontaneously gave me his copy of Gerber and Greef's *Lexicon Taciteum*, which I had previously only been able to consult in libraries, and Matthew Robinson patiently provided specialised computing expertise which made a huge difference. I was also lucky to spend the academic year 2002–3 teaching at Cornell University, where I have fond memories of a life free of administrative duties amongst congenial colleagues and bright students. Over that year, Dave Mankin, a 'Green and Yellow' veteran himself, discussed many specific questions with me, but he was particularly helpful in talking through the infamous textual crux at *Histories* 2.40 and the whole strategy of the first battle of Bedriacum. More general conversations with Fred Ahl about Latin literature also helped to focus my thinking, and Judy Ginsburg gave me access to her specialised collection of books and offered advice on the structure of the commentary. My pleasure in being able to acknowledge publicly my debt to this trio of Cornell Latinists is mixed with great sadness that Judy Ginsburg did not live to see the end result.

Completion of this commentary was only made possible by the Department of Greek and Latin at UCL awarding me a term of sabbatical leave in 2005, which was then extended by a 'matching leave' grant from the Arts and Humanities Research Council. I am indebted both to UCL and the AHRC for this invaluable opportunity. Michael Sharp, the Classics editor at CUP, has been consistently helpful, as has my copy editor Muriel Hall. I am very grateful to them both. It is unusual in the preface of a commentary on a Latin text to offer thanks to a Regius Professor of Greek. Then again, Chris Pelling is no ordinary Hellenist. He patiently read through and commented on a large portion of the commentary, which has been immeasurably improved and sharpened by his suggestions. I owe similar thanks to Philip Hardie, who was typically supportive and generous with his time while I was finding my feet as a commentator. However, my most substantial debt is to E. J. Kenney. It is something of a convention for those working on Latin texts in this series to offer him warm thanks, but I now know at first hand what an extraordinary privilege and pleasure it is to work with someone whose erudition, humour and patience has such a beneficial impact on every word of the commentary.

Finally, I dedicate this book to the memory of my mother Elanwy. Her passion for languages and sound advice twenty-five years ago first persuaded me that studying Greek and Latin would be absorbing and fun. I had no idea then how true this would turn out to be.

ABBREVIATIONS

AE	*L'année épigraphique*
CIL	*Corpus Inscriptionum Latinarum* (1863–). Berlin
EJ	Ehrenberg, V. and Jones, A. H. M. (1955) *Documents illustrating the reigns of Augustus and Tiberius.* Oxford
G-G	Gerber, A. and Greef, A. (1962) eds. *Lexicon Taciteum.* Hildesheim
GL	Gildersleeve, G. L. and Lodge, G. (1895³) *Latin grammar.* London
ILS	Dessau, H. (1892–1916) *Inscriptiones Latinae Selectae.* Berlin
K-S	Kühner, R. and Stegmann, C. (1955) *Ausführliche Grammatik der lateinischen Sprache.* Hanover
L-H-S	Leumann, M., Hofmann, J. B. and Szantyr, A. (1965) *Lateinischer Grammatik: Syntax und Stilistik,* vol II. Munich
LSJ	Liddell, H. G. and Scott, R. (1940) eds. *A Greek–English lexicon.* 9th edn, rev. H. S. Jones. Oxford
mod.	modern
MW	Martin, R. H. and Woodman, A. J. (1989) *Tacitus Annals Book IV.* Cambridge
M-W	McCrum, M. and Woodhead, A. G. (1961) *Select documents of the principates of the Flavian emperors.* Cambridge
NLS	Woodcock E. C. (1959) *A new Latin syntax.* London
*OCD*³	Hornblower, S. and Spawforth, A. (2003) eds. *Oxford classical dictionary.* Oxford
OGIS	Dittenberger, S. (1903–5) *Orientis Graecae Inscriptiones Selectae.* Leipzig
OLD	Glare P. W. (1968–82) ed. *Oxford Latin dictionary.* Oxford
RE	Pauly, A. and Wissowa, G. et al., (1894–1979) *Paulys Real-Encylopädie der classischen Altertumswissenschaft.* Stuttgart
RIC	Mattingly, H., and Sydenham, E. (1923, 1926) *The Roman imperial coinage,* vol I *and* II. London
SHA	*Scriptores Historiae Augustae*
TLL	*Thesaurus linguae latinae* (1900–). Munich
WM	Woodman, A. J. and Martin, R. H. (1996) eds. *The Annals of Tacitus Book 3.* Cambridge

The names and titles of classical authors and texts are generally abbreviated in accordance with *OLD* and LSJ, with the following exceptions for Tacitus (T.) and his works: *Annals* (*A.*), *Agricola* (*Agr.*), *Germania* (*G.*) and *Dialogus* (*D.*). Journal titles are abbreviated in accordance with *L'année philologique.*

Map 1. The Roman Empire

Map 1. (*cont.*)

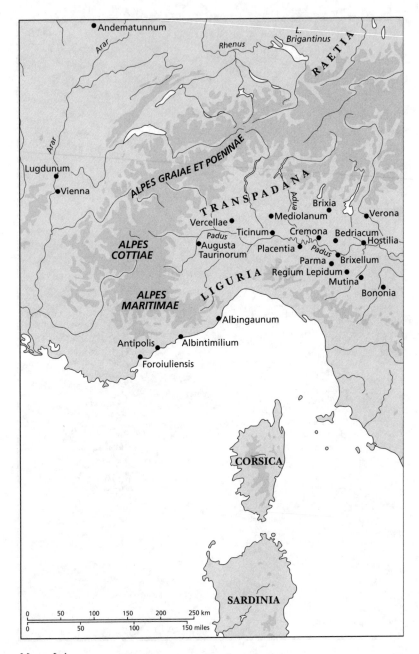

Map 2. Italy

ALPES IULIAE
or ALPES PANNONICAE

Aquileia

Patavium

HISTRIA

Ravenna

Ariminum

D A L M A T I A

Tiberis

VIA FLAMINIA

Interamna

Ferentium

Pons Mulvius

Roma
Campus Martius
Capitol
Lacus Curtius

Arpinum

Ostia

Aquinum

Capua

Brundisium

CALABRIA

LUCANIA

Tarentum

Map 2. (cont.)

INTRODUCTION

1. TACITUS

In general, Roman historians give away personal details in their narratives less often than their Greek counterparts do.[1] Yet we still know a certain amount about T., especially in comparison with other authors, such as his elusive contemporary Juvenal, even if much evidence still has to be teased out of T.'s own works.[2]

Born in 56 or 57 when Nero was emperor, T. was perhaps the son of Cornelius Tacitus, the equestrian procurator of Gallia Belgica, mentioned by Pliny the Elder as the father of a mentally impaired and short-lived dwarf child (*Nat.* 7.76).[3] The family itself came either from Transpadane Italy or (more likely) Gallia Narbonensis;[4] but by 75, T. was in Rome, learning rhetoric and listening to court cases conducted by the leading barristers of his day (*D.* 2.1), with a view to embarking on a senatorial career.[5] He attests to a certain *iuuenilis ardor* (*D.* 2.1) for these activities, and in due course Vespasian granted him the *latus clauus*, the broad purple stripe on his tunic which designated the right to stand for senatorial office (*H.* 1.1.3). That would have been followed by a minor magistracy, serving as one of the *uigintiuiri* (*OCD*[3]), and by a military appointment as a *tribunus laticlauius* (*OCD*[3] *tribuni militum*). He had made a good start to his career. In 77, he married the daughter of Agricola (*Agr.* 9.6), a *uir militaris* who came from Forum Iulii in Gallia Narbonensis and was suffect consul at the time. Agricola's prominent position suggests that he must have sensed T.'s promise. We assume that T. reached the quaestorship in *c.* 81, which allowed him membership of the senate, but we know for sure that in 88, he was praetor and a priest, one of the *quindecimuiri sacris faciundis* responsible for organising Domitian's secular games (*A.*11.11.1). Those who had held the praetorship usually then went abroad on military service and T. was indeed out of the country when Agricola died in 93 (*Agr.* 45.5). He must have returned soon afterwards to witness the tense atmosphere in Rome which culminated in the assassination of Domitian in 96.[6] His selection as suffect consul in the second half of 97 meant that he was close to the centre of power during Nerva's short principate. This was when he delivered the funeral oration in honour of Verginius Rufus (Plin. *Ep.* 2.1.6), who appears in the *H.* as a protagonist. The acme

---

[1] Marincola (1997) 264.

[2] Syme (1958a) 59–74, Martin (1981) 26–35 and Birley (2000) discuss T.'s biography in detail. See too Alföldy (1995) on *CIL* VI 1574.

[3] T.'s approximate date of birth is calculated from what we know of his subsequent appointments on the *cursus honorum* and from what he says about himself in the *Dialogus*.

[4] Syme (1958a) 618–24; 806–7 for T.'s knowledge of Gallia Narbonensis.

[5] The dramatic date of the *Dialogus* is 75 (Syme (1958a) 670–1, Mayer (2001) 16), when T. was *iuuenis admodum* (*D.* 1.2). He may have been taught by Quintilian (Ogilvie and Richmond (1967) 8).

[6] Juvenal, talking about Domitian's principate, refers to *tempora saeuitiae, claras quibus abstulit Vrbi* | *illustresque animas impune et uindice nullo* (4.151–2). In practice, the years 93–6 appear to have been the most tense and dangerous for the aristocracy.

1

2 INTRODUCTION

of T.'s undoubtedly successful career was being awarded the proconsulship of Asia in 112/13.[7] He died at some point after 115/16.[8]

During his life, T. wrote five works. In chronological order, these are the *Agricola* (a spirited biography of his father-in-law) and the *Germania* (an ethnographical study of the German tribes), both published in 98, the *Dialogus* (a dialogue about the state of contemporary oratory, published at some point early in the second century AD, possibly 102, but set in 75), and then the historical works, the *Histories* (published in *c.* 109) covering the Flavian dynasty over the years 69–96, and finally the *Annals* (published after 115/16), covering the Julio-Claudian dynasty (though interestingly omitting Augustus) over the years 14–68.[9]

These skeletal details of a literary career can be fleshed out. One extraordinary aspect of T.'s publications is the late stage at which they first appeared: in 98, T. was *c.* 42 years old and as far as we know had not published anything previously, but the appearance in quick succession of the *Agricola* and the *Germania* shows that he must have been preparing these works before that. Yet his decision to publish them only in 98 was a brilliant way to endorse a central ideological aspect of the *Agricola*, namely the extent to which the tyranny of Domitian had stifled literary creativity in the years leading up to his death. That decision, a brilliant coup, has had a fundamental impact on modern assessments of Domitian's principate and of the calibre of literature produced before his assassination in 96.[10]

The other striking aspect of T.'s literary career is its well-judged and deliberately plotted trajectory. Writers and readers in the ancient world acknowledged that there was a hierarchy of genres, moving from lighter areas such as epigram, love poetry and biography, to the heavy-weights, epic, tragedy and historiography. If an author tried to embark too early on the most serious genres, then he risked compromising his credibility. Pliny the Younger, for instance, pokes gentle fun at himself for having written a tragedy at the tender age of fourteen (*Ep.* 7.4.2). In contrast, T. methodically earns his spurs in 'lesser' genres before trying his hand at historiography. In tracing this generic arc, he resembles predecessors such as Virgil (pastoral, didactic poetry,

[7] An inscription (*OGIS* 487) gives us the post; Syme (1958a) 664–5 the date.

[8] This date is calculated from T.'s reference to Roman control over the Red Sea (*A.* 2.61.2 with Goodyear (1981) 387–93), which was achieved during Trajan's Parthian campaign of 115/16. Bowersock (1993) suggests caution in positing a date for the *A.*'s composition (itself relevant to determining when he died).

[9] For the composition dates see Ogilvie and Richmond (1967) 10–1 (*Agr.*), Rives (1999) 47 (*G.*), Mayer (2001) 22–7 (*D.*), Damon (2003) 4–5 (*H.*), and WM 12 (*A.*). Pliny's letters supplying evidence for the *H.* (6.16, 6.20, 7.33) show T. at work in *c.*106–7. Publication may have been in instalments, with public readings of books preceding the final appearance of the completed work (Syme (1958a) 119–20).

[10] It is ironic that damage done to Domitian's posthumous reputation, shaped by the *Agr.*, has been compounded by the loss of the relevant books of the *H.* (as our surviving evidence for his principate from other authors is scarce). Martial, Silius Italicus and Statius are the main Domitianic authors, each of whom has laboured under accusations of being 'puppets' of a tyrannical *princeps*, although recently their writings have been assessed more positively. Ahl (1984) and Newlands (2002) are important.

epic) and Ovid (elegiac poetry, verse epistles, didactic poetry, a calendrical poem and epic, before reverting to more serious elegiacs after his exile). We can see how the pair 'ascended' through the hierarchy of genres as they became more established.[11] Historiography, a competitive genre whose practitioners often made polemical sallies against their predecessors, was not something to be attempted by the novice.[12] T. sensibly reserved it for a point in his career when his reputation already had strong foundations laid down by the so-called 'minor works'.

2. ANCIENT HISTORIOGRAPHY

When T. turned to writing history, he faced all the advantages and disadvantages of operating in a well-established genre, shaped by the Greeks and refined by his Roman predecessors. Even so, although the foundation of Rome was traditionally dated to 753 BC, it was not until the third century BC that the Romans began to produce written narratives of their own history: Fabius Pictor was the first Roman historian, but significantly he wrote in Greek, primarily to introduce Rome (growing rapidly in influence) to the Greek-speaking peoples of the eastern Mediterranean.[13] It was not until Cato the Censor (234–149 BC) composed his *Origines* (now fragmentary) that an account of Roman history in Latin was available, but even this text, influential though it was, provides uneven historical coverage, devoting much more attention to the foundation of the city and to the recent Punic wars than to the intervening period of the early republic.

Yet Roman historiography involves much more than telling a comprehensive story. Whether in the form of a monograph or an extensive annalistic account, its corner-stones were utility and pleasure, the latter ideally provided in pursuit of the former. Indeed, historians were very reluctant to provide items just to entertain.[14] In the second century AD, Lucian likens accomplished historiography to an athlete with good looks, in whom what is pleasurable enhances the basic utility of athletic prowess (*How to write history* 9), but a handsome athlete is pointless if he cannot throw a javelin. In a historical narrative, enjoyment could be furnished in two main ways. First, the quality of the Latin used to relay events could captivate readers. Cicero recommends a style for history that is 'copious and extended, flowing out in a measured way and devoid of that roughness of the law-courts and the stinging aphorisms belonging to forensic oratory' (*De orat.* 2.64).[15] Pliny the Younger too distinguishes between the appropriate styles for orators and historians (*Ep.* 5.8.9–10). In practice, there were differing types of

---

[11] See further Conte (1994) and Barchiesi (2001) on genre.
[12] Pliny the Elder also embarked on historiography only when his literary career was established. His nephew's chronological survey of his works shows that his history of the German wars in twenty books comes only after a technical manual on the art of throwing a javelin from horseback and a biography of Pomponius Secundus (Pliny the Younger *Ep.* 3.5).
[13] Marincola (1997) 26–7.
[14] 50.2n. *fictis oblectare legentium animos*; Dion. Hal. 7.70.1, Liv. 9.17.1–2.
[15] See Woodman (1988) 94–5 on this passage, Kraus (1994) 17 n.72 on the relationship of Cicero's recommendations to Livy's style.

historiographical language, as the contrasting styles of Livy and Sallust demonstrate, and of course any good historian will vary his style depending on the nature of the subject matter at any given point.[16] In particular, speeches often manifest a different style from the rest of the narrative and are attractive in their own right. Yet whatever choices were made by an individual author, the language of a work was a fundamental way to enhance an audience's enjoyment of historiography.

The other way to captivate was in the selection and presentation of the subject matter, particularly if the narrative included set pieces like exotic geographical and ethnographical material or tense battle-scenes. T. himself observes how the *situs gentium, uarietates proeliorum, clari ducum exitus* (*A.* 4.33.3) keep readers interested and eager for more. Historians were expected to indulge in a certain amount of creative but plausible embellishment of particular scenes for the entertainment of their audience.[17] Yet that is not the same as making up something from scratch: historians often express frustration at inadequate evidence in establishing a true record, as when Livy grumbles about the difficulties of reconstructing historical events before the Gallic sack in 390 BC (6.1.2), and protestations of truthfulness from historians were so common that they could be parodied (*haec ita uera*, Sen. *Apoc.* 1.1). At the same time, historians were addressing a cultivated and widely read audience, and they could build on that sophistication to borrow techniques and motifs from other genres, such as epic and tragedy. So, Quintilian famously comments that historiography is *proxima poetis* (10.1.31): its elevated diction and predominantly martial focus naturally result in (and stem from) an especially close relationship with hexameter epic.[18]

As Romans read historical accounts of their ancestors overcoming adversities or defeating foreign enemies, the experience could instil intense feelings of national pride, and even a healthy spirit of competition with their dead forebears' achievements.[19] The landscape of the past was very much alive in Roman eyes, and written history, just as much as physical monuments, funeral speeches and wax portrait-masks, was a way to preserve and shape the collective memory. This brings us to the utility of history. Sallust puts it simply, saying that of all possible intellectual pursuits, *in primis magno usui est memoria rerum gestarum* (*Jug.* 4.1).[20] Building on the legacy of Cato the Censor, Roman historians wrote their narratives of the past to bring about practical

---

[16] In stylistic terms, Servilius Nonianus called Sallust and Livy *pares . . . magis quam similes* (Quint. 10.1.102). Livy was thought to evoke the style of Herodotus and Sallust Thucydides (Vell. 2.36.2, Quint. 10.1.101). For a comprehensive discussion of Livy's language, see Oakley (1997) 111–51, and for an analysis of one sample passage, see Kraus and Woodman (1997) 62–70. Sallust's style is known for its *breuitas et abruptum sermonis genus* (Quint. 4.2.45) and its *amputatae sententiae et uerba ante exspectatum cadentia et obscura breuitas* (Sen. *Ep.* 114.17). For Statius he is just *Sallustius breuis* (*Silu.* 4.7.55).

[17] Woodman (1988) 87–9, Marincola (1997) 161–2.

[18] See further Ash (2002) on the cross-fertilisation between epic and historiography regarding battle narratives.

[19] See Sall. *Jug.* 4.5–6.

[20] Lucian, *How to write history* 53, advises historians to emphasise the usefulness of their work in the preface. Polybius 1.1.1 says that almost all his predecessors do this.

improvements in their own contemporary world. For one thing, history could provide cogent *exempla*, models of behaviour to be emulated or avoided, and the concept of 'exemplarity' is a pervasive element in many historical accounts. So, Livy plays up this valuable function of history in his preface: 'This especially is what renders the study of history beneficial and fruitful, that you look upon the teachings of every kind of example, set forth in an illustrious "monument"' (*Ab vrbe condita*, preface 10). Ancient historiography, conceptualised by Livy architecturally as a physical monument, allows readers to see for themselves the useful lessons of the past, and thus improves the general 'health' of the state.[21] Hand in hand with this aspect of ancient historiography goes a broad moralising agenda, delivered in part by the incorporation of *sententiae*, pithy epigrams which the audience could detach from the narrative and apply to their own lives.[22] Such touches lend *grauitas* to a historical narrative, allowing it to rise above the chronological constraints of the immediate subject matter.

Ancient historiography had different aims and characteristics from its modern counterpart, but its practitioners all knew the importance of striking the right balance between what was *utile* and *dulce*. In the *Histories*, T. sets himself a particularly hard task in this respect by writing about relatively recent events, including a harrowing set of civil wars. Yet he had learned much from his predecessors in the genre and in addition, he refined some brilliant techniques of his own to render his narrative enjoyable, despite its grim subject matter. His own oxymoron, *misera laetitia* (2.45.3), describing victors and vanquished contemplating civil war after the battle of Bedriacum, could apply equally well to the experience of reading his historical narrative.

3. *QVO QVO SCELESTI RVITIS?* CIVIL WAR AND ROMAN IDENTITY

Civil war lies at the very heart of Roman culture and identity. Indeed, the very myth of foundation, the story of the fratricidal twins Romulus and Remus, gives a central place to fatal internecine conflict. Romulus was the *conditor urbis* (*A.* 4.9.2), but in an increasingly popular version of the myth, the city was founded at the cost of his brother Remus' life.[23] This is a curiously grubby story on which to build Roman identity, but its pessimistic notes eloquently reflect the traumatic events of the late

---

[21] T. famously says: *praecipuum munus annalium reor, ne uirtutes sileantur utque prauis dictis factisque ex posteritate et infamia metus sit* (*A.* 3.65.1 with WM 451–6, Woodman (1998) 86–103). Chaplin (2000) discusses exemplarity in Livy. Cicero, *Arch.* 14 acknowledges the importance of literature for illuminating *exempla*.

[22] Sinclair (1995).

[23] The original version of the myth apparently had the brothers founding the city together, but was modified to include the fratricidal aspect relatively early, perhaps as a result of 'the desperate crisis that ended with the battle of Sentinum in 295 BC' (Wiseman (2004) 140), before which Roman dominance in central Italy was threatened by a coalition of Gauls, Samnites and Etruscans. Yet by the time Livy was writing, 'after more than fifteen years of constant civil war, the story most Romans accepted was that Romulus killed his twin brother with his own hand' (Wiseman (2004) 142).

republic: as so often, myth and history interconnect. In the 30s BC the poet Horace, gloomily anticipating the onset of yet another civil war (probably between Octavian and Antony), sees the latest round of self-destruction as directly resulting from the 'curse' of the innocent Remus' murder (*acerba fata Romanos agunt | scelusque fraternae necis, Epod.* 7.17–18).[24] After the relentless succession of civil wars over the first century BC (Marius vs Sulla, Caesar vs Pompey, Octavian vs Antony), it is easy to see why the more pessimistic version of the Romulus and Remus myth gained ascendancy. The notion that Romulus' descendants were being belatedly punished was one way, however unsatisfactory, to try and make sense of the almost uninterrupted chain of civil wars which ultimately saw the republican system of government make way for the principate.[25] As one critic observes, 'where Romulus and Remus were involved, fratricide expressed not just battlefield trauma but a more pervasive sense of loss, a loss of social cohesion and civic identity rooted in shared moral assumptions'.[26]

Even if some Romans were ambivalent about the merits of the new imperial system, the spectre of further civil wars made them willing to tolerate their new *princeps*. As the pseudo-Senecan Nero says of Augustus' creation of the principate, *continuit imperium metus* (*Oct.* 526). This reflects not just the *princeps'* methods of control, but also collective fears about a reversion to civil war. Augustus at *Res gestae* 34 boasts of 'exstinguishing' the civil wars, after which he was given absolute control *per consensum uniuersorum*.[27] As a piece of self-promotion and a timely reinforcement for the institution of the principate at a vulnerable moment (the transfer of power to Tiberius), this observation is well judged: long after the Augustan settlement, Romans were still alive to the possibility of a deadly regression into civil war. So T. attributes the outbreak of the Pannonian mutiny in 14 to *nullis nouis causis, nisi quod mutatus princeps licentiam turbarum et ex ciuili bello spem praemiorum ostendebat* (*A.* 1.16.1). Even emperors themselves were not immune to such fears, as when the sly Sejanus claims to Tiberius that the state is riven *ut ciuili bello* (*A.* 4.17.3) by supporters of Agrippina the Elder. This is a powerful motif for the minister to conjure up, in a bid to get the emperor to eliminate members of his own family. The idea that civil war was somehow being replayed under the principate is

---

[24] Mankin (1995) 151, contemplating when Romans began to interpret their foundation myth as a paradigm of civil strife, detects initial traces in Sall. *Hist.* 1.55.5, Cic. *Off.* 3.41 and perhaps Lucr. 3.70–3 and Catul. 29.9, 58.5, 64.397–9, then Virg. *G.* 2.533, *A.* 1.292–3, after which 'it is almost a commonplace in later writers'.

[25] The real explanation for the sequence of civil wars lies in the evolution of Rome from a city state with a citizen army to an extensive realm on an imperial scale controlled by a professional army susceptible to the cult of personality when led by men such as Marius and Caesar. Traces of the Horatian viewpoint can arguably be seen in T.'s assertion that the civil wars of 68–9 prove that *non esse curae deis securitatem nostram, esse ultionem* (1.3.2). Innocent descendants being punished for an ancestral crime is a fundamental motif in tragedy.

[26] Bannon (1997) 159, but see too her whole discussion of the myth (158–73).

[27] When Lepidus formed a plot to assassinate Augustus, Maecenas allegedly *noui et resurrecturi belli ciuilis restinxit initium* (Vell. 2.89.3). It was easy and natural for Roman authors to analyse an event in counterfactual terms as a narrowly averted civil war. Another metaphor for ending the civil wars involves 'burial' (Vell. 2.90.1, *sepultis . . . bellis ciuilibus*; also the *Senatus consultum de Pisone patre* 47, [Sen.] *Oct.* 523, Luc. 8.529–30).

also articulated in some scurrilous verses written about Tiberius, popularly casting him as a latterday Sulla, Marius and Antony (Suet. *Tib.* 59.2).[28] For Romans, these men were still expressive historical models, even though by Tiberius' principate the people who had directly suffered under them were almost all dead. Yet they had left their mark on the generations that followed.

One especially subtle response to the legacy of civil conflict can be seen in Virgil's *Aeneid.* Some critics see the whole second half of the poem (the war between Aeneas and Turnus) as an encoded replay of the republican civil wars. Certainly Juno's angry reference to Aeneas and his future father-in-law Latinus (*hac gener atque socer coeant mercede suorum, A.* 7.317; cf. *A.* 12.192–3) recalls the earlier bloody depiction of Caesar and Pompey as *socer* and *gener* (*A.* 6.830–1).[29] We can see how the 'veiled' device of an epic narrative allows the poet to confront recent history in a subtle and less overtly painful way than a direct treatment would have done. The educated Roman élite, its numbers depleted by the brutal proscriptions, was not quite ready for that. It was only under Nero that such a poem would be written, in the form of Lucan's *Bellum Ciuile.* This unfinished epic poem about the civil war between Caesar and Pompey written during Nero's principate is curiously prescient, although its author Lucan was forced to kill himself in 65. When civil war finally broke out after Nero's suicide in 68, it was the realisation of deeply embedded fears that had been alive for the last century, ever since Augustus defeated Antony at Actium in 31 BC.

In literary terms, there were many possible responses to civil war (not all mutually exclusive): denial,[30] dissimulation,[31] assimilating the conflict to previous civil wars or even to mythical models,[32] and writing works that moralise or commemorate the events, so as either to justify conduct retroactively or else to prevent any recurrence of such wars.[33] In essence, T. wrote the *Histories* as a moralising record of an intensely self-destructive and shameful period of history. Yet in shaping his narrative, his techniques embrace some of the broad responses just identified. For instance, we can see dissimulation in T.'s characterisation of the participants: he identifies the Othonians (12.2n. *tamquam externa . . . hostium*) and especially the Vitellians (83.2n. *atque . . . protegeret,* 87.2n. *ut hostile solum,* 89.1n. *ut captam urbem,* 90.1n. *tamquam . . . populumque*) with foreign invaders, making it easier for readers to rationalise the civil war by perceiving the morally flawed protagonists as outsiders. In defining their dubious conduct against an idealised model of Roman identity, T. (however counterintuitively) positively bolsters his readers' sense of what it means to be Roman. In addition, T. musters previous

[28] Cf. Pompey's slogan, *Sulla potuit: ego non potero?* (Cic. *Att.* 9.10.2).
[29] Caesar and Pompey are labelled *socer* and *gener* also at Catul. 29.24, Luc. 1.290, Mart. 9.70.3.
[30] Vespasian's associate Licinius Mucianus wrote a work on *mirabilia* (now fragmentary), which falls into this category.
[31] E.g. Virgil's *Aeneid.*
[32] E.g. Varius Rufus' *Thyestes,* performed in 29 BC for the games celebrating Actium, Seneca's *Thyestes* and Statius' *Thebaid.*
[33] Caesar's *Bellum ciuile* is an instance of commemorative propaganda; Horace's *Epodes* 7 and 16 are 'deterrents'.

civil wars as a yardstick, either analysed by internal protagonists in the text (1.50.2–4,
3.66.3) or by T. himself (2.38, 3.51.2, 3.83.3), as a way to indicate continuity or decline
in collective conduct. Roman orators were trained to use historical *exempla* to make
their arguments more pointed: T., an accomplished rhetorician himself, had a rich
fund of relevant comparative material available to him from previous civil wars and
he uses it to add a broad chronological and moral perspective to the specific events
of this particular civil war.[34] Even when T. does not explicitly compare an incident
with previous civil wars, his readers would probably have done so spontaneously, as
when the Flavians sent envoys to the Parthians, just as Pompey had done in the civil
war against Caesar (82.3n. *missi . . . legati*). The *Histories* is a text which can be located
within a broader tradition of literary responses to civil war; and despite the traumatic
subject matter, T. could count on a receptive audience, simultaneously horrified and
fascinated by his narrative, particularly after the recent 'near miss' of another narrowly
averted civil war during the principate of Nerva.[35]

4. HISTORIES 2

There was clearly huge potential for T.'s narrative in *Histories* 2 to run aground,
overwhelming readers with its geographically diverse spheres of activity, politically
complex events and constantly evolving cast of characters. The challenge of producing a clear and coherent account of the civil war was made harder by chronological
difficulties. Annalistic history conventionally dated events to a particular year by giving
the names of consuls, and relating events in an organised way within that framework,
but the scale of the narrative in the *Histories* is so detailed that this hardly helps:
T. does use consular dates for 1 Jan. 69 (1.1.1) and 1 Jan. 70 (4.38.1), but a great deal
happens between those two points in the narrative, so that a much finer chronological calibration is needed.[36] Even that is not always possible, since T.'s sources (and
T. himself) often had to date events relative to one another, without pinning them
down to a particular point.[37]

Yet what at first appears to be a considerable difficulty also has historiographical advantages. The 'unanchored' chronological status of many episodes left

[34] This is a common device, as when Lucan depicts an elderly survivor of the civil war
between Marius and Sulla recollecting earlier horrors to compare with the current conflict
between Caesar and Pompey (2.67–233). This poetic construct may reflect the historical reality
of citizens prompted to reminisce about Marius and Sulla by Caesar's crossing of the Rubicon
(App. *BC* 2.35, 2.41, Dio 41.5.8, 16).
[35] The elderly Nerva had no children and a praetorian mutiny in the summer of 97 signalled
a deepening crisis. In October 97 he adopted Trajan, the governor of upper Germany, and
trouble was averted (Grainger (2003) 96–100).
[36] In the *Histories*, the events of a single day, such as the final clash between Galba and Otho
on 15 Jan. 69 (1.27–47), can be narrated on a more extensive scale than whole years in the *Annals*
(e.g. 15.23–32, the year 63).
[37] For broad chronological markers see 8.1n. *Sub idem tempus*; 23.3n. *Isdem diebus*; 58.1n. *Isdem
diebus*; 85.2n. *In eo motu*; and 87.2n. *maturis iam frugibus*. There are only three precise dates in
Histories 2 (79n. *kalendis Iuliis*).

T. considerable freedom to incorporate them (within reason) at whatever point in his own narrative he saw fit. This gave him full scope for exploiting suggestive juxtaposition. A good example is his inclusion of the story about the emergence of a false Nero (2.8–9) immediately after his account of the incipient Flavian plans for an imperial challenge (2.1–7). That juxtaposition reminds us that these are uncertain times indeed and that Vespasian's bid for power is just one distinctive element in the wider chaos, rather than being predestined to succeed. That pattern is repeated in the appearance of an episode about a Boian pretender, Mariccus (2.61), in the extended narrative of the aftermath of Vitellius' victory and progress to Rome (2.52–73), raising the question of how different from one another these men really are.

The structure of *Histories* 2 is unconventional in traditional annalistic terms (obviously there can be no neat alternation between domestic and foreign events), but it is still carefully organised. The book opens (appropriately enough) with a section on the dawning of the Flavian challenge in the east (2.1–7). This carefully plants the seeds for the extensive narrative of its germination later in the book (2.74–86), pulling against the prevailing emphasis of pro-Flavian propaganda which cast the challenge as a spontaneous movement by the soldiers. In aesthetic terms, it also forms an obvious contrast with the darker notes at the end of the book, which focuses on Vitellius' arrival in Rome and his first dubious moves as *princeps* (2.87–101). Then there are two 'interludes', both apparently unrelated to the main narrative, but in fact casting suggestive light on those events (and *vice versa*). First, the story of the false Nero who unsettled Achaea and Asia (2.8–9), which leads (via an ingenious transitional device of a severed head carried back to Rome) to a vignette of warped activity in the senate (2.10), hopelessly trying to steer a faltering course back to normal life in a sea of military incursions, but failing utterly. The futility of senatorial activity in a turbulent military climate where pretenders are being thrown up left, right and centre is made brutally clear.

The next portion of the book (2.11–45) is overwhelmingly military in its emphasis. There follows a résumé of Otho's military forces (2.11), which has several characteristics suggestive of the opening of a book: such catalogues usually come early in a work (commentary, 11 intro.). Yet despite the upbeat tone, the resumed coverage of the Othonian campaign (left in suspended animation at the end of *Histories* 1) is pessimistically overshadowed by the emerging Flavian challenge (2.1–7). This adds a feeling of futility to the whole campaign (T.'s readers, knowing that Otho will lose the civil war, would be receptive to hints of tragic patterning). Then T. narrates (uniquely) Otho's diversionary campaign in Gallia Narbonensis (2.12–15), designed to allow time for him to set up a defensive line along the Po. Although the Othonians emerge as morally flawed, in strategic terms the mission is a success, setting up a pattern familiar from epic, where an initial victory of one side often serves as a prelude to disaster. Next, for entertainment and *uariatio*, and also to add moral fibre, T. punctuates his main narrative with turbulent events on the island of Corsica, which culminate in the murder of its procurator (2.16). The segment is connected by a loose chronological strand to the central account of the civil war, but again allows readers time for reflection: normal activities in the provinces are being dangerously disrupted by the impetus of civil war, and the Corsican affair demonstrates this eloquently.

T.'s account of military affairs before the final battle (2.17–30.1) may at first feel chaotic, but there is a meaningful structure to it. An Othonian mutiny at the start (2.17–20.1) is neatly mirrored by a Vitellian mutiny at the end of the section (2.27.1–30.1), showing the common problem in civil war of maintaining discipline amongst troops, a phenomenon which transcends individual sides.[38] Then T. further develops the dramatic device of Othonian successes being a prelude to a final defeat, as the Vitellian general Alienus Caecina faces a series of disasters: we see first, his failed assault on the northern Italian town of Placentia (2.20.2–23.2), second, a successful Othonian attack on some Vitellian auxiliaries near Cremona (2.23.3–5) and third, a failed Vitellian ambush at Castores (2.24–27.1). Caecina is desperate to retrieve some glory amidst his continuing military misfortunes, but to no avail.

After this sequence, T. deploys the useful device of *syncrisis*, a comparison of the two Vitellian generals, which in turn is followed by one of Otho and Vitellius (2.30.2–31.1). These comparisons could have been placed at any point, but the advantage of having them here is that they establish a pause in the narrative before the final battle, allowing readers time to reflect, and in the case of the imperial *syncrisis*, reminding us of the flawed figureheads for whom all of this fighting is happening. Neither Otho nor Vitellius will be present at the battle being fought in their names, which curiously marginalises them. This forms a contrast with the imperial biographies of Plutarch and especially Suetonius, where the emperors take centre stage in the narrative spotlight.

T. is now ready to move to the sequence of events leading to the telling final battle. An Othonian council scene (2.31.2–33) reveals serious divisions between the different generals in formulating an appropriate strategy: a long speech from the experienced general Suetonius Paulinus advocating delay is swiftly superseded by Otho's brother Salvius Titianus and the urban prefect Licinius Proculus proposing immediate action (T. significantly gives them no speech). Moreover, the decision is taken that Otho should not be present at the battle itself, a move that will prove disastrous for the morale of his soldiers. As if to underline the point, T. narrates a battle on the river Po where the Othonians are beaten, (2.34–36), reversing their prevailing military dominance of the clashes narrated so far and signalling a significant shift in their fortunes.

We have seen how effectively T. uses digressions such as the false Nero (2.8–9) to create dramatic pauses in his main narrative. He now masterfully freezes the action by the distinctive device of two authorial interventions, first challenging a report in his sources (2.37) and then analysing passion for power through the ages in a digression recalling his predecessor, the republican historian Sallust (2.38). This immediately heightens tension for readers by delaying the miserable finale of Otho's principate,

---

[38] The sandwiching effect of the two mutinies is created by T.'s deliberately narrating the second mutiny out of sequence (*neque enim rerum a Caecina gestarum ordinem interrumpi oportuerat*, 2.27.2).

but it also enhances T.'s own *auctoritas* as a historian (2.37) and satisfies the moralising agenda of ancient historiography (2.38).[39] T. has prepared the ground well for the two magnificent 'central panels' of the whole book, the first battle of Bedriacum (2.39–45) and Otho's moving suicide (2.46–51). Each in different ways engages with a reader's emotions. Everything so far has been building up to this battle as a decisive and climactic moment (and the description of a battle in ancient historiography was one of the main set pieces of the genre, so readers were primed to expect certain elements). Yet T. surprises us. His account of the battle is entirely unconventional: there is no enumeration of the armies' fighting-order and no pre-battle harangues, while the terrain proves bizarrely inappropriate for Roman fighting techniques, and the focus moves kaleidoscopically between different groups of soldiers. All of this makes the battle-narrative strangely messy and anti-climactic after the prolonged build-up. Even the expectation of decisive finality is undercut. It becomes clear after the defeat that the Othonians still have the military capability to continue their campaign and extend the civil war. Yet Otho himself puts an end to the struggle by his suicide, another sequence in which T. wrong-foots us. After all, the calibre of Otho's morally flawed life leaves us entirely unprepared for the nobility of his end, and T. pulls out all the emotional stops in narrating it, investing his subject with stoic traits and aligning him with such historical heavyweights as Cato the Younger (2.46–51 introduction).

It is a provocative arrangement (and expressive of the relentless momentum of civil war) that the suicide comes in the middle rather than at the end of a book. Otho's obituary (2.50) and funeral (2.51) are panels traditionally associated with closure, but what seems like an end-point is in fact only a step along the way and the prelude to the next *princeps*, Vitellius. Political and military beginnings and endings in the *Histories* are often messy, and T. makes full use of the structure of his books to reflect this.[40]

The second half of *Histories* 2 is arguably less complex than the first half of the book, since there are no direct military clashes between the victorious Vitellians and the new challengers, the Flavians. This allows a simpler alternating presentation of events unfolding in Italy and the east. Yet T. still brilliantly exploits the possibilities for tension and drama in presenting his material. First, the fickleness of the people and the powerlessness of the senate are ruthlessly articulated in a panel exploring reactions to news of Vitellius' victory (2.52–56). Meanwhile, Vitellius himself does not even know that he has won (2.57.1), crisply revealing his irrelevance to the movement which brought him to power. The carefree people in Rome (2.55.1), not directly affected by the violent military clashes that have been unfolding in northern Italy, look increasingly vulnerable as the marauding Vitellian soldiers move southwards towards the capital in a march where violence and the pursuit of pleasure escalate (2.57–73). T. pointedly decelerates the journey, splitting the narrative into two sections (2.57–73, 87–89), and interrupting it with disquieting digressions of murder in Mauretania (2.58–59.1), a

---

[39] Lucan uses a similarly powerful device when he suspends the momentum of his narrative before the battle at Pharsalus with an authorial intervention (7.387–459).

[40] Cf. 4.1.1 *Interfecto Vitellio bellum magis desierat quam pax coeperat.*

Gallic pretender (2.61), the execution of Dolabella (2.63–64) and a runaway slave who pretends to be a Roman noble (2.72). All of these episodes express the damage done to Roman identity and conventional power structures by the civil war. T. further builds up tension by deferring Vitellius' arrival in the city (2.89) until after the section on Vespasian's proclamation (2.74–86). This arrangement creates the impression that Vitellius' journey took time to complete, casting him as sluggish and lazy, whatever the real chronology of his march (2.57–73 intro.). Further tension is added by another 'purple passage', the scene of Vitellius' ghoulish visit to the battlefield forty days after his victory (2.70). It is almost as if he himself cannot believe what has happened until he sees the grim evidence with his own eyes.

The emergence of the Flavian challenge (2.74–86) is driven above all by T.'s interest in the psychology of the main protagonists, since there is little real 'action' in this section. Earlier character sketches of Vespasian and Mucianus (1.10, 2.5) are now fleshed out by internal focalisation elaborating Vespasian's worries about proclaiming himself emperor (2.74.2–75) and by a masterful hortatory speech from the charismatic Mucianus (2.76–77). Also, at 2.86 T. introduces the Flavian generals Cornelius Fuscus and (crucially) Antonius Primus, whose energetic intervention sabotages Flavian plans, but will secure victory for Vespasian. Shifting to introductory character sketches in the section's last chapter (2.74–86) is bold, but creates forward momentum and shows T.'s narrative artistry in whetting our appetites for these protagonists, who will reappear at the start of *Histories* 3. Moreover, the whole extended panel (2.74–86) repeats the dynamics of the book's opening, where the incipient Othonian campaign (2.11) is overshadowed by Flavian preparations (2.1–7): Vitellius has not even reached Rome, but T. has placed the Flavian threat firmly in our minds and invested Vitellius' early imperial activities with a sense of futility. In the final section (2.87–101), Vitellius goes through the motions of entering Rome in a meticulously regimented military procession (2.89), but the urban delights will quickly debilitate his pleasure-seeking soldiers (2.93) and the fragile collaboration between his generals Caecina and Valens will soon collapse (2.100). The army's chaotic departure from Rome (2.99) shows a complete transformation from the carefully orchestrated arrival. After all the energetic Flavian preparations in the east, the Vitellians look extraordinarily vulnerable. The book ends with a final digressionary pause, T.'s denunciation of pro-Flavian historians who rebranded Caecina's treachery as 'concern for peace' (2.101). This is a timely reminder of his objectivity as a historian on the threshold of *Histories* 3, the book which will narrate the ultimate Flavian victory and raise the most direct questions about possible bias towards the winners.

5. DRAMATIS PERSONAE

Histories 2 is populated by a dizzying array of protagonists and presents military activities taking place across a geographically huge area embracing both eastern and western extremes of the empire. It is arguably the most complex book of an already complex narrative, presenting as it does crucial phases of two civil wars (Othonians vs Vitellians, the Flavians vs Vitellians). Keeping track of the main players can be confusing, but a skeletal list may help. Family members are under (i), major supporters under (ii), other supporters under (iii):

(a) *Othonians*:

(i) Otho, Salvius Titianus (Otho's brother, 23.5n.), Salvius Cocceianus (Otho's nephew, 48.2n.).

(ii) Annius Gallus (Othonian general, 11.2n.), Vestricius Spurinna (Othonian general, 11.2n.), Suetonius Paulinus (Othonian general, 23.4n.), Martius Macer (Othonian general, 23.3n.), Marius Celsus (Othonian general, 23.4n.), Licinius Proculus (praetorian prefect, 33.1n.).

(iii) Suedius Clemens (Othonian general, 12.1n.), Antonius Novellus (Othonian general, 12.1n.), Aemilius Pacensis (Othonian general, 12.1n.), Turullius Cerialis (Othonian general, 22.3n.), Julius Briganticus (Othonian general, 22.3n.), Epiphanes (prince of Commagene, Othonian supporter, 25.2n.), Julius Fronto (tribune, 26.1n.), Plotius Firmus (praetorian prefect, 46.2n.), Orfidius Benignus (Othonian general, 43.1n.), Vedius Aquila (legionary commander, 44.1n.), Rubrius Gallus (general, later Vitellian, 51n.), Coenus (freedman, 54.1n.), Lucceius Albinus (governor of Mauretania, 58.1n.), Galerius Trachalus (orator, 60.2n.).

(b) *Vitellians*:

(i) Vitellius, Lucius Vitellius (Vitellius' brother, 47.2n.), Triaria (Lucius Vitellius' wife, 63.2n.), Galeria (Vitellius' wife, 47.2n.), Petronia (Vitellius' ex-wife, 47.2n., 64.1n.), Sextilia (Vitellius' mother, 64.2n.), Germanicus (Vitellius' son, 47.2n., 59.3n.).

(ii) Fabius Valens (Vitellian general), Alienus Caecina (Vitellian general), Lucilius Bassus (prefect of the fleets, 100.3n.).

(iii) Julius Classicus (Vitellian general, 14.1n.), Decumus Picarius (pro-Vitellian governor of Corsica, 2.16), Julius Gratus (camp prefect, 26.1n.), Alfenus Varus (camp prefect, 29.2n.), Salonina (Caecina's wife, 20.1n.), Junius Blaesus (governor of Gallia Lugdunensis, 59.2n.), Hilarus (Vitellius' freedman, 65.1n.), Asiaticus (Vitellius' freedman, 57.2n.), Publilius Sabinus (praetorian prefect, 93.1n.), Julius Priscus (praetorian prefect, 93.1n.).

(c) *Flavians*:

(i) Vespasian, Flavius Sabinus (Vespasian's brother, 55.1n.), Titus (son of Vespasian, 1.1n.), Domitian (son of Vespasian), Flavius Sabinus (Vespasian's nephew, 36.2n.).

(ii) Mucianus (governor of Syria, Vespasian's second-in-command, 5.1n.), Antonius Primus (Flavian general, 86.1n.), Cornelius Fuscus (general, 86.3n.), Tiberius Alexander (governor of Egypt, 74.1n.), Berenice (Jewish queen, 2.1n.), Sohaemus (king of Emesa, 81.1n.), Antiochus (king of Commagene, 81.1n.), Agrippa (Jewish king, 81.1n.).

(iii) Asiaticus (freedman, 57.2n.), Sostratus (priest of the temple of Venus at Paphos, 4.2n.), Seleucus (Vespasian's astrologer, 78.1n.).

(d) *Others*:

Verginius Rufus (general, 49.1n.), Tampius Flavianus (legate of Pannonia, 86.3n.), Pompeius Silvanus (legate of Dalmatia, 86.3n.), Tettius Julianus (legionary commander, 85.2n.), Valerius Festus (legionary legate, 98.1n.), Asinius Pollio (cavalry commander, 2.59.1), Festus (infantry commander, 2.59.1), Scipio (infantry commander, 2.59.1), Claudius Pyrrhicus (naval commander, 16.2n.).

Calpurnius Asprenas (governor of Galatia and Pamphylia, 9.1n.), Marius Maturus (governor of the Maritime Alps, 12.3n.), Hordeonius Flaccus (governor of upper Germany, 57.1n.), Cluvius Rufus (governor of Hispania Tarraconensis, 58.2n.), Trebellius Maximus (governor of Britain, 65.2n.), Vettius Bolanus (governor of Britain, 65.2n.), Aponius Saturninus (governor of Moesia, 85.2n.).

Caecilius Simplex (consul, 60.2n.), Valerius Marinus (consul designate, 71.2n.), Vibius Crispus (senator, 10.1n.), Licinius Caecina (senator, 53.1n.), Plancius Varus (senator, 63.1n.), Cornelius Dolabella (relative of Galba, 63.1n.), Annius Faustus (equestrian, 10.1n.), Quintius Certus (equestrian, 16.2n.).

Eprius Marcellus (informer, 53.1n.), Mariccus (pretender, 61n.), Geta (pretender, 72.2n.), Basilides (priest of Carmel, 78.3n.), Asiaticus, Flavus and Rufinus (Gallic chieftains, 94.2n.).

6. STYLE

Style as a carrier of historical meaning is a powerful weapon in T.'s hands. Through his selection of words and arrangement of clauses, he startles, engages and challenges the expectations of his readers at every opportunity. The frequent ellipse of verbs[41] and the often complex relationship between main and subordinate clauses[42] makes the experience of reading his narrative collaborative and intellectually stimulating: so, where another author might have used an unambiguous conjunction to introduce a subordinate clause, T. leaves us to work out for ourselves whether (e.g.) an ablative absolute has a causal, concessive or temporal connection with the main clause. Sometimes there is not a single, easy answer, but the process of analysing forces us to engage broadly with complex historical questions and to take nothing for granted.

In addition, T. regularly uses his syntax to peel back discrepancies between surface behaviour and inner motivation, and above all exploits it as a vehicle for ruthless wit, with 'stings in the tail' driving home his moral judgements about the protagonists and the times.[43] In a work where the debasement of language is a theme (101.1n.

---

[41] See Goodyear (1972) 346–50 on Tacitean ellipse.

[42] See Damon (2003) 16–19 on 'appendix sentences'; O'Gorman (2000) 1–10.

[43] See Plass (1988) on wit as 'a natural tool for dealing with absurdity in the special form of paranoid political logic' (103) under the principate. The best known example of T.'s witty syntax in the *H.* is the judgement of Galba, *omnium consensu capax imperii, nisi imperasset* (*H.* 1.49.4). The abrupt shift from Galba's potential to the disappointing reality of his principate is implemented by omitting a verb in the apodosis. This means that we only identify this as a contrary-to-fact conditional sentence in the protasis (if-clause).

curam pacis), T. demonstrates by the style of his own narrative how precision and delicacy in his vibrant Latin can reinvest language with power and meaning. In a reference to his (then) future historical narratives, T. pledges that he will not regret having recorded the previous servitude and current good times *uel incondita ac rudi uoce* (*Agr.* 3.3). That 'fiction' of literary powers diminished by Domitian's oppressive regime bears no resemblance to the sophisticated narrative of the *Histories*, in which T. develops a highly distinctive and devastatingly effective historical style. It is impossible to offer a comprehensive template of this, precisely because T. is so versatile, but an overview of some stylistic elements that are prominent in *Histories* 2 will at least offer readers a taste of things to come.

T.'s prose can be described as 'artificial', in that it admits words which were not, so far as we can tell, in ordinary use in the early empire. Examples include striking synonyms such as *cunctus* for *omnis* (1.3n.), *ingens* for *magnus* (4.2n.), *luxus* for *luxuria* (11.3n.), *repente* for *subito* (16.3n.) and *quando* for *quoniam* (33.3n), as well as poeticisms such as *iuuenta* (1.1n.), *praesagus* (1.2n.),[44] *ualidus* (19.1n.), *quatio* (22.1n.), *coepto* (29.1n.), *tempestas* for *tempus* (32.1n.), *amnis* for *flumen* (35.1n.), *attonitae mentes* (42.1n.), *maestus* for *tristis* (46.1n.), *inuiolabilis* (61n.), *flammo* (74.1n.), *recurso* (78.2n.), *classes* for *naues* (83.2n.), the neuter pl. *auia* as a substantive (85.2n.), and *fluito* (93.2n.).[45] The effect of such usage will naturally vary depending on context: incongruity of elevated words with the surrounding narrative can generate bathos, while a cluster of poeticisms (in combination with allusions to specific passages in a poet) can open up or enhance a heightened emotional register. T. is also fond of choosing strikingly simple verb forms for more familiar compounds, a touch which has poetic resonances (*memoro* for *commemoro*, 2.4.4, 50.2; *firmo* for *affirmo*, 9.2, 23.3; *propinquo* for *appropinquo*, 18.1, 24.1, 71.1; *flagro* for *conflagro*, 21.1; *mitto* for *committo*, 40; *solor* for *consolor*, 48.2; *nouo* for *renouo*, 51; *claresco* for *inclaresco*, 53.1; *traho* for *contraho*, 57.1; *traho* for *attraho*, 61; *terreo* for *deterreo*, 63.2; *fero* for *praefero*, 65.1; *crebresco* for *increbresco*, 67.1; *posco* for *exposco*, 68.4; *flammo* for *inflammo*, 74.1; *sumo* for *assumo*, 74.2; *tumesco* for *intumesco*, 77.3; *fero* for *transfero*, 79; *tardo* for *retardo*, 99.1). Yet he can also jump in the opposite direction, using choice compound verbs for more familiar simple forms (*exterreo* for *terreo*, 8.1; *conclamo* for *clamo*, 68.3; *consterno* for *sterno*, 70.2; *recognosco* for *cognosco*, 70.3; *resisto* for *sisto*, 87.1;) and his usage can sometimes shift within the surviving *corpus* (*struo* ~ *exstruo*, 34.2n.).

T. is also prone to using archaisms, a regular feature of Latin historical prose, in order to evoke the atmosphere of a past age through a register that is often jarringly incongruous with the morally flawed era being described in the narrative. In this, he follows his predecessor Sallust, a flagrant archaiser, although T. shies away from unduly conspicuous instances.[46] Examples include *igitur* as the first word in the sentence (2.2n.), the preposition *ob* for *propter* (4.3n.), abl. *diu* for *die* (5.1n.), *penes* (6.2n.), *super* for

---

[44] T. is especially fond of resonant compound adjectives with a *prae*– prefix (28.1n.).

[45] T. naturally also uses constructions and devices associated with poetry, such as the dative of the agent (80.3) and hypallage (5.2, 31.1, 34.1, 40).

[46] Asinius Pollio criticised Sallust for using archaisms in a mannered way (Suet. *Gram.* 10). See Goodyear (1972) 334–5.

de (8.1n.), *metuo* for *timeo* (8.2n.), *ni* (14.3n.), *socordius* (15.1n.), *occipio* (16.2n.), *reputo* (16.2n.), *mortales* for *homines* (20.1n.), *accedo* without *ad* (27.2n.), *tempestas* for *tempus* (32.1n.), *claritudo* for *claritas* (78.2n.), *egregie* + adj. (82.2n.), and *pone* + acc. (83.2n.). Such colourful choices often enable T. to avoid a more common word, just as he does when he strives to shun technical language (either as too prosaic or too hackneyed) in favour of lengthy and lofty periphrasis: so he rejects *conus* (3.2n.), *pinnae* (19.2n.), *phalaricae* (21.1n.) and *circumire uigilias* (29.2n.). Whether this reflects his desire to avoid terms inconsistent with the dignity of historiography or is just a natural consequence of his deeply entrenched desire for *uariatio* is probably best decided on a case-by-case basis.[47] Probably the most famous example is his periphrasis for *pala* 'spade' and *ligo* 'mattock' as tools *per quae egeritur humus aut exciditur caespes* (*A.* 1.65.7).[48] Yet we should not underestimate T.'s capacity for humour in such cases, and indeed he is quite happy to admit technical terminology elsewhere (*traduces*, 25.1n.; *reuocare ueteranos*, 82.1n.; *exauctoro*, 96.2n.; *nomen dare*, 97.2n.) or to redeploy it in striking metaphorical contexts (*argumentum fabulae*, 72.2n.; *caligo*, 80.2n.).

This makes arguments uncritically based on T.'s aversion to terms that are technical or *inhonesta dictu* problematic. When the narrative calls for it, he admits words that are distinctly prosaic, such as *uenter* and *gula* (31.1n.), and *ganea* (95.2n.), and he does so for good reasons: all these declassé words are associated damningly with the hedonistic *princeps* Vitellius. Yet in general, the linguistic register of individual words must be pinned down with care: a grandiloquent word used by an epic poet will trigger different resonances if used by a satirist or a writer of epigrams for a mock-serious effect, as with Martial's mischievously elevated description of *caluam trifilem semitatus unguento*, 'a bald pate with its three remaining hairs streaked with unguent' (6.74.2).[49] Context and genre are always relevant considerations. Furthermore, usage naturally changed over time. Words that may have struck the original readers of one author as poetic shifted their register, particularly if they were taken up enthusiastically by prose authors: so the verb *remeo* (79n.) was predominantly poetic down to the end of the Augustan era until Columella, Seneca the Younger and Pliny the Elder appropriated it for prose, and there is a similar story with *raptor* (86.2n.). We can see T. himself participating in the process, as when he takes the Ovidian coinage *refugus* (24.2n.) and introduces it to prose. Other words may at first seem to be intrinsically prosaic, but in fact constraints of scansion kept them out of reach of the poets: so, *inhabilis* (87.1n) is inadmissable to poetry for reasons of metre, and *officina* (82.1n.) does not scan in dactylic hexameters.

One affectation common in T. is to use abstract nouns as the subject of active verbs (*spes*, 2.1; *fors*, 8.2; *fortuna*, 12.1, 76.1; *gaudium*, 42.1; *pauor*, 44.1; *nox*, 44.2; *posteritas*, 47.2; *metus*, 52.1; *formido*, 63.2; *auctoritas*, 65.2; *mendacium*, 72.1; *quantum superbiae socordiaeque*, 73; *arrogantia*, 74.1; *ira odium ultionis cupiditas*, 77.3; *bellum*, 77.3; *fama*, 78.4; *infirmitas*, 99.1;

---

[47] Goodyear (1972) 342–5 is still salutary. See too Oakley (1998) 136–9.
[48] T. does not have *pala* elsewhere, but *ligo* is at *H.* 3.27.2.
[49] Watson and Watson (2003) 25, 319.

prauitas, 100.3). This is a technique which adds elevation, and in some cases, hints at personification of influential forces that have an impact on historical events. The effect is often to subordinate human protagonists to powerful but unpredictable entities and emotions, pointing up the importance of the 'unexpected' in historical events. T. also uses abstract nouns to designate people, another lofty touch drawing attention to those labelled in this way, which can introduce bathos, as the agents described fail to match up to the elevated vocabulary applied to them (*transfugium* for *perfuga*, 34.1n.; *ministerium* for *minister*, 59.2n.; *seruitium* for *serui* 78.3n.). Indeed, T. is often at his most stylistically lofty and creative when addressing base or hypocritical conduct. So, he uses a resonant and rare adjective ending in *–bundus* (85.2n.) for the centurion Tettius Julianus speeding up or delaying (*cunctabundus*) his journey according to the news he receives about Vespasian's chances of becoming *princeps*; he has extensive and ostentatious alliteration (91.2n. *sed comitia consulum cum candidatis ciuiliter celebrans*) for Vitellius' canvassing activities, despite already having selected his consuls; and he chooses a rare and expressive compound verb for the crowd's mindless adulation of their new *princeps* Vitellius (90.2n. *astrepo*).

An especially rich feature of T.'s language is his fondness for metaphor. The scale can range from a single word to an elaborate and interlocking set of images. These often have an interpretative bearing on the historical event being described and are not simply decorative.[50] For instance, when T. describes a quarrel at an extraordinary meeting of the senate at Mutina, he uses a number of nouns and verbs which have metaphorical associations with physical fighting (*iurgium*; *inuasit*; *dirempti*, 2.53.1). This language subtly underscores how gravely normal senatorial procedure based on discussion has been polluted by the eruption of military violence around the empire, and it captures well the degradation of the senate, a body that was ideally a beacon of the Roman national character. A similar metaphor of physical fighting is used to suggest the erosion of morals when the city prefect Flavius Sabinus is prevailed upon by Vitellius' sister-in-law Triaria to collude in the downfall of the innocent aristocrat Dolabella (63.2n. *ne alleuasse uideretur, impulit ruentem*). They are grimly cast as gladiators or boxers, with Triaria playing the part of a warped female *lanista*.

Sometimes T. uses a relatively common metaphor, but with the additional function of a structuring device: so metaphorical verbs associated with fire are used in ring-composition at the start (*seditio exarserat*, 27.2n.) and the end of the Vitellian mutiny (*deflagrante paulatim seditione*, 29.2n.).[51] Or else T. will use a familiar metaphor to add a disturbing twist: he has a fire metaphor to describe the still passionate feelings of the Othonian soldiers after their defeat (46.1n. *flagrabant*), but some 'burn' with such intense ardour that they will kill themselves at Otho's funeral pyre (2.49.4); and similarly, the fire metaphor applied to a narrowly averted battle (66.2n. *arsisset*) is given

---

[50] Woodman (2006) analyses the complex images of disease that pervade T.'s narratives of the mutinies in *A.* 1.

[51] Another fire metaphor marks a progression: (Cornelius Fuscus) *acerrimam bello facem praetulit* (2.86.3) and *flagrabat ingens bellum* (2.86.4)

a literal twist when real fires break out in Augusta Taurinorum on the night of the soldiers' departure (2.66.3).

T. can also use metaphorical language to raise questions about pro-Flavian propaganda. So after giving details of Vespasian's concerns about making an imperial challenge, he describes how his friends bolster him: *his pauoribus nutantem . . . firmabant* (76.1n.). The combination of *nuto + firmo* seems to activate the metaphor of Vespasian as a tottering building, which is suggestive, as elsewhere the robust Vespasian himself is cast as shoring up the tottering state (*nutantemque rem publicam stabilire*, Suet. *Ves.* 8.1).[52] Likewise, T. has the priest Basilides use metaphorical language involving the *domus* in his prediction of future success for Vespasian, but he adds disquieting notes involving the metaphor of imperial power as slavery (78.3nn. *domum exstruere* and *ampliare seruitia*).

Metaphor is also a deft way to bring out character, especially in speeches. So Otho pleads with his friends to leave quickly and not provoke the victor's anger (*iram uictoris asperarent* 48.1n.), but he uses a verb associated with the sharpening of weapons, hinting grimly perhaps at the possible dangers if they do not depart. Or when the dynamic Mucianus repeatedly calls money the sinews of civil war (84.1n. *eos esse belli ciuilis neruos*), he seems to trump the Othonian general Suetonius Paulinus' rather blander reference to *immensam pecuniam, inter ciuiles discordias ferro ualidiorem* (2.32.2), where the metaphor is arguably less effective and the epigram is less pithy. Mucianus' sparkling manipulation of language (as exemplified by his speech at 2.76–77) is a crucial part of his character and an important factor in driving the Flavians to war, while Paulinus' failure to convince his colleagues about the strategy of delay (2.32) is a prelude to the Othonian defeat. As such, their speeches are not just adornments, but play a part in helping us to understand the progression of this civil war.

Finally, metaphor in T. can also be a vehicle for wit, albeit of a grim sort. It is darkly apt that T. musters a military metaphor *custodire sermones* (52.1n.) for soldiers keeping watch on senators' conversations, an activity intrinsically at odds with normal military activities. In a similar vein, the general Caecina's efforts to undermine his soldiers' loyalties to Vitellius are described metaphorically with a verb usually associated with undermining ramparts or walls during a siege (101.2n. *subruebat*). The metaphor reminds us of the type of thing that a commander should be doing, but the treacherous Caecina is no normal general and the language underscores this point. T. also uses a darkly humorous financial metaphor (85.2n. *imputari Vespasiano*) for the Vitellian soldiers claiming 'credit' with Vespasian for their mutiny, in which the centrepiece had been the chaotic seizure of money from the legionary chest. Such

---

[52] Metaphors involving buildings recur: 57.2n. *concidisse bellum*, 76.2n. *fundatam . . . domum*, 86.2n. *labantibus Vitellii rebus*, 101.2n. *monimenta belli huiusce*. Other favourites include water (23.3n. *repente effudit*, 32.1n. *redundare*, 58.2n. *spargebatur*, 93.1n. *redundante multitudine*), agriculture (18.2n. *seditio mitesceret*, 30.3n. *quamuis uberrima . . . materia*, 76.4n. *noua . . . semina*, 86.2n. *serendae . . . inuidiae*) and disease or wounds (7.1n. *coalescere*, 56.1n. *Italia afflictabatur*, 67.1n. *addito . . . lenimento*, 73n. *proruperant*, 77.3n. *aperiet . . . uolnera*, 86.4n. *quidquid . . . aegrum*).

metaphorical touches are designed to be provocative and to point up the abnormal behaviour patterns that prevail in the warped world of civil war.[53] T.'s word-play reaches beyond the trope of metaphor. Despite his reputation for being an austere author, T.'s fondness for playful paronomasia is deep-seated.[54] Names are a favourite target. So, the *Legio XXI Rapax* (aptly) *rapuit* the enemy's standards (43.1n. *rapuit*). Or when T. says that Turullius Cerialis was *Caecinae haud alienus*, he apparently puns on Caecina's *cognomen* Alienus (22.3n.), and he indulges in name-play again when noting that with the arrival of Valens, the party *conualuerant* (93.2n.).[55] Such witty touches provide some respite in a predominantly grim narrative. They can, however, serve a serious purpose, as when T. stresses that after Vespasian's proclamation, he showed *nihil tumidum, arrogans aut in rebus nouis nouum* (80.1n.). The two different senses of *nouus* manifest paronomasia, but the linguistic playfulness also embraces a serious historical point, that Vespasian did not allow imperial power to go to his head. Other stylistic devices involving repetition can be useful for capturing the intrinsic absurdities of civil war: polyptoton (the repetition of a word with a morphological variation in the same clause) is often expressive, such as *remedium tumultus fuit alius tumultus* (68.3n.) and *unde metus et ex metu consilium* (85.1n.), or *uinctus . . . uinxisset* (26.1n.) for the two brothers fighting on opposite sides in the civil war, but arrested on the same charge.[56] Some readers may find such touches disconcerting in a serious narrative, but T. is a writer 'who consistently challenges the conventions of language and pushes against the boundaries of literary expression'.[57] His manipulation of language (*uerba*) enhances his presentation of the subject matter (*res*) and is a central way in which the reader becomes engaged in the historiographical process.

T.'s vocabulary is rich and expressive in its own right, but it gains huge impact from the distinctive and complex sentence structure in which it is displayed. Beyond the basic main clause devoid of additional subordinate clauses, many permutations are possible, but Kraus identifies three dominant patterns in historiography:[58] (1) the basic historiographical sentence, in which one or more grammatically subordinate clauses are followed by one or more main clauses, so that the sentence often ends with a main verb (Sb Mn; Sb Sb Mn; Sb Sb Mn Mn, and so forth). All clauses tend to move the action of the story forwards;[59] (2) the 'phrase à relance', which builds on the basic unit by adding a second such unit (subordinate clause(s) + main clause(s); Sb Mn, Sb Mn, and so forth);[60] and (3) the 'phrase à rallonge', where one or more main clauses are followed by one or more subordinate clauses, which tend to elaborate or

---

[53] A related example involving the metaphor of comedy and the blurring of boundaries between reality and the comic stage is the episode of Geta (72.2n. *in argumentum fabulae*).
[54] Woodman (1998) 218–29 deftly brings out this point.
[55] T. also likes suggestive names (16.2n. *Quintum Certum*, 60.2n. *Caecilio Simplici*, 65.1n. *Hilarus*).
[56] T. also likes *adnominatio*, word-play involving a change of spelling (17.2n. *capta . . . intercepti*, 60.1n. *perfidia et fidem*). Its impact depends on context.
[57] Woodman (1998) 228.   [58] Kraus (1994) 21.
[59] Chausserie-Laprée (1969) 129–247. An example from T. is *et ducibus Othonis iam pridem profugis Caecina ac Valens subsidiis suos firmabant* (2.43.2).
[60] Chausserie-Laprée (1969) 253–82.

analyse what has just been described, without necessarily moving the action forward (Mn Sb; Mn Sb Sb etc.).[61]

T.'s speciality is without doubt the third type. By jumping off with a pithy main clause and adding on a lengthy subordinate 'appendix', T. can take an apparently straightforward event or action and complicate it, either by highlighting (often dubious) motives, by revealing contradictions between appearance and reality, or by magnifying and illustrating the substance of the main clause with specific details. A powerful example comes during the Othonians' diversionary campaign in Gallia Narbonensis, when the soldiers attack Albintimilium (|| = end of main clause): *auxit inuidiam praeclaro exemplo femina Ligus, || quae filio abdito, cum simul pecuniam occultari milites credidissent eoque per cruciatus interrogarent ubi filium occuleret, uterum ostendens latere respondit, nec ullis deinde terroribus aut morte constantiam uocis egregiae mutauit* (2.13.2). Mention of an *exemplum* prepares us for a memorable scene, and the focus on *inuidia* in the main clause (6 words) sets up in advance the basic emotion that it will trigger. Yet in the elaborate subordinate clause (30 words), consisting of an ablative absolute, a *cum* clause, an indirect question, and two verbs dependent on the relative pronoun *quae*, incorporating a nominative participle clause and and two ablatives of means, T. paints a detailed and highly emotive scene which makes the broad generalisation of the main clause seem like an understatement: no wonder contemporaries felt *inuidia* towards the Othonian troops.

Another example is T.'s notice about Tiberius Alexander getting his troops to swear the oath of allegiance to Vespasian on 1 Jul.: *isque primus dies principatus dies in posterum celebratus, || quamuis Iudaicus exercitus quinto nonas Iulias apud ipsum iurasset, eo ardore ut ne Titus quidem filius exspectaretur, Syria remeans et consiliorum inter Mucianum ac patrem nuntius* (2.79). Here the simple notice of Vespasian's choice of *dies imperii* is deconstructed, as T. questions the convenient façade of that date by hinting at its arbitrariness. Vespasian could just as well have opted for 3 Jul., when the Jewish army took the oath, while his complete circumvention of the senate, the body supposed to confer imperial powers, is conspicuous; and the Flavians' worrying lack of complete control is suggested by the focus on the absent Titus, who was supposed to be present at the proclamation in Judaea. Of course, not all sentences of this type are so elaborate, but even a short version can have impact. T. opens one panel as follows: *discubuerat Vitellius Ticini || adhibito ad epulas Verginio* (2.68.1). Here the prominence of the main clause highlights Vitellius' gormandising, while the 'guest of honour' is almost an afterthought, relegated to an ablative absolute. This suggests a great deal about Vitellius' priorities in a context (the eruption of fighting amongst his own soldiers) implying that his conduct is having a detrimental impact on military discipline. This type of arrangement is only one of many different varieties of creative sentence structure in T., but it is the one which commentators identify as being the most powerful vehicle for T.'s edgy historiography, where things are so often not what they appear to be at first sight.[62]

[61] Chausserie-Laprée (1969) 283–336.
[62] For a different arrangement in sentence structure which eloquently reflects the confusion of the event being described, see 80.1n. *dum . . . salutauere*, the description of Vespasian's

Finally, a particularly distinctive aspect of T.'s style is his pursuit of *uariatio* at all levels, from the smallest phrase to the insertion of whole scenes. On a linguistic level, this is a technique evocative of Sallust, who strove to avoid neat balance and parallelism between clauses. So in attributing motives to some trierarchs, T. shifts from a participle to an ablative noun (*seu nutantes seu dolo*, 2.9.2); he varies his use of prepositions (*erga Neronem . . . in Othonem*, 2.11.1); uses four synonyms for 'hide' in one sentence (*abdo, occulto, occulo, lateo*, 2.13.2); varies an ablative clause and a causal subordinate clause (*nullo apud quemquam Othonis fauore, nec quia Vitellium mallent*, 2.17.2); has asyndeton in the main clause and polysyndeton in the subordinate clause (29.3n. *ut uero . . . fauor*); and shifts nouns from concrete to collective to abstract (*histrionibus . . . gregibus . . . ingenio*, 2.71.1). These are just a few examples. In fact, *uariatio* is such a mark of T.'s style that, paradoxically, lack of *uariatio* can itself be a form of *uariatio* (22.2n. *subruit muros, instruit aggerem, molitur portas*). In addition, T. innovates with his constructions, using *dispergo* as if it were a verb of speaking followed by an acc. and inf. (1.1.n.), replacing the usual prolative infinitive or *quin* clause after (*non*) *dubito* with a *quominus* clause (45.2n.), using an acc. + inf. after *aemulor* (62.2n.), following *insimulo* with *ut* (68.4n.), replacing the usual preposition *inter* after *discordia* with two genitives (88.1n.), and so forth. He also takes combinations which were probably by his time clichés and changes them for *uariatio*, such as the standard Latin terminology for describing extremes on a vertical plane (*summa~ima*), where T. replaces *ima* with the substantive adj. *praecipitia* (74.2n.). The cumulative effect of such touches is to push his readers into a constantly unfolding series of double-takes, as constructions and expressions which they expect to see are distorted and derailed. Such disjointed and unexpected language creates an atmosphere which aptly mirrors the confusing world of the narrative at every turn, and most importantly engages us with T.'s historiography.

7. *SENTENTIAE* AND MORALISING ALLUSIONS

(a) *Sententiae*

For a historian with a broad moralising agenda, peppering a narrative with *sententiae* was an invaluable rhetorical device. A *sententia* can be defined as a universalising pronouncement of a general truth, deriving from particular circumstances under discussion (Quint. *Inst.* 8.5.3).[63] It serves as a way to broaden out a historical narrative and to invest an account with a timeless relevance. The authoritative tone of such *sententiae* can also enhance an author's *auctoritas* and add conviction to the particular point being made: so, if readers accept the general truth, then they are more likely to concede the validity of the detail that forms the 'springboard' for the *sententia*. On

---

proclamation. Word-order mirroring the concept being described works on a smaller scale too (19.1n. *Caecina . . . paucas cohortes circumfudisset*, 55.1n. *congestis in modum tumuli coronis*, 59.2n. *circumdaret principi ministeria*).

[63] For *sententiae* in T. see Kirchner (2001) and Sinclair (1995) 33–77, in *Histories* 1 see Damon (2003) 15–16, 302–4 and Keitel (2006), and in *Histories* 2, Stegner (2004) 55–97.

a practical level, the *sententia* also has a punctuating effect, momentarily halting the main narrative (Quint. *Inst.* 8.5.27), and it is often expressed in the present tense (as opposed to epigrams, which share many characteristics with *sententiae*, but are usually tied to the timeframe and circumstances of the main narrative).[64] For Quintilian, *sententiae* should be used sparingly to gain the most impact, as in a painting where a figure stands out through contrast with the background (*Inst.* 8.5.26). They can either be articulated by the author, or put in the mouths of protagonists in the text, but if so, they ideally need to be delivered by someone with *auctoritas*, whose character can suitably endorse the concept (*Inst.* 8.5.8). In the *Histories*, T. uses them 'to articulate the principal features of the moral and political breakdown of Roman society – leaders, armies, and citizens – during civil war'.[65]

Given the subject matter of *Histories* 2, it is not surprising that most *sententiae* have a military flavour. What is more striking is the number of *sententiae* articulated not by T. himself, but by characters in the text. They come from Flavian generals (2.7.1a *bello ciuili uictores uictosque numquam solida fide coalescere*; 2.7.1b *rebus secundis etiam egregios duces insolescere*), the Vitellian generals Alienus Caecina (2.20.2 *gnarus ut initia belli prouenissent, famam in cetera fore*) and Fabius Valens (2.29.3 *gnarus ciuilibus bellis plus militibus quam ducibus licere*), the Othonian general Suetonius Paulinus (2.32.1a *nec exercitum sine copiis retineri posse*; 2.32.1b *multa bella impetu ualida per taedia et moras euanuisse*; 2.32.2 *pecuniam, inter ciuiles discordias ferro ualidiorem*), the Othonian centurion Plotius Firmus (2.46.2 *maiore animo tolerari aduersa quam relinqui*), Otho himself (2.47.1 *difficilius est temperare felicitati, qua te non putes diu usurum*), Vespasian (2.75 *facilius uniuersos impelli quam singulos uitari*) and his colleague Licinius Mucianus (2.77.3 *nam qui deliberant, desciuerunt*). In these *sententiae* we can see an unsettling pattern where characters in a highly abnormal situation (civil war) authoritatively appeal to general rules formed during normal military life, often to endorse dubious courses of action (2.7.1b, 20.2, 32.1 × 2), or else they formulate their own disturbing universal rules from the aberrant situation around them (2.7.1a, 29.3, 32.2, 75, 77.3), with an alarming potential for future application to new civil wars. It is striking too that probably the most impressive *sententia* articulated for the most laudable reason (to persuade Otho not to kill himself) comes from the centurion Plotius Firmus (2.46.2), the lowliest person in the military hierarchy amongst those who deliver *sententiae* in *Histories* 2. The dynamics of these individual situations are complex, but in allocating *sententiae* to characters in the text, T. opens our eyes to the potential for rhetorical devices to be misdirected (cf. 101.1n. *curam pacis* on the warping of language during civil war).

T. also appeals sparingly to *sententiae* in his own person as narrator. (i) He creates a humbling truism out of unpromising material, as onlookers in Italian country towns find fault with Caecina and his wife Salonina for their attire and mode of transport

---

[64] E.g. an epigram such as *nimius honos inter secunda rebus aduersis in supplicium cessit*, 2.59.3. The perfect tense of *cessit* is significant. If T. had used *cedit*, the epigram would have become a *sententia*.
[65] Keitel (2006) 220.

respectively (2.20.1 *insita mortalibus natura recentem aliorum felicitatem acribus oculis introspicere modumque fortunae a nullis magis exigere quam quos in aequo uiderunt*). Plutarch has similar details about Caecina and Salonina, but there is no *sententia* about jealousy (*Oth.* 6.6). T.'s addition enhances both the inner and outer frames: not only does he tacitly find fault with the jealous onlookers in the text, who are right to be ambivalent about these Vitellians, but not because of what they are wearing, but at the same time, he also offers readers a home truth about their attitude to others in their own contemporary world. (ii) Another *sententia* (2.35.1 *nec ea constantia gladiatoribus ad proelia quae militibus*) is concisely expressive: the fact that T. as author points out that gladiators are not as steadfast in battle as professional soldiers shows him intervening with a generalisation that should be self-evident. He thus highlights a dubious characteristic (resorting to gladiators as fighters) of the warped world of civil war, and implicitly draws a sharp contrast with the normal practices of his own era. (iii) One *sententia* grows naturally but disturbingly from the grim world of T.'s narrative, as he explains the unusual level of slaughter in the first battle of Bedriacum (44.1 *neque enim ciuilibus bellis capti in praedam uertuntur*). Plutarch has a similar *sententia* when pointing out that in civil wars 'there is no use for prisoners' (*Oth.* 14.3), but T. sharpens the point by referring explicitly to *praeda* as a motivation of the potential captors. *Sententiae* are supposed to be obviously true (Quint. *Inst.* 8.5.7), but this is indeed a disturbing truth. (iv) Other *sententiae* focus scornfully on one of T.'s favourite targets, the people (2.90.2 *uolgus tamen uacuum curis et sine falsi uerique discrimine*), who react sycophantically to their new emperor Vitellius. This sort of sententious swipe would have appealed to the aristocratic élite who made up his audience, but T. is generally interested in the behaviour of crowds, as when he observes that mobs tend to oscillate between emotional extremes (2.29.3 *uersi in laetitiam, ut est uolgus utroque immodicum*).

Some of T.'s *sententiae* are 'embedded', where an authorial gloss signals that we can view a particular phenomenon through a universalising lens. So, he designates frequent desertions as a general characteristic of civil war (*crebris, ut in ciuili bello, transfugiis*, 2.34.1) and wonders whether the treacherous Bassus recruited Caecina or whether they were independently bad (*quod euenit inter malos ut et similes sint*, 2.100.3). In such cases, T. adds a sententious tone without stopping the narrative by a separate *sententia*. This may be a sign of things to come in his narrative technique. Scholars detect a pattern, where in the *Annals* T. more regularly integrates his *sententiae* into the narrative, whereas in the earlier works they are often free-standing. This syntactical independence makes them striking, but potentially 'the *sententia* stands out too much from its context and is, if anything, too effective; the whole is obscured by the brilliance of a part'.[66] T.'s authorial persona is trenchant and moralising, but he may have decided over time that less overt sententiousness had more bite, as Quintilian suggests: 'crowded together, *sententiae* get in one another's way, just as with all crops

---

[66] Goodyear (1968) 27, who sees T. as being at his sharpest and most epigrammatic in the early books of the *Histories*. See also Martin (1981) 219–20, MW 98.

and fruit on trees nothing can develop to its proper size if it lacks room to grow' (*Inst.* 8.5.26).

(*b*) *Moralising allusions*

Another way for T. to satisfy the moralising agenda of historiography is to call on weighty and authoritative writers of the past, both poets and prose authors, by pointed allusion. This technique clearly depends on an educated readership, with sufficiently detailed knowledge of earlier texts to be able to recognise such meaningful allusions. Generally, T.'s moral tone in specific cases is clear enough without decoding the allusion, but the interaction between text and intertext adds weight, depth and moral authority to his narrative. It also enhances the enjoyment and intellectual stimulation for readers who can recognise the allusions, making the relationship between T. and his audience more robust by reinforcing a shared system of values.

These allusions can operate on different scales, either functioning in isolation or as part of a suggestive network of references within a passage; and they often cluster in emotionally heightened 'purple passages'. Some selected examples from *Histories* 2 show T.'s techniques in action. So, on a small scale, we have Vitellius' marching column accompanied by *spadonum gregibus* (2.71.1), where T. alludes to Horace's scornful description of Cleopatra's entourage of eunuchs (*contaminato cum grege turpium, morbo uirorum*, *Carm.* 1.37.9–10). Detecting the allusion is not necessary to see that T. is describing the antithesis of a proper imperial march, but recognising it inauspiciously aligns Vitellius with Cleopatra, someone who is foreign, female and ultimately a loser in civil war. Moral disapproval is thus reinforced by allusion (especially as T. 'trumps' Horace's *grege* with the plural *gregibus*).[67] Elsewhere, T. points up the erosion of traditional military discipline by *luxus*, comparing this with ancestors *apud quos uirtute quam pecunia res Romana melius stetit* (2.69.2) and thereby mustering the moralising weight of Ennius (*moribus antiquis stat res Romana uirisque*, *Ann.* 156 Sk.; quoted at Cic. *Rep.* 5.1, SHA *Auidius* 5.7). By changing Ennius' present tense *stat* to the perfect *stetit*, T. reinforces the distinction between the debased world of the civil war and the higher standards of the early republic. His disapproving tone is accessible without acknowledging the Ennian echo, but its resonances make his moralising more pointed.[68] T. also alludes fruitfully to Virgil, as during Vitellius' visit to the battlefield after Bedriacum, when he observes that *erant quos uaria sors rerum lacrimaeque et misericordia subiret* (2.70.3). Here T. recalls Aeneas, whose cathartic tears after seeing images of the Trojan war on Dido's temple reflect his bitter-sweet joy that even Carthaginians can empathise with him and his people: *hic etiam . . . sunt lacrimae rerum* (Vir. *A.* 1.461–2). The humanity of the Carthaginians, later the Romans' archetypal enemy, contrasts sharply with some of T.'s Roman voyeurs on the battlefield, who fail to empathise with dead fellow-citizens: *erant quos* implies that the emotional response came from only

---

[67] Further Horatian language is at 2.46.3, 55.1, 56.1, 62.1, 70.1, 80.3, 99.1, 101.2.
[68] Further Ennian language is at 2.25.2, 27.2, 29.2, 69.2, 73.

some of those present.[69] Such allusions as these progressively elevate and enrich T.'s narrative.

Other allusions are more extensive and operate in a dove-tailed and cumulative way within particular passages. In *Histories* 2, the most conspicuous instance is at 2.38, where T. incorporates a cluster of allusions to Sallust (*Cat.* 10–11, *Jug.* 41–2, *Hist.* 1.7, 1.12). Style can be used economically to reflect ideology, serving as a 'pledge of allegiance' with other writers, who have a similar view of the world: so, Sallust's distinctive Latin, with its love of imbalanced syntax and self-consciously archaic vocabulary, itself lays claim to the moralising heritage of Cato the Censor, who wrote the first historical work in Latin, the *Origines*, and whose *persona* is defined by exemplary parsimony and the desire to uphold high moral standards. For T. to evoke (at a pivotal moment) Sallust's programmatic sketch of morally flawed Romans diverging from the good practices of their ancestors and ruining themselves after the destruction of Carthage in 146 BC (*Jug.* 10–11) is highly expressive, adding historical depth and broadening the perspective in analysing the soldiers' conduct in 69.[70] Readers who knew their Sallust would also see T. being pointedly selective: he entirely omits the 'good' half of Sallust's sketch outlining the qualities that allowed Rome to rise (*Jug.* 6–9), concentrating instead on the self-destructive decline. The syntax, diction and vocabulary of T.'s Latin is pervasively rich in Sallustian echoes throughout: *Histories* 2.38 simply shows an unusual cluster.[71] To T., Sallust was quite simply the *rerum Romanorum florentissimus auctor* (*A.* 3.30.2).[72]

In another case, it is not so much specific allusions to individual texts, but broadly suggestive language evoking the genre of Roman comedy that becomes T.'s weapon (2.72), as he narrates the incident of a runaway slave who pretends to be a Roman aristocrat. In the 'drama' of the daring slave Geta, T. sets up a miniature Plautine comedy, uncomfortably blurring the boundaries between reality and pretence in both inner and outer frames. In so doing, T. prompts unflattering comparisons between Vitellius (the upstart emperor) and Geta (the runaway slave) and raises fundamental questions about Roman identity during civil war.[73] Finally, T. is also amenable to

---

[69] Further Virgilian language is at 2.2.1, 4.1, 4.2, 5.2, 8.1, 10.2, 11.3, 14.2, 14.3, 20.1, 21.3, 22.1, 22.2, 23.2, 27.2, 33.1, 33.2, 33.3, 34.1, 35.1, 41.1, 41.2, 41.3, 43.1, 45.3, 47.3, 48.2, 49.1, 55.1, 59.1, 62.1, 67.1, 70.1, 78.1, 78.2, 81.1, 81.3, 82.3, 83.2, 85.2, 86.2, 88.3, 89.2, 97.2, 100.2.

[70] That T. knew this passage well is clear from his later allusion to a pivotal phrase, *saeuire fortuna ac miscere omnia coepit* (*Jug.* 10.1), at *A.* 4.1.1.1, *cum repente turbare fortuna coepit, saeuire ipse.* MW 79 subtly draw out the nuances. T. also evokes the passage in his digression on the history of law (*A.* 3.25.2–28.2 with WM 236–59).

[71] Further Sallustian language is at 2.1.3, 2.2, 5.1, 5.2, 6.2, 7.1, 7.2, 8.2, 10.1, 12.2, 15.1, 19.1, 20.2, 23.1, 23.5, 25.1, 25.2, 27.2, 29.2, 30.1, 31.1, 32.1, 33.2, 37.1, 37.2, 39.2, 44.3, 46.3, 50.1, 55.1, 56.1, 56.2, 57.1, 62.1, 66.1, 69.2, 70.1, 70.2, 73, 74.1, 76.1, 77.3, 78.2, 78.3, 80.2, 82.1, 84.1, 86.2, 87.2, 88.2, 89.2, 93.1, 95.2, 95.3, 100.2.

[72] Syme (1958a) 196–200, 728–32. Mucianus' speech opens with an important double allusion to Sallust (76.1n. *omnes . . . adquiratur*). T. can also allude to Sallust in a slyly humorous way, though not without making a serious point (100.2n. *quem ipse ductauerat*).

[73] 72.1n. *quamquam . . . coeptum*, 72.2n. *deterrimo . . . assumpto*, 72.2n. *fugitiuus*, 72.2n. *sumptum . . . modum.*

imitating himself quite extensively: so, his memorable account of Vitellius' visit to the
battlefield at Bedriacum (2.70) will serve as a rich reference point for his later description of Germanicus' earlier visit in 15 to the site of Varus' defeat by Arminius in 9
(*A.* 1.61–2).[74] The nuances of such interlinked scenes provide much material for modern discussions of T.'s subtle narrative techniques.

8. THE SOURCES

The source material available to any ancient historian is often difficult to pin down,
not least because those writing historical accounts usually position themselves in an
agonistic relationship with their predecessors in a bid to secure 'immortality' for their
own works; and they do not always name their sources directly.[75] Even when this does
happen, it is often unclear how extensively or directly a source has been consulted:
so Sallust mentions books in Carthaginian, either belonging to or written by King
Hiempsal (*Jug.* 17.7), but he may not have read them directly, and perhaps highlights
the source (the only one he cites explicitly) largely in order to impress his readers
with a recondite and unusual work. At times, T. also likes to underscore his diligent
research in this way, as when he cites the *commentarii* of Agrippina the Younger for a
detail about her mother (*A.* 4.53.4).

The material treated by T. in the *Histories* presents a particular set of problems
regarding sources. For one thing, the subject matter, covering the years 68–96, is
uncomfortably close to the point at which T. was writing (the *Histories* was published
in *c.* 109). Some of the protagonists from the civil wars were still alive, even if the Flavian
dynasty had run its course with the death of Domitian in 96. Although a number of the
main players were dead, their descendants were still alive and could take issue with the
latest historical account of a vexed period. As Pliny the Younger says, when rejecting
the genre of history for himself, if you choose to write about recent times, 'the potential
for being offensive is grave, the opportunity to give pleasure is fleeting', particularly
since 'amidst such vast human corruption, more elements must be censured than
praised' (*Ep.* 5.8). Yet at the same time, the contemporary nature of the topic also
gave T. access to a unique wealth of information, in the form of biographies, histories,
generals' memoirs, and the oral tradition, all of which allowed him to check stories
about specific events against each other. We have evidence external to the text that
T. was actively engaged in this sort of meticulous research: Pliny the Younger wrote
two letters in response to Tacitus' request for information about the dramatic death
of his uncle in the eruption of Vesuvius in 79 (*Ep.* 6.16, 6.20) and another about a trial
in 93 in which he had played a part (*Ep.* 7.33).

---

[74] Woodman (1998) 70–85.
[75] On sources in ancient historiography, see Marincola (1997) 66–79, 95–112. T. himself later
says that unless there is a divergence between his sources on a particular point, he will not name
individual writers (*A.* 13.20.2).

The other distinctive aspect of the sources, especially for the civil wars of 68–9, is that there was potentially a great deal of material available.[76] Josephus says that many Greek and Roman authors wrote about this period (*BJ* 4.495–6) and T. refers generally to the *scriptores temporum* (2.101.1) who flourished under the Flavian dynasty. Yet quantity does not necessarily mean quality. Many traumatic events of the civil war understandably prompted tendentious and self-justifying accounts from writers subsequently wishing to please by distancing the new Flavian regime from embarrassing disasters such as the burning of the Capitoline temple in Rome.[77] In addition, although some individual generals, such as the Othonians Marius Celsus (23.4n.) and Vestricius Spurinna (11.2n.), wrote memoirs of particular campaigns, these were not balanced by contributions from their opposite numbers amongst the Vitellian commanders: Fabius Valens had been executed promptly and the turncoat Alienus Caecina had no incentive to reminisce about the civil wars before he too was put to death in 79. This sort of unevenness made it challenging for a historian to strike an equilibrium between the invitingly rich detail of his sources and their inevitable partiality. As Syme says, 'no active partisan of Vitellius is known to have written history or memoirs'.[78] Those who lost civil wars but survived were better off keeping a low profile.

So what was available? First, there were anonymous oral sources. So, T. records (with disapproval) a story about a strange bird which appeared on the day of the first battle of Bedriacum and vanished when Otho killed himself: the garrulous locals were still talking about it when he wrote the *Histories* (50.2n. *incolae memorant*). Similarly, T. cites eye-witnesses for Vespasian's miracle cures in Alexandria, (*utrumque qui interfuere nunc quoque memorant*, 4.81.3) and people who saw from a distance the meeting between Cluvius Rufus and Silius Italicus in Rome (*uoltus procul uisentibus*, 3.65.2). Such citations enable T. to invest his narrative with a certain vividness without having to take responsibility for what is claimed; and the anonymity of the sources would make it almost impossible for anyone to verify the reports.

A related category is when T. cites anonymous written sources, such as his sceptical report of the aborted armistice among the Othonian and Vitellian soldiers before the final battle (37.1n. *apud quosdam auctores*). By setting himself against the majority of (unnamed) writers, T. asserts his own independence and *auctoritas* as a historian. We see a similar strategy when T. lists the arrangement of the Vitellian troops at the second battle of Bedriacum (*alii tradidere*, 3.22.2), but underscores the level of chaos

---

[76] Much of this is no longer extant, but it included Vespasian's *Commentarii* (Jos. *Vit.* 65, *Ap.* 1.10), Domitian's poem on the siege of the Capitol (Mart. 5.5.7), memoirs of Otho's secretary Julius Secundus (Plut. *Oth.* 9.3), Claudius Pollio's life of Annius Bassus (Plin. *Ep.* 7.31.5), Herennius Senecio's life of Helvidius Priscus (*Agr.* 2.1, Plin. *Ep.* 7.19.5), Titinius Capito's work on the deaths of famous men (Plin. *Ep.* 8.12.4) and the memoirs of Vipstanus Messalla (*H.* 3.28). There may also have been some useful material embedded in Mucianus' work on wonders, cited frequently by Pliny the Elder as a source in his *Natural History*, but equally this could have been a pointedly escapist literary venture. See Ash (forthcoming).

[77] Dio 64.17.3 firmly blames the Vitellians for the fire; T. 3.71.4 is more ambivalent.

[78] Syme (1958a) 172.

and distances himself from the accuracy of the information relayed (cf. 3.2n. *ratio in obscuro* for the limits of historiographical knowledge). At other times, T. sceptically cites unnamed sources for a detail reeking of pro-Flavian propaganda, thereby giving himself a veneer of impartiality: so, he mentions at arm's length the story that Vitellius put to death the centurion Julius Agrestis, who brought him news of the Flavian victory (*quidam . . . tradidere*, 3.54.3). Alternatively, he appeals to anonymous sources (*multi tradidere*, 3.59.3) for the detail that the general Antonius Primus (the architect of the Flavian victory, but later frozen out of the power structure) set about giving Flavius Sabinus and Domitian the chance to escape from the Vitellian stronghold in Rome: pro-Flavian historians had evidently accused Primus of neglecting Vespasian's prominent relatives, so T. challenges the official version. Finally, T. can appeal in general terms to anonymous sources to endorse a detail that he sensed could be implausible to his readers, such as the fact that Otho slept soundly on the night before his suicide (*utque affirmatur*, 2.49.2). We have no way of retrieving the provenance of such material, but T. liberally uses anonymous sources, both oral and written, throughout his narrative to enhance his own credibility and to add vividness. No doubt the closer he advanced to his own era in the missing books of the *Histories*, the more pervasive such references would have become.[79]

In what survives of the *Histories*, T. names directly only two sources, Vipstanus Messalla (3.25.2, 3.28) and Pliny the Elder (3.28). Messalla, who had temporarily commanded a legion under Antonius Primus in the Flavian campaign, wins unusual praise from T. (*claris maioribus, egregius ipse et qui solus ad id bellum bonas artes attulisset*, 3.9.3) and was also one of the protagonists in the *Dialogus*. Yet his account, useful though it was, may have been restricted to the Flavian campaign in the autumn of 69, rather than offering a full-scale narrative.[80] Much more extensive in thirty-one books was Pliny the Elder's continuation of the history of Aufidius Bassus, cited by his nephew (Plin. *Ep.* 3.5.4). It covered some or all of Nero's principate, the civil wars, and at least some of Vespasian's principate, probably culminating in the Jewish triumph of 71.[81] Pliny the Elder judiciously postponed publication of this *temporum nostrorum historia*

---

[79]   There were other sources of information. The *acta senatus*, senatorial records, were useful perhaps for the clashes between Vibius Crispus and Annius Faustus (2.10) and between Vitellius and Helvidius Priscus (2.91.3), the senate's award of distinctions to the victorious Vitellius (2.55.2), and Vitellius' arrangements for the consulships. Yet the data provided would have been skeletal (T. only cites the *acta senatus* once in his surviving works at *A.* 15.74.3) and the important action of *Histories* 2 took place far beyond the senate. There were also various *fasti*, calendars, for exact dates, but there are only three in *Histories* 2 (79 × 2, 91.1) and arguably two of these are so well known that T. would not have needed to consult the *fasti*.

[80]   He is the likely source for the insidious activities of Aponius Saturninus in Moesia (2.85.2), but was probably consulted by T. mainly for the Flavian campaign in *Histories* 3.

[81]   The end-point of Aufidius Bassus' history is contentious. Syme (1958a) 697–9 suggests that it began in 8 BC (continuing Livy) and ended in AD 47 (with the *Ludi Saeculares* of that year, celebrating the 800th anniversary of Rome, as an effective conclusion). Marincola (1997) 292 n.7 agrees. Pliny the Younger says that the history was written *religiosissime* (*Ep.* 5.8.5). Its scale, with more than a year per book, was huge. Writing in 77, Pliny the Elder says that it was *iam pridem peracta* (*Nat. Preface* 20).

until after his death (*Natural History, Preface* 20), thinking that his work's contemporary focus left him open to charges of fostering *ambitio*. Yet despite this attempt to secure posthumous credibility for his history, it may still have been sharply pro-Flavian in its emphasis. Blaming Antonius Primus for the sack of Cremona, as Pliny did (3.28), was safe: the general was an easy target after falling from favour in the aftermath of the Flavian victory. Elsewhere, T. criticises Pliny directly for the plausibility of a detail in his history (*A.* 15.53.4). So, although T. apparently consulted Pliny the Elder, he did not do so uncritically. Indeed some scholars suggest that T. used instead either Fabius Rusticus (cited at *A.* 13.20.2, 14.2.2, 15.61.3) or Cluvius Rufus (58.2n.; cited at *A.* 13.20.2, 14.2.1): both wrote histories, but the scope of their works is unclear.

The identity of T.'s main source remains elusive (Syme dubbed him *ignotus*), even if the broad historiographical problems which he faced in confronting pro-Flavian bias in his evidence are clear.[82] Yet proving conclusively who his sources were is ultimately less important than analysing how creatively T. treats his raw material. In this task we are uniquely aided by the survival of other accounts relating to the same period in the parallel tradition.

9. THE PARALLEL TRADITION

The survival of texts from the ancient world is often a precarious business, but we are lucky to have extant works by several authors about the civil wars of 68–9. The most relevant for *Histories* 2 (in chronological order) are Josephus' *Bellum Judaicum*, Plutarch's biography of Otho, Suetonius' biographies of Otho, Vitellius, Vespasian, Titus and Domitian, and Cassius Dio's *Roman History*.[83] Together these make up the 'parallel tradition'. Josephus' account of the Jewish war, originally written in Aramaic but then published in a Greek version, appeared between 75 and 79 and narrated events in which he himself participated. It is often dismissed as hopelessly partisan, but is still useful for identifying pro-Flavian elements in accounts of the civil war. Since it only treats these events in a peripheral way, it is in rather a different category from the other works of the parallel tradition. Plutarch's *Otho* (in Greek), originally one of a sequence of imperial lives, was probably written under Domitian. It is a succinct biography intended to be read in a dovetailed way with his *Galba* (still extant) and *Vitellius* (which has not survived). Suetonius' twelve imperial biographies running from Caesar to Domitian, written (in Latin) early in the second century AD, were published probably under Hadrian. His narratives preserve intriguing details excluded by T. as incompatible with the grandeur of historiography, but the material is often chronologically unanchored. Finally, Dio's monumental *Roman History*, narrating (in Greek) events from the origins of Rome until 229, was originally an ambitious work, but the portions relating to the civil wars are unfortunately only preserved in fragments

---

[82] Syme (1958a) 674–6.

[83] Josephus (*c.* 37/38–100), Plutarch (before 50 – after 120), Suetonius (*c.* 70–130), Cassius Dio (*c.* 164–after 229).

or epitomes. Comparative analysis of all these texts can shed fascinating light on T.'s 'workshop' by revealing what has been omitted, modified or expanded.[84]

Some central scenes feature across the board. Otho's suicide is the most obvious example of a purple passage that must have appeared in the common source (T. 2.47–51, Plut. *Oth*. 15–17, Suet. *Otho* 9.3–12.2, Dio 64.11–15).[85] The broad pattern of events is similar in each account. Otho, waiting calmly for news of the battle, hears about his defeat and faces extraordinary protestations of loyalty from his soldiers. He addresses them and then retires, taking time to comfort his young nephew and his friends. His preparations are then interrupted by the troops, who are intimidating the departing senators, at which point he intervenes to secure their safety. After this, he goes to bed, sleeps well, and kills himself at dawn.

Yet within this narrative sequence, there are suggestive differences of detail and emphasis between the accounts which reflect the individual authors' distinctive concerns and interests: (i) In all versions except T.'s, a pivotal moment is the dramatic suicide of a soldier who kills himself before Otho to validate news of the defeat (Suet. *Otho* 10.1, Plut. *Oth*. 15.3, Dio 64.11). T. moves this entire scene to a Vitellian context (3.54), perhaps in order not to upstage Otho and diminish his heroism by having a soldier show him the way. Plutarch especially finds this suicide a powerful device, as it underscores his central thesis about the terrifying power of soldiers gripped by irrational passions (*Galb*. 1.4, *Oth*. 17.11–12. (ii) Suetonius seeks credibility for his account by citing the evidence of his own father, who had served as a tribune under Otho, for the emperor's attitude towards civil war and for his reaction to the soldier's public suicide. None of the other accounts refers directly to a source at this point. (iii) Only T. gives an expanded version of Otho's consolatory speech to his nephew, an ideal vehicle to enhance the emotive power of the whole suicide narrative. Suetonius gives no extended speeches, in keeping with his techniques elsewhere in his biographies. Plutarch *Oth*. 15 and Dio 64.13 give versions of Otho's final speech to the soldiers (47.1n. *inquit*), but unlike these two, T. blends touches that ennoble Otho with his recriminations of Vitellius (despite overtly claiming to blame nobody), encapsulating the emperor's peculiar mix of laudable and disreputable character traits; and where in the parallel tradition Otho speaks about specific *exempla* from the past, T.'s Otho boldly visualises himself as an *exemplum* for the future (47.2n. *penes me exemplum erit*). T.'s extensive and carefully constructed speeches contribute to his characterisation of protagonists and enhance his historical analysis. (iv) Where Plutarch says that Otho

---

[84] There are traces especially in Plutarch, Suetonius and T. of a 'common source'. T. probably did not consult Plutarch as his main source, while Suetonius is likely to have consulted both T. and the 'common source' (Syme (1958a) 674–6). See Martin (1981) 189–96 for close consideration of the parallel tradition in connection with *Histories* 2. Hardy (1890) and Mooney (1930) are still useful, as is Damon (2003) 24–30, 291–302, 304–6.

[85] Other cases relevant to *Histories* 2 are the final battle at Bedriacum (T. *H*. 39–44, Plut. *Oth*. 11–14, Suet. *Otho* 9, Dio 64.10.2–3), Vitellius' gruesome visit to the battlefield (T. *H*. 2.70, Suet. *Vit*. 10.3, Dio 65.1.3), Vespasian's proclamation as emperor (T. *H*. 2.80.1, Jos. *BJ* 4.601–4, Suet. *Ves*. 6.3, Dio 65.8.4) and Vitellius' sacrifices to Nero's spirit after arriving in Rome (T. *H*. 2.95.1, Suet. *Vit*. 11.2, Dio 65.7.3).

slept soundly enough for the attendants outside the room to hear him snoring (*Oth.* 17.3), T. avoids this point, perhaps considering it incompatible with the dignity of his genre (49.2n. *noctem . . . non insomnem*). Plutarch may have had special reasons for including the detail, in that it aligns his Otho with Cato the Younger, who also slept well (and snored loudly) on the night before his suicide (Plut. *Cat. Mi.* 70.3).

There are not many scenes across the parallel tradition which can be analysed quite so closely as Otho's suicide, since individual authors often treat material on very different scales (and in any case the loss of Plutarch's *Vitellius* reduces the scope for multiple points of comparison with the parallel tradition for *Histories* 2.52–101). Yet details shared between two or more authors that are given a different emphasis or framed in distinctive ways can often be revealing. Some examples (not an exhaustive list) will illustrate this: (i) Where Plutarch says that Otho's praetorians are keen for the final battle so that they can return to their pampered life in Rome (33.3n. *praetoriarum . . . manus*), T. omits the detail, instead casting the men's unquestioning loyalty to Otho as noble, avoiding the easy stereotype of hedonistic soldiers and anticipating their crucial future role as supporters of Otho's 'avenger', Vespasian. This slant in T. is part of a wider tragic patterning surrounding Otho's end. (ii) In the parallel tradition, Vitellius travels from the north in the most exquisite boats garlanded with wreaths (Suet. *Vit.* 10.2), evoking a mode of transport more usually associated with Cleopatra and the east. T., avoiding the obvious, plays down this element (2.59.2). This allows his account of Vitellius' decadent journey to build to a crescendo (2.87–8), adding narrative tension. (iii) When T. documents the early omen of the collapsing cypress tree that instantly took root again to foreshadow Vespasian's success (2.78.2), he is highly selective, passing over other omens recorded by Suetonius (78.2n. *uetera omina*). It is significant that he focalises the detail through Vespasian, enhancing his characterisation, whereas Suetonius presents it from an authorial viewpoint (*Ves.* 5.4). T. also specifies that the tree sprang up *eodem uestigio* (2.78.2), adding a detail not in Suetonius to sharpen the omen's significance. (iv) In T. Vespasian's proclamation is set in motion when he comes out of his quarters and the soldiers finally have access to him (80.1n. *egressum cubiculo*). The detail is not in Josephus or Suetonius, but such a mundane part of the daily routine triggers bathos after all the grand Flavian planning (which crucially precedes the proclamation, undercutting pro-Flavian versions suggesting that the coup was driven by a spontaneous move on the part of the soldiers). (v) In T. Mucianus drums up support during a public address in the theatre at Antioch through a well-judged fiction that Vitellius was planning to transfer soldiers from Germany to Syria and *vice versa*. A partial version of this strategic propaganda is in the parallel tradition (though only the German legionaries are ear-marked for transfer to the east), but it is not explicitly attributed to Mucianus (Suet. *Ves.* 6.4). Instead T. uses the detail to enhance the characterisation of Vespasian's invaluable and politically astute associate. (vi) In T., the *III Gallica* legion at Aquileia, distraught at news of Otho's defeat, tears Vitellius' name from the standards and seizes the funds kept in the camp (85.1n. *laceratis . . . praeferentibus*). Yet Suetonius explicitly says that the soldiers inscribed Vespasian's name on the standards (*Ves.* 6.3). T.'s violent and chaotic soldiers show no overt support for

Vespasian at this point, only turning to him later as an opportunistic way to excuse
their outburst. This detail further pulls against the keynote of pro-Flavian propaganda.

It is also revealing for T.'s historiographical concerns to clarify scenes included
by him that are entirely absent from the parallel tradition. Most conspicuously, the
parallel tradition shows much less interest in events taking place in the provinces. So
T. is our only source for events on Corsica (2.16), the murder of Lucceius Albinus, the
ambitious governor of Mauretania (2.58–59.1), the revolt of Mariccus (2.61) and the
murderous activities of Aponius Saturninus in Moesia (2.85.2). Moreover, the parallel
tradition has little time for detailed elements of the military campaign, so that T. alone
covers scenes such as the Othonians' diversionary raid on Gallia Narbonensis (2.12–
15). If Dio's historical narrative had survived intact, then the situation could have
been different, but Plutarch and Suetonius were writing biographies of emperors:
the activities of intermediate military commanders were therefore of little concern
to them, particularly if their imperial subjects were completely absent from these
campaigns. Indeed, in the *Vitellius*, Suetonius manages to get away without even once
mentioning Vitellius' generals, Caecina and Valens; and the Flavian general Antonius
Primus makes only a token appearance in the final chapter (*Vit.* 18; remarkably, he
is absent from the *Ves.*). Finally, the parallel tradition is much less concerned than T.
about senatorial business, such as Vibius Crispus' attack on Annius Faustus in Otho's
absence (2.10). Where the other authors do focus on Vibius Crispus (10.1n.), it is to
give his biting witticisms about particular emperors (Suet. *Dom.* 3.1, Dio 65.2.3). T.
instead wants to introduce a dubious figure who will play an increasingly important
part under the Flavians.

10. PRO-FLAVIAN HISTORIOGRAPHY

T. is clearly ambivalent about the tiresome flood of pro-Flavian accounts which positively 'spin' the events of the civil war after the event to flatter the new regime. Both
his measured denunciation of historians who recast the Vitellian general Caecina's
treachery as *cura pacis* and *amor rei publicae* (2.101.1) and his programmatic sketch of
the decline of historiography after the battle of Actium in 31 BC (1.1.1) are part of a
wider strategy designed to show his efforts to swim against the prevailing political tide.
Painstaking analysis of the sources and a consistently measured outlook were the only
ways for T. to avoid being duped into partiality and producing merely a superficially
repackaged version of the same old material.[86] What is at stake for T. is no less than
the credibility of his historical narrative and ultimately, his own posthumous fame.
Although his friend Pliny was brazenly confident about the enduring status of the

---

[86] T. still faces criticism for being fooled by pro-Flavian sources, particularly in his portrait of
Antonius Primus. Chilver (1979) 247 and Wellesley (1972) 15 suggest that T. used a hostile source
for the initial character-sketch at 2.86, but then switched to a more friendly source for the more
positive portrayal of the general in *Histories* 3, creating an inconsistent character as a result. Ash
(1999) 148–9 challenges this view.

Histories (auguror nec me fallit augurium, historias tuas immortales futuras, Ep. 7.33.1), T. faced a real challenge in writing a fresh new historical work, untainted by a pro-Flavian outlook. That he himself had enjoyed a flourishing career under the Flavians (1.1.3) hardly helped: it compromised his credibility for his readers from the very start, even if the outspoken tone of the *Agricola* had shown that he was more than ready to be critical of his former patron Domitian.[87]

Histories 2 presents material where the potential for producing an uncritically pro-Flavian account was especially rich.[88] The emergence of Vespasian's challenge (2.1–7) and his proclamation as emperor (2.74–86) is an obvious danger area, but so too is the centrepiece of the book, the Vitellians' defeat of Otho's army (2.39–45), as well as Vitellius' triumphant advance towards Rome (2.57–73) and establishment of his regime (2.87–101). Essentially, the worse the picture of the Vitellian victors, the more justified Vespasian's intervention will seem; and the fact that, at the time, Vespasian's side blatantly tried to woo the defeated Othonian soldiers to join them generated a lively propaganda campaign during the conflict, which cast the dead Otho as a hero emotively appealing to Vespasian to avenge him.[89]

T. uses a range of techniques to demonstrate to his readers that he is no tame Flavian puppet. The most cogent involves the arrangement of events within the narrative. So, although pro-Flavian accounts of Vespasian's rise to power judiciously post-date his challenge as the only possible response to Vitellius' 'decadent' principate (Jos. *BJ* 4.588–604), T. makes it clear that Otho is still *princeps* when the seeds for the Flavian challenge are first planted (1.3n. *se . . . obsidem*; also *nec referre Vitellium an Othonem superstitem fortuna faceret*, 2.7.1). T.'s decision to split the account of the Flavians' early musings about making an imperial challenge, as Titus is en route to congratulate Galba (2.1–7), from the main narrative of Vespasian's proclamation as emperor (2.74–86) is a powerful way to show that this campaign was well-planned and pre-meditated. Indeed, the suggestive chronological arrangement allows at least five and a half months for the Flavians to plan their challenge.[90] Thus, pro-Flavian images of the soldiers' 'spontaneous' demands that an 'unwilling' Vespasian should become emperor seem hollow and contrived in comparison.

That said, T. uses a similar technique of fragmentation to cast the Vitellians in a dim light. By splitting his account of their march from northern Italy to Rome into two parts (2.57–73, 87–89), he creates the impression of a sluggish, lazy journey aptly reflecting the passive and destructive personality of the new *princeps*. Whether

---

[87] See esp. *Agr.* 43–6. On the prologue to the *Histories*, see Christes (1995), Marincola (1999), and Damon (2003) 77–82.

[88] On pro-Flavian propaganda, see Briessmann (1955), Nicols (1978), and Ramage (1983).

[89] On the Flavians' attempts to woo the Othonian soldiers, see Ash (1999) 87. The letter (possibly forged) in which Otho in a final request instructed Vespasian to avenge him is particularly relevant (Suet. *Ves.* 6.4).

[90] Broad arrangement of the narrative is reinforced by smaller details including suggestive pluperfect tenses of strategic verbs (74.1n. *consilia sociauerat*).

this presentation accurately reflects the real duration of the journey has been questioned (57–73 introduction). Yet T.'s agenda is not to whitewash the Vitellians, nor to
address the problem of pro-Flavian sources by simply reversing the polarity. Instead,
in accordance with the moralising agenda of ancient historiography, he aims to
acknowledge the damage inflicted on Italy and her citizens by *all* sides in the civil
war, including the victors: Vitellian culpability was already well established in the
tradition, but the Flavians had tended to escape censure. That was where the balance
needed to be redressed and that is where T. is often at his most subtle in presenting material. So, when noting that Vitellius spent 900 million sesterces during his
short principate, he introduces the point with a cautious *creditur* (95.3n. *interuertisse
creditur*); and he remains commendably cautious about the victors' finances, reporting
that the Flavians arranged for a loan of 60 million HS from private sources, either
from real need or to make it seem that way (4.47), so as to cast aspersions on the
dead Vitellius. T. is nobody's fool. Similarly when observing that Vitellius used to
accompany Nero on his singing tours, he says that he did not do this under obligation, as *honestissimus quisque* did (2.71.1). Yet Suetonius explicitly attaches this story
positively to Vespasian (*Ves.* 4.4), who was coerced, but T. does not name him. This
is a small point, but typifies how T. resists the prevailing adulation of the victorious
dynasty. Even when T. is positive about Vespasian, there is often a sting in the tail
(82.2n. *quibusdam fortuna . . . fuit*). This 'muting' of praise is best exemplified in T.'s
lukewarm tribute to Vespasian as *solusque omnium ante se principum in melius mutatus est*
(1.50.4).[91]

11. THE TEXT

That we are able to read the *Histories* today in modern editions is an extraordinary piece
of luck. It is all thanks to the chance survival of a single manuscript, the so-called Codex
Laurentianus Mediceus 68.2, now preserved in the Biblioteca Mediceo-Laurentiana
in Florence.[92] This manuscript was written in Beneventan script at the monastery
of Montecassino in the eleventh century and contains *Histories* 1–5 and *Annals* 11–16,
as well as the major works of Apuleius.[93] In fact, the surviving books of the *Histories*
(even though they were written before the *Annals*) feature as *Annals* 17–21, a natural
arrangement given the relative subject matter of T.'s two historical works, which
were apparently combined by an editor at a relatively early stage. Indeed, Jerome

---

[91] Another effort to swim against the tide is T.'s acknowledgement that Civilis' Batavian revolt
is not straightforwardly a 'foreign' war, but one that developed from Flavian activities during
the civil war (69.1n. *interno . . . parantibus*).

[92] On this manuscript, see Lowe (1929), Heilig (1935), Zelzer (1973), Oliver (1976) and Tarrant
(1983) 407–9. Wellesley's edition (1989) ix–xx has a useful bibliography on the various *codices*, as
well as listing editions of the *Histories* and discussions of textual problems.

[93] On the Beneventan script, see Lowe (1980).

(*c.* AD 347–420) in his commentary on *Zacchariah* 14.1–2 refers to thirty books of (what he calls) Tacitus' *Lives of the Caesars*, showing that he was reading a consolidated edition of the *Annals* and the *Histories*.

The Codex Laurentianus Mediceus 68.2 is known today by the siglum **M**, or more accurately **M II**, 'the second Medicean', to distinguish it from the Codex Laurentianius Mediceus 68.1, 'the first Medicean', a manuscript written in Germany in the ninth century containing *Annals* 1–6.[94] How accurate **M II** is in relation to T.'s original text is unclear. There is a chronological gap of at least 950 years between T.'s autograph of the *Histories* and the point at which **M II** was copied, allowing scope for errors to creep in as the text was transmitted by various scribes. Scholars detect two stages of transmission. The first (and the closest to T.) involves a manuscript written in rustic capitals in the fifth century or earlier. We can deduce its existence from the sort of transcription errors in **M II** that are often made by later scribes copying manuscripts in rustic capitals. However, the scribe of **M II** himself was probably copying, not the early manuscript in rustic capitals, but a later 'intermediary' manuscript written in a minuscule hand.

Although **M II** is the closest that we can get to T.'s original text, the manuscript itself has suffered some physical damage, which has left gaps (1.69–75.2, 1.86.2–2.2.2), and there are also errors in the Latin deriving from scribes' mistakes. Many of these are relatively simple to correct, and involve straightforward supplements or excisions by later editors.[95] In other cases the correct reading is less immediately obvious, but suggested emendations of the text have been generally accepted by successive editors. Yet there are inevitably still instances where modern editors are at variance about the correct reading and interpretation of particular passages.[96] In tackling such problems, textual critics must turn to the so-called *recentiores*, the later manuscripts copied from **M II**, which offer an invaluable tool in restoring the text of **M II**.[97] These *recentiores* generally pre-date the *editio princeps*, the first printed edition of the *Histories* (combined with *Annals* 11–16), which was produced by the press of 'Spira' in Venice (undated, but generally assumed to be from 1468 or 1470). It was only in 1515 that Filippo Beraldo the Younger produced the first edition of Tacitus' *Annals* 'reuniting' books 1–6 with 11–16.

The text printed here uses the paragraph and sentence numbering of H. Heubner's Teubner text (Stuttgart 1978), but some spelling, punctuation and paragraphing are different, and there is no apparatus criticus.[98] Where the text is substantially different

---

[94] In the commentary, I refer throughout to **M**, as shorthand for **M II**.

[95] The modern convention is to indicate editorial supplements with angle brackets (< >) and excisions with square brackets ([ ]). An *obelus* or 'dagger' (†) indicates an unresolved corruption.

[96] On the process of editing texts, see *OCD*[3] 'textual criticism', West (1973), Reynolds and Wilson (1991) and Nisbet (1991).

[97] On the thirty-one *recentiores*, see Wellesley (1972) 28–31.

[98] The Teubner edition of K. Wellesley (Leipzig 1989) has the most substantial apparatus criticus of the modern editions.

from that of Heubner, there is explanation in the notes. The most important departures
are:

Heubner	Ash
1.1 *quo*	1.1 *quod*
7.1 *discordia militis ignauia luxurie et suismet uitiis*	7.1 *discordiam his ignauiam luxuriem; et suismet uitiis*
18.2 *[qui]*	18.2 *quin*
28.2 *sin uictoriae [sanitas sustentaculum] columen in Italia uerteretur*	28.2 *sin uictoria incolumi in Italia uerteretur*
40 *confluentes Padi et Aduae fluminum*	40 *confluentes †Padi et Aduae† fluminum*
59.3 *in solacium*	59.3 *in supplicium*
68.1 *inuidiam Vitellio auxisset*	68.1 *inuidiam †bello† auxisset*
76.2 *[tam] quam salutare*	76.2 *tam salutare*
88.1 *consensu*	88.1 *consensus*
100.3 *legiones, Cremonam, pars Hostiliam petere iussae*	100.3 *legiones, <pars> Cremonam, pars Hostiliam petere iussae*

The spelling has been regularised according to the *OLD* (so prepositional prefixes are
elided with initial consonants: e.g. *aggredior* for *adgredior*) and minuscule 'v' has been
replaced with consonantal 'u'. In the punctuation, a colon introduces an indirect
statement or text that refers back to what immediately precedes the colon. A semicolon
separates syntactically complete antitheses. Commas set off appositions and ablative
absolute clauses, especially at the end or in mid-sentence.

CORNELI TACITI HISTORIARVM

LIBER SECVNDVS

Struebat iam fortuna in diuersa parte terrarum initia causasque imperio, 1 quod uaria sorte laetum rei publicae aut atrox, ipsis principibus prosperum uel exitio fuit. Titus Vespasianus, e Iudaea incolumi adhuc Galba missus a patre, causam profectionis officium erga principem et maturam petendis honoribus iuuentam ferebat, sed uolgus fingendi auidum disperserat accitum in adoptionem. materia sermonibus senium et orbitas principis et intemperantia ciuitatis, donec unus eligatur, multos destinandi. augebat famam ipsius Titi ingenium quantaecumque fortunae 2 capax, decor <or> is cum quadam maiestate, prosperae Vespasiani res, praesaga responsa, et inclinatis ad credendum animis loco ominum etiam fortuita.

Vbi Corinthi, Achaiae urbe, certos nuntios accepit de interitu Galbae 3 et aderant qui arma Vitellii bellumque affirmarent, anxius animo paucis amicorum adhibitis cuncta utrimque perlustrat: si pergeret in urbem, nullam officii gratiam in alterius honorem suscepti, ac se Vitellio siue Othoni obsidem fore: sin rediret, offensam haud dubiam uictoris, set incertam adhuc uictoriam et concedente in partis patre filium excusatum. sin Vespasianus rem publicam susciperet, obliuiscendum offensarum de bello agitantibus.

His ac talibus inter spem metumque iactatum spes uicit. fuerunt 2 qui accensum desiderio Berenices reginae uertisse iter crederent; neque abhorrebat a Berenice iuuenilis animus, sed gerendis rebus nullum ex eo impedimentum. laetam uoluptatibus adulescentiam egit, suo quam patris imperio moderatior.

Igitur oram Achaiae et Asiae ac laeua maris praeuectus, Rhodum et 2 Cyprum insulas, inde Syriam audentioribus spatiis petebat. atque illum cupido incessit adeundi uisendique templum Paphiae Veneris, inclitum per indigenas aduenasque. haud fuerit longum initia religionis, templi ritum, formam deae (neque enim alibi sic habetur) paucis disserere.

Conditorem templi regem Aëriam uetus memoria, quidam ipsius deae 3 nomen id perhibent. Fama recentior tradita a Cinyra sacratum templum deamque ipsam conceptam mari huc appulsam; sed scientiam artemque haruspicum accitam et Cilicem Tamiram intulisse, atque ita pactum ut familiae utriusque posteri caerimoniis praesiderent. mox, ne honore nullo regium genus peregrinam stirpem antecelleret, ipsa quam intulerant scientia hospites cessere: tantum Cinyrades sacerdos consulitur. hostiae, ut 2 quisque uouit, sed mares deliguntur: certissima fides haedorum fibris.

37

sanguinem arac offundere uetitum: precibus et igne puro altaria adolentur, nec ullis imbribus quamquam in aperto madescunt. simulacrum
deae non effigie humana, continuus orbis latiore initio tenuem in ambitum metae modo exsurgens, et ratio in obscuro.

4 Titus spectata opulentia donisque regum quaeque alia laetum antiq-
uitatibus Graecorum genus incertae uetustati affingit, de nauigatione primum consuluit. postquam pandi uiam et mare prosperum accepit, de se
2 per ambages interrogat, caesis compluribus hostiis. Sostratus (sacerdotis
id nomen erat) ubi laeta et congruentia exta magnisque consultis annuere
deam uidet, pauca in praesens et solita respondens, petito secreto futura
aperit. Titus aucto animo ad patrem peruectus, suspensis prouinciarum
et exercituum mentibus, ingens rerum fiducia accessit.

3 Profligauerat bellum Iudaicum Vespasianus, oppugnatione Hierosoly-
morum reliqua, duro magis et arduo opere ob ingenium montis et peruica-
ciam superstitionis quam quo satis uirium obsessis ad tolerandas neces-
4 sitates superesset. tres, ut supra memorauimus, ipsi Vespasiano legiones
erant, exercitae bello: quattuor Mucianus obtinebat in pace, sed aemulatio et proximi exercitus gloria depulerat segnitiam, quantumque illis
roboris discrimina et labor, tantum his uigoris addiderat integra quies
et inexperti belli ardor. auxilia utrique cohortium alarumque et classes
regesque ac nomen dispari fama celebre.

5 Vespasianus acer militiae anteire agmen, locum castris capere, noctu
diuque consilio ac, si res posceret, manu hostibus obniti, cibo fortuito,
ueste habituque uix a gregario milite discrepans; prorsus, si auaritia abes-
set, antiquis ducibus par. Mucianum e contrario magnificentia et opes et
cuncta priuatum modum supergressa extollebant; aptior sermone, dispositu prouisuque ciuilium rerum peritus: egregium principatus temper-
2 amentum, si demptis utriusque uitiis solae uirtutes miscerentur. ceterum
hic Syriae, ille Iudaeae praepositus, uicinis prouinciarum administrationibus inuidia discordes, exitu demum Neronis positis odiis in medium
consuluere, primum per amicos, dein, praecipua concordiae fides, Titus
praua certamina communi utilitate aboleuerat, natura atque arte compositus alliciendis etiam Muciani moribus. tribuni centurionesque et uolgus militum industria licentia, per uirtutes per uoluptates, ut cuique ingenium, asciscebantur.

6 Antequam Titus aduentaret sacramentum Othonis acceperat uterque
exercitus, pernicibus, ut assolet, nuntiis et tarda mole ciuilis belli, quod
longa concordia quietus Oriens tunc primum parabat. namque olim
ualidissima inter se ciuium arma in Italia Galliaue uiribus Occidentis
coepta; et Pompeio, Cassio, Bruto, Antonio, quos omnes trans mare

secutum est ciuile bellum, haud prosperi exitus fuerant; auditique saepius in Syria Iudaeaque Caesares quam inspecti. nulla seditio legionum, tantum aduersus Parthos minae, uario euentu; et proximo ciuili bello turbatis aliis inconcussa ibi pax, dein fides erga Galbam. mox, ut Othonem ac 2 Vitellium scelestis armis res Romanas raptum ire uolgatum est, ne penes ceteros imperii praemia, penes ipsos tantum seruitii necessitas esset, fremere miles et uiris suas circumspicere. septem legiones statim et cum ingentibus auxiliis Syria Iudaeaque; inde continua Aegyptus duaeque legiones, hinc Cappadocia Pontusque et quidquid castrorum Armeniis praetenditur. Asia et ceterae prouinciae nec uirorum inopes et pecunia opulentae. quantum insularum mari cingitur, et parando interim bello secundum tutumque ipsum mare.

Non fallebat duces impetus militum, sed bellantibus aliis placuit 7 exspectari. bello ciuili uictores uictosque numquam solida fide coalescere, nec referre Vitellium an Othonem superstitem fortuna faceret. rebus secundis etiam egregios duces insolescere: discordiam his ignauiam luxuriem; et suismet uitiis alterum bello, alterum uictoria periturum. igi- 2 tur arma in occasionem distulere, Vespasianus Mucianusque nuper, ceteri olim mixtis consiliis, optimus quisque amore rei publicae, multos dulcedo praedarum stimulabat, alios ambiguae domi res: ita boni malique causis diuersis, studio pari, bellum omnes cupiebant.

Sub idem tempus Achaia atque Asia falso exterritae uelut Nero 8 aduentaret, uario super exitu eius rumore eoque pluribus uiuere eum fingentibus credentibusque. ceterorum casus conatusque in contextu operis dicemus: tunc seruus e Ponto siue, ut alii tradidere, libertinus ex Italia, citharae et cantus peritus, unde illi super similitudinem oris propior ad fallendum fides, adiunctis desertoribus, quos inopia uagos ingentibus promissis corruperat, mare ingreditur; ac ui tempestatum Cythnum insulam detrusus et militum quosdam ex Oriente commeantium asciuit uel abnuentes interfici iussit, et spoliatis negotiatoribus mancipiorum ualentissimum quemque armauit. centurionemque Sisennam dextras, concordiae 2 insignia, Syriaci exercitus nomine ad praetorianos ferentem uariis artibus aggressus est, donec Sisenna, clam relicta insula, trepidus et uim metuens aufugeret. inde late terror: multi ad celebritatem nominis erecti rerum nouarum cupidine et odio praesentium.

Gliscentem in dies famam fors discussit. Galatiam ac Pamphyliam 9 prouincias Calpurnio Asprenati regendas Galba permiserat. datae e classe Misenensi duae triremes ad prosequendum, cum quibus Cythnum insulam tenuit; nec defuere qui trierarchos nomine Neronis accirent. is in 2 maestitiam compositus et fidem suorum quondam militum inuocans, ut

eum in Syria aut Aegypto sisterent orabat. trierarchi, s<eu> nutantes
seu dolo, alloquendos sibi milites et paratis omnium animis reuersuros
firmauerunt. sed Asprenati cuncta ex fide nuntiata, cuius cohortatione
expugnata nauis et interfectus quisquis ille erat. caput, insigne oculis
comaque et toruitate uoltus, in Asiam atque inde Romam peruectum
est.

10 In ciuitate discordi et ob crebras principum mutationes inter libertatem ac licentiam incerta paruae quoque res magnis motibus agebantur.
Vibius Crispus, pecunia potentia ingenio inter claros magis quam inter
bonos, Annium Faustum equestris ordinis, qui temporibus Neronis delationes factitauerat, ad cognitionem senatus uocabat; nam recens Galbae
principatu censuerant patres, ut accusatorum causae noscerentur. id senatus consultum uarie iactatum et, prout potens uel inops reus inciderat,
2 infirmum aut ualidum, retinebat adhuc <aliquid> terroris. et propria
ui Crispus incubuerat delatorem fratris sui peruertere, traxeratque magnam senatus partem, ut indefensum et inauditum dedi ad exitium postularent. contra apud alios nihil aeque reo proderat quam nimia potentia accusatoris: dari tempus, edi crimina, quamuis inuisum ac nocentem
3 more tamen audiendum censebant. et ualuere primo dilataque in paucos
dies cognitio: mox damnatus est Faustus, nequaquam eo assensu ciuitatis
quem pessimis moribus meruerat: quippe ipsum Crispum easdem accu-
sationes cum praemio exercuisse meminerant, nec poena criminis sed
ultor displicebat.

11 Laeta interim Othoni principia belli, motis ad imperium eius e Dalmatia Pannoniaque exercitibus. fuere quattuor legiones, e quibus bina
milia praemissa; ipsae modicis interuallis sequebantur, septima a Galba
conscripta, ueteranae undecima ac tertia decima et praecipui fama quartadecimani, rebellione Britanniae compressa. addiderat gloriam Nero
eligendo ut potissimos, unde longa illis erga Neronem fides et erecta in
Othonem studia. sed quo plus uirium ac roboris e fiducia tarditas inerat.
2 agmen legionum alae cohortesque praeueniebant; et ex ipsa urbe haud
spernenda manus, quinque praetoriae cohortes et equitum uexilla cum
legione prima, ac deforme insuper auxilium, duo milia gladiatorum, sed
per ciuilia arma etiam seueris ducibus usurpatum. his copiis rector additus
Annius Gallus, cum Vestricio Spurinna ad occupandas Padi ripas praemissus, quoniam prima consiliorum frustra ceciderant, transgresso iam
3 Alpis Caecina, quem sisti intra Gallias posse sperauerat. ipsum Othonem
comitabantur speculatorum lecta corpora cum ceteris praetoriis cohortibus, ueterani e praetorio, classicorum ingens numerus. nec illi segne aut

corruptum luxu iter, sed lorica ferrea usus est et ante signa pedes ire, horridus, incomptus famaeque dissimilis.

Blandiebatur coeptis fortuna, possessa per mare et naues maiore Ital- **12** iae parte penitus usque ad initium maritimarum Alpium, quibus temptandis aggrediendaeque prouinciae Narbonensi Suedium Clementem, Antonium Nouellum, Aemilium Pacensem duces dederat. sed Pacensis per licentiam militum uinctus, Antonio Nouello nulla auctoritas: Suedius Clemens ambitioso imperio regebat, ut aduersus modestiam disciplinae corruptus, ita proeliorum auidus.

Non Italia adiri nec loca sedesque patriae uidebantur: tamquam **2** externa litora et urbes hostium urere uastare rapere, eo atrocius quod nihil usquam prouisum aduersum metus. pleni agri, apertae domus; occursantes domini iuxta coniuges et liberos securitate pacis et belli malo circumueniebantur. maritimas tum Alpes tenebat procurator Mar- **3** ius Maturus. is concita gente (nec deest iuuentus) arcere prouinciae finibus Othonianos intendit: sed primo impetu caesi disiectique montani, ut quibus temere collectis, non castra, non ducem noscitantibus, neque in uictoria decus esset neque in fuga flagitium.

Irritatus eo proelio Othonis miles uertit iras in municipium Albintim- **13** ilium. quippe in acie nihil praedae, inopes agrestes et uilia arma; nec capi poterant, pernix genus et gnari locorum: sed calamitatibus insontium expleta auaritia. auxit inuidiam praeclaro exemplo femina Ligus, **2** quae filio abdito, cum simul pecuniam occultari milites credidissent eoque per cruciatus interrogarent ubi filium occuleret, uterum ostendens latere respondit, nec ullis deinde terroribus aut morte constantiam uocis egregiae mutauit.

Imminere prouinciae Narbonensi, in uerba Vitellii adactae, classem **14** Othonis trepidi nuntii Fabio Valenti attulere; aderant legati coloniarum auxilium orantes. duas Tungrorum cohortes, quattuor equitum turmas, uniuersam Treuirorum alam cum Iulio Classico praefecto misit, e quibus pars in colonia Foroiuliensi retenta, ne omnibus copiis in terrestre iter uersis uacuo mari classis acceleraret. duodecim equitum turmae et lecti e cohortibus aduersus hostem iere, quibus adiuncta Ligurum cohors, uetus loci auxilium, et quingenti Pannonii, nondum sub signis.

Nec mora proelio: sed acies ita instructa ut pars classicorum, mixtis **2** paganis, in colles mari propinquos exsurgeret, quantum inter colles ac litus aequi loci praetorianus miles expleret, in ipso mari ut adnexa classis et pugnae parata conuersa et minaci fronte praetenderetur: Vitelliani, quibus minor peditum uis, in equite robur, Alpinos proximis iugis, cohortis

3 densis ordinibus post equitem locant. Treuirorum turmae obtulere se
hosti incaute, cum exciperet contra ueteranus miles, simul a latere saxis
urgeret apta ad iaciendum etiam paganorum manus, qui sparsi inter
milites, strenui ignauique, in uictoria idem audebant. additus perculsis
terror inuecta in terga pugnantium classe: ita undique clausi, deletaeque
omnes copiae forent ni uictorem exercitum attinuisset obscurum noctis,
obtentui fugientibus.

15 Nec Vitelliani quamquam uicti quieuere: accitis auxiliis securum
hostem ac successu rerum socordius agentem inuadunt. caesi uigiles, perrupta castra, trepidatum apud naues, donec sidente paulatim metu, occu-
2 pato iuxta colle defensi, mox irrupere. atrox ibi caedes, et Tungrarum
cohortium praefecti sustentata diu acie telis obruuntur. ne Othonianis
quidem incruenta uictoria fuit, quorum improuide secutos conuersi equites circumuenerunt. ac uelut pactis indutiis, ne hinc classis inde eques
subitam formidinem inferrent, Vitelliani retro Antipolim Narbonensis
Galliae municipium, Othoniani Albingaunum interioris Liguriae reuertere.

16 Corsicam ac Sardiniam ceterasque proximi maris insulas fama uictricis classis in partibus Othonis tenuit. sed Corsicam prope afflixit Decumi
Picarii procuratoris temeritas, tanta mole belli nihil in summam profutura, ipsi exitiosa. namque Othonis odio iuuare Vitellium Corsorum
2 uiribus statuit, inani auxilio etiam si prouenisset. uocatis principibus insulae consilium aperit, et contra dicere ausos, Claudium Pyrrichum trierarchum Liburnicarum ibi nauium, Quintium Certum equitem Romanum,
interfici iubet: quorum morte exterriti qui aderant, simul ignara et alieni
metus socia imperitorum turba in uerba Vitellii iurauere. sed ubi dilectum
agere Pacarius et inconditos homines fatigare militiae muneribus occepit,
laborem insolitum perosi infirmitatem suam reputabant: insulam esse
quam incolerent, et longe Germaniam uirisque legionum; direptos uas-
tatosque classe etiam quos cohortes alaeque protegerent. et auersi repente
3 animi, nec tamen aperta ui: aptum tempus insidiis legere. digressis qui
Pacarium frequentabant, nudus et auxilii inops balineis interficitur; trucidati et comites. capita ut hostium ipsi interfectores ad Othonem tulere;
neque eos aut Otho praemio affecit aut puniit Vitellius, in multa colluuie
rerum maioribus flagitiis permixtos.

17 Aperuerat iam Italiam bellumque transmiserat, ut supra memorauimus, ala Siliana, nullo apud quemquam Othonis fauore, nec quia
Vitellium mallent, sed longa pax ad omne seruitium fregerat faciles occupantibus et melioribus incuriosos. florentissimum Italiae latus, quantum
inter Padum Alpesque camporum et urbium, armis Vitellii (namque et

praemissae a Caecina cohortes aduenerant) tenebatur. capta Pannonio- 2
rum cohors apud Cremonam; intercepti centum equites ac mille classici
inter Placentiam Ticinumque. quo successu Vitellianus miles non iam flumine aut ripis arcebatur; irritabat quin etiam Batauos Transrhenanosque
Padus ipse, quem repente contra Placentiam transgressi raptis quibusdam
exploratoribus ita ceteros terruere ut adesse omnem Caecinae exercitum
trepidi ac falsi nuntiarent.

Certum erat Spurinnae (is enim Placentiam obtinebat) necdum uenisse 18
Caecinam et, si propinquaret, coercere intra munimenta militem nec tris
praetorias cohortes et mille uexillarios cum paucis equitibus ueterano
exercitui obicere. sed indomitus miles et belli ignarus correptis signis 2
uexillisque ruere et retinenti duci tela intentare, spretis centurionibus
tribunisque: quin pro<di> Othonem et accitum Caecinam clamitabant.
fit temeritatis alienae comes Spurinna, primo coactus, mox uelle simulans,
quo plus auctoritatis inesset consiliis si seditio mitesceret.

Postquam in conspectu Padus et nox appetebat uallari castra placuit. is 19
labor urbano militi insolitus contundit animos. tum uetustissimus quisque
castigare credulitatem suam, metum ac discrimen ostendere si cum
exercitu Caecina patentibus campis tam paucas cohortes circumfudisset.
iamque totis castris modesti sermones, et inserentibus se centurionibus
tribunisque laudari prouidentia ducis quod coloniam uirium et opum ualidam robur ac sedem bello legisset. ipse postremo Spurinna, non tam cul- 2
pam exprobrans quam rationem ostendens, relictis exploratoribus ceteros
Placentiam reduxit minus turbidos et imperia accipientes. solidati muri,
propugnacula addita, auctae turres, prouisa parataque non arma modo
sed obsequium et parendi amor, quod solum illis partibus defuit, cum
uirtutis haud paeniteret.

At Caecina, uelut relicta post Alpes saeuitia ac licentia, modesto 20
agmine per Italiam incessit. ornatum ipsius municipia et coloniae in superbiam trahebant, quod uersicolori sagulo, bracas, barbarum tegumen,
indutus togatos alloqueretur. uxorem quoque eius Saloninam, quamquam
in nullius iniuriam insignis equo ostroque ueheretur, tamquam laesi
grauabantur, insita mortalibus natura recentem aliorum felicitatem
acribus oculis introspicere modumque fortunae a nullis magis exigere
quam quos in aequo uiderunt.

Caecina Padum transgressus, temptata Othonianorum fide per collo- 2
quium et promissa, isdem petitus, postquam pax et concordia speciosis et
irritis nominibus iactata sunt, consilia curasque in oppugnationem Placentiae magno terrore uertit, gnarus ut initia belli prouenissent famam in
cetera fore.

21   Sed primus dies impetu magis quam ueterani exercitus artibus
transactus: aperti incautique muros subiere, cibo uinoque praegraues.
in eo certamine pulcherrimum amphitheatri opus, situm extra muros,
conflagrauit, siue ab oppugnatoribus incensum, dum faces et glandes et
missilem ignem in obsessos iaculantur, siue ab obsessis, dum regerunt.
2   municipale uolgus, pronum ad suspiciones, fraude illata ignis alimenta
credidit a quibusdam ex uicinis coloniis inuidia et aemulatione, quod
nulla in Italia moles tam capax foret. quocumque casu accidit, dum atro-
ciora metuebantur, in leui habitum, reddita securitate, tamquam nihil
grauius pati potuissent, maerebant.
3   Ceterum multo suorum cruore pulsus Caecina, et nox parandis
operibus absumpta. Vitelliani pluteos cratesque et uineas subfodiendis
muris protegendisque oppugnatoribus, Othoniani sudes et immensas
lapidum ac plumbi aerisque molis perfringendis obruendisque hostibus
4   expediunt. utrimque pudor, utrimque gloria et diuersae exhortationes
hinc legionum et Germanici exercitus robur, inde urbanae militiae et
praetoriarum cohortium decus attollentium; illi ut segnem et desidem et
circo ac theatris corruptum militem, hi peregrinum et externum increpabant. simul Othonem ac Vitellium celebrantes culpantesue uberioribus
inter se probris quam laudibus stimulabantur.
22   Vixdum orto die plena propugnatoribus moenia, fulgentes armis
uirisque campi: densum legionum agmen, sparsa auxiliorum manus
altiora murorum sagittis aut saxis incessere, neglecta aut aeuo fluxa comminus aggredi. ingerunt desuper Othoniani pila librato magis et certo
ictu aduersus temere subeuntes cohortes Germanorum, cantu truci et
2   more patrio nudis corporibus super umeros scuta quatientium. legionarius
pluteis et cratibus tectus subruit muros, instruit aggerem, molitur portas:
contra praetoriani dispositos ad id ipsum molares ingenti pondere ac
fragore prouoluunt. pars subeuntium obruti, pars confixi et exsangues
aut laceri: cum augeret stragem trepidatio eoque acrius e moenibus uol-
nerarentur, redi<e>re infracta partium fama.
3   Et Caecina pudore coeptae temere oppugnationis, ne irrisus ac uanus
isdem castris assideret, traiecto rursus Pado Cremonam petere intendit. tradidere sese abeunti Turullius Cerialis cum compluribus classicis et
Iulius Briganticus cum paucis equitum, hic praefectus alae in Batauis genitus, ille primipilaris et Caecinae haud alienus, quod ordines in Germania
duxerat.
23   Spurinna comperto itinere hostium defensam Placentiam, quaeque
acta et quid Caecina pararet, Annium Gallum per litteras docet. Gallus legionem primam in auxilium Placentiae ducebat, diffisus paucitati

cohortium, ne longius obsidium et uim Germanici exercitus parum tolerarent. ubi pulsum Caecinam pergere Cremonam accepit, aegre coercitam 2
legionem et pugnandi ardore usque ad seditionem progressam Bedriaci
sistit. inter Veronam Cremonamque situs est uicus, duabus iam Romanis
cladibus notus infaustusque.

Isdem diebus a Martio Macro haud procul Cremona prospere 3
pugnatum; namque promptus animi Martius transuectos nauibus gladiatores in aduersam Padi ripam repente effudit. turbata ibi Vitellianorum auxilia, et ceteris Cremonam fugientibus caesi qui restiterant: sed
repressus uincentium impetus ne nouis subsidiis firmati hostes fortunam
proelii mutarent. suspectum id Othonianis fuit, omnia ducum facta praue 4
aestimantibus. certatim, ut quisque animo ignauus, procax ore, Annium
Gallum et Suetonium Paulinum et Marium Celsum – nam eos quoque
Otho praefecerat – uariis criminibus incessebant. acerrima seditionum 5
ac discordiae incitamenta, interfectores Galbae scelere et metu uecordes
miscere cuncta, modo palam turbidis uocibus, modo occultis ad Othonem litteris; qui humillimo cuique credulus, bonos metuens trepidabat,
rebus prosperis incertus et inter aduersa melior. igitur Titianum fratrem
accitum bello praeposuit.

Interea Paulini et Celsi ductu res egregie gestae. angebant Caecinam **24**
nequiquam omnia coepta et senescens exercitus sui fama. pulsus Placentia, caesis nuper auxiliis, etiam per concursum exploratorum, crebra magis quam digna memoratu proelia, inferior, propinquante Fabio
Valente, ne omne belli decus illuc concederet, reciperare gloriam auidius
quam consultius properabat. ad duodecimum a Cremona (locus Casto- 2
rum uocatur) ferocissimos auxiliarium imminentibus uiae lucis occultos
componit: equites procedere longius iussi et irritato proelio sponte refugi
festinationem sequentium elicere, donec insidiae coorerentur.

Proditum id Othonianis ducibus, et curam peditum Paulinus, equitum 3
Celsus sumpsere. tertiae decimae legionis uexillum, quattuor auxiliorum
cohortes et quingenti equites in sinistro locantur; aggerem uiae tres praetoriae cohortes altis ordinibus obtinuere; dextra fronte prima legio incessit
cum duabus auxiliaribus cohortibus et quingentis equitibus: super hos ex
praetorio auxiliisque mille equites, cumulus prosperis aut subsidium laborantibus, ducebantur.

Antequam miscerentur acies, terga uertentibus Vitellianis, Celsus doli **25**
prudens repressit suos: Vitelliani temere exsurgentes cedente sensim Celso
longius secuti ultro in insidias praecipitantur; nam a lateribus cohortes,
legionum aduersa frons, et subito discursu terga cinxerant equites. signum 2
pugnae non statim a Suetonio Paulino pediti datum: cunctator natura

et cui cauta potius consilia cum ratione quam prospera ex casu placerent, compleri fossas, aperiri campum, pandi aciem iubebat, satis cito
incipi uictoriam ratus ubi prouisum foret ne uincerentur. ea cunctatione
spatium Vitellianis datum in uineas nexu traducum impeditas refugiendi;
et modica silua adhaerebat, unde rursus ausi promptissimos praetorianorum equitum interfecere. uolneratur rex Epiphanes, impigre pro Othone
pugnam ciens.

26   Tum Othonianus pedes erupit; protrita hostium acie, uersi in fugam
etiam qui subueniebant; nam Caecina non simul cohortes sed singulas
acciuerat, quae res in proelio trepidationem auxit, cum dispersos nec
usquam ualidos pauor fugientium abriperet. orta et in castris seditio
quod non uniuersi ducerentur: uinctus praefectus castrorum Iulius Gratus, tamquam fratri apud Othonem militanti proditionem ageret, cum
fratrem eius, Iulium Frontonem tribunum, Othoniani sub eodem crimine uinxissent.

2   Ceterum ea ubique formido fuit apud fugientes occursantes, in acie
pro uallo, ut deleri cum uniuerso exercitu Caecinam potuisse, ni Suetonius Paulinus receptui cecinisset, utrisque in partibus percrebru<er>it.
timuisse se Paulinus ferebat tantum insuper laboris atque itineris, ne Vitellianus miles recens e castris fessos aggrederetur et perculsis nullum retro
subsidium foret. apud paucos ea ducis ratio probata, in uolgus aduerso
rumore fuit.

27   Haud proinde id damnum Vitellianos in metum compulit quam ad
modestiam composuit: nec solum apud Caecinam, qui culpam in militem
conferebat seditioni magis quam proelio paratum: Fabii quoque Valentis copiae (iam enim Ticinum uenerat) posito hostium contemptu et
reciperandi decoris cupidine reuerentius et aequalius duci parebant.

2   Grauis alioquin seditio exarserat, quam altiore initio (neque enim
rerum a Caecina gestarum ordinem interrumpi oportuerat) repetam.
cohortes Batauorum, quas bello Neronis a quarta decima legione digres-
sas, cum Britanniam peterent, audito Vitellii motu in ciuitate Lingonum
Fabio Valenti adiunctas rettulimus, superbe agebant, ut cuius<que>
legionis tentoria accessissent, coercitos a se quartadecimanos, ablatam
Neroni Italiam atque omnem belli fortunam in ipsorum manu sitam iactantes. contumeliosum id militibus, acerbum duci; corrupta iurgiis aut
rixis disciplina; ad postremum Valens e petulantia etiam perfidiam sus-
pectabat.

28   Igitur nuntio adlato pulsam Treuirorum alam Tungrosque a classe
Othonis et Narbonensem Galliam circumiri, simul cura socios tuendi et
militari astu cohortes turbidas ac, si una forent, praeualidas dispergendi,

partem Batauorum ire in subsidium iubet. quod ubi auditum uolga-
tumque, maerere socii, fremere legiones. orbari se fortissimorum uirorum 2
auxilio; ueteres illos et tot bellorum uictores, postquam in conspectu sit
hostis, uelut ex acie abduci. si prouincia urbe et salute imperii potior sit,
omnes illuc sequerentur; sin uictoria incolumi in Italia uerteretur, non
abrumpendos ut corpori ualidissimos artus.

Haec ferociter iactando, postquam immissis lictoribus Valens coercere 29
seditionem coeptabat, ipsum inuadunt, saxa iaciunt, fugientem sequuntur. spolia Galliarum et Viennensium aurum, [et] pretia laborum suorum, occultare clamitantes, direptis sarcinis tabernacula ducis ipsamque
humum pilis et lanceis rimabantur; nam Valens seruili ueste apud decurionem equitum tegebatur. tum Alfenus Varus praefectus castrorum, defla- 2
grante paulatim seditione, addit consilium, uetitis obire uigilias centurionibus, omisso tubae sono, quo miles ad belli munia cietur. igitur torpere
cuncti, circumspectare inter se attoniti et id ipsum quod nemo regeret
pauentes; silentio patientia, postremo precibus ac lacrimis ueniam quaerebant. ut uero deformis et flens et praeter spem incolumis Valens processit, 3
gaudium miseratio fauor: uersi in laetitiam, ut est uolgus utroque immodicum, laudantes gratantesque circumdatum aquilis signisque in tribunal
ferunt. ille utili moderatione non supplicium cuiusquam poposcit, ac ne
dissimulans suspectior foret, paucos incusauit, gnarus ciuilibus bellis plus
militibus quam ducibus licere.

Munientibus castra apud Ticinum de aduersa Caecinae pugna alla- 30
tum, et prope renouata seditio tamquam fraude et cunctationibus Valentis
proelio defuissent: nolle requiem, non exspectare ducem, anteire signa,
urgere signiferos; rapido agmine Caecinae iunguntur.

Improspera Valentis fama apud exercitum Caecinae erat: expositos 2
se tanto pauciores integris hostium uiribus querebantur, simul in suam
excusationem et aduentantium robur per adulationem attollentes, ne ut
uicti et ignaui despectarentur. et quamquam plus uirium, prope duplicatus legionum auxiliorumque numerus erat Valenti, studia tamen militum in Caecinam inclinabant, super benignitatem animi, qua promptior
habebatur, etiam uigore aetatis, proceritate corporis et quodam inani
fauore. hinc aemulatio ducibus: Caecina ut foedum ac maculosum, ille 3
ut tumidum ac uanum irridebant. sed condito odio eandem utilitatem
fouere, crebris epistulis sine respectu ueniae probra Othoni obiectantes,
cum duces partium Othonis quamuis uberrima conuiciorum in Vitellium materia abstinerent. sane ante utriusque exitum, quo egregiam 31
Otho famam, Vitellius flagitiosissimam meruere, minus Vitellii ignauae
uoluptates quam Othonis flagrantissimae libidines timebantur: addiderat

huic terrorem atque odium caedes Galbae, contra illi initium belli nemo imputabat. Vitellius uentre et gula sibi inho<ne>stus, Otho luxu saeuitia audacia rei publicae exitiosior ducebatur.

2 Coniunctis Caecinae ac Valentis copiis nulla ultra penes Vitellianos mora quin totis uiribus certarent: Otho consultauit trahi bellum an for-
32 tunam experiri placeret. tunc Suetonius Paulinus dignum fama sua ratus, qua nemo illa tempestate militaris rei callidior habebatur, de toto genere belli censere, festinationem hostibus, moram ipsis utilem disseruit: exercitum Vitellii uniuersum aduenisse, nec multum uirium a tergo, quoniam Galliae tumeant et deserere Rheni ripam irrupturis tam infestis nationibus non conducat; Britannicum militem hoste et mari distineri: Hispanias armis non ita redundare; prouinciam Narbonensem incursu classis et aduerso proelio contremuisse; clausam Alpibus et nullo maris subsidio transpadanam Italiam atque ipso transitu exercitus uastam; non frumentum usquam exercitui, nec exercitum sine copiis retineri posse: iam Germanos, quod genus militum apud hostes atrocissimum sit, tracto in aestatem bello, fluxis corporibus, mutationem soli caelique haud toleraturos.

2 multa bella impetu ualida per taedia et moras euanuisse. contra ipsis omnia opulenta et fida, Pannoniam Moesiam Dalmatiam Orientem cum integris exercitibus, Italiam et caput rerum urbem senatumque et populum, numquam obscura nomina, etiam <si> aliquando obumbrentur; publicas priuatasque opes et immensam pecuniam, inter ciuiles discordias ferro ualidiorem; corpora militum aut Italiae sueta aut aestibus; obiacere flumen Padum, tutas uiris murisque urbes, e quibus nullam hosti cessuram Placentiae defensione exploratum: proinde duceret bellum. paucis diebus quartam decimam legionem, magna ipsam fama, <cum> Moesicis copiis adfore: tum rursus deliberaturum et, si proelium placuisset, auctis uiribus certaturos.

33 Accedebat sententiae Paulini Marius Celsus; idem placere Annio Gallo, paucos ante dies lapsu equi afflicto, missi qui consilium eius sciscitarentur rettulerant. Otho pronus ad decertandum; frater eius Titianus et praefectus praetorii Proculus, imperitia properantes, fortunam et deos et numen Othonis adesse consiliis, adfore conatibus testabantur, neu quis obuiam ire sententiae auderet, in adulationem concesserant.

2 Postquam pugnari placitum, interesse pugnae imperatorem an seponi melius foret dubitauere. Paulino et Celso iam non aduersantibus, ne principem obiectare periculis uiderentur idem illi deterioris consilii auctores perpulere ut Brixellum concederet ac dubiis proeliorum exemp-
3 tus summae rerum et imperii se ipsum reseruaret. is primus dies Othonianas partis afflixit; namque et cum ipso praetoriarum cohortium et

speculatorum equitumque ualida manus discessit, et remanentium fractus animus, quando suspecti duces et [ut] Otho, cui uni apud militem
fides, dum et ipse non nisi militibus credit, imperia ducum <in> incerto
reliquerat.

Nihil eorum Vitellianos fallebat, crebris, ut in ciuili bello, transfugiis; 34
et exploratores cura diuersa sciscitandi sua non occultabant. quieti intentique Caecina ac Valens, quando hostis imprudentia rueret, quod loco
sapientiae est, alienam stultitiam opperiebantur, inchoato ponte transitum
Padi simulantes aduersus oppositam gladiatorum manum, ac ne ipsorum
miles segne otium tereret. naues pari inter se spatio, ualidis utrimque 2
trabibus conexae, aduersum in flumen dirigebantur, iactis super ancoris
quae firmitatem pontis continerent, sed ancorarum funes non extenti
fluitabant, ut augescente flumine inoffensus ordo nauium attolleretur.
claudebat pontem imposita turris et in extremam nauem educta, unde
tormentis ac machinis hostes propulsarentur. Othoniani in ripa turrim
struxerant saxaque et faces iaculabantur.

Et erat insula amne medio, in quam gladiatores nauibus molientes, 35
Germani nando praelabebantur. ac forte plures transgressos completis
Liburnicis per promptissimos gladiatorum Macer aggreditur: sed neque
ea constantia gladiatoribus ad proelia quae militibus, nec proinde nutantes
e nauibus quam stabili gradu e ripa uulnera derigebant. et cum uariis 2
trepidantium inclinationibus mixti remiges propugnatoresque turbarentur, desilire in uada ultro Germani, retentare puppes, scandere foros aut
comminus mergere: quae cuncta in oculis utriusque exercitus quanto
laetiora Vitellianis, tanto acrius Othoniani causam auctoremque cladis
detestabantur.

Et proelium quidem, abruptis quae supererant nauibus, fuga 36
diremptum: Macer <ad> exitium poscebatur, iamque uolneratum eminus lancea strictis gladiis inuaserant, cum intercursu tribunorum centurionumque protegitur. nec multo post Vestricius Spurinna iussu Otho- 2
nis, relicto Placentiae modico praesidio, cum cohortibus subuenit. dein
Flauium Sabinum consulem designatum Otho rectorem copiis misit,
quibus Macer praefuerat, laeto milite [et] ad mutationem ducum et
ducibus ob crebras seditiones tam infestam militiam aspernantibus.

Inuenio apud quosdam auctores pauore belli seu fastidio utriusque 37
principis, quorum flagitia ac dedecus apertiore in dies fama noscebantur, dubitasse exercitus num, posito certamine, uel ipsi in medium
consultarent, uel senatui permitterent legere imperatorem, atque eo
duces Othonianos spatium ac moras suasisse, praecipua s<pe> Paulini,
quod uetustissimus consularium et militia clarus gloriam nomenque

2 Britannicis expeditionibus meruisset. ego ut concesserim apud paucos tacito uoto quietem pro discordia, bonum et innocentem principem pro pessimis ac flagitiosissimis expetitum, ita neque Paulinum, qua prudentia fuit, sperasse corruptissimo saeculo tantam uolgi moderationem reor ut qui pacem belli amore turbauerant, bellum pacis caritate deponerent, neque aut exercitus linguis moribusque dissonos in hunc consensum potuisse coalescere, aut legatos ac duces magna ex parte luxus egestatis scelerum sibi conscios nisi pollutum obstrictumque meritis suis principem passuros.

38 Vetus ac iam pridem insita mortalibus potentiae cupido cum imperii magnitudine adoleuit erupitque; nam rebus modicis aequalitas facile habebatur. sed ubi subacto orbe et aemulis urbibus regibusue excisis securas opes concupiscere uacuum fuit, prima inter patres plebemque certamina exarsere. modo turbulenti tribuni, modo consules praeualidi, et in urbe ac foro temptamenta ciuilium bellorum; mox e plebe infima C. Marius et nobilium saeuissimus Lucius Sulla uictam armis libertatem in dominationem uerterunt. post quos Cn. Pompeius occultior non melior, et 2 numquam postea nisi de principatu quaesitum. non discessere ab armis in Pharsalia ac Philippis ciuium legiones, nedum Othonis ac Vitellii exercitus sponte posituri bellum fuerint: eadem illos deum ira, eadem hominum rabies, eaedem scelerum causae in discordiam egere. quod singulis uelut ictibus transacta sunt bella, ignauia principum factum est. sed me ueterum nouorumque morum reputatio longius tulit: nunc ad rerum ordinem uenio.

39 Profecto Brixellum Othone honor imperii penes Titianum fratrem, uis ac potestas penes Proculum praefectum; Celsus et Paulinus, cum prudentia eorum nemo uteretur, inani nomine ducum alienae culpae praetendebantur; tribuni centurionesque ambigui quod spretis melioribus deterrimi ualebant; miles alacer, qui tamen iussa ducum interpretari 2 quam exsequi mallet. promoueri ad quartum a Bedriaco castra placuit, adeo imperite ut quamquam uerno tempore anni et tot circum amnibus penuria aquae fatigarentur. ibi de proelio dubitatum, Othone per litteras flagitante ut maturarent, militibus ut imperator pugnae adesset poscentibus: plerique copias trans Padum agentes acciri postulabant. nec proinde diiudicari potest quid optimum factu fuerit, quam pessimum fuisse quod factum est.

40 Non ut ad pugnam sed ad bellandum profecti confluentes †Padi et Aduae† fluminum, sedecim inde milium spatio distantes, petebant. Celso et Paulino abnuentibus militem itinere fessum, sarcinis grauem obicere hosti, non omissuro quo minus expeditus et uix quattuor milia passuum

progressus aut incompositos in agmine aut dispersos et uallum molientes aggrederetur, Titianus et Proculus, ubi consiliis uincerentur, ad ius imperii transibant. aderat sane citus equo Numida cum atrocibus mandatis, quibus Otho, increpita ducum segnitia, rem in discrimen mitti iubebat, aeger mora et spei impatiens.

Eodem die ad Caecinam operi pontis intentum duo praetoriarum **41** cohortium tribuni, colloquium eius postulantes, uenerunt: audire condiciones ac reddere parabat, cum praecipites exploratores adesse hostem nuntiauere. interruptus tribunorum sermo, eoque incertum fuit insidias an proditionem uel aliquod honestum consilium coeptauerint.

Caecina dimissis tribunis reuectus in castra datum iussu Fabii Valentis **2** pugnae signum et militem in armis inuenit. dum legiones de ordine agminis sortiuntur, equites prorupere; et mirum dictu, a paucioribus Othonianis quo minus in uallum impingerentur, Italicae legionis uirtute deterriti sunt: ea strictis mucronibus redire pulsos et pugnam resumere coegit. disposita Vitellianarum legionum acies sine trepidatione: etenim quamquam uicino hoste aspectus armorum densis arbustis prohibebatur. apud Oth- **3** onianos pauidi duces, miles ducibus infensus, mixta uehicula et lixae, et praeruptis utrimque fossis uia quieto quoque agmini angusta. circumsistere alii signa sua, quaerere alii; incertus undique clamor accurrentium, uocantium: ut cuique audacia uel formido, in primam postremamue aciem prorumpebant aut relabebantur.

Attonitas subito terrore mentes falsum gaudium in languorem uertit, **42** repertis qui desciuisse a Vitellio exercitum ementirentur. is rumor ab exploratoribus Vitellii dispersus, an in ipsa Othonis parte seu dolo seu forte surrexerit, parum compertum. omisso pugnae ardore Othoniani ultro salutauere; et hostili murmure excepti, plerisque suorum ignaris quae causa salutandi, metum proditionis fecere.

Tum incubuit hostium acies, integris ordinibus, robore et numero **2** praestantior: Othoniani, quamquam dispersi pauciores fessi, proelium tamen acriter sumpsere. et per locos arboribus ac uineis impeditos non una pugnae facies: comminus eminus, cateruis et cuneis concurrebant. in aggere uiae collato gradu corporibus et umbonibus niti, omisso pilorum iactu gladiis et securibus galeas loricasque perrumpere: noscentes inter se, ceteris conspicui, in euentum totius belli certabant.

Forte inter Padum uiamque patenti campo duae legiones congressae **43** sunt, pro Vitellio unaetuicensima, cui cognomen Rapaci, uetere gloria insignis, e parte Othonis prima Adiutrix, non ante in aciem deducta, sed ferox et noui decoris auida. primani, stratis unaetuicensimanorum principiis, aquilam abstulere; quo dolore accensa legio et impulit rursus

primanos, interfecto Orfidio Benigno legato, et plurima signa uexillaque
2 ex hostibus rapuit. a parte alia propulsa quintanorum impetu tertia decima legio, circumuenti plurium accursu quartadecimani. et ducibus Othonis iam pridem profugis, Caecina ac Valens subsidiis suos firmabant.
accessit recens auxilium, Varus Alfenus cum Batauis, fusa gladiatorum
manu, quam nauibus transuectam oppositae cohortes in ipso flumine
trucidauerant: ita uictores latus hostium inuecti.

44 Et media acie perrupta, fugere passim Othoniani, Bedriacum petentes.
immensum id spatium, obstructae strage corporum uiae, quo plus caedis
fuit; neque enim ciuilibus bellis capti in praedam uertuntur. Suetonius Paulinus et Licinius Proculus diuersis itineribus castra uitauere.
Vedium Aquilam tertiae decimae legionis legatum irae militum inconsultus pauor obtulit. multo adhuc die, uallum ingressus clamore seditiosorum
et fugacium circumstrepitur; non probris, non manibus abstinent; desertorem proditoremque increpant, nullo proprio crimine eius sed more
uolgi suum quisque flagitium aliis obiectantes.

2 Titianum et Celsum nox iuuit, dispositis iam excubiis conpressisque
militibus, quos Annius Gallus consilio precibus auctoritate flexerat, ne
super cladem aduersae pugnae suismet ipsi caedibus saeuirent: siue finis
bello uenisset seu resumere arma mallent, unicum uictis in consensu
3 leuamentum. ceteris fractus animus: praetorianus miles non uirtute se
sed proditione uictum fremebat: ne Vitellianis quidem incruentam fuisse
uictoriam, pulso equite, rapta legionis aquila; superesse cum ipso Othone militum quod trans Padum fuerit, uenire Moesicas legiones, magnam
exercitus partem Bedriaci remansisse: hos certe nondum uictos et, si ita
ferret, honestius in acie perituros. his cogitationibus truces aut pauidi
extrema desperatione ad iram saepius quam in formidinem stimulabantur.

45 At Vitellianus exercitus ad quintum a Bedriaco lapidem consedit, non
ausis ducibus eadem die oppugnationem castrorum; simul uoluntaria
deditio sperabatur: sed expeditis et tantum ad proelium egressis munimentum fuere arma et uictoria.

2 Postera die haud ambigua Othoniani exercitus uoluntate, et qui
ferociores fuerant, ad paenitentiam inclinantibus, missa legatio; nec
apud duces Vitellianos dubitatum quo minus pacem concederent. legati
paulisper retenti: ea res haesitationem attulit ignaris adhuc an impe-
3 trassent. mox remissa legatione patuit uallum. tum uicti uictoresque in
lacrimas effusi, sortem ciuilium armorum misera laetitia detestantes;
isdem tentoriis alii fratrum, alii propinquorum uolnera fouebant: spes
et praemia in ambiguo, certa funera et luctus, nec quisquam adeo mali

expers ut non aliquam mortem maereret. requisitum Orfidii legati corpus
honore solito crematur; paucos necessarii ipsorum sepeliuere, ceterum
uolgus super humum relictum.

Opperiebatur Otho nuntium pugnae nequaquam trepidus et consilii **46**
certus. maesta primum fama, dein profugi e proelio perditas res patefaciunt. non exspectauit militum ardor uocem imperatoris; bonum haberet
animum iubebant: superesse adhuc nouas uires, et ipsos extrema passuros ausurosque. neque erat adulatio: ire in aciem, excitare partium
fortunam furore quodam et instinctu flagrabant. qui procul adstiterant, **2**
tendere manus, et proximi prensare genua, promptissimo Plotio Firmo.
is praetorii praefectus identidem orabat ne fidissimum exercitum, ne
optime meritos milites desereret: maiore animo tolerari aduersa quam
relinqui; fortes et strenuos etiam contra fortunam insistere spei, timidos
et ignauos ad desperationem formidine properare. quas inter uoces ut **3**
flexerat uultum aut induruerat Otho, clamor et gemitus. nec praetoriani
tantum, proprius Othonis miles, sed praemissi e Moesia eandem obstina-
tionem aduentantis exercitus, legiones Aquileiam ingressas nuntiabant,
ut nemo dubitet potuisse renouari bellum atrox lugubre incertum uictis et
uictoribus.

Ipse auersus a consiliis belli 'hunc' inquit 'animum, hanc uirtutem **47**
uestram ultra periculis obicere nimis grande uitae meae pretium puto.
quanto plus spei ostenditis, si uiuere placeret, tanto pulchrior mors erit.
experti in uicem sumus ego ac fortuna. nec tempus computaueritis: difficilius est temperare felicitati qua te non putes diu usurum. ciuile bellum **2**
a Vitellio coepit, et ut de principatu certaremus armis initium illic fuit: ne
plus quam semel certemus penes me exemplum erit; hinc Othonem posteritas aestimet. fruetur Vitellius fratre coniuge liberis: mihi non ultione
neque solaciis opus est. alii diutius imperium tenuerint, nemo tam fortiter
reliquerit. an ego tantum Romanae pubis, tot egregios exercitus sterni rur- **3**
sus et rei publicae eripi patiar? eat hic mecum animus, tamquam perituri
pro me fueritis, sed este superstites. nec diu moremur, ego incolumitatem
uestram, uos constantiam meam. plura de extremis loqui pars ignauiae
est. praecipuum destinationis meae documentum habete quod de nemine
queror; nam incusare deos uel homines eius est qui uiuere uelit.'

Talia locutus, ut cuique aetas aut dignitas, comiter appellatos, irent **48**
propere neu remanendo iram uictoris asperarent, iuuenes auctoritate,
senes precibus mouebat, placidus ore, intrepidus uerbis, intempestiuas
suorum lacrimas coercens. dari nauis ac uehicula abeuntibus iubet; libellos epistulasque studio erga se aut in Vitellium contumeliis insignes abolet;
pecunias distribuit parce nec ut periturus. mox Saluium Cocceianum, **2**

fratris filium prima iuuenta, trepidum et maerentem ultro solatus est,
laudando pietatem eius, castigando formidinem: an Vitellium tam immitis animi fore ut pro incolumi tota domo ne hanc quidem sibi gratiam
redderet? mereri se festinato exitu clementiam uictoris; non enim ultima
desperatione sed poscente proelium exercitu remisisse rei publicae nouissimum casum. satis sibi nominis, satis posteris suis nobilitatis quaesitum.
post Iulios Claudios Seruios se primum in familiam nouam imperium
intulisse: proinde erecto animo capesseret uitam, neu patruum sibi Othonem fuisse aut obliuisceretur umquam aut nimium meminisset.

49 Post quae dimotis omnibus paulum requieuit. atque illum supremas
iam curas animo uolutantem repens tumultus auertit, nuntiata consternatione ac licentia militum; namque abeuntibus exitium minitabantur,
atrocissima in Verginium ui, quem clausa domo obsidebant. increpitis
seditionis auctoribus, regressus uacauit abeuntium alloquiis, donec omnes
inuiolati digrederentur.

2 Vesperascente die, sitim haustu gelidae aquae sedauit. tum allatis
pugionibus <duobus>, cum utrumque pertemptasset, alterum capiti sub-
didit. et explorato iam profectos amicos, noctem quietam, utque affir-
3 matur, non insomnem egit: luce prima in ferrum pectore incubuit. ad
gemitum morientis ingressi liberti seruique et Plotius Firmus praetorii
praefectus unum uolnus inuenere.

Funus maturatum; ambitiosis id precibus petierat ne amputaretur
caput ludibrio futurum. tulere corpus praetoriae cohortes cum laudibus
4 et lacrimis, uolnus manusque eius exosculantes. quidam militum iuxta
rogum interfecere se, non noxa neque ob metum, sed aemulatione decoris
et caritate principis. ac postea promisce Bedriaci, Placentiae aliisque in
castris celebratum id genus mortis. Othoni sepulchrum exstructum est
modicum et mansurum. hunc uitae finem habuit septimo et tricensimo
aetatis anno.

50 Origo illi e municipio Ferentio, pater consularis, auus praetorius;
maternum genus impar nec tamen indecorum. pueritia ac iuuenta,
qualem monstrauimus. duobus facinoribus, altero flagitiosissimo, altero
egregio, tantundem apud posteros meruit bonae famae quantum malae.
2 ut conquirere fabulosa et fictis oblectare legentium animos procul graui-
tate coepti operis crediderim, ita uolgatis traditisque demere fidem non
ausim. die, quo Bedriaci certabatur, auem inuisitata specie apud Regium
Lepidum celebri luco consedisse incolae memorant, nec deinde coetu
hominum aut circumuolitantium alitum territam pulsamue, donec Otho
se ipse interficeret; tum ablatam ex oculis: et tempora reputantibus initium
finemque miraculi cum Othonis exitu competisse.

In funere eius nouata luctu ac dolore militum seditio, nec erat qui 51
coerceret. ad Verginium uersi, modo ut reciperet imperium, nunc ut
legatione apud Caecinam ac Valentem fungeretur, minitantes orabant:
Verginius per auersam domus partem furtim digressus irrumpentes frustratus est. earum quae Brixelli egerant cohortium preces Rubrius Gallus
tulit, et uenia statim impetrata, concedentibus ad uictorem per Flauium
Sabinum iis copiis quibus praefuerat.

Posito ubique bello, magna pars senatus extremum discrimen adiit, 52
profecta cum Othone ab urbe, dein Mutinae relicta. illuc aduerso de
proelio allatum: sed milites ut falsum rumorem aspernantes, quod infensum Othoni senatum arbitrabantur, custodire sermones, uoltum habi-
tumque trahere in deterius; conuiciis postremo ac probris causam et
initium caedis quaerebant, cum alius insuper metus senatoribus instaret,
ne praeualidis iam Vitellii partibus cunctanter excepisse uictoriam crederentur. ita trepidi et utrimque anxii coeunt, nemo priuatim expedito 2
consilio, inter multos societate culpae tutior. onerabat pauentium curas
ordo Mutinensis arma et pecuniam offerendo, appellabatque patres conscriptos intempesti<uo> honore.

Notabile iurgium fuit quo Licinius Caecina Marcellum Eprium 53
ut ambigua disserentem inuasit. nec ceteri sententias aperiebant: sed
inuisum memoria delationum expositumque ad inuidiam Marcelli nomen
irritauerat Caecinam, ut nouus adhuc et in senatum nuper ascitus magnis
inimicitiis claresceret. moderatione meliorum dirempti. et rediere omnes 2
Bononiam, rursus consiliaturi; simul medio temporis plures nuntii sperabantur. Bononiae, diuisis per itinera qui recentissimum quemque per-
contarentur, interrogatus Othonis libertus causam digressus habere se
suprema eius mandata respondit; ipsum uiuentem quidem relictum, sed
sola posteritatis cura et abruptis uitae blandimentis. hinc admiratio et
plura interrogandi pudor, atque omnium animi in Vitellium inclinauere.

Intererat consiliis frater eius L. Vitellius seque iam adulantibus offere- 54
bat, cum repente Coenus libertus Neronis atroci mendacio uniuersos perculit, affirmans superuentu quartae decimae legionis, iunctis a Brixello
uiribus, caesos uictores; uersam partium fortunam. causa fingendi fuit ut
diplomata Othonis, quae neglegebantur, laetiore nuntio reualescerent. et 2
Coenus quidem raptim in urbem uectus paucos post dies iussu Vitellii poenas luit: senatorum periculum auctum credentibus Othonianis militibus
uera esse quae afferebantur. intendebat formidinem quod publici consilii
facie discessum Mutina desertaeque partes forent. nec ultra in commune
congressi sibi quisque consuluere, donec missae a Fabio Valente epistulae
demerent metum. et mors Othonis quo laudabilior eo uelocius audita.

55 At Romae nihil trepidationis; Ceriales ludi ex more spectabantur. ut cessisse Othonem et a Flauio Sabino praefecto urbis quod erat in urbe militum [in] sacramento Vitellii adactum certi auctores in theatrum attulerunt, Vitellio plausere; populus cum lauru ac floribus Galbae imagines circum templa tulit, congestis in modum tumuli coronis iuxta lacum Curtii, quem locum Galba moriens sanguine infecerat.

2 In senatu cuncta longis aliorum principatibus composita statim decernuntur; additae erga Germanicum exercitum laudes gratesque et missa legatio quae gaudio fungeretur. recitatae Fabii Valentis epistulae ad consules scriptae haud immoderate: gratior Caecinae modestia fuit quod non scripsisset.

56 Ceterum Italia grauius atque atrocius quam bello afflictabatur. dispersi per municipia et colonias Vitelliani spoliare, rapere, ui et stupris polluere: in omne fas nefasque auidi aut uenales non sacro, non profano abstinebant. et fuere qui inimicos suos specie militum interficerent. ipsique milites regionum gnari refertos agros, dites dominos in praedam aut, si repugnatum foret, ad exitium destinabant, obnoxiis ducibus et pro-

2 hibere non ausis. minus auaritiae in Caecina, plus ambitionis: Valens ob lucra et quaestus infamis eoque alienae etiam culpae dissimulator. iam pridem attritis Italiae rebus, tantum peditum equitumque, uis damnaque et iniuriae aegre tolerabantur.

57 Interim Vitellius uictoriae suae nescius ut ad integrum bellum reliquas Germanici exercitus uires trahebat. pauci ueterum militum in hibernis relicti, festinatis per Gallias dilectibus, ut remanentium legionum nomina supplerentur. cura ripae Hordeonio Flacco permissa; ipse e Britan-

2 nico <exercitu> delecta octo milia sibi adiunxit. et paucorum dierum iter progressus prosperas apud Bedriacum res ac morte Othonis concidisse bellum accepit: uocata contione, uirtutem militum laudibus cumulat. postulante exercitu ut libertum suum Asiaticum equestri dignitate donaret, inhonestam adulationem compescit; dein mobilitate ingenii, quod palam abnuerat, inter secreta conui<ui>i largitur, honorauitque Asiaticum anulis, foedum mancipium et malis artibus ambitiosum.

58 Isdem diebus accessisse partibus utramque Mauretaniam, interfecto procuratore Albino, nuntii uenere. Lucceius Albinus a Nerone Mauretaniae Caesariensi praepositus, addita per Galbam Tingitanae prouinciae administratione, haud spernendis uiribus agebat. decem nouem cohortes, quinque alae, ingens Maurorum numerus aderat, per latrocinia et raptus apta bello manus. caeso Galba in Othonem pronus nec Africa contentus

2 Hispaniae angusto freto diremptae imminebat. inde Cluuio Rufo metus, et decimam legionem propinquare litori ut transmissurus iussit; praemissi centuriones qui Maurorum animos Vitellio conciliarent. neque arduum fuit, magna per prouincias Germanici exercitus fama; spargebatur insuper spreto procuratoris uocabulo Albinum insigne regis et Iubae nomen usurpare.

Ita mutatis animis Asinius Pollio alae praefectus, e fidissimis Albino, **59** et Festus ac Scipio cohortium praefecti opprimuntur: ipse Albinus dum e Tingitana prouincia Caesariensem Mauretaniam petit, appulsu litoris trucidatus; uxor eius cum se percussoribus obtulisset, simul interfecta est, nihil eorum quae fierent Vitellio anquirente: breui auditu [ui] quamuis magna transibat, impar curis grauioribus.

Exercitum itinere terrestri pergere iubet: ipse Arare flumine deuehi- **2** tur, nullo principali paratu, sed uetere egestate conspicuus, donec Iunius Blaesus Lugudunensis Galliae rector, genere illustri, largus animo et par opibus, circumdaret principi ministeria, comitaretur liberaliter, eo ipso ingratus, quamuis odium Vitellius uernilibus blanditiis uelaret. praesto **3** fuere Luguduni uictricium uictarumque partium duces. Valentem et Caecinam pro contione laudatos curuli suae circumposuit. mox uniuersum exercitum occurrere infanti filio iubet, perlatumque et paludamento opertum sinu retinens Germanicum appellauit cinxitque cunctis fortunae principalis insignibus. nimius honos inter secunda rebus aduersis in supplicium cessit.

Tum interfecti centuriones promptissimi Othonianorum, unde prae- **60** cipua in Vitellium alienatio per Illy<ri>cos exercitus; simul ceterae legiones contactu et aduersus Germanicos milites inuidia bellum meditabantur. Suetonium Paulinum ac Licinium Proculum tristi mora squalidos tenuit, donec auditi necessariis magis defensionibus quam honestis uterentur. proditionem ultro imputabant, spatium longi ante proelium itineris, fatigationem Othonianorum, permixtum uehiculis agmen ac pleraque fortuita fraudi suae assignantes. et Vitellius credidit de perfidia et fidem absoluit. Saluius Titianus Othonis frater nullum discrimen adiit, **2** pietate et ignauia excusatus. Mario Celso consulatus seruatur: sed creditum fama obiectumque mox in senatu Caecilio Simplici, quod eum honorem pecunia mercari, nec sine exitio Celsi, uoluisset: restitit Vitellius deditque postea consulatum Simplici innoxium et ine<m>ptum. Trachalum aduersus criminantes Galeria uxor Vitellii protexit.

Inter magnorum uirorum discrimina, pudendum dictu, Mariccus **61** quidam, e plebe Boiorum, inserere sese fortunae et prouocare arma Romana simulatione numinum ausus est. iamque assertor Galliarum et deus (nam id sibi indiderat) concitis octo milibus hominum proximos Aeduorum pagos trahebat, cum grauissima ciuitas electa iuuentute,

adiectis a Vitellio cohortibus, fanaticam multitudinem disiecit. captus in
eo proelio Mariccus; ac mox feris obiectus quia non laniabatur, stolidum
uolgus inuiolabilem credebat, donec spectante Vitellio interfectus est.

62 Nec ultra in defectores aut bona cuiusquam saeuitum: rata fuere eorum
qui acie Othoniana ceciderant, testamenta aut lex intestatis: prorsus, si
luxuriae temperaret, auaritiam non timeres. epularum foeda et inexplebilis libido: ex urbe atque Italia irritamenta gulae gestabantur, strepentibus ab utroque mari itineribus; exhausti conuiuiorum apparatibus
principes ciuitatum; uastabantur ipsae ciuitates; degenerabat a labore ac
uirtute miles assuetudine uoluptatum et contemptu ducis.

2   Praemisit in urbem edictum quo uocabulum Augusti differret, Caesaris
non reciperet, cum de potestate nihil detraheret. pulsi Italia mathematici;
cautum seuere ne equites Romani ludo et harena polluerentur. priores
id principes pecunia et saepius ui perpulerant, ac pleraque municipia et
coloniae aemulabantur corruptissimum quemque adulescentium pretio
illicere.

63 Sed Vitellius aduentu fratris et irrepentibus dominationis magistris
superbior et atrocior occidi Dolabellam iussit, quem in coloniam
Aquinatem sepositum ab Othone rettulimus. Dolabella audita morte Othonis urbem introierat: id ei Plancius Varus praetura functus, ex intimis
Dolabellae amicis, apud Flauium Sabinum praefectum urbis obiecit,
tamquam rupta custodia ducem se uictis partibus ostentasset; addidit
temptatam cohortem quae Ostiae ageret; nec ullis tantorum criminum
probationibus in paenitentiam uersus seram ueniam post scelus quaere-
2   bat. cunctantem super tanta re Flauium Sabinum Triaria L. Vitellii uxor,
ultra feminam ferox, terruit ne periculo principis famam clementiae
affectaret. Sabinus suopte ingenio mitis, ubi formido incessisset, facilis
mutatu et in alieno discrimine sibi pauens, ne alleuasse uideretur, impulit
ruentem.

64 Igitur Vitellius metu et odio quod Petroniam uxorem eius mox Dolabella in matrimonium accepisset, uocatum per epistulas uitata Flaminiae
uiae celebritate deuertere Interamnium atque ibi interfici iussit. longum
interfectori uisum: in itinere ac taberna proiectum humi iugulauit, magna
cum inuidia noui principatus, cuius hoc primum specimen noscebatur.
2   et Triariae licentiam modestum e proximo exemplum onerabat, Galeria imperatoris uxor non immix<ta> tristibus; et pari probitate mater
Vitelliorum Sextilia, antiqui moris: dixisse quin etiam ad primas filii sui
epistulas ferebatur, non Germanicum a se sed Vitellium genitum. nec ullis
postea fortunae illecebris aut ambitu ciuitatis in gaudium euicta domus
suae tantum aduersa sensit.

Digressum a Luguduno Vitellium [M.] Cluuius Rufus assequitur 65
omissa Hispania, laetitiam et gratulationem uoltu ferens, animo anxius
et petitum se criminationibus gnarus. Hilarus Caesaris libertus detulerat
tamquam audito Vitellii et Othonis principatu propriam ipse potentiam
et possessionem Hispaniarum temptasset, eoque diplomatibus nullum
principem praescripsisset; <et> interpretabatur quaedam ex orationibus
eius contumeliosa in Vitellium et pro se ipso popularia. auctoritas Cluuii 2
praeualuit ut puniri ultro libertum suum Vitellius iuberet. Cluuius comitatui principis adiectus, non adempta Hispania, quam rexit absens exemplo L. <Arruntii. sed> Arruntium Tiberius Caesar ob metum, Vitellius
Cluuium nulla formidine retinebat. non idem Trebellio Maximo honos:
profugerat Britannia ob iracundiam militum; missus est in locum eius
Vettius Bolanus e praesentibus.

Angebat Vitellium uictarum legionum haudquaquam fractus animus. 66
sparsae per Italiam et uictoribus permixtae hostilia loquebantur, praecipua quartadecimanorum ferocia, qui se uictos abnuebant: quippe Bedri-
acensi acie uexillariis tantum pulsis uires legionis non adfuisse. remitti
eos in Britanniam, unde a Nerone exciti erant, placuit atque interim
Batauorum cohortes una tendere ob ueterem aduersus quartadecimanos
discordiam.

Nec diu in tantis armatorum odiis quies fuit: Augustae Taurinorum, 2
dum opificem quendam Batauus ut fraudatorem insectatur, legionarius
ut hospitem tuetur, sui cuique commilitones aggregati a conuiciis ad caedem transiere. et proelium atrox arsisset, ni duae praetoriae cohortes
causam quartadecimanorum secutae his fiduciam et metum Batauis fecis-
sent. quos Vitellius agmini suo iungi ut fidos, legionem Grais Alpibus 3
traductam eo flexu itineris ire iubet quo Viennam uitarent; namque et
Viennenses timebantur. nocte, qua proficiscebatur legio, relictis passim
ignibus pars Taurinae coloniae ambusta, quod damnum, ut pleraque belli
mala, maioribus aliarum urbium cladibus obliteratum. quartadecimani
postquam Alpibus degressi sunt, seditiosissimus quisque signa Viennam
ferebant: consensu meliorum compressi et legio in Britanniam transuecta.

Proximus Vitellio e praetoriis cohortibus metus erat. separati primum, 67
deinde addito honestae missionis lenimento, arma ad tribunos suos deferebant, donec motum a Vespasiano bellum crebresceret: tum resumpta
militia robur Flauianarum partium fuere. prima classicorum legio in 2
Hispaniam missa ut pace et otio mitesceret, undecima ac septima suis
hibernis redditae, tertiadecimani struere amphitheatra iussi; nam Caecina
Cremonae, Valens Bononiae spectaculum gladiatorum edere parabant,
numquam ita ad curas intento Vitellio ut uoluptatum obliuisceretur.

68 Et \<uictas\> quidem partes modeste distraxerat: apud uictores orta
seditio, ludicro initio \<ni\> numerus caesorum inuidiam †bello† auxis-
set. discubuerat Vitellius Ticini adhibito ad epulas Verginio. legati tribunique ex moribus imperatorum seueritatem aemulantur uel tempestiuis
conuiuiis gaudent; proinde miles intentus aut licenter agit. apud Vitellium
omnia indisposita, temulenta, peruigiliis ac bacchanalibus quam disci-
2 plinae et castris propiora. igitur duobus militibus, altero legionis quintae,
altero e Galli auxiliaribus, per lasciuiam ad certamen luctandi accensis,
postquam legionarius prociderat, insultante Gallo et iis qui ad spectan-
dum conuenerant in studia diductis, erupere legionarii in perniciem auxiliorum ac duae cohortes interfectae.
3 Remedium tumultus fuit alius tumultus. puluis procul et arma
aspiciebantur: conclamatum repente quartam decimam legionem uerso
itinere ad proelium uenire; sed erant agminis coactores: agniti dempsere
4 sollicitudinem. interim Verginii seruus forte obuius ut percussor Vitellii
insimulatur: et ruebat ad conuiuium miles, mortem Verginii exposcens.
ne Vitellius quidem, quamquam ad omnes suspiciones pauidus, de innocentia eius dubitauit: aegre tamen cohibiti qui exitium consularis et
quondam ducis sui flagitabant. nec quemquam saepius quam Verginium
omnis seditio infestauit: manebat admiratio uiri et fama, sed oderant ut
fastiditi.
69 Postero die Vitellius senatus legatione, quam ibi opperiri iusserat,
audita transgressus in castra ultro pietatem militum collaudauit, frementibus auxiliis tantum impunitatis atque arrogantiae legionariis accessisse. Batauorum cohortes, ne quid truculentius auderent, in Germaniam
remissae, principium interno simul externoque bello parantibus fatis.
reddita ciuitatibus Gallorum auxilia, ingens numerus et prima statim
2 defectione inter inania belli assumptus. ceterum ut largitionibus affectae
iam imperii opes sufficerent, amputari legionum auxiliorumque numeros
iubet uetitis supplementis; et promiscae missiones offerebantur. exitiabile
id rei publicae, ingratum militi, cui eadem munia inter paucos periculaque
ac labor crebrius redibant: et uires luxu corrumpebantur, contra ueterem
disciplinam et instituta maiorum apud quos uirtute quam pecunia res
Romana melius stetit.
70 Inde Vitellius Cremonam flexit et spectato munere Caecinae insistere
Bedriacensibus campis ac uestigia recentis uictoriae lustrare oculis concupiuit, foedum atque atrox spectaculum. intra quadragensimum pugnae
diem lacera corpora, trunci artus, putres uirorum equorumque formae,
2 infecta tabo humus, protritis arboribus ac frugibus dira uastitas. nec minus
inhumana pars uiae quam Cremonenses lauru rosaque construerant,

exstructis altaribus caesisque uictimis regium in morem; quae laeta in praesens mox perniciem ipsis fecere.

Aderant Valens et Caecina, monstrabantque pugnae locos: hinc 3 irrupisse legionum agmen, hinc equites coortos, inde circumfusas auxiliorum manus: iam tribuni praefectique, sua quisque facta extollentes, falsa uera aut maiora uero miscebant. uolgus quoque militum clamore et gaudio deflectere uia, spatia certaminum recognoscere, aggerem armorum, strues corporum intueri mirari; et erant quos uaria sors rerum lacrimaeque et misericordia subiret. at non Vitellius flexit oculos nec tot 4 milia insepultorum ciuium exhorruit: laetus ultro et tam propinquae sortis ignarus instaurabat sacrum dis loci.

Exim Bononiae a Fabio Valente gladiatorum spectaculum editur, 71 aduecto ex urbe cultu. quantoque magis propinquabat, tanto corruptius iter immixtis histrionibus et spadonum gregibus et cetero Neronianae aulae ingenio; namque et Neronem ipsum Vitellius admiratione celebrabat, sectari cantantem solitus, non necessitate, qua honestissimus quisque, sed luxu et saginae mancipatus emptusque.

Vt Valenti et Caecinae uacuos honoris menses aperiret, coartati alio- 2 rum consulatus, dissimulatus Marci Macri tamquam Othonianarum partium ducis; et Valerium Marinum destinatum a Galba consulem distulit, nulla offensa, sed mitem et iniuriam segniter laturum. Pedanius Costa omittitur, ingratus principi ut aduersus Neronem ausus et Verginii exstimulator, sed alias protulit causas; actaeque insuper Vitellio gratiae consuetudine seruitii.

Non ultra paucos dies quamquam acribus initiis coeptum men- 72 dacium ualuit. extiterat quidam Scribonianum se Camerinum ferens, Neronianorum temporum metu in Histria occultatum, quod illic clientelae et agri ueterum Crassorum ac nominis fauor manebat. igitur deter- 2 rimo quoque in argumentum fabulae adsumpto uolgus credulum et quidam militum, errore ueri seu turbarum studio, certatim aggregabantur, cum pertractus ad Vitellium interrogatusque quisnam mortalium esset. postquam nulla dictis fides et a domino noscebatur condicione fugitiuus, nomine Geta, sumptum de eo supplicium in seruilem modum.

Vix credibile memoratu est quantum superbiae socordiaeque Vitellio 73 adoleuerit, postquam speculatores e Syria Iudaeaque adactum in uerba eius Orientem nuntiauere. nam etsi uagis adhuc et incertis auctoribus, erat tamen in ore famaque Vespasianus ac plerumque ad nomen eius Vitellius excitabatur: tum ipse exercitusque, ut nullo aemulo, saeuitia libidine raptu in externos mores proruperant.

74 At Vespasianus bellum armaque et procul uel iuxta sitas uires circumspectabat. miles ipsi adeo paratus ut praeeuntem sacramentum et
fausta Vitellio omnia precantem per silentium audierint; Muciani animus nec Vespasiano alienus et in Titum pronior; praefectus Aegypti
<Ti.> Alexander consilia sociauerat; tertiam legionem, quod e Syria in
Moesiam transisset, suam numerabat; ceterae Illyrici legiones secuturae
sperabantur; namque omnis exercitus flammauerat arrogantia uenientium a Vitellio militum, quod truces corpore, horridi sermone ceteros ut
impares irridebant.

2 Sed in tanta mole belli plerumque cunctatio; et Vespasianus modo
in spem erectus, aliquando aduersa reputabat: quis ille dies foret quo
sexaginta aetatis annos et duos filios iuuenes bello permitteret? esse priuatis cogitationibus progressum et, prout uelint, plus minusue sumi ex
fortuna: imperium cupientibus nihil medium inter summa aut praecipi-
75 tia. uersabatur ante oculos Germanici exercitus robur, notum uiro militari:
suas legiones ciuili bello inexpertas, Vitellii uictrices, et apud uictos plus
querimoniarum quam uirium. fluxam per discordias militum fidem et
periculum ex singulis: quid enim profuturas cohortes alasque, si unus
alterue praesenti facinore paratum ex diuerso praemium petat? sic Scribonianum sub Claudio interfectum, sic percussorem eius Volaginium e
gregario ad summa militiae prouectum: facilius uniuersos impelli quam
singulos uitari.

76 His pauoribus nutantem et alii legati amicique firmabant et Mucianus,
post multos secretosque sermones iam et coram ita locutus: 'omnes,
qui magnarum rerum consilia suscipiunt, aestimare debent an quod
inchoatur rei publicae utile, ipsis gloriosum, an promptum effectu aut
certe non arduum sit; simul ipse qui suadet considerandus est, adiciatne
consilio periculum suum, et, si fortuna coeptis adfuerit, cui summum
2 decus adquiratur. ego te, Vespasiane, ad imperium uoco, tam salutare
rei publicae, quam tibi magnificum. iuxta deos in tua manu positum
est.

Nec speciem adulantis expaueris: a contumelia quam a laude propius
fuerit post Vitellium eligi. non aduersus diui Augusti acerrimam mentem
nec aduersus cautissimam Tiberii senectutem, ne contra Gai quidem
aut Claudii uel Neronis fundatam longo imperio domum exsurgimus;
cessisti etiam Galbae imaginibus: torpere ultra et polluendam perdendamque rem publicam relinquere sopor et ignauia uideretur, etiam si
3 tibi quam inhonesta, tam tuta seruitus esset. abiit iam et transuectum est
tempus quo posses uideri concupisse: confugiendum est ad imperium.
an excidit trucidatus Corbulo? splendi<di>or origine quam nos sumus,

fateor, sed et Nero nobilitate natalium Vitellium anteibat. satis clarus est
apud timentem quisquis timetur.

Et posse ab exercitu principem fieri sibi ipse Vitellius documento, nullis   4
stipendiis, nulla militari fama, Galbae odio prouectus. ne Othonem quidem ducis arte aut exercitus ui, sed praepropera ipsius desperatione uictum, iam desiderabilem et magnum principem fecit, cum interim spargit
legiones, exarmat cohortes, noua cotidie bello semina ministrat. si quid
ardoris ac ferociae miles habuit, popinis et comissationibus et principis
imitatione deteritur: tibi e Iudaea et Syria et Aegypto nouem legiones
integrae, nulla acie exhaustae, non discordia corruptae, sed firmatus usu
miles et belli domitor externi: classium alarum cohortium robora et fidissimi reges et tua ante omnis experientia.'

'Nobis nihil ultra arrogabo quam ne post Valentem et Caecinam   77
numeremur: ne tamen Mucianum socium spreueris, quia aemulum non
experiris. me Vitellio antepono, te mihi. tuae domui triumphale nomen,
duo iuuenes, capax iam imperii alter et primis militiae annis apud Germanicos quoque exercitus clarus. absurdum fuerit non cedere imperio
ei cuius filium adoptaturus essem, si ipse imperarem. ceterum inter nos   2
non idem prosperarum aduersarumque rerum ordo erit: nam si uincimus,
honorem quem dederis habebo: discrimen ac pericula ex aequo patiemur.
immo, ut melius est, <tu> tuos exercitus rege, mihi bellum et proeliorum
incerta trade. acriore hodie disciplina uicti quam uictores agunt. hos ira   3
odium ultionis cupiditas ad uirtutem accendit: illi per fastidium et contumacia hebescunt. aperiet et recludet contecta et tumescentia uictricium
partium uolnera bellum ipsum; nec mihi maior in tua uigilantia parsimonia sapientia fiducia est quam in Vitellii torpore inscitia saeuitia. sed
meliorem in bello causam quam in pace habemus; nam qui deliberant,
desciuerunt.'

Post Muciani orationem ceteri audentius circumsistere, hortari,   78
responsa uatum et siderum motus referre. nec erat intactus tali superstitione, ut qui mox rerum dominus Seleucum quendam mathematicum
rectorem et praescium palam habuerit. recursabant animo uetera omina: 2
cupressus arbor in agris eius conspicua altitudine repente prociderat ac
postera die eodem uestigio resurgens procera et latior uirebat. grande
id prosperumque consensu haruspicum et summa claritudo iuueni
admodum Vespasiano promissa, sed primo triumphalia et consulatus et
Iudaicae uictoriae decus implesse fidem ominis uidebatur: ut haec adeptus est, portendi sibi imperium credebat.

Est Iudaeam inter Syriamque Carmelus: ita uocant montem deumque.   3
nec simulacrum deo aut templum – sic tradidere maiores – : ara tantum

et reuerentia. illic sacrificanti Vespasiano, cum spes occultas uersaret
animo, Basilides sacerdos inspectis identidem extis 'quicquid est' inquit,
'Vespasiane, quod paras, seu domum exstruere seu prolatare agros siue
ampliare seruitia, datur tibi magna sedes, ingentes termini, multum
4 hominum.' has ambages et statim exceperat fama et tunc aperiebat; nec
quicquam magis in ore uolgi. crebriores apud ipsum sermones, quanto
sperantibus plura dicuntur. haud dubia destinatione discessere Mucianus
Antiochiam, Vespasianus Caesaream: illa Syriae, hoc Iudaeae caput est.
79 Initium ferendi ad Vespasianum imperii Alexandriae coeptum, fes-
tinante Tiberio Alexandro, qui kalendis Iuliis sacramento eius legiones
adegit. isque primus principatus dies in posterum celebratus, quamuis
Iudaicus exercitus quinto nonas Iulias apud ipsum iurasset, eo ardore ut
ne Titus quidem filius exspectaretur, Syria remeans et consiliorum inter
Mucianum ac patrem nuntius.
Cuncta impetu militum acta non parata contione, non coniunctis
80 legionibus. dum quaeritur tempus locus quodque in re tali difficillimum
est, prima uox, dum animo spes timor, ratio casus obuersantur, egressum cubiculo Vespasianum pauci milites, solito adsistent<es> ordine ut
legatum salutaturi, imperatorem salutauere: tum ceteri adcurrere, Caesarem et Augustum et omnia principatus uocabula cumulare. mens a
metu ad fortunam transierat: in ipso nihil tumidum, arrogans aut in rebus
2 nouis nouum fuit. ut primum tantae altitudinis obfusam oculis caliginem
disiecit, militariter locutus laeta omnia et affluentia excepit; namque id
ipsum opperiens Mucianus alacrem militem in uerba Vespasiani adegit.
tum Antiochensium theatrum ingressus, ubi illis consultare mos est, concurrentes et in adulationem effusos alloquitur, satis decorus etiam Graeca
facundia, omniumque quae diceret atque ageret arte quadam ostentator.
3 nihil aeque prouinciam exercitumque accendit quam quod asseuerabat
Mucianus statuisse Vitellium ut Germanicas legiones in Syriam ad militiam opulentam quietamque transferret, contra Syriacis legionibus Germanica hiberna caelo ac laboribus dura mutarentur; quippe et prouin-
ciales sueto militum contubernio gaudebant, plerique necessitudinibus et
propinquitatibus mixti, et militibus uetustate stipendiorum nota et famil-
iaria castra in modum penatium diligebantur.
81 Ante idus Iuli<as> Syria omnis in eodem sacramento fuit. accessere
cum regno Sohaemus haud spernendis uiribus, Antiochus uetustis opibus
ingens et inseruientium regum ditissimus. mox per occultos suorum nuntios excitus ab urbe Agrippa, ignaro adhuc Vitellio, celeri nauigatione
2 properauerat. nec minore animo regina Berenice partes iuuabat, florens aetate formaque et seni quoque Vespasiano magnificentia munerum

grata. quidquid prouinciarum alluitur mari Asia atque Achaia tenus, quantumque introrsus in Pontum et Armenios patescit, iurauere; sed inermes legati regebant, nondum additis Cappadociae legionibus.

Consilium de summa rerum Beryti habitum. illuc Mucianus cum 3 legatis tribunisque et splendidissimo quoque centurionum ac militum uenit, et e Iudaico exercitu lecta decora: tantum simul peditum equitumque et aemulantium inter se regum paratus speciem fortunae principalis effecerant.

Prima belli cura agere dilectus, reuocare ueteranos; destinantur ual- 82 idae ciuitates exercendis armorum officinis; apud Antiochenses aurum argentumque signatur, eaque cuncta per idoneos ministros suis quaeque locis festinabantur. ipse Vespasianus adire hortari, bonos laude, segnes exemplo incitare saepius quam coercere, uitia magis amicorum quam uirtutes dissimulans. multos praefecturis et procurationibus, plerosque 2 senatorii ordinis honore percoluit, egregios uiros et mox summa adeptos; quibusdam fortuna pro uirtutibus fuit. donatiuum militi neque Mucianus prima contione nisi modice ostenderat, ne Vespasianus quidem plus ciuili bello obtulit quam alii in pace, egregie firmus aduersus militarem largitionem eoque exercitu meliore. missi ad Parthum Armeniumque 3 legati, prouisumque ne uersis ad ciuile bellum legionibus terga nudarentur. Titum instare Iudaeae, Vespasianum obtinere claustra Aegypti placuit: sufficere uidebantur aduersus Vitellium pars copiarum et dux Mucianus et Vespasiani nomen ac nihil arduum fatis. ad omnes exercitus legatosque scriptae epistulae praeceptumque ut praetorianos Vitellio infensos reciperandae militiae praemio inuitarent.

Mucianus cum expedita manu, socium magis imperii quam ministrum 83 agens, non lento itinere, ne cunctari uideretur, neque tamen properans, gliscere famam ipso spatio sinebat, gnarus modicas uires sibi et maiora credi de absentibus; sed legio sexta et tredecim uexillariorum milia ingenti agmine sequebantur. classem e Ponto Byzantium adigi iusserat, ambiguus 2 consilii num omissa Moesia Dyrrachium pedite atque equite, simul longis nauibus uersum in Italiam mare clauderet, tuta pone tergum Achaia Asiaque, quas inermes exponi Vitellio, ni praesidiis firmarentur; atque ipsum Vitellium in incerto fore quam partem Italiae protegeret, si sibi Brundisium Tarentumque et Calabriae Lucaniaeque litora infestis classibus peterentur.

Igitur nauium militum armorum paratu strepere prouinciae, sed nihil 84 aeque fatigabat quam pecuniarum conquisitio: eos esse belli ciuilis neruos dictitans Mucianus non ius aut uerum in cognitionibus, sed solam magnitudinem opum spectabat. passim delationes, et locupletissimus quisque in

2　praedam correpti. quae grauia atque intoleranda, sed necessitate armorum excusata etiam in pace mansere, ipso Vespasiano inter initia imperii
ad obtinendas iniquitates haud perin<de> obstinante, donec indulgentia fortunae et prauis magistris <di>dicit aususque est. propriis quoque
opibus Mucianus bellum iuuit, largus priuatim, quo auidius de re publica
sumeret. ceteri conferendarum pecunia<ru>m exemplum secuti, rarissimus quisque eandem in reciperando licentiam habuerunt.

85　　　Accelerata interim Vespasiani coepta Illyrici exercitus studio transgressi in partes. tertia legio exemplum ceteris Moesiae legionibus praebuit:
octaua erat ac septima Claudiana, imbutae fauore Othonis, quamuis
proelio non interfuissent. Aquileiam progressae, proturbatis qui de Othone nuntiabant laceratisque uexillis nomen Vitellii praeferentibus, rapta
postremo pecunia et inter se diuisa, hostiliter egerant. unde metus et ex
metu consilium, posse imputari Vespasiano quae apud Vitellium excusanda erant. ita tres Moesicae legiones per epistulas alliciebant Pannonicum exercitum aut abnuenti uim parabant.

2　　　In eo motu Aponius Saturninus Moesiae rector pessimum facinus
audet, misso centurione ad interficiendum Tettium Iulianum septimae
legionis legatum ob simultates, quibus causam partium praetendebat.
Iulianus comperto discrimine et gnaris locorum ascitis per auia Moesiae ultra montem Haemum profugit; nec deinde ciuili bello interfuit,
per uarias moras susceptum ad Vespasianum iter trahens et ex nuntiis
cunctabundus aut properans.

86　　At in Pannonia tertia decima legio ac septima Galbiana, dolorem
iramque Bedriacensis pugnae retinentes, haud cunctanter Vespasiano
accessere, ui praecipua Primi Antonii. is legibus nocens et tempore Neronis falsi damnatus inter alia belli mala senatorium ordinem reciperauerat.

2　praepositus a Galba septimae legioni scriptitasse Othoni credebatur,
ducem se partibus offerens; a quo neglectus in nullo Othoniani belli usu
fuit. labantibus Vitellii rebus Vespasianum secutus grande momentum
addidit, strenuus manu, sermone promptus, serendae in alios inuidiae
artifex, discordiis et seditionibus potens, raptor largitor, pace pessimus,
bello non spernendus.

3　　Iuncti inde Moesici ac Pannonici exercitus Dalmaticum militem
traxere, quamquam consularibus legatis nihil turbantibus. Tampius
Flauianus Pannoniam, Pompeius Siluanus Dalmatiam tenebant, diuites
senes; sed procurator aderat Cornelius Fuscus, uigens aetate, claris natalibus. prima iuuenta quietis cupidine senatorium ordinem exuerat; idem
pro Galba dux coloniae suae, eaque opera procurationem adeptus, sus-
ceptis Vespasiani partibus acerrimam bello facem praetulit: non tam

praemiis periculorum quam ipsis periculis laetus pro certis et olim partis noua ambigua ancipitia malebat. igitur mouere et quatere, quidquid 4
usquam aegrum foret, aggrediuntur. scriptae in Britanniam ad quartadecimanos, in Hispaniam ad primanos epistulae, quod utraque legio pro Othone, aduersa Vitellio fuerat; sparguntur per Gallias litterae; momentoque
temporis flagrabat ingens bellum, Illyricis exercitibus palam desciscen-
tibus, ceteris fortunam secuturis.

Dum haec per prouincias a Vespasiano ducibusque partium gerun- 87
tur, Vitellius contemptior in dies segniorque, ad omnes municipiorum
uillarumque amoenitates resistens, graui urbem agmine petebat. sexaginta milia armatorum sequebantur, licentia corrupta; calonum numerus
amplior, procacissimis etiam inter seruos lixarum ingeniis; tot legatorum
amicorumque comitatus inhabilis ad parendum, etiam si summa modestia rege<re>tur. onerabant multitudinem obuii ex urbe senatores equi- 2
tesque, quidam metu, multi per adulationem, ceteri ac paulatim omnes
ne aliis proficiscentibus ipsi remanerent. aggregabantur e plebe flagitiosa
per obsequia Vitellio cogniti, scurrae histriones, aurigae, quibus ille amicitiarum dehonestamentis mire gaudebat. nec coloniae modo aut municipia
congestu copiarum, sed ipsi cultores aruaque maturis iam frugibus ut hostile solum uastabantur.

Multae et atroces inter se militum caedes, post seditionem Ticini coep- 88
tam manente legionum auxiliorumque discordia; ubi aduersus paganos
certandum foret, consensus. sed plurima strages ad septimum ab urbe
lapidem. singulis ibi militibus Vitellius paratos cibos ut gladiatoriam saginam diuidebat; et effusa plebes totis se castris miscuerat. incuriosos milites 2
– uernacula utebantur urbanitate – quidam spoliauere, abscisis furtim
balteis an accincti forent rogitantes. non tulit ludibrium insolens contumeliarum animus: inermem populum gladiis inuasere. caesus inter alios
pater militis, cum filium comitaretur; deinde agnitus et uolgata caede
temperatum ab innoxiis.

In urbe tamen trepidatum praecurrentibus passim militibus; forum 3
maxime petebant, cupidine uisendi locum in quo Galba iacuisset. nec
minus saeuum spectaculum erant ipsi, tergis ferarum et ingentibus telis
horrentes, cum turbam populi per inscitiam parum uitarent, aut ubi
lubrico uiae uel occursu alicuius procidissent, ad iurgium, mox ad manus
et ferrum transirent. quin et tribuni praefectique cum terrore et armatorum cateruis uolitabant.

Ipse Vitellius a ponte Muluio insigni equo, paludatus accinctusque, sen- 89
atum et populum ante se agens, quo minus ut captam urbem ingrederetur, amicorum consilio deterritus, sumpta praetexta et composito agmine

incessit. quattuor legionum aquilae per frontem totidemque circa e legionibus aliis uexilla, mox duodecim alarum signa et post peditum ordines eques; dein quattuor et triginta cohortes, ut nomina gentium aut species
2 armorum forent, discretae. ante aquilas praefecti castrorum tribunique et primi centurionum candida ueste, ceteri iuxta suam quisque centuriam, armis donisque fulgentes; et militum phalerae torquesque splendebant: decora facies et non Vitellio principe dignus exercitus. sic Capitolium ingressus atque ibi matrem complexus Augustae nomine honorauit.

90 Postera die tamquam apud alterius ciuitatis senatum populumque magnificam orationem de semet ipso prompsit, industriam temperantiamque suam laudibus attollens, consciis flagitiorum ipsis qui aderant
2 omnique Italia, per quam somno et luxu pudendus incesserat. uolgus tamen uacuum curis et sine falsi uerique discrimine solitas adulationes edoctum clamore et uocibus astrepebat; abnuentique nomen Augusti expressere ut adsumeret, tam frustra quam recusauerat.

91 Apud ciuitatem cuncta interpretantem funesti ominis loco acceptum est quod maximum pontificatum adeptus Vitellius de caerimoniis publicis xv kalendas Augustas edixisset, antiquitus infausto die Cremerensi Alliensique cladibus: adeo omnis humani diuinique iuris expers, pari libertorum
2 amicorum socordia, uelut inter temulentos agebat. sed comitia consulum cum candidatis ciuiliter celebrans omnem infimae plebis rumorem in theatro ut spectator, in circo ut fautor adfectauit: quae grata sane et popularia, si a uirtutibus proficiscerentur, memoria uitae prioris indecora et uilia accipiebantur.

Ventitabat in senatum, etiam cum paruis de rebus patres consulerentur. ac forte Priscus Heluidius praetor designatus contra studium eius
3 censuerat. commotus primo Vitellius, non tamen ultra quam tribunos plebis in auxilium spretae potestatis aduocauit; mox mitigantibus amicis, qui altiorem iracundiam eius uerebantur, nihil noui accidisse respondit quod duo senatores in re publica dissentirent; solitum se etiam Thraseae contra dicere. irrisere plerique impudentiam aemulationis; aliis id ipsum placebat quod neminem ex praepotentibus, sed Thraseam ad exemplar uerae gloriae legisset.

92 Praeposuerat praetorianis Pub<li>lium Sabinum a praefectura cohortis, Iulium Priscum tum centurionem: Priscus Valentis, Sabinus Caecinae gratia pollebant; inter discordes Vitellio nihil auctoritas. munia imperii Caecina ac Valens obibant, olim anxii odiis, quae bello et castris male dissimulata prauitas amicorum et fecunda gignendis inimicitiis ciuitas auxerat, dum ambitu comitatu et immensis salutantium

agminibus contendunt comparanturque, uariis in hunc aut illum Vitellii inclinationibus; nec umquam satis fida potentia, ubi nimia est. simul 2
ipsum Vitellium, subitis offensis aut intempestiuis blanditiis mutabilem,
contemnebant metuebantque. nec eo segnius inuaserant domos hortos opesque imperii, cum flebilis et egens nobilium turba, quos ipsos
liberosque patriae Galba reddiderat, nulla principis misericordia iuuarentur. gratum primoribus ciuitatis etiam plebs approbauit, quod reuer- 3
sis ab exilio iura libertorum concessisset, quamquam id omni modo
seruilia ingenia corrumpebant, abditis pecuniis per occultos aut ambitiosos sinus, et quidam in domum Caesaris transgressi atque ipsis dominis
potentiores.

Sed miles, plenis castris et redundante multitudine, in porticibus aut 93
delubris et urbe tota uagus, non principia noscere, non seruare uigilias neque labore firmari: per illecebras urbis et inhonesta dictu corpus otio, animum libidinibus imminuebant. postremo ne salutis quidem
cura: infamibus Vaticani locis magna pars tetendit, unde crebrae in uolgus
mortes, et adiacente Tiberi Germanorum Gallorumque obnoxia morbis
corpora fluminis auiditas et aestus impatientia labefecit. insuper con- 2
fusus prauitate uel ambitu ordo militiae: sedecim praetoriae, quattuor
urbanae cohortes scribebantur, quis singula milia inessent. plus in eo
dilectu Valens audebat, tamquam ipsum Caecinam periculo exemisset.
sane aduentu eius partes conualuerant, et sinistrum lenti itineris rumorem
prospero proelio uerterat. omnisque inferioris Germaniae miles Valentem
adsectabatur, unde primum creditur Caecinae fides fluitasse.

Ceterum non ita ducibus indulsit Vitellius ut non plus militi liceret. sibi 94
quisque militiam sumpsere: quamuis indignus, si ita maluerat, urbanae
militiae adscribebatur; rursus bonis remanere inter legionarios aut alares
uolentibus permissum. nec deerant qui uellent, fessi morbis et intemperiem caeli incusantes; robora tamen legionibus alisque subtracta, conuolsum castrorum decus, uiginti milibus e toto exercitu permixtis magis
quam electis.

Contionante Vitellio postulantur ad supplicium Asiaticus et Flauus et 2
Rufinus duces Galliarum, quod pro Vindice bellassent. nec coercebat eius
modi uoces Vitellius: super insitam [mortem] animo ignauiam conscius
sibi instare donatiuum et deesse pecuniam omnia alia militi largiebatur.
liberti principum conferre pro numero mancipiorum ut tributum iussi: 3
ipse sola perdendi cura stabula aurigis exstruere, circum gladiatorum
ferarumque spectaculis opplere, tamquam in summa abundantia pecuniae illudere. quin et natalem Vitellii diem Caecina ac Valens, editis tota 95

urbe uicatim gladiatoribus, celebrauere, ingenti paratu et ante illum diem
insolito.

Laetum foedissimo cuique apud bonos inuidiae fuit quod exstructis in campo Martio aris inferias Neroni fecisset. caesae publice uictimae cremataeque; facem Augustales sub<di>dere, quod sacerdotium,
2 ut Romulus Tatio regi, ita Caesar Tiberius Iuliae genti sacrauit. nondum quartus a uictoria mensis, et libertus Vitellii Asiaticus Polyclitos
Patrobios et uetera odiorum nomina aequabat. nemo in illa aula probitate aut industria certauit: unum ad potentiam iter, prodigis epulis
3 et sumptu ganeaque satiare inexplebiles Vitellii libidines. ipse abunde
ratus si praesentibus frueretur, nec in longius consultans, nouiens miliens
sestertium paucissimis mensibus interuertisse creditur. magna et misera
ciuitas, eodem anno Othonem Vitellium passa, inter Vinios Fabios, Icelos
Asiaticos uaria et pudenda sorte agebat, donec successere Mucianus et
Marcellus et magis alii homines quam alii mores.

96   Prima Vitellio tertiae legionis defectio nuntiatur, missis ab Aponio Sat-
urnino epistulis, antequam is quoque Vespasiani partibus aggregaretur;
sed neque Aponius cuncta, ut trepidans re subita, perscripserat, et amici
adulantes mollius interpretabantur: unius legionis eam seditionem, ceteris
2 exercitibus constare fidem. in hunc modum etiam Vitellius apud milites
disseruit, praetorianos nuper exauctoratos insectatus, a quibus falsos
rumores dispergi, nec ullum ciuilis belli metum asseuerabat, suppresso
Vespasiani nomine et uagis per urbem militibus qui sermones populi
coercerent. id praecipuum alimentum famae erat.

97   Auxilia tamen e Germania Britanniaque et Hispaniis exciuit, segniter
et necessitatem dissimulans. perinde legati prouinciaeque cunctabantur,
Hordeonius Flaccus suspectis iam Batauis anxius proprio bello, Vettius
Bolanus numquam satis quieta Britannia, et uterque ambigui. neque ex
Hispaniis properabatur, nullo tum ibi consulari: trium legionum legati,
pares iure et prosperis Vitellii rebus certaturi ad obsequium, aduersam
2 eius fortunam ex aequo detrectabant. in Africa legio cohortesque delec-
tae a Clodio Macro, mox a Galba dimissae, rursus iussu Vitellii militiam
cepere; simul cetera iuuentus dabat impigre nomina. quippe integrum
illic ac fauorabilem proconsulatum Vitellius, famosum inuisumque Vespasianus egerat: proinde socii de imperio utriusque coniectabant, sed
experimentum contra fuit.

98   Ac primo Valerius Festus legatus studia prouincialium cum fide iuuit;
mox nutabat, palam epistulis edictisque Vitellium, occultis nuntiis Vespasianum fouens et haec illaue defensurus, prout inualuissent. deprehensi cum litteris edictisque Vespasiani per Raetiam et Gallias militum et

centurionum quidam ad Vitellium missi necantur: plures fefellere, fide
amicorum aut suomet astu occultati. ita Vitellii paratus noscebantur, 2
Vespasiani consiliorum pleraque ignota, primum socordia Vitellii, dein
Pannonicae Alpes praesidiis insessae nuntios retinebant. mare quoque
etesiarum flatu in Orientem nauigantibus secundum, inde aduersum
erat.

Tandem irruptione hostium atrocibus undique nuntiis exterritus 99
Caecinam ac Valentem expedire ad bellum iubet. praemissus Caecina,
Valentem e graui corporis morbo tum primum assurgentem infirmitas
tardabat. longe alia proficiscentis ex urbe Germanici exercitus species:
non uigor corporibus, non ardor animis; lentum et rarum agmen, fluxa
arma, segnes equi; impatiens solis pulueris tempestatum, quantumque
hebes ad sustinendum laborem miles, tanto ad discordias promptior.

Accedebat huc Caecinae ambitio uetus, torpor recens, nimia fortunae 2
indulgentia soluti in luxum, seu perfidiam meditanti infringere exercitus uirtutem inter artes erat. credidere plerique Flauii Sabini consiliis
concussam Caecinae mentem, ministro sermonum Rubrio Gallo: rata
apud Vespasianum fore pacta transitionis. simul odiorum inuidiaeque
erga Fabium Valentem admonebatur ut impar apud Vitellium gratiam
uiresque apud nouum principem pararet.

Caecina e complexu Vitellii multo cum honore digressus partem equi- 100
tum ad occupandam Cremonam praemisit. mox uexilla primae, quartae,
quintaedecimae, sextaedecimae legionum, dein quinta et duoetuicensima secutae; postremo agmine unaetuicensima Rapax et prima Italica
incessere cum uexillariis trium Britannicarum legionum et electis auxiliis.

Profecto Caecina scripsit Fabius Valens exercitui, quem ipse duc- 2
tauerat, ut in itinere opperiretur: sic sibi cum Caecina conuenisse. qui
praesens eoque ualidior mutatum id consilium finxit ut ingruenti bello
tota mole occurreretur. ita accelerare legiones, <pars> Cremonam 3
pars Hostiliam petere iussae: ipse Rauennam deuertit praetexto classem
alloquendi; mox patuit secretum componendae proditionis quaesitum.
namque Lucilius Bassus post praefecturam alae Rauennati simul ac Misenensi classibus a Vitellio praepositus, quod non statim praefecturam
praetorii adeptus foret, iniquam iracundiam flagitiosa perfidia ulcisce-
batur. nec sciri potest traxeritne Caecinam, an, quod euenit inter malos
ut et similes sint, eadem illos prauitas impulerit.

Scriptores temporum, qui potiente rerum Flauia domo monimenta 101
belli huiusce composuerunt, curam pacis et amorem rei publicae, corruptas in adulationem causas, tradidere: nobis super insitam leuitatem
et prodito Galba uilem mox fidem aemulatione etiam inuidiaque, ne ab

aliis apud Vitellium anteirentur, peruertisse ipsum Vitellium uidentur.
2 Caecina legiones assecutus centurionum militumque animos obstinatos
pro Vitellio uariis artibus subruebat: Basso eadem molienti minor diffi-
cultas erat, lubrica ad mutandam fidem classe ob memoriam recentis pro
Othone militiae.

COMMENTARY

1–7 TITUS, VESPASIAN AND A BID FOR POWER

The previous book ended at Rome (rather darkly) with a fervent *libido seruitii* (1.90.3) more familiar from stereotypical images of the east. T. now turns to the east itself, specifically to the incipient Flavian challenge. To locate an account of the *initia causasque imperio* (2.1.1) at the start of a book is structurally and artistically appropriate, but by this arrangement T. also asserts his independence as a historian. Pro-Flavian accounts of Vespasian's rise to power had judiciously post-dated the challenge as the only possible response to Vitellius' 'decadent' principate (Jos. *BJ* 4.588–604). Instead, T. makes it amply clear that Otho is still *princeps* when the seeds for the Flavian challenge are first planted: *se Vitellio siue Othoni obsidem fore* (2.1.3), *nec referre Vitellium an Othonem superstitem fortuna faceret* (2.7.1). Although Vespasian was officially proclaimed emperor in Egypt on 1 Jul. 69 (2.79, Jos. *BJ* 4.592–604, Suet. *Ves.* 6.3), T. makes Titus' abortive journey to Galba, rendered obsolete by the emperor's death on 15 Jan. 69 (1.27.1), the significant turning-point for the Flavians. This suggestive chronological framework allows at least five and a half months for the Flavians to plan their challenge (narrated in full at 2.74–86). So pro-Flavian images of the soldiers' 'spontaneous' demands that an 'unwilling' Vespasian should become emperor seem hollow and contrived in comparison.

Even so, Vespasian himself has a peculiarly low profile in this section, as T. points the spotlight firmly at his elder son, the affable Titus. His anxious debate with his friends about whether or not to continue his journey (2.1.3) and his surreptitious questioning of the priest Sostratus about himself (2.4.1) are revealing about his personality and ambitions. In contrast, Vespasian's inner thoughts are not elaborated at all at this point. T. momentarily gives us a glimpse of an 'alternative history', in which Titus himself could have become emperor, according to some observers (2.1.2; cf. 1.50.4. See O'Gorman (2006) on 'virtual history' and Pagán (2006) on 'side-shadowing'). Yet at the same time T. also makes it clear that Titus has no imperial ambitions (cf. Germanicus in the *Annals*, with whom Titus shares many traits). Titus, acutely aware of the dangers, thinks purely in terms of his father as a potential challenger: *sin Vespasianus rem publicam susciperet* (2.1.3). This is perhaps not entirely altruistic, but it coheres with a recurrent pattern in the *H.* where third parties in the background act as facilitators or prompt others to act: e.g. the astrologer Ptolemy and Otho (1.22.2–3), Fabius Valens and Vitellius (1.52.3–4), and Mucianus and Vespasian (2.76–7). T. certainly alludes to the hedonistic personality of Titus (2.2.1, 2.4.1), who may have preferred to enjoy the fruits of imperial power without facing the risks of being a direct challenger. Yet whether Vespasian himself is the right sort of man for this rôle is another question implicitly posed in this section. T. casts Vespasian as an ideal general, marred only by a tendency towards *auaritia* (2.5.1). This portrait at first seems comforting, but a man who is *antiquis ducibus par* (2.5.1) should strike readers as being a mismatch for these treacherous times. Slippery operators like his colleague Mucianus appear to have a better chance of success, or indeed the pragmatic and ruthless Antonius Primus (2.86.1–2), who eventually secures victory for the Flavians.

T. fleshes out this section with a suggestive account of Titus' visit to the temple of Paphian Venus (not in Jos.; but see Suet. *Tit.* 5.1), which prompts a digression on the cult of the goddess (2.3). Some question its relevance: Syme calls it 'frankly exotic, almost extraneous' ((1958a) 310), and Wellesley is uneasy, since 'the abortive trip seems hardly worth a mention' ((2000) 44). Yet this digression slows down the narrative at a significant moment, raising the stakes by providing a dramatic religious backdrop to the inauguration of the Flavian challenge. Unlike Otho, who has no time to linger over rituals (1.89.3), the Flavians can afford to wait. We can also see a contrast between the digression's inner frame and the surrounding narrative: whereas the families of the local man Cinyras and the outsider Tamiras cordially co-operate with each other in presiding over the rites of the temple (with the descendants of the latter eventually stepping down), the contenders for the principate destructively resort to war to settle their differences. It is ironic too that Venus is the goddess of love, and the mother of Aeneas, from whom Augustus, the founder of another imperial dynasty, traced his descent. Finally, the digression is also a prelude to Titus' consultation of the priest Sostratus. This is one of three related narrative segments, where members of the Flavian dynasty successively consult priests: cf. Vespasian's visit to Carmel and consultation of Basilides (2.78) and Vespasian's visit to temple of Serapis (4.82–4). Vespasian and Titus clearly share similar concerns, but Domitian (though young) is conspicuously absent from such scenes (a tacit sign of rifts to come, perhaps; 4.86). So while there is certainly not much formal action in this section, it helps to characterise the fledgling Flavian dynasty, introducing important themes to be expanded subsequently in the narrative.

1.1 Struebat . . . imperio 'Fortune was already establishing in a different part of the world the origins and causes for a dynasty.' T. successively evokes *fortuna* and *fatum* during the Flavian rise to power (1.10.3, 2.82.3, 3.1.1, 3.59.2, 3.82.3; Scott (1968) 70–84), but thereby implies neither that Vespasian was a flawless challenger (cf. *solus . . . omnium ante se principum in melius mu<ta>tus est*, 1.50.4) nor that *fortuna* was benign or purposeful (cf. *magna documenta instabilis fortunae summaque et ima miscentis*, 4.47). *Fortuna* had had a temple in Rome since the regal period (North (2000) 36); cf. Lucan's Caesar, rashly pledging himself to Fortune (1.226) without being abandoned by her, despite his impiety (Weinstock (1971) 112–27 on Caesar's *fortuna*). Pro-Flavian propaganda exploited *fortuna*, an important concept both during and after the civil wars, to cast Vespasian as a superior, yet reluctant, candidate (Levick (1999) 67). *fortuna* differs from *fatum* (Sage (1990) 946–8 and Levene (1993) 13–15), since '*fatum* denoted the future as decreed by the gods, while *fortuna* referred to something like the chance element in the world' (Levene (1993) 13). 'The words belong to literature, not dogma' (Syme (1958a) 527n.2). T. previously combined *initia causasque* to introduce the Vitellian challenge (1.51.1). The pair, which has an obvious opening function, features 'at significant points' (MW 80) e.g. *A.* 4.1.1. Ancient historians were naturally concerned to shed light on the causes of events.   **quod uaria sorte laetum rei publicae**

uel atrox 'which was, with varying lot, happy for the state or terrible'. T.'s Eprius Marcellus subsequently emphasises the random calibre of emperors: *bonos imperatores uoto expetere, qualescumque tolerare* (4.8.2). The Lucretian coinage *uaria sorte* (4.1223) is only in the *H.* (2.70.3, 2.95.3, 3.80.1), here in a subordinate clause undercutting the book's apparently optimistic opening and confirming that *fortuna* is capricious. T.'s subordinate clauses often suggestively outweigh his main clauses (Martin (1981) 221, O'Gorman (2000) 3–4).   **ipsis principibus . . . fuit:** Vespasian and Titus prospered, but imperial power was deadly for Domitian, assassinated on 18 Sept. 96. Cf. *A.* 3.24.2 (with WM 224) for Augustus' principate as *ualida* for the state, but *improspera* domestically. T. uses the predicative dat. *exitio* elsewhere only in the *A.* (3.28.1, 3.55.3, 6.30.3, 11.24.4). For *uariatio* of adj. + dat., see Sörbom (1935) 89.   **Titus Vespasianus:** although Vespasian's elder son Titus has already featured twice (1.1.3, 1.10.3), T. formally marks his entry into the text as a protagonist by using both *praenomen* (Titus) and *cognomen* (Vespasianus). His full name was Titus Flavius Vespasianus, while his younger brother Domitian was Titus Flavius Domitianus. Under the empire, individuals were usually referred to by their *cognomen*, but in literary texts Titus is generally known by his *praenomen* alone to distinguish him from his father, whose *cognomen* (Vespasianus) he shared (Suet. *Tit.* 1.1).   **e Iudaea . . . patre:** T. has already mentioned Titus' mission to congratulate Galba for becoming emperor (1.10.3), but reserves the full story for its proper place, which (T. judges) has now arrived (Fuhrmann (1960) 267). The date of the mission is difficult to establish. Since popular rumour speculated that the journey was a prelude to Titus' adoption by Galba, who adopted Piso on 10 Jan. 69 (1.18.1), he probably set off before then. Nero killed himself on 9 Jun. or (possibly) 11 Jun. 68 (Murison (1993) 6). It must have taken time for the news to reach Vespasian and Titus in Judaea, so Titus perhaps began his journey late in 68 or early in 69, turning back at the end of January. The season indicates the importance of the mission, since winter sea-journeys were unpopular: *est enim hiberna nauigatio odiosa* (Cic. *Att.* 15.25 with Rougé (1952)). Suetonius also mentions Titus' journey (*Tit.* 5.1). Josephus says that Berenice's brother King Agrippa II, the client-king of eastern Palestine, accompanied Titus on this mission (*BJ* 4.498) and continued the journey to Rome, but T. postpones his introduction (81.1n. *Agrippa*). That T. narrates the journey here, when Titus turns back, rather than earlier (1.10.3) is historiographically important (Büchner (1964) 84). The hint that Titus was even now thinking about empire undercuts pro-Flavian propaganda, which post-dated Vespasian's bid for power as a reaction against Vitellius.   **causam profectionis** 'as the reason for the journey' (predicative acc.).   **officium erga principem:** other sources suggest that visiting Galba was not just a polite gesture. Vespasian allegedly feared assassination by Galba's agents (Suet. *Gal.* 23, only here). If so, the decision to send his son to Rome was a bold insurance policy. Titus' main aim was probably to secure harmony between his father and the new emperor (Levick (1999) 44), whose recent dismissal of Vespasian's brother Flavius Sabinus as *praefectus urbi* no doubt alarmed the family (Nicols (1978) 61–2). Josephus suggests another possibility, that the practical Vespasian sought orders from Galba about the Jewish war (*BJ* 4.498).   **maturam . . . iuuentam:** Titus (born 30 Dec., 39), currently legionary legate of the *XV Apollinaris* in Judaea, was probably seeking a praetorship (Chilver (1979) 162, Levick (1999) 44). '*adulescentia* was the usual word, *iuuenta* a poeticism' (Adams (1973) 137).   **ferebat** 'alleged, claimed' (*OLD* 32). The formulation hints at a (typically Tacitean) gulf between professed and hidden reasons for the trip.   **uolgus fingendi auidum** 'the people, eager to fab-ricate stories'. Although T. disdains the gossipy *uolgus*, the previous sentence still hints (*causam . . . profectionis*) that Titus' journey has a hidden agenda. T. uses rumours extensively to evoke the atmosphere of the times (Shatzman (1974), Gibson (1998); cf. Laurence (1994)). Rome is characterised as a hotbed of rumours (cf. 1.12.2, 1.19.2, 1.85.2, *A.* 11.27.1, 13.6.2); her inhabitants' tendency to gossip is integral to the dra-matic beginning of the *Dialogus* (*D.* 2.1).   **disperserat:** *dispergo* used as if it were a verb of speaking followed by an acc. + inf. construction is peculiarly Tacitean (cf. *A.* 14.38.3, *TLL* s.v. *dispergo* 1410.44–6), although it often takes nouns such as *rumor* and *fama* as direct objects (*TLL* s.v. *dispergo* 1410.36–44). The 'instantaneous' pluper-fect indicates the rapidity of the change effected (Roby (1879) §1492; also *aboleuerat* 2.5.2; *cinxerant* 2.25.1; *proruperant* 2.73, *transierat* 2.80.1; *effecerant* 2.81.3). Here it nicely undercuts Titus' claims in the previous sentence about the reasons for his journey. The *uolgus* (typically) had already cooked up and circulated their own explanation for his trip.   **accitum in adoptionem:** sc. *esse*. Assonance emphasises a rumour perhaps invented later to flatter the Flavian dynasty (Levick (1999) 44).   **materia sermonibus:** sc. *erat*. The Ciceronian phrase (*Q.fr.* 1.2.3; cf. *Fam.* 3.6.4) recurs in T. (4.4.1) for gossip amongst the senators. *materia*, 'basis', for gossip is aptly metaphorical (*OLD* 4d 'fuel for a fire'), since fire-imagery is often linked with rumour: cf. *hos uolgi ser-mones . . . incendit* (*A.* 2.82.3).   **senium . . . destinandi** 'the old-age and childlessness of the emperor and the extravagance of the city in designating many candidates until one is selected'. In T. *ciuitas* often = the city of Rome (G-G 173–4), but *intemperantia* features only once more (*A.* 4.18.2), where Gaius Silius' *intemperantia* apparently left him vulnerable to attack by Sejanus. Actions dangerous for an individual are often safer for a group (2.29.3, 2.52.2, 3.31.2, *A.* 5.4.3, *A.* 14.49.3, Caes. *BG* 1.27.4, Plin. *Ep.* 2.11.7). Cf. 23.5n. *palam . . . occultis*. T. comments on futile public speculation about Claudius, whom nobody predicted would become emperor (*A.* 3.18.4). Not only the *uolgus* speculated about imperial candidates (cf. *A.* 1.13.2–3 for Augustus designating *capaces imperii*).

    1.2 quantaecumque fortunae: *fortuna*, 'greatness' (*OLD* 11b), here with specific resonances of imperial power, as *post fortunam* (1.10.3), *inserere se fortunae* (2.61), and *mens . . . ad fortunam transierat* (2.80.1).   **decor . . . maiestate:** Suetonius describes Titus' appearance, marred only by a slight pot-belly, but enhanced by his physical attractiveness and authoritative presence (*non minus auctoritatis quam gratiae, Tit.* 3.1). The implicit contrast is with Galba. Such physical comparisons between emperors were popular (Galba and Nero, 1.7.3). Seneca describes Nero's beauty (*Apoc.* 4.31–2), in sharp contrast with his predecessor Claudius' defects (*Apoc.* 5.2, 6.2).   **praesaga responsa:** *praesagus* 'portentous' (*OLD* 2) is poetical, though Cicero and Livy use the verb *praesagio* (Kuntz (1962) 23–5). Suetonius lists omens in detail (*Ves.* 5), but T. is more selective (2.78.2). *responsum* refers to an answer received from an oracle, astrologer or diviner (cf. 4.65.4). **et inclinatis ad credendum animis loco ominum etiam fortuita** 'as well as the coincidences which a credulous society took as omens'. *fortuita* = nom.; *animis* = dat. (*OLD* 2a for *animus* substituted for persons). Cf. Cic. *Diu.* 2.27.58 for similar gullibility during wartime. In T., *locus* ('as' *OLD* 18c) with the gen. in the context of omens usually implies misguided interpreters or at best, that they are right, but for the wrong reasons (2.91.1, 4.26.2, *G.* 8.3, *A.* 11.11.2, 13.58). The phrasing is Livian: *inclinatis . . . ad credendum animis* (40.21.10; cf. 1.51.7, 7.21.5, 24.31.6, 28.15.16, 30.43.1, 31.32.1).

1.3 Corinthi: locative case. Corinth, on the isthmus joining central Greece to the Peloponnese, a flourishing centre of commerce, administration and entertainment during the Roman period (Wiseman (1979) 509–21), was a convenient and pleasant place for Titus to break his journey. Commercial construction had flourished particularly under Claudius (Williams (1993)), but it was devastated by an earthquake in 77. **Achaiae urbe:** contemporary readers knew where Corinth was, so the gloss suggests T.'s expectation that the *H.* would be read in the future by readers not so conversant with ancient topography (Kenney). **certos nuntios:** the adj. is not superfluous. T. is sensitive to inaccurate reports and rumours about 'dead' emperors who were really alive (1.34.2–35) or *vice versa* (*A.* 1.5.4); and a 'false Nero' is imminent (2.8–9). **de interitu Galbae:** Galba was killed in Rome on 15 Jan. 69 (1.27.1). **anxius animo:** cf. *anxius animi atque incertus* (Sall. *Hist.* 4.68 Maurenbrecher). T. calls Cluvius Rufus *animo anxius* (2.65.1) and Domitian *pectore anxius* (*Agr.* 39.1), but both explicitly deceive onlookers by showing happiness on their faces. **paucis amicorum adhibitis:** cf. *paucis familiarium adhibitis* (*A.* 2.57.3, of Germanicus, *A.* 3.10.3, of Tiberius). Titus' desire to consult others contrasts with his more secretive brother Domitian (*talibus curis exercitus, quodque saeuae cogitationis indicium erat, secreto suo satiatus, Agr.* 39.3; cf. Plin. *Pan.* 48, Juv. 4.72–5). The difference is later made explicit (4.86.2; Bannon (1997) 181–2). T., seeing Titus' potential as a foil for Domitian, may play down his bad qualities (Urban (1971) 107–19). **cuncta utrimque perlustrat:** *perlustro*, 'ponder' (*OLD* 2c), only here in T.'s extant works, is in Cicero and Seneca the Younger. *cunctus*, an artificial alternative to *omnis*, was 'not in everyday educated use during the early empire' and in the *H.* '*cuncta* is used only in the narrative', not in the speeches (Adams (1973) 129–31). **si pergeret . . . fore:** future conditional sentence in indirect speech in secondary sequence of tenses. The verb in the protasis (if-clause), following an implied *dixit*, changes from future indicative to imperfect subjunctive. The verb in the apodosis changes from future indicative to future infinitive (GL §595). T., our only source for Titus' concerns here, probably draws on his imagination to recreate the debate. Suetonius simply says *redit ex itinere* (*Tit.* 5.1). **nullam . . . suscepti** '(there would be) no gratitude for a duty undertaken to honour another man'. **se . . . obsidem:** possibly an over-reaction, albeit revealing about Flavian imperial ambitions. If Otho or Vitellius sought a hostage, Vespasian's brother Flavius Sabinus, the city prefect, was already in Rome (1.46.1). In fact neither man harmed or took hostages from the other's family (1.75.2). **offensam haud**

dubiam uictoris '(it would be) a definite affront (*OLD offensa* 5a) to the victor' (*uictoris* = objective gen.). Titus may over-estimate his own importance. T. says that Otho was quite forgiving (1.47.1). **sed . . . excusatum** (sc. *iri*, an unusual ellipse, perhaps explained by *iri* dropping out of the manuscripts by haplography, as Kenney suggests) 'but victory (was) still uncertain, and if his father went over to the (winning) party, the son (would be) excused'. Cf. Tiberius' argument that *patris quippe iussa nec potuisse filium detrectare* (*A.* 3.17.1; cf. *A.* 1.6.1). Titus is prepared to play on public perceptions of his youth, but his calculations here suggest political shrewdness. Cf. *A.* 1.47.2 for a father (Tiberius) hiding behind his (real and adopted) sons, despite public disapproval. **sin . . . susciperet:** the adversative conditional particle *sin*, 'if however', is generated by the hidden conditional implicit in the abl. absolute of the previous sentence, *concedente . . . patre.* 'When two conditions exclude each other, *si* is used for the first; *sin* . . . for the second' (GL §592; cf. 2.28.2, 4.20.1, 5.25.1). The first *si* need not be expressed explicitly, but context usually implies it (cf. 3.26.2). This pronouncement, focalised through Titus, pulls against pro-Flavian propaganda, which (misleadingly) post-dated Vespasian's challenge to Vitellius' principate. Nor is this Titus' private thought: his readiness to discuss the possibility of an imperial challenge with friends is significant. **obliuiscendum . . . agitantibus** 'men pondering war would have to forget about causing offence'. T. unusually uses a gerund, *obliuiscendum*, rather than an infinitive. Titus' pragmatism in this apodosis cuts through the complex debate so far, suggesting a link with his father's reputedly practical personality. Cic., Sall., and Liv. have *agito* (*OLD* 16c, 17c) + *de.*

    2.1 inter . . . iactatum: T. often combines *spes* + *metus* (G-G 1536–9), 'a natural coupling' (Oakley (1998) 537–8), but the language cumulatively evokes Virgil (*spemque metumque inter*, *A.* 1.218), who 'constantly' has *iacto* (Austin (1971) 30). The echoes heighten the tone, but need not cast Titus as Aeneas and Berenice as Dido (Guerrini (1986)). **spes uicit:** T. often makes an abstract noun the subject. In practical terms T. just means that Titus chose to abandon his journey, but *spes* also suggests a grander frame of reference i.e. hope of imperial power. Cf. Vitellius, driven *ut concupisceret magis quam ut speraret* (1.52.4), and Vespasian's *spes occultae* (2.78.3). **fuerunt qui . . . crederent:** the perfect tense indicates contemporary rumour rather than retroactive speculation by T.'s sources. Unattributed beliefs recur throughout *H.* as T. recreates the atmosphere of the times (with particularly close verbal parallels for the phrasing at 1.7.2, 3.11.4, *A.* 4.57.2, 14.10.3, and 15.43.5). The orthodox view casts T. as deviously reporting unattributed rumours to denigrate individuals, without himself taking responsibility for the views expressed. Yet in some cases T. wholly or partially confirms the rumour, as here (Pauw (1980), Marincola (1997) 93–4). **accensum desiderio:** the verb *accendo* is a Sallustian favourite (Horsfall (2000) 362) and recalls the Numidian King Syphax, *accensum cupiditate* (Liv. 29.23.4; also *accensum recenti amore*, 29.23.7) for Hasdrubal's daughter. Pliny tells his wife that by reading her letters *magis ad desiderium tui accendor* (*Ep.* 6.7.2). Titus' romance with Berenice (Suet. *Tit.* 7.1, Dio 66.15) perhaps began while visiting Agrippa's palace at Caesarea Philippi in the summer of 67 (Jos. *BJ* 3.444). 'Imagery derived from fire and flames is much favoured by

T.' (Martin (2001) 153; Fantham (1972) 86–8 analyses fire imagery for love, a pervasive feature of Virg. *A.* 4). **Berenices reginae:** Berenice (*OCD³* 'Berenice (4)'), daughter of Agrippa I, married her uncle Herod, king of Chalcis in Syria, in 46 aged 18, and then Polemon, king of Olba in Cilicia, in 53/4 (partly to quell rumours of incest from living with her brother). She tried unsuccessfully to help her brother Agrippa II (81.1n.) settle problems in Jerusalem in 66, but joined him in offering support to the nascent Flavian dynasty (2.81.2). After the civil war, she came to Rome in 75 to live with Titus, but was eventually dismissed (Suet. *Tit.* 7.2, Dio 66.15.3–4; Racine wrote a play, *Bérénice*, about this *peripeteia*), perhaps because the damage she was doing to Titus' reputation (Crook (1951), Rogers (1980), Braund (1984b), Levick (1999) 192–5, Keaveney and Madden (2003)). Two cynic philosophers, Diogenes and Heras, had denounced her in a crowded theatre in Rome (Dio 66.15.5). A prominent eastern queen, she risked evoking the image of 'dubious' predecessors such as Cleopatra, and her fabulous wealth and influence may have caused resentment in straitened times: Vespasian's 'professor of rhetoric' Quintilian mentions pleading a case on her behalf (4.1.19), so she could clearly afford the best; Juvenal describes a fabulously valuable ring belonging to Berenice on sale in Rome (6.157).   **iuuenilis animus:** T. as narrator confirms that Titus was fond of Berenice, but urbanely undercuts sensational popular gossip that the young man was enslaved to his passion. T. elsewhere uses this phrase only of Nero (*A.* 12.64.3, 13.11.1), with whom Titus was often linked (Suet. *Tit.* 7.1). Using an adj. instead of a dependent noun in the gen. (i.e. *iuuenis*), frequent in T. (Goodyear (1972) 117–18, WM 156–7), contributes to a lofty style: cf. *hostilem libidinem* (*Agr.* 31.1), *militarem largitionem* (2.82.2). Cf. Shakespeare, *Julius Caesar* I ii 11: 'sterile curse' = curse of sterility.   **neque abhorrebat a Berenice** 'was far from insensible to Berenice's charms'. The elegant litotes (Lausberg (1998) §586–8) initially seems to confirm the popular rumour in elevated language suitable for historiography, but T. modifies this impression in the subsequent *sed* clause.   **gerendis . . . impedimentum:** sc. *erat.* For the phrasing, cf. *magnum utrisque impedimentum ad rem gerendam fuit* (Liv. 33.6.7). **laetam uoluptatibus adulescentiam:** Romans indulged hedonistic young men, provided this did not continue indefinitely; when young, even Cato the Younger spent the night drinking (Plut. *Cat. Mi.* 6.2). T. judges similar behaviour in Otho (1.13.3) and Domitian (4.2.1) more harshly.

  2.2 Igitur as the first word in a sentence is 'the norm in the historical works (167 occurrences), where it is perhaps an archaism' (Mayer (2001) 113; Adams (1973) 132–3).   **Achaiae et Asiae:** Achaea is the 'official name for the Roman province of Greece, commemorating Rome's defeat of the Achaean Confederacy in 146 BC' (*OCD³* 'Achaia'). T. himself was subsequently (112–13) proconsul of Asia, a prestigious post.   **laeua maris praeuectus** 'having sailed by the coastal areas to his left'. T. is devoted to the neuter substantive adj. + defining gen. (Goodyear (1972) 202–3, Nisbet and Hubbard (1978) 24, Constans (1893) §23b, WM 82); cf. *laeua moenium* (Sall. *Hist.* 2.54), *laeua Italiae* (Liv. 32.29.6) and *laeua fluminis* (Pliny *Nat.* 6.145).   **audentioribus spatiis** 'by a bolder crossing'. T. means that Titus, after hugging the coast, rashly sailed across greater stretches of open sea. This illustrates a general point, that sailors in antiquity lacking navigational aids liked to stay close to the coast: by contemporary standards, Titus was running risks. For the phrasing cf. *modo breuioribus modo longioribus spatiis* (Liv. 5.27.2).   **atque** 'And thereupon' (*OLD atque* 5c); cf. 2.49.1.   **illum cupido incessit:** some see Titus' *cupido* as evoking Alexander the Great's *pothos* for seeing famous sites (e.g. Arr. *An.* 2.3.1, 3.3.1, Curt. 4.7.8, 4.8.3, 10.1.16, [Call.] 3.27–8 with Guerrini (1986) 28 n.3 for bibliography). Yet T. (4.82.1, 5.23.1, *A.* 1.61.1 with Woodman (1998) 218–29, *A.* 2.54.1), Liv. (1.56.10, 24.13.5) and Sall. (*Cat.* 7.3) have similar language. *cupido* (cf. *cupiditas*, used exclusively by Cic. and Caes.) is Sallustian (WM 147).   **templum Paphiae Veneris:** Aphrodite's temple on Cyprus in Old Paphos overlooked the wealthy city of New Paphos, which contained the Roman proconsul's residence and the main port for those en route to Syria and Egypt. Horace calls her *regina . . . Paphi* (*Carm.* 1.30.1). During her annual festival, people processed *c.* 10 miles (Strabo 14.6) from the new city to the old city. The Flavians probably rebuilt Aphrodite's temple, seriously damaged in the earthquake of 77. There was a sugar-mill on the site in medieval times (Mitford (1980a) 1314 n.99). Archaeologists think that the foundations currently surviving in the area belong to two sanctuaries used concurrently, 'the southern, in essentials Mycenean, but re-paved with Roman slabs; the northern, which in part overlies it, a Roman construction seemingly of Flavian date . . . incorporating *in situ* megalithic blocks of Bronze Age origin' (Mitford (1990) 2179). Our sanctuary is the northern one. A sardonyx gem found in the House of Theseus in New Paphos and engraved with a legionary eagle and the inscription *LEG. XV APOLLINARIS* (W. A. Daszewski, *Reports of the Department of Antiquities, Cyprus* (1973) 202–11) offers an extraordinary piece of material evidence for Titus' visit. **inclutum . . . aduenasque:** T. uses *inclutus* less often after the *H.*, 'perhaps because it was the very kind of word a historian was expected to use: he is always counter-suggestible' (Goodyear (1981) 353; cf. Kuntz (1962) 99–101). Other historians relate the dedication of famous shrines and temples (esp. Liv. 1.45.2, 2.8.7, 24.3.6), a crucial part of annalistic history (Oakley (1997) 60–1), but T.'s digressions on the rites of Venus and (later) Serapis (4.82–4) are unusual, both in extent and in historiographical impact. The digressions link the personalities of Titus and Vespasian, contrasting them with Vitellius' insensitive attitude to religion (2.91.1). Sall., Liv., and T. are more likely than other prose writers to end a sentence with an enclitic *–que* (8 × in *H.* 2), perhaps a choice feature of the republican historiographical style (Kraus (1992)). **haud fuerit longum . . . disserere** 'It may be of some interest to discuss' (*OLD longus* 8a, 9c). The perfect subj. = potential, with a future aspect (*NLS* §119, MW 104). An apologetic formula formally opens the digression: cf. *haud fuerit absurdum tradere* (*A.* 4.65.1 with MW 238). There are three substantial excursuses in the *H.* (2.3, 4.83, 5.2–10: Syme (1958a) 310), but 1.89, 2.38, 3.34, 3.51, 3.68, 3.72 and 3.83 also have digressive qualities (Hahn (1933) 78–85). Pliny the Elder may be T.'s source here (Townend (1962a) 361–2).   **neque enim alibi sic habetur** 'for she is not presented in this way anywhere else' (*TLL* s.v. *habeo* 2461.1–15; cf. *A.* 1.73.2, 6.8.4, 13.30). T. will substantiate (2.3.2). This proleptic device prompts interest and further justifies the digression.

3.1 Conditorem . . . Aëriam: Aerias is not mentioned outside T. (Pirenne-Delforge (1994) 330–3). In an alternative tradition, Agapenor, leader of the Arcadian forces who fought with Agamemnon at Troy (Hom. *Il.* 2.609), founded the temple (Paus. 8.5.2, 53.7, Strabo 14.682). Venus' 'scented altar' on Paphos is already in Homer (*Od.* 8.363), but no founder features there. T. later reiterates that Aerias founded the temple, identifying his son as Amathus (*A.* 3.62.4), also the name of an ancient coastal city on Cyprus. Aerias' 'son' was perhaps invented as the city's eponymous founder, a common phenomenon in the ancient world. Stephanus of Byzantium, *s.v. Amathous*, says that the city is named after Amathus, son of Heracles, or Amathousa, mother of Cinyras.   **uetus memoria . . . fama recentior:** T. often highlights such divergences between sources in his digressions; cf. *Liuius ueterum, Fabius Rusticus recentium eloquentissimi auctores (Agr.* 10.3).   **quidam . . . perhibent:** Crates says that the island of Crete itself was first called Aeria (Plin. *Nat.* 4.58), making Aerias an apt (if predictable) name for the founder of such an important temple.   **a Cinyra:** a legendary king of Cyprus (Pind. *Pyth.* 2.15–16, *Nem.* 8.18) and father of Myrrha. An incestuous relationship between the pair produced Adonis (Antimachus of Colophon *Lyde* fr. 102 Wyss, with Matthews (1996) 256–7, Apoll. 3.14.3, Hyginus 58, Liberalis 34, Ov. *Met.* 10.298–502). Pliny says that Cinyras lived to be 160 (*Nat.* 7.154) and invented tiles and copper-mining (*Nat.* 7.195); he also gave Agamemnon a corselet (Hom. *Il.* 11.20). 'In reality Cinyras is nothing but the mythical eponymous ancestor of the Kinyradai, the guild of temple musicians who controlled the Paphian cult' (West (1997) 57; also Ribichini (1981) 45–54).   **deamque . . . appulsam:** T. violates the natural sequence of events by placing this second (*hysteron proteron:* the temple's consecration followed Venus' arrival, rather than *vice versa*). In one version of the myth Venus was born in the sea (*mari* is locative) from the severed genitals of the jealous sky-god Uranus after his wife Gaia persuaded their son Cronus to castrate him (Hes. *Th.* 188–206 with West (1966) 211–13, Varro *LL* 5.63, Cic. *ND* 3.59, Ov. *Fast.* 4.62, Luc. 8.457–9). Aphrodite often bears the title *Ourania* in cult (Hdt. 1.105, with Farnell (1977) 629–31, Pirenne-Delforge (1994) 15–25), which connects her with an older goddess: 'the Greek goddess's title *Ourania* corresponds to the Phoenician goddess's title Queen of Heaven' (West (1997) 56). The sixth Homeric hymn narrates Aphrodite's arrival on Cyprus (Hansen (2000)).   **artemque haruspicum:** Cicero *Diu.* 1.6.11 distinguishes between divination based on *ars* (observation of birds, weather phenomena, entrails of sacrificial victims) and on *natura* (inspired utterances and dreams). On divination see North in Beard and North (1990).   **accitam** 'brought in from abroad'. The word can be pejorative (*per accitam lasciuiam, A.* 14.20.4), but not here.   **et Cilicem Tamiram intulisse** 'and Tamiras the Cilician was the one who imported it'. This clause after *scientiam . . . accitam* seems oddly jerky, even for T., so some emend *et Cilicem* to *e Cilicia*. Yet emphasising Tamiras through *et Cilicem* is apt, as his descendants will preside over the rites for some time (*intulerant*, below, hammers home the point). Cilicia in southern Asia Minor was famous for piracy and divination (Cic. *Diu.* 1.1.2, 1.15.25, 2.38.80). Mopsus and Calchas allegedly held a contest of divination there (Hes. fr. 278 M–W).   **familiae utriusque posteri:** the families of the native king

Cinyras and the foreigner Tamiras.   **mox** 'later' (*OLD* 2).   **ne . . . antecelleret**
'lest the royal family should not outrank the foreign stock by any mark of esteem'. *antecello* (a Ciceronian favourite, also in Sempronius Gracchus, *Orationes* 37.1 Malcovati)
takes the dat. until Val. Max., the younger Sen., Apul. and T., who have the acc. (cf.
A. 14.55.5; Draeger (1882) §40c, *TLL* s.v. *antecello* 146.25–35).   **ipsa quam intulerant scientia hospites cessere:** *cedo*, 'resign the ownership of' (*OLD* 12) + abl.;
cessere = alternative third person pl. perfect of *cesserunt* (GL §131). In the *H.*, the ratio
of *–erunt* (32) to *–ere* (294) endings is 1: 9.2 (Martin (1946) 17). *intulerant* echoes *intulisse*
above, emphasising the altruistic withdrawal. *hospes*, 'foreign' (*OLD* 3), refers to the
descendants of Tamiras, but at least one tradition also casts Cinyras as a settler from
Cilicia (Apoll. 3.14.3).

    3.2 hostiae . . . deliguntur '(there are) sacrificial victims, of whatever kind
people have vowed, but male ones are chosen'. The animals are killed so that the
haruspex can inspect their entrails. Female victims for female deities are normal, so
the divergence draws explicit comment from T. (cf. Cic. *Leg.* 2.29 on the rigid rules;
Ovid specifies female animals for Venus on Cyprus, *Met.* 10.271–2). A male sacrificial
victim for extispicy is also required at Lucan 1.609. Cicero cynically attributes the
selection of sacrificial victims to chance, not to *aliquid diuini* (*Diu.* 2.15.38–9). *ut quisque*
expresses 'a recurrent situation to which there is a constant response' (*OLD ut* 19; also
1.29.1, 1.36.2, 1.85.2, 2.27.2).   **certissima . . . uetitum:** a sharp contrast with
the British druids, who spill human blood on their altars (*A.* 14.30.3).   **haedorum
fibris:** *fibrae*, 'entrails' (*OLD* 5), is used by the poets (*TLL* s.v. *fibra* 642.75–643.56). The
haruspices used various animals (Thulin (1906) 17–20), including sheep (Ov. *Fast.* 4.908,
4.935), cattle (Plin. *Nat.* 11.195, Cic. *Diu.* 1.52.119, 2.12.29, Luc. 1.633), chickens (Plin.
Nat. 10.49, Cic. *Diu.* 2.12.29) and even dogs (Ov. *Fast.* 4.908, 4.936; cf. Paus. 6.2.5).
A bronze liver (3rd century BC) with markings to aid *haruspices* interpreting a victim's
organ was found in 1877 in Placentia (Van der Meer (1987)).   **precibus et igne
puro altaria adolentur** 'the altars are venerated with prayers and pure fire'. This
is a type of syllepsis (Lausberg (1998) §702), with the verb used in a different sense with
each noun. Poets and early historians like *adoleo* (Kuntz (1962) 126–7), 'to burn ritually'
(*OLD* 1), which here suits *igne puro* rather than *precibus*. Lucretius already extends the
verb's meaning (*adolentque altaria donis*, 4.1237), but T.'s abstract *precibus* is bolder. Venus'
hundred altars on Paphos *Sabaeo ture calent* (Virg. *A.* 1.416–17; cf. Ov. *Met.* 10.273).   **nec
ullis imbribus:** *non* or *nec ullus* emphatically varies *nullus* (*OLD* 1c). Cf. *celebre fanum
habet Veneris Paphos, in cuius quandam aream non impluit* (Plin. *Nat.* 2.210). Polybius 16.12.3
reports that no rain falls on the statues of Artemis Kindyas at Bargylia and Artemis
Astias at Iasus, despite being in the open air, but accuses people (including historians)
who believe such things of childish simplicity. T. is less judgemental.   **quamquam in
aperto:** likewise at Eryx on Sicily Aphrodite's largest altar is in the open air (Aelian *NA*
10.50). *quamquam* without a finite verb (common in T.) is largely post-Ciceronian (MW
139).   **simulacrum . . . exsurgens:** the adversative asyndeton after a negative in
the first clause typifies T.'s compact style (cf. *non Italia . . . rapere*, 2.12.2; *nec tamen . . . legere*,
2.16.3; *nec simulacrum . . . reuerentia*, 2.78.3).   **continuus . . . exsurgens** 'a circle

rising without interruption from a rather broad starting-point into a narrow circuit, like a conical turning-post'. This elaborate description of a relatively simple object (cf. the famous periphrasis for 'spade', *A.* 1.65.7) avoids the technical term *conus* (prosaic in the strictly geometrical sense; cf. 21.1n. *faces . . . missilem ignem*) and climactically closes the digression (Oakley (1998) 136–9 on avoiding some terms in historiography; Lausberg (1998) §592 on the purpose of periphrasis). T.'s readers could have seen this conical representation of Paphian Venus on coins (Hill (1904) plates XV–XVI and cxxvii–cxxxiv). Servius *ad A.* 1.720 has the same image. The analogy from the race-track is perhaps incongruous in the context, but other authors found the *meta* (only here in T.) useful for clarification (Liv. 37.27.7, Curt. 8.11.6 for steep hills; Columella *RR* 9.15.12 for a bag used in honey-production).   **tenuem in ambitum:** T. often places monosyllabic prepositions between the adj. and noun, which emphasises the adj. (WM 172–3). This word order is a poeticism (L-H-S 216 §114), which Cicero uses in his early works, particularly with monosyllabic prepositions.   **ratio in obscuro:** T. can be candid about the limits of his knowledge (2.41.1, 2.42.1, 2.100.3), but religious ritual often leads authors to admit *aporia* (Plut. *Art.* 3.2). 'Statements of "unsuccessful enquiry" are a literary device for maintaining an author's credibility' (WM 93): *adfert aliquem fidem ueritatis et dubitatio* (Quint. 9.2.19).

　　4.1 spectata opulentia: Titus apparently plays the polite tourist, but T. else-where emphasises his weakness for riches (5.11.2); the young Titus' playboy lifestyle features in the biographical tradition (Suet. *Tit.* 7.1–2).   **quaeque alia** = *et aliis quae* (also 1.23.1, *A.* 3.43.2, 11.3.1 as the last item in a list of three, after two simple nouns). The long subordinate clause allows T. to snipe at the Greeks. The antecedent *alia* is rather dismissive.   **quaeque . . . affingit:** *affingo* = 'ascribe to' (*OLD* 4). T. elsewhere portrays the Greeks as obsequious (*A.* 2.53.3), self-obsessed (*A.* 2.88.3), and *promptis . . . animis ad noua et mira* (*A.* 5.10.1), and his Piso disparagingly calls the Athenians *conluuies* (*A.* 2.55.1). More positively T. laments the destruction of *Grae-carum artium decora* (*A.* 15.41.1) in the fire of Rome in 64. Livy uses similar language of the locals at Croton, who concoct marvellous stories about the altar of Lacinian Juno's temple: *ac miracula aliqua affingunt, ut plerumque tam insignibus locis* (24.3.7).   **de nauigatione . . . consuluit:** Suetonius' almost identical language (*de nauigatione consulit* (*Tit.* 5.1) suggests that this was in the common source, though he must have read the *H.* (Mooney (1930) 36–9, Shotter (1993) 32–5).   **pandi uiam et mare prosperum:** sc. *esse.* The chiastic phrase, marked off by enveloping alliteration, makes the clause cohere and functions 'indexically, pointing and calling attention to a sense already present semantically' (Wills (1996) 7). The idiom *uiam pandere* (Liv. 10.5.11, Virg. *A.* 6.96–7, 12.626) also features in later poets (Ov. *Fast.* 4.449, Luc. 3.467, Stat. *Theb.* 12.266).   **per ambages:** normally, the oracular or haruspical response, not the question, was described in these terms (2.78.4, 5.13.2, *A.* 2.54.4, Virg. *A.* 6.99, Ov. *Met.* 7.761, Sen. *Oed.* 214).   **interrogat:** a historic present (Chausserie-Laprée (1969) 369–73, Leigh (1997) 315–24) put to vivid effect, as are *uidet, aperit* (2.4.2).   **caesis compluribus hostiis:** T. only uses *complures* twice again (2.22.3, also alliterative, *G.* 8.3), otherwise preferring *plures*. Killing several victims could indicate manipulation of extispicy: e.g. Liv. 41.14.7 (the senate has animals continually sacrificed until a victim with satisfatory organs is found, guaranteeing a favourable omen), Cic. *Diu.* 2.15.36, Suet. *Iul.* 81.4. That possibility is not excluded here. On divination to legitimate a man's position, see North in Beard and North (1990) 69.

4.2 Sostratus . . . erat: claims of efforts made in researching a historical work can be implicit or explicit. T.'s parenthetical format drawing attention to a name emphatically underscores his diligence (cf. *Agr.* 22.1, *A.* 11.30.1, 12.51.4, 14.4.2, 15.37.4, 16.30.2). **magnisque . . . deam:** *annuo,* '(of the gods) grant favour' (*OLD* 6), often features in poetry. The phrasing combines two Virgilian echoes (*A.* 9.625, 11.410). **petito secreto:** *secretum* has a substantival sense, 'privacy' (*OLD* 3a; cf. 2.100.3, *A.* 3.8.2, 11.30.1, and 13.18.2). Sostratus, aware that this was a significant exchange with Titus, sought privacy, a wise precaution, since such predictions could unsettle a current emperor. Josephus also delivered his predictions to Vespasian in private (*BJ* 3.399–408). **futura aperit:** Virgilian phrasing (*A.* 6.12) enhances an already dramatic moment. Galba had also been encouraged to join Vindex against Nero by a priest's pronouncement that *oriturum quandoque ex Hispania principem dominumque rerum* (Suet. *Gal.* 9.2). 'Galba made reference to the Clunia oracle on no less than five distinct varieties of sestertii struck at Rome (*RIC I*², p. 254, nos. 469–73)' (Sutherland (1987) 116). **aucto animo:** ring-composition. Titus was initially *anxius animo* (2.1.3), but no longer. Yet confidence generated by extispicy could be misplaced. Pompey, who *admodum extis et ostentis mouebatur* (Cic. *Diu.* 2.24.53), still lost the civil war. **suspensis . . . mentibus** 'with the feelings of the provinces and armies on tenterhooks' (*OLD suspensus* 2). Cf. *suspensa . . . mens* (Virg. *A.* 5.827–8). **ingens rerum fiducia:** in apposition to *Titus* (cf. *praecipua concordiae fides* 2.5.2). *fiducia* used in apposition to refer to a person or thing on which one's safety rests is poetical (*OLD* 2c; Ov. *Trist.* 5.6.1, Sil. 2.342, 8.607). *ingens* is an elevated synonym for *magnus*, also favoured by Sallust, Livy and Virgil (MW 102). Its distribution (minor works = 11×; *H.* = 24×; *A.* 1–6 = 18×; *A.* 11–16 = 13×) is striking for its clustering in *H.*, and for the preponderance of appearances (13×, more than half) in book 2 (Goodyear (1981) 124–5).

4.3 Profligauerat 'had given the decisive turn to' (*OLD* 2b), implying that the war is not yet ended. Gellius *NA* 15.5 complains that this verb is often misused to mean 'almost completed' (Cicero, Livy and T. all have it in this sense). A pluperfect verb in the emphatic initial position often introduces an informative flashback, usually when shifting to new material (*addiderat,* 2.11.1; *aperuerat,* 2.17.1; *discubuerat,* 2.68.1; *extiterat,* 2.72.1; *praeposuerat,* 2.92.1). **bellum Iudaicum:** the Jewish revolt began in May 66 and was eventually suppressed on 2 Sept. 70 (Jos. *BJ* 6.407, 6.435), when Titus overran Jerusalem and destroyed the Temple (Levick (1999) 25–42, Ball (2000) 56–60). Masada, the final fortress to hold out after the fall of Jerusalem, capitulated in Apr. 73, but Vespasian and Titus still held their joint triumph in Rome in 71 (Jos. *BJ* 7. 119–57, Suet. *Ves.* 8.1, *Tit.* 6.1, *Dom.* 2.1, Dio 66.12.1ª). Vespasian's combination of military experience and non-senatorial background led Nero to entrust the war to him in 67 (Suet. *Ves.* 4.5) after the elderly Cestius Gallus, legate of Syria, died (5.10.1, Jos. *BJ* 2.540–55). **oppugnatione Hierosolymorum reliqua:** the abl. absolute has a concessive force.   **ob:** an archaism, which T. 'almost always employs for *propter* in the historical works' (Adams (1973) 125).   **ingenium montis:** T. later describes the topography of Jerusalem, *ardua situ* and containing two walled *colles* (5.11.3). Josephus is naturally much more detailed (*BJ* 5.136–83; Asali (1997) 87 has a map of Jerusalem in 68). For *ingenium*, 'inherent quality or character (of things)' (*OLD* 2) with a gen., cf. *ingenio loci caelique* (1.51.2) *ingenio umentium* (5.14.2), *collisque propinqui | ingenium* (Sil. *Pun.* 4.90–1).   **peruicaciam superstitionis:** T. elaborates in his ethnographical excursus on the Jews (5.4–5 with Schäfer (1997) 185–92 and Bloch (2002)). See Feldman (1993) 149–53 on pagan writers' attitudes to Judaism. *superstitio* (pejorative here, *OLD* 1b; cf. the Jews as a *gens superstitioni obnoxia*, 5.13.1) was applied elsewhere to Jews (Cic. *Flac.* 67, Ulpian *Dig.* 50.2.3.3), Christians (Plin. *Ep.* 10.96.9, Suet. *Nero* 16.2) and Druids (4.54.2).   **quam quo . . . superesset:** subjunctive of rejected reason (GL §541 n.2; 3.72.2, Cic. *Fam.* 10.3.4, Caes. *Gal.* 4.2.1, with L-H-S §375 on *quam quo = quam eo quod*).   **satis uirium** 'enough strength' (*uirium =* defining gen.).   **ad tolerandas necessitates:** *tolero* (a synonym for *fero* and *perfero*) belonged to the higher genres of prose (Adams (1973) 133).   *necessitas*, a 'constraint imposed by external circumstances' (*OLD* 3), is an evasive way to denote the hardships of a siege (cf. Jos. *BJ* 5.420–564). T. would certainly have described these in the missing part of the *H.*, whetting our appetites at 5.2.1 *quoniam famosae urbis supremum diem tradituri sumus*. Describing assaults on cities was a traditional historiographical motif (*A.* 4.32.1; Paul (1982), Kraus (1994) 15–16, Purcell (1995)).

4.4 ut supra memorauimus: T. often provides helpful markers for his readers (1.10.3, 1.59.1, 1.64.2, 2.17.1, 2.50.1, 2.63.1, 3.76.1, 4.15.1, 4.70.5, 5.19.3), always preferring the grander 1st person plural form of the verb in the *H.* (cf. the 1st person singular in *Agr.*, *G.*, *D.* and the *A.*). Perhaps T. was especially keen to adopt the appropriate style for his first formal historical work (WM 189, Starr (1981)). T. (with Sall., Ov., Virg., Vitr., Val. Flac.) overwhelmingly prefers the simple form *memoro* to the compound *commemoro* (WM 230); likewise Livy in his first decade, but the pattern is then reversed (Adams (1974) 55).   **tres . . . legiones:** the *X Fretensis* (named after the *fretum*, 'channel' between Italy and Sicily; *RE* XII 1672–8), *V Macedonica* (so named having served in Macedonia, 30 BC–AD 6; *RE* XII 1572–86), and *XV Apollinaris* (named after Octavian / Augustus' patron god Apollo; *RE* XII 1747–58).   **exercitae bello:** all three legions had been fighting the Jewish war since 66.   **quattuor:** T. also implies that Mucianus commanded four legions at 1.10.1, 2.6.2 and 2.76.4, but *III Gallica* was transferred to Moesia by Nero (1.79.1, 2.74.1, Suet. *Ves.* 6.3) which left only three, the *IV Scythica*, *VI Ferrata* (2.83.1), and *XII Fulminata* (5.1.2). Chilver (1979) 18–19 lists where legions were stationed on 1 Jan. 69. The *III Gallica*'s recent victory over the Rhoxolani in Moesia (1.79), made it a useful, battle-ready force, as did earlier service (54–66) in Armenia under Corbulo (3.24.2, *A.* 15.6.3, 15.26.1).   **Mucianus:** 5.1n.   **aemulatio** 'rivalry' (*OLD* 2) could usefully inspire soldiers to fight better (*Agr.* 36.2), but in this dysfunctional world, destructive competition between soldiers (2.23.4, 3.60.1) and even generals (2.30.3, 3.52.2) on the same side is common (with McGillicuddy (1991) 48–62 on *aemulatio* in the *H.*).   **proximi . . . gloria:** the army's successes included capturing Jotapata on 2 Jul. 67 (Jos. *BJ* 3.142–339) and Gamala on 21 Oct. 67 (Jos. *BJ* 4.1–53, 62–83), and assaulting Tarichaeae on 6 Sept. 67 (Jos. *BJ* 3.462–542). Vespasian's campaigns in Galilee were part of a systematic plan to isolate Jerusalem by capturing troublespots to her north.   **segnitiam:** cf. Corbulo's soldiers, who had come from Syria in 58, *pace longa segnes* (*A.* 13.35.1). Troops based in the east were often portrayed as incapacitated by the enervating environment (Liv. 9.18.3, Alexander's army in Persia, Sall. *Cat.* 11.5–6, Sulla's army in Asia; Wheeler (1996)). These tough Flavian troops contrast with the sluggish Vitellians, debilitated by their victory and the delights of Rome (2.69.2, 2.93.1, 3.2.1–2).   **quantumque illis roboris discrimina et labor, tantum his uigoris addidit integra quies et inexperti belli ardor** 'danger and hard work had generated just as much strength in Vespasian's men (*illis*) as unbroken inaction and passion for the war which they had not experienced had produced energy in Mucianus' soldiers (*his*)'. For *ardor*, our main manuscript, M, reads *labor*, repeated in error, but just as *discrimina* is contrasted with *integra quies*, the contested reading (*inexperti belli* + ?) should contrast with *labor*. Rhenanus (1533) substituted *ardor*, accepted by Heubner: where Vespasian's soldiers had been campaigning hard, Mucianus' men wanted active service that had so far been denied them in the Jewish war. Morgan (2004) revives Andresen's *rubor* (1914), which also has its merits; absolute certainty is impossible.   **auxilia . . . alarumque** 'auxiliary units of infantry and cavalry' (Saddington (1982) 38–40 on the terms *cohors* and *ala* in the *H.* and 114–16 on the auxiliaries' contribution to the Flavian cause). In the republic, an *ala* consisted of both cavalry and infantry, but in the imperial army, it exclusively indicated auxiliary cavalry (with *cohors* for auxiliary infantry). *cohors* can also refer to legionary cohorts, but if so, T. often clarifies with an adj., *Romana* (*A.* 3.20.1, 15.5.1) or *legionaria* (*A.* 12.38.3).   **nomen dispari fama celebre:** *dispar* = 'dissimilar' (*OLD* 2). Accius described Oedipus as *nomine celebri* (*Trag.* 521), but later prose authors (Liv., Vell., Sen., Curt.) regularly combine the noun and adj., as does Silius Italicus (*TLL* s.v. *celeber* 740.14–30). T. shifts from the two men's concrete resources to something abstract, their different reputations, nicely preparing for the *syncrisis* of the next chapter. Such formal comparisons between two figures are common in ancient historiography (cf. Sall. *Cat.* 53.6–54.6 on Caesar and Cato). By giving readers 'two for the price of one', historians economically used polarities to enhance understanding of both men (cf. Batstone (1988) 3 on *syncrisis* as 'essentially agonistic'), no doubt mirroring and deepening comparisons made by contemporary observers in 69: e.g. *imperatores forma ac decore corporis, ut est mos uolgi, comparantibus* (1.7.3). T. likes using *syncrisis* in paired obituary notices (MW 268–9, Moles (1988) 19–26).

   5.1 acer militiae 'every inch the soldier', 'energetic with regard to military service'. Cf. Otho's supporter Licinius Proculus, *urbanae militiae impiger* (1.87.2) and Vespasian's adherent Valerius Paulinus, *strenuus militiae* (3.43.1; with K-S I §85.2f for adjectives + *militiae*). Velleius Paterculus has *acer belli iuuenis* (1.3.1).   **anteire agmen** 'preceded the army on the march'. This idealised description of Vespasian leading from the front suggests bravery and confidence, since under attack, the middle of the column is safest. Josephus is more realistic: as the army marches to Galilee,

Vespasian precedes the legions, but is himself preceded by auxiliary troops, heavily armed Roman infantry and cavalry, and road-clearers, as well as his personal
baggage and senior officers (*BJ* 3.115–26, with Goldsworthy (1996) 105–11 on the
order of the march). The image of the general fraternising with his men on the
march varies this theme: 1.23.1 (Otho), 5.1.1 (Titus), *Agr.* 20.2 (Agricola), *A.* 13.35.4
(Corbulo), Sall. *Jug.* 45.2 (Metellus), *Jug.* 96.3 (Sulla). Otho (surprisingly perhaps)
leads from the front (2.11.3); Vitellius (predictably) does not (2.59.2), until he wants
to create a good impression (2.89.1).   **anteire . . . capere . . . obniti:** historic
infinitives feature especially in historians for rapid sequences of events (GL §647). T.
has striking clusters: 1.81.1, 2.5.1, 2.12.2, 2.56.1, 2.93.1, 3.25.3, 3.36.1, 3.84.2, 5.22.1
(three), 2.30.1, 2.35.2, 2.70.3, 2.82.1, 4.34.4, 4.46.3 (four), 1.36.2, 4.29.2 (five), 1.45.1
(six), 3.73.1 (eight), and most extraordinarily, *Agr.* 38.1 (ten; Chausserie-Laprée (1969)
377–8). The rapid-fire syntax (historic infinitives, asyndeton) aptly mirrors Vespasian's
military dynamism, perhaps conveying his functional ubiquity. Kenney compares Ov.
Met. 13.211–15, Ulysses enumerating his different roles in the Greek army.   **locum
castris capere:** the ideal general typically chooses a safe place to camp on the
march. Cf. *loca castris ipse capere* (*Agr.* 20.2), Cic. *Rab. Post.* 15.42, Liv. 9.17.15, Veg. 1.21–
5 (Woodman (1977) 165, Oakley (2005) 219).   **noctu diuque:** *diu* = archaism of
the abl. *die* (also *A.* 15.12.4), used by the archaiser Sallust in reverse order: *diu noc-
tuque* (*Jug.* 38.3, 44.5). Cf. Tiberius, accessible day and night on campaign (Suet. *Tib.*
18.2).   **consilio . . . manu:** in fact, imperial writers thought it risky for generals to enter battle (cf. Liv. 2.6.8 *decorum erat tum* (509 BC) *ipsis capessere pugnam ducibus,*
Onas. *Strat.* 33.6, Plut. *Pel.* 2.4), hence T.'s qualifying *si* clause. 'A commander who
chose to fight throughout a battle automatically lost the ability to direct his reserves
or indeed issue any orders for the duration of the action' (Goldsworthy (1996) 155).
T. has Antonius Primus call *ratio* and *consilium* the 'proper arts of the general' (3.20.2;
cf. *A.* 13.6.4).   **consilio ac, si res posceret, manu hostibus obniti** 'struggling
against the enemy by strategy (*OLD* 7) and, if the occasion demanded it, by fighting
(*OLD* 9f)'. This is a type of syllepsis (3.2n. *precibus*): *consilio* and *manu* = abl. of manner
with *obnitor*, used most often either for struggling physically (*TLL* s.v. *obnitor* 121.60–
122.11) or metaphorically (*TLL* s.v. *obnitor* 122.12–44), but rarely both together. The
two nouns are frequently paired (3.17.1, Cic. *Font.* 44, Nep. *Paus.* 1.2, Sall. *Jug.* 96.3, Liv.
2.33.5, Ov. *Met.* 13.205, Sen. *Ben.* 3.29.7). *consilium* is an attribute of the ideal general
(Oakley (1997) 605; cf. *diu magnum inter mortalis certamen fuit uine corporis an uirtute animi res
militaris magis procederet,* Sall. *Cat.* 1.5). *posceret* is a subjunctive in a generalising condition,
containing an idea of repetition (*NLS* §196).   **cibo fortuito** 'eating whatever food
happened to be available'. Sometimes this was a necessity, as when Caecina's soldiers
can only eat *infectos caeno aut cruore cibos* (*A.* 1.65.7), but food could be revealing about
morals: cf. Cato the Elder's maxim *magna cura cibi, magna uirtutis incuria* (Amm. 16.5.2).
Ideal generals traditionally ate frugally: Liv. 21.4.6, Justin 32.4.10, Sall. *Jug.* 89.8, Plut.
Mar. 7.4, *Ant.* 4.4, *Caes.* 17.3, Plin. *Pan.* 13.1, Luc. 2.384, Vell. 2.114.3 (with Woodman
(1977) 176), 2.41.2, Suet. *Tib.* 18.2, Diod. Sic. 33.1.1, 33.7.2, Amm. 16.5.3, 25.4.4,
SHA *Hadrian* 10.2). T. later stresses the austere Vespasian's exemplary lifestyle as

princeps (antiquo ipse cultu uictuque, A. 3.55.4, with WM 406).   **ueste habituque:** Vespasian's pragmatic attitude to the trappings of military life (and his real martial talents) contrasts with the other civil war emperors, who all dress up in military uniform with varying degrees of implausibility: cf. Galba (1.35.1), Otho (2.11.3) and Vitellius (2.89.1). **uix . . . discrepans:** the 'general who resembles the common soldier' is a topos (Pelling (1988) 124–5; Xen. *Cyr.* 1.6.25, Cic. *Mur.* 38, Plin. *Pan.* 15, Vell. 2.114.1–3 with Woodman (1977) 174–7, and esp. Plut. *Mar.* 7.3–6; also Plut. *Cat. Mi.* 9.9, *Art.* 24.6, Curt. 7.2.33). Titus is said to mingle with common soldiers, but (crucially) *incorrupto ducis honore* (5.1.1).   **prorsus** 'all in all' (*OLD* 4b) sums up after an enumeration of points (Sall. *Jug.* 76.4, *Cat.* 15.5). Such particles are comparatively rare in T.'s historical works: 'of the 14 examples of *prorsus* only 5 are in the narrative, and of these 4 are in the first three books of the *Histories* and the other is in a digression (*A.* 4.6.3)' (Adams (1973) 132).   **auaritia** is often associated with Vespasian (Suet. *Ves.* 16, Dio 66.8) and also Mucianus (2.84.2, Dio 66.2.5): 'The numerous anecdotes on avarice that have made their contribution to Vespasian's "character", masquerading as factual, show how hard pressed the Empire was to pay its way' (Levick (1999) 103; 95–106). Nero's extravagance (Griffin (1984) 197–207) and the donatives offered to the soldiers during the civil wars necessitated Vespasian's stringency. At the start of his principate, he claimed to need 40,000 million HS to restore the state finances (Suet. *Ves.* 16.3). His methods for recouping the money included the *quadragensima* ($2\frac{1}{2}$% customs duty) and the re-provincialisation of previously 'free' provinces (Sutherland (1987) 126–8). Cf. the bad reputation of Henry VII, King of England, who had to develop ruthlessly efficient financial practices after the Wars of the Roses. Romans particularly disliked avarice: cf. *nullum igitur uitium taetrius est . . . quam auaritia, praesertim in principibus et rem publicam gubernantibus* (Cic. *Off.* 2.77).   **antiquis ducibus par:** is a 'match for the generals of old' what the corrupt atmosphere of the civil wars requires? Cf. the sketch of the Flavian general Antonius Primus (2.86.1–2). Pliny calls Trajan *Romanum ducem unum ex illis ueteribus et priscis (Pan.* 12.1).   **Mucianum:** T. has already introduced the 'kingmaker' Licinius Mucianus (1.10.1–2), (again) coupled with Vespasian (1.10.3). The four sketches (1.10, 2.5) are arranged chiastically. 'Mucianus stands forth, at the expense of Vespasian. That is artistic, and historically correct . . . In January of 69, the governor of Syria seemed the stronger candidate' (Syme (1958a) 195). Antonius Primus outstripped Mucianus in invading Italy, but his arrival in Rome a few days after its capture (4.11.1) conveniently distances him from the atrocities. Mucianus, having been suffect consul three times (probably in 64, 70 and 72), died, 'perhaps already by 74, certainly by 77' (Levick (1999) 194). He was a man *notae impudicitiae* (Suet. *Ves.* 13), his writings about natural curiosities are often a source for Pliny the Elder's *Nat.*, and he may have had Spanish roots (Syme (1958a) 791).   **magnificentia . . . supergressa:** after the asyndeton of the previous tightly-wrought section follows a more leisurely tricolon joined by *et . . . et.* The stylistic difference implicitly reflects the contrasted characters of the two men. Mucianus contributes to the Flavian cause from his personal fortune, albeit *quo auidius de re publica sumeret* (2.84.2), but after victory, he quickly embraces *domos hortosque* in Rome (4.11.1). As governor of Lycia in Asia Minor, Mucianus held a banquet for 18 friends inside a huge hollow plane tree, and, spending the night there, for once got more pleasure from the pattering rain than from 'gleaming marble, diversity of painting or golden panelling' (Plin. *Nat.* 12.9). *cunctus* = a synonym for *omnis* (1.3n. *cuncta . . . perlustrat*). T. redeploys his own language for the accusations against Nero's minister, Seneca the Younger: *tamquam ingentes et priuatum modum euectas opes adhuc augeret* and *hortorum quoque amoenitate et uillarum magnificentia quasi principem supergrederetur* (*A.* 14.52.2). 'The author T. most imitates is himself' (Goodyear (1981) 90).   **extollebant** 'distinguished' (*OLD* 5). Cf. 4.28.1.   **aptior . . . peritus** 'a better speaker, a skilled and far-sighted adminstrator' (Irvine). The chiasmus incorporates an unusual noun *prouisus*, used only by T. in extant Latin.   **aptior sermone:** T. recreates a speech of Mucianus (2.76–7), *satis decorus etiam Graeca facundia* (2.80.2). The comparative adj. (indirectly) suggests another link between Vespasian and ideal generals, frequently portrayed as gruff and succinct (cf. 4.73.1, *Rhet. Her.* 4.65, Liv. 2.56.8, 4.41.1, 10.24.4, Quint. 11.1.33). Some authors privileged competence at both warfare and speaking (Plut. *Phoc.* 7.5–6): the Flavian general Antonius Primus is ambidextrous in this respect (86.2n. *strenuus manu, sermone promptus*). Suetonius says that studying language and literature was unknown in early Rome, a state 'devoted to warfare' (*Gram.* 1.1). Portraits of generals devoting more energy to warfare than to clever speeches implicitly hark back to this idealised past. **dispositu,** here first in extant Latin (for the usual word, *dispositio*), did not appeal widely to other authors (*TLL* s.v. *dispositus* 1436.47–51).   **egregium principatus temperamentum:** *temperamentum* = 'a blend' (*OLD* 1). The ellipse of a main verb in the present subjunctive in this apodosis momentarily suggests that T. endorses Mucianus as a possible emperor, until the protasis (specifically *utriusque*) clarifies that the blend is between Vespasian's martial and Mucianus' administrative skills. The most famous temporarily misleading apodosis + a ruthlessly revealing protasis is T.'s epigram about Galba, *omnium consensu capax imperii, nisi imperasset* (1.49.4).   **demptis utriusque uitiis:** T. owes the start of his career to Vespasian (1.1.3), but is willing to criticise him. He has already called him the first emperor to change for the better (1.50.4).

   5.2 ceterum . . . moribus is a particularly complex sentence. Mucianus (*hic*) and Vespasian (*ille*) are the subjects, but T. shifts (with *uariatio*) from the nom. singular past participle (*praepositus*) to the nom. plural adj. (*discordes*), which is first modified (without significant *uariatio*) by two abl. constructions (abl. of attendant circumstances, causal abl.) in asyndeton. The main verb (*consuluere*), itself preceded by two further abl. constructions (abl. of time, abl. abs.), is then qualified first by a prepositional phrase (*per amicos*) and second by a long co-ordinate clause (*praecipua . . . moribus*).   **uicinis prouinciarum administrationibus:** this abl. of attendant circumstances shows hypallage, the poetic device where an adj. (*uicinis*) is attracted to a substantive to which it does not properly belong (*administrationibus*). 'Hypallage is not unknown in prose . . . but it is mostly poetic' (Coleman (1999) 85).   **inuidia discordes** 'at odds through jealousy'; *inuidia* = causal abl. The parallel tradition also cites the pair's enmity before Nero's death (Suet. *Ves.* 6.4). The hostility was perhaps partly caused by Vespasian maintaining his base camp for the Jewish war in Ptolemais in Syria, Mucianus' province (Jones (2000) 51). Lucretius likens the destructive force of *inuidia* to a thunderbolt (5.1131).   **in medium consuluere** 'they took counsel for the common good' (*OLD consulo* 3b, *medium* 4b). The phrase is also at Liv. 24.22.15, 26.12.7, Virg. *A.* 11.335 and Curt. 8.14.21. For *consuluere*, see 3.1n. *ipsa . . . cessere*. T. has similar language with slight variants: *in medium consultarent* (2.37.1), *in unum consulere* (4.70.1), *in commune consulere* (*Agr.* 12.2, *A.* 12.5.3). This metaphorical sense of *in medium* has precedents (Cic. *Off.* 1.22, Virg. *G.* 1.127, 4.157, Liv. 6.6.18, Ov. *Met.* 4.41, Luc. 4.491). **praecipua concordiae fides** is in apposition to *Titus* (cf. 4.2n); *fides* = 'assurance' (*OLD* 2). Titus had visited Mucianus in Oct. 67 during the siege of Gamala (Jos. *BJ* 4.32).   **aboleuerat:** 'instantaneous' pluperfect (1.1n. *dispersera*t).   **natura atque arte compositus alliciendis etiam Muciani moribus** 'inclined (*OLD compositus* 5) by nature and by training also to win the compliance (*OLD mos* 5e) of Mucianus'. For the phrasing, cf. *spe uolgum alliciendi* (1.78.2), *aptus alliciendis feminarum animis* (*A.* 5.2.2). Titus, eloquent in Greek and Latin (Suet. *Tit.* 3.2) and fond of luxurious living while young (Suet. *Tit.* 7.1–2), was temperamentally similar to Mucianus, and thus suited to win him over. As a boy, Titus was taught with Claudius' son Britannicus (Suet. *Tit.* 2) in an environment where charm could be a survival technique. Titus' peacemaking between his elders reverses the topos of hotheaded young men being restrained by wiser and more senior colleagues (Eyben (1992), Nerandeau (1979) 249–58), but tensions remain (2.74.1). Josephus in the *BJ* contrasts a cautious Vespasian and an impetuous Titus (Jones (1992)). T. reminds us of Titus' role as an intermediary at 2.79.   **industria . . . uoluptates:** two ablatives of means are followed by two prepositional phrases in a clause marked by asyndeton. Anaphora of *per* is fairly common (*TLL* s.v. *per* 1167.31–52, Oakley (2005) 501).   **ut cuique ingenium** is also applied to the Flavians during the second battle of Bedriacum (3.17.2). Similar phrases are in Sall. (*Jug.* 57.4, 58.2) and Liv. (8.21.1, with Oakley (1998) 618, 9.3.1, 26.3.4, 38.50.5).   **asciscebantur** 'the support of the tribunes etc. was being secured'. The imperfect tense reminds us that the Flavian challenge was carefully prepared over time, contrary to pro-Flavian propaganda that the movement to make Vespasian emperor was a spontaneous outburst from the soldiers (Jos. *BJ* 4.601–4). The verb *ascisco* is associated with the challenges of both Otho (1.25.2) and Vitellius (1.54.3).

6.1 Antequam . . . aduentaret: Titus' journey 'can hardly have been completed before mid-February' 69 (Chilver (1979) 169).   **sacramentum Othonis:** the oaths administered by Vespasian and Mucianus to their armies were motivated more by respect for Rome than enthusiasm for Otho, who was simply *prior auditus* (1.76.2), but the pair apparently sent 'friendly letters' to Otho (Plut. *Oth.* 4.3). On the military oath in the imperial period, see *OCD³* '*sacramentum* (military)'. T. in the *H.* 'consistently employs *sacramentum* in a military context, in reference only to the oath taken by soldiers. The one exception involves the use of *sacramentum* in a metaphorical sense (2.81)' (Campbell (1984) 26; 23–32). It was normally the most strictly observed of all Roman oaths (Dion. Hal. 10.18); and the Roman army was 'a highly sacralised community' (Lendon (1997) 253).   **pernicibus . . . nuntiis:** Heubner (1978) accepts *pernicibus*, Jacob's emendation (1842) of M's *precibus* (*praecipitibus*, Wellesley (1989); *properis*, Cernjak (1976) 111). The phrase recurs in T. (3.40.1), again for speedy news explicitly contrasted with physical slowness. The adj. *pernix* is often applied to *fama*, *nuntius* etc. (*TLL* s.v. *pernix* 1596.3–7); and writers regularly attribute speed to *fama* (Virg. *A.* 4.174 with Pease (1967) 211–14, Luc. 1.471, Curt. 4.1.24, Val. Flac. 2.124–5, Stat. *Theb.* 3.425–30). *nuntii* here may refer to actual messengers (*OLD* 1) or oral communications (*OLD* 2), but G-G prefer the former.   **ut assolet:** the present tense prompts a 'gnomic moment', as T. nudges readers to use their contemporary world as a yardstick to judge past events (cf. 1.31.1, *A.* 1.24.3, 1.28.2, 3.1.3, 6.12.2, 13.44.3). **tarda mole ciuilis belli** 'while civil war is slow and cumbersome'. Historians regularly have *moles belli* (first in Accius, *Trag.* 610), even if the precise sense of *moles* varies (Ogilvie (1965) 278 comparing the Homeric μῶλος Ἄρηος, Woodman (1977) 102, Oakley (1997) 515–16, (1998) 291–2, *TLL* s.v. *moles* 1346.1–7). The formula usually involves *tota* (1.61.2) or *tanta mole belli* (2.16.1, 2.74.2), or *mole* without *belli* (2.100.2, 3.46.2), so even within the *H.* the addition of *ciuilis* is novel. The adj. *tarda* contrasts with *pernicibus* in the previous clause.   **longa concordia quietus Oriens:** cf. *mota Orientis regna* (*A.* 2.1.1), *turbari res Orientis* (*A.* 2.5.1), *motum Orientem* (*A.* 2.43.1), *distractis Orientis uiribus* (*A.* 11.9.1). In the civil wars, Galba challenged the emperor from Spain, Otho from Rome and Vitellius from Germany; cf. *Oriens adhuc immotus* (1.10.1), anticipating Vespasian's campaign. There had been some foreign disturbances in the east, such as Corbulo's war against Parthia for control of Armenia and Vespasian's Jewish war, both under Nero. Once this latter campaign was finished, the east was peaceful under the Flavians.   **parabat:** for the implications of the imperfect, cf. 5.2n. *asciscebantur*.   **olim** 'previously' (*OLD* 1). T. contrasts the current civil wars with their republican counterparts, conceiving the former as eclipsing the latter, certainly in their geographical extent (cf. 1.50.2–3).   **ualidissima . . . arma:** *arma* = *bellum* by synecdoche (*TLL* s.v. *arma* 599.11–600.43). T. naturally strives for *uariatio* after *ciuile bellum* above and following.   **trans mare . . . ciuile bellum:** the war between Pompey and Caesar was effectively settled at Pharsalus in Thessaly (48 BC), Brutus and Cassius were defeated by Antony and Octavian in two separate battles at Philippi in eastern Macedonia (42 BC), and Antony and Octavian fought at Actium at the entrance to the Ambracian gulf (31 BC). The personified *ciuile bellum* (*TLL* s.v. *bellum* 1834.19–27, Furneaux (1896) 66; 2.77.3, *G.* 1.1) and the list of names in asyndeton at the start of the sentence, suggesting the war's merciless progress, creates the impression that it dwarfs the individual protagonists who initiate it.   **haud prosperi exitus** 'disastrous outcomes', both personally and for the various campaigns (with litotes for emphasis).   **auditi saepius . . . quam inspecti:** Germanicus died at Antioch in Syria in 19 BC, *ingenti luctu prouinciae et circumiacentium populorum* (*A.* 2.72.2). Since then, members of the imperial household had not visited the region.   **nulla seditio legionum:** the obvious points of comparison are the mutinies in Pannonia (*A.* 1.16–30) and Germany (*A.* 1.31–52) in 14, to which Tiberius dispatched Germanicus and Drusus.   **tantum aduersus Parthos minae** 'only demonstrations against the Parthians' (Irvine). This convenient understatement glosses over Nero's general

Corbulo, who fought several campaigns to recover Armenia from Parthia, notably in 58–9 (*A.* 13.34–41) and in 62–3 (*A.* 15.1–17, 24–31). T. used Corbulo's memoirs as a source (*A.* 15.16.1) in *A.* 12–15. See Campbell (1993) and Rives (1999) 275–6 for relations between Rome and Parthia in the early imperial period.   **uario euentu:** standard Livian phrasing (Oakley (1998) 173). Corbulo eventually managed to re-establish Roman influence over the Parthian ruler of Armenia, Tiridates, but there had been some setbacks, such as the defeat at Rhandeia of the Roman general Caesennius Paetus, rashly keen to impose *tributa ac leges et . . . ius* (*A.* 15.6.4; Gilmartin (1973), Ash (2006)).   **proximo ciuili bello:** i.e. the conflicts leading to Nero's suicide and Galba's accession.   **inconcussa ibi pax:** cf. *proximorum certaminibus inconcussi* (*A.* 2.43.6) of Germanicus and Drusus. The adj. *inconcussus* is Senecan (Goodyear (1981) 329).   **fides erga Galbam:** Vespasian apparently bore Galba no ill-will (1.10.3), but distance from the centre rather than active devotion perhaps kept the eastern provinces loyal in the short term. The legions in Britain, *procul et Oceano diuisae* (1.9.2), were unusually loyal, while Aquitania's defection from Otho to Vitellius prompts T. to say that *nusquam fides aut amor* (1.76.1).

   6.2 scelestis armis: T. first combines this noun and adj., varying the more familiar *scelerata arma* (Luc. 6.406, Ov. *Met.* 5.102) and *impia arma* (Virg. *A.* 6.612–3, 12.31, Luc. 6.781, Sen. *Phoen.* 402, *Ag.* 78–9, Sil. 1.74–5, 3.501).   **res Romanas raptum ire:** expressive alliteration stresses the implied sacrilege; cf. 8.1n. *credentibus . . . contextu.* The supine in -*um* for purpose after a verb of motion (*NLS* §152), rare in Cicero and Caesar (MW 81), is Sallustian (*Jug.* 31.27, 68.1, 85.42, *Cat.* 28.1, 36.4, 52.12, *Hist.* 1.55.20, 3.48.16). Cf. *quo facinore dominationem raptum ierit* (*A.* 4.1.1).   **penes:** this preposition 'though found in Plaut. and Ter. (only with a pronoun), is non-vulgar, appearing mostly in verse, elevated prose and archaising literature' (MW 80). The anaphora (also at 1.30.1, 2.39.1, 4.81.2, *A.* 15.14.2) heightens the petulant contrast drawn by the disgruntled soldiers.   **imperii praemia . . . seruitii necessitas:** Caesar usually has *necessitas* (cf. *necessitudo* in Sall.). T. favours *seruitium* in his narrative, rather than the normal term *seruitus*, which is almost entirely confined to the speeches (similarly in Sall.). 'Outside the historians Sallust (13×), Livy (11×) and Curtius (once), *seruitium* is found elsewhere in pre-Tacitean prose only once in a letter of Brutus, in a highly rhetorical passage (*ad Brut.* 24.9)' (Adams (1973) 129; WM 347). The contrast between *imperii praemia* and *seruitii necessitas* is provocative; *libertas* (often paired with *seruitium* by T.) is conspicuously absent. T. does not idealise the Flavian soldiers, who are just as materialistic as the other armies. Legions in the east were often characterised as soft, greedy and undisciplined (cf. *A.* 13.35.1, Plin. *Ep.* 8.14.7), although Wheeler (1996) suggests that this does not reflect historical reality.   **fremere miles . . . circumspicere:** *fremere* and *circumspicere* are historic infinitives (5.1n., *anteire . . . obniti*). The onomatopoeic *fremo*, 'muttered' (*OLD* 2a), with *ne* is 'relatively rare . . . ; *TLL* s.v. *fremo* 1284.66–9' (WM 345); cf. *A.* 3.45.1. The verb (also at 2.28.1, 2.69.1, followed by indirect speech) is a Livian favourite (Oakley (1998) 531). The combination *uires circumspicere* is also Livian: *circumspectis omnibus imperii uiribus* (23.20.6). 'The collective singular *miles* (for *milites*) occurs in prose from Quadrigarius, but is common only in Livy, Tacitus and Ammianus' (MW 88).   **septem legiones:** cf. 4.4n. *quat-tuor*.   **statim** 'immediately at hand'.   **ingentibus:** 4.2n. *ingens . . . fiducia*.   **inde continua Aegyptus duaeque legiones** 'on one side they were bordered by Egypt with its two legions'. These were the *III Cyrenaica* and the *XXII Deiotariana* (named after the client king Deiotarus, tetrarch of Galatia, who trained soldiers to help Caesar in his campaign against Pharnaces, [Caes.] *Alex.* 34.4). Cf. *cetera Africae per duas legiones parique numero Aegyptus . . . coercita* (*A.* 4.5.2) with MW 101.   **Cappadocia Pontusque:** Cappadocia was annexed by Tiberius in 17 as a procuratorial province, while Pontus Polemonaicus was only annexed in 64 (Suet. *Nero* 18; Griffin (1984) 228). Neither area served as a legionary base (cf. *nondum additis Cappadociae legionibus*, 2.81.2), though auxiliaries were present (*A.* 12.49.1, 15.6.3). Vespasian made major changes, establishing one legion (*XII Fulminata*) at Melitene on the river Euphrates and another (*XVI Flavia Firma*) further north (probably) at Satala, and putting a consular *legatus* in charge, rather than an equestrian governor (Suet. *Ves.* 8.4; Bosworth (1976), Mitford (1980b)). His motive for reorganising Cappadocia-Galatia thus was partly to minimise the risk of fresh civil war by providing a 'natural counterweight' to any commander based in Syria (Levick (1999) 166).   **quidquid . . . praetenditur** 'whatever camps are stationed on the Armenian frontier'. Cf. *nostris prouinciis late praetenta [Armenia]* (*A.* 2.56.1). This verb features in geographical descriptions (Virg. *A.* 3.692, 6.60, Plin. *Nat.* 3.6, 4.100, 5.48, 5.130, 6.9).   **nec uirorum inopes:** litotes adds emphasis (as at *A.* 1.35.2, 14.62.4). T. follows *inops* by the gen. (2.16.3, 3.22.1, 3.68.3, *D.* 12.3, *A.* 4.23.2, 6.34.1, 13.55.1, 14.10.1, 15.16.1), rather than by the abl. (as at Liv. 21.50.3 and elsewhere). There is paronomasia (word-play; Woodman (1998) 218–29) between *inopes* and the next adj. *opulentae*.   **pecunia opulentae:** adding *pecunia* is not pleonastic, since *opulentus* can indicate abundant resources other than money (cf. *pecunia dites*, *A.* 3.46.2 with WM 350). Ritter (1848) suggested *pecunia* here for *pecuniae* of the manuscripts. See *TLL* s.v. *opulentus* 839.29–60 for different ablatives of respect after *opulentus*. Mucianus (2.84.1) and Paulinus (2.32.2) both stress that money is crucial for the civil war; cf. *uectigalia opulentissimarum prouinciarum* (3.8.2), referring to Egypt, Syria and Asia.   **quantum insularum mari cingitur . . . secundum tutumque ipsum mare** 'As for all the islands, they are surrounded by sea . . . and the sea itself offers favourable protection.' The sea is 'clearly the Aegean' (Wellesley (1991) 166f). *quantum* + the defining gen. (GL §369, *NLS* §77) conveys the numerous islands involved. The passive voice of *cingo* is often used in this way to refer to islands (*TLL* s.v. *cingo* 1066.5–14). Chilver (1979) 171 worries that T.'s description is superfluous, (presumably) because all islands are surrounded by water, but the sea is defensively important for the Flavians in preparing their challenge, and the emphasis is carefully managed; Kenney proposes that the repetition of *ipsum mare* after *mari* (and the present tense of *cingitur*) perhaps conveys the soldiers thinking aloud. The expansive phrasing helps to convey the general idea of the ample resources available.   **secundum . . . mare:** cf. *mare . . . secundum* (2.98.2, 4.83.4), *flumen secundum* (5.23.2). There is a thin line between the landscape offering strategic advantages and nature (personified) aiding a particular cause (cf. 1.86.3, 4.26.2, *A.* 1.28.1–2).

7.1 Non fallebat . . . militum 'The generals could not fail to notice (*OLD fallo* 6) the ardour of the soldiers.' The idea in pro-Flavian propaganda that a surprised Vespasian was swept to power by enthusiastic soldiers is undercut. '*impetus* was characteristic of children, of youth, of animals, of the Roman mob' (Winterbottom (1995) 316). It also typifies soldiers, whose collective zeal off the battlefield is a common denominator (1.56.1: Vitellians, 1.82.1: Othonians, 2.79: Flavians). **exspectari** 'that the outcome should be awaited'. The impersonal passive voice is supported by *A.* 11.26.3, 12.7.2, but Wellesley (1989) suggests *exspectare*, which has merits. Otho apparently believed in the Syrian legions' loyalty until his death (Plut. *Oth.* 15.8). **bello ciuili . . . periturum:** T. switches to *oratio obliqua* for the Flavian generals' views. A verb of saying (or thinking) is to be inferred from the context. **uictores uictosque:** an alliterative pair (also in Caes., Sall., Liv.) favoured by T. throughout the *H.* (usually in the reverse order). **solida fide:** *solidus*, 'lasting' (*OLD* 7), is a Ciceronian favourite (paired with *fides* at Plaut. *Merc.* 378, Sen. *Thy.* 972). **coalescere** 'unite' (*OLD* 3); cf. *coalescentium in dies magis duorum populorum* (Liv. 1.2.5, of Trojans and Latins). The verb can also apply to a wound (*OLD* 1a), a potentially suggestive metaphor in the context of a civil war. Uneasy co-existence of victors and vanquished after a civil war can be seen (e.g.) in the relationship between Augustus and the historian Asinius Pollio (*A.* 4.34.4). **nec referre** 'it did not matter whether . . .'. **fortuna:** as focalised through the Flavian generals, this is pejorative. *fortuna* often attends successful generals (Thuc. 3.97.2, Vell. 2.55.3, Luc. 4.121–2), but here Vitellius and Otho are cast as utterly subordinate to her whims. Yet Otho presents his relationship with her more impressively: *experti in uicem sumus ego ac fortuna* (2.47.1). **rebus secundis . . . insolescere:** *insolescere*, 'become overbearing', is Sallustian (*Cat.* 6.7). The idea that success leads first to arrogance and then failure is commonplace (*ferme fit ut secundae res neglegentiam creent* Liv. 21.61.2; *mox sic labere secundis* Sil. 9.352; Nisbet and Hubbard (1978) 163, Kraus (1994) 192), but is especially dangerous in a military context (Liv. 5.44.6, 6.3.5, 23.27.3). It is ironic that the Flavian general Antonius Primus' conduct after victory validates this *sententia* (*superbia uiri* 4.80.1). **discordiam his ignauiam luxuriem; et suismet uitiis alterum bello, alterum uictoria periturum:** so Shotter (1968) and Morgan (1995a) read, rejecting the correction of Madvig (1884) 264 (*discordia militis, ignauia, luxurie et suismet uitiis*) for M's problematic *discordiam his ignauiam luxurie et suismet uitiis*. To retain M's dat. *his* (rather than introducing *militis*) seems desirable as it accentuates the adversative asyndeton at the start of the sentence, highlighting the implicit contrast between *egregii duces* and *these* disreputable leaders (i.e. Otho and Vitellius). The Flavian generals thereby cast *discordia* ('dissension within an army', Morgan (1995a) 337), *ignauia* and *luxuries* as problems and attributes of *both* Otho and Vitellius. Certainly, in the narrative, *ignauia* is often attributed to Vitellius (1.50.1, 2.31.1, 2.94.2, 3.36.1, 3.86.1), whereas Otho denounces it (2.47.3), while *luxuria* (Otho: 1.21.1, 1.30.1, 1.71.1, Vitellius: 2.62.1) and *luxus* (Otho: 1.13.3, 1.22.1, 2.11.3, 2.31.1, Vitellius: 2.71.1, 2.90.1) are associated with both men. Yet the Flavian generals are denigrating Otho and Vitellius, so accuracy does not concern them. The abl. of means *suismet uitiis* (with the enclitic particle -*met* added to the pronoun *suus* for emphasis; cf. 3.16.2) has caused undue controversy: the generals simply mean that if they wait, the rival emperors will conveniently fall victim to their own vices, rather than requiring immediate Flavian intervention.   **7.2 igitur:** 2.2n.   **in occasionem** 'until the right time' i.e. 1 Jul. 69 (2.79), when Tiberius Alexander has his troops in Alexandria swear allegiance to Vespasian. **mixtis consiliis** 'having come to an understanding'; cf. *miscere . . . consilia* (*Agr.* 38.1).   **optimus quisque:** in such lists T. often puts the collective singular, 'the best sort', first, contrasting it with the more numerous *multi*, *plures* or *pessimi* (1.83.1, *Agr.* 41.4, *A.* 3.44.2).   **amore rei publicae:** T. later criticises historians who say that Caecina betrayed Vitellius through *amor rei publicae* (2.101.1). The motivation of these proto-Flavians is cast more positively.   **dulcedo praedarum:** T. elsewhere attributes this discreditable motivation to German tribes (*praedae dulcedine*, *G.* 33.1). Livy 6.41.11, 9.38.2 and 10.2.8 has similar phrasing (with Oakley (1997) 713 on the pejorative aspect of *dulcedo*). Desire for booty marks out the Flavian soldiers in the second battle of Bedriacum (3.19.2, 3.25.3, 3.26.3).   **stimulabat:** cf. Sallust's Piso *quem ad perturbandam rem publicam inopia atque mali mores stimulabant* (*Cat.* 18.4). The verb derives from goading animals with a *stimulus*, perhaps hinting at the soldiers' bestial qualities (cf. *fremere* 2.6.2).   **ambiguae domi res** 'domestic uncertainties'. i.e. personal financial problems, often seen as a catalyst for rebellion (cf. 1.88.3, 3.50.3, 4.23.4, 4.26.1, *G.* 29.4, *A.* 14.57.3, Sall. *Cat.* 18.4, 28.4, *Hist.* 1.77.7). Sallust's Catiline contrasts the wealthy ruling élite with his impoverished supporters (*nobis est domi inopia*, *foris aes alienum*, *Cat.* 20.13). Otho is motivated *inopia uix priuato toleranda* (1.21.1), Vitellius is *uetere egestate conspicuus* (2.59.2, cf. Suet. *Vit.* 7.2, Plut. *Galb.* 22.7), and Vespasian had to mortgage his lands to his brother during Nero's principate (3.65.1, Suet. *Ves.* 4.3).   **causis diuersis, studio pari:** T. (1.32.1, *A.* 4.55.1, 14.19) and other authors (*TLL* s.v. *diuersus* 1582.14–17 and 10.1.278.24–8; WM 323) often contrast *diuersus* and *par*.   **bellum omnes cupiebant:** the hexameter ending may enhance the sense of closure. For the phrasing, cf. *bellum . . . alii cupere* (*A.* 1.4.2), *bellum cupiens* (Sall. *Hist.* 1.55.16), *uidi . . . nostros amicos cupere bellum* (Cic. *Fam.* 9.6.2). T. ends this section as he started it (*struebat* 2.1.1), with a verb in the imperfect tense, suggesting the looming Flavian threat in the east, to be activated once the war between Otho and Vitellius is over. T. now leaves the Flavian challenge in 'hibernation' until 2.74.1, where he shifts from the Flavian soldiers collectively desiring war to Vespasian's contemplation of it: *Vespasianus bellum armaque . . . circumspectabat* (2.74.1).

8–9 A FALSE NERO

This excursus has a digressionary feel, but as so often, T. illuminates the main narrative by an event which has an indeterminate chronological relationship with the outer frame. Although readers already know which challenge from the east will eventually succeed, the appearance of the 'false Nero' (2.8–9), suggestively juxtaposed with the incipient Flavian challenge (2.1–7), eloquently captures the uncertainty of the times. It perhaps seems absurd that a *seruus e Ponto* or a *libertinus ex Italia* (2.8.1) could ever successfully impersonate Nero, but the incident shows how easily new challengers could be disgorged at any time around the empire. If a pretender was determined enough, then lowly origins were no obstacle: we can compare here the extraordinary Prussian clockmaker, Karl Wilhelm Naundorff, who, from 1831 onwards, successfully convinced many people that he was Louis XVII, who had died in 1793 (Cadbury (2002) 209–34; cf. Val. Max 9.15 on low-born men falsely trying to infiltrate illustrious families). In any case, Vespasian's own pedigree was not all that impressive, since his father Flavius Sabinus had been a tax-collector (Levick (1999) 4–8). Furthermore, although the Flavians have sensibly decided to play a waiting game, this excursus emphasises the risks inherent in that strategy and graphically illustrates how easily the unexpected can jeopardise even carefully considered plans: *fortuna* (2.1.1) is certainly crucial in generating the Flavian principate, but likewise *fors* (2.8.2) played its part in the dramatic story of the opportunistic pretender. If Galba's governor Calpurnius Asprenas had not happened to stop at the tiny island of Cythnus, then this movement could have gained momentum. Moreover, the excursus highlights a paradox: the sources present Nero in a dim light, but some still found him attractive, so we must ask whether Vespasian will be able to satisfy the empire's craving for a particular kind of emperor. Is he a mismatch for the times in which he is operating? Finally, the story of the false Nero cogently illustrates the power of rumour, particularly during times of civil war. Gibson (1998) 115 calls this 'an example of the "chain" effect of rumours: uncertainty about Nero's death lends credibility to reports of his survival; in turn such rumours give rise to alarm on the appearance of the false Nero in the provinces of Achaea and Asia'. The Flavians will be particularly adept at harnessing the power of rumours as their challenge comes to fruition (e.g. 2.80.3), and although the false Nero is abortive, the incident shows that rumours potentially play a crucial role in driving events.

8.1 Sub idem tempus: this formula indicating a hazy chronological relationship with what precedes recurs in T. (once in *H.*, 9 times in *A.*), but has caused uncertainty about dating. The false Nero possibly emerged between mid Feb. and early Apr. 69 (Morgan (1993a) 795).   **Achaia atque Asia falso exterritae:** sc. *sunt*. There are marked similarities with T.'s later account of the false Drusus, son of Germanicus, in 31: *per idem tempus Asia atque Achaia exterritae sunt acri magis quam diuturno rumore* (*A.* 5.10.1). In both narratives there is much 'circumstantial detail . . . especially on geography' (Martin (2001) 107). T. himself was subsequently proconsul of Asia in 112–13. Achaea's fear is odd, since the real Nero, a notorious philhellene (Griffin (1984) 208–15), had liberated Greece from Roman administration and taxation at the Isthmian games at Corinth (28 Nov. 67). Vespasian reversed the policy, saying that the Greeks had forgotten how to be free (Paus. 7.17.4). '*exterreo* is a recherché equivalent of the simple *terreo* and a favourite word of Virgil; T. has an increasing preference for it' (WM 166). Asia and Achaea, often alliteratively paired by T. (2.2, 81.2, 83.2), are personified, adding further colour.   **falso** 'mistakenly' (*OLD* 1). The adverb shows from the start that the rumour was unfounded, hinting at the frightened observers' gullibility. **uelut Nero aduentaret** 'as though (*OLD* 5a) Nero were at hand'; *uelut* 'as though' + the subjunctive 'is first in Nepos, then often in Livy' (MW 247). **uario . . . credentibusque:** the multiple abl. constructions, four in 11 words, are striking (abl. of attendant circumstances enclosing a preposition + abl., an abl. co-ordinating conjunction, abl. absolute). They dwarf the main clause, but allow T. to achieve an extraordinarily compressed expression. On sentence terminal *–que*, see 2.2n. *aduenasque*. **uario . . . rumore:** Nero killed himself on 9 June or (possibly) 11 June 68 (Murison (1993) 6; Suet. *Nero* 47–50, Dio 63.27.3–29). Only Nero's nurses and mistress witnessed his burial, so the idea of a false Nero was plausible. Dio of Prusa says (21.10) that '. . . even now, everyone wishes that Nero were alive, and most people actually believe that he is, although in a sense he has died not once, but many times, in the company of those who particularly believed in his being alive'. *uario rumore* recurs in T. (*A.* 3.14.5, 3.19.2; cf. *A.* 1.4.2, 11.23.1). **super exitu eius:** T. regularly uses the preposition *super* for *de*, an archaising effect (WM 183). It appears with a noun other than *res* only here in the *H.* (Adams (1972) 358–9). Cf. Sall. *Jug.* 71.5, Cic. *Att.* 10.8.10. **fingentibus credentibusque** is another verbal intersection with the false Drusus episode (*fingebant simul credebantque*, *A.* 5.10.2. Cf. *H.* 1.51.5). **credentibusque . . . contextu:** emphatic alliteration highlighting the authorial intervention perhaps 'marks the adoption of a . . . mock epic tone' (Morgan (1993a) 784). There is further extensive alliteration in T. (2.91.2, *A.* 4.27.2, both with *c*; 2.65.1, 2.92.1, *A.* 1.3.2, all with *p*) and in Livy (29.36.12, 32.29.1, 37.3.1 all with *p*). Yet 'if alliteration is to have expressive significance, then something more is required than that a series of words should begin with the same letter' (Goodyear (1972) 336). **ceterorum . . . dicemus:** at least one and more probably two other men claimed to be Nero (*ceteri* suggests the latter; Gallivan (1973) 365, Tuplin (1989)). One pretender, Terentius Maximus, appeared during Titus' principate (Dio 66.19 = Zonaras 11.18, Jos. *AJ* fr. 106M) and another surfaced in 88 or 89 (Suet. *Nero* 57.2). Both sought help from Parthia, since Nero considered fleeing there in May / June 68 (Suet. *Nero* 47.2). The *H.* breaks off before these points, but T. anticipates the disruption caused by one of these pretenders: *mota prope etiam Parthorum arma falsi Neronis ludibrio* (1.2.1). T. often gives advance notice of episodes, partly to stimulate his readers, partly to enhance historical understanding (3.46.1, 4.5.1, 4.67.2, *A.* 1.58.6, 2.4.3, 4.71.1, 6.22.4, 11.5.3). **contextu** 'course' (*OLD* 3) is only here in T., but perhaps appealed because it extends the alliteration. For the (Senecan) pairing *contextus operis* see Val. Max. 5.4.7, Sen. *Dial.* 1.1.1, *Ep.* 106.1, *Nat.* 6.1.3. **seruus e Ponto . . . libertinus ex Italia:** Dio wryly says (63.12.2) that Nero as *princeps* played the role of lyre-player and tragic actor, while his freedman Helius acted the part of Caesar. When a slave called Clemens impersonates Agrippa Postumus, Tiberius asks him after his capture how he had done this, and Clemens replies 'Just as you made yourself into Caesar' (*A.* 2.40.3). Cf. Otho's accession: *omnia seruiliter pro dominatione* (1.36.3). **citharae et cantus peritus:** *cithara* (not in Caes., Sall., Liv.) and *cantus* is an alliterative pairing, exemplifying a general tendency in Latin to associate *cithara* with words beginning with *c*, (Hor. *Carm.* 1.15.15, 3.1.20, Virg. *A.* 1.740, Val. Flac. 3.158, Stat. *Theb.* 6.355–6, Plin. *Nat.* 9.28). Nero's singing and lyre-playing is ubiquitous in the literary tradition, but these skills would not endear the impostor to the military: the military tribune Subrius Flauus disparagingly refers to Nero as a *citharoedus* (*A.* 15.65). **unde** 'because of which' (*OLD* 11). **super similitudinem oris** 'in addition to a facial resemblance'. *super = praeter*, as often in T. (G-G 1595–6). Nero apparently had yellowish hair, handsome rather than attractive features, greyish-blue but rather weak eyes, and a stout neck (Suet. *Nero* 51). His distinctive hairstyle, with its tiered rows of curls, was easy to imitate, and recognisable since it appeared on Nero's coinage from 64 onwards. For a physiognomical reading of Nero's appearance see Barton (1994a) 57. **adiunctis desertoribus:** some generals (e.g. Corbulo) punished desertion by death (*A.* 13.35.4), but it was impossible to eliminate it completely. Campbell (1984) 303–4, 307–10 discusses the legal penalties for desertion.   **inopia uagos:** 7.2n. *ambiguae domi res.*   **ingentibus promissis:** cf. *A.* 2.67.1, 12.9.1. The pretender was no doubt charismatic, the deserters desperate and gullible. The chances of the plan (such as it was) succeeding were slim, despite his resemblance to Nero, but the technique is typical in civil war: Otho (1.25.1), Caecina (2.20.2), Antonius Primus (3.24.1), Vitellius (3.58.3), Mucianus (4.39.4) all make promises to win support. See 4.2n. *ingens . . . fiducia* for *ingens.*   **Cythnum insulam detrusus** 'driven in to the island of Cythnus'. Cythnus = 'a minor island of the Cyclades group famous chiefly for its cheeses and hot springs' (Wellesley (2000) 46 with Plin. *Nat.* 13.134, Ath. 12.516e). Tiberius proposes it as a (relatively mild) place of exile for Junius Silanus (*A.* 3.69.5). It is ironic that the pretender's '"kingdom" is a small island . . . with a total area of 85.2km² and a population not over a few thousand' (Morgan (1993a) 785). *detrudo* is applied most often to those on dry land, but *TLL* s.v. *detrudo* 844.56–8 lists examples at sea (by hypallage). With towns and small islands, the 'place to which' is expressed by the acc. without a preposition. The pretender's original destination, whether he was from Italy or Pontus, is unclear, but he later mentions Syria or Egypt (2.9.2). Dio-Zonaras (11.15) says that, even before the pretender stopped at Cythnus, he was travelling to the legions of Syria.   **militum . . . commeantium:** *commeo* = 'travel on leave' (*OLD* 1b). These soldiers had perhaps been fighting the Jewish war. There was a lull in Vespasian's campaigning between mid-68 to mid-69, which may have allowed scope for leave (Levick (1999) 38).   **interfici iussit:** the pretender's violent tactics do not bode well for the mission. An immediate consequence may be Sisenna's panic (2.8.2). There is poetic justice perhaps, with the dismissive *interfectus quisquis ille erat* (2.9.2).   **spoliatis negotiatoribus:** the pretender needed money to finance his plans. Merchants were often seen as fair game in such circumstances (cf. 4.15.3, *A.* 2.62.3, 3.42.1).   **mancipiorum ualentissimum quemque:** the superlative of *ualens* occurs again only in T.'s minor works (*G.* 40.1, 43.3, *Agr.* 24.1). To enlist slaves is often presented as a sign of desperation: Caes. *Civ.* 1.24.2, 1.75.2, 3.4.4 (Pompey and his supporters), Cic. *Cat.* 1.27, 2.19, 4.4, 4.13, Dio 37.33.2 (Catiline). Catiline was allegedly reluctant to enlist slaves, worried about the bad publicity *causam ciuium cum seruis fugitiuis communicauisse* (Sall. *Cat.* 56.5).

8.2 centurionem Sisennam: he features only here. By naming him, T. adds authority to his account. The pretender remains nameless, diminishing his status. **dextras:** cf. 1.54.1. These clasped right hands of bronze or silver were tokens of alliance or hospitality (*OLD* 1c) and also appeared on coinage. There is 'irony inherent in an encounter between an emissary of peace and an agent of disruption' (Morgan (1993a) 786). **dextras . . . ad praetorianos ferentem:** T. again shows the Flavians planning in advance. The Vitellians also try to win over the praetorians in Rome, as Valens sends them letters from the German army (1.74.3). Yet the men dubbed *propius Othonis miles* (2.46.3) remain fiercely loyal to Otho (cf. their mutiny on his behalf, 1.80–2, Plut. *Oth.* 3.2–3, Suet. *Otho* 8.2). After victory Vitellius discharges those of doubtful loyalty (2.96.2), who have been approached again by the Flavians (2.82.3).   **uariis artibus:** such phrasing, implying a mix of threats and cajolery, recurs (2.101.2, 3.59.3, 4.41.1, *A.* 4.1.2, 12.68.2, 13.22.1).   **aggressus est** 'tried to influence' (*OLD* 3c).   **donec . . . aufugeret** 'until he escaped'. *donec* usually takes the subjunctive when suspense and design are involved (GL §572), but 'in T. the subjunctive is used after *donec* with and without the implication of purpose' (Wellesley (1972) 90; *NLS* §224 n.ii); cf. *mansere infensi . . . donec magistratu abirent* (*A.* 5.11.2).   **uim metuens:** understandable, if Sisenna knew about the pretender killing the soldiers (2.8.1). *metuo* (preferred by Sall.) = an archaising equivalent of *timeo* (preferred by Liv.). T. is 'almost alone' (Adams (1973) 135, WM 130) in preferring *metuo* in his historical works (except in direct speech).   **inde late terror:** the psychological impact of the short-lived rebellion 'must ironically have been generated when the impostor was actually dead' (Tuplin (1989) 370).   **ad celebritatem nominis:** *celebritas*, 'renown' (*OLD* 3), is often associated with *nomen* (*TLL* s.v. *celebritas* 741.63–78). Nero apparently had a *fauorabile nomen . . . apud Parthos* (Suet. *Nero* 57.2). T. says that the senators and equestrians were happy at Nero's death, but that the *plebs sordida* and *deterrimi seruorum* were *maesti et rumorum auidi* (1.4.3).   **erecti** 'excited by' (*OLD erigo* 7, *ad* 33a). **rerum nouarum cupidine et odio praesentium:** the chiasmus highlights their dubious motives. Similarly (and unexpectedly) many in Rome rejoice at the Gallic revolt in 21 *odio praesentium et cupidine mutationis* (*A.* 3.44.2). WM 342 suggest that T. alludes to Catiline's followers: *uetera odere, noua exoptant, odio suarum rerum mutari omnia student* (Sall. *Cat.* 37.3). The phrase *rerum nouarum cupido* recurs once more in T. (3.4.2). **Gliscentem in dies famam:** Virgil has the classic description of *fama* (*A.* 4.173–90 with Pease (1967) 211–22; cf. Ov. *Met.* 12.39–63, Sil. 4.5–7, 6.63, 10.578, Val. Flac. 2.116–25), including *parua metu primo, mox sese attollit in auras* (*A.* 4.176). T. may allude to this in describing *fama*'s daily growth. Cf. *cuncta (ut mos famae) in maius credita* (*A.* 3.44.1). *glisco* is 'a choice and colourful replacement for *cresco* . . . In T. there are 23 examples, 19 of them in the *Annals*, where *glisco* has driven out *cresco* altogether (*Hist. cresco* 3, *glisco* 4; *A. cresco* 0, *glisco* 19)' (Goodyear (1972) 96). Livy links the verb particularly with sedition (e.g. 6.14.1 with Kraus (1994) 170, Oakley (1997) 516–17). There may be irony in T.'s associating *glisco* with *fama* rather than with the rebellion itself.   **fors discussit:** T. signposts the *peripeteia* within the miniature drama; for the abstract noun as subject, see 2.1n. *spes uicit. discutio*, 'dispelled' (*OLD* 4), is only here in T.'s extant work.

9.1 Galatiam ac Pamphyliam prouincias: the plural *prouincias* points to a new but fleeting organisation. Galba detached Pamphylia from Lycia (Claudius' arrangement), joining it instead to Galatia (Augustus' arrangement). Vespasian reunited Pamphylia and Lycia early in his principate (Levick (1999) 146), creating the huge province of Cappadocia-Galatia (Suet. *Ves.* 8.4, with Jones (2000) 60–1, Syme (1937a), Sherk (1980); also 6.2n. *Cappadocia Pontusque*). **Calpurnio Asprenati:** Nonius Calpurnius Asprenas, from a distinguished consular family, was related to Galba's adopted son, Piso Licinianus. He was suffect consul at some time between 70–74, and proconsul of Africa in 83. T. probably knew his son, proconsul of Asia in 109/110. Asprenas' confrontation with the false Nero is his moment in the sun, at least in the literary tradition.   **e classe Misenensi:** the fleet at Misenum later deserts Vitellius (2.100.3, 3.56.2, 3.60.2).   **ad prosequendum** 'as his escort'. An escort enhanced an official's prestige (Rougé (1981) 130).   **Cythnum insulam tenuit** 'he docked at the island of Cythnus'; cf. *Agr.* 38.4.   **trierarchos:** the Romans adopted Greek titles for ship's officers. The *trierarchus* captained an individual ship, manned by a crew with both military and naval functions. A centurion aided him in military matters, which were 'left almost entirely to the centurion, for the trierarch did not even carry a sword' (Starr (1975) 59).

9.2 in maestitiam compositus: emotive appeal through appearance recurs in T.: cf. the Lingonian envoys, *in squalorem maestitamque compositi* (1.54.1), Agrippina the Elder, *cunctis ad tristitiam compositis* (*A.* 3.1.3) and Paris, *compositus ad maestitiam* (*A.* 13.20.1), bringing 'news' of a fake plot to Nero. The verb *compono*, 'put on a masked expression' (*OLD* 11) + *ad* or *in*, is peculiarly suited to T.'s narratives, where dissimulation is often a survival technique (*TLL* s.v. *compono* 2128.71–9). On clothing used to stir pity in the law-courts, see 2.60.1 *tenuit tristi mora squalidos*.   **fidem suorum quondam militum:** a sensible appeal (if a shade desperate).   **Syria aut Aegypto:** 8.1n. *Cythnum . . . detrusus*. There was a rumour that Nero himself had planned to flee to Alexandria at the end of his principate (Dio 63.27.2, Plut. *Galb.* 2.1; cf. Suet. *Nero* 47.2). Legions were stationed in both Syria (*IV Scythica, VI Ferrata, XII Fulminata*) and Egypt (*III Cyrenaica, XXII Deiotariana*).   **seu nutantes seu dolo** 'either hesitating or through trickery'; *uariatio* of participle + abl. noun (cf. 1.28.1, *A.* 2.1.2, *A.* 2.22.1, *A.* 15.56.3). *nuto* = 'hesitate' (*OLD* 6; also 1.31.3, 2.76.1), rather than 'waver in allegiance' (*OLD* 6b; also 2.98.1, 3.40.1).   **alloquendos . . . reuersuros:** a sensible way to bargain for time. Cf. Caesar *Gal.* 4.9.1, though Caesar, unlike the pretender, is not fooled.   **firmauerunt:** the simple verb form for *affirmo* is a poetical usage (cf. 1.22.1).   **cuncta:** *cunctus* = a synonym for *omnis* (1.3n. *cuncta . . . perlustrat*). **cuius cohortatione:** that Asprenas, the most senior Roman official present, in an alliterative phrase, encourages (rather than orders) the trierarchs does not necessarily discredit him (*contra* Morgan (1993a) 787–8). The trierarchs and their soldiers have not seen much active service in recent months, so Asprenas boosts their confidence; and anyway, he may not technically have commanded the escort himself. Cf. the legionaries in Britain, overcoming a momentary loss of confidence *cohortationibus ducis* (*A.* 14.30.2).   **expugnata nauis:** *expugno* for the capture of ships is Livian (*TLL* s.v.

expugno 1808.46–55).   **interfectus quisquis ille erat:** T.'s dismissive formulation enacts a sort of literary *damnatio memoriae*. 'The false Nero's anonymity . . . proved his worthlessness in a world where names counted' (Morgan (1993a) 789).   **caput:** the MS has *corpus* (preferred by Wellesley (1991) 1660), but many editors (following Würm (1853) 366) print *caput*. Morgan (1993a) 789–91 argues that in T. only important men were decapitated (1.44.1, 1.47.2, 1.49.1, 3.62.1, 3.74.2), so *corpus* deflates the pretender by denying him a 'distinction' paid otherwise only to lofty men. Yet the subsequent emphasis on the features supports *caput*. Deterioration of the body must also have been a concern. So, senators take Augustus' body from Nola to Rome, a much shorter journey, at night, presumably because a hot August day would have hastened decomposition (Suet. *Aug.* 100.2); Germanicus' body was cremated before being taken from Antioch to Rome (*A.* 2.73.4). It would have been pointless to take back the pretender's body anyway.   **insigne oculis comaque et toruitate uoltus** 'remarkable for its eyes, hair and grimness of expression'. T. elsewhere describes hair only in ethnographical passages (*G.* 4.2, *Agr.* 11.2), but often focuses on eyes (1.44.1, 2.70.4, 3.3, 3.39.1, 4.72.3). Cf. eyes and ears *quasi fenestrae . . . animi* (Cic. *Tusc.* 1.46). *toruitas* is only here in T., although the adj. *toruus* is more common (*A.* 2.14.3, 4.60.2, 16.29.1). The characteristic recalls Caligula rather than Nero (*A.* 15.72.2, Sen. *Cons. sap.* 18.1).   **in Asiam:** this route helped to dispel Asia's *terror*, as the decapitated head proved that the pretender was dead. Such grim trophies were not always conclusive: the severed head of the satrap Spitames was unrecognisable (Curt. 8.3.13).   **Romam peruectum est:** Domitian sent severed heads back to Rome to prove his enemies' demise (Dio 67.11.3; cf. Suet. *Dom.* 6.2) and Augustus did so with Brutus' head for revenge (Suet. *Aug.* 13.1). Here the dispatch of the remains to Rome elegantly switches the narrative from east to west, a device which T. likes enough to redeploy almost immediately (2.16.3, a severed head again). Less gory transitional devices include Othonian deserters used to move the narrative back to the Vitellians (*crebris . . . transfugiis*, 2.34.1) and messengers arriving from Syria and Judaea to see Vitellius, a prelude to switching the narrative back to the east (2.73). Livy also uses a journey to effect a narrative transition (Walsh (1961) 180–1).

10 A QUARREL IN THE SENATE

With the arrival of the pretender's severed head in Rome, T. elegantly introduces a revealing narrative about how the senatorial 'body' conducts business while the 'head of state' is absent from the city. The picture is not reassuring. Although the senate now has more freedom, its efforts misfire: measures to prosecute informers are applied inconsistently, so that an individual's personal power and influence are more weighty than his guilt or innocence. Vibius Priscus' prosecution of the Neronian *delator* Annius Faustus (relatively small fry) exemplifies this. Any chance of real debate is short-circuited by Priscus, who is so influential that his peers demand that Faustus should be executed *indefensus et inauditus* (2.10.2). Some senators feel uncomfortable, but even they assume that the defendant is *nocens* (2.10.2). T. as narrator implies

Faustus' guilt, but his concern is that no senator is prepared to challenge Priscus' hypocrisy: he too had profited hugely from being an informer. Men to champion freedom of speech are conspicuously absent, and the senate emerges as hierarchical, morally flawed and dominated by bullies. All of this is a far cry from Otho's eulogy of the senate as the *caput imperii et decora omnium prouinciarum* (1.84.3). If the senate is the centrepiece of the Roman empire, then its current troubled incarnation mirrors the warped world around it, riven by civil war. T.'s concerns with senatorial voicelessness in this section should be compared with the *Agricola: memoriam quoque ipsam cum uoce perdidissemus, si tam in nostra potestate esset obliuisci quam tacere* (*Agr.* 2.3). There Domitian is represented as having shrivelled the senate's capacity to embrace *libertas:* here 'T. wants to illustrate the way in which Nero's shadow continued to fall across the struggle for power' (Morgan (1993a) 794–5).

   10.1 ciuitate: *ciuitas* = the city of Rome (1.1n. *senium . . . destinandi*). **liber-tatem ac licentiam:** an alliterative antithesis (cf. *licentia ac libidine* 1.12.2) used by Cicero, Livy and Quintilian (*TLL* s.v. *licentia* 1356.73–5). *licentia* = 'disorderliness' (*OLD* 2). **incerta:** *incertus* + the preposition *inter* is also in Livy (*TLL* s.v. *incertus* 884.72–7). **paruae quoque res magnis motibus agebantur** 'even trivial affairs were being transacted amidst heightened emotions'. The polarised adjectives add rhetorical force. T. may count the episode as *parua* (at least compared with the fighting), but it raises important questions. How will the senate heal the rifts of the past while guaranteeing justice? Will the senate control its emotions and make balanced decisions? Cf. Sallust's Caesar, opening the debate about the Catilinarian conspirators by saying that those deliberating difficult questions must free themselves from all emotions (*Cat.* 51.1), a Thucydidean motif with rich potential for *sententiae:* 'Nature has treated human character badly, because we tend to weigh up acts, not beforehand, but after they have been done' (Curt. 8.2.1). So T.'s focus on *magni motus* in the senate is worrying. **Vibius Crispus** from Vercellae in north Italy (*D.* 8.1) was suffect consul in 61 (probably), 74 and 83, proconsul of Africa probably under Nero, *curator aquarum* from 68 to 71 (Front. *Aq.* 102.13), and legate of *Hispania Tarraconensis* in *c.* 71–3 (Bosworth (1973) 71–2). T. casts him as a typical *delator* (4.41.3, 4.42.5), but he still became an *amicus* of Vespasian (*D.* 8.3). 'Friendship with him became a thing for decent men like Pliny the Younger to conceal after the [Flavian] dynasty fell' (Levick (1999) 91). T.'s Aper (*D.* 8.1) cites him as the model of a successful speaker, while Quintilian calls him 'smooth, agreeable, born to please' (10.1.119). Unlike Eprius Marcellus, another *delator* with whom he is often paired, Crispus allegedly survived to the age of 80 by not speaking his mind (Juv. 4.89–93) or by doing so only when it was safe (cf. *cum clamant omnes, loqueris tunc, Naeuole, tantum,* Mart. 1.97.1). He was dead by 93. **pecunia potentia ingenio:** the asyndeton accentuates the factors that made him notorious, with the most striking item placed first. Crispus' brother Vibius Secundus, accused of extortion in 60, apparently avoided a harsh penalty, *Vibii Crispi fratris opibus enisus* (*A.* 14.28.2). Crispus, whose wealth was proverbial (Mart. 4.54.7), was worth 200 million HS (*D.* 8.2, scholiast on Juv. 4.81). 'Such wealth was staggering, especially when it is recalled that eight million sesterces is estimated as the appropriate capital for a senator' (Mayer (2001) 110). He had a *mite ingenium* (Juv. 4.82–3), and was a *uir ingenii iucundi et elegantis* (Quint. 5.13.48; cf. 8.5.15). He made a famous joke about Domitian's habit of stabbing flies (Suet. *Dom.* 3.1, with Jones (1996) 29), and another about illness keeping him from Vitellius' feast: 'if I hadn't fallen ill, I would certainly have died' (Dio 65.2.3).   **inter claros:** to be *clarus* in T. is not always bad (cf. 1.71.1 Marius Celsus, 3.75.1 Flavius Sabinus, *clarus et magnus haberi Agricola, Agr.* 18.5), and the adj. memorably appears at the start of Cato the Elder's *Origines* (Powell (1988) 258–9); but here, notoriety lacks a moral component.   **magis quam** is something of a formula in T., who here 'muffles a potential compliment through invidious comparison' (Plass (1988) 53; cf. 3.62.2). Sallust (*clari magis quam honesti, Jug.* 8.1) and then Livy (8.27.6) have similar formulations, 'a staple of the declaimers' paradoxical language' (Kraus (1994) 146).   **inter bonos:** Cato famously defined the ideal orator as a *uir bonus dicendi peritus* (Quint. 12.1.1), a standard which Crispus implicitly fails to match. The criticism anticipates the uneasy finale. Cf. Livy's Manlius (*famaeque magnae malle quam bonae esse*, 6.11.7), highlighting the gulf between specious appearance and true worth (Kraus (1994) 154, Oakley (1997) 499).   **Annium Faustum:** this equestrian *delator* is only here in T., despite the emphasis on his notoriety.   **equestris ordinis:** so Faustus is lower in the social scale than the senators proposing to prosecute him. Other equestrians tried in the senate include Clutorius Priscus (executed, *A.* 3.51.1), two *equites* called Petra (executed, *A.* 11.4.1), and Vinicius Rufinus and Terentius Lentinus (convicted under the *lex Cornelia, A.* 14.40).   **qui . . . delationes factitauerat:** the pluperfect tense of *factito*, 'make a profession of' (*OLD* 1b), suggests that Faustus is no longer an active *delator*.   **ad cognitionem senatus uocabat** 'summoned him to trial before the senate'. Augustus introduced the 'momentous change' whereby 'cases involving the interest, security, or welfare of the senate as a whole or of individual members were to be tried in the House' (Levick (1976) 184 with 199–200 for the 'inherent faults' of the senatorial court). T. stresses his own guilt over (mis)trials in the senate under Domitian (*Agr.* 45.1).   **recens:** adverbial, a use which 'enjoys particular favour with historians. T. is predictably partial to it' (Goodyear (1981) 241). Cf. 1.77.3, 4.68.4.   **Galbae principatu:** for the senate's relatively unfettered conduct just after Nero's death, see 1.4.3 (with Damon (2003) 102), but Plutarch mentions its sycophantic treatment of the praetorian prefect Nymphidius Sabinus (*Galb.* 8.4–5).   **ut accusatorum causae noscerentur** 'that the cases of informers (*OLD* 2b) should be brought to trial'. The senators' purpose was (presumably) to settle old scores against those who had profited unduly from legal cases under Nero, but in practice, prosecuting informers could prove traumatic. So, the case later brought by Musonius Rufus renewed the 'bitterness aroused by the period of accusations' (4.10 with Chilver and Townend (1985) 31; cf. 4.40.3). Pliny makes the process seem all too easy, as exiled informers fill islands recently occupied by exiled senators (*Pan.* 35.2).   **uarie iactatum** 'was bandied about in different ways'.   **et:** epexegetic, introducing a clause explaining what has preceded (*OLD* 11).   **prout potens uel**

inops reus inciderat 'depending on whether it was a case of a powerful or a helpless defendant' (*OLD incido* 11). Annius Faustus was (now) *inops*; powerful Neronian *delatores* included Eprius Marcellus, who won five million HS for prosecuting Thrasea Paetus (*A.* 16.33.2), and Aquilius Regulus, whose attacks allegedly got him seven million HS and a priesthood (4.42.4). Both were currently shielded by money, influential friends and family. Faustus was not in their league. Cf. *A.* 4.36.3.

10.2 propria ui . . . incubuerat . . . peruertere 'had done his utmost to ruin'. *incumbo* can be followed by *in* + acc., *ad*, *ad* + gerundive, dat. noun or dat. of the gerundive (*OLD* 6) or by an *ut*-clause (*OLD* 6c). *incumbo* + an infinitive is extremely rare: *TLL* s.v. *incumbo* 1074.40 lists in addition only Virg. *G.* 4.249.   **delatorem fratris sui:** Crispus' brother Vibius Secundus, procurator of Mauretania in 60, was convicted of extortion and expelled from Italy (*A.* 14.28.2). Yet 'a Roman audience was susceptible to the moral claim of fraternal duty and to the emotional appeal of brotherly affection' (Damon (1997) 127).   **traxeratque** 'had won over' (*OLD* 9c).   **indefensum et inauditum:** the alliteration (8.1n. *credentibus . . . contextu*) accentuates the travesty of justice in the senate's demand. T. pairs these words elsewhere (*D.* 16.4, *H.* 1.6.1, *A.* 2.77.3), but later authors did not follow him. T. is 'the first to employ *indefensus* in a judicial context' (Goodyear (1981) 424; *TLL* s.v. *indefensus* 1129.79–1130.22); the normal context is military (as 3.71.4).   **dedi ad exitium:** instead of a simple dat. (cf. Ov. *Met.* 13.259 with Bömer (1982) 267), T. uses *ad* + acc. The death penalty (Garnsey (1970) 105–11) seems severe, especially since the precise charges remain unclear. When accusers are themselves accused, the punishment is not usually so severe (banishment to islands, *A.* 6.30.1; exile from the city, *A.* 6.30.2). Thrasea Paetus rejects a suggested death penalty because *carnificem et laqueum pridem abolita* (*A.* 14.48.4). **nimia potentia accusatoris** suggests hypocrisy, since Crispus attacks Faustus from a position of power similar to that which the defendant once held. As T. says elsewhere, *factum esse scelus loquuntur faciuntque* (3.25.3), a point not lost on observers (2.10.3).   **dari tempus, edi crimina:** 'Once an accusation had been accepted for hearing in the senate, the normal procedure was for a date to be fixed and for the defendant to be informed of the charges . . . To arrange a hearing and to summon witnesses would take some days at least, so that a defendant could usually count on this amount of notice' (Talbert (1984) 482).   **quamuis inuisum ac nocentem:** even Faustus' supporters presuppose his guilt. Cf. Publius Celer, *uilis et nocens reus* (4.10), and Lepida, *quamuis infami ac nocenti* (*A.* 3.22.1). See Adams (1972) 357–8 on *nocens*.   **more** 'in the traditional way' (*OLD* 3).   **audiendum** challenges *inauditum* in the other side's proposal.

10.3 dilata . . . cognitio: that hasty decisions motivated by hatred are flawed is a topos (10.1n. *paruae res*), but here the postponement makes little difference to the outcome.   **damnatus est Faustus:** the penalty is unknown.   **nequaquam eo assensu ciuitatis, quem pessimis moribus meruerat** 'but the condemnation was not in any way greeted by that approval from the citizenry which a man of his evil character had deserved' (*OLD ciuitas* 2). The *ciuitas discors* (2.10.1) may have hoped to be united by common hatred of a corrupt man, but the mode of Faustus' downfall denies them this satisfaction. Cf. the moral clarity of the senatorial *cognitio* investigating the unruly conduct of the people of Sena (4.45). **quippe . . . meminerant:** a mark of the senate's deterioration is that only outsiders see the hypocrisy. *quippe* (often = *nam, OLD* 1a, 4b) typically introduces an explanatory clause or sentence. **cum praemio:** Quintilian criticises those who prosecute others hoping for rewards and calls it 'little better than highway robbery' (12.7.3). **nec poena . . . displicebat:** a lapidary ending to the chapter (cf. Cic. *Phil.* 2.96, Plin. *Pan.* 46.3, Just. 31.6.2 for the sentiment).

11 OTHO'S FORCES

With this section, T. ends the narrative *mora* and broad geographical sweep that have characterised the book's opening (2.1–10) to focus on Otho, left in suspended animation since T. outlined his preparations for leaving Rome on 14 Mar., 69 (1.90.1). If T. had been a different kind of historian, he could have neatly begun the book with this chapter, which has several characteristics suggestive of an opening: so, the enumeration of military forces, an appropriate flourish for a campaign's start, naturally tends to fall near the start of a narrative (cf. Hom. *Il.* 2; Harrison (1991) 106–11 on epic catalogues) or book (Caes. *Civ.* 3.3–4), or stands as a discrete narrative unit in the build-up to a battle (Hdt. 7.61–99, 9.28.2–32.2, Thuc. 7.57–8). Otho's own prominence on the march as he leads his troops, *horridus, incomptus famaeque dissimilis* (2.11.3), temporarily makes him coalesce with republican generals of old embarking on foreign wars (e.g. Liv. 5.19.7). Even the opening word, *laeta*, contrasting sharply with the last word of the previous chapter, *displicebat*, seems to shift the narrative to an upbeat mood. Yet this opening frame is still palpably fragile: in the ancient world, happy beginnings often have embedded in them the notion of darker endings, and Otho's conspicuous presence on this march only underscores the devastating impact that his later absence will have on the final campaign. Moreover, that this section of narrative is so forcefully overshadowed by the incipient Flavian challenge adds poignant undercurrents of futility to all of this busy Othonian activity.

11.1 Laeta . . . principia: this formulation has embedded in it the contrasting idea of a dismal end: 'We must look to the end of every matter and see how it will turn out. For god gives a glimpse of happiness to many, and then utterly ruins them' (Hdt. 1.32). **motis . . . exercitibus:** when precisely Otho started his military preparations is a vexed question. Murison (1993) 96–9, extrapolating dates from the distances to be travelled to Bedriacum by the Pannonian and Dalmatian legions, proposes 3 Mar. 69 for Otho sending orders to the legions, with the orders arriving on 9 Mar. 69 and the legions setting out *c.* 19 or 20 Mar. 69. Chilver (1979) 270 agrees with the 3 and 9 Mar. dates, but has the legions set out on 15 Mar. 69. **quattuor legiones:** i.e. the Pannonian legions *VII Galbiana* (originally *Hispana*, later *Gemina*, and based perhaps at Carnutum; *RE* xii 1629–41) and *XIII Gemina* (based at Poetovio, 3.1.1; *RE* xii 1710–27), and the Dalmatian legions *XI Claudia* (based at Burnum; *RE* xii 1690–1705) and *XIV Gemina* (*RE* xii 1727–47). The *XIV Gemina*, intensely loyal to Otho (2.66.1, 2.86.4), had not been in the east for long. The location of its camp in Dalmatia is unknown; its previous base was at Viroconium in Britain, from where Nero summoned it in 67 for his intended eastern campaign. These legions included some interesting personnel, Antonius Primus, legate of *VII Galbiana* (*cuius flagrantissimus in Antonium amor* 4.39.4), and Suetonius' father, tribune of the *XIII Gemina* (*Otho* 10).   **bina milia praemissa:** i.e. an advance force (vexillation) of 2,000 men from each legion, rather than 2,000 men in total (Levick (1999) 46). 'The Roman army's use of vexillations emphasizes its essential flexibility more than any other aspect of its organization' (Goldsworthy (1996) 27). T. mentions a vexillation from the *XIII Gemina* participating in the battle at Castores (2.24.3) and men from the *XIV Gemina* (from the advance force) being surrounded during the battle of Bedriacum (2.43.2).   **modicis interuallis:** of the four legions, only the *XIII Gemina* definitely arrived in time for the battle of Bedriacum. The expression is Livian (25.22.9, 28.20.4, 44.33.2, pl. form).   **septima a Galba conscripta:** 1.6.2 with Damon (2003) 109. The *VII Galbiana*, having come from Spain to Rome, was then sent to Pannonia. Galba raised the legion, but this did not inculcate special loyalty to him.   **praecipui fama:** cf. *magna . . . fama* (2.32.2). *praecipuus* 'almost always has full superlative rather than intensive force (= "special") in Tacitus. In the *Annals* it replaces *maximus*, which Tacitus may have regarded as hackneyed' (Adams (1972) 361).   **rebellione Britanniae compressa:** Boudicca's revolt broke out in the late summer of 60, but Suetonius Paulinus suppressed it in 61 (*Agr.* 15–16.3, *A.* 14.29–39, Dio 62.1–12, though see Syme (1958a) 765). The *XIV Gemina* was the main Roman force at the decisive battle (*A.* 14.34). Cerialis later calls the men of the fourteenth *domitores Britanniae* (5.16.3) to stir their pride before confronting the rebel Julius Civilis.   **addiderat:** 4.3n. *profligauerat*.   **eligendo ut potissimos:** in 66 Nero planned an expedition to the 'Caspian gates' in the Caucasus to fight the Albani (1.6.2, Suet. *Nero* 19.2, Dio 63.8.1), or to the 'Caucasian gates' to fight the Alani (Plin. *Nat.* 6.40). The *XIV Gemina* left Britain for the east in 67 (Griffin (1984) 228–9).   **erga Neronem . . . in Othonem:** *uariatio* of prepositions (Sörbom (1935) 48).   **erecta in Othonem studia:** Nero's supporters, perceiving Otho as similar, tended to support him (1.13.4, 1.78.2, Suet. *Otho* 7.1).   **sed quo plus uirium ac roboris, e fiducia tarditas inerat** 'the greater their strength and power, the more tardiness they showed as a result of confidence'. In the second part of the sentence T. has omitted *eo* and a comparative, to be supplied by the reader. Cf. . . . *quo suspectior sollicitis, adoptanti placebat* (1.14.2); *quantoque incautius efferuerat paenitentia patiens tulit absolui reum* (*A.* 1.74.6). The *tarditas* of these crack troops is inauspicious. Otho's decision to mobilise the Danubian and Pannonian legions came at 'the latest possible moment at which the intervention of these troops could be effective against an invading force expected over the Alps in the course of April' (Wellesley (2000) 61).

    11.2 ales cohortesque: 4.4n. *auxilia . . . alarumque*. Auxiliary forces often preceded the legionaries on the march (Goldsworthy (1996) 106–7).   **et ex ipsa urbe:** T. postpones until now details of the soldiers leaving Rome (cf. 1.90.3). The force 'was assembled in great haste and will have left Rome about 4th March' (Murison (1993) 105).   **haud spernenda manus:** cf. the *haud spernenda . . . manus* of Roman troops (*A.* 4.72.3). This Livian litotes (30.45.5) involving *spernendus* (not in Sall.) is a favourite of T. (2.58.1, 2.81.1, 2.86.2, 3.75.1, *A.* 2.52.3, 12.39.3, 15.4.2). **equitum uexilla** 'detachments of cavalry'. 'This metonymy for *uexillatio* is already in Livy and relatively common in T. (G-G 1764b)' (WM 206). On metonymy, see Quintilian 8.6.23–9. **cum legione prima:** i.e. the *prima Adiutrix, ferox et noui decoris auida* (2.43.1), enlisted by Nero from sailors at Misenum (1.6.2), but probably awarded their eagle by Galba (Dio 55.24.2; Chilver (1979) 53, Damon (2003) 109). Their support for Otho was a confidence booster (1.36.3), even if they lacked military experience. Vitellius wisely sends these turbulent soldiers to Spain *ut pace et otio mitesceret* (2.67.2), but the Flavians still try to convert them to their cause (2.86.4), a ploy which succeeds (3.44). **deforme insuper auxilium, duo milia gladiatorum:** to enlist gladiators (or slaves; 8.1n. *mancipiorum . . . quemque*) was perceived negatively (Caes. *Civ.* 1.14.4, App. *BC* 3.49), but could be practical, since 'there was a very close link between gladiatorial combats and military training' (Wiedemann (1992) 39; cf. Cic. *De orat.* 2.84). These gladiators initially perform well under Martius Macer (2.23.3), but *neque ea constantia gladiatoribus ad proelia quae militibus* (2.35.1; cf. 2.43.2). The adverb *insuper* (31× in T., never in Cicero, once in Sallust, 4× in Caesar, 48× in Livy) often conveys exasperation and vehemence (Damon (2003) 175). **etiam seueris ducibus:** T. is sensitive to the impact of civil war on the techniques of military leadership (cf. 2.7.1). In the *H.*, *seueri duces* tend not to flourish. **usurpatum** 'made use of' (*OLD* 4). **rector** potentially has a wide range of meanings, but in the *H.* often indicates the commander of an army (1.87.2, 2.36.2, 3.22.1, 3.25.1, 4.37.1). **Annius Gallus:** suffect consul in *c.* 66, Gallus was sent 'to keep open the road north-eastward to Aquileia at the head of the Adriatic and provide a rallying point for the reinforcements expected from the armies in Pannonia, Dalmatia and Moesia' (Syme (1958a) 159). In 70 he became legate of Upper Germany to deal with the rebellion of Julius Civilis: T. calls him an *egregius dux* (4.68.1; cf. Plut. *Oth.* 5.5) and he can control the troops in difficult circumstances after their defeat (2.44.2), but his injury after falling from a horse (2.33.1) left him unable to contribute meaningfully to Otho's campaign (Damon (2003) 284). **Vestricio Spurinna:** Gallus' subordinate, born in *c.* 25 (Plin. *Ep.* 3.1.10) and later suffect consul under Vespasian, imposed a puppet king on the German tribe, the Bructeri, under Domitian (or soon after his death). For this, he was awarded a triumphal statue (Plin. *Ep.* 2.7.1). He became suffect consul for a second and third time in 98 and 100. Pliny praises his way of life, adding that he was a learned writer of lyric verse in Latin and in Greek (*Ep.* 3.1.7). T. perhaps consulted him directly: 'What he says of Spurinna's operations is not only much more full and explicit than the other account surviving. It looks apologetic' (Syme (1958a) 177; Levick (1999) 160, Syme (1991a)). **ad occupandas Padi ripas:** the Po (Plin. *Nat.* 3.117–22), Italy's longest (and richest; *Nat.* 3.49) river, was a natural line of defence in the north. Livy highlights the potential difficulties of crossing it (21.47.5), but Caecina does it twice unopposed (2.20.2, 2.22.3; cf. 2.34, bridge-building across the Po). Authors often exploited the dramatic potential of transgressing by crossing rivers (Luc. 1.185–227, the Rubicon), which could also be seen as gods (*A.* 1.79.3, Diod. Sic. 4.35.3–4). 'The crossing of rivers

had been fraught with religious significance at least since the time of Hesiod' (Braund
(1996) 46). Rivers could serve as boundaries (Liv. 34.13.7, the Ebro; Plin *Nat.* 3.115, the
Rubicon; Caes. *Gal.* 1.33.4, the Rhône; *Gal.* 4.16, the Rhine; Dion. Hal. 1.9.2, Tiber
and Liris) and natural lines of defence (*G.* 1.1, 40.1 *H.* 2.32.2, 3.9.1, *A.* 12.14.1). Military handbooks advised generals how to cross large rivers (Veg. 3.7; Konstan (1985)
201–2, Austin and Rankov (1995) 173–80). **transgresso iam Alpes Caecina:**
T.'s description of Caecina's march (1.67–70) problematically lacks geographical (and
chronological) detail. The plan was to cross the Alps via the Great St Bernard pass
(1.61.1). Although he contemplated crossing the Raetian Alps into Noricum (1.70.2),
he stuck to the original itinerary, *hibernis adhuc Alpibus* (1.70.3), having sent across some
forces in advance (2.17.1). 'The area north of the Po and west of Cremona had gone
over to Vitellius before the first of his forces emerged from the Alpine passes' (Murison
(1993) 114). By *c.* 8 Mar. Caecina had reached Augusta Praetoria at the Italian end
of the Great St. Bernard pass (Chilver (1979) 265). Wellesley (2000) 42 suggests 'early
March'.   **sperauerat:** sc. Otho.

   11.3 speculatorum lecta corpora 'chosen detachments of his bodyguards'.
The *speculatores*, part of the praetorian guard, protected the emperor in Rome, on
journeys and military expeditions (Campbell (1984) 109–14). Otho was first hailed as
emperor by 23 *speculatores* (1.27.2). For *corpus* denoting a man, see Liv. 6.11.8.   **cum
ceteris praetoriis cohortibus:** Sejanus had raised the number of praetorian
cohorts to 12 (93.2n. *sedecim scribebantur*). Since 5 cohorts had been sent ahead, T.
could mean here anything up to 7 cohorts (though some of these had already been
sent to Narbonese Gaul, 1.87.1). The praetorians were especially devoted to Otho
(8.2n. *dextras . . . ferentem*).   **ueterani e praetorio:** praetorians normally enlisted
for 16 years (*A.* 1.17.6), a shorter period than a normal legionary would serve. These
men had probably completed their military service, but were serving in a special
unit assembled to meet the immediate crisis.   **classicorum ingens numerus:**
their identity and role in the civil wars have caused controversy (Chilver (1979) 52–4,
Damon (2003) 282). Nero had brought some oarsmen to Rome to form a new legion,
the *prima Adiutrix* (1.6.2, Plut. *Galb.* 15.6, Suet. *Gal.* 12.2 with Shotter (1993) 120; cf.
Dio 64.3.2), which was a potential improvement in their lot (Rougé (1981) 128), but
it is unclear how far this process had gone before he died. Whatever their status,
these oarsmen (or marines?) confronted Galba as he entered the city (keen perhaps
that the new emperor should finish what the old one had started). Some were put
to death (1.6.2) and others were arrested (1.87.1), which naturally predisposed them
to support Otho (1.31.2, 36.3), but Galba himself may have granted an eagle (i.e.
formally founded the legion) to those who were not dead or in prison. Otho released
the arrested men and enlisted them in a legion (1.87.1), probably allowing them to join
their comrades in the *prima Adiutrix* (4.2n. *ingens . . . fiducia* for *ingens*).   **nec illi segne
aut corruptum luxu iter:** this rapid march could 'place Otho at Brixellum after
17–18 days of travel, i.e. on about 1st April', but the senators may have slowed him
down, so that realistically 'he will have reached Brixellum about 8th April' (Murison (1993) 106–7). Although Otho apparently endeared himself to Nero *aemulatione*

luxus (1.13.3) and is partly driven to seize power by the attraction of *luxus* (1.22.1), the crisis brings out the best in him. Marches disgraced by excess typify the Vitellians after their victory (2.71.1, 2.87.1) and Vitellius himself is often linked with *luxus* (2.71.1, 3.36.1, 3.55.2; and *luxuria*, 1.50.1). 'For the Romans . . . luxury was a political question because it signified the presence of the potentially disruptive power of human desire, a power which must be policed' (Berry (1994) 63). See too T.'s digression on *luxus* (A. 3.52–5 with WM 376–413, Edwards (1993) 27–8). *luxus* is 'a rare and artificial variant for *luxuria*' (Adams (1974) 57; *TLL* s.v. *luxus* 1935.30–6), and cf. *luxuries* (2.7.1). **lorica ferrea:** Otho's iron breastplate, typical of the common soldier, is significant (Chilver (1979) 176). The Roman infantry soldier wore different types (and weights) of body armour (Goldsworthy (1996) 216). This was perhaps the *lorica segmentata*, 'a cuirass made of strips of iron sheet articulated on leather straps, with copper alloy fittings' (Bishop and Coulston (1993) 85).   **ante signa pedes ire** 'he marched on foot before the standards', indicating bravery and confidence (5.1n. *anteire agmen*). Cf. Agricola before battle: *pedes ante uexilla constitit (Agr.* 35.4).   **horridus, incomptus famaeque dissimilis:** Otho's appearance was notoriously effeminate (1.22.1, Suet. *Otho* 12.1, Juv. 2.99–109, Mart. 6.32.2 with Edwards (1993) 69–70), but here he plays the rugged soldier. To describe Otho's appearance as *horridus*, 'rough' (*OLD* 3; cf. *TLL* s.v. *horridus* 2992.49–53, in a good sense), counteracts Suetonius' image of the emperor shaving every day and using face-packs (*Otho* 12.1). For the public-relations hazards of foppish dress, see Gell. 1.5. Livy has Roman generals observe that *horridum militem esse debere* (9.40.4); for *horridus* used for soldiers' appearance, see Oakley (2005) 516–17, citing Virg. *A.* 7.669, Homer. Lat. 374, 433, our passage and *A.* 6.34.3.

12–15 OTHO MOVES NORTH. HIS DIVERSIONARY ATTACK ON GALLIA NARBONENSIS

T. is our only source to preserve an account of this Othonian expedition (1.87.1, 2.12–15, with Murison (1993) 101), so there has been much speculation about its aims and scope: 'The Ligurian campaign has been dismissed by historians as a pointless and ill-conducted foray, or elevated into a totally incredible attempt at a grandiose Othonian pincers movement. The truth lies somewhere in between' (Wellesley (2000) 52). T. says that the catalyst for the expedition is Otho's recognition that the Pennine and Cottian Alps and all other passes into Gaul are being held by Vitellius' troops (1.87.1). While Caecina took the Upper German army over the St. Bernard pass (the Pennine pass) to the north (1.67–70), Valens led the Lower German army via Lugdunum and Mount Genèvre (the Cottian pass) to the south (1.64–6). Otho's expedition to Gallia Narbonensis was probably meant to hamper the progress of Valens' army, allowing time for the Othonian forces to set up a defensive line along the river Po. Although the chronology of Valens' march is elusive, he 'may have been in a position to cross the Cottian pass some time in the second week of March' (Murison (1993) 89). However, thanks to Otho's diversionary expedition, Valens was delayed: having heard about the Othonian attacks on *c.* 10–11 Mar. (2.14.1), before he had crossed the Cottian Alps, he eventually learned of the stalemate between his own men and the Othonians on *c.* 25–26 Mar. (2.15.2). By then Caecina had already crossed the Alps and was advancing to Placentia. Valens 'must have been in a frenzy of impatience' (Murison (1993) 103), as Caecina's army was ideally placed to monopolise the glory of the campaign.

Yet even if the Othonians had valid strategic reasons for this expedition, T. problematises the moral conduct of these 'Romans' by aligning them with foreign invaders, who wreak havoc on a peaceful pastoral environment (12.2). The searing *exemplum* of the unnamed Ligurian woman enduring torture to protect her son (13.2) allows T. further scope to show the Othonian soldiers abusing others and demeaning themselves to procure money. In this context, the Vitellians are momentarily 'heroised' when Valens sends some troops to rescue the stricken province. Yet although the Vitellians briefly seize the moral high ground, they still fail to defeat the Othonians: all the sufferings of the innocent civilian population and the bloodshed of the battle itself only bring an uneasy stalemate (15.2).

12.1 Blandiebatur coeptis fortuna 'to begin with fortune smiled upon their enterprises'; abstract noun as subject, (2.1n. *spes uicit*). *blandior* (*OLD* 5 + dat.) casts *fortuna* as an alluring but capricious mistress (cf. Plaut. *Men.* 193, Ov. *Am.* 1.15.18, Sen. *Con.* 1.2.12 for the *blanditiae* of a *meretrix*; Fantham (1998) 257). *coepta* (+ the inceptive imperfect) anticipates a time when fortune will abandon Otho (11.1n. *laeta . . . principia*). Porcius Latro highlights that *omnis blandientis fortunae speciosus . . . nitor* is dangerous (Sen. *Con.* 2.1.1).   **possessa . . . parte:** the abl. absolute is marked off by chiastic alliteration.   **per mare et naues** 'through command of the sea'. This hendiadys is 'standard coupling' in Livy (Oakley (1998) 317). T. means the fleets at Misenum and Ravenna, which have not so far participated much in the civil war. Otho retained a freedman called Moschus as naval commander (1.87.2).   **penitus usque ad initium** 'right up to the foot'. *initium* can refer to a geographical starting-point (*OLD* 2b, *TLL* s.v. *initium* 1657.18–39). *penitus* + *ad* is in Caesar and Livy (*TLL* s.v. *penitus* 1079.33–47). T. elsewhere has *usque ad* or *penitus ad*, but *penitus usque ad* only here, perhaps reflecting the Othonians' optimism as the campaign opens.   **initium maritimarum Alpium:** the homoioteleuton (Lausberg (1998) §725–8, 965) distinguishes the phrase. In 14 BC (Dio 54.24) Augustus created the *Alpes Maritimae*, a small province which, together with the *Alpes Cottiae* (annexed by Nero) to the north, formed a buffer zone between *Gallia Narbonensis* and Italy, demarcated by a natural boundary, the river Varus (Plin. *Nat.* 3.31). Augustus celebrated the achievement with an inscribed monument erected in 7–6 BC at La Turbie (Plin. *Nat.* 3.136–7). Nero awarded the inhabitants of the *Alpes Maritimae* the Latin right in AD 63 (*A.* 15.32). 'From AD 70 onwards the province . . . seems to have remained peaceful and figures very little in history' (Rivet (1988) 337).   **quibus temptandis** 'to try to get possession of it' (*OLD* 9). The verb presents the *Alpes Maritimae* as an incidental objective in comparison with *Gallia Narbonensis* (Heubner (1968) 64).   **aggrediendaeque prouinciae Narbonensi:** the Othonian mission to *Gallia Narbonensis* was 'purely diversionary' to allow time for the troops to get into position along the Po (Murison (1993) 100). *Gallia Narbonensis* supported Vitellius through fear (1.76.1); T. has already cited Otho's plan to attack the area by sea (1.87.1).   **Suedium Clementem:** Clemens was a *primipilaris*, a senior centurion (1.87.2). He disappears from T.'s narrative after this campaign, but later became a tribune under Vespasian (M-W 339) and *praefectus castrorum* in Egypt (M-W 405).   **Antonium Nouellum:** Novellus was also a *primipilaris* (1.87.2). His future career is unknown.   **Aemilium Pacensem:** Otho had restored him as tribune of the urban cohorts, after Galba demoted him (1.20.2, 1.87.2). Pacensis later supported Vespasian and was killed fighting bravely on the Capitol (3.73.2). His *cognomen* seems to be unparalleled (Birley (1977) 279).   **per licentiam militum uinctus:** soldiers who fetter their commanders recur throughout the *H.* (1.56.1, 2.26.1, 3.36.2, 4.27.2). **ambitioso imperio regebat** 'was serving as commander in a manner designed to bring him popularity', 'commanded only for popularity' (Irvine). Cf. 1.83.1 and Sallust's Marius (*neque facto ullo neque dicto abstinere, quod modo ambitiosum foret, Jug.* 64.5). **ut aduersus modestiam disciplinae corruptus, ita proeliorum auidus** '(being) as corrupt with regard to (*OLD aduersus*[4] 11) military discipline as he was eager for battle' (with Goodyear (1972) 257, Christes (1993) on *modestia*). The gen. pl. *proeliorum* suggests Clemens' grandiose ambitions.

12.2 Non Italia . . . rapere: punchy adversative asyndeton (3.2n. *simulacrum . . . exsurgens*).   **tamquam externa . . . hostium:** T. links the Othonians with foreign invaders for dramatic and emotional effect. Cf. T. applying the *urbs capta* motif to the principates of Tiberius and Nero, an eloquent denunciation of civil war (Keitel (1984)). The motif is often introduced by *uelut* (1.82.2, *A.* 6.1.2), *ut* (2.87.2, 2.89.1, 3.49.1), *tamquam* (2.90.1, *A.* 16.9.2) or *quasi* (1.40.2, *A.* 15.72.1). Cf. 4.1.3. **urere uastare rapere:** historic infinitives in asyndeton (5.1n., *anteire . . . obniti*) mirror the brutally methodical attack, with echoes of Sallust and Naevius (Ash (1997)). **nihil usquam prouisum aduersum metus** 'no preparation had been undertaken to meet the threat' (*OLD metus* 5). Cf. *constans aduersus metus* (4.5.2).   **pleni agri, apertae domus:** cf. *apertae portae, repleta arua cultoribus* (Sall. *Hist.* 1.14). War's impact on agriculture is a topos (Ov. *Fast.* 1.697–700, Luc. 5.403–4, Virg. *G.* 1.506–7). Cf. Isaiah 2:4 'They shall beat their swords into ploughshares, and their spears into pruning hooks'.   **domini** 'the landowners' (*OLD* 1). Cf. 2.56.1.   **iuxta . . . liberos:** the presence of women and children stresses that the Othonians attack unexpectedly, enhancing pathos.   **securitate pacis et belli malo circumueniebantur** 'were being lured to their doom through the security of peace and the evil of war'. The chiasmus links a curious pairing, pregnant even for T., who refers simultaneously to the feeling of security and the actuality of war.

12.3 procurator Marius Maturus: the *eques* Marius Maturus Arrianus was loyal to Vitellius for as long as possible, offering refuge to Fabius Valens (3.42.2), but eventually had to switch his allegiance to Vespasian (3.43.2; Syme (1991b) 530). He was still in post in 78 (*AE* (1952) 122) and refused Vespasian's offer of praetorian rank, preferring 'a peaceful, respected life to high position and struggles' (Levick (1999) 172, Pflaum (1960) 95–8).   **iuuentus** 'men of military age' (*OLD* 1b). Cf. *iuuenta*, used almost always in the abstract sense (as at 2.86.3).   **intendit** 'set about' (*OLD* 11b). The auxiliary verb *intendo* (GL §423.2) + the infinitive (also *Agr.* 18.3, *H.* 2.22.3, *A.* 11.32.2)

is first in Plautus *Mil.* 380, then Lucr. 5.385, Caes. *Gall.* 3.26.5, Sall. *Rep.* 2.6.3 and
Liv. (9×). **primo impetu:** swift collapse in battle after initial enthusiasm typifies
barbarians (Fron. *Str.* 2.1.8), but the emphasis on youth here adds poignancy. The
scene evokes T.'s description of the unlucky Helvetii (1.68), inexperienced fighters who
refused to acknowledge Vitellius and were massacred by Caecina's men. Differences
between Othonians and Vitellians are thereby elided. The phrase is also symptomatic
of Livy's interest in the results of the first charge of a battle (Oakley (1997) 431).
caesi disiectique: sc. *sunt. -que* = 'or' (*OLD* 7); cf. *iuuenes capti caesique* (Liv. 23.1.9).
T. links these verbs again (*A.* 12.31.2).   **montani:** *montanus* is only here in T.'s extant
work. Shaped by the environment, mountain-dwellers are traditionally portrayed as
hardy (if erratic) fighters (Caes. *Civ.* 1.57.3, Liv. 9.13.7, 21.34.9, 21.60.4, Luc. 7.225),
but not here.   **ut quibus temere collectis . . . decus esset** 'since there was
no pride in victory for men who had been assembled in rash haste'. The relative
pronoun introducing a causal clause with the subjunctive is often preceded by *ut*
(*NLS* §157).   **non . . . non . . . neque . . . neque:** emphatic anaphora typifies
descriptions of military collapse (1.68.1, 2.93.1, *A.* 4.25.2, Sall. *Jug.* 99.2).   **neque in
fuga flagitium:** for *pudor* as a driving-force in battle, see *utrimque pudor, utrimque gloria*
(2.21.4), *Romanos pudor excitauerat* (5.15.2); cf. *pudor ire retro* (Stat. *Theb.* 8.522), *uertere terga
pudor* (Sil. 4.329) with Oakley (1997) 595. Yet T. presents these men of the Maritime
Alps as devoid of shame, despite fighting on home territory before *coniuges* and *liberi*
(Calgacus argues that fighting near home enables watching parents to shame their
sons to win by reproaching any flight, *Agr.* 32.2; cf. 4.18.2). Cf. Caesar on the power
of shame and pride in battle: *neque recte aut turpiter factum celari poterat, utrosque et laudis
cupiditas et timor ignominiae ad uirtutem excitabant* (*Gall.* 7.80.5).

13.1 Irritatus eo proelio 'goaded by that battle'. *irritatus*, 'used of the physical
provocation of animals' (Martin (2001) 142), coheres with similar metaphorical language elsewhere to suggest soldiers' bestial qualities (cf. 6.2n. *fremere*, 7.2n. *stimulabat*).
proelium is hyperbolic for the short-lived attack on the disorganised *montani*.   **miles:**
collective singular (6.2n. *fremere miles*).   **uertit iras:** *uerto* can designate directing
either weapons or anger at a target (*OLD* 13). These two registers are elegantly appropriate, as the soldiers' anger is a prelude to attacking the town physically.   **Albintimilium**, also known as *Intimilium* (= mod. Ventimiglia), is in the *H.* only here. This
pleasant Ligurian coastal town, situated below the Cottian Alps and reachable by the
Via Iulia Augusta, saw a brief uprising in March 49 BC, after a local celebrity, who had
once entertained Caesar, was murdered (Cic. *Fam.* 8.15.2), but otherwise it had not
seen much trouble until now.   **quippe:** explanatory (10.3n. *quippe . . . meminerant*).
nihil praedae: cf. Livy 39.1.6, on Liguria in 187 BC as an *inops regio*, which offered
praedae haud multum.   **in acie** 'in the battle'. *acies* (*OLD* 7) = *proelium.*   **inopes
agrestes et uilia arma** forms a hidden causal clause in apposition, explaining
the lack of booty. It also accentuates the unfair fight between Othonian troops and
the *montani*. Cf. the people of Ariminum, who grab decrepit shields, javelins with
bent points, and rusty swords to confront Caesar's army, with predictable results
(Luc. 1.239–43). The traditional *agrestis* is often cast as materially poor, but morally

rich. Environmental determinism should have toughened these Ligurians (cf. Cic. *Agr.* 2.95 *Ligures duri atque agrestes*; cf. Diod. Sic. 5.39), but they are helpless before the Othonian invaders. Ligurian weapons were originally lighter than Roman arms (Diod. Sic. 5.39.7), but the point here is that these 'domesticated' farmers only had improvised weapons, which were worthless as booty.   **nec capi poterant:** the *montani*, even if captured, would not have provided booty, since citizens could not be sold as slaves (cf. 2.44.1, 3.34.2).   **pernix genus:** Ligurians were traditionally speedy (Liv. 39.1.6, Sil. 8.605, Flor. 1.19.4). Rome had fought them continuously until the 150s BC. Livy's Aemilius Paullus disparagingly calls them *latrones* rather than a real enemy (40.27.10; cf. Plut. *Aemil.* 6, Diod. Sic. 5.39). For Cato the Elder, they were *fallaces* (F32 Peter) and *mendaces* (F31 Peter), and Virgil has a trickster Ligurian attack Camilla (*A.* 11.699–724). Yet T. casts them as innocent victims.   **gnari locorum:** T. increasingly likes the choice adj. *gnarus*: 2× (*Agr.*), 15× (*H.*), 30× (*A.*). It is in Sallust (2×) and Livy (10×), but not in Caesar. This particular combination is at Livy 38.12.6 (cf. *gnaritatis locorum* Sall. *Hist.* 3.84) and Val. Flac. 4.208. T. has it again (*Agr.* 37.4, *H.* 2.85.2), but then abandons it.   **calamitatibus insontium** 'at the cost of disasters inflicted on the innocent'. T. reserves *calamitas* for moments of heightened emotion: e.g. the devious entrapment of Titius Sabinus (*A.* 4.68.3). *insons* (not in T.'s minor works, 2× in the *H.*, 16× in the *A.*) is eye-catching (WM 463, Adams (1972) 357–8). Cf. *innocens* (2× in *Agr.*, ix *D.*, 10× in *H.*, 9× in *A.*). T. polarises greedy, abusive Othonians and innocent Ligurian civilians.   **expleta auaritia:** in the *H.* avarice marks out both individuals (Galba 1.5.2, 1.37.4, 1.38.1, Fonteius Capito 1.7.2, 1.52.1, Titus Vinius 1.37.5, Calpurnius Piso 1.38.1, Trebellius Maximus 1.60.1, Ofonius Tigellinus 1.72.1, Cadius Rufus, Pedius Blaesus, Saevinus Propinquus 1.77.3, Vespasian 5.in. *auaritia*, Vitellius 2.62.1, Antonius Primus 3.49.1) and groups (Vitellians 1.51.4, 1.57.2, 1.67.1, 4.14.1, Flavians 4.1.2, Germans 4.73.3, emperors 4.74.2, Romans 5.12.2). Elsewhere only Cicero combines *auaritia* and *expleo* (*S. Rosc.* 150, *Red. Pop.* 13). *auaritia* can be seen as as 'a foreign immigrant which causes the Romans themselves to adopt the values of their defeated opponents' (Feldherr (1997) 274). It may further align the Othonians with foreign invaders.

13.2 praeclaro exemplo: exemplarity is pervasive in ancient historiography (MW 162; Aubrion (1985) 237–46, Chaplin (2000); also Lausberg (1998) §410–26 for *exempla* in oratory). The Ligurian woman illustrates 'the principle that the story of a sympathetic individual affects us more even than large human statistics – Ann Frank contrasted with the round figures of Auschwitz-Birkenau' (Powell (1998) 125). Some people in T. self-consciously enact exemplarity (Otho 2.47.2, Tarsa *A.* 4.50.3, Corbulo *A.* 13.35.4, Arria *A.* 16.34.2) or actively appeal to it (Vocula 4.58.2). T. signals his plan to include appropriate *exempla* (1.3.1, 3.51.2), but we have only two other references in the *H.* to an *exemplum* about a woman (Epponina 4.67.2, Galeria 2.64.2. Cf. Epicharis *A.* 15.57.2, Arria *A.* 16.34.2). T. also presents negative *exempla* (the fratricidal *eques* 3.51, Tigellinus *A.* 15.37.1). With this particular *exemplum*, T. exerts self-control and enhances his credibility as a historian by not narrating the murder of Julia Procilla, Agricola's mother (*Agr.* 7.1), killed in this very attack. For other *exempla* of loyalty and betrayal in a civil war, see Appian *BC* 4.12–30 (especially 4.30, Atilius and his mother).   **femina Ligus:** she remains unnamed, but her gender and status as a mother add emotive power and novelty (ancient narratives about war naturally focus more on men than on women, Hom. *Il.* 6.490–3, cited by WM 293 with useful bibliography). Ligurian women were famously hardy (Diod. Sic. 5.39.2, 39.7).   **quae** introduces a complex and climactic subordinate clause, which fills the rest of the chapter and dwarfs the short initial main clause (a typical 'appendix sentence', Damon (2003) 16–19).   **filio abdito:** the son's age is unclear. An example of family loyalty is striking in a narrative where such bonds are usually betrayed: cf. *nec eo segnius propinquos adfines fratres trucidant spoliant* (3.25.3). For the opposite scenario (sons betraying mothers), see *A.* 15.56.4 (Lucan / Acilia) and 15.67.2 (Nero / Agrippina).   **cum . . . credidissent:** cf. the Flavian soldiers in Rome, also driven by greed, who enter houses searching for money, *Vitellianos occultari simulantes* (4.1.2).   **eoque:** 'and therefore' (2.8.1, 22.2, 41.1, 56.2, 65.1, 82.2, 100.2).   **per cruciatus:** interrogation by torture was normally reserved for slaves (*OCD³* 'torture'). Descriptions of torture were a staple of the declamation schools (e.g. Sen. *Con.* 2.5, 8.3, 10.5) and dramatic narratives (Plut. *Art.* 16), but T. usually withholds gory details, in accordance with the dignity of history (cf. *A.* 11.22.1). Elsewhere, torture of women involved sensational details (e.g. Plut. *Art.* 19.6, Plin. *Nat.* 7.87, 34.72).   **occuleret:** T. increasingly prefers *occulto*, rather than *occulo* (*H.* 5 : 3, *A.* 21 : 2). The subordinate clause shows marked *uariatio* of vocabulary (Sörbom (1935) 39) with synonyms for 'hide' (*abdo, occulto, occulo, lateo*).   **uterum ostendens latere respondit:** the Ligurian woman reinforces her word (presumably *latet*) with a defiant gesture reasserting the primeval bond between mother and son. Wombs can symbolise loyalty (Luc. 1.377), treachery (*A.* 14.8.5, with O'Gorman (2000) 141, where Agrippina tells her son Nero's assassins, *protendens uterum, 'uentrem feri'*), fratricide (Stat. *Theb.* 11.408), corruption (T. *D.* 29.3, Vell. 2.93.2), sycophancy (*A.* 15.23.2) and fertility; the womb even prompts a Ciceronian joke (Quint. 8.3.54). The scene perhaps alludes to the cruel Achilles consigning to death *etiam latentem | matris in aluo* (Hor. *Carm.* 4.6.19–20; cf. Hom. *Il.* 6.55–60). *latere* (only here in T.'s extant work) with ellipse of *eum* is bold, but the meaning is clear from what precedes (Hardie).   **nec ullis deinde terroribus aut morte** 'from then on, not by means of any terrors, even fear of death'. It is unclear if the woman was eventually killed.   **constantiam uocis egregiae** 'the consistency of her excellent utterance'. T. often gives brave words spoken in the face of death (Galba 1.41.2, Vitellius 3.85, Subrius Flauus *A.* 15.67.4), a regular feature of *exitus* literature, but the speaker's gender here adds power (cf. Messalina's *questus irriti, A.* 11.37.4).

14.1 Imminere 'threaten' (*OLD* 6 + dat.). An intimidating Roman fleet can inspire fear (*Agr.* 25.2) or, at times, defiance, as in Calgacus' speech to the Britons (*imminente nobis classe Romana, Agr.* 30.1). Yet *longa pax* and contact with the Romans had softened these Gauls, who no longer resemble the hardy Britons (cf. *Agr.* 11.4).   **prouinciae Narbonensi:** 12.1n.   **in uerba Vitellii adactae** 'bound by an oath to Vitellius' (*OLD adigo* 9b). See 1.76.1 for the circumstances; the expression recurs at 2.73. Such oaths to the emperor, an extension of the military *sacramentum* (6.1n.), but sworn by the provinces and the people, were usually administered annually on New Year's day or on the anniversary of the emperor's accession (Plin. *Ep.* 10.52, *A.* 1.34.1; Mommsen (1887–8) 792–3). In the *H.*, oaths, sworn with increasing frequency to different emperors, are progressively devalued. **classem Othonis:** this fleet, commanded by the freedman Moschus, is *ualida et partibus fida* (1.87.1). Its mission to create a diversion on the coast and to stir fear among the Vitellians was a success (*fama uictricis classis* 2.16.1, 2.28.1, *contremuisse* 2.32.1). **trepidi nuntii:** 1.39.2, 4.18.1; 'an absolutely standard Livian expression' (Oakley (1997) 630), but not Sallustian. The idea of a *nuntius* terrified by his own message features in Senecan tragedy (*Thy.* 634–5). **Fabio Valenti:** Vitellius' general, a legionary legate of equestrian rank from Anagnia *c.* 40 miles south-east of Rome (3.62.2), had marched through Gallia Narbonensis to cross the Alps via the Cottian pass (1.61.1), after leaving Colonia Agrippinensis on *c.* 12 / 13 Jan. (Murison (1993) 86–90). This was a longer route than that taken by Vitellius' other general, Alienus Caecina. Valens' location on receiving the news about Otho's fleet is unclear: perhaps he was at Lucus (Chilver (1979) 267) or Vapincum (Murison (1993) 101). Both are before the pass through the Cottian Alps. **attulere:** the news reached Valens on 10 or 11 Mar. (Murison (1993) 102). **legati coloniarum:** the colonies were perhaps Forum Iulii, Aquae Sextiae and Arelate (Chilver (1979) 178). The legates may not have known about the Othonian fleet, but the raids on Albintimilium no doubt prompted nearby communities to seek help. **auxilium orantes:** cf. the Saguntine *legati . . . auxilium . . . orantes* (Liv. 21.6.2) from Rome in 219 BC against the Carthaginian general Hannibal. Yet in this civil war, the *coloniae* must plead for help against a Roman (Othonian) enemy. **Tungrorum:** the Tungri (first mentioned at Plin. *Nat.* 4.106) came from north-east Gaul, but were perhaps a new grouping of a tribe annihilated by Caesar, the Eburones (*G.* 2.5 with Rives (1999) 117–18). One Tungrian cohort deserted to join the rebel Julius Civilis in 70 (4.16.2), but that was a temporary aberration: two Tungrian cohorts fought for Agricola at the battle of Mons Graupius in 84 (*Agr.* 36.1, with Ogilvie and Richmond (1967) 78). **turmas:** the average *turma* was *c.* 30 men (Goldsworthy (1996) 19). **Treuirorum:** after clashes with Caesar, the Treveri (from north-east Gaul) had remained quiet (Agrippina even chose them as a haven from the mutinous legionaries, *A.* 1.41.1) until 21, when a Treveran noble Julius Florus started a short-lived revolt (*A.* 3.40–2 with WM 327–37). Galba, by confiscating their land, drove them to support Vitellius (1.53.3, 1.57.2). Subsequently 'they at first refused to join the revolt of Civilis, and fought against the Germani who were allied with him (4.32.2, 37.3); later, under the leadership of Classicus and Tutor, they did join, but were brought back under Roman rule relatively quickly and easily (4.55–9, 68–74)' (Rives (1999) 236). This *ala* 'had returned to the Rhine by the time of Civilis' rebellion' (Chilver (1979) 179). **alam:** 4.4n. **Iulio Classico praefecto:** Julius Classicus was a wealthy and high-ranking noble from Augusta Treverorum (4.55.1). His ancestors 'must have been granted citizenship by Caesar or Augustus as an attempt to win their loyalty' (Wightman (1970) 44), but he still joined Civilis' rebellion. T. casts him as arrogant (4.55.1) and self-satisfied (4.70.1). **retenta:** sc. *est.* **in colonia Foroiuliensi:** Forum Iulii (Fréjus), a *uetus et illustris . . . colonia* (*Agr.* 4.1) and a coastal port of Gallia Narbonensis, was originally a colony for veterans of the *Legio VIII Hispana* (Plin. *Nat.* 3.35). Augustus deposited there the ships captured at Actium (*A.* 4.5.1). It was the birthplace of T.'s father-in-law Agricola and the Flavian general Valerius Paulinus (3.43.1).   **omnibus copiis . . . uersis uacuo mari:** the two abl. absolutes function as two conditional clauses.   **in terrestre iter uersis** 'marching inland' (Irvine). *terrestre iter* (not in Sall.) is Livian (5×). T. has it 5× (2.59.2, 4.35.1, 4.79.3, *A.* 1.70.1, *A.* 2.23.1), often in contexts contrasting journeys by water.   **acceleraret** 'might advance quickly' (intransitive).   **aduersus hostem:** i.e. the Othonians, focalised through the Vitellians.   **Ligurum cohors:** these Vitellians were no doubt motivated by the recent Othonian attacks on their people.   **uetus loci auxilium** 'a long-standing local auxiliary force'.   **quingenti Pannonii:** Chilver (1979) 180 raises the possibility that T. wrongly assigns these men to the Vitellians, suggesting that these recruits were more likely to be destined for Otho's Pannonian cohort in northern Italy (2.17.2). Whether this a mistake or a deliberate switch, T. paves the way for a colourful battle scene, with Otho's *ueterani milites* fighting a heterogeneous Vitellian force (Tungrians, Treveri, Ligurians, Pannonians). T. was prepared to distort 'the truth' for literary impact: e.g. he moves Arminius' death from 21 to 19 (*A.* 2.88), to juxtapose it with Germanicus' obituary (Ginsburg (1981) 37–8).   **nondum sub signis** 'not yet regularly enrolled' (Irvine).

14.2 Nec mora: a Livian opening for a battle-description (28.33.4, 29.36.7, 31.33.8), which is also in epic (Virg. *A.* 9×, Ov. *M.* 16×, Stat. *Theb.* 8×, Sil. 9×). Yet T. still tantalisingly suspends the action until he has explained the arrangement of the troops for battle.   **acies:** sc. the Othonian (Morgan (1994–5) 225–31).   **classicorum:** 11.3n.   **mixtis paganis:** T. does not use *paganus* ('civilian') outside the *H.* (absent from Caes., Sall., Liv.). *pagani* are cast as a bad influence on the troops (1.53.3), a target for soldiers' anger (2.88.1), and a term of abuse (3.24.3; Wellesley (1972) 110). The presence of civilians in battle reflects the chaos of civil war (3.77.2, 4.20.2).   **in colles . . . exsurgeret** 'was occupying the rising ground of the hills' (cf. 4.23.1). The effect is almost amphitheatrical (cf. Kraus (1994) 232 on another battle 'played out in a depression between two hills'), but these spectators will also participate in the battle. The effect of this curious and striking use of the verb is perhaps that of a total wave of bodies breaking and overtopping the rising ground (Kenney).   **quantum . . . aequi loci:** 6.2n. *quantum insularum.* Roman troops traditionally fought more efficiently on level ground (5.14.2, *A.* 1.68.3, Liv. 2.64.4, 9.19.15, Caes. *Gall.* 2.10.4, 3.17.7), so the detail anticipates an Othonian victory.   **praetorianus miles:** Otho's crack troops (8.2n.).   **ut** continues the consecutive clause.   **conuersa et minaci fronte** 'with menacing prows turned shorewards'. These ships would have had animal figure heads (Williams (1985)), so *frons* is not simply a metaphor. Ships were often named after them, creating 'an ambiguity between ship and homonymous figure head' (Harrison (1991) 127; Casson (1971) 344–60).   **minor peditum uis, in equite robur:** cf. the Parthians (*sola in equite uis, A.* 6.34.1), the Britons (*in pedite robur, Agr.* 12.1), the Germans (*plus penes peditem roboris, G.* 6.4 with Rives (1999) 142), the Chatti (*omne robur in pedite, G.* 30.3). Such touches accentuate differences between combatants, add variety and enhance enjoyment.   **Alpinos**

proximis iugis: locating the Ligurians on higher ground was perhaps meant to intimidate the Othonians visually. Cf. the Britons similarly positioned *in speciem simul ac terrorem* (*Agr.* 35.3). **densis ordinibus:** 3.17.2, 3.63.1; a Livian combination (30.34.8, 33.8.14, 35.5.7). **post equitem:** the Vitellians naturally put their stronger cavalry in front, ready to charge the enemy infantry. 'The cavalry had to persuade the infantry to run away before they had reached them, frightened by their appearance and noise.' (Goldsworthy (1996) 230). Yet if the infantry held their ground, then (despite what one might think) the charging horses instinctively avoided colliding with them (cf. 4.33.2).

14.3 incaute: Gauls and Germans attacking recklessly at first, but then fading is a topos (Liv. 5.43.3, 7.12.11, 10.28.3, 38.17.7, Dion. Hal. 14.8, Jos. *AJ* 19.120, T. *G.* 4.2, *A.* 2.14.3, Dio 38.49.5, Flor. 1.38.5, Fron. *Str.* 2.1.8; Oakley (1998) 158–9, Rives (1999) 129). T. also associates this mode of attack with the Vitellians (2.22.1, 3.17.2), a device which accentuates their northern identity. **cum** 'given that'. **exciperet:** sc. *eos*. **saxis:** instrumental abl. **apta ad iaciendum:** a disparaging observation about the civilians: the professional soldiers will engineer the victory. T. has *apta + ad* again (*G.* 6.4, *H.* 3.41.1; also Cic. *Att.* 16.2.2, Caes. *Civ.* 1.30.5), but usually prefers *aptus +* a simple dat. (1.79.2, 2.16.3, 2.58.1, 3.75.3, *A.* 2.6.2, 2.14.1, 3.31.4 with WM, 5.2.2). Here the preposition allows scope for assonance (Woodman (1998) 223–4 on such sound effects in T., sometimes underestimated by commentators). **sparsi inter milites:** the excited civilians must have moved down from the rising ground by the sea to mix with the professional soldiers. **strenui ignauique** 'whether they were energetic or cowards'. *strenuus* can be negative (1.52.3) or ironic (3.57.1, *A.* 3.53.2), but more often positive (1.46.3, 1.62.2, 2.46.2, 2.86.2, 3.6.1, 3.43.1, 4.69.1, *A.* 1.70.3, 6.35.2, 13.35.4, 14.44.4). **in uictoria idem audebant:** T. implies that defeat is a more telling test of a man's bravery. **deletae . . . forent:** WM 163. T. especially favours this alternative to *essent* in the *H.* (51 : 17). Cf. *Agr.* (4 : 8); *A.* 1–12 (62 : 31); *A.* 13–16 (1 : 29). **ni**, 'a commonplace of Hellenistic battle-descriptions' (Ogilvie (1970) 402), is an archaism, used dramatically to introduce a near *peripeteia* (1.26.1, 2.26.2, 66.2, 68.1, 3.15.1, 3.23.2, 3.71.2, 3.81.1, 4.39.3 with Chausserie-Laprée (1969) 598–617, 636–7). Josephus has the parallel Greek construction in the *BJ* to add epic grandeur to Titus (Paul (1993) 56–64). *ni* (or *nisi*) is a useful device for concluding battle-descriptions (*Agr.* 26.2). T. abandons it in *A.* 11–16, and it also fades out in the later decades of Livy (Adams (1974) 60). **obscurum noctis:** neuter substantive adj. + defining gen. (2.2n. *laeua maris*). Virgilian phrasing (*G.* 1.478; cf. *A.* 6.268) introduces the topos of night halting a battle (Kraus (1994) 143). **obtentui fugientibus** 'a covering for the fugitives'; predicative dat. (*NLS* §68).

15.1 quamquam uicti: victory can breed complacency, but defeat is sometimes salutary (cf. 2.27.1). *quamquam* lacks a finite verb (3.2n. *quamquam in aperto*). **quieuere** 'refrained from violence' (*OLD quiesco* 6a); 3.1n. *ipsa . . . cessere.* **accitis auxiliis:** a Livian expression (also at 3.45.2, 4.13.2). They were summoned from Forum Iulii (2.14.1), where they had wisely been left in reserve. 'Since the distance from Forum Iulii to Albintimilium, the probable site of the camp, is 64 miles, the attack on this camp would have come probably 3 days at least after the 1st battle i.e. *c.* 24–25 Mar.'

(Murison (1993) 103).   **hostem . . . inuadunt:** a phrase common in Sallust and Livy (Kraus (1994) 236). The vivid present tense reflects the Vitellians' current dynamism. **socordius agentem** 'taking their ease'. '*socors* and *socordia* are not found in verse after Terence . . . and outside the historians they are rare in prose . . . It seems reasonable to regard them as archaisms, obsolescent by Cicero's time but favoured by historians' (Oakley (1997) 681–2).   **caesi . . . naues:** the tricolon + asyndeton mirror the speedy attack, perhaps recalling the abrupt style of military dispatches. Cf. *trucidati ueterani, incensae coloniae, intercepti exercitus* (*Agr.* 5.2), *domitae gentes, capti reges* (*Agr.* 13.3), *trahi, occidi, capi* (*A.* 4.25.2). 'Passive verbs and short sentences are characteristic of "military communiqué" style' (Kraus (1994) 108; Ogilvie and Richmond (1967) 188). **trepidatum:** the impersonal passive is 'perfect . . . for putting things briefly' (Pinkster (1992) 174); cf. *bellatum* 1.1.1, *placitum* 2.33.2, *conclamatum* 2.68.3.   **sidente . . . metu:** *sido* (for the compound *resido*; 18.1n. *si propinquaret*) is metaphorical, either from winds abating (Sil. 14.623) or sediment sinking in liquid (Plin. *Nat.* 33.120).   **iuxta colle:** the adverb in this position functions as an adj. (cf. 2.34.2 *ualidis utrimque trabibus*, 2.39.2 *tot circum amnibus*). On the desirability of occupying higher ground, see Caes. *Gall.* 1.24, 2.22, Fron. *Str.* 2.2.2–4.   **defensi** 'they defended themselves'.   **irrupere:** 3.1n. *ipsa . . . cessere.* The alternative third person plural is apt for a fast-moving military narrative.

15.2 atrox ibi caedes: also at 2.88.1, *A.* 14.17.1. '*atrox* and its cognates were much affected by the historians' (Oakley (1998) 246; cf. 170).   **sustentata diu acie** 'after long maintaining their battle formation', a priority for a skilled general (e.g. *A.* 1.65.6, Caes. *Afr.* 82.3); Vegetius (1.26) suggests practical ways to keep the *acies* in order.   **telis obruuntur:** eliminating leaders disorientates the common soldiers; cf. *A.* 4.25.3 (Tacfarinas). T. claims that it is a mark of *Romana disciplina* to rest more hope in the general than in the army (*G.* 30.2).   **ne . . . quidem incruenta uictoria:** cf. 2.44.3, 4.37.3 (also with litotes). This is 'a characteristic comment at the end of a Livian battle, usually with a list of Roman casualties following' (Oakley (1998) 170). **quorum improuide secutos** 'those of them who had followed rashly', with the participle doing duty for a relative clause. The rare adverb is a Livian coinage (21.53.7, 27.27.11) and appealed to his imitator Curtius Rufus (3.11.8, 4.16.17).   **uelut pactis indutiis:** they lack authority to agree to a proper armistice, hence the modifying *uelut*. All this bloodshed leads only to stalemate. Cf. *uelut pacta exercitus licentia ducis salute* (*Agr.* 16.4), *uelut communi pacto commercio* (Liv. 34.19.8). *indutiae* 'armistice' is in the *H.* only here.   **hinc . . . inde:** this pairing (instead of *hinc / illinc*, Constans (1893) §47) recurs (1.68.1, 1.84.3, 2.21.4, 4.19.3, 5.24.2).   **Antipolim:** modern Antibes on the French riviera (only here in T.). Founded by the Greeks of Massilia, it was famous for its *muria*, brine used for pickling and as a cheap relish (Plin. *Nat.* 31.94, Mart. 13.103).   **Albingaunum** = modern Albenga (only here in T.). The two places are *c.* 70 miles apart.   **interioris Liguriae** '(a town) within Liguria'. This phrase has sometimes been misinterpreted to mean 'further from the coast', but the contrast, on an east-west axis, is with Antipolis in Narbonese Gaul.   **retro . . . reuertere:** the enveloping pleonasm (Lausberg (1998) §502) + asyndeton sharpen the contrast between the withdrawing Vitellians and Othonians. Pleonasm with *retro* is Livian (Petzke (1888) 58, Oakley (2005) 61).

16 TROUBLE ON CORSICA

For *uariatio* and entertainment, T. peppers his narrative with miniaturised dramas, often involving murder (or attempted murder) of Roman officials around the empire: cf. 2.58–59.1 (murder of Albinus, procurator of Mauretania), 2.85.2 (attempted murder of Tettius Iulianus, legate of the Seventh Legion in Moesia), and 4.48–50.3 (murder of Lucius Piso, proconsul of Africa). This distinct category of digression is often linked to the main narrative by loose chronological formulae: *isdem diebus* (2.58.1), *in eo motu* (2.85.2), *sub idem tempus* (4.48.1). Here the link is especially tenuous: the rumour of Otho's victorious fleet is said to have kept Sardinia and Corsica loyal (2.16.1). So the events must have occurred after the first battle on 21–22 Mar., but before Otho's suicide on 17 Apr. at Brixellum, since the severed heads were brought to him in person (2.16.3). Such episodes vividly illustrate the impact of civil war on the normal workings of the Roman empire. Assaults on Roman *auctoritas* would usually have been challenged and punished, as at 4.45, the trial after an assault on a senator, Manlius Patruitus, in the colony of Sena (mod. Sienna), committed with the collusion of local magistrates. In Corsica, 'the sideshow attracted no attention from either side [sc. the Othonians and Vitellians]' (Levick (1999) 62), but T. includes it both to entertain and to show how the provinces were disrupted while normal activity was suspended by civil war.

16.1 Corsicam ac Sardiniam: *OCD³* 'Corsica', 'Sardinia'. 'The two islands had been made into a single senatorial province in 27 BC (Strabo 17.3.25); but in AD 6 Sardinia was put under an equestrian governor (Dio 55.28.1) and Corsica was perhaps detached from it' (Chilver (1979) 181). In ancient texts Sardinians are cast as dishonest (Cic. *Scaur.* 42–3, Paus. 10.17.1–7) and prone to brigandage (*A.* 2.85.4, Varro *RR* 1.16.2, Dio 55.28.1, with Rowland (1974)), while the Corsicans are reputedly savage (Sen. *Helu.* 6.5, Strabo 5.2.7). The Romans still held only nominal control over Corsica's wild, mountainous interior (Diod. Sic. 5.13.5, Strabo 5.2.7). It was a destination for exiles such as Seneca the Younger (Dio 60.8), who bitterly calls it *hoc saxum* (*Helu.* 6.5), and Mettius Pompusianus (Dio 67.12.4). Its main products were wood and bitter honey (Plin. *Nat.* 16.197, Diod. Sic. 5.13.4, 5.14.3).   **ceteras proximi maris insulas** 'the other islands of the Tyrrhenian sea', e.g. Sicily, and the much smaller island of Ilua (Elba), off the coast of Etruria (Strabo 5.2.6).   **fama uictricis classis:** Otho's dominant fleet holds a special relevance for these islands, which could be reached quickly by sea at this time of year. The combination of noun + dependent gen. noun and adj. (or participle) is an economical mode of expression favoured by T. (*famaque aucti exercitus* 3.61.1, *obsessi Capitolii fama* 3.78.3, *captarum legionum fama* 4.62.3, *uenientis exercitus fama* 4.68.5, *fama dediti benigneque excepti Segestis*, *A.* 1.59.1, *circumuenti exercitus fama*, *A.* 1.69.1), but Livy has a precedent (34.12.8; also for the combination *uictrix classis*, 21.41.11, 28.6.8).   **tanta mole belli nihil in summam profutura**

'in such a colossal war not at all useful for the struggle as a whole' (cf. *A.* 13.38.1; 6.1n. *tarda mole ciuilis belli*), agreeing with *temeritas.*   **ipsi exitiosa:** the adj. artfully anticipates an exciting narrative in miniature, culminating in a sensational death; cf. *quattuor principes ferro interempti* (1.2.1). Such advance notices are designed to stir readers' interest.   **Othonis odio:** this alliterative phrase gives no precise motivation for this hatred. Picarius will not survive long enough for it to matter.   **inani auxilio etiam si prouenisset** 'which would have had no effect on the outcome, even if the help had been forthcoming'.

16.2 principibus insulae: the island's leading figures clearly included Roman officials, but there may also have been some locals involved.   **Claudium Pyrrichum:** only here in T.'s works. T. often names a minor character conspicuous for some act of bravery, thereby commemorating and celebrating the person and the act.   **trierarchum:** 9.1n.   **Liburnicarum ibi nauium:** the *Liburna* or *Liburnica* ship, originally a small, fast vessel with one or two banks of oars, was named after the Liburnians, an Illyrian people famous for piracy; Octavian successfully used it at Actium and the small ship features in the 'David and Goliath' style imagery of that naval conflict (Florus 2.21.6; Panciera (1956), Rougé (1981) 124–5, Wilkes (1992) 187). **Quintium Certum:** only here in T.'s extant works. It may be a 'suggestive name' (93.2n. *sane . . . uerterat*) as Certus ('Resolved') speaks out confidently against the bully Picarius.   **exterriti:** 8.1n.   **alieni metus socia** 'sharing the others' fear'. *alienus*, the possessive form of *alius*, enhances brevity (2.18.2, 2.34.1, 2.39.1, 2.56.2, 2.63.2). It is used in a different sense at 2.22.3 and 2.74.1.   **dilectum agere**, a post-Augustan alternative for *dilectum habere* (*A.* 13.35.2, 16.13.3; *TLL* s.v. *dilectus* 1169.46–70; for Liv. 2.48.1, see Ogilvie (1965) 358), recurs at *Agr.* 7.3, *H.* 2.82.1, *A.* 1.31.4 (*OLD ago* 29; *TLL* s.v. *dilectus* 1169.75–80). There were three stages to a military levy, 'the *dilectus* or choosing of those eligible, the oath-taking (*OLD iuro* 5a), the division into fighting units' (Kraus (1994) 97). The process could cause trouble (4.14.1, *A.* 1.31.4), and buying exemption was possible (Cic. *Man.* 2), but Agricola, to his credit, conducts it *integre . . . ac strenue* (*Agr.* 7.3). Sertorius was also good at levying troops (Plut. *Sert.* 4.1, Veg. 1.7.4). Vegetius values judicious recruitment: 'Suitable recruits should be levied with great care by great men' (1.7.9).   **inconditos homines** 'undisciplined men'; cf. *inconditi . . . ac militiae nescii oppidani* (*A.* 3.46.1). *inconditi* = 'standard depreciation of the un-Roman(ised) enemy' WM 204, perhaps with a hint of environmental determinism: the Corsicans have wilted in the island's enervating climate.   **occepit:** 'a recherché synonym for *inire* and *incipere*, after the second century BC almost exclusively historiographical (Sis. Sall. L. Tac.); the archaizing Apul. revives it' (Kraus (1994) 117).   **laborem insolitum:** the notion of recruits, or even enlisted men, flagging under rigorous training and military work is a topos (1.23.2, 1.51.2, 2.19.1, *A.* 13.35.1), but the capacity to tolerate *labor* marks out an ideal general (Woodman (1983) 198–9, Kraus (1994) 123). Vegetius recommends that recruits should frequently carry burdens of up to 60lbs on route marches 'since on arduous campaigns they have necessarily to carry their rations together with their arms' (1.19.1).   **infirmitatem**

suam reputabant: elsewhere in the *H.*, groups tend to consider their strength (e.g. 1.62.1, 2.6.2), rather than their weakness. The internal focalisation recreates their motives, but modern historians would demand firmer evidence. *infirmitas* can refer to bodily weakness (2.99.1, *D.* 16.6), but also T. extends it to mental weakness (*D.* 19.1) and lack of military authority (1.9.1). T. usually prefers the archaising *reputo* (also 2.50.2, 2.74.2; avoided by Caes., rare in Cic.) for *cogito* in the narrative as opposed to speeches (Adams (1973) 136; WM 146).   **insulam:** elsewhere an island location could be seen as a strategic advantage: cf. 2.6.2 (the sea as *secundum tutumque* for those preparing war), *Agr.* 15.3 (the Britons regard the sea as a defence mechanism).   **longe:** sc. *abesse.* The relatively isolated and short-lived rebels perhaps did not know that the Vitellian forces under Caecina and Valens (*c.* 35,000 from the total Vitellian force of 65,000 men, 1.61.2 with Damon (2003) 225) were much closer than Germany. The *ala Siliana* was also impressed by the *robur aduentantium legionum et famam Germanici exercitus* (1.70.1).   **etiam quos . . . protegerent:** strictly speaking, Otho's attack on Gallia Narbonensis came when the Vitellian forces were not protecting the area. Help was only requested (2.14.1) once the raids had begun, and after the Vitellians respond, the Othonians pull back to Albingaunum. They are either ignorant of the full picture (known to T.'s readers), or deliberately exaggerate to justify their change of heart. **uastatos** for people (2.87.2, *Agr.* 22.1, *A.* 14.23.3, 15.1.2), rather than countries or cities, is an innovation, inspired perhaps by Seneca's *gentium uastator* (*Ben.* 1.13.3).

16.3 repente: T. regularly uses this 'stylistically elevated synonym for *subito*' (Kraus (1994) 119).   **nec tamen . . . legere:** punchy adversative asyndeton (3.2n. *simulacrum . . . exsurgens*). The phrase *nec tamen aperta ui* is Livian (Oakley (1998) 750–1). **auxilii inops** (6.2n. *inops*) is Livian (3.7.7). The lofty periphrasis accentuates the underhand nature of the attack, rendering Picarius' death pathetic and the conspirators cowards.   **balineis:** a popular place for murdering men while naked and vulnerable (Plin. *Ep.* 3.14, Larcius Macedo). It had such potential that when Domitian's assassins ponder *quando et quo modo*, they consider only two possibilities: *id est lauantemne an cenantem aggrederentur* (Suet. *Dom.* 17.1). The *locus classicus* for murder while bathing is the case of Agamemnon (Seaford (1984); cf. Charlotte Corday's murder of Jean-Paul Marat in his bath (1793), painted by David.   **interficitur:** the ring-composition (2.16.2 *interfici iubet*) conveys a sense of poetic justice.   **trucidati:** *uariatio*, as T. finds another verb for killing; cf. *trucidatus . . . interfecta est* (2.59.1), *interfecto . . . trucidatis* (4.1.1). Synonyms for killing and dying are especially varied in T. (Sörbom (1935) 34–5).   **ut** 'as though' (*OLD* 8). T. favours *ut* in this sense for conduct that would be natural against an enemy, but is shocking against Romans (2.87.2, 2.89.1, 3.49.1).   **praemio affecit:** severed heads furnish grisly evidence for rewards during the triumviral proscriptions (App. *BC* 4.13, 4.15, 4.22) and on other occasions (App. *BC* 1.26).   **neque . . . puniit Vitellius:** cf. Caesar avenging those who, keen for a reward, decapitate Pompey (App. *BC* 2.86), and Artaxerxes punishing a man who lyingly boasts that he has killed two enemies (Plut. *Art.* 14.2).   **maioribus flagitiis permixtos** 'utterly lost in the confusion amongst more significant crimes'.

To murder a procurator and his entourage would normally entail a significant penalty.

17–20.1 VITELLIAN DOMINANCE BETWEEN THE ALPS AND THE PO; AN OTHONIAN MUTINY

Some think that T. describes this mutiny too extensively, but the transformation of the Othonians from *indomitus miles et belli ignarus* (2.18.2) to men who are *minus turbidi et imperia accipientes* (2.19.2) offers an important psychological and causal backdrop to what follows: 'as Tacitus has organised his narrative, it explains how a small force of Othonians was able to beat back the attempt to storm Placentia made by a much larger, battle-hardened army' (Morgan (1997) 354). An army's state of mind was at least as important as strategic and material advantages in winning victory. The experienced commander Tiberius knew this when he questioned Germanicus' decision to take his troops to bury the remains of Varus' army, the sight of which might make the army *tardatum ad proelia et formidolosiorem hostium* (*A.* 1.62.2). Yet the mutiny sequence also coheres with a broader theme, namely the Othonian soldiers' growing mistrust of their superior officers, which plays a direct causal role in their subsequent defeat at the first battle of Bedriacum (Ash (1999) 29–35). The soldiers' fear at Placentia that *prodi Othonem et accitum Caecinam* (2.18.2) is not an isolated phenomenon: cf. *fremit miles et tribunos centurionesque proditionis arguit* (1.80.2), *Otho, cui uni apud militem fides, dum et ipse non nisi militibus credit* (2.33.3). All emperors tried to foster loyalty from their soldiers, whether through oaths or personal contact, but the Othonians' devotion becomes so intense that it threatens to jeopardise the military hierarchy. There are parallels with the πόθος ('desire') felt by Antony's soldiers for their general (Pelling (1988) 125, 288).

17.1 Aperuerat . . . transmiserat: the chiasmus and enclitic *-que* allow the emotive juxtaposition of *Italiam / bellum*. The Livian *aperio* + a direct object (a country or people), also at *Agr.* 22.1, *H.* 4.64.3, is a compact alternative (*OLD aperio* 9) to *aperio uiam in* + acc. On the tense and position, see 4.3n. *profligauerat.* **ut supra memorauimus:** 1.70.1; 4.4n. **ala Siliana:** probably in 60–61 this cavalry unit had served under Vitellius as proconsul in Africa (T. briefly commends him, 2.97.2). Its name came perhaps from Gaius Silius, governer of Upper Germany under Tiberius (Chilver (1979) 132). The enthusiasm stems (unusually) from real loyalty to Vitellius: the fervent *decuriones* are said to be *Vitellio obstricti* (1.70.1). **nullo apud quemquam Othonis fauore, nec quia Vitellium mallent** 'with nobody there (i.e. no civilian) supporting Otho, although this was not because they preferred Vitellius'; *nullo . . . fauore* = abl. of attendant circumstances. *uariatio* of an abl. noun or phrase + a causal clause is most common in *A.* 13–16, but this example is particularly complex and elegant (Martin (1953) 91–2, Sörbom (1935) 127). The negative element in both clauses is unusual, but *nec quia* adds a twist, underlining the provincials' supine attitude: lack of support for Otho does not necessarily mean passion for Vitellius. 'A plain statement to the effect that they had no enthusiasm for either side would be by Tacitean standards a bit flat' (Kenney). **longa pax:** the correlation between prolonged peace and moral and military decline is traditional (Ogilvie and Richmond (1967) 178), but T. is especially interested in the link between peace and acclimatisation to slavery: e.g. *plus tamen ferociae Britanni praeferunt, ut quos nondum longa pax emollierit* (*Agr.* 11.4; cf. *Agr.* 21.2, *G.* 14.3, 36.1). T. uses the backdrop of prolonged peace as a dramatic device: it makes people ill-prepared to fight (senators as *longa pace desides* 1.88.2; cf. *A.* 13.35.1), enables places such as Aquae Helveticae to grow prosperous, offering the soldiers a tempting target (1.67.2), and even allows a small town to develop near the military camp of Vetera (4.22.1).   **ad omne seruitium fregerat** 'had crushingly prepared them for every kind of slavery' (6.2n. *seruitii necessitas*).   **faciles occupantibus et melioribus incuriosos** '(people who were) easy pickings for those who arrived first and were unconcerned about the better side'. The sentence ends, as it began, with chiasmus. *melioribus* is dat. (as at *A.* 14.38.2), but elsewhere T. favours the gen. case after *incuriosus* (a novelty that did not appeal to later authors; Constans (1893) §90f): the (less adventurous) dat. accentuates the chiasmus.   **florentissimum Italiae latus** implies a jarring clash between this fertile tract of Italy and the military destruction about to hit the area (mainly *Regio XI*; Morgan (1996a) 384). In the climactic battles of books 2 and 3, T. emphasises the normal agricultural backdrop against which the abnormal civil wars unfold (*per locos arboribus uineis impeditos* 2.42.2, *densis arbustis intersaepta* 3.21.2). T. 'is generally sparing in his use of superlatives' (WM 271), so they have greater impact when deployed. This one recurs (3.60.1, *A.* 2.88.2, 3.30.2; once in Caes., 4× in Liv.). The people of the Transpadane region developed a special method of ploughing under the republic because of damage caused by wars (Plin. *Nat.* 18.182). **quantum inter Padum Alpiumque camporum et urbium** 'all the farmland and cities between the Po and the Alps' (6.2n. *quantum insularum*), an exaggeration, as Vitellian control extended only as far east as Cremona (Chilver (1979) 182). The gen. plurals continue to accentuate the area's prosperity, but the Transpadane region, fertile in itself, imported further products by the 'fruitful channel' of the Po (Plin. *Nat.* 3.123). The *ala Siliana* had originally handed over to Vitellius four *municipia:* Mediolanum, Novaria, Eporedia and Vercellae (1.70.1).   **praemissae . . . cohortes:** Caecina had sent ahead a miscellaneous force, namely cohorts of Gauls, Lusitanians, and Britons, plus some *uexilla* of Germans and the *ala Petriana* (1.70.2).

    17.2 capta . . . intercepti: sc. *est . . . sunt*. This contrast between related simple and compound verb forms is a type of *adnominatio*, word-play involving a change of spelling, 'an old pattern' (Adams (1992) 296).   **Pannoniorum cohors:** it is unclear how long these Othonians had been in the area. They may have been 'troops left in Italy since Nero's mobilisation in 68' (Chilver (1979) 183; Morgan (1996a) 384 n.13). Their provenance is less important than the increasing sense of Vitellian dominance, itself a dramatic prelude to the unexpected Othonian resurgence at Placentia (2.20.2–22).   **apud Cremonam:** this need not mean that the Vitellians had already taken Cremona (*pace* Morgan (1996a) 383). Caecina advances towards the city after his defeat at Placentia (2.22.3, 23.2, Plut. *Oth.* 7.1), and the Cremonese may have capitulated to the Vitellians relatively quickly after that, but the level of Cremonese collaboration with the Vitellians during this phase of the war is left open (3.32.2 *credebantur*). There were stories that they co-operated, but the Flavians could have been trying to justify their destruction of the city. **Placentiam:** although Placentia (mod. Piacenza), established as a Latin colony in 218 BC (Plb. 3.40.3–10, Liv. 21.25.1–7 with Gargola (1990)), had faced attacks from Carthaginians (207 BC, Liv. 27.39), Gauls (200 BC, Liv. 31.10.2–3) and Ligurians (193 BC, Liv. 34.56.10), this pleasant *campestre oppidum* ('town on the plain', Liv. 27.39.12) prospered, particularly once the Via Aemilia, built in 187 BC, connected it with Ariminum on the Adriatic coast (Liv. 39.2.10). It was apparently 'more flourishing than any in Italy' (Plut. *Oth.* 6.4). Pagliani (1991) discusses its history (11–15) and architecture (15–59). **Ticinumque:** sentence-terminal *–que* (2.2n. *aduenasque*). Hannibal had defeated the Romans in 218 BC at Ticinum (*OCD³*), a flourishing town in Gallia Transpadana on the confluence of the rivers Ticinus and Po (Plin. *Nat.* 3.124). It kept a low profile thereafter, until Augustus went there to meet those escorting the body of Germanicus' father, Drusus (*A.* 3.5.1). Vitellius held a celebratory feast here after his victory (2.68.1). **quo successu:** causal abl. **Vitellianus miles:** collective singular (6.2n. *fremere miles*). **non . . . arcebatur:** rivers (especially the Po) were natural boundaries (11.2n.). **quin etiam:** this anastrophe of conjunctions (once in *D.*, once in *Agr.*, 5× in *G.*, 2× in *H.*, 2× in *A.*) is found in the poets (Lucr. 15×, Prop. 5×, Virg. 9×) and post-Augustan prose writers. **Batauos:** Roman recruits were trained to swim (Veg. 1.10), a useful skill (*Agr.* 18.4, Dio 69.9.6), but the Batavians were especially talented (Hassall (1970), Speidel (1991), *CIL* III 3676); cf. 2.35.1, 4.12.3. **raptis quibusdam exploratoribus:** 'a major concern for Otho must have been his lack of knowledge of the overall strategy which his opponents had devised for the period after their arrival in Italy' (Murison (1993) 105). Spurinna must have sent out these (and other) *exploratores* to find out when Caecina was likely to arrive (a component of the ideal general: cf. *prouidentia* 2.19.1). On reconnaisance, see Goldsworthy (1996) 125–31 (Roman), Pritchett (1971) I 127–33 (Greek), Austin and Rankov (1995) 16–38. **adesse omnem Caecinae exercitum:** 11.2n. *transgresso . . . Caecina* for the chronology and route of Caecina's march. The Othonian soldiers' fear is unfounded, but not irrational, since Caecina will soon arrive and try to take Placentia (perhaps 30–31 Mar., Murison (1993) 108).

18.1 Certum erat: the expression is applied with slightly different meanings to the infinitives which follow (syllepsis; 3.2n. *precibus*). With *uenisse*, it means 'Spurinna was convinced that' (*TLL* s.v. *certus* 913.80–914.2), but with *coercere* and *obicere*, it means 'he had resolved to' (*TLL* s.v. *certus* 911.25–33). **Spurinnae:** 11.2n. **is enim:** especially in the swift-moving *H.*, T. adds helpful explanations in parenthesis (1.10.3, 1.49.1, 2.88.2, 3.2.1, 3.45.1, 3.57.2, 4.18.1, 4.83.4), often introduced by *enim* (1.79.4, 2.27.1, 3.37.2, 4.11.3, 4.68.1, 4.77.1) or *nam* (2.23.4). So he shows consideration for his readers, who might otherwise have unanswered questions (cf. *octaua erat*, 2.85.1). On parenthesis (or *interpositio / interclusio*), see Quint. 9.3.23 with Lausberg (1998) §860. **obtinebat:** Spurinna arrived *c.* 23 / 24 Mar. (Murison (1993) 105). **necdum uenisse Caecinam:** Spurinna's gut reaction is endorsed by the adj. *falsi* (2.17.2). **si propinquaret:** if people are the subject, T. usually prefers the simple form *propinquo* (2.24.1, 4.70.3, 5.12.4) over *appropinquo* (14 : 4 in his extant works; cf. 15.1n.

sidente . . . metu), a divergence from normal prose usage (but cf. Sall. *Hist.* 4.74, Liv. 21.46.4, 28.37.7, Col. 7.6.6 for *propinquo*).   **intra munimenta:** Placentia's defensive walls are in disrepair (cf. 2.22.1, where some sections are *neglecta aut aeuo fluxa*). Even a city with high walls, Noviodunum, was vulnerable before Roman siege technology and the right general (Caes. *Gal.* 2.12).   **militem:** collective singular (6.2n.). **tris praetorias cohortes . . . cum paucis equitibus:** the detailed enumeration only underscores the inadequate numbers. One can almost see Spurinna nervously counting up his men on his fingers. These troops were part of the contingent (*haud spernenda manus* 2.11.2) sent from Rome to hold the banks of the Po. The remainder (a larger force), including the *Prima Adiutrix*, was with Annius Gallus, east of Cremona. **ueterano exercitui:** Caecina's men mostly came from the *Legio XXI Rapax* (1.61.2), originally raised by Octavian in 41–40 BC and based in Upper Germany at Vetera from 9, then at Vindonissa from 46. After the first battle of Bedriacum, it went to Rome, and then brought up the rear of Caecina's column which set out to confront the Flavians (2.100.1). It did not do well in the battle (3.18.1), but performed better against Julius Civilis (4.68.4, 4.70.2, 4.78.1). It was heavily involved in the mutiny at the start of Tiberius' principate (*A.* 1.31.3).

     18.2 indomitus miles 'uncontrollable troops' (*TLL* s.v. *indomitus* 1224.68ff.). The phrase recurs (4.35.3). Some of Spurinna's praetorians had participated in the mutiny in Rome (1.80–5), so their unruliness is consistent.   **belli ignarus:** this was because these troops had come from Rome. The phrase is Sallustian (*Jug.* 28.5, 96.1). Cf. Pindar fr. 110 'War is sweet to the inexperienced, but an experienced man fears it as it approaches with all his heart, extraordinarily.'   **correptis signis uexillisque:** the military standards (Campbell (1984) 96–9, Webster (1985) 133–9) were emotive objects (cf. the topos where the general in battle throws the *signum* into enemy lines to shame his troops to fight; Oakley (1997) 462–3), whose loss was the ultimate disgrace for a legion (Liv. 7.13.4, 9.15.7; Oakley (1998) 161–2). The most important standard bore the image of an eagle (43.1n. *aquilam*), and they generally had pieces of cloth suspended from a cross-piece at the head of a pole and emblazoned with the emperor's name. They 'resembled sails, with purple letters upon them to distinguish the army and its commander-in-chief' (Dio 40.18.3). Standards served a practical purpose in battle, indicating to the troops where they should go, as the colours did well into the modern era: the last British Regiment to carry its colours into battle was the 58th Regiment at Laing's Nek (South Africa) in 1881. They also had a religious function: kept in a special shrine (*sacellum*), they were anointed with special oils and garlands (Plin. *Nat.* 13.23, Suet. *Cl.* 13.2), and served as a focal point for oaths (*A.* 15.16.2). Quintilian draws an analogy between impromptu speaking inspired by a large audience and soldiers enthused by the massed standards (10.7.16). Their value is eloquently expressed by Augustus' efforts to retrieve the standards lost with Crassus in 53 BC, finally recovered in 20 BC and celebrated on his coinage (Aug. *RG* 29.1–2, Prop. 3.5.48, Ov. *Fast.* 5.584–90, Vell. 2.91, Luc. 8.358, Suet. *Aug.* 21.3, *Tib.* 9.1).   **retinenti duci:** the present participle is conative (*NLS* §102).   **tela intentare:** so the disruptive Vitellian soldiers *tela ac manus in ora legatorum intentant* (1.69). In the parallel tradition the soldiers

almost kill Spurinna (Plut. *Oth.* 5.9).   **spretis centurionibus tribunisque:** the
Othonian soldiers' hostility towards their officers is recurrent (1.36.1, 1.80.2, 1.82.1). T.
almost always links these nouns with the conjunction *-que.*   **pro<di> Othonem:**
this recalls the accusation during the praetorian mutiny *tamquam familiae senatorum ad
perniciem Othonis armarentur* (1.80.2). Plutarch's Othonians also call Spurinna a traitor
(*Oth.* 5.9). Bekker (1825) corrected *pro* to *prodi,* a reading accepted by the *OCT* and
Heubner's Teubner edition, but Wellesley prefers *proditione* (and deletes *Othonem*); either
way, the general sense is clear.   **accitum Caecinam clamitabant:** the alliteration aptly underscores the soldiers' angry outburst (8.1n. *credentibus . . . contextu*). T.
always uses the more striking frequentative *clamito* rather than *clamo* (MW 152, WM
96).   **temeritatis alienae comes:** 16.2n. *alieni . . . socia.*   **primo coactus, mox
uelle simulans:** sc. *se.* The ellipse is a sign of things to come: 'In the *Histories* T.
rarely omits *se* with tenses other than the future, but in the *Annals* he becomes progressively less restrictive' (Adams (1972) 370–1). Spurinna's strategy was hazardous,
as soldiers sometimes detect such ruses (*A.* 1.37.1).   **plus auctoritatis:** Spurinna's
strategy is practical, but any *auctoritas* secured by apparent collusion with the soldiers
is vulnerable.   **si seditio mitesceret** 'if the mutiny should deteriorate'. T. uses
this verb selectively and after the *H.* drops it. Its primary frame of reference is agricultural, of ripening produce (*OLD* 1): [sc. *fruges*] *tarde mitescunt, cito proueniunt* (*Agr.* 12.
5). T. uses it metaphorically again (*OLD* 3): *prima classicorum legio in Hispaniam missa, ut
pace et otio mitesceret* (2.67.2). Pacuvius has the alliterative combination *mitescit metus* (fr.
350, D'Anna). Cf. *eoque mitescere discordiae intestinae metu communi . . . coeptae* (Livy 5.17.10),
positis mitescent saecula bellis (Virg. *A.* 1.291), *furore mitescente* (Amm. 16.3.2).

   19.1 Postquam in conspectu Padus: sc. *erat.* The phrasing (including the ellip-
sis) is Livian (6.29.1), but contentious. The Po was visible from Placentia, so why has
it disappeared from view? The accepted solution is that Spurinna, marching his men
west from Placentia along the road that branched from the Via Postumia to Ticinum,
crossed the river at Ad Padum (*c.* 20 miles west of Placentia). Since the river makes a
large bend to the north between Placentia and Ad Padum, it briefly disappears from
view along this stretch of road (Passerini (1940) 194, Wellesley (1960) 274).   **nox
appetebat:** further Livian phrasing (5.44.6, 8.38.3, 10.42.1, 38.40.15). The two-day
expedition was perhaps on 26–27 Mar. (Murison (1993) 105).   **uallari castra:**
entrenching a marching-camp for the night, a regular job for soldiers on campaign,
took about 3 hours (Harmand (1967) 132 n.240). Constructing it could both instil
a reassuring sense of order in legionaries and intimidate the enemy (Goldsworthy
(1996) 113). The general Corbulo claimed that battles were won with the *dolabra,* the
pick-axe with which the marching-camps were built (Fron. *Str.* 4.7.2).   **placuit:** this
impersonal verb masks a delicate moment. Spurinna must have persuaded rather
than ordered his urban troops to entrench camp, since they were not accustomed to
do it automatically.   **is labor:** 'A standard remedy for defeat was to toughen the
troops with toil (Val. Max. 2.7, Fron. *Str.* 4.1; cf. Sall. *Jug.* 45, Liv. *Per.* 57, App. *Hisp.*
85)' (Rives (1999) 129). One way to calm mutinous soldiers was to segregate them
from camp and get them to build fortresses (Veg. 3.4.7). Or you could simply abandon

them to avoid corrupting the decent fighting men (Plut. *Phoc.* 12.3).   **contundit animos:** the combination, first in Accius, appealed to Cicero (*Att.* 12.44.3), Valerius Maximus (2.17.11, 3.7.1c, 7.3 *ext.* 10) and Pliny (*Pan.* 44.6) amongst prose authors (*TLL* s.v. *contundo* 806.28–34). The movement from beating the chest externally to crushing the spirit internally is logical.   **uetustissimus quisque** 'each longest-serving soldier' (also at 1.23.1). *uetustissimus* in T. (*G.* 1×; *H.* 3×; *A.* 15×) normally has connotations of reverence and the correlation between age and wisdom is a topos (Powell (1988) 147; cf. 5.2n. *natura atque arte*), but the context here undercuts the grandiloquent superlative: long-serving soldiers should have known better than to disobey their general.   **castigare credulitatem suam:** the alliteration adds bite to their self-criticism (8.1n. *credentibus . . . contextu*). Their gullibility lies in believing that Caecina's whole army was present (2.17.2) and leaving the relative safety of Placentia. **metum ac discrimen ostendere** 'pointed out the threatening danger'. *discrimen* + *ostendere* is only here (*TLL* s.v. *discrimen* 1359.76), though cf. *discrimen ac dedecus ostentantes* (3.66.1).   **Caecina . . . circumfudisset:** the word-order mirrors the concept, as nom. noun and verb syntactically and alliteratively envelop the *tam paucas cohortes*. The verb *circumfundo* + *Caecina* shows synecdoche of the leader for the group under his command (*TLL* s.v. *circumfundo* 1147.74–1148.53; Hardie (1986) 252).   **patentibus campis:** Livian phrasing (24.41.6, 29.32.6, 44.39.8). The open country would have offered strategic advantages to the more numerous Vitellian force (14.2n.). The Flavians point to the *patentes campi* around Verona as being especially suited to a cavalry battle (3.8.1).   **iamque . . . modesti sermones:** sc. *erant*. Ellipse of the verb is common in T. with adverbs of time (*Agr.* 33.1, *H.* 1.65.2). *modestus* 'compliant' has a military tinge to it (cf. 20.1), prevalent above all in the *H.* (*TLL* s.v. *modestus* 1225.52–7), but also in Sallust, *milites modesto imperio habiti* (*Jug.* 92.2). The military context is much more common for the noun *modestia* (*TLL* s.v. *modestia* 1223.3–15; Sall., Caes., Liv., T. with 12.1n. *ut . . . disciplinae*); in favouring the adj., T. follows Sallust in extending the usage of the noun.   **inserentibus se:** 'the verb is often used of persons joining a group of men in order to work upon its feelings' (Wellesley (1972) 103); 2.61, 3.20.1, *A.* 1.28.4. The reflexive use of *inserere* begins with Livy 3.17.10, but was quickly taken up by others (Ov. *Met.* 3.117, Val. Max. 9.15 *ext.* 1, Sen. *Ep.* 66.6; Bömer (1969) 480 and *TLL* s.v. *insero* 1872.71–1873.7).   **laudari:** the historic infinitive (5.1n. *anteire . . . obniti*) in the passive voice is a Livian affectation (Kraus (1994) 154, Constans (1893) §175). **prouidentia ducis:** foresight is a quality often assigned to the ideal general (5.17.2, *A.* 13.39.2, Vell. 2.115.5, with Woodman (1977) 182–3: military *prouidentia* was especially associated with Tiberius).   **quod . . . legisset:** the verb = subjunctive, as T. gives the officers' explanation (GL §541), rather than his own, which would need the indicative (GL §540).   **coloniam uirium et opum ualidam** 'a powerful and wealthy colony'. In this chiastic clause, the officers' emphasis on Placentia's wealth as an advantage reveals much about these urbanised soldiers' priorities. Spurinna himself had pondered the town's defences (2.18.1). *ualidus*, 'common in poets and writers of artificial prose, was not in ordinary use in the late Republic or early Empire' (Adams (1974) 59; WM 188). T. innovates by combining the adj. with gen. nouns, a stylistic

trait which he increasingly favours (Constans (1893) §90).   **robur ac sedem** 'as a
strong base'. The phrase (manifesting hendiadys) is in apposition to *coloniam.*

19.2 ipse postremo Spurinna: bathetic perhaps, since in military contexts
ipse without the proper noun 'frequently designates a commander' (Kraus (1994) 98),
often in idealised terms (MW 158). Yet here Spurinna, who needs to be named,
unglamorously mops up a mutiny, only entering the scene once his officers have safely
prepared the way.   **non tam culpam exprobrans:** Spurinna, like his emperor
Otho (1.85.1), is circumspect in reproaching and punishing his soldiers. This can
(paradoxically) be the mark of a good general (*Agr.* 19.3, Plin. *Pan.* 70.2, 80.3, Suet.
Jul. 67.1), but only when a man with solid control over his men allows this leeway
(Woodman (1977) 176).   **rationem ostendens** 'making clear his purpose' (Irvine).
That Spurinna explains his strategy to the soldiers shows his fragile *auctoritas* as a
general and illustrates the constraints imposed by civil war on normal military practice.
Such explanations are impractical during war, as Otho has already made clear in his
earlier speech to the mutinous praetorians (1.83.3). One of the first principles of
generalship was keeping plans secret. So, 'the image of the Minotaur is included
among military standards because the plans of generals should be not less secret than
was the labyrinth' (Paul. Fest. 135.21 L.; cf. Plb. 9.13.2–5, Onas. *Strat.* 10.22–4, Veg.
3.6.9).   **Placentiam** without *ad*, as this is the name of a town (GL §337).   **minus
turbidos et imperia accipientes:** *uariatio* of adj. and participle (Sörbom (1935)
93–4).   **solidati muri, propugnacula addita, auctae turres:** the asyndeton
aptly reflects the soldiers' new-found efficiency. Vitruvius, Lucan, Seneca, Statius and
Apuleius favour *solido*, 'strengthen' (*OLD* 2a), a novel substitute for *firmo.* T. uses it
again of building-work only at *A.* 15.43.3. The eye-catching *propugnacula* 'ramparts'
features instead of the technical term *pinnae* (in Caes., Virg. and T. himself, 3.29.1). It
was especially urgent to heighten the defences, as the attackers could use the nearby
amphitheatre 'as a ready-made, if immovable, siege tower' (Morgan (1997) 345). Cf.
the Plataeans' counter-measure of heightening their wall with a wooden frame during
the siege by the Peloponnesian army (Thuc. 2.75.4). On Roman sieges in general, see
Kern (1999) 251–322.   **prouisa parataque:** sc. *sunt.* Livy has similar alliterative
phrases: *prouidendum praecauendumque* (22.42.4), *prouidendum ac praecauendum* (24.8.13),
prouisum atque praecautum est (36.17.12). Foresight and advance preparation are qualities
of the ideal general (19.1n. *prouidentia ducis*).   **non arma modo sed obsequium:**
concrete + abstract noun (Sörbom (1935) 75–6; WM 283) generates a kind of syllepsis
(3.2n. *precibus*), as the verbs are used in a slightly different sense with each noun.
This movement from concrete to abstract underscores the difficulty of inculcating
obedience as opposed to preparing weapons.   **obsequium et parendi amor:** the
pleonasm (Lausberg (1998) §502), generally used sparingly by T., here underscores the
peripeteia, as passion for mutiny is unexpectedly superseded by passion for obedience
(the striking *amor parendi* is only here); cf. *amor obsequii* (*A.* 1.28.6), which returns once the
Pannonian mutiny implodes.   **quod solum . . . defuit:** 'the only thing missing'
is a topos (Kraus (1994) 189–90, citing Liv. 23.5.5, Virg. *A.* 12.643, Sen. *Con.* 1.3.1.
Vell. 2.67.3 with Woodman (1983) 154, [Quint.] *Decl.* 1.15, 2.38; also Caes. *Civ.* 3.2).

cum uirtutis haud paeniteret: T.'s grudging praise anticipates their good conduct during the siege, which might otherwise seem inconsistent with their stereotypically unruly behaviour so far.

20.1 At: T. uses *at* + proper names (2.55.1, 2.70.4, 2.74.1) and nouns (2.45.1, 2.86.1) to signal a transition (Ginsburg (1981) 59, 117n.9) and to mark a contrast (e.g. between Rome and elsewhere, G-G 106).   **uelut** qualifying an abl. absolute is first in Livy, and 'it is highly likely that he influenced subsequent writers' (Oakley (1998) 564). The adverb here ominously indicates appearance (*OLD* 5), rather than reality, hinting that *saeuitia ac licentia* will soon return.   **post Alpes** 'north of the Alps' (*OLD post* 1b).   **saeuitia ac licentia:** i.e. the attacks on the Helvetians (1.67–9): *plus praedae ac sanguinis Caecina hausit* (1.67.1), (his army) *immodicum saeuitia* (1.69). T. combines the two nouns again (4.72.2), when the Flavian general Petillius Cerialis fears getting a bad reputation if he gives his soldiers a taste for *licentia saeuitiaque*.   **modesto agmine:** the adj. mirrors *modesti sermones* (19.1n.; cf. 12.1n. *ut . . . disciplinae*). Discipline seems to have been restored temporarily on both sides, with the Vitellians perhaps being sobered by the salutary backdrop of Italy.   **ipsius:** *TLL* s.v. *ipse* 325.36–84, *OLD ipse* 10b for other genitives of *ipse* used for the reflexive or possessive pronoun, from Plautus and Terence onwards. It need not be especially emphatic by T.'s time (Lebreton (1901) 143–5). T. uses it again (2.27.2, 34.1, 45.3, 76.4, *A.* 2.41.3).   **municipia et coloniae:** 'the container for the thing contained, a kind of metonymy' (Kraus (1994) 229 with Quint. 8.6.24). The petty-minded inhabitants are rightly worried about Caecina's presence, but this should not be because of his clothing.   **in superbiam trahebant:** *trahere in* 'attribute to' (*OLD traho* 20, WM 314) is in Sall. *Jug.* 92.2 and Liv. 44.37.7. Romans were especially sensitive to the negative connotations of clothing: e.g. Caesar's high, reddish shoes, in the style of the kings of Alba, caused talk (Dio 43.43.2). 'Caecina's garb arouses unfavourable comment upon his first appearance in Italy in 69 and upon his last (3.31.4), in the one case because he disregards propriety and in the other because he insists on it' (Morgan (1996a) 386 n.20).   **uersicolori sagulo:** Caecina's multicoloured cloak is stereotypically associated with Gauls (Plb. 2.28.7, 2.30.1, Virg. *A.* 8.660, Strabo 4.4.3), marking him out as 'other'. Plutarch pushes this association further by highlighting Caecina's huge body (*Oth.* 6.6), another stereotypical trait of Gauls. Manlius' opponent is a huge Gaul, dressed *uersicolori ueste* (Liv. 7.10.7, with Oakley (1998) 141); in the second century BC the comic poet Afranius mocks a Gaul 'dressed in a cloak (*sagatum*) and stuffed with fatty lard' (Williams (2001) 47). Probably 'the Romans borrowed not only the word *sagum* but the garment itself from the Celts of north Italy' (Rives (1999) 196).   **bracas, barbarum tegumen:** trousers were also seen as typically barbarian clothing (esp. Gauls, Medes, Sarmatians) and were even blamed for causing Scythian impotence (Hipp. *Airs, Waters, Places* 22). Gallic breeches were apparently more tightly fitting than the eastern type (Luc. 1.430; Cic. *Fam.* 9.15.2, *Font.* 33, Diod. Sic. 5.30.1) and featured in a line of poetry when Gauls were admitted to the senate: *Galli bracas deposuerunt, latum clauum sumpserunt* (Suet. *Jul.* 80.2). Some editors omit *barbarum tegumen* as an unnecessary gloss (Chilver (1979) 185 finds it 'incredible' that *bracae* should need explanation), but the periphrasis well captures the indignation of the bigoted townspeople whose viewpoint is expressed here (and may evoke Virgil, *barbara tegmina crurum, A.* 11.777 with Horsfall (2003b) 416–17). Others, arguing that T. avoids calling a spade a spade, omit *bracas* (though Plut. *Oth.* 6.6 also has the trousers, which were perhaps in the common source). Yet *barbarum tegumen* alone is not enough to indicate trousers unambiguously. **indutus** has a strong reflexive element, functions like a Greek middle and takes an accusative object (a poetical or post-Augustan usage, GL §338 n.2; Harrison (1991) 290–1 on *exuuias indutus Achilli*, Virg. *A.* 2.275). **togatos:** the toga, the ultimate symbol of *Romanitas*, was often associated with peace (Kraus (1994) 239); subjects craving to assimilate themselves (albeit unsubtly) with their Roman conquerors also wore it (*Agr.* 21.2, *A.* 1.59.4). How common it was in reality is another question: *pars magna Italiae est, si uerum admittimus, in qua | nemo togam sumit nisi mortuus* (Juv. 3.171–2; Vout (1996)). **alloqueretur** is subjunctive as T. gives the townspeople's reason, not his own (19.1n. *quod . . . legisset*). In Plutarch's text (quite possibly corrupt), Caecina communicates even with Roman officials using sign-language (*Oth.* 6.6; cf. *<s>cito sermone*, 1.53.1). **Saloninam:** T. often names minor characters to accentuate his *auctoritas*. Plutarch does not name her (*Oth.*. 6.6). **quamquam . . . ueheretur:** cf. 92.3n. *quamquam . . . corrumpebant.* **in nullius iniuriam** 'not intended to offend anyone'. *in* + acc. + gen. here indicates purpose or intention, a usage much favoured by T. (GL §418, 1a, *NLS* §151.6). **insignis equo ostroque** 'conspicuous on her purple-decked horse'. Plutarch also puts her on a horse (*Oth.* 6.6), but T. adds colour: *ostrum* (metonymy for material dyed purple, *OLD ostrum* 2) is only here in his extant work (not in Sall., Caes., Liv.). Whether it was Salonina herself or (more likely, by hendiadys) her horse who was decked out in purple, her eye-catching presence transgresses accepted female behaviour: cf. Piso's wife, Plancina, attending cavalry exercises *nec . . . intra decora feminis* (*A.* 2.55.6 with WM 296). Severus argues that women *Romanum agmen ad similitudinem barbari incessus conuertant* (*A.* 3.33.2). 'The notion of women accompanying men to war usually, though not always (cf. Luc. 2.338–48), has pejorative overtones' (WM 294–5). T. perhaps alludes to the description of Dido's horse, *ostro . . . insignis et auro | stat sonipes* (Virg. *A.* 4.134–5, with Pease (1967) 184–8). **tamquam laesi:** a pointed over-reaction, given the real casualties soon to be inflicted by Caecina and his army in northern Italy (cf. *dispersi per municipia et colonias Vitelliani spoliare, rapere, ui et stupris polluere*, 2.56.1). **grauabantur:** the construction with the acc. (*OLD* 4b; *TLL* s.v. *grauo* 2314.17–49; also at *A.* 3.59.4) is first in Plautus, but became increasingly popular with writers of the first century AD (especially Sen. and Stat.). **insita mortalibus natura:** (causal abl.) T. uses this formula (1.55.1; cf. 2.38.1, Liv. 28.24.1) to move swiftly from the particular to the general, investing his historical narrative with the sort of timeless truths about human psychology that implement a moralising agenda and add contemporary relevance. T. likes *sententiae* about a person's fortune, or lack of it (Kirchner (2001) 167). *mortales* (9× in the *H.*, including 2.38.1, 2.72.2, 26× in the *A.*), a substantive adj. for *homines*, is a dignified 'archaism popular with historians (Gell. 13.29)' (MW 196, Oakley (1997) 536–7). **acribus oculis introspicere:** for the inf. after *natura*, see GL §422. The notion of *inuidia* is closely linked (both etymologically and practically) with sight, which first triggers, then intensifies the jealousy. So, Lucretius depicts jealous people *in tenebris*, who complain about the object of their envy: *ante oculos illum esse potentem | illum aspectari* (3.75–6). Cf. Vitellius, jealous of Blaesus being honoured at a party, upon seeing from his sickbed that a *turrim . . . collucere per noctem crebris luminibus* (3.38.1). Excellence attracting *inuidia* is a topos (Kraus (1994) 125). *introspicere* + acc. is here first, then at *A.* 3.60.3 (Heubner (1968) 91).   **modum fortunae:** yet Caecina has actively toned down his conduct after crossing the Alps (*modesto agmine*, 2.20.1).   **in aequo:** Cicero advises the socially lofty to treat their socially inferior friends as if they were on the same level: *exaequare se cum inferioribus debent* (*Amic.* 71).   **uiderunt** further accentuates the visual register.

20.2–23.2 CAECINA'S ASSAULT ON PLACENTIA AND ITS AFTERMATH

After the short-lived mutiny of Spurinna's wayward soldiers, T. now has a scene with huge scope for traditional historiographical motifs, the Vitellian assault on Placentia. Plutarch also has a version (*Oth.* 6.1–4), but it differs significantly. It is much shorter than T.'s, but dwells on the colourful insults hurled by the Vitellians at the Othonian soldiers, who are so humiliated that they are driven to win the siege. Plutarch avoids central elements of T.'s version: the deceptive talks before the assault (2.20.2), the incidental burning of the amphitheatre (2.21.1–2), the lengthy duration over two days, the technical military preparations made overnight by both sides (2.21.3), and the graphic physical injuries involved in the Vitellian defeat (2.22.2, where Plutarch simply has φόνῳ πολλῷ, *Oth.* 6.4). For Plutarch, the main interest lies in the touchy and volatile Othonians' response to the insults. T. is less interested in their collective psychology, focusing instead on the Vitellians and their general Caecina. They handle the incident unimpressively (*impetu magis quam ueterani exercitus artibus* 2.21.1, *pudore coeptae temere oppugnationis* 2.22.3), despite the terror inspired by their imminent arrival (2.17.2). T., unlike Plutarch, tells the story from a Vitellian perspective (Morgan (1997) 348 n.41, 356), focusing on Caecina's hopes (2.20.2) and ultimate disappointment (2.22.3, 24.1). This dovetails with a broader theme of the first two books, the growing rivalry between Vitellius' generals, Caecina and Valens, each anxious about his own standing in relation to the other (92.1n.). After Vitellius' victory, that sense of *aemulatio* subsides, leading to sluggishness and complacency. The other significant divergence from Plutarch is that the Othonian general Spurinna has vanished from T.'s account (Morgan (1997) 356). T. may be sparing the feelings of Pliny, a friend to Spurinna (an *optimus uir*, Plin. *Ep.* 1.5.9; cf. 2.7.1–3, 3.1, 4.27.5), who perhaps failed to excel during the siege (Wellesley (1960) 275). That could be, but a small Othonian contingent still defeated a seasoned (and sizeable) Vitellian force, and that must have reflected well on the victorious general. The omission could instead reflect T.'s concerns with his own credibility as a historian: if Spurinna was a source (11.2n.), then a glowing account of the general's activities during the assault risked charges of partiality.

20.2 isdem petitus 'attacked with the same weapons' (Irvine).   **pax et concordia . . . iactata sunt:** the neut. pl. agreeing with two feminine nouns (also *pacem*

et concordiam . . . utilia, 3.70.3) recalls Sallust (Constans (1893) §73; Heubner (1968) 92).
Misappropriation of this language is a theme in the *H*.: Vitellius exploits the 'great
civic blessings' (Kraus (1994) 247) *concordia et pax* in his imperial challenge (1.56.3; also
3.80.1), while T. criticises writers who attribute Caecina's betrayal of Vitellius to *cura
pacis* (2.101.1). 'As a political slogan, especially used as a coin legend, *pax* occurs from
Sulla onwards, often linked with *concordia* and always in the context of civil war' (Woolf
(1993) 176). Both had temples in Rome (*OCD³* '*Concordia*' and '*Pax*'). For *pax* being
abused in negotiations, see [Caes.] *Alex.* 36, 37.   **speciosis et irritis nominibus**
'fine-sounding but useless phrases'.   **consilia curasque in oppugnationem . . .
uertit:** T. combines two Livian expressions, *magna pars curae . . . in Samnites uersa est*
(10.11.8) + *consiliis ab oppugnanda urbe ad obsidendam uersis* (2.11.1). The alliterative *consilia
curasque* (8.1n. *credentibus . . . contextu*) and the vivid present *uertit* add bite, marking a shift
from ineffectual talk to real action.   **in oppugnationem Placentiae:** 4.3n. for the
historiographical motif.   **magno terrore** 'inspiring great fear'. The plan was sensible as Spurinna only had *c.* 4,000 men (2.18.1), whereas Caecina had *c.* 15–16,000
of the 30,000 soldiers from Upper Germany (1.61.2 with Murison (1993) 85). Vitellius
had *c.* 30,000 troops himself, while Valens had *c.* 20,000.   **gnarus . . . famam in
cetera fore:** Caecina and his army already have a formidable reputation (2.17.2).
Yet the gamble in assaulting Placentia does not pay off (cf. *infracta partium fama* 2.22.2).
Indeed it becomes a positive *exemplum* for the Othonians (2.32.2). Maximising first
impressions in warfare is a topos (Thuc. 6.49.2, 7.42.3, *Agr.* 18.3, *A.* 12.31.2, 13.8.3).
'For appearances count, from the start of the chapter to its conclusion' (Morgan (1996a)
386). On *gnarus*, see 13.1n. *gnari locorum*.   **fore:** T. almost always has *fore* for *futurum*
(*esse*) (only at 3.32.3, *A.* 14.48.4). He prizes brevity.

21.1 primus dies . . . transactus: sc. *est*. The adj. instantly reveals that this
attack will take longer than Caecina hopes. T. has *transigo* + *dies* (also *A.* 16.18.1), instead
of his more usual *exigo* (WM 174).   **ueterani exercitus artibus:** Spurinna had
originally not wanted to expose his paltry force to a *ueteranus exercitus* (2.18.1), but the
Vitellians do not fulfill their potential. The initial absence of siege equipment (implied
by *artes*) may suggest the Vitellians' barbarian identity; cf. *nihil tam ignarum barbaris
quam machinamenta et astus oppugnationum: at nobis ea pars militiae maxime gnara* (*A.* 12.45.3
with Morgan (1997) 342).   **aperti incautique** 'unprotected and careless'. *aperti*
is a military term, i.e. the soldiers lack screens, fascines and mantlets (cf. Caes. *Gal.*
7.25.1). Antonius Primus, restraining his men from attacking Cremona, asks whether
any troops could break through walls *gladiis . . . et pilis* (3.20.3) i.e. without the proper
equipment.   **muros subiere:** perhaps the Vitellian approach was not so reckless,
if Caecina was covering them from the amphitheatre (Morgan (1997) 345).   **cibo
uinoque praegraues:** the novel expression develops Livy's *cibo uinoque grauatum*
(1.7.5; Heubner (1968) 92; the compound adj. *praegrauis* is found since Liv. 44.4.10,
Ov. *Ep.* 9.98). An ideal general feeds his troops before combat (Ash (1999) 43), but the
Vitellians have over-indulged, as soldiers should eat before fighting 'moderately, so as
not to put a huge load into their stomachs' (Onas. *Strat.* 12.2). Excessive drinking of
wine before battle (transferred by Plut. to his version of the Othonian mutiny, *Oth.* 5.10)

was associated with barbarians (Ash (1999) 42), which discredits the Vitellians. Otho has already snubbed Vitellius' supporters as *Germani* (1.84.3). **in eo certamine:** T. tantalises by leaving the vulnerable Vitellians and embarking on a digression, only narrating their fate at 2.21.3 (*multo suorum cruore pulsus Caecina*); cf. 14.2n. *nec mora*. **pulcherrimum amphitheatri opus:** the superlative adj. (used sparingly: 17.1n. *florentissimum*) anticipates the citizens' civic pride. Wasteful destruction of fine buildings in the civil war is thematic (part of Augusta Taurinorum, 2.66.3; the Capitoline temple, 3.72; Cremona, 3.33.2). Yet Otho distinguishes between the (replaceable) physical buildings of Rome (1.84.4; cf. the restoration of the Capitol, 4.53) and the senators, the true repository of Roman values. **situm extra muros:** amphitheatres usually lay outside a city's walls. This was practical, as they required space, but it was also symbolic: 'the arena . . . symbolized the margin between culture and the wild' (Wiedemann (1992) 91, 46). Placentia's amphitheatre was to the north-west. **conflagrauit:** this compound verb features only twice in T. at emotive points (also 3.71.4, the burning of the Capitol): T. generally prefers the simple form *flagro*. The amphitheatre must have been mostly wooden, like the one at Fidenae (*A.* 4.62.1). **siue . . . siue:** for similar *aporia* in T. about allocating blame for a destructive fire, see 3.71.4 (*oppugnatores . . . an obsessi*). **dum . . . iaculantur:** *dum* + present indicative here has 'causal overtones' (Goodyear (1972) 218; Draeger (1882) §168, Heubner (1963) 135, WM 197). **missilem ignem:** 'a deliberate attempt to avoid the technical term *phalaricae*' (Morgan (1997) 345 n.30; 3.2n. *continuus . . . exsurgens*). Such devices cause the besieged difficulties, as at Uspe, where the wicker walls quickly catch fire (*A.* 12.16.2). **dum regerunt** 'because they were hurling fire in return'. Puteolanus (1475) emended *reportans gerunt* of the MS, transmitted in a gloss, to *regerunt*, generally accepted (Wellesley (1989) 191).

21.2 pronum ad suspiciones: Placentia's population was 'more interested in indulging its *suspiciones* than . . . in helping to defend the town' (Morgan (1997) 346). T. often regards the *uolgus* pejoratively: *fingendi auidum* (2.1.1), *stolidum* (2.61), *credulum* (2.72.2, 4.49.3), *uacuum curis et sine falsi uerique discrimine* (2.90.2). **ignis alimenta** 'food for the fire'. Cf. *id mercimonium . . . quo flamma alitur* (*A.* 15.38.2), *alimenta uorat . . . Vulcanus* (Sil. 17.97). The singular *alimentum* is common in Livy (27.3.4, 27.4.12, 38.18.4): T. has the plural. **a quibusdam ex uicinis coloniis:** Placentia had a special rivalry with neighbouring Cremona (Morgan (1996a) 387–8). This was typical of a *longa pax* (2.17.1), since in the past, the two towns had faced constant incursions from the north, which united them (Liv. 33.23.2, 37.46.9–10). Without more pressing distractions, gladiatorial shows and their venues could become the focus for intense civic antagonism (*A.* 14.17). Other neighbouring towns squabbled: Lugdunum and Vienne (1.65.1), Puteoli and Capua (3.57.1), Leptis and Oea (4.50.4). T. casts this as a general truth: *solito inter accolas odio* (5.1.2). **nulla in Italia moles tam capax foret:** *foret* = *esset* (14.3n. *deletae . . . forent*). Before 69, Italy's most capacious amphitheatres were at Pola (capacity 22,000), Verona (30,000) and Aquileia (26,000), all built by the Julio-Claudians (Golvin (1988) 219–23 for dating, 284–88 for capacity). By T.'s time, the Flavian amphitheatre in Rome (capacity 50,000) surpassed them. As Placentia's amphitheatre (mentioned only by T.) has not survived, we cannot validate the citizens' claim. There are later examples of very capacious wooden structures: George Lewis Rickard's temporary wooden structure in Toledo, Ohio could hold 80,000 people for a boxing match in 1919 (Kahn (1999) 54), and another built in 1921 in Jersey City, New Jersey, had room for 90,000 (Kahn (1999) 235). **quocumque casu accidit:** this alliterative phrase questions the citizens' theory of a deliberate fire. **metuebantur:** 8.2n. *uim metuens*. **in leui habitum:** sc. *est*. This expression, the direct object of the verb *maerebant*, only recurs at *A.* 3.54.4 in Classical Latin (WM 395). **tamquam . . . potuissent:** *tamquam* 'on the grounds that' + subj. (typical of Latin in the first century AD) adds subjective colour to the reason (GL §602 n.4.) Cf. 2.26.1, 30.1, 47.3, 63.1, 65.1, 93.2 for similar *tamquam* clauses. **maerebant:** T. will include 'obituaries' (Pomeroy (1991) 255–7) for Cremona (*propugnaculum aduersus Gallos*, 3.34.1) and the Capitoline temple (*sedes Iouis Optimi Maximi*, 3.72.1). Yet mourning the loss of an amphitheatre (an entertainment venue) seems trite in comparison.

21.3 Ceterum marks the end of the digression on the amphitheatre (cf. 2.26.2). **multo suorum cruore:** Cicero first has *cruor* metonymically for bloodshed, but it becomes a favourite of Seneca the Younger (*TLL* s.v. *cruor* 1244.34–71); cf. *ceterae ad noctem cruore hostium satiatae sunt* (*A.* 2.21.2). For the combination with *multus*, first at Ov. *Met.* 12.382 (Bömer (1982) 130), see Liv. 22.36.7, Val. Max. 9.5.2, Luc. 3.627, 4.567 (*TLL* s.v. *cruor* 1245.18–19). **nox . . . absumpta:** verbal *uariatio* after *dies . . . transactus* (2.21.1; Sörbom (1935) 40). The notion of toiling night and day during a siege is a topos (Oakley (1997) 432). **parandis operibus** 'in preparing siege equipment' (*OLD opus* 10b). The term collectively designates the offensive and defensive devices prepared by both sides. **pluteos:** movable wooden or wickerwork screens on wheels, used for protection during sieges (Veg. 4.15.5–6). T. has them only in the *H.* (2.22.2, 3.20.3; cf. 3× in Livy). **crates:** fascines (i.e. bundles of brush), used for building fortifications, for cover (2.22.2, 3.20.3) and for filling in ditches (*A.* 1.68.2, 4.51.1, Caes. *Gal.* 3.18.6). **uineas:** movable towers for sheltering besiegers as they undermine walls (Liv. 23.18.8, 38.7.6, Caes. *Gal.* 2.12.3, Amm. 24.4.13, 24.4.21–2). They could be covered with raw and freshly flayed hides to stop them from catching fire (Veg. 4.15.4). For their efficient deployment, the terrain should ideally be level (Liv. 21.7.6), so ground near walls could be excavated in advance to counter them (Ain. Tact. 32.8, Veg. 4.20). **oppugnatoribus:** for this agent-noun, see Nep. *Milt.* 7.3, Liv. 27.15.8, 44.13.6, Cic. *Balb.* 51 (used figuratively), *Planc.* 76. **sudes:** the besieged used these defensively, embedding sharpened stakes in the walls beforehand to stop attackers from scaling them (Caes. *Gal.* 2.29.3). **immensas lapidum ac plumbi aerisque moles:** Aineias Tacticus advises against indiscriminate stone-throwing by the besieged, but if stones are thrown, men should be lowered from the walls in baskets to collect them (38.6–7). The pleonastic *immensas + moles* (Virg. *A.* 2.185, Sen. *Ag.* 626) hammers home the missiles' size. **perfringendis obruendisque hostibus:** the Othonians can afford to prepare offensive weapons, since Spurinna previously made them reinforce their defences before the Vitellians arrived (2.19.2).

21.4 utrimque pudor, utrimque gloria: sc. *erat*. Anaphora of *utrimque* is only here in T., emphasising the identical motives of both sides (apt for a civil war). Polarised stimuli before battle are more usual: *pro gloria atque imperio his, illis pro salute certantibus* (Sall. *Jug.* 94.5; also 5.15.2, *A.* 4.51.2). Both nouns are pregnant i.e. used alone, without modification to clarify the meaning (Constans (1893) §272), but *gloria* '[desire for] glory' is especially bold (cf. *militaris gloriae cupido, Agr.* 5.3; *cupido gloriae,* 4.6.1; *gloriae cupido, A.* 4.50.2). T. has a comparable pregnant use of *gloria* again: [sc. *milites*] *quos iam pudor et gloria intrat* (*A.* 1.43.3). Soldiers under the Republic ideally indulged in a *gloriae . . . certamen* (Sall. *Cat.* 7.6). On *pudor* as a motivation in battle see 12.3n. *in fuga flagitium.*   **et diuersae exhortationes** 'but with differing sorts of exhortation on each side'. *diuersae* implicitly contrasts with *utrimque* in the previous clause; *et* = epexegetic.   **diuersae exhortationes . . . attollentium:** noun and participle are combined pleonastically, as T. gives minimal details of the officers' exhortations (*hinc* = the Vitellians; *inde* = the Othonians; 15.2n. *hinc . . . inde*). Each side will soon identify their enemy's source of pride (the strength of the Vitellian army from Germany ~ the Othonians' urban identity) and twist it to become an insult (*illi . . . hi*). Military *exhortationes* were a familiar part of historiography (Goldsworthy (1996) 145–9, WM 346), but some standard motifs (e.g. 'past victories', WM 346) were unavailable to generals in a civil war.   **urbanae militiae:** the urban Othonians are in a city (their natural environment) when their generals exhort them, but their service in Rome would not have given them much experience of siege warfare. Augustus first created the urban cohorts, notionally less prestigious than the praetorians (Suet. *Aug.* 49), but they now shared the praetorian camp in Rome and their numeration was intertwined with that of the praetorians (cohorts I-IX were praetorian, X and above urban; Freis (1967) 36–46, Le Bohec (1994) 21–2).   **illi** = the Vitellians.   **segnem et desidem et circo ac theatris corruptum:** taunting the enemy is a Homeric device (Keith (1923–4), Kraus (1994) 227). Near synonyms often feature in such contexts (e.g. *desertorem proditoremque,* 2.44.1; *resides ipsi ac segnes* Liv. 25.6.21). Plutarch's jeering Vitellians call the Othonians 'actors, dancers, spectators at the Pythian and Olympic games, men who had not experienced or seen war and fighting, big-heads, who had decapitated an unarmed old man (meaning Galba), and who would not openly enter a contest and battle of real men' (*Oth.* 6.2). This tirade spurs the indignant Othonians to victory. Ironically the Vitellians in Rome will themselves be corrupted by the city's temptations (2.93.1, 99.1). The Flavian general Antonius Primus calls them *circo quoque ac theatris et amoenitate urbis emollitos* (3.2.2).   **hi** = the Othonians.   **peregrinum et externum:** Plutarch records no Othonian taunts (*Oth.* 6.2). Yet T.'s Othonians voice something that has perhaps already struck readers, after the Vitellians' typical barbarian fighting methods. 'National hatred . . . is a substitute for personal hostility in the breast of individual opposed to individual' (von Clausewitz (1968) 186), but the Vitellians are still Roman: 'In fact many of them were North Italians' (Chilver (1979) 186). There is irony in mocking the Vitellians as foreigners when their Othonian comrades *tamquam externa litora et urbes hostium urere uastare rapere* (2.12.2).   **increpabant:** the imperfect suggests insults being exchanged for some time (possible, with the Othonians on the walls and the Vitellians outside; cf. the slanging match of Arminius and Flavus, prolonged as the two are separated by a river, *A.* 2.10.2). The Aduatuci stand on the walls of their town, mocking their puny Roman attackers (Caes. *Gal.* 2.30.4).   **uberioribus . . . laudibus:** *uberioribus* involves an agricultural metaphor. *uber*, also of a speaker's style (WM 282), hints at verbal creativity in concocting insults about the rival emperor. *inter se* = 'between each other' i.e. between the two groups.   **stimulabantur:** 7.2n.

    22.1 Vixdum orto die: *dies* stands for *lux* (*OLD dies* 2a), though T. also has *luce orta* (*A.* 13.21.1). The gender of *dies* can fluctuate (masc. here and at *A.* 1.29.1, fem. at *A.* 1.68.2; WM 128). T. generally prefers the masc. form (*TLL* s.v. *dies* 1024): 126 masc.:31 fem.; cf. 805 : 143 (Liv.), 29 : 2 (Sall.), 133 : 17 (Caes.), 66 : 2 (Amm.).   **plena propugnatoribus moenia:** from Lucretius onwards the adj. *plenus* increasingly takes the abl. instead of the gen. case (GL §405 n.3, Constans (1893) §113). The agent noun *propugnator* is a Livian favourite (15×; 2× in Caes., not in Sall.). *moenia* shows *uariatio* for *muri* (3× in the previous chapter).   **fulgentes armis uirisque campi** 'the plains gleaming with men in armour'. In a variant of the more familiar *fulgentibus armis*, the plains themselves seem to shine (again at 2.89.2), a Virgilian flourish (*A.* 11.854). The element of display is meant to make the besieged panic: 'the side wishing to enter the walls doubles the sense of panic in hopes of forcing a surrender by parading its forces equipped with terrible apparatus in a confused uproar of trumpets and men' (Veg. 4.12.2). The gleam of the Vitellian armour is enhanced by the new day dawning: cf. *propinqua luce fulsere signa* (*Agr.* 26.1). The combination *armis uirisque* (evoking the *Aeneid*'s opening and signalling a miniaturised epic narrative, Ash (2002)) with *fulgentes* is a hendiadys. The *fulgor armorum* is a topos (Kraus (1994) 164). Cf. Shakespeare *Henry V*, 4.ii.1 (also before a crushing defeat): 'The sun doth gild our armour. Up, my lords!'   **legionum:** technically only one legion (*XXI Rapax*) is present, but T. often uses *legiones* for *legionarii* (Chilver (1979) 65, 186).   **altiora murorum:** neut. substantive adj. + defining gen. noun (2.2n. *laeua maris*); for the comparative adj. cf. *propiora Syriae* (5.2.3).   **sagittis aut saxis:** throwing rocks at town walls is apparently a trait of Gallic besiegers (Caes. *Gal.* 2.6.2), so the deployment of this method here may be a way to barbarise the Vitellians (unless foreign auxiliaries are responsible). Estimates for the range of the Roman archer's composite bow vary between 55–65 and 250 yards (Goldsworthy (1996) 184).   **neglecta aut aeuo fluxa:** Lucretius highlights the vulnerability of rocks and structures made from them (5.306–8); cf. *fragiles aeuo . . . muros* (Stat. *Theb.* 2.700). *fluxus* applied to walls appears only here (*TLL* s.v. *fluxus* 983.51–2), though cf. *longinquo fluere omnia . . . aeuo* (Lucr. 2.69). *aeuum* for *uetustas* is reasonably common (*TLL* s.v. *aeuum* 1169.19–36).   **comminus aggredi** 'they attacked at close quarters'.   **ingerunt desuper Othoniani pila:** the 7-foot-long javelin (*pilum*), the Roman weapon *par excellence*, accentuates the Othonians' *Romanitas* (Goldsworthy (1996) 197–201 on the '*pila* volley'). Greater accuracy was achieved by throwing *pila* downhill or from walls (Caes. *Gal.* 1.25.2, 3.2.4, 4.23.3, Liv. 7.23.8, 30.10.13, Plut. *Mar.* 20.5): cf. *maiore Flauianorum pernicie, in quos tela desuper librabantur* (3.27.1). Firm footing was needed to exploit the weapon's potential (*A.* 1.64.2).   **librato magis et certo ictu** 'with more deliberate and sure effect'.

libro is regular in epic for throwing javelins and other projectiles (Oakley (1998) 223, *TLL* s.v. *libro* 1352.11–43). Roman military expertise contrasts with German rashness. **temere subeuntes cohortes Germanorum:** approaching city-walls like this was risky (14.3n. *incaute* for reckless northern barbarians). Gaius Atinius dies *dum incautius subit muros* (Liv. 39.21.3), while Hannibal is wounded *dum murum incautius subit* (Liv. 21.7.10).   **cantu truci:** Germans in their battle-cries strive after *asperitas soni et fractum murmur* (*G.* 3.2), sometimes raising their shields to their mouths as a sort of megaphone (*G.* 3.2; Rives (1999) 123–4 for the German *barditus* 'war-song'). Noisy Germans and Gauls are an ethnographical commonplace in Roman literature: 'their ululations became a ubiquitous feature of the historical tradition even when there was no specific evidence for them' (Oakley (1998) 142). Yet Romans can also make unsettling noise during battle (*Agr.* 26.1) and boast about it afterwards (*Agr.* 34.1). **more patrio:** such phrases are typical in ethnographical contexts: *more gentis* (4.15.2, *A.* 4.47.2), *ut mos barbaris* (*A.* 4.49.3) *ubi . . . mos est* (2.80.2), *ita in Syria mos est* (3.24.3), *ita illis mos* (5.17.3). Cf. Caes. *Gal.* 5.43.1, 56.2, Liv. 29.16.6, Vell. 2.107.1 (WM 339). **nudis corporibus** 'lightly clad', i.e. without wearing the *sagulum* (*G.* 6.2 with Rives (1999) 140, Caes. *Gal.* 1.25.4, Liv. 22.46.6).   **super umeros scuta quatientium:** this was not just for show. The auxiliaries raise their shields for protection from the *pila* being hurled from the walls (cf. *elatis super capita scutis* 3.27.2). If they were struck, it was still tricky: 'If a *pilum* penetrated a shield, its soft shank was intended to bend. The barbs on the point made it difficult to draw out the *pilum*, and its weight prevented the shield from being used properly' (Goldsworthy (1996) 198). *quatio* (11× in T.), a deliberate poeticism in Livy, 'generally belongs to poetical language in pre-Antonine Latin' (Oakley (1998) 237).

    22.2 pluteis et cratibus tectus: 21.3n. *pluteos* and *crates* (also paired at Livy 10.38.5, Caesar *Civ.* 1.25.9, 3.24.1). T., seeking novelty, consistently reverses the order used by his predecessors.   **subruit muros, instruit aggerem, molitur portas:** the lack of *uariatio*, as an acc. predictably follows each verb, is itself a form of *uariatio* (cf. *Batauus . . . tuetur* 2.66.2; *lacera . . . uastatis* 2.70.1). From a total of 250 tricola in *H.* 1–2, 116 are asyndetic (Fanetti (1983) 27–9). This one aptly mirrors the Vitellian legionaries' methodical techniques. Livy (21.11.8, 33.17.9, 34.29.6) and Caesar (*Gal.* 2.6.2) both have *subruit muros* (cf. 3.20.3, 4.23.3). Though Caesar regularly uses *exstruo* + *agger* (*Gal.* 2.30.3, 7.72.4, *Civ.* 2.1.4), T. varies with *instruo*. *molior* 'is used regularly by L. and other historians' (though not by Caesar) 'of trying to shift a gate: 6.33.11, 23.18.2, 24.46.5, 25.36.13, 27.28.10' (Oakley (1997) 644; *TLL* s.v. *molior* 1362.20–33). **dispositos ad id ipsum molares:** just as Caesar's Aduatuci did in preparing for a siege (*Gal.* 2.29). The formulation reinforces the general's foresight.   **ingenti pondere ac fragore** 'with a huge weighty crash'; 4.2n. *ingens . . . fiducia* for *ingens*. Livy has *ingens* + *fragor* (8.6.3, 21.8.6, 32.24.3, 40.58.4) and *ingens* + *pondus* (24.34.8, 31.46.10, 37.36.2), but T. caps this by combining all three. T. only has *fragor* once again (*A.* 12.57.2, for an accident at a gladiatorial show).   **pars subeuntium obruti:** sc. *sunt*. *obruti* is pl. as *pars subeuntium* implies a group of men. *pars . . . pars* with a pl. features again (3.63.1, *A.* 1.23.1, 2.15.1, though sing. at 3.82.2, *A.* 2.20.1). Livy likes *obruti*, normally adding an instrumental abl., but here *molares* are clearly involved.

obruo is regular in battle-scenes for men struck by missiles (*TLL* s.v. *obruo* 151.64–75). **pars confixi:** *confixi* suggests wounds from a pointed projectile, an arrow or javelin; cf. *sagittis confixus* (*A.* 13.40.3), *confixa telis* (*A.* 14.37.1). **exsangues aut laceri** 'bleeding to death and mangled'. T. uses the pair again (3.27.3), also in the context of a siege. *exsanguis* originally = 'bloodless' (*OLD* 1) or 'pale' (*OLD* 2), but Cicero used it for 'wounded' or 'dying' (*Sest.* 79; also Liv., Sil., Pliny the Younger, *TLL* s.v. *exsanguis* 1825.1–14). **trepidatio** 'panic'. Caecina had hoped to inflict *magnus terror* (2.20.2) on the Othonians; the tables have been turned. **eoque:** 13.2n. **infracta partium fama:** shifting from the Vitellians' physically broken bodies to their metaphorically shattered reputation is most effective (a Virgilian combination: *infracta . . . fama A.* 7.332–3; cf. *ueritas . . . infracta*, 1.1.1, *fides . . . infracta*, 3.42.2, *infracta auaritia*, *A.* 15.21.4). This closural abl. absolute in ring-composition with *gnarus . . . famam in cetera fore* (2.20.2) reminds us that Caecina's main aim in attacking Placentia had been to enhance his reputation.

22.3 pudore coeptae temere oppugnationis: Plutarch has onlookers criticising Caecina for acting rashly (*Oth.* 6.8), but T. makes Caecina berate himself. The *pudor* is disturbingly warped: he is ashamed that this defeat diminishes his reputation, but has no qualms about attacking Romans in Italy during a civil war. *temere* picks up on the *temere subeuntes cohortes Germanorum* (2.22.1), reinforcing the Vitellian 'otherness' with which the siege-description is riddled. **ne irrisus ac uanus isdem castris assideret** 'afraid of looking ridiculous and useless if he stayed put in the same camp'. The earlier mockery by the Othonian soldiers (2.21.4) seems to have riled Caecina, as well as his men. Roman generals found it notoriously difficult to remain inactive, as men of action were expected to be constantly busy. Movement alone may not salvage his reputation: cf. *castrorum autem mutatio quid habet nisi turpem fugam . . . ?* (Caes. *Civ.* 2.31.4). **Cremonam petere intendit:** 17.2 n. *apud Cremonam*. For *intendo* + inf., see 12.3n. *intendit*. **Turullius Cerialis:** this *primipilaris*, only here in the *H.*, is not in the other sources. **cum compluribus classicis:** 4.1n. *caesis compluribus hostium*. The alliteration (8.1n. *credentibus . . . contextu*) helps to link the marines with their commander Cerialis as a grammatical (as well as a military) unit. **Iulius Briganticus . . . in Batauis genitus:** Briganticus, the nephew (and enemy) of the rebel Civilis (4.70.2), later dies fighting against his uncle under the Flavian general Petillius Cerialis (5.21.1). Briganticus' men were apparently not deeply loyal to Vitellius: his *ala* was *excita olim a Vitellio, deinde in partes Vespasiani transgressa* (4.70.2). Yet Briganticus himself is still *fidus Romanis* (5.21.1). Briganticus the Batavian probably felt a natural affinity with Caecina and his German auxiliaries, but T. cites the incident here to emphasise the Vitellians' 'otherness' (Morgan (1997) 353). **Caecinae haud alienus:** T. puns on Caecina's *cognomen* (*Alienus*) (Morgan (1997) 354). T. likes *alienus* 'averse' with a negative (2.74.1, 4.68.2), a type of litotes. **primipilaris** = a senior centurion (Dobson (1974)).

23.1 comperto itinere hostium: 17.2n. *raptis . . . exploratoribus*. The lull after a battle is a good time for gathering intelligence: so Agricola sends out *exploratores* after the battle at Mons Graupius to locate the defeated enemy (*Agr.* 38.2; cf. *Agr.*

26.1). *comperto itinere* is a unique combination (*TLL* s.v. *comperio* 2052.68). Livy has *exploratis itineribus* (4×).   **quaeque acta:** sc. *essent*.   **quid Caecina pararet:** this means only Caecina's immediate plan to head for Cremona (2.22.3), not any broader Vitellian strategy.   **Annium Gallum . . . docet:** Spurinna's exemplary co-operation with Gallus (11.2n.) contrasts sharply with the worsening relationship between the Vitellian commanders Caecina and Valens (92.1n. *olim . . . dissimulata*). **in auxilium Placentiae** 'to bring help to Placentia'; *in* + acc. + gen. to express purpose (20.1n. *in nullius iniuriam*). For *in auxilium* see 2.91.3, 3.35.2, 3.57.2. If one group of Roman soldiers marches to help another, the motives are not always altruistic, as the helpers enhance their reputation at the expense of their comrades (e.g. *Agr.* 26.2, *A.* 15.10.4).   **diffisus paucitati cohortium:** this echoes Spurinna's own fears before the siege (2.18.1). 'One Roman = many barbarians' is a motif in historiography (Kraus (1994) 131), but Gallus fears that *these* few Romans will be no match for the mighty German army.   **obsidium** (not in Cic. or Liv.) is Sallustian. T. uses it in *A.* 1–6 for *obsidio* (MW 158, WM 326).

  23.2 aegre coercitam . . . usque ad seditionem progressam: the *legio prima Adiutrix* (11.2n. *cum legione prima*), formed by Nero in 66 or 67 from sailors, was in Rome at the start of Otho's challenge (1.6.2, 1.31.2, 1.36.3), but had not so far seen action, so it was especially keen to fight.   **Bedriaci:** the village of Bedriacum (*OCD³*), notorious, yet curiously obscure, gave its name to two crucial battles of the civil wars, although both took place closer to Cremona. Ancient geographers do not mention it and even the spelling of the place-name fluctuates: Suetonius prefers Betriacum (*Oth.* 9.2), while Juvenal has *Bebriacis campis* (2.106). Pliny refers to *nouae aues* like thrushes, found there after the civil wars (*Nat.* 10.135), but this curiosity, and the two battles, are its only claim to fame. Bedriacum lay two days' march (= 40 Roman miles) west of Verona (3.15.2) on the *uia Postumia* (Wellesley (1972) 198–9), and 20 Roman miles east of Cremona (scholiast on Juvenal 2.99, citing Pompeius Planta; Wellesley (1971) 28–9).   **duabus iam Romanis cladibus:** the first battle was on 14 Apr. 69, the second on 24–5 Oct. 69. The contrast between the tiny village and the huge disasters associated with it is dramatic.   **infaustusque:** *infaustus* features in Roman poetry first in Virgil, and then in Ovid onwards. T. likes it, using it 12× in his extant works (*TLL* s.v. *infaustus* 1355.64–1356.12; MW 262). On sentence terminal *-que*, see 2.2n. *aduenasque*.

23.3–5 THE OTHONIAN GENERAL MARTIUS MACER WINS A SKIRMISH

This brief episode (not in the other sources) adds to the cumulative psychological pressure placed on Caecina, who sees it as further personal humiliation after Placentia (2.22.3, 24.1). It also allows T. to elaborate the dysfunctional relationship between the Othonian soldiers and their generals, which will ultimately cause disaster in contributing to their final defeat (Morgan (2005) 572). The precise agenda of the Othonian general Macer is unclear, and made more contentious by T.'s hazy dating of the incident.

Whatever the historical reality, the positioning of the episode in the narrative suggests that Macer's well-timed but opportunistic attack took place as Caecina marched from Placentia to Cremona: some *Vitellianorum auxilia* (2.23.3, possibly an advance force from Caecina's army) are certainly present near Cremona on the northern bank of the Po (which Caecina had already crossed, 2.22.3), but the possibility that *noua subsidia* (2.23.3) might arrive implies that Caecina and his main force are still en route. Indeed, if Caecina had already reached Cremona, Macer's attack would have been 'unintelligible, or rather nonsensical' (Heubner (1968) 83). At least the mission of Macer's Othonians in the area is clear: they are part of the general force intended to hold the banks of the Po (2.11.2). One feature of the incident is the prominence of the Othonian gladiators. This destabilises the temporarily reassuring polarisation of the previous chapter between 'German' Vitellians and 'Roman' Othonians: collective identities in the *H.* are never static, and Otho's deployment of a rogue force of gladiators qualifies our sense of Othonian *Romanitas*. See further Morgan (2005).

23.3 Isdem diebus: the imprecise chronological formula allows 'any one of three possible time-frames: while Caecina was attacking Placentia; while Caecina was marching from Placentia back to Cremona, the commonest view; or after Caecina had reached Cremona, an option usually dismissed' (Morgan (1996a) 383 n.9; (2005) 574). **a Martio Macro:** the success of Macer's current plan depends on the element of surprise and cannot be replicated without it (2.35–6). Macer is brave (*uolneratum eminus lancea* 2.36.1) and enterprising, but his soldiers will demand his death (2.36.1). Otho had designated him for a consulship (2.71.2), but this was ignored after Vitellius' victory. This Macer is probably not the same man who was legate of Moesia before 44 and proconsul of Achaea at some point between 44–54 (*CIL* xi 1835). His namesake would now be quite old (Chilver (1979) 188). **pugnatum:** sc. *est.* **promptus animi Martius:** if an adj. is followed by a complementary genitive, 'the seat of the feeling is put in the gen., chiefly with *animi* and *ingenii*' (GL §374 n.7). T. likes the gen. rather than the abl. after various adjectives (Constans (1893) §90); cf. *promptissimos belli* (Sall. *Hist.* 2.91 Reynolds). T. engages in name play, calling the general Martius (= warlike, sacred to Mars) during a military success, but Macer (= lean, scraggy) during defeat (2.35–6). **gladiatores:** these 2000 gladiators came from Rome (11.2n. *deforme . . . auxilium*). **in aduersam Padi ripam:** 'Macer, apart from his sudden sally across the Po, seems to have remained on the *south* bank of the river in the general vicinity of Cremona (cf. 2.34–36)' (Murison (1993) 106). **repente effudit:** *effundere* 'let loose' (*OLD effundo* 8; *TLL* s.v. *effundo* 219.82–220.18, of men) is at Cic. *Sest.* 95 (also Virg. *A.* 7.522, Liv. 30.11.8, 30.32.3, 38.17.7, Sen. *Suas.* 2.7, Luc. 6.292, Sil. 2.151), suggesting the metaphor of water (especially apt here, as the gladiators cross the river and 'pour out' onto the river-bank like a flash flood). Cf. Fenno (2005) on 'hydropolemic' imagery in Homer. **Vitellianorum auxilia:** Caecina had either sent these auxiliaries ahead (a common practice; cf. 2.11.2), or posted them earlier to guard the area (Wellesley (2000) 64). **repressus:** sc. *est.* **impetus uincentium:** restraining ardent soldiers after victory was difficult, but typically Agricola does so after Mons Graupius (*Agr.* 37.4). The one Roman casualty, Aulus Atticus, who pursues the enemy *iuuenili ardore* (*Agr.* 37.6), enhances the achievement. Vegetius warns that 'over-confidence and too little caution are used against fugitives' (3.22.10). For the expression, cf. *fortiter uincentium impetum sustinuit* ([Caes.] *Alex.* 40.3).   **nouis subsidiis firmati:** a Livian expression (4.37.8, 4.40.6, 9.17.15; also [Caes] *Alex.* 37.4). T. combines *firmo + subsidia* again (*Agr.* 23, 2.43.2, *A.* 2.45.2).   **firmati . . . mutarent:** WM 435 on *A.* 3.60.3; see 9.2n. *firmauerunt* on the simple for compound form. We also see the arrival of fresh forces changing a battle's fortune when Julius Civilis fights Vocula: *nouo auxilio fortuna pugnae mutatur* (4.33.2; Vell. 2.79.4). The element of chance in warfare is crucial: *multum cum in omnibus rebus tum in re militari potest fortuna* (Caes. *Gal.* 6.30.2; cf. *Civ.* 3.68.1). T. has *fortuna + proelii* again (3.18.2, 4.20.2), but (surprisingly) is alone in doing so (*TLL* s.v. *fortuna* 1189.6); *fortuna belli* or *pugnae* are much more common.

23.4 suspectum id Othonianis fuit: i.e. not just the gladiators, but the Othonian soldiers in general, who critically watch every aspect of the campaign. They presumably suspect that Martius Macer, secretly supporting Vitellius, withdrew his men, thus aiding the rival cause: similar collective mistrust plagues generals whose actions seem to 'help' the other side (Suetonius Paulinus 2.26.2). In some cases, suspicious conduct is a real prelude to treachery (Caecina 3.9.2).   **omnia ducum facta praue aestimantibus** 'who put a bad construction on all that their generals did' (Fyfe / Levene). *praue aestimare* is novel (only here in extant Latin, *TLL* s.v. *aestimo* 1104.6). The adverb *praue* is only here in the *H.*, used in a more pregnant way than *praue facundus* (*A.* 1.53.3) or *praue detorta* (*A.* 6.5.2). Cf. *uirtutes . . . optime aestimantur* (*Agr.* 1.3).   **certatim:** this adverb, prominently opening the sentence, signals a warped rivalry among the soldiers, perversely echoing the healthy competition that should exist (e.g. *Agr.* 25.1); cf. *certatim ostentantibus cruentas manus qui occiderant* (1.44.2).   **quisque animo ignauus, procax ore** 'every cowardly big-mouth'. *animo* and *ore* = abl. of respect (*NLS* §55). Both are slightly pleonastic, but pointedly contrast inner reality and outward show. The chiasmus and adversative asyndeton neatly accentuate a stereotype (cf. *ignauissimus quisque . . . nimii uerbis, linguae feroces*, 1.35.1).   **Suetonium Paulinum:** Paulinus (*OCD*[3], Birley (1981) 54–7), a senior officer trusted by Otho (1.90.2), had commanded troops in Mauretania in 41 (Dio 60.9). He was suffect consul in the 40s and consul in 66 (*A.* 16.14.1). While Paulinus, made governor of Britain in 58, was subduing the stronghold of Mona (Anglesey) in 60, Boudicca rebelled to his rear, so he initially abandoned Londinium and Verulanium to their fate (*A.* 14.33.1). He quelled the revolt (*unius proelii fortuna*, *Agr.* 16.2), but was recalled in 61. T.'s father-in-law Agricola served under Paulinus, a *diligens ac moderatus dux* (*Agr.* 5.1) often compared with Corbulo (*A.* 14.29.2), but T. in the *H.* is less positive about him. We know that he travelled to Africa (Plin. *Nat.* 5.14–15), but not when and how he died.   **Marium Celsum:** Celsus was an experienced officer, after his legateship of the *Legio XV Apollinaris* under Corbulo in Pannonia and Syria in 63 (*A.* 15.25.3). Galba made him consul-designate (1.14.1), a wise move, as he stayed faithful to the end (1.45.2); loyalty also marked his relationship with Otho (1.71.2). The dubious Licinius Proculus criticises his *uigor* (1.87.2), but Otho trusted him as an adviser (1.90.2). In T., who probably used his writings as a source (Syme (1958a) 682–3), he is a man of integrity. He survived the civil wars to serve on the Lower Rhine in 71

(Levick (1999) 164) and govern Syria in 73 (*ILS* 8903). **eos quoque:** i.e. Paulinus and Celsus (T. has recently noted Annius Gallus' command, 2.11.2). The trio's command over the cavalry and infantry for the attack on Gallia Narbonensis features earlier (1.87.2), but the parenthesis (18.1n. *is enim*) shows T. makes a concession to his readers, who had perhaps forgotten it. **uariis criminibus incessebant:** *incesso* can apply to real missiles (2.22.1 *incessere*, *A.* 3.41.3), but another kind of 'weapon' features here, accusations; cf. *incessere dictis* (Ov. *Met.* 13.232), *conuiciis incesserat* (Suet. *Nero* 35.3).

23.5 incitamenta, (in apposition to *interfectores*), 'much favoured by T., is used of humans only' here and *A.* 6.29.4 (Martin (2001) 163). **interfectores:** T. uses this Ciceronian coinage (*Brut.* 128, *Phil.* 1.35), found 12× in Livy, only in the major works, but grew less fond of it (9× in *H.*, 6× in *A.*). **scelere et metu uecordes:** 'the notion that (consciousness of) crime leads to madness . . . is standard tragic psychology' (MW 164). T. uses *uecors* sparingly in the *H.*, applying it to men only here (cf. *uecordi facundia* 4.68.5). Collective military madness was a popular way to explain these civil wars (especially in Plutarch, who perhaps drew the notion from Cluvius Rufus; Godolphin (1935), Townend (1964)). Yet T. aims to explore the complex causes of civil wars, as well as to illustrate their devastating effects. **miscere cuncta** *uel sim.* is in Cic. *S. Rosc.* 91, Liv. 42.13.9, Sen. *Phoen.* 342, Plin. *Ep.* 1.20.19 and above all Sall. *Cat.* 2.3, 10.1, *Jug.* 5.2, 12.5. T. also applies it to Caecina (1.53.2); cf. *mixtis omnibus* (*D.* 36.2). *cunctus* = a synonym for *omnis* (1.3n. *cuncta utrimque perlustrat*). **palam . . . occultis:** *uariatio* of adverb and adj. (Sörbom (1935) 96). T. often combines *palam* with polarised adjectives showing the gulf between appearance and reality (G-G 1049–50). The inconcinnity demonstrates the Othonian soldiers' cowardice, happy to denounce their generals *en masse* while hidden in the crowd (cf. 1.1n. *senium . . . destinandi*). **ad Othonem:** Otho was still travelling north from Rome, having been preceded by Suetonius Paulinus and Marius Celsus '(perhaps leaving Rome at the same time as Otho but travelling on horseback with a cavalry escort and taking about ten days to reach the front), since complaints . . . began to reach Otho either upon his arrival at Brixellum or perhaps while he was still on his way north (*H.* 2.23.5)' (Murison (1993) 106). **humillimo cuique credulus:** during his challenge Otho trusted *liberti*, *serui* and *mathematici* (1.22.1), while his freedman Onomastus co-ordinated the plot (1.25.1). So his trust in *humillimi* is understandable, even if it now leaves him vulnerable. **inter aduersa melior** foreshadows Otho's impressive decisiveness in handling his defeat and suicide. *aduersa* = substantival adj. (WM 165–6). **igitur** (2.2n.) masks a discrepancy. Plutarch locates the change of command after the clash at Castores (*Oth.* 7.6), as Paulinus fails to consolidate his victory, but T. places it immediately before that episode (Klingner (1940) 3–27, Sage (1990) 892). Yet Plutarch 'surely misunderstood the common source' (Chilver (1979) 189), since the post-Castores timetable would not allow Titianus to arrive before the final battle. **Titianum fratrem:** L. Salvius Otho Titianus, consul in 52 (*A.* 12.52.1, *CIL* IV 2029) and proconsul of Asia in 63–4, with Agricola as his quaestor, is *in omnem auiditatem pronus* (*Agr.* 6.2). On leaving Rome, Otho had entrusted the *quietem urbis curasque imperii* (1.90.3) to his older brother, his fellow consul until 1 Mar. (1.77.2). The notice that Titianus is now summoned to war is part of a broader pattern where the normal business of empire is neglected (e.g. 1.79.1). Yet his leadership in the campaign remains decorative (2.39.1), and Vitellius ultimately spares him (2.60.2). The complex relationship between imperial brothers is a theme in the *H.* (Lucius + Aulus Vitellius, Vespasian + Flavius Sabinus, Titus + Domitian), but Titianus remains rather colourless, conspicuous largely for his *ignauia* (2.60.2).

24–27.1 CAECINA'S FAILED AMBUSH AT CASTORES

'This battle produced by far the most significant of the minor victories won by Otho . . . and on the Vitellian side its consequences were considerable' (Murison (1993) 110). Both T. and Plutarch (*Oth.* 7.2–7) relate it, but do so (as often) with differing emphases. T. links the ambush with the psychology and morale of Caecina, who desires *reciperare gloriam* (2.24.1) amidst his continuing military misfortunes, but Plutarch only describes the clash briefly, focusing instead on the excessive reaction of the Othonian soldiers, who call Suetonius Paulinus a traitor and maliciously try to turn Otho against him (*Oth.* 7.5). This picture coheres with Plutarch's general thesis in the *Galba* and *Otho* that nothing is more frightening than soldiers gripped by irrational impulses (*Galb.* 1.4). However, in T. the accusations are made *utrisque in partibus* (2.26.2), without the boasting and malice of Plutarch's Othonians, and Paulinus tries to justify his conduct (2.26.2). Yet in an artful twist, T. has already hinted that Paulinus' delay during the battle did indeed help the Vitellians: *ea cunctatione spatium Vitellianis datum . . . refugiendi* (2.25.2). If Paulinus had not delayed, he could have eliminated (or severely weakened) Caecina's army; and then the outcome of the whole civil war might have been very different. All of this casts doubts on the suggestion that T. had 'an obvious desire to exculpate [Suetonius Paulinus]' (Murison (1993) 110). If anything, Plutarch's account is kinder to Paulinus, with the hyperbolic accusations of treachery from the Othonian soldiers, which Otho himself does not believe (*Oth.* 7.5–6). Heubner (1968) 99–104, Chilver (1979) 189–91, and Murison (1993) 107–10 discuss the ambush. It took place on *c.* 5 Apr. 69 (Murison (1993) 98).

24.1 Paulini et Celsi ductu . . . gestae: 23.4n. for Paulinus and Celsus. Annius Gallus (11.2n.), the third commander, was perhaps already injured after his horse fell (2.33.1; Chilver (1979) 191). The adverb *egregie*, used sparingly by T. (1.83.2, 2.82.2, 4.68.2; 4 × in *A.*), pointedly undermines both the Othonians' criticisms (2.23.4) and Titianus' promotion over the other generals (2.23.5). The phrasing is Livian (cf. *ductu C. Sulpici legati res per occasionem gesta egregie est* 7.7.1), but the abl. *ductu* (+ a gen. or pronoun, and common in prose authors in military contexts: *TLL* s.v. *ductus* 2170.52–80) may also evoke triumphal inscriptions; cf. *L. MVMMI(VS) L. F. CO(N)S(VL). DVCT(V) AVSPICIO IMPERIOQVE EIVS ACHAIA CAPT(A) . . . (CIL* 1² 626). **gestae:** sc. *sunt.* **angebant:** this graphic verb, originally 'throttle' (*OLD* 1), came to mean 'vex' mentally (*OLD* 3; first in Plaut. *Cas.* 153, Ter. *Phorm.* 160). A Ciceronian favourite, it is also in Livy, always in the imperfect, often + a *quod* clause as the subject (24.2.4, 26.38.1, 39.23.6; *TLL* s.v. *ango* 48.32–60). For the abstract subject, see *OLD* 3b.   **senescens . . . fama:** T. uses the verb metaphorically again: *relinquendum etiam rumoribus tempus, quo senescant* (*A.* 2.77.1). Cf. *Fului senescere fama*, Liv. 27.20.10; *Hannibalem ipsum iam et fama senescere et uiribus*, 29.3.15. The implicit personification of the army's *fama* through the metaphor of old age is especially striking, given the incongruity between the concept of deterioration and soldiers, ideally showing *uirtus* in the prime of life. Juxtaposing *senescens* + *exercitus* subtly underlines this.   **exercitus sui:** with the possessive adj., Caecina's concerns are laid bare: his own reputation is inextricably bound up with his army's standing.   **caesis nuper auxiliis:** i.e. by Martius Macer's gladiators (2.23.3–5).   **per concursum exploratorum** 'in clashes between patrols'.   **crebra . . . proelia:** in apposition to *per concursum exploratorum*. T. stresses that a historian needs to be selective, and also dims the army's *fama* by not recording these *proelia* in detail (Hardie). The status of minor clashes as *proelia* is also questioned at *A.* 3.39.2. The Livian *digna memoratu* (4.43.2, 25.1.5, also T. *Agr.* 1.2; cf. *leuia memoratu*, *A.* 4.32.1) becomes especially prominent in Pliny the Elder and Aulus Gellius.   **propinquante:** simple for compound form (18.1n. *si propinquaret*).   **ne omne belli decus illuc concederet** 'lest all the glory of war should fall to him'. *illuc* = *in illum* (also 4.18.3, 79.2). *belli decus* is Livian (Oakley (1997) 559).   **reciperare gloriam . . . properabat:** the auxiliary verb *propero* takes an infinitive, from Plautus onwards (GL §423 note 2). *reciperare gloriam* recurs in the context of a battle (3.24.1).   **auidius quam consultius:** in the campaign, haste typifies Caecina (*turbidum ingenium* 1.67.1, *belli auidus* 1.67.2, *propere* 1.67.2, *statim* 1.68.2), but he is sluggish after victory (*Caecinae ambitio uetus, torpor recens* 2.99.2, *per uarias moras* 3.9.2).

24.2 ad duodecimum a Cremona 'near (*OLD ad* 13b) the 12th milestone from Cremona', i.e. on the Via Postumia, between Cremona and Bedriacum.   **locus Castorum uocatur:** Castores (Suet. *Otho* 9.2) was named after the twin gods Castor and Pollux. The plural of one name to refer to a differently named pair is also at Plin. *Nat.* 7.86, 10.121, 35.27, and Apul. *Met.* 10.31. The divine twins probably had a shrine there, perhaps the ancient temple surrounded by corpses, seen by Plutarch while visiting the battlefield with Mestrius Florus (*Oth.* 14.2; Chilver (1979) 191). The divine twins are an apt focus for the civil war, when telling two sides apart is difficult, and fraternal strife becomes a synecdoche for civil conflict (cf. Gratus and Fronto, 2.26.1).   **ferocissimos auxiliarium:** these auxiliaries were Germans (1.61.2), traditionally good at ambushes (*A.* 1.63.1), but also rash (2.22.1), so Caecina, already cast as impulsive (24.1n. *auidius quam consultius*), takes a gamble. Their haste soon manifests itself (*temere exsurgentes* 2.25.1).   **imminentibus uiae lucis:** standard descriptions of sites for ambush often have wooded terrain looming over a central path (cf. Virg. *A.* 11.522–31, Liv. 9.2.7–8), so T. can be sparing. Further topographical details emerge from the narrative (*modica silua adhaerebat; uineas nexu traducum impeditas* 2.25.2).   **equites:** Plutarch allocates the cavalry the same role (*Oth.* 7.2). The cult of Castor and Pollux was originally linked with the equestrian order, but these Vitellian horsemen will not impress their divine patrons (cf. Fron. *Str.* 1.11.8 for Castor and Pollux inspiring soldiers).   **iussi:** sc. *sunt*.   **sponte refugi:** 'deliberately retreating' (*OLD sponte* 4).

Feigned retreat was used pervasively to lure an enemy into a trap (Liv. 6.24.4, 42.47.5, Fron. 2.5.1–2, 5–8, 23–4, 32–5, 37, 40, 44, Flor. 1.3.4, Tac. *A.* 2.11.2, 13.40.1). Other methods included deploying fake deserters and false rumours. *refugus* is an Ovidian coinage (*Ep.* 18.182, *Met.* 10.42; Luc., Stat., Val. Flac. and Sil. also liked it). T. intro-duced it to prose (also 3.61.2; and as a substantive, *A.* 13.40.2). **festinationem sequentium elicere** 'to draw the enemy into a hasty pursuit' (Irvine). *elicio* is often thus used in a military context, but not usually with an abstract noun as the direct object (*TLL* s.v. *elicio* 366.72–367.14).

24.3 Proditum id: Plutarch specifies that 'deserters' (*Oth.* 7.2) brought word of the plan (suggesting that Caecina's low morale extended to his men). **Paulinus . . . Celsus sumpsere:** T. often allocates two (or more) singular subjects a plural verb (2.30.3, 2.31.1, 2.67.2, 2.81.1, 2.86.3), following Livy: *Palatium Romulus, Remus Auentinum . . . capiunt* (1.6.4). **tertiae decimae uexillum . . . mille equites:** the detailed, methodical catalogue of the Othonian marching-order contrasts sharply with the bare references to the Vitellian auxiliary and cavalry, hinting at the likely outcome of the 'ambush'. The Othonians, forewarned and outnumbering their enemy, should prevail. The *uexillum* from the *XIII Gemina* was the first arrival from Pannonia. **super** = *praeter* (8.1n. *super . . . oris*). **cumulus prosperis aut subsidium laborantibus**, 'to provide the finishing-touch to success or assistance if they were struggling', is in apposition to the *mille equites*. The polarised possibilities suggest that the Othonians are not complacent about their chances of victory. T. uses *cumulus* metaphorically elsewhere (*cumulum dignitatis* 1.77.3).

25.1 Antequam miscerentur acies: a poetic combination of noun + verb (Sil. 12.394, Stat. *Theb.* 12.717–18; cf. *cohortes miscentur*, Luc. 1.578–9). T. also has *mis-cuerint manus* (*A.* 2.15.2) and *miscere ictus* (*Agr.* 36.2). *antequam* + the imperfect sub-junctive is common for a subordinate verb denoting action which did not happen (GL §577). **terga uertentibus Vitellianis:** the Vitellian cavalry fail to execute Caecina's plan competently, since they were ordered to flee after provoking an engage-ment (*irritato proelio* 2.24.2). Turning tail at a distance reveals the ruse. **Celsus doli prudens repressit suos:** *dolus* was purportedly the 'least Roman art' (Liv. 1.53.4), but Frontinus cites plenty of Roman examples (*Str.* 2.5.1, 2.5.2, 2.5.8, 2.5.20, 2.5.29, 2.5.32, 2.5.33, 2.5.34, 2.5.35, 2.5.37, 2.5.38, 2.5.39). The shrewd general is implictly contrasted with his over-eager men, who could have been fooled despite the Vitel-lians' half-hearted attempt at deception. *prudens* 'having foreknowledge of' (*OLD* 1b) + the gen. is Sallustian (*Hist.* 1.71, 2.87B). **Vitelliani temere exsurgentes:** i.e. the hidden auxiliary forces. **cedente sensim Celso:** alliteration marks off the abl. absolute. *sensim* is only here in T.'s extant works. **longius secuti:** repeated vocabulary underscores that the tables have been turned (cf. *longius* + *sequentium* 2.24.2). **ultro** 'themselves' (*OLD* 4). **in insidias praecipitantur:** this com-bination of prepositional phrase + verb is a Livian favourite (2.51.5, 3.43.5, 5.18.7, 7.6.9, 21.25.9, 25.16.15; Oakley (1997) 626). T., like Livy (Oakley (1998) 104–5), uses the verb reflexively (3.29.2, 4.23.2, 4.71.5, *A.* 2.23.4, *A.* 6.21.1). Ammianus Marcellinus echoes the phrase: *in perniciosas praecipitatus insidias* (24.4.3). **subito discursu terga**

cinxerant equites 'the [Othonian] cavalry had closed in on their [the Vitellians']
backs in a sudden dividing movement'; 'instantaneous' pluperfect (1.1n. *disperserat*).
These must be the 500 Othonian cavalry on the left wing and 500 on the right wing,
rather than the reserve force. The Vitellian auxiliaries had been lured forwards as
the Othonian centre withdrew, which enabled the remaining Othonians, especially
the two groups of cavalry, to envelop the Vitellians by a swift pincer movement. For a
similar manoeuvre, see Fron. *Str.* 1.6.1.

    25.2 Suetonio Paulino: 23.4n.   **datum:** sc. *est.*   **cunctator natura:** Pauli-
nus, a *diligens ac moderatus dux* (*Agr.* 5.1), can move quickly if necessary: *nisi Paulinus . . . propere subuenisset* (*Agr.* 16.2). At the council of war, he advises delay before
fighting the Vitellians (2.32.1). The term *cunctator* evokes the republican past, above
all the honorific name given to Fabius Maximus (Quint. 8.2.11): *unus homo nobis cunc-
tando restituit rem* (Ennius *A.* 363 Sk.; Liv. 30.26.9). Yet Paulinus is no Fabius Maximus,
and these Romans are not fighting Hannibal. Likewise the Flavian general Tampius
Flavianus is a *natura ac senecta cunctator* (3.4.1).   **et:** epexegetic (*OLD* 11).   **cui cauta
potius consilia cum ratione quam prospera ex casu placerent** 'the sort of
man who liked cautiously reasoned measures rather than accidental success'. The
relative pronoun + the subjunctive indicates the general character of the antecedent
(Paulinus). Josephus says that good Roman generals prefer a solid plan to a stroke of
fortune, since accidental success can lead to rashness (*BJ* 3.100). One of Augustus'
favourite aphorisms was 'A safe commander is better than a bold one' (Suet. *Aug.*
25.4 = Eur. *Phoen.* 599).   **compleri fossas, aperiri campum, pandi aciem
iubebat:** this was done to enable the Othonian troops to move easily on either side
of the road. The three subordinate clauses in asyndeton suggest efficiency, even if the
orders hinder the battle's progress. The imperfect *iubebat* also suggests delay.   **satis
cito . . . ne uincerentur:** *foret* for *esset* (14.3n. *deletae . . . forent*). Strangely jerky and
expansive phrasing, as the impersonal passive shifts to a third person plural passive
verb, itself slowing down the narrative.   **spatium . . . refugiendi** 'time to take
refuge'.   **datum:** sc. *est.*   **in uineas nexu traducum impeditas** 'amidst vines
that had become entangled because of their criss-crossed side-branches'. *uinea* = vines
collectively (cf. *uitis*, a single grape-vine). Vines were cultivated on trees for support
(Col. *Arb.* 4.1), usually poplars or elms (Col. *Arb.* 16.1). The vines' side-branches, *traduces*,
were trailed across the space between trees in a vineyard, creating a covered walkway.
T. (unusually) does not avoid the technical term *traduces* (3.2n. *continuus . . exsurgens*), a
hapax in his extant works. Cf. *per locos arboribus ac uineis impeditos* (2.42.2).   **modica
silua adhaerebat** 'a little wood adjoined [the vineyard]'. This sense of *adhaereo* is a
Livian innovation (*TLL* s.v. *adhaereo* 635.33–45).   **unde:** in the shelter of the over-
grown vineyard the Vitellians first regroup, then use the adjoining wood as a base for
attacking the Othonian cavalry (hampered while fighting on horseback amongst the
trees). Agricola dismounts his cavalry when pursuing Britons into a dense wood (*Agr.*
37.4).   **rursus ausi:** this picture of the reinvigorated Vitellian auxiliaries coheres
with the notion that Germans like fighting in enclosed spaces such as forests (1.68.2,
A. 1.63.1, 2.5.3, 2.16.2, 2.19.2).   **promptissimos praetorianorum equitum:**
i.e. the roving Othonian reserve force, designated to help in the event of surprise

developments (2.24.3).   **rex Epiphanes** (C. Iulius Antiochus Epiphanes) is only
here in the *H.*, but naming an individual humanises the battle description. Epiphanes,
son of the wealthy king of Commagene, Antiochus IV (2.81.1) and Iotape (brother and
sister), was probably a hostage in Rome before joining the Othonians on campaign.
Despite his injuries he led auxiliary troops to Judaea for his father in May or June 70
(Jos. *BJ* 5.460–5). This capable and warlike man (Jos. *BJ* 5.462) had two children,
Balbilla, a poetess, and Philopappus, suffect consul under Trajan.   **impigre:** the
adverb (first in Plaut. *Rud.* 915, then introduced to prose by Sall. *Jug.* 88.2, 101.6;
48 × in Liv.) recurs in T. (*Agr.* 13.1, *H.* 1.53.1, 2.97.2).   **pugnam ciens:** *'ciere*
pugnam and related expressions were largely the property of the historians (especially Livy) and the epic poets (especially Silius)' (Oakley (1998) 329, with helpful
table).

26.1 Tum often marks the climax of a battle when one side begins to retreat
(Oakley (1998) 330). The Othonian infantry should have charged before now. It is
unclear whether Suetonius Paulinus had given orders.   **uersi in fugam etiam**
qui subueniebant: probably the Vitellian auxiliary cohorts, but T. could mean
some Vitellian legionaries from the camp.   **cum dispersos nec usquam uali-**
dos pauor fugientium abriperet 'since the fugitives' rout was dragging away
reinforcements who were scattered and not pooling their strength'.   **orta:** sc. *est.*
On T.'s ellipse of the auxiliary verb in deponent forms, see Goodyear (1972) 346–50.
in castris: i.e. in the main Vitellian camp at Cremona *c.* 12 miles away (2.22.3); cf.
Othoniano bello Germanicus miles moenibus Cremonensium castra sua, castris uallum circumiecerat
(3.26.1). It was probably built close to the 'walls and suburbs of Cremona . . . on
the north-east, between the converging road from Brixia and the Via Postumia, and
near their junction' (Wellesley (1972) 203). Caecina had not used all his men for the
ambush. In 1887 metal facing from the legionary chest of the *Legio IV Macedonica*,
abandoned while its bearer was fleeing from the northern gate of the Vitellian camp,
was discovered (Wellesley (1971) 31–2).   **quod non uniuersi ducerentur:** 19.1n.
quod . . . legisset. The original plan (a surprise ambush) undermined the credibility of
the Vitellian soldiers' excuse for mutiny, but now that a full-scale battle is taking place,
their complaint seems more valid, especially since T. has just criticised Caecina's generalship (*nam . . . abriperet*). As elsewhere in the *H.*, mutiny is morally complex, rather
than unambiguously wrong.   **uinctus** (sc. *est*) **. . . uinxissent:** 12.1n. *per . . . uinctus.*
The repeated vocabulary (also *fratri . . . fratrem; Iulius . . . Iulium*), here emphasised
by enclosing word-order, aptly underscores the brothers' parallel dilemmas. Yet both
charges of treachery clearly cannot simultaneously be valid. The accusers assume that
the fraternal bond transcends political allegiance to Otho or Vitellius, but perversion
of such family and fraternal ties is increasingly common in the *H.* (esp. 3.51). Stylistic
devices involving repetition (e.g. polyptoton) are useful for capturing the perversity of
civil war (Wills (1996) 206).   **praefectus castrorum Iulius Gratus**, left in the
camp to supervise the troops in Caecina's absence, features in the *H.* only here. He
and his brother were perhaps originally from Gallia Narbonensis (Birley (1977) 279).
The *praefectus castrorum* was a senior officer in charge of discipline, building, training,
payment, supplies and medical care (Veg. 2.10). Minucius Iustus, another *praefectus*

castrorum, enrages the Flavian troops because his standards of discipline are too strict
(3.7.1). **tamquam fratri . . . proditionem ageret** 'on the grounds that he was
engaging in treachery in the interest of his brother'; 21.1n. *tamquam . . . potuissent*. The
combination *proditionem agere* is only here. Whether Iulius Gratus was the culprit is
unclear, but someone betrayed the Vitellian plan for a surprise ambush: *proditum id*
(2.24.3). **cum . . . uinxissent:** *cum* 'while' (*OLD cum* 7b) suggests the paradox
that these events were happening simultaneously on the opposing sides. **Iulium
Frontonem:** Fronto, a tribune *e uigilibus* (seven cohorts serving as a fire brigade and
police force in Rome), was discharged by Galba (1.20.3), but restored to office by
Otho. His fate is unknown.

26.2 Ceterum resumes the battle-narrative after the miniature digression on
the mutiny. **apud fugientes occursantes, in acie pro uallo:** asyndeton of
opposed concepts contrasts the different groups (cf. *comminus eminus* 2.42.2, *falsa uera*
2.70.3). The *fugientes* are the main group of Vitellian auxiliaries (2.24.2), while the
occursantes are either some of Caecina's reinforcements (2.26.1), although the Othonians have already routed most of these, or perhaps some Vitellian reserves from the
main camp (Murison (1993) 109). Yet what does T. mean by *pro uallo*? It must refer
to the Vitellian camp outside Cremona, almost 12 miles away (cf. *uallum* 3.26.1), as
opposed to *in acie*, the site of the battle, but the Othonians certainly did not pursue the
Vitellians that far (Paulinus notoriously sounded the retreat). Instead T. dramatically
highlights how far the *formido* was spreading (and panic in the Vitellian camp is already
suggested by the mutiny). T.'s account is vivid rather than muddled (Murison (1993)
110). **cum uniuerso exercitu:** *c.* 15,000 to 16,000 men (20.2n. *magno terrore*). **ni:**
14.3n. **receptui cecinisset:** common Livian phrasing. In the parallel tradition
(Plut. *Oth.* 7.3–4), Marius Celsus, in charge of the cavalry, summons the Othonian
infantry from the camp. Paulinus brings the reinforcements too slowly and damages his
reputation by excessive caution. **utrisque in partibus percrebu<er>it** 'it was
common talk on both sides'. Significantly, both sides emphasise that Caecina's army
was almost destroyed (a detail not in Plut.). If even the defeated Vitellians admit that
only Paulinus' signal to retreat saved them, it adds corroboration. Defeated soldiers
generally wanted to salvage some dignity, but the Vitellians, faced with overwhelming
evidence, must concede their narrow escape. The 'aoristic' perfect subjunctive in the
consecutive clause denoting the final result (after a main verb in the perfect tense) is
not found in early Latin, Cicero or Caesar, but features in Livy and is common in
T. (GL §513 n.1). **ferebat** 'used to maintain' (*OLD* 32). Paulinus wrote memoirs
about his Mauretanian campaign in 41 (Plin. *Nat.* 5.14), but T. may have consulted
him directly (or via Agricola) about the controversial events at Castores. **tantum
insuper laboris atque itineris** 'so much additional labour and marching', the
direct object of *timuisse*. An army's ability to endure extended labour was fundamental
to its efficiency (Cic. *Tusc.* 2.37; cf. 16.2n. *laborem insolitum*). On the adverb *insuper*, see
11.2n. *deforme insuper auxilium*. **ne . . . aggrederetur . . . foret:** the subordinate
clause is epexegetic, giving further details about what Paulinus fears. It shows brachylogy, since the verb of fearing is not repeated. Cf. *diffisus paucitati cohortium, ne . . . parum*

tolerarent (2.23.1), *nec hostes modo timebant, sed suosmet ipsi ciues, ne Romana plebs metu per-culsa . . . pacem acciperet* (Liv. 2.9.5). **Vitellianus miles recens e castris fessos aggrederetur:** the clash at Castores took place *c.* 5 Apr. and the Vitellians had been assaulting Placentia on 30–31 Mar. (Murison (1993) 108), so Caecina's men were probably not as well-rested as Paulinus implies. Paulinus' legionaries had travelled from different places: the *prima Adiutrix* had left Rome on 14 Mar., travelling 345 miles to Brixellum (Otho's headquarters), whereas the *uexillum* from the *XIII Gemina* had marched *c.* 338 miles from Pannonia (11.1n. *quattuor legiones*), after setting out between 15–20 Mar. (11.1n. *motis . . . exercitibus*). The *uexillum* from Pannonia can only have arrived recently and was no doubt tired after the march. **perculsis** 'if they were repulsed'. **nullum retro subsidium:** this argument sits oddly with the detail that 1,000 cavalry from the praetorians and auxiliary were serving as a *subsidium laborantibus* (2.24.3). **foret:** *foret* for *esset* (14.3n. *deletae . . . forent*). **aduerso rumore:** descriptive abl. (GL §400), also *A.* 14.11.3, Liv. 27.20.10. The episode ends with the *uolgus* seeking to blame one individual, a familiar phenomenon in warfare: *iniquissima haec bellorum condicio est: prospera omnes sibi uindicant, aduersa uni imputantur* (Agr. 27.1); cf. *quippe res humanae ita sese habent: in uictoria uel ignauis gloriari licet, aduorsae res etiam bonos detractant* (Sall. *Jug.* 53.8).

27.1 Haud proinde . . . quam 'not so much . . . as'. T. especially likes *proinde* + *quam* (2.35.1, 39.2, 3.58.2, 4.72.3; otherwise only in Plaut. *Truc.* 324, Gell. 9.3.5) where earlier authors prefer *ac* or *atque*. MSS often disagree whether to read *proinde* or *perinde* (4.69.3). **in metum compulit . . . ad modestiam composuit:** T. uses structuring sound-effects so that the two clauses being compared mirror one another. For *modestia* see 12.1n. *ut . . . corruptus*. T. has prepositional *uariatio* of *ad / in* again (1.44.2, 1.83.2, 2.44.3, 2.56.1, 3.61.1, *A.* 1.28.5, *A.* 4.51.2; Sörbom (1935) 46–9). **nec solum** is balanced by a simple *quoque* instead of *sed etiam* (cf. *non modo . . . sed quoque D.* 2.1, 37.3, 1.50.1, *nec modo . . . sed quoque* 1.57.2, *nec solum . . . sed quoque D.* 10.4, *G.* 13.4; L-H-S 518 §284c). **qui culpam in militem conferebat, seditioni magis quam proelio paratum:** Caecina's accusation is especially unfair, as the mutiny in the camp happened precisely because the soldiers were *not* being led to battle (*quod non uniuersi ducerentur* 2.26.1). Others in the narrative blame their soldiers (*Vitellius . . . culpam in militem conferens* 3.70.4), but soldiers can reciprocate (*miles culpam cladis in Hordeonium uertebat* 4.25.1). **Ticinum:** 17.2n. Valens' troops, after reaching Ticinum on *c.* 6 Apr. (Murison (1993) 87), were now only 50 miles away from Cremona and Caecina's camp. From Lucus (arrival date = *c.* 28 Feb., 1.66.3), they had crossed the Cottian Alps and arrived at Augusta Taurinorum in Italy (*c.* 30 Mar.). The last marker of Valens' position was very general: *propinquante Fabio Valente* (2.24.1). The itinerary before Valens crosses the Alps is much more detailed (Damon (2003) 229). **posito hostium contemptu** 'their contempt for the enemy laid aside'. *contemptus* (not in Cicero) appears only once in Caesar. It is 'greatly preferred to *contemptio* by Livy (21 : 1), the younger Seneca (34 : 5), Quintilian (18 : 0) and T. (9 : 2)' (WM 392). **reciperandi decoris cupidine:** T. probably means the troops' unruly march from Lower Germany to the Cottian Alps (1.62.3–66), spreading *terror* throughout Gaul

(1.63.2), rather than a single battle.   **reuerentius et aequalius:** a striking pair, as T. uses both comparative adverbs only here. Columella, Celsus and Seneca the Younger are the only other authors to use *aequalius*.

27.2–30.1 MUTINY ERUPTS AMONGST VALENS' TROOPS

Mutinies (Othonian 1.80–5, 2.18–19, 2.51, Vitellian 2.68–9, 3.12, Flavian 3.10–11) or near-mutinies (2.30.1, 4.48.1), confronted with varying degrees of (in)efficiency by different leaders, pepper T.'s narrative of the civil war. Valens initially confronts the trouble well (*militari astu* 2.28.1), but his plan to separate the troublesome Batavian auxiliaries from the legionaries backfires. After failing to subdue the men by lictors, Valens even resorts to disguising himself as a slave to protect himself (2.29.1). Only the intervention of the camp prefect Alfenus Varus (2.29.2), when the mutiny is naturally subsiding, averts trouble. The Vitellian soldiers are cast as inconsistent (although mocked by the Batavians (2.27.2), they complain when Valens sends away the auxiliaries) and greedy (craving *spolia Galliarum et Viennensium aurum* 2.29.1). Such stereotypically mutinous conduct is no surprise perhaps, after the soldiers' unruly march from Lower Germany. Yet the Vitellians' standing will progressively improve as the narrative continues (Ash (1999) 37–55). This mutiny should be compared with the earlier Othonian sedition (2.18–19): in particular, the Othonian general Spurinna pointedly emerges with more dignity than the Vitellian Valens.

This segment has been strikingly displaced within the narrative. The mutiny, which had been brewing for some time, broke out before the Vitellians reached Ticinum on *c.* 6 Apr., but perhaps after they had crossed the Alps and arrived in Augusta Taurinorum (*c.* 30 Mar.), as is implied by *postquam in conspectu sit hostis* (2.28.2). This may explain why Valens and his army took more than a week to cover the 89 miles between Augusta Taurinorum and Ticinum. So, T. could have narrated the mutiny (2.27.2–29) *before* the Castores incident (*c.* 5 Apr. 69; 2.24–27.1), but did not to do so. Why? First, T. avoids interrupting Caecina's military setbacks (defeats at Placentia 2.20.2–23.3 and at Castores 2.24–27.1), helping us to understand the general's desperation. Second, it shows how obsessed Caecina is with himself: his main reason for arranging the ambush at Castores was to make sure that not all the glory of the war fell to Valens (2.24.1). Yet now it emerges (with a jolt) that Caecina was so immersed in his own problems that he did not know about Valens recently losing control of his men. Such tunnel vision could have jeopardised the whole campaign. This suspicion and lack of communication between the two Vitellian generals is a theme which T. will explore (2.30.2–3). On 2.27.2–30.1 see Herzog (1996) 84–99.

27.2 Grauis alioquin seditio exarserat 'But as a matter of fact, a serious mutiny had blazed up' (*OLD alioqui(n)* 4). *exardesco*, often coupled with wars and battles (*TLL* s.v. *exardesco* 1181.63–76), less frequently with mutinies (*TLL* s.v. *exardesco* 1181.69–71), is conventionally linked with anger and emotions (Fantham (1972) 10, 130): *exarserat . . . iracundia exercitus* (1.58.2), *certamina exarsere* (2.38.1), *proelium atrox arsisset* (2.66.2), *militaris seditio prope exarsit* (4.46.1). Cf. *subdere ignem ac materiam seditioni* (Liv.

8.32.16). T. creatively applies the metaphor of fire to the mutinies in *Annals* 1 (Goodyear (1972) 215–16; cf. Woodman (2006)), but it can appear in more positive contexts: *omnis exercitus flammauerat* (2.74.1).   **quam altiore initio . . . repetam** 'which I will trace back from its start earlier on'. T. often uses *repeto* in 'flashbacks' (1.4.1, 4.5.1, 4.48.1, *A*. 3.24.1, 15.72.2, 16.18.1), reserving for the appropriate moment information which could otherwise confuse a reader.   **neque enim . . . oportuerat:** the defensive parenthesis (18.1n. *is enim*) shows T.'s sensitivity towards the proper order of events, whether in digressions (2.38.2, *A*. 4.33.4), specific incidents (*A*. 2.27.1) or foreign campaigns (*A*. 6.38.1, 12.40.5). Yet dislocated narrative sequence can generate suggestive historiographical juxtapositions: cf. *ordo ipse annalium mediocriter nos retinet quasi enumeratione fastorum* (Cic. *Fam.* 5.12.5).   **cohortes Batauorum:** in 67, Nero withdrew the *XIV Gemina* and eight Batavian cohorts (1.59.1), including horsemen (4.19.1), from Britain for his eastern campaign. He then recalled them to help suppress the rebellion of Vindex, who had revolted from Nero in early March 68 (1.6.2). The Batavians joined Valens while en route back to Britain and contributed to the Vitellian victory in northern Italy (2.43.2), but the *XIV Gemina* was intensely pro-Othonian. Next the Batavians were ordered to escort the restive legionaries of the *XIV Gemina* back to Britain (2.66.1), but a riot almost broke out (2.66.2). The Batavians later joined Civilis' revolt (4.19.2).   **bello Neronis:** i.e. the vexed, complex period between early Mar. and June 68 (Murison (1993) 1–26), when C. Iulius Vindex, governor of Gallia Lugdunensis, revolted from Nero. Verginius Rufus (49.1n.), governor of Upper Germany, put down the revolt at Vesontio in mid-May, but Galba, governor of Hispania Tarraconensis, had emerged to challenge Nero in early April. On 9 or 11 June Nero killed himself. **audito Vitellii motu:** cf. *initia causasque motus Vitelliani* (1.51.1). Fabius Valens had sworn allegiance to Vitellius on 2 Jan., 69 (1.57.1) and the army of Upper Germany joined him on 3 Jan. 69 (1.57.2).   **a quarta decima legione:** the *XIV Gemina* (11.1n. *quattuor legiones* and *rebellione Britanniae compressa*).   **rettulimus:** 1.59.1, 64.2. On the 1st person plural form, see 4.4n. *ut . . . memorauimus.*   **superbe agebant:** these troublesome Batavians (*cohortes turbidas*, 2.28.1) have already shown *intemperies* (1.64.2) by brawling with Valens' legionaries. They will soon fight with the legionaries from the *XIV Gemina* (2.66.2), and shortly before they join the rebel Civilis, *intumuere statim superbia ferociaque* (4.19.1).   **ut cuiusque legionis tentoria accessissent** 'whenever they approached the tents of a legion'; *ut* + a generalising subjunctive (*OLD ut* 19). Cf. *ut quemque nuntium fama attulisset* (1.85.2). *accedo* without the preposition *ad* is an archaism, recalling Sallust and Virgil. Cf. *ut quosque accesserat* (3.24.2).   **coercitos a se quartadecimanos, ablatam Neroni Italiam:** the men of *XIV Gemina* were loyal to Nero in the *bellum Neronis*: cf. *longa illis erga Neronem fides* (2.11.1). The Batavian cohorts' boast (that they had deprived Nero of Italy by stopping these legionaries from helping him) must be an exaggeration. Nero's forces in northern Italy (including *XIV Gemina*) under Petronius Turpilianus did not fight Vindex, who was defeated by Verginius Rufus (49.1n.) and the German armies. Nero was paradoxically toppled *nuntiis magis et rumoribus quam armis* (1.89.2).   **omnem belli fortunam . . . iactantes:** 20.1n. *ipsius.* Similar language is used either to claim influence (Mucianus boasts that *in manu sua fuisse imperium donatumque Vespasiano*, 4.4.1; the mutinous soldiers in Germany assert, with more justification, that *sua in manu sitam rem Romanam*, *A.* 1.31.5) or to flatter (Piso says to the troops that the outcome of his adoption *in uestra manu positum est*, 1.29.2, and Mucianus tells Vespasian that the impact of his principate on the state *in tua manu positum est*, 2.76.2). The phrasing is Sallustian (*in uostra manu situm est, Jug.* 31.5), but the appended nom. present participle (also 2.45.3, 2.54.1, 2.68.4, 2.88.2) is Livian (Chausserie-Laprée (1969) 311–14). *ipsorum* = 'their own' (*OLD ipse* 10). *belli fortunam* is Ennian (*A.* 199 Sk.).   **contumeliosum id militibus:** the Batavians' boasts were especially offensive to Valens' soldiers from Lower Germany, who had been pivotal in Nero's downfall. News of the German armies' defection was decisive, after Verginius Rufus (49.1n.), general of the army in Upper Germany, was offered the principate by these soldiers. *contumeliosus* features from Cicero onwards (but the adverb is in Ter.). T. uses this sonorous adj. only in the *H.* (2.65.1, 4.4.1, 4.64.1). It also takes a dat. in Livy: *id demum contumeliosum plebi est* (4.4.9).   **acerbum duci:** the Batavians' boasting annoyed Valens in a different way from the legionaries: it had the potential to disrupt military discipline. Yet he himself presented the German auxiliaries to Vitellius as an asset: *secutura Germanorum auxilia* (1.52.3).   **corrupta:** sc. *est.* **iurgiis et rixis:** *iurgium* 'quarrel' is the natural prelude to the physical violence of a *rixa* 'brawl' (also 1.64.2, Ov. *Ars* 3.374, Juv. 15.51–2, Sen. *De ira* 2.34; cf. *ad iurgium, mox ad manus et ferrum transirent* (sc. *milites*), 2.88.3; *iurgium inde et clamor, pugna postremo orta*, Liv. 29.9.3). Germans, often fuelled by drink, stereotypically indulged in *rixae* (*G.* 22.2; cf. 2.88.3).   **ad postremum** 'ultimately'.   **e petulantia etiam perfidiam:** the enveloping alliteration (4.1n. *pandi . . . prosperum*) marks a downward progression (cf. *a conuiciis ad caedem* 2.66.2). After the *H.* T. drops *petulantia* 'insolence' (Syme (1958a) 714), a typical trait of unruly soldiers (*Agr.* 16.5, 3.11.2, 4.1.3, [Caes.] *Afr.* 54.2, Suet. *Vit.* 10.2). It 'signifies aggression that falls short of dangerous' (Damon (2003) 131).

          28.1 Igitur: 2.2n.   **Treuirorum alam Tungrosque:** i.e. the forces dispatched by Valens at 2.14.1. He heard on 10 or 11 Mar. (Murison (1993) 102) that the Othonian fleet was threating Gallia Narbonensis and on *c.* 25–6 Mar. (2.15.2) about the stalemate between his own men and the Othonians.   **Narbonensem Galliam circumiri** 'that Gallia Narbonensis was being blockaded'. T. as narrator is less forceful about the impact of the Othonian victory (2.15.2), although it keeps Corsica and Sardinia loyal to Otho (2.16.1). Valens perhaps artfully magnified the Othonian success to make it easier to remove the Batavians from his main force, or else initial reports of the battle were too pessimistic (Chilver (1979) 194). The two possibilities are not mutually exclusive.   **simul** links the two abl. noun + gen. gerund phrases (*cura . . . tuendi* and *astu dispergendi*), emphasising a gulf between Valens' apparently respectable motives (protecting the allies) and his real aim (separating turbulent cohorts). Since the *legati coloniarum* have already made their presence felt (2.14.1), further concern for allies adds plausibility to his scheme.   **militari astu:** the striking pairing is only here (*TLL* s.v. *astus* 984.20). *astus* (Wheeler (1988) 73–4) is often associated with barbarians (cf. 5.17.2), but the general Valens must use it to control his own men. *militaris* = 'typical of a soldier' (*OLD* 4b).   **cohortes turbidas ac, si**

una forent, praeualidas: *forent* = *essent* (14.3n. *deletae . . . forent*). A cohort usually consisted of six centuries of 80 men. With eight cohorts in total, Valens has to consider *c.* 3,840 Batavian auxiliaries, about one-fifth of his force of *c.* 20,000 men (20.2n. *magno terrore*). *praeualidus* (3× in *H.*, 6× in *A.*, 6× in Liv.) is a choice alternative to *ualidus*. T. likes compound adjectives with a *prae-* prefix and has some especially unusual ones in the *A.* (*praegracilis*, *A.* 4.57.2; *praecalidus*, *A.* 13.16.2; *praeferuidus*, *A.* 14.64.2). 'Compounds with *per-* and *prae-* could be created with the utmost facility' (Syme (1958a) 723).   **ire in subsidium:** T. prefers *in* + acc. (also *A.* 12.55.2, 14.32.3) over the predicative dat. *subsidio* (favoured by Caes. *Gal.* 1.52.7, 5.58.5, *Afr.* 39.2, *Alex.* 21.3). Cf. 23.1n. *in auxilium Placentiae.* The mutinous element in an army should ideally be sent off to perform other duties 'with such subtlety that they seem to have been specially selected, although they are being cast off' (Veg. 3.4.7). Valens was not subtle enough. **maerere socii, fremere legiones:** 6.2n. *fremere miles.* Historic infinitives (5.1n., *anteire . . . obniti*) in asyndeton boil down the army's hostile reactions (*socii* = auxiliary troops).

28.2 orbari se: the rest of the chapter gives in indirect speech the complaints of the legionaries. Their sudden desire not to be deprived of these auxiliaries seems mercurial after the Batavians' earlier insults. *orbo* takes an abl. of separation.   **fortissimorum . . . auxilio:** the Batavians (17.2n.), despite being unruly, had a good reputation from their service in Britain (4.12.3). Their support of one side or the other was potentially important (*grande momentum* 1.59.1) and Civilis tries to entice them *occultis nuntiis* (4.15.1). 'The power of these eight cohorts is vividly illustrated at 4.19–20 where, caught between two (admittedly weakened) Roman legions, they frighten one into inaction and defeat the other' (Damon (2003) 222). T. has the superlative (17.1n. *florentissimum*) of *fortis* less and less often in his extant work (minor works: 5×, *H.*: 8×, *A.*: 4×). The homoioteleuton of *fortissimorum uirorum* sounds doleful.   **tot bellorum uictores**, an emotive phrase, is also in Vocula's speech (4.58.4).   **uelut ex acie:** *uelut* softens an audacious turn of phrase. Valens' men will only fight the Othonians at the battle on the river Po (2.34–6).   **prouincia** = Gallia Narbonensis, an administrative unit created by Augustus, but originally (121 BC) encompassing southern France from the Mediterranean to Lake Geneva (simply known as *prouincia* under the republic).   **potior** 'more important'.   **sit . . . sequerentur:** mixed sequence of tenses in an unreal conditional sentence. The imperfect subj. in the apodosis is historic, while the present subj. in the protasis is primary. The *uariatio* of *si . . . sit* and *sin . . . uerteretur* seems especially arbitrary.   **sin:** 1.3n. *sin . . . susciperet.*   **sin uictoria incolumi in Italia uerteretur** 'If however the victory depended on Italy being safe'; (*OLD uerto* 2 for the verb used figuratively). This is the reading of Wellesley (1973), reinstating Hadley's emendation (1899). M has *uictoriae [sanitas, sustentaculum] columen*, but Nipperdey omitted the bracketed words (which Meiser and W. Heraeus pointed out were a gloss in Placidus). The *columen* was 'the horizontal pole which supported the roof of a house; but the word was used fairly often in a metaphorical sense to mean "support" or "corner-stone"' (Oakley (1997) 683; also Kraus (1994) 291). Wellesley argues that *uictoriae columen* 'the mainstay of victory' combined with *uerteretur* (involving the metaphor of a hinge or pivot) is incongruous since, 'it is not the habit of tops or mainstays to turn or pivot' (Wellesley (1973) 7; cf. Fantham (1972) 45–6).   **non abrumpendos ut corpori ualidissimos artus** 'the strongest limbs, so to speak, should not be severed from the body'. In Livy, Ov. and Curt. *corpus* = 'a body of troops' (*OLD corpus* 15b), but T. plays creatively with the metaphor of the body for an army. Elsewhere, usually the general = the head, the soldiers = the body (Dion. Hal. 1.48.3, Plut. *Galb.* 4.5, Curt. 6.9.28, Sil. 10.309–11). Here (more elaborately) the auxiliaries = the 'limbs', the legionaries = the 'trunk', but the 'head' is pointedly ignored (and silent). Plutarch *Pel.* 2.1 has an even more elaborate metaphor (light-armed troops = hands, cavalry = feet, phalanx = chest and breast-plate, and general = head).

   29.1 Haec ferociter iactando 'fiercely hurling out these words'. *iacto* (*OLD* 10) has a different sense here from *iactantes* at 2.27.2 (*OLD* 11). A gerund in the instrumental abl. can often be virtually equivalent to a present participle agreeing with the subject (*NLS* §205).   **coercere seditionem coeptabat** 'he tentatively began to restrain the mutiny'; *coeptabat* = inceptive imperfect. *coepto* + an infinitive (also at 3.10.3, 3.81.1, 5.10.1) predominates in poetry, rather than in prose (*TLL* s.v. *coepto* 1432.61–70). 'Though rare elsewhere and mostly poetical, the frequentative form is common in T.' (MW 149).   **ipsum inuadunt, saxa iaciunt, fugientem sequuntur:** the asyndeton of these verbs in the vivid present tense mirrors the soldiers' frantic actions. The verbs are in the same position in each clause, but the objects shift from pronoun, to noun, to acc. participle (*uariatio*). Plutarch transposes this detail about the stoning to his brief notice of Valens' soldiers' anger after the failed ambush at Castores (*Oth.* 7.9).   **spolia Galliarum et Viennensium aurum:** in chiastic phrasing the soldiers' true motives are revealed, undercutting the respectable reasons for their disaffection articulated at 2.28.2. Petillius Cerialis points to Gallic gold as a particular incentive for invasion over the years (4.74.3; cf. *A.* 16.1.2) and Seneca talks of *aurum non minore periculo quaerendum quam possidendum* (*Nat.* 5.15.3; cf. Plin. *Nat.* 33.58–63 on the allure of gold). T.'s Claudius even suggests Gauls should be admitted to the senate as they will bring their gold with them (*A.* 11.24.6). Valens' men already have assets from their march through Gaul (1.64.3, 1.66.1).   **pretia laborum suorum:** Valens' soldiers have not yet fought a proper battle against the Othonians, so *labores* seems boastful. The original motives of the German armies for civil war apparently included desire for illicit rewards (*praemia quam stipendia malebat* 1.51.1).   **occultare:** sc. *eum* (cf. 13.2n. *uterum ostendens latere respondit*, a similar ellipse). T. increasingly prefers *occulto* for *occulo* (13.2n. *occuleret*). Valens' poverty prompted rumours that he had been bribed by the citizens of Vienne (1.66.2 with Damon (2003) 235). He profited from planning his route (1.66.3) and later from his powerful position in Rome (2.92.2), and is generally cast as rapacious (2.56.2, Plut. *Oth.* 6.7, Dio 64.15.3).   **clamitantes**, a verb naturally associated with the heightened emotions of mutiny narratives (18.2n. *accitum . . . clamitabant*, 3.10.2, *A.* 1.18.3, 1.21.2, 1.30.4, 1.35.4, 1.38.2).   **tabernacula ducis:** the rhetorical pl. for singular noun is striking. Cf. *intra tabernaculum ducis* (*A.* 1.29.4).   **ipsamque humum pilis et lanceis rimabantur:** a vivid misappropriation of the weapons of war, emphasised by citing *pilum* and *lancea. ipsam* hints at the soldiers' desperation. Since the camp was struck each day on the march, burying the gold under or near the commander's tent would not have been especially practical. Suetonius uses *rimor* only once (*Vit.* 17.1), possibly inspired by T.'s phrasing here (Shotter (1993) 189). **nam** explains why the soldiers had such freedom to search. Valens had already fled (cf. *fugientem* 2.29.1). **seruili ueste:** (cf. *seruili habitu* 3.73.3, 4.36.2) T. has an adj. instead of a dependent noun in the gen. (2.1n. *iuuenilis animus*). The stylistically lofty touch contrasts with Valens' degrading action, while the slave's garb symbolises the role-reversal perpetrated by the soldiers. High-ranking people compromising their dignity, either by disgraceful hiding-places (Piso 1.43.2, Otho's dinner guests 1.81.2, Aponius Saturninus 3.11.3, Vitellius 3.84.4, the senators in the ceiling *A.* 4.69.1; cf. Hiempsal at Sall. *Jug.* 12.5) or degrading disguises (Flavians on the Capitol 3.73.3, Vocula 4.36.2) recurs in T. **decurionem equitum:** i.e. a commander of a *turma* (14.1n. *turmas*) of cavalry (Caes. *Gal.* 1.23.2, Liv. 4.38.2). Each *turma* had three *decuriones*, one being the senior commander (Plb. 6.25.1).

29.2 Alfenus Varus participates energetically in the first battle of Bedriacum, leading the Batavian auxiliaries (2.43.2, Plut. *Oth.* 12.7). Vitellius appoints him as praetorian prefect in Rome (3.36.2), after removing Caecina's friend Publilius Sabinus, and sends him to hold the Apennines (3.55.1). Varus abandons camp (3.61.3), and after the Flavian victory, *ignauiae infamiaeque suae superfuit* (4.11.3). **deflagrante paulatim seditione:** the fire metaphor (Fantham (1972) 130) suggests ring-composition (cf. *seditio exarserat* 2.27.2). The eye-catching *deflagro*, only here in T., appears from Ennius onwards, but the metaphorical use (*TLL* s.v. *deflagro* 357.25–31) is a Livian innovation: cf. *deflagrare iras uestras* (Liv. 40.8.9), *sic deflagrare minaces | incassum et uetito passus languescere bello* (Luc. 4.280–1). Ammianus imitates T.: *tumore iam deflagrante* (29.6.16). **consilium:** this corresponds chiastically to the earlier Othonian mutiny (2.18–19; Herzog (1996) 88). Where Spurinna made the city-troops, not used to hard work, entrench the camp to restore discipline (19.1n. *is labor*), the non-urban Vitellian troops are restrained by the startling cessation of the normal camp routine. **uetitis obire uigilias centurionibus:** the officers' secession implies that the soldiers' bad conduct has set them outside the boundaries of the martial community (Lendon (1997) 240). With *obire uigilias* T. avoids the normal technical expression *circumire uigilias*, common in Liv. and Sall. (*TLL* s.v. *circumeo* 1137.65–6). **omisso tubae sono:** 'Times for sleep, guard-duty, and reveille are announced by trumpet-calls' (Jos. *BJ* 3.86; cf. Veg. 2.22). **igitur:** 2.2n. **torpere cuncti, circumspectare inter se:** the historic infinitives (5.1n., *anteire . . . obniti*) suggest ring-composition: cf. *maerere socii, fremere legiones* (2.28.1) at the start of the mutiny. T. recalls Livy on the troops caught in the ambush at the Caudine Forks: *uelut torpor quidam insolitus membra tenet, intuentesque alii alios* (9.2.10, with Oakley (2005) 62). *cunctus* = a synonym for *omnis* (1.3n. *cuncta . . . perlustrat*). **id ipsum, quod nemo regeret, pauentes** 'fearing the very fact that no-one was in charge'. Varus' plan to create a vacuum in the military hierarchy has worked. In the *A.*, mutinies usually have named leaders (e.g. Percennius, *A.* 1.16.3; Vibulenus, *A.* 1.22.1), but *seditiones* in the *H.* are often leaderless, so seditious soldiers can find it difficult to persevere at moments of crisis. *id ipsum, quod* (placed emphatically at the start of the clause) + causal subjunctive in the relative clause (*NLS* §156) recurs (1.86.3, 2.91.3, 4.76.3). *pauere* + acc. is Sallustian. T. later recasts his language pithily and paradoxically: *id ipsum pauentes, quod timuissent* (*A*. 4.70.2). **silentio, patientia, postremo precibus ac lacrimis:** ablatives of means in tricolon crescendo. Generals elsewhere in T. use such methods to try to control unruly soldiers (1.82.1, 2.44.2, *A*. 1.66.2). Shedding tears was apparently no stigma for soldiers (2.45.3, 2.49.3, 3.31.2, 4.46.3, 4.72.3, *A*. 15.16.4).

   29.3 ut uero . . . fauor: polysyndeton in the subordinate clause (*et . . . et*) + asyndeton in the main clause creates *uariatio*. **deformis et flens** 'unsightly and weeping'. Valens is still dressed as a slave, not intrinsically ugly (cf. *nigra . . . ueste deformis*, Petr. 133.4). His weeping mirrors the soldiers' tears and is perhaps manipulative. **gaudium miseratio fauor:** the asyndeton captures the mercurial soldiers' rapid succession of paradoxical emotions upon seeing Valens, so recently their target. For a similar transformation cf. *pro metu repente gaudium mutatur: milites alius alium laeti appellant* (Sall. *Jug*. 53.8). Yet the Vitellians' mood is unpredictable: when they hear about Caecina's defeat, mutiny nearly breaks out again (2.30.1) and they quickly snub their general: *non exspectare ducem* (2.30.1). **ut est uolgus utroque immodicum** 'just as a crowd always veers from one emotional extreme to the other'. The extreme emotional fluctuations of the *uolgus* is a topos (1.69, 1.80.2, 5.8.3, Liv. 2.7.5, Plut. *Mor*. 800c, *Brut*. 21.1), often especially marked in soldiers (Curt. 9.4.22). **aquilis:** the two eagles, from the *V Alaudae* (1.61.2) and the *I Italica* (1.64.3), will be carried prominently as Vitellius enters Rome (2.89.1). These supremely Roman symbols and the soldiers' happy mood after the mutiny recall (but challenge) the *laetum augurium* (1.62.3) of a real eagle flying beside Valens' column as it set out. **utili moderatione non supplicium cuiusquam poposcit:** Valens' leniency is practical, but could set a bad precedent. Selectively punishing leaders of mutinies is common: 'But if extreme necessity urges the medicine of the sword, it is juster to follow ancestral custom and punish the ringleaders of crimes, so that fear extends to all, but punishment to few' (Veg. 3.4.9). In the praetorian mutiny, Otho only punishes two men (1.85.1), as the soldiers wish (1.82.3), while Spurinna (2.19.2), Vitellius (2.69.1) and Antonius Primus (3.10.3) discipline none of their mutinous men. Drusus orders the ringleaders in Pannonia to be put to death (*A*. 1.29.4), while under Germanicus, the contrite mutineers themselves demand punishment for the guilty (*A*. 1.44.1). **ne dissimulans suspectior foret paucos incusauit** 'to avoid arousing further mistrust by pretending to ignore (the mutiny), he reproached a few men' (*OLD dissimulo* 3); *foret* for *esset* (14.3n. *deletae . . . forent*). If Valens completely ignored the mutiny, then the soldiers might think that he was being insincere and only planning to punish them after the *seditio* had subsided. This compromise shows his deteriorating authority: earlier he averted violence between his legionaries and auxiliaries by physical punishment: *animaduersione paucorum* (1.64.2). **gnarus . . . licere:** the phrasing recalls Caecina's thoughts before the assault on Placentia (*gnarus . . . fore* 2.20.2), and is a transitional device in the narrative. His point about men having more licence than their generals in civil war is illustrated by Antonius Primus' careless remark before the violent sack of Cremona by 40,000 Flavian soldiers (3.32.3–33.1), where the *inuidia* for the city's destruction falls to the general. On *gnarus*, see 13.1n. *gnari locorum*.

30.1 aduersa . . . pugna: a Livian periphrasis (18×) for military defeat. The reaction of Valens' men to news of 'an indecisive battle with which neither side was happy' (Morgan (1996b) 359) continues the chain of recriminations. The Othonians and Vitellians held Suetonius Paulinus responsible (2.26.2), Caecina had blamed his men (2.27.1), and now Valens is criticised.   **pugna . . . proelio:** 'sometimes *proelium* ("skirmish" or "fray", with particular reference to the actual fighting) and *pugna* ("fight" or "battle" in a broader sense) are distinguished: e.g. Liv. 27.2.7–8, 33.36.9, Caes. *Gal.* 3.4.3, Tac. *Histories* 2.30.1, 1.39.2' (Oakley (1998) 152).   **allatum** (sc. *est*) 'news was brought' (also 2.52.1). The arrival of news about Caecina's defeat at Castores (2.24–27.1) resumes the narrative's proper chronological order.   **prope renouata** (sc. *est*) **seditio:** this observation initially seems odd after T.'s assertion that the defeat prompted Valens' men to obey their general (2.27.1), but it is not necessarily inconsistent. Rather, it vividly pinpoints a momentary crisis from which the soldiers (of their own accord) pull back.   **tamquam . . . defuissent:** *tamquam* + subj., giving the soldiers' reasoning (21.1n. *tamquam . . . potuissent*).   **fraude et cunctationibus Valentis** 'thanks to the treacherous delays of Valens'. The hendiadys + rhetorical pl. (*cunctationibus*; cf. *fraude . . . cunctatione*, Liv. 27.21.2) accentuate the soldiers' resentment, although the charge is not substantiated. Plutarch also depicts the anger of Valens' men on hearing about the failed ambush at Castores, but gives no hint (either as narrator or through the soldiers) that Valens deliberately delayed to humiliate Caecina (*Oth.* 7.8). Valens' progress to the Alps was certainly slow (*lento . . . agmine* 1.66.3). Later on, Valens does delay with damaging results (*inutili cunctatione* 3.40), though the reason is indecisiveness, not treachery. Even the famous general Corbulo was vulnerable to accusations of dawdling to intensify a dramatic rescue (*A.* 15.10.4).   **nolle . . . urgere signiferos:** the four historic infinitives (5.1n., *anteire . . . obniti*) in asyndeton aptly mirror the bustling impatient soldiers. *anteire signa* recalls Vespasian (*anteire agmen* 2.5.1), reinforcing the idea that these Vitellian soldiers are playing the role of their side-lined commander. *anteeo* + the acc. is a Sallustian poeticism (*Hist.* 1.75) avoided by Caesar. **Caecinae iunguntur:** Caecina was at Cremona on the Po's north bank, while Otho was at Placentia on the south bank. Valens and his men arrived on 7. Apr. (Murison (1993) 110).

30.2–31.1 CAECINA AND VALENS; OTHO AND VITELLIUS

T. suspends the action to analyse the evolving relationship between Vitellius' two generals, Caecina and Valens. This section could have come earlier, but postponing it until now means that author's observations (and even the generals' mutual recriminations) are endorsed by the previous narrative. The two men could not be more different: where Caecina is young, charismatic and arrogant, Valens is older, sordid and unpopular. Even in their respective marches to the Alps (1.61–70), T. creates

a 'diptych', prompting readers to compare the generals (Morgan (1994a) 103–25).
They apparently have little in common, except for supporting Vitellius as an imperial
challenger, but *metus hostilis* in miniature prompts them to bury their differences for
now so that they can secure the prize. That fragile bond will soon disintegrate after
victory (92.1n. *olim . . . dissimulata*). In historiography and elsewhere, authors often
dramatically pair younger and older generals on the same side, conspicuous for their
contrasting methods: e.g. Marcus Minucius ∼ Fabius Maximus (Liv. 22.27–30, Plb.
3.103–5); Xerxes ∼ Darius (Aesch. *Persae*); Adrastus ∼ Theseus (Aesch. *Supp.*); Alcibiades ∼ Nicias (Thuc. 6); Hector ∼ Polydamas (Hom. *Il.* 18). In such cases, age and
experience usually triumph over youthful enthusiasm, but Caecina and Valens will
each fall short of the model, particularly when Vespasian rises to challenge Vitellius: an
increasingly sluggish Valens is only surpassed by the spectacular treachery of Caecina.
Yet for now, it is an advantage that there are only two of them, compared with the
multiple Othonian generals (Annius Gallus, Marius Celsus, Vestricius Spurinna, Suetonius Paulinus, Salvius Titianus), who are dangerously mistrusted by their soldiers
(*suspecti duces* 2.33.3), even if they are not riven by such intense internal rivalries. The
contrasting Vitellian pair will in turn be superseded by the single dynamic Flavian
general, Antonius Primus (*uni Antonio apertae militum aures* 3.10.2).

    From one *syncrisis* (4.4n. *nomen . . . celebre*), T. naturally moves to another, Otho
and Vitellius (cf. Jos. *BJ* 4.592–600 on Vitellius and Vespasian). Whatever these men's
real characters, T. compares them in terms of their reputations at the time (*timebantur . . . ducebatur* 2.31.1). This further refines his earlier assessment of public opinion
about the pair (1.50), which initially elided the differences between them. Yet although
Otho is here cast as more terrifying than Vitellius, this hostile public assessment could
easily be wrong (cf. *famaeque dissimilis* 2.11.3, with Ash (1999) 83–94). The *egregia . . . fama*
(2.31.1) and narrative (2.46–50) of Otho's death shows how sharply reputations can
fluctuate. Mucianus will wryly claim that Vitellius' conduct as emperor has made even
Otho *iam desiderabilem et magnum principem* (2.76.4).

    30.2 Improspera Valentis fama apud exercitum Caecinae erat:
although Caecina had blamed his soldiers for the defeat at Castores (2.27.1), his
men did not simply blame him in return (Morgan (1996b) 360). *improspera* (+ *fama*
only here) is T.'s coinage (also *A.* 3.24.2 with WM 224, 4.44.3, 14.65.2).   **expositos se tanto pauciores integris hostium uiribus** 'that despite being greatly
inferior in numbers, they had been exposed to the full force of the enemy'. The past
participle *expositos* leaves the agent unclear, but the context suggests the soldiers mean
that Valens (not Caecina) let them down. Even immediately afterwards, the Vitellians
focus on the Othonian general Suetonius Paulinus, rather than on Caecina, to explain
the battle's outcome (2.26.2). Critics disagree over the point of comparison in *tanto
pauciores*. Does T. mean that Caecina's men are inferior in numbers relative to Valens'
men or to the enemy Othonians? Morgan (1996b) 363 argues that the contrast is primarily with Valens' army, although this is unclear until the end of the sentence. The
key lies in how one takes *integris*, whether 'complete' (*OLD integer* 5) or 'having suffered
no losses' (*OLD integer* 9); 'fresh' (*OLD integer* 1) is possible, but less likely, as Paulinus

himself called his soldiers *fessi* (2.26.2). It seems best to take *integris* as 'complete' and to see *tanto pauciores* as contrasting Caecina's men and the enemy Othonians. Caecina's soldiers complain that, despite their inferior numbers, they have been rashly exposed to the full force of the enemy, but implicit in *integris*, 'complete', is the reason why their numbers are inferior (and another cause for complaint): Valens' sluggish response means that the two wings of the Vitellian army have not been reunited.   **in suam excusationem** '(speaking) to excuse themselves'. T. could have written *se excusantes*, but avoids the obvious for *uariatio*: a verb of speaking is to be understood with *in* indicating purpose (20.1n. *in nullius iniuriam*). There is deliberate inconcinnity with the following participle *attollentes*, to which the prepositional phrase corresponds.   **et aduentantium robur per adulationem attollentes** 'and magnifying by flattery the strength of the reinforcements'. The flattery is delicately judged. By exaggerating the size of Valens' army, Caecina's soldiers cast the reinforcements as their (belated) saviours, but also celebrate their own bravery, as a numerically smaller force holding out in a tricky spot. Their *adulatio* may have worked too well: Valens later boasts of having 'saved' Caecina after Castores (2.93.2). Cf. *augendo rumoribus uirtutem copiasque hostium, quo amissi praesidii dedecus lenirent* (3.61.2).   **despectarentur** is first used in this metaphorical sense here (again at *A.* 2.43.3), a choice alternative to *contemno* (*TLL* s.v *despecto* 736.35).   **prope duplicatus legionum auxiliorumque numerus erat Valenti:** Caecina originally had *c.* 15–16,000 and Valens 20,000 men (20.2n. *magno terrore*), but Caecina had lost some men in the battles fought so far in northern Italy.   **super benignitatem animi:** *super* = *praeter* (8.1n. *super . . . oris*). *benignitas* is a striking characteristic, attributed elsewhere by T. to the gods (4.85.2, *A.* 11.15.2, 12.43.2, 14.6.2) or *fortuna* (*A.* 13.41.4). The focus on *animus* will form a familiar pairing with *corpus* (93.1n. *corpus . . . imminuebant*).   **qua promptior habebatur** 'which they thought he readier to show'.   **uigore . . . proceritate . . . fauore =** causal ablatives. T. often uses *et* to introduce one or more items after asyndeton (G-G 390–1, Draeger (1882) §106, §140, Goodyear (1981) 430), a feature liked by Cato, Varro and Sallust, though Cicero avoids it (Kroll (1927) 282–3). The expression *uigore aetatis* is Livian (6.23.9; cf. *uiget aetas* Sall. *Cat.* 20.10). T. repeatedly emphasises Caecina's appearance (1.53.1, 2.20.1, 3.31.4) and huge body (1.53.1; also Plut. *Oth.* 6.6). His youthful vigour contrasts sharply with Valens, the *senex prodigus* (1.66.2), who falls ill later in the year (2.99.1). The *eloquentia corporis* (Cic. *Orat.* 55; Quint. 11.3.1) is potentially expressive: an orator can learn tricks, but some people are just physically impressive. The combination *inanis fauor* is only here (*TLL* s.v. *favor* 385.63), but the soldiers' fickle *fauor* towards their general is already clear when Valens emerges from hiding to *gaudium miseratio fauor* (2.29.3), only to be ignored by his men (2.30.1).

30.3 aemulatio: 4.4n.   **foedum ac maculosum:** T. uses similar language for popular opinion about Fonteius Capito (*auaritia et libidine foedum ac maculosum* 1.7.2; cf. 3.38.2, *A.* 13.33.2) and endorses Caecina's charge about Valens' dirty and dishonest ways (involving sexual and financial misconduct) in the earlier narrative. On the march to the Alps, Valens *quotiens pecuniae materia deesset, stupris et adulteriis exorabatur* (1.66.3). Mud continued to stick. As Vitellius' principate collapsed, Valens was believed *rapere illicitas uoluptates adulteriisque ac stupris polluere hospitum domus* (3.41.1). In T.'s damning obituary Valens is *procax moribus* and under Nero acted in farces *scite magis quam probe* (3.62.2). **tumidum ac uanum:** the surrounding narrative also endorses this insult, but it hardly gives Valens the *fama urbanitatis* which he sought (3.62.2). Caecina appears self-obsessed, both in his fears that he will seem *irrisus ac uanus* (2.22.3) and in his desire *reciperare gloriam* (2.24.1). The Flavian soldiers later charge him with *superbia* and *saeuitia* (3.31.4). **irridebant:** pl. verb with two singular subjects (24.3n. *Paulinus . . . Celsus sumpsere*). **condito odio:** *condere odium* is only here. 'The imagery (like that of *iram condiderat*, of Tiberius at *A.* 2.28.1) is surely taken from the laying down of wine. Once the enmity has matured, it will reappear (2.92–93)' (Morgan (1996b) 364 n.14). **eandem utilitatem fouere:** the combination occurs only here (*TLL* s.v. *foueo* 1223.78). The temporary suppression of Caecina and Valens' mutual dislike for the sake of the campaign recalls a similar situation between Vespasian and Mucianus, engineered by Titus *communi utilitate* (2.5.2). The *utilitas* bonding Caecina and Valens is ultimately self-serving (cf. *quamquam fas sit priuata odia publicis utilitatibus remittere, A.* 1.10.3) and they have no equivalent of Titus to intervene. **crebris epistulis:** insulting letters and proclamations were standard in civil war (Lendon (1997) 119). Caecina and Valens no doubt wrote to the Othonian commanders trying to undermine their loyalty (Murison (1993) 94): a later incident (2.41.1) raises the possibility that they succeeded. Otho and Vitellius were also exchanging increasingly abusive letters at this time (1.74.1, Plut. *Oth.* 4.5). Octavian and Antony had done the same (Ov. *Pont.* 1.1.23, Plut. *Ant.* 75.1, 78.3, Suet. *Aug.* 7.1, 16.2, 63.2, 69.2, Tac. *A.* 4.34.5, Dio 50.1; Scott (1933)). When Cocceius tried to mediate between Antony and Octavian, Antony supposedly replied: 'Now what could we write to one another, since we are enemies, except mutual taunts?' (App. *BC* 5.60). It was always possible for such letters to be forged (App. *BC* 5.29). **sine respectu ueniae** 'without any consideration for the possibility of future pardon'. **probra Othoni:** Otho was potentially open to slurs about his effeminacy (1.22.1, 1.30.1), hedonism (1.30.1, 1.50.1, 2.31.1) and association with Nero (1.30.1, 1.78.2). It rarely mattered whether such insults were based on fact, as Rome had a deeply-entrenched culture of colourful invective. The worst elements of the propaganda against Otho lie relatively dormant in the literary tradition because Vespasian set himself up as Otho's avenger, and fought directly against Vitellius (Ash (1999) 87). Traces remain in Juvenal, Martial and Suetonius. **cum duces partium Othonis . . . abstinerent:** of course Otho still received abusive letters about Vitellius. On the night before his suicide, we see him burning them to spare their authors from being punished by the victors (2.48.1, Suet. *Otho* 10.2, Dio 64.15), a gesture also made by Octavian (App. *BC* 5.132). **quamuis uberrima conuiciorum in Vitellium materia:** a powerful snub, based on *praeteritio* and an agricultural metaphor, liked by T. (cf. *D.* 37.6, 1.1.4; cf. 21.4n. *uberioribus . . . probris*). *quamuis* + the superlative (rare, GL §609 n.2) is also at 3.28 (*quamuis pessimo flagitio*). The *materia* for insulting Vitellius included his drunkenness and gluttony (Jos. *BJ* 4.651, Plut. *Galb.* 22.11, Plin. *Nat.* 35.163, Dio 65.2, Suet. *Vit.* 13.2, T. *H.* 1.62.2, 2.62.1) and association with Nero (Suet. *Vit.* 4, 11.2, Dio 65.7.3, T. *H.* 2.95.1, Phil. *Vit. Apol.* 7.33,

SHA *Elagabalus* 1.1). Plutarch has a similar snub, but applies it to both men ([they wrote] 'not telling lies, but it was foolish and ridiculous for one to mock the other with reproaches which applied to both men' *Oth.* 4.5).

31.1 sane often 'indicates a concession . . . , a rhetorical device used as a foil, *reculer pour mieux sauter*' (WM 101). It can introduce a clause with a sting in the tail (G-G 1429–30 B), but sometimes (as here) just confirms a point from the author's perspective (G-G 1429 A).   **egregiam . . . famam:** Otho's suicide (2.46–50) is a *facinus . . . egregium* that earned him *bona fama* (50.1).   **Otho . . . Vitellius . . . Vitellii . . . Othonis . . . huic** (sc. *Othoni*) **. . . illi** (sc. *Vitellio*) **. . . Vitellius . . . Otho:** the comparisons in the chapter are elegantly organised in an alternating chiastic pattern of names in different cases, beginning and ending with Otho.   **flagitiosissimam:** this superlative adj. (used sparingly) is only in this book (also 2.37.2, 2.50.1). In Vitellius' death (3.84.4–86 with Levene (1997)), T. includes degrading aspects such as the *pudenda latebra* (3.84.4) and *laniata ueste* (3.84.5), but also admirable moments, such as Vitellius' fine last words. **meruere:** pl. verb with two singular subjects (24.3n. *Paulinus . . . Celsus sumpsere*). **Vitellii ignauae uoluptates** 'the slothful pleasures of Vitellius'. The combination occurs only here (*TLL* s.v. *ignauus* 281.4–6), but cf. *ignauus amor* (Stat. *Silu.* 3.2.99) and *ignauum corrumpant otia corpus* (Ov. *Pont.* 1.5.5). The adj. applies more strictly to Vitellius than to his pleasures, a form of hypallage (5.2n. *uicinis . . . administrationibus*).   **Othonis flagrantissimae libidines timebantur:** the metaphor of fire is applied to Otho again: *flagrantissimus in amicitia Neronis habebatur* (*A.* 13.45.4). Before seizing power, Otho is cast as greedy for *adulteria matrimonia ceterasque regnorum libidines* (1.22.1), while Piso scorns his daydreams about *stupra nunc et comissationes et feminarum coetus* (1.30.1). Once Otho is *princeps*, Rome fears his *ueteres . . . mores* (1.50.1), and dreads his *falsae uirtutes et uitia reditura* (1.71.1) when he behaves well. In the parallel tradition Otho's initial good conduct as emperor quells earlier fears (Plut. *Oth.* 1.5).   **terrorem atque odium:** this inauspicious pair recalls Accius' tag about the archetypal tyrant's attitude to his people, *oderint dum metuant* 'let them hate me as long as they fear me' (Cic. *Off.* 1.28.97, *Sest.* 48.102, *Phil.* 1.14.34, Sen. *De ira* 1.20.4, *Clem.* 1.12.4, 2.2.2, Suet. *Cal.* 30.1).   **caedes Galbae:** there are many versions (1.41, Plut. *Galb.* 27.1–4, Suet. *Gal.* 19.2–20, Dio 64.6).   **contra illi initium belli nemo imputabat:** yet Otho makes this very accusation: *ciuile bellum a Vitellio coepit* (2.47.2). The idea that nobody accused Vitellius of starting the war initially seems positive, but reminds us that he was passive and pushed to act by his generals (*segne ingenium* 1.52.4). Reluctant challengers claiming that the soldiers forced them to intervene is a leitmotiv of this civil war. So, Otho says that the soldiers took him to the camp against his will (Dio 64.8; Vespasian uses the same line, Jos. *BJ* 4.601–4). Claudius is the *locus classicus* (Suet. *Cl.* 10).   **uentre et gula** 'because of his gluttonous appetite'. The deployment of two nouns, both used selectively by T. (also paired by the younger Sen., Quint. and Mart.), adds impact to the metonymy. Sallust has *gula* (4×), but Liv. and Caes. avoid it: T. uses it once more (*irritamenta gulae*, 2.62.1), again about Vitellius' greed, while *uenter* is only here in the *H.* (2× in *A.*: 3.52.1, 14.8.5). These prosaic nouns pull against the elevated diction of history and degrade Vitellius as a character ('*tapeinosis*', Quint.

8.3.48). On sending Vitellius to govern Lower Germany, Galba apparently said that *posse prouincialibus copiis profundam gulam eius expleri* (Suet. *Vit.* 7.1; Ash (1999) 96–105 for his gluttony).   **sibi inhonestus . . . ducebatur:** *sibi* is balanced by *rei publicae* in the next clause. It is warped that onlookers feel shame that Vitellius himself does not. Cicero urges the need to hide one's appetites for modesty's sake: *si quis est paulo ad uoluptates propensior . . . occultat et dissimulat appetitum uoluptatis propter uerecundiam (Off.* 1.30.105). Piso contrasts Otho's guilt-free indulgence and the collective shame: *libido ac uoluptates penes ipsum sit, rubor ac dedecus penes omnes* (1.30.1).   **luxu saeuitia audacia:** the causal ablatives in asyndeton after the more expansive *uentre et gula* show *uariatio.* Otho's *luxus* (11.3n. *nec . . . luxu iter*) included putting perfume on his feet (Plin. *Nat.* 13.22).

31.2–33 OTHO'S COUNCIL OF WAR

Council scenes proliferate in the *H.* (extensive ones at 1.32–3, 3.1–2; abridged ones at 2.1.3, 2.16.2, 2.81.3) and Suetonius Paulinus' speech at the Othonian council of war on *c.* 10 Apr. (Murison (1993) 95) is the first of three in this book. Unlike the other two speeches by Otho (2.47) and Mucianus (2.76–7), Paulinus' words are given in *oratio obliqua.* This does not intrinsically make it less vivid than a speech in *oratio recta* (Laird (1999) 138–43), but it is clear from the content of the speech that Paulinus is a much less fiery and successful orator than the Flavian general Antonius Primus, whose speech (3.2) at the Flavian council of war T. shapes in such a way that readers must compare the two (Courbaud (1918) 112–13). Paulinus divides his speech in two, focusing first on the strengths of Vitellius' army (2.32.1) and then elaborating the Othonian position (2.32.2). Primus mirrors this structure, first outlining the situation for the Vitellians (3.2.1–2) and then turning to the Flavians (3.2.3–4), but he invests his words with powerful metaphors, vivid images and rhetorical questions, speaking *flagrans oculis, truci uoce* (3.3). The two men use some of the same arguments, but paradoxically, Primus 'seems to answer Paulinus' [speech] and comes to the opposite conclusions from the same reasons' (Keitel (1991) 2793).

    T. gives Paulinus' arguments extensively and puts them first, despite Otho's brother Titianus being overall commander (2.23.5) and Licinius Proculus holding real power (2.39.1). In contrast Plutarch (*Oth.* 8.2) summarises the views of Titianus and Proculus first, and only then gives Paulinus' arguments. T.'s arrangement (and the fact that he skims over the counter-arguments of Titianus and Proculus) vividly draws out Otho's almost perverse impatience: after all, Paulinus does not want an extensive delay, but simply suggests waiting a few days until reinforcements from Moesia arrive *(paucis diebus* 2.32.2). This they poignantly do just in time to miss the final battle *(praemissi e Moesia* 2.46.3). Although the common soldiers understandably mistrust Otho's immediate circle of advisers for leading him astray, Otho himself, *pronus ad decertandum* (2.33.1), must bear some blame. So Paulinus' speech sets up a dominant and powerful theme: Otho's defeat was far from inevitable.

    Although Paulinus is a less brilliant orator than Primus, the substance of his argument is cast in an interesting light by Galba's council scene. This also hinges on the question of immediate action or delay (1.32.2–33). After the advocates of speed prevail, Galba, *nec diutius . . . cunctatus* (1.34.1), is dead by the end of the day. T.'s readers also knew that the danger of speed as opposed to delay is a historiographical topos, particularly in a military context (Caes. *Gal.* 5.28–30, Liv. 22.14.4–15, App. *BC* 2.66–7, 2.103, Jos. *BJ* 4.366–78; Ash (1999) 149). So Josephus gives Vespasian some spirited words: 'If anyone thinks that victory without a fight won't taste so sweet, he had better realise that to win success by biding your time is a sounder policy than courting disaster by plunging into battle' (*BJ* 4.372; cf. *bellantibus aliis placuit exspectari*, 2.7.1). Military handbooks too endorse the potential advantages of delay: 'But most important of all, the general should deliberate whether it is expedient for the crisis to be prolonged or fought out more swiftly. For sometimes the enemy hopes that the campaign can be ended quickly, and if it becomes long-drawn-out, is either reduced by hunger, or called back to his own country by his men's homesickness, or through doing nothing significant is compelled to leave in despair' (Veg. 3.9.9). Hasty action can look good, but is pointless if it leads to defeat. In some ways Paulinus recalls Herodotus' 'wise adviser' figure (Lattimore (1939) 24–35, Flower and Marincola (2002) 7). Yet T. adds a twist: Paulinus correctly advocates *mora*, but some of his detailed arguments are distinctly flawed (see below). On 2.32–3, see Keitel (1991) 2792 and especially Herzog (1996) 99–191.

31.2 Coniunctis Caecinae ac Valentis copiis: the close pairing of the names nestling inside an enclosing abl. absolute (marked off by alliteration) aptly expresses the reintegration of the Vitellian army. The generals' names (paired 9× in *H.* 2, but then only mentioned separately) have not been so closely linked since their introduction (*Alienus Caecina et Fabius Valens* 1.52.3). **trahi bellum an fortunam experiri** 'whether the war should be prolonged or fortune should be put to the test'. The two possibilities are balanced by chiasmus, but the second option sounds more attractive than the first. In any case, Otho is predisposed to shun delay (*nec cunctatione opus*, 1.21.2; *nullus cunctationis locus est*, 1.38.2; *ire praecipites et occupare pericula iubet*, 1.40.1; *aspernatus est omnem cunctationem*, 1.89.3). Even his suicide (*festinato exitu* 2.48.2) and burial (*funus maturatum* 2.49.3) are quick. Suetonius has the same phrase (*trahi bellum*, *Otho* 9.1), possibly drawn from the common source. Cf. μεθεῖναι τὰ πράγματα πρὸς τὸ συντυχόν (Plut. *Oth.* 9.2).

32.1 Suetonius Paulinus: 23.4n. Marius Celsus, Salvius Titianus, Licinius Proculus, with Annius Gallus also consulted by messenger (the same group in Plut. *Oth.* 8) also participate in the council (as well as Otho and Paulinus). This selective group contrasts with the more open Flavian councils, where legates, tribunes, centurions and even soldiers attend (2.81.3, 3.3). So, Paulinus' advice should have special weight, as he is the most experienced general in this small council. **ratus** + the acc. (*dignum*) and infinitive (*censere*) + *de*. T. is also careful to describe Paulinus' personal motives during the clash with the Vitellians at Castores (*satis cito incipi uictoriam ratus . . .* 2.25.2). Such touches cast him as forceful and confident. **qua** = abl. of respect with *fama* as its antecedent. **nemo . . . militaris rei callidior habebatur:** T. elsewhere accentuates his *auctoritas* (1.87.2) and *prudentia* (2.39.1), but his recent conduct at Castores raises questions about his reputation. Paulinus' current pre-eminence was no doubt enhanced by Corbulo's enforced suicide late in 66 or early in 67. T. calls Paulinus the *concertator* 'rival' of Corbulo (*A.* 14.29.2).   **illa tempestate:** *tempestas* for *tempus* is 'archaic and poetical, but also firmly domiciled in the historians . . . *qua tempestate* is cited from Coelius Antipater by Cicero in discussion of *inusitata uerba* in prose' (Goodyear (1972) 115; Oakley (1998) 251).   **de toto genere belli** 'about the general conduct of the war' (Fyfe / Levene).   **festinationem hostibus, moram ipsis utilem disseruit:** Antonius Primus argues at the Flavian council of war that *festinationem ipsis utilem, Vitellio exitiosam* (3.2.1). Where Paulinus has two polarised concepts (*festinatio, mora*) linked to the same adj. (*utilis*), Primus uses a single noun (*festinatio*) linked to two polarised adjectives (*utilis, exitiosa*). So Primus, a more fiery orator than Paulinus, eliminates delay from the debate, but Paulinus considers the question from both sides. Paulinus' blanket term *hostes* contrasts with Primus' personal and emotive focus on Vitellius. *mora* is apt advice from the *cunctator natura* (2.25.2), although T. will later consider a more selfish reason for Paulinus' stance (2.37.1).   **exercitum Vitellii . . . nec multum uirium a tergo:** Paulinus opens provocatively, since Vitellius is supposed to be following his two generals *tota mole belli* (1.61.2; *c.* 30,000 men, 20.2n. *magno terrore*). Plutarch's Titianus and Proculus (silent in T.) use precisely this point to advocate a speedy engagement (*Oth.* 8.2; cf. Suet. *Otho* 9.1 for Otho hoping to settle the matter *ante Vitelli aduentum*). The exact timetable of Vitellius' journey from Colonia Agrippinensis to northern Italy is disputed, but he was perhaps near Andematunnum, 518 miles from Cremona (Murison (1993) 144). Is Paulinus twisting the truth or just ill-informed?   **quoniam Galliae tumeant** 'since Gaul was bursting with unrest'. The name of a country is used collectively for its inhabitants (Lebreton (1901) 75–7). T. uses metaphor and metonymy together for impact. Cf. *ciuitates . . . bello tument* (Sen. *Con.* 10.1.8).   **et . . . non** = *neque* (also 2.34.1, 2.56.1).   **deserere Rheni ripam . . . non conducat:** Paulinus may be too optimistic about the Vitellians' concern for foreign affairs. Cf. *conuersis ad ciuile bellum animis externa sine cura habebantur* (1.79.1). Trouble will erupt in Germany when Julius Civilis exploits the diversion of civil war (3.46.1), after Antonius Primus instructs him to create a diversion *tumultus Germanici specie* (4.13.2). Cf. Augustus' fears that the Germans will invade Italy in AD 9 after Varus' disaster (Dio 56.23.1), although in fact they did not even advance to the Rhine (Dio 56.24.1).   **irrupturis tam infestis nationibus:** the abl. absolute with a future participle (not in Cic.) is first in Livy. T. uses it sparingly (2.86.4, 3.56.3, 4.39.3, *A.* 2.80.2, 15.52.2).   **Britannicum militem . . . distineri:** T. calls the legions in Britain (*II Augusta, IX Hispana, XX Valeria*) *Oceano diuisae* (1.9.2), but Vitellius already has many of them with him when he begins his march (1.61.1; cf. 2.57.2, 2.100.1) and later summons further auxiliary reinforcements from Britain (2.97.1; cf. 2.57.1). Since it is now *c.* 10 Apr., crossing the Channel will be less problematic than in winter. Antonius Primus, arguing for speed, stresses the closeness of Britain, divided only *freto* 'by a narrow channel' (3.2.2).   **Hispanias armis non ita redundare:** Galba had taken the *VII Galbiana* with him (1.6.2) and sent it to Pannonia (2.11.1), so only two legions (*VI Victrix, X Gemina*) remained in Spain. *redundo* 'abound in' (*OLD* 8) suggests the metaphor of water (also 2.93.1: cf. Cic. *Pis.* 11.25, *Prov.* 31). Again, Primus depicts

Spain differently, as rich in resources (*uiros equos tributa*, 3.2.2).   **prouinciam Nar-bonensem . . . contremuisse:** Paulinus perhaps exaggerates the impact of the Othonian victory (2.14–15). Applying the compound *contremesco* to a country is Sallustian (*quo metu Italia omnis contremuerat, Jug.* 114.2; cf. Lucr. 3.835) and suggests personification. Ennius uses the simple form in this way: *Africa terribili tremit horrida terra tumultu* (*A.* 309 Sk.).   **clausam Alpibus . . . transpadanam Italiam:** Galba's soldiers from Spain complain about struggling over the Alps (1.23.2), but the mountains hardly cause trouble to the Vitellians, despite the wintry conditions (1.70.3, 2.11.2). The Transpadane region, fertile in itself, was accessible to imports via the Po (17.1n. *quantum . . . urbium*), so Paulinus' claim is questionable. The argument about the Vitellians being penned in between the Alps and the Po was probably in the common source: *quando et fame et angustiis locorum urgeretur hostis* (Suet. *Otho* 9.1).   **ipso transitu exercitus uastam** 'laid waste by the very passage of their army': *uastus* in this sense (*OLD* 1c) is in Plautus and Accius, but Livy has it in prose (10.12.8). T. does not suggest elsewhere that the Vitellians ravaged the Transpadane region through military attacks (cf. the Othonians in the Maritime Alps, 2.12.2), but Paulinus is more likely to mean the drain on resources (food and water) by the passage of a large army, a Herodotean motif (7.119–120, 187).   **non frumentum . . . exercitui:** the parallel tradition also says that the Vitellian soldiers lacked food (*fames*, Suet. *Otho* 9.1), but without attributing this to a named speaker. Plutarch formulates Paulinus' argument differently: the passing of time would leave the Vitellians short of supplies in hostile territory (*Oth.* 8.5), but the implication is that this is not a problem now. Cf. Pompey's argument for postponing battle at Pharsalus: Caesar only wants to fight because he lacks supplies (App. *BC* 2.67). Vegetius suggests that a council of war should specifically consider 'which side has more food or lacks it, for hunger, they say, fights from within, and often conquers without a blow' (3.9.8; cf. Caes. *Civ.* 1.72.1, Fron. *Str.* 4.7.1, Amm. 25.7.4).   **nec exercitum sine copiis retineri posse:** Paulinus, concerned with his own reputation, tends to inject his speech with *sententiae* when not addressing the tactics of the immediate campaign (*multa bella impetu ualida per taedia et moras euanuisse* 2.32.1; *pecuniam, inter ciuiles discordias ferro ualidiorem* 2.32.2). Quintilian advises that *sententiae* must not be used too often or be obviously false, and that the speaker's character should add weight to the concept (8.5.7–8).   **atrocissimum:** the Batavian auxiliaries are turbulent (27.2n. *superbe agebant*), but potentially invaluable in battle (28.2n. *fortissimorum . . . auxilio*).   **fluxis corporibus mutationem soli caelique haud toleraturos** '[that the Germans] as their bodies wilt, will be unable to tolerate the change of climate and weather'. The idea that northern constitutions cannot tolerate Mediterranean heat (environmental determinism) is a topos (Liv. 5.48.3, 27.48.17, 34.47.5, 35.5.7, 38.17.7, Dion. Hal. 14.8, Plut. *Cam.* 28.2, *Mar.* 26.8, T. *G.* 4.3, Florus 1.38.13, Polyaen. 8.10.3, with Kremer (1994) 33–4). T. may allude to Livy: *Gallorum quidem, etiam <u>corpora</u> intolerantissima laboris atque aestus <u>fluere</u>* (10.28.4). Paulinus is right (2.93.1): the German Vitellians will be unable to stand the summer heat in Rome.   **multa bella impetu ualida per taedia et moras euanuisse** 'that many campaigns which were forceful at the first onset had dwindled to nothing through tedious delays'. This *sententia* gains in point after Paulinus' observation about the German Vitellians. The other standard cliché about northern fighters involves initial ferocity in battle, but no staying power (14.3n. *incaute*): Paulinus implies that the Vitellians will fight their whole campaign in this way. The (decelerating) hendiadys *per taedia et moras* is apt for a *sententia* about delay; and the pl. nouns enhance this effect (the pl. of *taedium* is only here and at *A.* 4.41.3). *bella + euanuisse* are combined only here (*TLL* s.v. *bellum* 1833.19).

32.2 contra is the 'hinge' of the speech, as Paulinus turns from the Vitellian to the Othonian situation.   **opulenta** is 'rich in resources', but it may antici-pate the emphasis on *pecunia* that follows.   **Pannoniam Moesiam Dalmatiam Orientem:** the asyndeton buoyantly celebrates the range of places supporting Otho (cf. *iurasse in eum Dalmatiae ac Pannoniae et Moesiae legiones* 1.76.1, 2.11.1), but the sweep-ing *Oriens* reveals with tragic irony a gap in Paulinus' understanding: the eastern troops already favour Vespasian (2.6.2).   **cum integris exercitibus** 'with their fresh armies'; i.e. the *VII Galbiana* and *XIII Gemina* from Pannonia, the *XI Clau-dia* and *XIV Gemina* from Dalmatia (11.1n. *quattuor legiones* and *rebellione Britanniae compressa*), and the *III Gallica, VII Claudia* and *VIII Augusta* from Moesia. Only the *XIII Gemina* will be there at the final battle. Whether or not three whole legions were really en route from Moesia is unclear. Suetonius specifies only vexillations of 2,000 men from each legion (*Ves.* 6.2), but an advance guard from Moesia tells Otho shortly before his suicide that the legions had reached Aquileia (2.46.1). The three legions had apparently returned to Moesia when they declared for Vespasian (2.85.1).   **caput rerum urbem:** 'the metaphor *caput / corpus* for Rome and her empire appears precisely in the period of Augustus' (Nicolet (1991) 9).   **numquam obscura nomina, etiam si aliquando obumbrentur:** Paulinus awkwardly challenges a dominant theme in T., that such names (SPQR) are irrelevant in a power struggle based on military dominance: *res publica et senatus et populus uacua nomina* (1.30.2), *senatus populique Romani obliterata iam nomina* (1.55.4); cf. Caesar's assertion that *nihil esse rem publicam, appellationem modo sine corpore ac specie* (Suet. *Jul.* 77). Paulinus' qualifying protasis almost suggests that he does not believe his own words, but per-haps he is trying to appeal to Otho, whose own speech referred to the senate as *caput imperii et decora omnium prouinciarum* (1.84.3). T. only uses *obumbro* here, but the metaphor of veiling something in shadows retroactively draws out the metaphori-cal tinge (*OLD* 1) of *obscura* 'insignificant' (*OLD* 5).   **immensam pecuniam . . . ferro ualidiorem:** Mucianus also stresses money's importance in civil war, but uses a bolder metaphor (*eos esse belli ciuilis neruos* 2.84.1). Paulinus degradingly places money above valour as a defence mechanism, but it reflects the corrupt times that a general can even make such an argument: cf. T. on Roman ancestors, *apud quos uirtute quam pecunia res Romana melius stetit* (2.69.2). Ovid is a powerful intertext: *iamque nocens ferrum ferroque nocentius aurum | prodierat: prodit bellum, quod pugnat utroque* (*Met.* 1.141–2; Herzog (1996) 147).   **corpora militum aut Italiae sueta aut aestibus** 'that the soldiers' constitutions were accustomed either to Italy or to (other) hot climates'. Roman soldiers are often cast as resilient to heat (Plut. *Cat. Ma.* 20.6, Liv. 5.6.4), but the east could still debilitate by other means (4.4n. *segnitiam*). Environmental determinism held that inhabitants of Italy, geographically located in a temperate central region, were physically and mentally well-balanced (Vitr. 6.1.3–11, Virg. *G.* 2.167–72, Plin *Nat.* 37.201) and better able than those on the extremes to tolerate excessive cold and heat (32.1n. *fluxis corporibus*). **obiacere flumen Padum** 'that the river Po served as a barrier'. The Po has defensive potential (11.2n. *ad . . . ripas*), but Caecina easily crossed it twice (2.20.2, 2.22.3), undermining Paulinus' point; and given evocation of ethnographical stereotypes, he risks activating another i.e. Germans as talented swimmers (17.2n. *Batauos*). **tutas uiris murisque urbes . . . Placentiae defensione:** this is a peculiar conclusion to draw. Placentia's walls were imperfect (18.1n. *intra munimenta*) and her inhabitants apparently did not help the Othonians against the Vitellian attackers (2.20.2–22). Yet the assertion does reflect the growing confidence of the Othonians after that encounter (2.17–20.1). **exploratum:** sc. *esse.* **proinde duceret bellum** 'therefore Otho should prolong the war'. **paucis diebus quartam decimam legionem . . . adfore:** cf. *praecipui fama* (11.1). Paulinus saves for a dramatic coda his most crucial argument about the famous *XIV Gemina* (11.1n. *quattuor legiones* and *rebellione Britanniae compressa*), about to arrive. *paucis diebus* does not over-dramatise: some *quartadecimani* feature in the final battle of Bedriacum (2.43.2), so at least a vexillation from this legion had arrived, and the main force only just missed it (2.54.1). **auctis uiribus:** cf. the Othonian soldiers' plea to Otho that *superesse adhuc nouas uires* (2.46.1). The expression is Livian (Oakley (1998) 107).

33.1 idem placere: acc. + inf. after *rettulerant.* **lapsu equi afflicto:** a hazard for generals on campaign (cf. Liv. 22.3.11). Tiberius' brother Drusus died after such a fall (Liv. *Per.* 142), either from gangrene or internal injuries. T. has lofty language (*infrenis equi lapsu*, Virg. *A.* 10.750) for a degrading fall (again, *lapsu equi prostratus* 4.34.5). Acquiring the ability to handle a horse was an important part of military training (Veg. 1.18 with Hyland (1990) 111–21). On a horse's ideal qualities, see Col. *Rust.* 6.29.2–4, Virg. *G.* 3.79–88. **missi, qui consilium eius sciscitarentur:** Plutarch also says that Gallus was consulted, specifying that his advice was 'not to hurry, but to await the force from Moesia, which was already on the road' (*Oth.* 8.6). **Otho pronus ad decertandum:** Suetonius has similar phrasing, but omits the whole council scene (*decertare statuit, Otho.* 9.1). *decerto* (4× in Liv., including *animi . . . obstinati ad decertandum fuerant*, 6.3.9) is only twice in T. (also *A.* 15.7.2). Otho's predisposition to fight detracts from his status as a competent commander: cf. Aemilius Paulus' maxim that a good general should avoid a pitched battle unless utmost necessity or opportunity presented itself (Gell. 13.3.6). **frater eius Titianus et praefectus praetorii Proculus:** *frater* and *praefectus* precede (rather than follow) the names only here. Through emphatic word-order, T. casts doubts on whether the fraternal relationship or the urban prefecture make Titianus (23.5n.) and Proculus as well qualified to give advice as the three experienced generals; and Titianus, as a brother, should have been more sensitive about Otho's best interests. Proculus was apparently ill-equipped to give strategic advice on this scale. Although he was good at urban garrison duty (*urbanae militiae impiger*), he was also *bellorum insolens* and hostile to Paulinus, Celsus and

Gallus (1.87.2). The praetorian soldiers themselves chose him as prefect (1.46.1): 'T. gives the impression that friendship with Otho was his only recommendation for the job' (Damon (2003) 191). Yet he still claimed that he actively betrayed Otho (2.60.1). Two equestrians usually served as praetorian prefect (e.g. Afranius Burrus and Ofonius Tigellinus under Nero). Since Tiberius' principate, they had controlled twelve cohorts (either 500 or 1000 men each) in a permanent camp between the Colline and Viminal gates (MW 87–8, Campbell (1984) 109–20, Keppie (1984) 153–4). The position attracted ambitious men. When Galba dismissed the praetorian prefect Nymphidius Sabinus, he plotted to seize power, but was killed by his own soldiers (1.5, Plut. *Galb.* 13–14). **imperitia properantes** 'impetuous through inexperience'. The causal abl. *imperitia* is a damning touch absent from Plutarch's version of the council. The participle *properantes* sharply aligns the pair against Paulinus, the *cunctator natura* (2.25.2). **fortunam et deos et numen Othonis:** the words are superficially soothing, but *fortuna*, an alluring but fickle mistress for the Othonians (12.1n. *Blandiebatur . . . fortuna*), has already been linked with the Flavian rise to power (1.1n. *struebat . . . imperio*). Otho wryly claims to have come to know *fortuna* after his defeat: *experti in uicem sumus ego ac fortuna* (2.47.1). Gods in T. are often angry (1.38.1, 2.38.2, 5.25.3) and vengeful (1.3.2, 5.24.2), but whatever T.'s personal beliefs, his gods can eloquently indicate manipulation by humans (1.38.1, 3.10.4) or signal an ignorant individual's impending doom (*Galba . . . fatigabat alieni iam imperii deos* 1.29.1; cf. 2.70.4). Here Titianus and Proculus manipulate the doomed protagonist Otho, whose *numen* will soon be defunct. What *numen* means here is debatable (*RE* XVII 1273–91 offers a useful survey). Most take it as 'divine power exercised on Otho's behalf' (*OLD* 3b) i.e. his protecting genius, 'the generative power of a man, . . . his divine protector from birth to death' (Weinstock (1971) 205); and the peculiar omen of the bird (2.50.2) perhaps symbolises this. Yet *numen Othonis* may also have a hybristic undercurrent, claiming (prematurely?) the divine power residing in Otho. Only under Augustus was *numen* ascribed to individuals (Ov. *Tr.* 3.8.13, *Pont.* 3.1.163), while Rome even had an *ara numinis Augusti*. T. refers to Augustus' *numen* being assailed (*A.* 1.73.2, 3.66.1; cf. *NVMINI AVGVSTI VOTVM SVSCEPTVM*, *CIL* XII 4333), but Otho has only had three months to establish his imperial credentials. Cf. the pretender Mariccus, who *prouocare arma Romana simulatione numinum ausus est* (2.61). Plutarch says that initially the Roman aristocracy considered Otho ἢ Ποινῆς ἢ παλαμναίου δαίμονος 'either a genius of retribution or an avenging spirit' (*Oth.* 1.5). **adesse consiliis, adfore conatibus:** *praesens* (*RE* XVII 1289) is a common epithet for *numen* and *deus*, so the verbs are apt. The asyndeton and anaphora (with interlinked alliteration and assonance) nicely suggest the speakers' heightened emotions. Both devices feature together again in animated speeches: *mansisse . . . mansisse . . . mansuram fuisse* (1.50.3), *moriendum uictis, moriendum deditis* (3.66.5). **neu** adding a final clause (GL §543.4) is the equivalent of *et ne*, an Ovidian twist. *neue* or *neu* was originally only used in a *subordinate* clause to co-ordinate an introductory final clause (whether positive or negative) and an additional negative final clause. Yet in Ovid *neu* links two *main* clauses, with the negation belonging to the subordinate part of the second main clause (*Met.* 4.716 with Bömer (1976) 358; *OLD neue* 2b).   **in**

adulationem concesserant 'they had sunk to flattery'. Yet a council of war needed 'an atmosphere from which all flattery, which does so much harm, has been banished' (Veg. 3.9.4).

33.2 Postquam pugnari placitum: sc. *est*. Alliteration underscores the forceful decision, while the impersonal passive verb (with ellipse) heightens the sense of speed (cf. 15.1n. *trepidatum*).   **interesse pugnae . . . an seponi:** ancient military handbooks (Onas. *Strat.* 33.4) often ask whether generals should participate in the fighting or hold back to oversee the strategy of the battle (Goldsworthy (1996) 150–63). Commanders can simultaneously serve as soldier and general, though it is often risky (Sall. *Cat.* 20.16, 60.4, Caes. *Gal.* 5.33.2, Suet. *Aug.* 10.4, Luc. 7.87–8, App. *BC* 2.57, [Caes] *Alex.* 21.1, Curt. 3.11.7, T. *H.* 4.66.2; cf. 15.2n. *telis obruuntur*). Otho will play neither role, despite the council's current concern. *seponi* occurs in descriptions of Otho's removal to Lusitania before he became *princeps* (*seposuit* 1.13.3, *sepositus est* Suet. *Otho* 3.2).   **imperatorem:** 'a term which strategically straddles that ambivalent divide betweem "victorious general" and "reigning emperor"' (Beard (2003) 554). T. pointedly accentuates the *princeps*' military dimension just when the council considers whether to withdraw Otho from the fighting (with similar irony used of Galba: *imperatorem suum inermem et senem* 1.40.2).   **foret:** *foret* for *esset* (14.3n. *deletae . . . forent*). **obiectare periculis:** also at Sall. *Jug.* 7.1, Virg. *A.* 2.751, Amm. 21.13.2.   **idem illi . . . auctores:** *idem* = *iidem* by synizesis (GL §103.2, §727). T. substitutes a periphrasis for proper names (*pronominatio* or *antonomasia*; Lausberg (1998) §580), condemning Titianus and Proculus without interrupting the flow of the narrative. Otho receives good advice, but stubbornly rejects it: cf. *uideo meliora proboque | deteriora sequor* (Ov. *Met.* 7.20–1).   **perpulere** 'prevailed over him', sc. *eum*.   **Brixellum** was *c.* 20 miles south of Bedriacum, where the council was taking place. Otho probably arrived there on *c.* 8 Apr. (Murison (1993) 95, 107, Plut. *Oth.* 5.5), but T. first mentions the base now for dramatic effect. There were strategic reasons for choosing it: 'Brixellum was also in a commanding position for the line of the *Via Aemilia* to Rome, and the road from the Danube' (Shotter (1993) 153).   **dubiis proeliorum exemptus:** *OLD dubius* 9a for the neuter used as a substantive, although the pl. is unusual. Emperors were expected, despite the risks, to take part in military campaigns. So, Tiberius is criticised for not personally suppressing the mutinies in Germany and Pannonia, despite being resolved *neque se remque publicam in casum dare* (*A.* 1.47.1), and Claudius feels obliged to go over to Britain, albeit only for 16 days (Dio 60.23.1). Otho himself had little experience of warfare. For ten years under Nero he was governor of Lusitania, a province with no legionary garrison (1.13.3–4, *A.* 13.46.3, Suet. *Otho* 3.2).   **summae rerum et imperii** 'the supreme control of the campaign and of the empire' (Fyfe / Levene).

33.3 is primus dies . . . afflixit: T. personifies *dies* (22.1n. *uixdum orto die* for the gender) again (*Agr.* 38.2, *H.* 4.29.3, 4.62.2, *A.* 1.49.1, 14.41.1). The notion of a dramatic *peripeteia* on a single day derives from epic (Hom. *Il.* 19.294, 21.100, 22.212, Virg. *A.* 2.249, 324, 4.169, 9.759, Luc. 6.312, 7.195; cf. Ov. *Fast.* 2.570). Yet *primus* sets up a *peripeteia* in 'slow motion', extending painfully between the council (*c.* 10 Apr.) and the final battle (14 Apr.). The contrast between the protagonists in the text, unaware of their looming fate, and the knowledgeable narrator and readers is powerful (cf. *Veientes, ignari se iam a suis uatibus . . . proditos seque ultimum illum diem agere,* Liv. 5.21.5). Plut. *Oth.* 10.1 acknowledges Otho's mistake in going to Brixellum, but does not have the *primus dies* (*uel sim.*) device (cf. Oakley (1997) 599).   **praetoriarum cohortium . . . ualida manus:** the praetorians are Otho's special soldiers (8.2n. *dextras . . . ferentem*), in the parallel tradition apparently keen to fight as they craved a return to their pampered life in Rome (Plut. *Oth.* 9.1).   **remanentium fractus animus:** sc. *est.* In T. the immediate collapse of Othonian morale even before the battle differs from Plutarch, who identifies a problem, but locates it as still in the future. Plutarch suggests that Otho's absence removes the shame and rivalry, which his soldiers would have felt on the battlefield, if he had been watching (*Oth.* 10.1; cf. 12.2n. *in fuga flagitium*).   **quando** for *quoniam* is 'an artificial usage rarely found in the ordinary prose of either the Republic or early Empire' (Adams (1972) 361).   **Otho . . . non nisi militibus credit:** the strong symbiotic relationship between Otho and his soldiers will be a central theme, but so far T. has largely elaborated the soldiers' enthusiasm for Otho (not *vice versa*). So, Otho acknowledges their extraordinary affection for him, which he tries to keep in check (*ueni postulaturus . . . erga me modum caritatis* 1.83.2). Whether Otho really trusted only his soldiers is unclear: he did suspect Paulinus, Celsus and Gallus (2.23.4), but Titianus (2.23.5; cf. 2.39.1) and Proculus (*plurima fides . . . Proculo* 1.87.2; cf. 2.39.1) apparently did not forfeit his trust. T. perhaps thinks ahead to Otho's paradoxical suicide, motivated in part by altruistic concern for his soldiers (2.47.1). With *cui uni,* cf. *uni Antonio apertae militum aures* (3.10.3).   **imperia ducum** 'the authority of the commanders'. Otho continued to manage the campaign (2.36.2, 2.40), but his officers' ability to implement his orders was compromised.   **in incerto reliquerat:** cf. *in incerto relictum sit* (Liv. 8.6.3). *in* (*OLD in* 37) + the abl. of the neuter singular adj. functions as a predicate, as *spes et praemia in ambiguo* (2.45.3), as often in T., Livy and Ovid.

34–36 BATTLE ON THE RIVER PO

This whole controversial sequence has exposed T. to charges of being a bad military historian, with debate concentrating largely on the Vitellians *transitum Padi simulantes* (34.1n.). Is T. right that Caecina and Valens only pretend to cross the Po from the north bank of the river, or is it a serious attempt? In either event, what is their agenda? Part of the problem is that the operation is abruptly abandoned when the Othonians start the final battle (2.41.1). If the attempt is a bluff, then its aim must be either to divert some Othonian troops from preparing for battle (the Vitellians now know about this, 2.34.1) or to maintain pressure, so that the Othonian generals do not change their minds about fighting. In these two respects, the operation succeeds: 'for it evoked Macer's counter-action from the southern bank of the Po and appears to have lured the Othonian army westward from Brixellum towards Bedriacum, Cremona and defeat' (Wellesley (1991) 1663). For Syme (1958a) 160–1, T. is 'probably right' about the crossing being a feint, although the operation could 'have become serious'. One strategic advantage for the Vitellians (if they really are trying to cross to the south bank of the Po) is the threat to Othonian communications with Rome and the Danube (the source of reinforcements). Even without pressure exerted by the Vitellians, Otho perhaps bases himself at Brixellum to protect these routes (33.2n.). Plutarch's brief parallel account of the incident (*Oth.* 10.2–5) gives no hint that the Vitellians are bluffing. On balance, however, it seems preferable to accept T.'s assertion that the crossing was mainly a feint, rather than to emend the text (Heubner (1968) 128–33).

Yet we should not just consider the incident from the point of view of tactics. Where Plutarch has one sentence about the battle on the river (*Oth.* 10.5), T. creates a richly entertaining episode: the Vitellian Germans and Othonian gladiators are sharply differentiated, both by their fighting techniques and their collective identities, while the scene of gladiators fighting from precariously wobbly boats, so different from a land battle, adds novelty (cf. Liv. 21.5.7–17, fugitives attack Hannibal's army in the river Tagus; Curt. 8.13.7–27, Alexander and Porus fight in the river Hydaspes, with significant clashes on mid-river islands). The element of *enargeia* is also important, as the battle happens *in oculis utriusque exercitus* (2.35.2), so it has an impact on the morale of both sides before the main battle. The whole episode is a novel 'appetiser' before the 'main course', the battle of Bedriacum. We see similar *uariatio* in the move from the ambush at Lake Trasimene (Liv. 22.4–6) to the main land battle at Cannae (Liv. 22.47–49).

34.1 Nihil eorum . . . transfugiis: so the Vitellians get some recompense for the earlier betrayal of Caecina's ambush at Castores (2.24.3). The phrasing is Livian (*neque quicquam . . . eum* (sc. *Hannibalem*) *fallebat et perfugis multa indicantibus et per suos explorantem* (22.28.1), but T. has the abstract *transfugium* 'desertion' (also 3.61.3; cf. *diffugia* 1.39.2) for Livy's *perfuga* 'deserter'. The word executes an especially elegant transition from the Othonians to the Vitellians (Chilver (1979) 198; cf. 9.2n. *Romam peruectum est*). **ut in ciuili bello** 'as is natural in a civil war'. *ut* adds an explanation by indicating a general tendency, usually without a verb (*OLD ut* 21; also 1.55.4, 3.33.2, 3.59.1, 3.71.3 and 4.33.1). It is a useful way for historians to enhance their *auctoritas* by locating particular events within broader patterns. The generalisation's validity rests on the underlying assumption that one side very much resembles the other. **et . . . non** for *neque* (32.1n.). **exploratores cura diuersa sciscitandi sua non occultabant** 'the scouts in their anxiety to learn the enemy's plans were not concealing their own'. Othonian scouts have had their problems before (17.2n. *raptis . . . exploratoribus*). The substantive neuter pl. *diuersa*, lit. 'the things of the opposing side' (*OLD diuersus* 7), is balanced by *sua*. T. increasingly prefers *occulto* for *occulo* (13.2n. *occuleret*). **quieti intentique . . . opperiebantur** 'quietly concentrating on when the enemy would rashly burst out, Caecina and Valens [did something] that is a substitute for (*OLD locus* 20) shrewd action: they waited for other people to make stupid mistakes'. The simple, pithy main clause (*alienam stultitiam opperiebantur*) is dwarfed by the sentence's complex 'wings' on either side: first there are adjectives, proper nouns, an indirect question, and a proleptic *quod* clause, and afterwards an abl. absolute, and co-ordinated participial and final clauses. For *intenti* + an indirect question, see *A.* 1.22.1, Liv. 5.45.1, 6.6.13, and

35.11.9. The positioning of T.'s proleptic *quod* clause qualifies what could otherwise reflect quite positively on Caecina and Valens and their strategy of waiting for others to make mistakes. This coheres with a broad theme in the narrative: the Vitellians do not so much win the war as the Othonians lose it. So T. here stresses the Othonians' *imprudentia*, complains that nobody used the *prudentia* of Celsus and Paulinus (2.39.1), notes that the Othonians camped where there was no water (2.39.2), and claims that they could have renewed the war even after their defeat (2.46.3). On *alienam* see 16.2n. *alieni . . . socia.*   **inchoato ponte:** 'the bridge . . . must be near Cremona, since it is opposite the force of Othonian gladiators described at 2.23.3 as *haud procul Cremona*' (Wellesley (1960) 279). Constructing temporary bridges over rivers was a crucial part of ancient military technology (Veg. 2.25.5, 3.7). Famous cases include Xerxes bridging the Hellespont with boats (Hdt. 7.36) and Caesar rapidly bridging the Rhine (*Gal.* 4.17–18, not using boats; cf. *Gal.* 7.58.4, *Civ.* 1.61.6, using boats). Arrian praises Romans for using interconnected boats to bridge rivers quickly (*An.* 5.7.3–5). Vitellius (*A.* 6.37.3) and Corbulo (*A.* 15.9) cross the Euphrates in this way (cf. Amm. 21.7.7 with Webster (1985) 234–9).   **transitum Padi simulantes:** Wellesley (1991) 1663 reads *simul copulantes* for *simulantes*, as both Plutarch and T. cover the episode in detail and the elaborate bridge building seems out of proportion to the relatively minor objectives, intimidating the gladiators on the opposite bank and occupying the soldiers (also Wellesley (1960) 279–82). Yet to emend the text seems drastic (*transitum* is an odd object for *copulantes*; cf. *hedera . . . platanos transitu suo copulat,* Plin. *Ep.* 5.6.32). By bluffing the Vitellians could draw the main part of the Othonian army westwards along the *Via Postumia* from their current position near Bedriacum and towards the Vitellian base-camp at Cremona. T. does not spell this out, but the text as it stands is not absurd.   **oppositam . . . manum:** i.e. the men serving under Martius Macer, who had launched a surprise attack across the Po (2.23.3).   **ac** co-ordinates a present participle + final clause (Martin (1953) 93–4); cf. 3.46.2 (co-ordination of an adj. + final clause).   **ne ipsorum miles segne otium tereret** 'so that their own troops should not waste time in idleness' (20.1n. *ipsius*). *segne otium* manifests hypallage, the transfer of an adj. (from *miles* to *otium*) to a substantive to which it does not properly belong (5.2n. *uicinis . . . administrationibus*). T. likes this combination (4.5.1, 4.70.1, *A.* 14.39.3), which indicates cause by effect (Quint. 8.6.27). *otium terere* (Liv. 1.57.5, Virg. *A.* 4.271, Sen. *Ep.* 113.1, Luc. 2.488, Stat. *Silu.* 3.5.61, 4.6.2; cf. Aesch. *Ag.* 1055) is a more pregnant, pithy construction for *ne segni otio tempus tereret*. Soldiers typically deteriorate through *otium* (2.67.2, Sall. *Jug.* 44.4–5, Liv. 37.5.4, 39.2.6, 40.21.1, Vell. 2.78.2, Fron. *Str.* 4.1.15).

34.2 naues . . . ualidis utrimque trabibus conexae: timbers could be attached at each boat's prow and the stern, with planks placed across them to connect them (Arr. *An.* 5.7.4). Cf. Corbulo's bridge across the Euphrates: *naues . . . conexas trabibus* (*A.* 15.9.1).   **aduersum in flumen** 'pointing upstream' (3.2n. *tenuem in ambitum* for the 'sandwiching' of the preposition). Arrian also recommends this position (*An.* 5.7.4), presumably so that the ships' broadsides are not exposed to the current's full force, which would jeopardise the makeshift bridge. Opposing the sharp end to the current stabilises the structure.   **iactis super ancoris** 'with anchors cast out besides'. A special anchor, a wicker crate full of rough stones cast from the bow of each ship, secured the bridge against the current (Arr. *An.* 5.7.3; cf. Hdt. 7.36). **firmitatem pontis:** this choice combination is only here (*TLL* s.v. *firmitas* 807.25–6). *firmitas* features again (*D.* 23.3, *A.* 4.63.1), but in the *A.* T. generally prefers the alternative noun *firmitudo* (neither noun is in Sall. or Liv.; Caesar has *firmitas* once and *firmitudo* 4×).   **ut augescente flumine inoffensus ordo nauium attolleretur** 'so that as the river rose, the line of ships might rise in safety'. In the spring, the rivers would be in spate, as the melting winter snows dispersed. *augesco* is often linked with rivers (*TLL* s.v. *augesco* 1358.46–55; *A.* 1.79.1). The waters of other rivers increase the Po's volume: *mox aliis amnibus adeo augescit atque alitur, ut se per septem . . . ostia effundat* (Mela 2.62).   **in extremam nauem educta** 'moved out to whichever was the last ship'. Presumably the tower is on the penultimate ship to cover the Vitellians while linking the next ship in the chain, and is then shifted. The task gets more difficult as the southern bank of the Po gets closer.   **tormentis ac machinis:** '*machina* may refer to any kind of mechanical apparatus, *tormentum* more specifically to a machine which hurls projectiles' (Oakley (1997) 469). Artillery and siege engines were often put on ships and pontoons (Plb. 10.12.1, Caes. *Civ.* 1.25.5–10, 1.26.1, Liv. 26.26.3, 26.44.10, 30.4.10, Diod. Sic. 20.76.3 with Marsden (1969) 169–73). For ancient treatises on artillery, see Marsden (1971).   **struxerant:** in the *H. struo* (when used literally to mean 'build') features less often than the compound *exstruo* (7 : 10). In *A.* 1–6, T. prefers the simple form rather than the compound, but that situation is reversed by the last hexad (Adams (1972) 363–4; WM 479).   **saxaque et faces iaculabantur:** the Othonians remain on the south bank of the Po. Plutarch adds that after the failed initial attack, the Othonians load boats with torches covered in sulphur and pitch. These accidentally catch fire, so the crews leap overboard (*Oth.* 10.3–4 with Veg. 4.44 for such missiles used during naval warfare).

35.1 insula: Vitellius' auxiliaries, the Batavians, were from an island in the middle of the Rhine (Caes. *Gal.* 4.10.4, Plin. *Nat.* 4.101, T. *G.* 29.1, *H.* 4.12.2), so the terrain was likely to suit them. Scholars have tried to locate this island, but the course of the Po has changed and there are many small islands around: it was probably to the south-east of Cremona (Chilver (1979) 199).   **amne medio:** cf. *medio amni* (Liv. 23.19.12, 32.10.8). '*amnis*, frequent in early Latin, is rare in Classical prose – only once in the archaist Sallust – but it is frequent in Livy, another instance of *historia proxima poetis*' (Coleman (1999) 56). In the *H.*, the occurrences of *flumen* to *amnis* are 28 : 17 and in the *A.* 33 : 37 (cf. Livy 185 : 158, Sallust 22 : 1). T. prefers *amnis* over *flumen* in the last hexad of the *A.* (Adams (1972) 360).   **in quam gladiatores nauibus molientes, Germani nando praelabebantur** 'to which, while the gladiators were struggling in boats, the Germans were gliding forward by swimming'. Is *praelabebantur* governed by both subjects and does the *prae-* prefix involve anticipation (Heubner (1955) 105–7)? It is perhaps best to take the verb with *Germani* alone and to see *prae-* as referring to space, not time. T. implies that the skilful German swimmers (17.2n. *Batauos*) exploit the current, which works against the gladiators. These Germans are the Batavian auxiliaries led by Alfenus Varus (2.43.2), omitted here so as not to distract from the Othonian general, Martius Macer, and his soldiers' anger towards him after defeat. They are perhaps called *Germani* here rather than *Bataui* either to enhance sound-effects or to accentuate their barbarian identity, despite being Roman auxiliaries. *molientes* and *nando* shows *uariatio* of a nom. plural participle + an abl. gerund (Sörbom (1935) 91). *praelabor* (only here in T.; absent from Sall., Caes., Liv.) perhaps reflects Livy's affectation of verbs compounded with *prae-* (Oakley (1998) 347). **Liburnicis:** 16.2n. **ea constantia:** sc. *est.* This *sententia* is validated by the narrative that follows (and 2.43.2), but undermined by 2.23.3, where Macer's gladiators do well against auxiliary soldiers (cf. 11.2n. *deforme . . . auxilium*). *constantia* is a common military virtue (*Agr.* 18.4, 41.3, *H.* 3.54.2, 4.78.2, *A.* 14.33.1, [Caes.] *Alex.* 26.2, *Hisp.* 17.1, Liv. 3.19.5, Vell. 2.85.4). In Plutarch the gladiators have experience and courage in close fighting (*Oth.* 12.7). **nec proinde nutantes e nauibus quam stabili gradu e ripa:** 27.1n. *haud proinde quam.* The repeated preposition *e* accentuates *uariatio* of a present participle + abl. of manner. Descriptions of land-battles have *stabili gradu* to convey the resilient *acies* confronting the enemy (Liv. 6.12.8, Amm. 31.7.10). Here it appears in a novel military context. **uolnera derigebant:** this Virgilian coinage (*A.* 10.140) is only here in a prose author (*TLL* s.v. *dirigo* 1242.32–4). 'It seems to be a combination of *derigere* of throwing weapons . . . with the use of *uulnus* for "prospective wounds residing in missiles, blows, etc." (*OLD* 1c)' (Harrison (1991) 98). Cf. *derigit . . . uulnera* (Sil. 2.92).

35.2 uariis trepidantium inclinationibus 'thanks to the erratic (*OLD uarius* 5) lurching of the quivering boats'. For *inclinatio* used of boats, cf. *inclinatio, qua in latera nutat alternis nauigii more* (Sen. *Nat.* 6.21.2). For *trepido* and cognates applied to ships (the noun is omitted here for brevity), see *trepidant . . . puppes* (Val. Flac. 3.132), *rector trepidae . . . ratis* (Luc. 5.568). **mixti remiges propugnatoresque turbarentur:** 22.1n. *plena propugnatoribus moenia.* Rowers and soldiers should play distinct roles, but the unfavourable surroundings cause chaos: cf. *miles ministeria nautarum, remex militis officia turbabat* (Curt. 4.3.18). **desilire . . . retentare . . . scandere . . . mergere:** after the leisurely subordinate clause marked by polysyllabic vocabulary and describing gradually unfolding action (*cum* + imperfect subjunctive), the abrupt historic infinitives (5.1n., *anteire . . . obniti*) in asyndeton underscore the Batavians' methodical attack. The adverb *ultro* can mark the shift from a defensive to an offensive mode of fighting (3.2.2, 4.23.4, 4.79.3): Fyfe and Levene translate it as 'took the initiative'. The boats evidently hold back, so that the initial engagement is an exchange of missiles, but the Batavians unexpectedly take the fight to close quarters. In catching hold of the ships' sterns to prevent any evasive manoeuvre, the Batavians themselves perform a task more usually accomplished by grappling-irons (Caes. *Civ.* 1.58.4). T. thereby tacitly activates the 'giant Germans' stereotype (*G.* 4.2, Caes. *Gal.* 1.39.1, 4.1.9, Vell. 2.106.1, Manil. 4.715, Mela 3.26, Col. *Rust.* 3.8.2, Jos. *BJ* 2.376, Amm. 16.12.47, Veg. 1.1.3; WM 351, Rives (1999) 129), also suggested by *comminus mergere* 'they sank them with their own hands'. The Liburnicae were relatively small, but sinking them without special equipment is still impressive. Poets often use *scando* for climbing on board a boat (*OLD scando* 2b); the *fori* are the narrow gangways running around the sides.

quae cuncta: *cunctus* = a synonym for *omnis* (1.3n. *cuncta . . . perlustrat*).   **in oculis utriusque exercitus:** the *in oculis* formula occurs again (1.37.3, 4.77.1). The picture of opposing sides watching a battle (or a single combat) is a historiographical topos designed to generate *enargeia* (Quint. 6.2.32, Davidson (1991) 10–24, Walker (1993) 353–77). The *locus classicus* is Thucydides' Athenians and Sicilians on dry land watching the naval battle in the harbour at Syracuse (7.71). Yet T. exaggerates the scale by referring to 'armies', when the main Othonian and Vitellian forces are elsewhere. His interest in 'warped spectatorship' recurs (1.40.1, 2.70, 3.83.1; cf. 2.55.1): here the presence of gladiators and their polarisation with the Germans suggests spectatorship for entertainment's sake, especially since naval battles were often re-enacted in the amphitheatre (Coleman (1993) 48–74). Augustus' *naumachia* of 2 BC recreated the battle of Salamis, represented by an island in the lake (Aug. *RG* 23, Ov. *Ars* 1.171–2, Fron. *Aq.* 11, Dio 55.10.7), and in 80 Titus replayed Athens' attack on Syracuse in 414 BC, with an island representing Ortygia (Dio 66.25.2–4).   **quanto . . . tanto:** ablatives of the measure of difference (GL §403).   **laetiora:** sc. *erant*.   **Othoniani . . . detestebantur:** Macer previously restrained the gladiators after victory, but the Othonians' silent suspicion (*suspectum id* 2.23.4) now turns into curses (*OLD detestor* 1). To call this minor skirmish a *clades* seems histrionic: T.'s *proelium quidem . . . fuga diremptum* (2.36.1) questions the Othonians' description. Macer may not be that culpable: he showed apt caution in only deploying the *promptissimi gladiatorum* (2.35.1), reserving the others in case the Vitellians crossed the river, but he had to take that threat seriously.

36.1 proelium . . . fuga diremptum: in the parallel tradition, many gladiators are killed (Plut. *Oth.* 10.5), but T. excludes this detail, making the Othonian response to the battle seem excessive.   **abruptis quae supererant nauibus** 'once the remaining boats had been detached'. *nauis* + *abrumpo* is only here (*TLL* s.v. *abrumpo* 140.55–6), so some editors prefer *abreptis* (cf. *nauem abripiunt* 4.27.1). Whichever is correct, the abl. absolute leaves the agent unspecified, but T. must mean the Othonians: otherwise the gladiators could not flee from a conflict taking place on an island. There is a further hint here of how strong the Germans are who were holding back the boats. **Macer:** suggestive naming (23.3n. *promptus . . . Martius*).   **iamque uolneratum eminus lancea strictis gladiis inuaserant:** Macer could have been wounded in battle, but juxtaposing *lancea* and *strictis gladiis* (with the implicit progression from long-range combat to an attack at close quarters) suggests that one of his own soldiers is to blame. If so, it is ironic that an Othonian soldier is perfectly adept when attacking his own commander, although the gladiators on the boats could not wound their enemies: *uolneratum* here picking up on the striking *uolnera derigebant* (2.35.1) emphasises the point.   **cum intercursu tribunorum centurionumque protegitur:** this is an inverse *cum* clause, used for dramatic effect. 'The sentence introduced by *cum* is always the more important, so that it looks as if the *cum*-clause and the main clause have changed places' (*NLS* §237; also 2.41.1, 54.1, 61, 72.2). T. uses the Livian *intercursus* (5×) only here. Cf. (*sc.* Lentulus) *iamque . . . accursu multitudinis . . . protectus est* (*A.* 1.27.2).

36.2 relicto Placentiae modico praesidio 'after leaving behind a small garrison at Placentia'. If the Vitellians' attempt to bridge the Po was a feint to draw the Othonians closer to their main stronghold at Cremona, then the plan seems to be

working. *modico praesidio relicto* features 12× in Liv., but otherwise only in his imitator
Curt. (3×) and here (Oakley (1997) 417).   **cum cohortibus subuenit:** yet this
reinforcement has a chequered history, since the cohorts had taken part in the mutinies
at Rome (1.80–5) and Placentia (2.18.2–19).   **Flauium Sabinum:** not Vespasian's
brother, the urban prefect, but probably that man's son (i.e. Vespasian's nephew),
who had been designated as consul until 1 Jul. (1.77.2), after taking up the post on
1 Apr. (so he is now consul). He surrenders his troops to Vitellius (2.51), probably
served as curator of public works in 70 or 71 (Jones (1996) 45 on *CIL* VI 814) and
held a second consulship with Mucianus in 72 (Townend (1961) 54–62, Gilmartin
Wallace (1987) 343–58, Jones (1996) 44–7). He died before 81.   **rectorem:** 11.2n.
laeto milite . . . ducibus . . . aspernantibus: *uariatio* of adj. + present participle
(Sörbom (1935) 93–4) with the abl. components arranged chiastically. *laetus + ad* (*OLD
ad* 33) is very unusual ('M. has *et ad*, so a word may be missing' Irvine 161), but Seneca
the Younger has a precedent (*nos, laeti ad omnia, D.* 1.5.8; *TLL* s.v. *laetus* 886.20–2). Cf.
laetantes . . . ad noua imperia (*A.* 2.2.1). *tam infestam militiam* = 'such a hostile command'.

37–38 TWO DIGRESSIONS

T. decelerates his narrative, stepping back to challenge a report in his sources (2.37)
and to analyse passion for power through the ages in a digression recalling Sallust
(2.38). This is a well-timed reflective pause before the climactic account of the first
battle at Bedriacum (2.39–45). Its advantages are clear: not only does T. heighten
tension for his readers by delaying the miserable finale of Otho's principate, but he
also enhances his own *auctoritas* as a historian (2.37) and satisfies the moralising agenda
of ancient historiography (2.38). In a similarly powerful device Lucan suspends the
momentum of his narrative before describing the battle at Pharsalus (7.387–459).

Plutarch gives three main reasons why the Othonians fight (*Oth.* 9): (i) the praetorians want to settle the war swiftly, so as to return to their hedonistic life in Rome (cf.
Suet. *Otho* 9.1), (ii) Otho himself is impatient and careworn (cf. 2.40, Suet. *Otho* 9.1),
(iii) although Marius Celsus and his supporters try to delay the final battle (since both
armies want to confer), Otho fears this and hastens the battle (cf. 2.37). T. typically
rearranges and reshapes this material to reflect his own historiographical agenda.
First, he postpones his focus on the praetorians until after the battle, concentrating
not (as Plutarch does) on their flawed calibre, but on their passionate loyalty to Otho
(2.46.3). This enhances the paradox and poignancy of his suicide. Second, T. postpones the point about Otho's impatience and anxiety until his generals have slowly
started to manoeuvre the troops (2.40). T. is critical of the generals in this phase,
so the rearrangement allows us to understand Otho's frustration, which in Plutarch
feels rather arbitrary and unanchored. Third, T. reads the rumour about the two
armies' inclination to confer in a diametrically opposed way to Plutarch, making it
the main focus of the digression. Where Plutarch speculates that the flawed characters
of Otho and Vitellius make it plausible that the soldiers conferred, T. introduces the
story only to refute it. In his version, the two morally flawed armies are incapable of

stopping a war (which they themselves had started) through concern for peace. T. also siphons off elements of Plutarch's version for use elsewhere: (i) the *syncrisis* of Otho and Vitellius is moved to 2.31.1 and presented as general public perceptions of the pair, rather than being filtered through the military, (ii) the comparison of Otho and Vitellius with protagonists from previous civil wars first appears at 1.50 and is made by the general population in Rome (stressing *decline* in the quality of leaders between republic and empire). It is then redeployed at 2.38, where T. analyses Marius, Sulla and Pompey (stressing *continuity* in the armies' selfish conduct between republic and empire). Plutarch focalises the comparison through the soldiers (*Oth.* 9.5), not through the general population (1.50.1) or his own narrative voice (2.38).

T.'s digression (2.38) locates this latest power struggle in a dark moralising framework, opening up a broad sweep of history for comparison. The clash between Otho and Vitellius is seen as part of a repeating historical pattern, illuminated by his audience's familiarity with the central motifs of Sallustian historiography. T.'s 'marriage' of Sallustian ideology and style came to fruition in the *A.*, a work which declares its Sallustian agenda from the outset (*urbem Romanam a principio reges habuere*, *A.* 1.1.1 with Woodman (1992); cf *urbem Romam . . . habuere initio Troiani*, Sall. *Cat.* 6.1, *a principio urbis*, Sall. *Hist.* 1.8) and imitates Sallust at principal points (e.g. *A.* 4.1.3 and Sall. *Cat.* 5.3–6, the character sketches of Sejanus and Catiline). Yet such elements also feature in all three of the minor works (Syme (1958a) 198) and in the *H.*, where civil war is ripe for filtering through his predecessor's distinctive language: 'a crabbed, difficult, elliptical style may reinforce a critical view of war or of the behaviour of political factions, and can create a linguistic atmosphere imitating the contradictions and hypocrisies of the "real" world' (Kraus and Woodman (1997) 12). Yet for a historian early in the second century AD to take up a Sallustian stylistic agenda was still bold: it took a sophisticated readership to appreciate the allusions (cf. *doctorum corda uirorum*, Mart. 14.191.1, *apud aures uacuas atque eruditas*, Quint. 10.1.32) and Sallust had had his critics (Sen. *Ep.* 114.17–18). In the current digression, T. especially draws on themes and language from Sallust (*Cat.* 10–11, *Jug.* 41–2, and *Hist.* 1.7, 1.12). See further Syme (1958a) 198–9, 728–32.

37.1 Inuenio: the 1st person singular introducing this historiographical digression is striking (Sinclair (1995) 54). For cross-references in the *H.*, T. exclusively has the 1st person plural (4.4.n. *ut supra memorauimus*). The chapter's discursive tone is enhanced by consisting structurally of only two long, elaborate sentences.   **apud quosdam auctores:** T. implies diligent consultation of multiple sources in an effort to enhance his historiographical *auctoritas*. Plutarch cites Secundus the rhetorician (whether through writings or oral report is unclear) for one explanation for the Othonian decision to fight immediately (*Oth.* 9.3), but Otho's secretary *ab epistulis* must have been supplementary to the main source. The events of the civil war had been narrated by many Greek and Roman authors (Jos. *BJ* 4.496), but scholars focus on three possible candidates as the common source (Cluvius Rufus, Fabius Rusticus and Pliny the Elder). T. perhaps also consulted Vestricius Spurinna (11.2n.) and Marius Celsus (23.4n.; Syme (1958a) 674–6). Absolute certainty is impossible: 'It is more

productive to examine the parallel tradition to learn how T. used this source' (Damon
(2003) 23). **pauore belli:** the causal abl. (+ objective gen.) points to a different
motivation from that identified by Plutarch, where the soldiers consider postponing
battle as they know its hardships (*Oth.* 9.5). **seu:** T. often omits *siue / seu* in the
first part of alternative explanations (G-G 1516–17, Sörbom (1935) 125). **fastidio
utriusque principis** 'through scorn for both emperors'. Yet *princeps* strictly speaking
only applies to Otho, declared emperor by the senate in Rome on 15 Jan. (1.47.1). The
armies of Upper and Lower Germany saluted Vitellius as emperor on 2–3 Jan. (1.57.1),
but the senate did not recognise him until 19 Apr. after Otho's suicide (2.55.2). The
notion that the soldiers felt scorn for Otho sits oddly with the theme of their passionate loyalty to him (2.33.3, 39.2, 44.3, 46, 47.3, 49.3–4), but T. rehearses an argument
made by *quidam auctores*, without endorsing it. **flagitia ac dedecus** 'scandalous
misconduct' (hendiadys). **apertiore in dies fama** 'through increasingly candid
daily reports'. *fama + apertior* is only here (*TLL* s.v. *fama* 208.16, 223.78). For the
substance of such reports, see 2.31.1. **dubitasse exercitus num** 'that the armies
wondered whether they should not'. The acc. + inf. depends on *inuenio.* **uel . . . uel:**
Plutarch also has these two alternatives (*Oth.* 9.4), but explicitly says that the candidate should be chosen from commanders present. **in medium consultarent:**
5.2n. *in medium consuluere.* The phrase is Sallustian: *neque in medium consultare* (Sall. *Hist.*
4.37). It was difficult for different armies to reach a consensus about selecting an
emperor: the army of Upper Germany tells the praetorians that Galba, an emperor
created in Spain, displeased them (Suet. *Gal.* 16.2; cf. 1.12.1, Plut. *Galb.* 22.8). Not every
man chosen by the armies would take the job: Verginius Rufus (49.1n.) consistently
refused (1.8.2, 2.51, Plut. *Galb.* 6.3, Dio 63.25.1). **senatui permitterent legere
imperatorem:** yet Otho's praetorians are previously cast as mistrusting the senate
(1.80.2), for whose safety the emperor fears during the mutiny: *discrimine senatus . . . ter-
ritus* (1.81.2), *periculo senatus anxius* (1.83.1). Otho in his speech says that the soldiers even
demanded the senators *ad sanguinem et caedem* (1.84.3). Also, although the legions of
Upper Germany briefly entrust choosing a new emperor to the senate and people
(*senatui ac populo Romano arbitrium elegendi permittere*, 1.12.1), within two days they drop
this façade in favour of their own candidate, Vitellius (*speciosis senatus populique Romani
nominibus relictis*, 1.57.1). This all raises further questions about the plausibility of the
story. **eo:** 13.2n. **duces Othonianos:** Plutarch centres the story on Celsus and
his supporters (*Oth.* 9.6), whereas T. will focus on Paulinus. **quod . . . meruisset**
gives Paulinus' reasons (19.1n. *quod . . . legisset*). **uetustissimus consularium et
militia clarus:** this chiastic phrase contains 'the only real evidence that he attained
the *fasces* in the 40s, but he might have had to wait until 47 or later' (Birley (1981) 55).
T. uses *militia clarus* of Titus (5.1.1). **gloriam nomenque** 'a brilliant name' (hendiadys). **Britannicis expeditionibus** (abl. of means) refers to Paulinus' three
years (58–61) as governor (Birley (1981) 55; 11.1n. *rebellione Britanniae compressa*, 23.4n.
Suetonium Paulinum). Generals could use the term *expeditio* for self-aggrandisement (*Agr.*
18.6); and the plural is perhaps hyperbolic, as his main campaign was against Boudicca
(cf. *unius proelii fortuna, Agr.* 16.2).

37.2 ego . . . passuros: *ego* emphatically shows T. disagreeing with the argument just summarised. It recurs again in an emphatic authorial assertion: *ego sicut . . . concesserim ita . . . reor* (5.7.2; cf. *Agr.* 12.6). T. now has one long, elaborate sentence: the first subordinate clause (*ut . . . expetitum*), which initially seems quite lengthy, is eventually dwarfed by the massive main clause (*ita . . . passuros*). After a subordinate clause introduced by the first *ut*, the main clause begins with *ita* and is articulated through *neque . . . reor . . . neque*, where the main verb is tucked away between an acc. + inf. construction (*Paulinum . . . moderationem*) and its continuation, a consecutive clause introduced by a second *ut* (*ut . . . deponerent*). T. then prolongs the main clause with a second sequence of acc. + inf. clauses (*aut exercitus . . . coalescere, aut legatos ac duces . . . passuros*). The complex structure is held together by verbs placed at the end of their sub-clauses.   **ut . . . ita** 'although . . . nevertheless' (*OLD ut* 5b).   **concesserim** 'I am prepared to admit'. The perfect potential subjunctive (GL §257) recurs (1.83.4, 2.50.2 *crediderim*; 2.76.2 *fuerit*).   **tacito uoto** 'with an unexpressed desire', but the abl. of manner is perhaps better translated with a verb, 'they hoped on the quiet'. Enforced silence for the sake of survival elsewhere stirs T.'s criticism: *memoriam quoque ipsam cum uoce perdidissemus, si tam in nostra potestate esset obliuisci quam tacere* (*Agr.* 2.3).   **quietem . . . expetitum:** T.'s Eprius Marcellus is more realistic: *bonos imperatores uoto expetere qualescumque tolerare* (4.8.2). T. shifts from pithiness, two unmodified single nouns in the first clause (*quietem pro discordia*), to expansiveness, a noun modified by two adjectives followed by two superlative adjectives (*bonum . . . flagitiosissimis*, trumping *flagitia* at 2.37.1). Asyndeton and alliteration of *p* and *s* in the second clause add bite. Anachronistic associations with Nerva and Trajan are perhaps at play here: *quies* was a notable characteristic of Nerva (Mart. 5.28.4, 8.70.1, Plin. *Ep.* 10.58.7, Syme (1958a) 2 n.3), while *innocentia* was attributed to Trajan (Plin. *Pan.* 28.3, 49.3). Some hoped for an emperor who was *bonus*, but eventually they acquired Trajan, called *optimus* early in his principate (Syme (1958a) 36). Before his succession, Pliny claims that dispirited people could only pray for an emperor who was better than the worst: *summa uotorum melior pessimo princeps* (*Pan.* 44.2).   **corruptissimo saeculo:** good and bad behaviour, like history itself, was thought to run in cycles (*A.* 3.55.5 with WM 407). Vespasian's principate marked a turning-point (*A.* 3.55.4), although there was deterioration under Domitian, then the *beatissimum saeculum* (*Agr.* 3.1), which started with Nerva and continued with the *felicitas temporum* of Trajan (*Agr.* 3.1, *H.* 1.1.4; cf. Plin. *Ep.* 10.58.7).   **ut . . . deponerent:** this is a consecutive clause after *tantam . . . moderationem*.   **pacem belli amore . . . bellum pacis caritate:** antimetabole, the figure whereby words are repeated with different inflections: cf. the Elder Curio insulting Caesar by calling him *omnium mulierum uirum et omnium uirorum mulierem* (Suet. *Jul.* 52.3). It reinforces T.'s argument by emphasising the absurdity of warmongerers suddenly embracing peace (Quint. 9.3.85, Plass (1992) 427, Wills (1996) 272–9). The author of the *Rhetorica ad Herennium* sees elegance when words are transposed in juxtaposing contrasting ideas (4.39). Cf. *ut prius in bello pacem, sic in pace bellum quaerens* (Liv. 1.27.2), *stupra caedibus, caedes stupris miscerentur* (*H.* 3.33.1), *quae iusserat uetare, quae uetuerat iubere* (*H.* 3.73.1). Yet there is also *uariatio* of vocabulary in the causal ablatives *amore* and *caritate* (cf. Cic. *Fam.* 11.8.1, Plin. *Pan.* 20.1). *amor* may suggest something more passionate than *caritas:* so, *amor* πάθος, *caritas* ἦθος (Quint. 6.2.12). *pacis caritate* is only here (*TLL* s.v. *caritas* 461.73); Otho's soldiers will kill themselves after his suicide *caritate principis* (2.49.4).   **exercitus . . . dissonos:** each army is heterogeneous in language and morals, but T. also polarises 'German' Vitellians (cf. Otho's scornful *Germani*, 1.84.3; 21.4n. *peregrinum et externum*) and more 'Roman' Othonians. This is probably an exaggeration. The German Arminius, after serving in the Roman army, insults his brother Flavus *Latino sermone* (*A.* 2.10.3) and T. 'has no friction or failure of communication to record in his description of victors and vanquished mingling after First Cremona' (Powell (1972) 839). This linguistic heterogeneity recalls Hannibal's army (*non lex, non mos, non lingua communis* Liv. 28.12.3, Sil. 3.221, 16.19–22) and the Pompeians (Luc. 3.288–90, App. *BC* 2.75), but the idea goes back to Homer's Trojans (*Il.* 2.804, 4.437–8).   **in hunc consensum . . . coalescere:** '*coalescere* + *in* is regular, and its metaphorical use, as exemplified at Liv. 1.8.1 . . . is straightforward. T. elsewhere seems to extend this usage (11.24.2)' (WM 324).   **magna ex parte luxus egestatis scelerum sibi conscios** '(who were) nearly all guiltily aware of progressing from hedonism, to poverty, to crimes' (*OLD conscius* 3b for the dat. of the reflexive pronoun, here adding alliteration). The carefully ordered nouns in asyndeton plot the downward spiral: *luxus* leads to *egestas*, which in turn means men commit *scelera*. Vitellius exemplifies this pattern.   **nisi pollutum . . . meritis suis:** yet a *princeps* feeling obliged to a general for his position was not always generous. Following Mucianus' lead (4.39.3–4), Vespasian slowly excluded Antonius Primus as the Flavian regime became established: *paulatim leuior uiliorque haberi, manente tamen in speciem amicitia* (4.80.3). Sallust also has the metaphor of pollution, but qualifies it: *quasi pollutus* (*Jug.* 63.7).   **passuros:** sc. *fuisse*.

38.1 Vetus ac iam pridem insita mortalibus potentiae cupido: 20.1n. *insita mortalibus natura*; 2.2n. *illum cupido incessit.* This varies *primo pecuniae, deinde imperi cupido creuit* (Sall. *Cat.* 10.3; also *Jug.* 19.1), but recalls a crucial point in Sallust's 'map' of moral decline in the Roman character. T.'s slightly pleonastic combination *uetus* + *iam pridem insita* is emphatic: cf. *uetere ac iam pridem recepta . . . consuetudine* (*Agr.* 14.1), *uetere atque insita . . . superbia* (*A.* 1.4.3).   **cum . . . adoleuit erupitque:** T. likes *adolesco* used metaphorically, which Ammianus later imitates (*TLL* s.v. *adolesco* 1424.1–55). Cf. *cupiditas agendi . . . adolescit* (Cic. *Fin.* 5.55). The combination *cupido* + *erumpo* is unusual: Lucretius has *se erupit neruis coniecta cupido* (4.1115, referring to ejaculation). Asinius Gallus argues that *auctu imperii adoleuisse etiam priuatas opes, idque non nouum, sed e uetustissimis moribus* (*A.* 2.33.2). T. condemns this as a *confessio uitiorum* (*A.* 2.33.4), but the senators support him.   **rebus modicis** 'when resources were limited'. So T. highlights the *modicae adhuc populi Romani res* (3.72.2) when Tarquinius Priscus laid the foundations for the Capitoline temple.   **aequalitas facile habebatur** 'equal standing was easily maintained' (*TLL* s.v. *habeo* 2439.73). *aequalitas* (not in Sall.) is only here in the *H.*, but recurs in T.'s assessment of collective subservience under the principate: *omnes exuta aequalitate iussa principis aspectare* (*A.* 1.4.1; 4× elsewhere in T.). In both cases the noun refers to equality under the law (WM

242). **subacto orbe et aemulis urbibus regibusue excisis:** the phrasing recalls Lucan: *mundo . . . subacto* (1.160). Like T., Sallust points to the acme of Rome's achievements before the inevitable decline: *reges magni bello domiti, nationes ferae et populi ingentes ui subacti, Carthago aemula imperi Romani ab stirpe interiit* (*Cat.* 10.1). Yet T. economically uses abl. absolutes, moving quickly to the corruption, and veils Carthage by generalising about the destruction of rival cities. His audience would certainly have thought of Carthage, whose destruction in 146 BC obliterated the beneficial *metus hostilis* which previously kept Rome's citizens morally upright (Sall. *Jug.* 41.2, *Hist.* 1.12). The historiographical tradition identified different points in the second century BC for the onset of degeneration (McGushin (1992) 78–9) and Sallust's own version of the theory of *metus hostilis* was not static (Paul (1984) 124–5). Yet for T. these details are less important than the theory that securing the empire by destroying foreign enemies led to moral decline. Cf. *orbem iam totum uictor Romanus habebat* (Petr. 119.1) with Connors (1998) 105 on Roman representations of the world and the empire as coextensive; also Sall. *Cat.* 36.4, Cic. *Arch.* 10.23.   **securas opes concupiscere** 'to covet wealth in safety'. T. echoes Sallust (*auaritia pecuniae studium habet, quam nemo sapiens concupiuit, Cat.* 11.3), but simplifies his more complex scheme whereby first *ambitio*, then *auaritia* corrupts men. Sallust uses *concupisco* 3× (cf. 17× in T., 2× in Liv., absent from Caes.), but generally prefers forms of *cupio* (24×). *concupisco* occurs from Lucilius onwards, but Seneca the Younger especially favours it.   **uacuum fuit** 'there was leisure to'. Cf. *uacuom fuit* (Sall. *Hist.* 1.12).   **prima inter patres plebemque certamina:** this alliterative phrase evokes Sallust on the adversarial relationship between the *nobilitas* and *populus* after Carthage's destruction (*Jug.* 41–2, esp. *ita omnia in duas partis abstracta sunt, res publica, quae media fuerat, dilacerata,* 41.5, *Cat.* 36.4–39.4, *Hist.* 1.11–12). Although our sources suggest that tension between these two groups flared up repeatedly before 146 BC, T.'s *prima certamina* probably means the conflicts which caused the death of Tiberius Gracchus in 133 BC, 'the first outbreak of civil strife in Rome which ended in bloodshed and the death of citizens since the expulsion of the kings' (Plut. *TG* 20.1). T. carefully indicates the chronological progression in this chapter: *prima / modo . . . modo / mox / post quos / nunc.*   **exarsere:** 27.2n. *grauis . . . exarserat* on the metaphor; 3.1n. *ipsa . . . cessere* on the verb form.   **turbulenti tribuni:** although tribunes of the *plebs* were supposed to protect liberty, T. can criticise them, calling Appuleius Saturninus (tribune 103 BC, 100 BC), Tiberius Gracchus (133 BC) and Gaius Gracchus (123 BC) *turbatores plebis* (*A.* 3.27.2 with WM 252). T. has *turbulentus* only here.   **praeualidi:** a choice form (28.1n. *cohortes . . . praeualidas*).   **temptamenta ciuilium bellorum** 'trial-runs for civil war' (Fyfe / Levene), sc. *erant. temptamentum*, only here in T., and elsewhere very rare (Ov. *Met.* 15.629, Val. Flac. 1.102) features in this sense only in the plural. T. likes nouns with the weighty ending *-mentum* (Syme (1958a) 341).   **mox e plebe infima C. Marius** (157–86 BC; *OCD³* 'Marius, Gaius') is in the *H.* only here. The idea that Marius came from a poor farming family in or near Arpinum recurs (Plut. *Mar.* 3.1, Plin. *Nat.* 33.150, Val. Max. 2.3.1, 6.9.14, Juv. 8.245–6, Sall. *Jug.* 63.3), but really he was a *nouus homo* (Sall. *Jug.* 63.7, 85.13) from an equestrian family (Vell. 2.11.1, Val. Max. 8.15.7). No doubt the declamation schools liked to play up

Marius' humble origins, as he already exemplified the mutability of fortune through
his later political career (Sen. *Con.* 1.1.3, 1.1.5, 1.6.4, Val. Max. 6.9.14). Plutarch also
uses Marius and Sulla as a reference point, but for the soldiers contemplating the
choice of a new emperor (*Oth.* 9.5). **nobilium saeuissimus Lucius Sulla:** the
savagery of Sulla (138–78 BC; *OCD³* 'Cornelius Sulla Felix') had erupted during the
proscriptions in Rome in 82 BC (App. *BC* 1.95, Liv. *Per.* 87, Plut. *Sull.* 31): *ille quod exiguum
restabat sanguinis urbi | hausit* (Luc. 2.140–1). Since his *crudelitas* was quickly assimilated
by the rhetorical and historical tradition (Cic. *Att.* 9.14.2, Val. Max. 6.8.2, 9.2.1, Sen.
Con. 9.2.19, *Suas.* 6.3, Sen. *Clem.* 1.12.1–2, *Prou.* 3.7–8, Luc. 2.139–222, Mart. 11.5.9),
saeuissimus would trigger familiar associations for the audience. So he is a concise
but chilling reference point when Tiberius predicts that Caligula will have all Sulla's
vices, but none of his virtues (*A.* 6.46.4) and during the fighting in Rome between the
Vitellians and Flavians (3.83.3). **uictam armis libertatem in dominationem
uerterunt** 'substituted tyranny for the liberty vanquished by war'. Yet *non Sullae longa
dominatio* (*A.* 1.1.1 with Goodyear (1972) 93; cf. *post dominationem L. Sullae*, Sall. *Cat.* 5.6);
and Sulla voluntarily abdicated (App. *BC* 1.103). T. injects further Sallustian echoes:
ubi regium imperium . . . in superbiam dominationemque se conuortit (*Cat.* 6.7), *namque coepere
nobilitas dignitatem, populus libertatem in lubidinem uortere* (*Jug.* 41.5). **Cn. Pompeius
occultior, non melior** '(there was) Gnaeus Pompey, more guarded, but no better'
(*OCD³* 'Pompeius Magnus'). T. casts Pompey (106–48 BC) as a dissimulator, craving
power just as Marius and Sulla did, but disguising his ambitions (cf. *modestus ad alia
omnia, nisi ad dominationem*, Sall. *Hist.* 2.17; cf. Sen. *Ep.* 94.64). Pompey's friends apparently found his dissimulation taxing (Plut. *Pomp.* 30.6). T. later criticises him as *grauior
remediis quam delicta erant suarumque legum auctor idem ac subuersor, quae armis tuebatur armis
amisit* (*A.* 3.28.1 with WM 255–6). Caesar (named by Plut., *Oth.* 9.5) is conspicuously
absent, but T.'s selected trio reflects a tendency for historical *exempla* to be grouped in
threes (Mayer (1991) 155–6). **quaesitum:** sc. *est.* Cf. *A.* 2.74.1, where *quaero* is also
used virtually in the sense of *certo*.

38.2 non discessere ab armis: yet in the republican civil wars, rival armies
did sometimes discuss reconciliation, e.g. at Ilerda in 49 BC (App. *BC* 2.42, Suet.
Jul. 75.2). The phrasing recalls Sall. (*Cat.* 34.1, 36.2, *Jug.* 21.4), Cic. (*Phil.* 5.41, 8.33),
Caes. (*Gal.* 5.41.8) and Liv. (3.17.2). **in Pharsalia ac Philippis:** 6.11. *trans mare.*
ciuium legiones, nedum Othonis ac Vitellii exercitus: by adding *ciuium*, T.
hints at an (artificial) contrast between legions of citizens in the first century BC (who
still insisted on fighting) and the bastardised, barbarised armies of the current civil
war (who would, by implication, be much less likely than concerned citizens to stop
fighting). The conjunction *nedum* 'still less', takes the subjunctive when used with a
verb (*OLD* 1) and 'is found first and only once in Terence, never in Caesar or Sallust, in
Cicero only after negative sentences; from Livy on it is used after affirmative clauses
as well' (GL §482.5). **sponte posituri bellum fuerint** 'would have willingly
laid aside war' (*OLD* s.v. *pono* 10; *uariatio* after so recently using the compound form
bellum . . . deponerent (2.37.2)). The periphrastic perfect subjunctive (fut. participle + perf.
subj.) after *nedum* serves as the apodosis of an unreal conditional sentence (GL §515)

instead of *non posuissent*. There is a 'tension between the perf. subj., denoting an actual result . . . , and the fut. participle, denoting a potential occurrence' (Damon (2003) 155). *sponte* (in this sense) without *sua* is first in Augustan poetry and post-Augustan prose (WM 171).   **eadem . . . eadem . . . eaedem:** expressions such as *deum ira* are 'devices of style, calculated to enhance his presentation of particular scenes and serving as convenient ways of expressing pathos and indignation' (Goodyear (1972) 276), here enhanced by triple anaphora and asyndeton. Cf. Germanicus on the mutiny in Germany: *fatalem . . . rabiem neque militum sed deum ira resurgere* (*A.* 1.39.6). For T. the disasters of the current civil wars already prove that *non esse curae deis securitatem nostram, esse ultionem* (1.3.2; cf. 33.1n. *fortunam et deos*), but here he extends blame to the human sphere. Collective madness is a common way for authors to describe outbreaks of civil war (Hor. *Epod.* 7.13, Val. Max. 5.8.5, Plut. *Galb.* 1.4), although this often curtails explanation of the phenomenon.   **singulis uelut ictibus . . . ignauia principum:** T. directly tackles a crucial difference between the current civil wars (lasting a year and a half) and those of the republic (lasting decades). With typical cynicism, he attributes this to the *ignauia* 'lack of spirit' (*OLD* 2) of the current *principes:* even leaders of civil wars are not what they used to be (cf. 1.50.3). The (qualified) metaphor of *ictus* alludes to the battles (one in Rome, two near Bedriacum) that terminated each principate (although even these are less impressive than their republican counterparts). It also reminds us that all three *principes* succumbed to violent death-blows by the sword (each showing bravery belittled by the causal abl. *ignauia principum*). A soldier called Camurius killed Galba (*impresso gladio iugulum eius hausisse*, 1.41.3), Otho *in ferrum pectore incubuit* (2.49.2), and Vitellius *ingestis uolneribus concidit* (3.85). 'The Romans felt metaphorical usages of their language more strongly than we do in ours, and commonly qualified any novel departure' (Mayer (2001) 102 on *uelut*).   **reputatio** (only here in T.) is a Plinian coinage (*Nat.* 7.52).   **longius tulit:** apologetic formulae often accompany digressions (2.2n. *haud fuerit longum . . . disserere*).   **nunc ad rerum ordinem uenio** 'now I move to the proper sequence of events'. Cf. *ad temporum ordinem redeo* (*A.* 12.40.5). Some editors (C. Heraeus, 1885) emend the text to *redeo* unnecessarily (Heubner (1968) 149).

39–45 THE FIRST BATTLE OF BEDRIACUM AND ITS AFTERMATH

Thanks to a notorious textual problem (40n. *confluentes Padi et Aduae fluminum*) and uncertainty about the Othonian plan (probably superseded by the Vitellians' actions), T.'s account of this chaotic battle is perhaps the most controversial part of *H.* 2 (cf. Plut. *Oth.* 11–12, Dio 64.10.3, Suet. *Otho* 9.2). The broad picture is that after Otho decides at the council meeting to join battle (*c.* 10 Apr.), the main Othonian force at Bedriacum sets out westwards (13 Apr.), advancing cautiously towards the Vitellian base at Cremona and setting up camp after covering only 4 miles (2.39.2). That evening, the generals discuss again how to confront the Vitellians, but Otho (in dispatches) urges speed. On the next day (14 Apr.) the Othonians aim to cover 16 miles, leaving themselves much closer to the Vitellians, but whether they intended to

engage in battle on that day is uncertain: Celsus and Paulinus certainly are unwilling
to expose their tired men to the Vitellians immediately, but Titianus and Proculus
overrule them. Whatever the Othonian plan, some scouts alert the Vitellian generals
to the danger, Valens gives the signal for battle, and all debate ceases. The reader is as
surprised at the outbreak of fighting as the Othonians themselves are (Herzog (1996)
305).

T.'s account of the battle is unconventional: there is no enumeration of the armies'
fighting-order and no pre-battle harangues, the terrain proves bizarrely inappropriate for Roman fighting techniques, and the focus moves kaleidoscopically between
different groups of soldiers (rather as does Caesar's account of the unusual battle
against the Nervii, *Gal.* 2.21–7). All of this makes the battle narrative strangely messy
and anti-climactic after the prolonged build-up. Yet if fighting methods in ancient
historiography reflect collective identity, this narrative epitomises the damage done
to normal Roman efficiency by civil war and even shows that the calibre of battle
has declined since the republican civil wars. It also contrasts sharply with the much
more conventional account of the battle between the Romans under Cerialis and
the Germans under Civilis (5.16–18). In addition, a narrative frustrating for military
historians can still delight readers for other reasons. Courbaud memorably calls T. 'le
peintre [de la guerre]' (1918) 113 and argues that T. zooms in on particular episodes as
'c'est ce qui parle à l'imagination' ((1918) 115). Also, depicting a battle in a fragmented
way arguably mirrors the experiences of the combatants: 'those who are present (in
a battle) do not know everything that happens, but each man barely knows what
happens near himself' (Thuc. 7.44.1). On the battle see Mommsen (1871), Passerini
(1940), Syme (1958a) 162–5, 676–82, Koestermann (1961), Schwinge (1970), Chilver
(1970–1), Wellesley (1971), Murison (1993) 110–19 and Wellesley (2000) 74–89.

39.1 Profecto . . . Othone initiates the plan formed earlier (33.2n. *Brixellum*).
In this chapter T. methodically analyses the military hierarchy, from Otho at the top,
down to the common soldiers, relentlessly identifying the problems at each level. It
is like watching a crash in slow motion.   **honor imperii . . . uis ac potestas
penes Proculum praefectum:** 6.2n. for anaphora of *penes*, 23.5n. for Titianus,
33.1n. for the ill-prepared Proculus. Alliteration draws attention to where real power
lies in the military hierarchy. T.'s interest in real power versus the trappings re-emerges
in the *A.*: *sublatisque inanibus ueram potentiam augeri* (4.41.2), *sed inane nomen apud imbellem
externa mollitia, uim in Abdagaesis domo* (6.43.3), [sc. *Romanos*] *apud quos uis imperii ualet,
inania tramittuntur* (15.31).   **Celsus et Paulinus:** 23.4n.   **alienae culpae praetendebantur** 'served as a screen for the faults of others' (16.2n. *alieni metus socia*). Cf.
hoc praetexit nomine culpam (Virg. *A.* 4.172), *praetendens culpae splendida uerba tuae* (Ov. *Rem.*
240). Yet after the civil wars Celsus (23.4n.) has a better reputation than Paulinus
(23.4n.), who retroactively admits treachery (probably a lie) and is pardoned by Vitellius (2.60.1).   **ambigui** 'were unreliable', sc. *erant*. The following *quod* clause must
indicate that the adj. is passive (*OLD* 9 'unreliable'; also 4.56.2), not active (*OLD* 2
'wavering').   **miles alacer:** sc. *erat*. It fleetingly looks as if T. identifies an Othonian
strength (cf. *Mucianus alacrem militem in uerba Vespasiani adegit*, 2.80.2), but the following

qui clause crushes this sense (cf. 5.1n. *egregium principatus temperamentum*). *alacritas* is a positive attribute of Roman soldiers in Livy (6.8.10, 7.33.4, 9.41.17, 26.9.5, 41.3.8). **iussa ducum interpretari quam exsequi mallet** 'preferred to interpret their generals' orders to suit their own purposes, rather than to carry them out'. *interpretari* in this sense (*OLD* 5) is applied to laws (Cic. *Inu.* 2.127, Liv. 3.20.5), *iniuriae* (*Agr.* 15.1) and priestly writings (5.13.2). The clause deconstructs idealised images of the Roman army elsewhere: 'their generals are held in even greater awe than their laws' (Jos. *BJ* 3.103) and (of the soldiers) 'so quick are their ears for orders' (Jos. *BJ* 3.105); cf. Crassus, who punishes an engineer for interpreting an order *non obsequio debito, sed consilio non desiderato* (Gell. 1.13.13).

39.2 ad quartum: sc. *miliarium*. Plutarch specifies 50 stades (*Oth.* 11.1), just over 6 miles, perhaps from a source where IV was written as (or mistaken for) VI (Wellesley (1971) 34), even though he had himself explored the site of the battle (*Oth.* 14.2). This marching-camp is now 16 miles away from the Othonian objective, the confluence of the Po and another river (2.40). **castra:** the marching-camp is near mod. Voltido (Wellesley (1971) 31). **adeo imperite ut . . . penuria aquae fatigarentur:** 35.1n. *amne medio*. Plutarch makes the same criticism more expansively (*Oth.* 11.1), also stressing the spring season and well-watered environs. A general's obligation to secure good drinking water for his soldiers is a topos (Plb. 6.27.3, [Caes.] *Alex.* 8.1, Veg. 1.22.1, 3.8.3), so the device damningly captures Othonian incompetence. *penuria aquae* (also *A.* 14.24.1; cf. *aquarum penuria*, 4.26.2) is Sallustian (*Jug.* 17.5), with *penuria* as a more poetic alternative to *inopia*. Abl. phrases qualified with *quamquam* (3.2n.) or *quamuis* (also 2.41.2, 2.72.1, 2.86.3), first in Cic. and Liv., are increasingly common in post-Augustan Latin (GL §609 n.1). **de proelio dubitatum** (sc. *est*) 'there was hesitation about (how to handle) the battle'. The Othonians intend to fight the Vitellians (*postquam pugnari placitum*, 2.33.2), but still have to work out the best tactics. A central question was how far to advance along the Via Postumia, before taking a side-road: the main road, ideal for transporting a large body of men, would naturally be scrutinised by Vitellian scouts (Wellesley (2000) 76). The debate is also in Plutarch (*Oth.* 11.2). **flagitante . . . poscentibus . . . postulabant:** *uariatio* of three synonymous verbs in different forms. The asyndeton between the two abl. absolutes only emphasises the distance and deadlock between Otho and his soldiers. The emperor's communication *per litteras* reminds us of his absence and anticipates the futility of the soldiers' demands for his presence. **militibus ut . . . poscentibus:** *posco* + *ut* (4.5.1, Liv. 5.28.9, Sil. 13.268, Quint. 9.4.57, Juv. 5.112) is unusual. T. implicitly activates the topos of troops inspired by seeing their commander (Liv. 6.8.6, 9.27.13, 21.43.17, Dio 43.36, Plin. *Pan.* 15.5), to which T. will return (42.2n. *ceteris conspicui*). **copias trans Padum agentes** 'the troops operating across the Po' (*OLD ago* 20). The remaining soldiers are now based south of the Po, one group at Brixellum with Otho (2.33.3) and another group near Cremona with Flavius Sabinus (2.36.2). The main army north of the Po presumably wants the Brixellum contingent to be brought forward. **quid optimum factu fuerit, quam pessimum fuisse quod factum est:** antimetabole (37.2n. *pacem belli amore*), enhanced by alliteration. Elegantly placed negatives (*Vitellius . . . quae non dabantur remisit* 3.58.4) or contrasting superlatives can amuse and add bathos.

40 Non ut ad pugnam sed ad bellandum profecti: the scornful *ut* 'as if' (*OLD* 8) captures the chaotic nature of the Othonian campaign. It is still unclear whether the Othonians intend to fight the Vitellians in battle on this same day (14 Apr.). The appearance of their marching column suggests not, but Otho's impatience and the dominance of Proculus implies that a battle is looming. How imminent is it? With *ad pugnam* T. (perhaps disingenuously) hints that the plan is to fight on that very day, but the immediate Othonian objective is the confluence of the rivers, from where they will fight the Vitellians, perhaps on the next day. Either way, the Othonian generals emerge as irresponsible: their route passes close to the Vitellian camp at Cremona so stealth and a defensive marching formation (both conspicuously absent) are still needed.   **confluentes †Padi et Aduae† fluminum sedecim inde milium spatio distantes petebant:** a satisfactory solution to the worst crux in T. remains elusive (Syme (1958a) 676–80, Wellesley (1971)). The problem is that if the Othonians are now 16 miles east of Cremona, the confluence of the rivers Po and Addua, 7 miles west of Cremona, is much too far away (Wellesley (1971) 36). So either T. has made a serious topographical mistake or there is a textual problem with *Aduae*. To complicate matters, the Po's course is not the same today as it was in 69, and in Plutarch the distance between the temporary marching camp and the Othonian objective to the west is lower, 'no less than 100 stades' (12 and a half miles) (*Oth.* 11.2), even if this discrepancy is partly explained by his higher figure (50 stades or 6 and a quarter miles) for the distance of the marching camp from Bedriacum (*Oth.* 11.1). There are two main contenders for the mysterious river, (i) the original reading *Adua* or *Addua* by an alternative spelling (Puteolanus, 1475), entering the Po 7 miles west of Cremona; (ii) *Arda* (Valmaggi, 1896) or *Adra* by metathesis, entering the Po 8 miles south of Cremona. Wellesley (1971) 38 proposes the alternative reading *Padi et accolae fluminum*. Yet Murison (1993) 116 n.58 offers the simplest solution to the whole problem, reviving Nipperdey's proposal that T. originally wrote *confluentes fluminum* and that the whole phrase *Padi et Aduae* (or an alternative second river) was added as a gloss. On this reading, *sedecim . . . distantes* is a predicate to *confluentes fluminum*. The tense and meaning of *petebant* perhaps offers a key: in strategic terms T. implies that the Othonians are (sensibly) seeking <u>any</u> confluence of the Po and another river located (within 16 miles) before Caecina's infamous bridge south of Cremona. This tributary will thus serve to defend the main Othonian army as they muster their forces (whether north or south of the Po) to confront the Vitellians encamped at Cremona. Otho at Brixellum with his crack troops offers a safety-net: if the Vitellians do manage to cross the Po before the main Othonian battle force confronts them, then Otho can attack the Vitellians before they sweep down to Rome.   **Celso et Paulino . . . aggrederetur:** 23.4n. for Celsus and Paulinus. This elaborate subordinate clause (32 words), where an abl. abs. triggers an acc. + inf. construction (itself a springboard for a long *quo minus* construction attached to a dat. noun), dwarfs the simple main clause (7 words). In such sentences, 'the looseness of the syntactic connection between the main clause . . . and the appendix demands that the reader determine how the two are related in content' (Damon (2003) 19). Here the intricate strategic arguments of the 'appendix' (significantly placed first) are ruthlessly crushed by the steamroller of *ius imperii* described concisely in the main clause. The sentence structure is expressive: powerless but reflective generals confront dominant but short-sighted generals with predictable results.   **itinere fessum:** T. reinforces this point in the account of the battle (*fessi* 2.42.2). Generals should not 'force to a pitched battle soldiers who are tired after a long march' (Veg. 3.11.7; cf. Onas. *Strat.* 6.9).   **sarcinis grauem:** the generals' fears will be confirmed (*mixta uehicula et lixae*, 2.41.3). Similarly in the parallel tradition Paulinus and his followers object to the impending march westwards in a column hampered by pack-animals and camp followers (Plut. *Oth.* 11.2).   **expeditus et uix quattuor milia passuum progressus:** in Plutarch Paulinus and his followers call the enemy 'armed and drawn up at their leisure' (*Oth.* 11.2) without the detail that the Vitellians will only have 4 miles to cover. T. arranges his points chiastically: *expeditus* picks up *sarcinis grauem* and *uix . . . progressus* responds to *itinere fessum*. The first-century BC historian Cornelius Sisenna similarly polarises unencumbered and laden troops: *impeditos expediti . . . interficiunt* (*H.* fr. 73). **incompositos in agmine:** technical writers suggest ways to minimise the dangers to troops (often heavily laden, Jos. *BJ* 3.115–26) on the march ('Those who have made a careful study of the art of war assert that more dangers tend to arise on the march than in battle itself', Veg. 3.6.1; cf. Onas. *Strat.* 6.5–6, Fron. *Str.* 1.4, Arr. *Ect.* 1–10).   **uallum molientes** 'constructing the rampart'.   **Titianus:** 23.5n. **ubi consiliis uincerentur:** *ubi* + subjunctive of repeated action (GL §567 n.; also 2.63.2, 2.88.1, 2.88.3). *uinco* in non-military contexts is common, but is ironic here, since the 'victory' of Titianus and Proculus will soon lead to military defeat.   **citus equo Numida:** hypallage, the poeticism where an adj. is attracted to a substantive to which it does not properly belong (5.2n. *uicinis . . . administrationibus*). In Plutarch too a Numidian courier arrives with Otho's demand (*Oth.* 11.3). Numidian cavalry, who had served Rome since the Jugurthine war (Sall. *Jug.* 68.2, Dio fr. 89.4), were used as couriers and outriders under the empire (Sen. *Ep.* 123.7; cf. Mart. 10.14.2). *Numida* no longer had to designate nationality.   **atrocibus mandatis:** in a work that is *atrox proeliis* (1.2.1), Otho's harsh directives trigger a *bellum atrox* (2.46.3) whose gory aftermath will be an *atrox spectaculum* (2.70.1).   **increpita ducum segnitia:** after the council, Otho knew that disagreements between his generals could still cause delay, so he galvanises them with the insult *segnitia* (Opelt (1965) 190 on the shaming potential of *segnis* in military contexts; e.g. Liv. 4.28.4). He himself eschews *segnitia* (1.13.4, 2.11.3).   **rem in discrimen mitti** 'that the matter be brought to the critical point'. Cf. *nec in tantae discrimina mittere pugnae | . . . agmen* (Luc. 2.599–600), *committendam rerum summam in discrimen utcumque ratus* (Liv. 33.7.10). T. prefers the simple *mitto* to Livy's compound *committo*.   **aeger mora et spei impatiens:** T. echoes Lucan (*impatiensque morae uenturisque omnibus aeger*, 6.424; cf. *aeger quippe morae*, 7.240), but his chiasmus is more pithy. Here and in the parallel tradition, Otho's fatalism transcends some complex events: two Othonian officers, perhaps intending to abort the final conflict, were asking to meet Caecina when battle erupted (2.41.1). The emperor may have discovered this and wanted to act quickly (Wellesley (2000) 78). In Plutarch, Otho's secretary, the rhetorician Secundus, claims that the emperor, worn out by anxiety (cf. *impatiens longioris sollicitudinis*, Suet. *Otho* 9.1), cannot bear the uncertainty any longer, and uses the vivid image of him leaping from a cliff (Plut. *Oth.* 9.2–3). Cf. Pompey's advisers, who are 'utterly exhausted with the war and preferred a quick decision rather than a sound one' (App. *BC* 2.67), and overturn his decision not to fight Caesar at Pharsalus.

41.1 Eodem die: 14 Apr. 69; 22.1n. *uixdum orto die.*   **operi . . . intentum:** the combination is first in Livy (Kraus (1994) 240).   **duo praetoriarum cohortium:** these officers came from Spurinna's praetorians who had joined the gladiators south of the Po opposite Cremona (2.36.2). The mysterious abortive meeting with Caecina is not in Plutarch.   **audire condiciones ac reddere:** cf. *audire et reddere uoces* (Virg. *A.* 1.409).   **cum** introduces an inverse *cum*-clause for dramatic effect (36.1n. *cum intercursu*).   **praecipites exploratores:** these scouts probably come to Caecina since he is closest, but the lack of communication with Fabius Valens is striking. Plutarch says that Caecina was 'disturbed' (*Oth.* 11.4) on hearing the news, but T. says nothing about his emotional state.   **interruptus:** sc. *est.*   **eoque:** 13.2n. **insidias an proditionem uel aliquod honestum consilium:** a compact list of possibilities. The first (*insidiae*) is a trap for the Vitellians, the second indicates betraying Otho, while the third means a discussion taking place with Otho's knowledge. Yet the praetorians are intensely pro-Othonian (2.46.3), so *insidiae* (perhaps a disingenous offer of peace) seems more likely than *proditio*. If the idea was to distract Caecina while their comrades made the dangerous journey along the Via Postumia, it worked. The *honestum consilium* suggests an attempt to end the war without bloodshed (2.37.1), already dismissed by T. as implausible. The later rumour during the battle that Vitellius' army had abandoned his cause (2.42.1) could have been fuelled by knowledge of this meeting.   **coeptauerint:** with the perfect subjunctive, there is a vivid shift to primary sequence of tenses after *incertum fuit*, suggesting that it was uncertain at the time and is still uncertain. Cf. *nequiuerint* 1.7.2, *uolgauerint* 1.34.2, *fuerit* 2.44.3, *fuderint strauerintque* 3.13.2, *composuerint* 3.53.3.

41.2 datum . . . signum et militem in armis: this is also in the parallel tradition (Plut. *Oth.* 11.5). Fabius Valens had to act quickly, but it is still striking that he ignores Caecina in preparing for battle. On the practicalities of giving the signal for battle (usually by horn or trumpet), see Goldsworthy (1996) 149–50.   **de ordine agminis sortiuntur:** the order of Vitellian troops in the battle-line, usually standard in such narratives (e.g. Caes. *Civ.* 3.88–9), is not given, but this will be no ordinary battle. Military handbooks advise on techniques for arranging battle-lines (Veg. 2.15, 3.14; Goldsworthy (1996) 133–41).   **equites prorupere:** 3.1n. *ipsa . . . cessere.* In Plutarch Caecina and Valens trigger this manoeuvre ('they sent out in advance the best of the cavalry' *Oth.* 11.5), but T. is ambiguous about whether it was spontaneous or in response to orders. Shock cavalry charges are regular (and often decisive) in Livian battle narratives (Oakley (1997) 620). Caecina and Valens will refer to the

incident during Vitellius' tour of the battlefield: *hinc equites coortos* (2.70.3).   **mirum
dictu** is adverbial. T. opens by highlighting a promising moment for the side that will
eventually lose, a common historiographical and epic technique. *mirum dictu* recurs
in discursive digressions on the east (4.84.3, 5.6.2) and again in a battle-narrative
(*A.* 2.17.3).   **a paucioribus Othonianis:** the phrase is placed emphatically, but
belongs grammatically to the *quo minus* subordinate clause. These are the *duae . . . Pannonicae ac Moesicae alae* (3.2.4) to whom Antonius Primus later refers.   **quo minus
in uallum impingerentur** 'from being hurled back on the rampart'. On *quo minus*
+ the subjunctive after verbs of hindering and preventing, see GL §549 (also 2.89.1,
4.71.5). T. may evoke Virgil: *cum Troia Achilles | exanimata sequens impingeret agmina muris*
(*A.* 5.804–5).   **Italicae legionis uirtute:** the *legio prima Italica* (*RE* xii 1408–17),
originally recruited by Nero in 66 or 67 and sent against Vindex, joined Vitellius
under the auspices of Junius Blaesus (1.59.2). Fabius Valens brought it to Italy from
Lugdunum (1.64.3). It performed less well against the Flavians (3.18.1, 3.22.2), and
after the Vitellian defeat, was sent to Illyricum (3.35.1), where it confronted a Sarmatian invasion.   **redire pulsos et pugnam resumere coegit** 'forced the beaten
men to go back and resume the fight'. The *prima Italica* performs a duty often associated with the ideal general (cf. Antonius Primus: *retinere cedentes*, 3.17.1). This highlights
a broad problem, the absence of dynamic commanders on both sides: Caecina and
Valens are only mentioned when the fighting is effectively over and Otho's generals
have fled long before then (2.43.2). *pugnam resumere* is an innovation, formed on the
analogy of *arma resumere*, and enhances the structuring sound effects.   **disposita:**
sc. *est.*   **quamquam** lacks a finite verb (3.2n. *quamquam in aperto*).   **aspectus
armorum:** in this phrase, marked by assonance, *arma* probably indicates the Othonians by synecdoche, but T. may also evoke the topos of *fulgor armorum* (Hom. *Il.* 3.83,
Plaut. *Mil.* 1–4, Prop. 4.6.26, Hor. *Carm.* 1.7.19–20, 2.1.19, Liv. 33.10.2, Luc. 1.244,
7.214–17, T. *H.* 3.82.1). 'The polished spear-points and flashing swords . . . send ahead
a terrible lightning-flash of war' (Onas. *Strat.* 29.2; Kraus (1994) 164). The shambolic
Othonian advance fails to live up to this standard. T. elsewhere accentuates the visual
dimension in battle: *primi in omnibus proeliis oculi uincuntur* (*G.* 43.6), as in Britain when
Druidaeque circum . . . nouitate aspectus perculere militem (*A.* 14.30.1).   **densis arbustis**
'by the thick plantations' (25.2n. *uineas . . . impeditas*), also at 3.21.2. These promote the
growth of vines (*si pinguis agros metabere campi, | densa sere; in denso non segnior ubere Bacchus,*
Virg. *G.* 2.274–5), but the difficult terrain will have an impact on the battle (2.42.2).

   41.3 mixta uehicula et lixae 'a jumble of carts and camp-followers' (30.2n.
uigore . . . fauore). This develops the earlier point that the Othonians set off *non ut ad pugnam sed ad bellandum* (2.40). *lixae* are civilians accompanying an army to make money,
usually by selling food to the soldiers or hiring out wagons. Elsewhere they are cast
as insolent (2.87.1), cruel (3.33.1) and cowardly (4.20.2). Sallust has them facilitate
the decadence of the Roman army in Africa (*Jug.* 44.5, 45.2). For T. mixing troops
with other elements is a symptom of civil war (Damon (2003) 180).   **praeruptis
utrimque fossis:** Roman roads were built up to create a central *agger* between two
drainage ditches (*fossae*). Paulinus at Castores wanted *compleri fossas* (2.25.2) to enable

his soldiers to move freely. For the complexities of road construction, see Stat. *Silu.* 4.3.40–55 (with Coleman (1988) 112–18, Chevallier (1976) 86–93). **uia:** sc. Postumia. **quieto quoque agmini** 'even for a peaceful march' (also at 3.59.2). **circumsistere . . . quaerere** are historic infinitives in asyndeton (5.1n., *anteire . . . obniti*). The rapid syntax here contrasts with the Othonian soldiers' hesitant actions. **incertus . . . clamor:** in Livy *incertus clamor* marks soldiers who are reluctant to fight (10.36.3; cf. *undique simul clamor ingens oritur*, Sall. *Jug.* 57.3) and a military column trying to find its way in bad weather (33.7.2). **uocantium** is J. F. Gronovius' emendation (accepted by Fisher, Heubner and Wellesley) of M's *clamantium*, although *cla-* is deleted and *uo-* added in the left-hand margin to give *uomantium* (Wellesley (1989) 192). **ut cuique audacia uel formido, in primam postremamue aciem prorumpebant aut relabebantur:** three artfully interlaced antithetical pairs have the item placed first (*audacia, in primam . . . aciem, prorumpebant*) for the brave, while the second item (*formido, in . . . postremam . . . aciem, relabebantur*) indicates the cowards. This distributive dove-tailing of antithetical pairs is 'found in poetry before it appears in Tacitus' rhetorical prose' (Brink (1944) 44 with examples, including *ille uel hic classis poterant uel perdere muros*, Prop. 2.22.33). Another case features at 1.6.1 (Damon (2003) 107). There is *uariatio* of conjunctions (*uel, -ue, aut*), while *relabor* is only here in the *H.* (used elsewhere for water: *A.* 1.76.1, 2.24.3; cf. 23.3n. *repente effudit*, 93.1n. *redundante multitudine*).

42.1 Attonitas subito terrore mentes: this section (2.42.1) is full of details about the Othonians' shifting feelings (*terrore / gaudium / languorem / omisso pugnae ardore / metum proditionis*), but the Vitellians' emotions are left opaque. This adds to the pathos of the impending Othonian defeat and subtly prepares for the passionate response to Otho's suicide. In battle, morale can be just as important as physical and numerical strength (17–20.1 introduction), in which the Vitellians also have the advantage (*robore et numero praestantior*, 2.42.2). Yet the Othonians' fear is only brief (*proelium . . . acriter sumpsere*, 2.42.2). *attonitas . . . mentes* is poetic (Tib. 1.9.47, Sen. *Tro.* 442, Luc. 5.476). The *subitus terror* must refer to the Vitellians' lightning charge that forced the Othonians' rapid call to arms. Such initial charges could potentially terrify an enemy ([Caes.] *Hisp.* 31.1). **falsum gaudium** 'baseless delight'. The abstract noun as subject (2.1n. *spes uicit*) suggests personification, and recalls the opening of the Othonian campaign (*blandiebatur coeptis fortuna* 2.12.1). **in languorem:** T. has *languor* only here, preferring to use the verb *languesco* (9×). **is rumor:** although this rumour serves the Vitellians well, the tables will turn during the second battle of Bedriacum when a *uagus . . . rumor* (3.25.1) that Mucianus has arrived boosts the Flavian assault. Announcing good news (even if false) during battle can be beneficial (Onas. *Strat.* 23). For rumours influencing fighting, see 4.33.3, *A.* 1.66.1, 6.35.2, Caes. *Gal.* 2.1. **dispersus:** sc. *sit*. The verbal ellipse momentarily suggests that this is the definitive explanation for the rumour's source (an impression undermined by *an*). **seu dolo seu forte:** for Suetonius the rumour directly caused Otho's defeat: *fraude superatus est* (*Otho* 9.2; cf. Plut. *Oth.* 12.1–2). It served a purpose after the battle: so the praetorians complain about being beaten *proditione* (2.44.3) and later Antonius Primus calls the

Pannonian legions *deceptae magis quam uictae* (3.2.3). The notion of the deceptive story was useful to pro-Flavian historiography, as it allowed ex-Othonians (many of whom went on to support Vespasian) to save face and cast the Vitellians as underhand. By acknowledging that the rumour could have started by chance. T. asserts his independence as a historian. **parum compertum:** sc. *est.* **ultro** 'spontaneously'. **hostili murmure** is a unique combination (*TLL* s.v. *hostilis* 3052.49). Plutarch has a similar detail, as the Vitellians answer μετὰ θυμοῦ καὶ φωνῆς πολεμικῆς 'with anger and hostile shouting' (*Oth.* 12.2). **plerisque . . . salutandi:** *plerisque . . . ignaris* = dat. (indirect object of *metum . . . fecere*). This is typical of a crowd (T. is a shrewd observer of such behaviour) as people are driven to act in unison by the impetus of others, despite not knowing the reason for their action. **metum proditionis:** the Othonian soldiers' fear of betrayal and mistrust of their officers is a powerful theme (1.80.2, 2.18.2, 2.23.4, 2.26.1, 2.33.3, 2.44.1, 2.44.3).

42.2 hostium acies: by calling the Vitellians *hostes*, T. focalises the narrative with the Othonians. **quamquam** lacks a finite verb (3.2n. *quamquam in aperto*). **dispersi pauciores fessi:** the three adjectives in asyndeton articulate the polarisation of Othonians and Vitellians in strategic terms. *dispersi* picks up *integris ordinibus*, while *pauciores + fessi* correspond chiastically to *numero praestantior + robore . . . praestantior*. Estimates of the troops available to Otho at the battle include just over 50,000 Othonian soldiers (Passerini (1940) 200–10) or 57,000 (Chilver (1970–1) 105–6). Yet the force which marched towards Cremona is not the entire Othonian army (the rest is south of the Po) and from the four legions from Pannonia and Dalmatia (32.2n. *cum integris exercitibus*, with Syme (1958a) 680–2), only the *XIII Gemina* and a vexillation from the *XIV Gemina* are present at the battle (Murison (1993) 110–13). On balance 'there are simply too many unknowns' to enumerate the Othonian force with any certainty (Murison (1993) 118 n.63). **per locos . . . impeditos:** the landscape is changed by the battle (*protritis arboribus ac frugibus*, 2.70.1), but Antonius Primus still exploits the terrain during the second battle of Bedriacum (*densis arbustis*, 3.21.2). Plutarch says that it was full of trenches and pits (*Oth.* 12.3). **non una pugnae facies:** sc. *erat.* The heterogeneous spectacle of this messy battle is clear from the start. This must partly reflect T.'s sources (some were probably eye-witnesses), but there is also a historiographical agenda, as T. adds variety and vividness to the battle-narrative for an audience well-versed in such scenes (a stock element of ancient historiography: Ash (2002)). The emphasis on varied fighting is also in Sallust's description of the battle at the river Muthul: *facies totius negoti uaria incerta, foeda atque miserabilis* (*Jug.* 51.1). **comminus eminus cateruis et cuneis concurrebant:** *caterua* = a loose cluster of soldiers; *cuneus* = a closely packed wedge-shaped group of men. The forceful alliteration facilitated by ablatives of manner (instead of *per cateruas*, *A.* 14.34.2) and a compound verb suggests clashing armies. **collato gradu** 'hand to hand' (*A.* 2.20.3, Sil. 12.382). Livy has the expression for infantry fighting (7.33.11), but generally prefers *pedem conferre* (not in T.), which means the same thing (Oakley (1998) 328). Cf. *fer pedem, confer gradum* (Plaut. *Men.* 554), *fer gradum et confer pedem* (Plaut. *Merc.* 882). **corporibus et umbonibus niti** 'pushing forwards with the weight of their bodies and shields' (Oakley (1997)

510–11 on *nitor* in battles). *umbo* 'shield boss', indicating the whole shield by synecdoche (also 4.29.3), refines *scutis corporibusque ipsis obnixi urgebant* (Liv. 34.46.10). The Roman *scutum* was 'very effective for striking an enemy and unbalancing him' (Goldsworthy (1996) 208; *Agr.* 36.2, *A.* 14.36.2). It measured 4 × 2.5 feet, was made of two layers of wood glued together, and was covered with canvas and calfskin, with the top and bottom edge protected by iron binding and an iron boss in the centre to deflect weapons (Goldsworthy (1996) 209; Plb. 16.23).   **omisso pilorum iactu:** this standard part of a Roman battle is usually a prelude to fighting at close quarters (22.1n. *ingerunt . . . pila*). Cf. *pila omittunt, gladiis res geritur* (Sall. *Cat.* 60.2).   **securibus:** it was not standard for legionaries to carry axes in battle, but the novel weapon (also *A.* 3.46.3) is a marker of the unusual fighting. The axes, normally used in siege warfare (3.20.3, 3.29.1) or camp construction (19.1n. *uallari castra*), presumably came from the baggage train.   **galeas loricasque perrumpere:** 11.3n. *lorica ferrea*. Over time the Roman infantry helmet developed more robust defensive features (e.g. strips of metal fixed to the front, and wider neckguards) to protect against sword-thrusts. The usual helmet in the first century AD was the iron Imperial Gallic model (Goldsworthy (1996) 215). Helmets did not always offer complete protection: Crastinus was killed by a sword-thrust full in the mouth (Caes. *Civ.* 3.99.2).   **noscentes inter se** 'recognising each other'. Cf. *Cicerones pueri amant inter se* (Cic. *Att.* 6.1.12), *uix inter sese . . . noscunt* (Stat. *Theb.* 6.413) with GL §221. Catching sight of friends and relatives on the opposing side in a civil war is a motif (Luc. 4.169–79, 7.460–9, Plut. *Pomp.* 70.1, Dio 41.58). Recognition will also be important in the second battle of Bedriacum, but in a different way, as Antonius Primus gains an advantage *ubi noscere suos noscique poterat* (3.24.1).   **ceteris conspicui** 'visible to their comrades'. The visual dimension has potential for stirring shame or pride, since 'in battle, soldiers fight harder where their comrades can see them' (Lendon (1997) 239 with [Caes.] *Gal.* 8.42.4; cf. 39.2n. *militibus ut . . . poscentibus*). Yet these soldiers must rely on themselves for inspiration, not on the gaze of their generals, who have a low profile in the battle. This contrasts with the Flavian general Primus, *conspicuus suis* (3.17.1), who will stir his men. **in euentum totius belli:** *in* + acc. + gen. to express purpose (20.1n. *in nullius iniuriam*).

43.1 Forte as a narrative device often introduces an episode, a new element in an episode or an ecphrasis (Harrison (1991) 229). Here it also underscores the lack of planning in the battle and bolsters the impression that this is not a proper old-style war (2.39–45 introduction), as this clash between legions on more standard terrain is an exception to the surrounding chaos. Plutarch has no equivalent expression in his version of the encounter (*Oth.* 12.4–6).   **patenti campo:** open terrain suits Roman fighting techniques (14.2n. *quantum . . . aequi loci*). Plutarch calls the area 'exposed and extended' (*Oth.* 12.4).   **unaetuicensima, cui cognomen Rapaci:** 18.1n. *ueterano exercitui*. The name *Rapax* means 'greedy, in the sense of sweeping everything before it' (Webster (1985) 105). Although the legion has already featured (1.61.2, 1.67.1), T. postpones its name until now, perhaps for paronomasia (43.1n. *rapuit*).   **uetere gloria insignis:** when T. was writing, the legion had already been annihilated while fighting the Sarmatians in 92. 'The erasure of its name on two tombstones at Vindonissa (*CIL* XIII 5201 and 11514) may indicate that it had seriously disgraced itself' (Webster (1985) 107 n.32). Although it fought a difficult battle against Arminius in 15 (*A.* 1.64.5), T. perhaps exaggerates its stature, especially after its involvement in the mutiny in 14 (*A.* 1.31.3) and in Saturninus' uprising in 88 or 89. After that, it was moved from Mogontiacum to Pannonia (Levick (1999) 162). Apparently its legionaries were experienced, but old and past their prime (Plut. *Oth.* 12.5).   **prima Adiutrix:** 11.2n. *cum legione prima*; 11.3n. *classicorum . . . numerus.*   **non ante . . . decoris auida:** T. similarly contrasts experienced and novice troops in introducing the Flavian legions, *exercitae bello* ∼ *inexperti belli ardor* (2.4.4). Plutarch also says that Otho's legionaries had not previously been in battle (*Oth.* 12.5), but in fact they recently fought at Castores (2.24.3). The detail was probably in the common source, who polarised the two legions to add excitement.   **stratis unaetuicensimanorum principiis** 'after the front ranks of the men from the twenty-first had been overcome'.   **aquilam abstulere:** the eagle gracing the legionary's most important standard (18.2n. *correptis . . . uexillisque*) was hugely emotive. So the centurion Atilius Verus dies while retrieving the *VII Galbiana*'s eagle (3.22.4). If the eagle was moved (or thrown) into the enemy's lines, then the legion would follow, despite the danger (Caes. *Gal.* 4.25.3, Fron. *Str.* 2.8.1–5). Its loss 'was equated with that of the legion itself' (Webster (1985) 133). The eagle, made of silver (Dio 43.35, App. *BC* 4.101), was carried by the senior standard-bearer, the *aquilifer*, who wore an animal skin for effect. Under the republic four other animals were associated with the standards (wolf, minotaur, horse and boar), but the eagle, linked with Jupiter, gradually superseded them (Plin. *Nat.* 10.16). Generals could exploit soldiers' knowledge of an individual eagle's history to inspire them (Sall. *Cat.* 59.3). See Speidel (1984) 3–43.   **dolore accensa:** 27.2n. *grauis . . . exarserat.* Cf. *accensa dolore* (Virg. *A.* 11.709), *accendit . . . animos dolor* (Liv. 21.44.4). The fire-imagery is not in Plutarch's version. At least something worthy fires the Vitellian legion, the sting of losing their eagle (cf. Antonius Primus, *omnes spe promissisque accendens*, 3.24.1).   **interfecto . . . legato:** the detail is also in Plutarch (*Oth.* 12.6). Focusing on a named individual humanises the battle description (25.2n. *rex Epiphanes*). T. will record his cremation (2.45.3).   **plurima . . . uexillaque:** 18.2n. *correptis . . . uexillisque.*   **rapuit:** with playful paronomasia, the *legio XXI Rapax* (aptly) *rapuit* the enemy's standards (Woodman (1998) 221–2 and n.12).

43.2 propulsa: sc. *est.* The clash between these two legions is not in Plutarch. **impetu quintanorum:** the *legio V Alaudae* (Gallic for 'larks'; *RE* XII 1564–70), created by Caesar (Suet. *Jul.* 24.2) and based in Vetera (mod. Xanten) in Lower Germany, started the mutiny in Germany in 14 (*A.* 1.31.3). It marched to Italy with Fabius Valens (1.61.2), and after the battle at Bedriacum, went to Rome with Vitellius (2.68.2). Then it headed north to fight the Flavians (2.100.1). The legion, fiercely loyal to Vitellius (3.14), was at the centre of the line in the second battle of Bedriacum (3.22.2). It was besieged at Vetera by Julius Civilis (4.18.1), who set up a treacherous ambush (4.60.2), and was eventually sent to Moesia.   **tertia decima legio:** i.e. the Othonian *legio XIII Gemina* (11.1n. *quattuor legiones*; 26.2n. *Vitellianus miles*).   **quartadecimani:** i.e.

the Othonian *legio XIV Gemina* (11.1n. *quattuor legiones* + *rebellione . . . compressa*). The main force only just missed the battle (2.54.1) and refused to acknowledge defeat, as only a detachment had been beaten (2.66.1).   **ducibus Othonis . . . profugis:** this shocking revelation endorses the soldiers' earlier fears about their officers (42.1n. *metum proditionis*). Plutarch, less interested than T. in the middle ranks of the military hierarchy, omits this point.   **subsidiis suos firmabant:** reserve forces should be held in readiness 'to prevent the line being broken, reinforce any weak points and, with this additional strength, break the enemy's onset' (Veg. 3.17.1). Caesar uses such reinforcements decisively during the battle at Pharsalus (*Civ.* 3.94.1).   **Varus Alfenus:** 29.2n.   **cum Batauis:** 27.2n. *cohortes Batauos.*   **fusa . . . manu:** in T., these gladiators cross the Po from the south, but are killed in the river before they can properly disembark. In Plutarch, the gladiators briefly fight the Batavians, but then flee *back* to the river where they are killed by enemy cohorts (*Oth.* 12.7–8). This is the third and final clash between Otho's gladiators and the Batavians: the defeat replays their recent encounter (2.35), suggesting that replacing Martius Macer with Flavius Sabinus (2.36.2) was not a success. Only under Macer did the gladiators win a victory (2.23.3). The gladiators' attack was probably synchronised with the main Othonian advance by a prearranged timetable (Wellesley (1971) 41).   **nauibus transuectam:** the phrase recalls the gladiators' initial success (*transuectos nauibus* 2.23.3), but ships have also been problematic for them: *gladiatores nauibus molientes* + *nutantes e nauibus* (2.35.1).   **in ipso flumine trucidauerant:** episodes of fighting in a river had potential for novelty, but T. curtails his description to avoid repetition (cf. 5.21, 5.23). **ita uictores latus hostium inuecti** (sc. *sunt*) 'having won the day there, they fell upon the enemy's flank' (*OLD ita* 6a) i.e. the Othonians' left flank. Caecina and Valens refer to this incident in their tour of the battlefield with Vitellius (2.70.3).

44.1 fugere passim Othoniani: military handbooks recommend that an escape route should be offered to the enemy to facilitate their destruction while fleeing (Veg. 3.21, Fron. *Str.* 2.6.1–10, 4.7.16). The reasoning is that trapped men gain courage from desperation. Catiline warns his men before the final battle: *nam in fuga salutem sperare, quom arma quibus corpus tegitur ab hostibus auorteris, ea uero dementia est* (Sall. *Cat.* 58.16). Plutarch especially blames the praetorians for cowardly flight during the battle (*Oth.* 12.9–10), but T. is not so critical.   **Bedriacum petentes:** the Othonians fleeing towards Bedriacum are aiming for their main camp just outside the village (cf. *oppugnationem castrorum*, 2.45.1), not the temporary marching-camp 4 miles to the west of Bedriacum.   **immensum id spatium:** sc. *erat.* T. has similar expressions elsewhere (*Agr.* 10.3, *G.* 1.1, 1.23.2, 3.38.3). Bedriacum was 20 miles east of Cremona (23.2n. *Bedriaci*), but the battle took place four miles east of Cremona, leaving 16 miles to cover. A legion on the march could travel *c.* 15 miles in a day (Wellesley (1971) 41), but these Othonians are not so heavily laden and probably drop any expendable gear in their panic.   **obstructae strage corporum uiae:** sc. *sunt. strages* (16× in T.), a Livian favourite (Oakley (1998) 223–4), is generally rare in prose. It recalls Otho in the forum being carried *per stragem iacentium* (1.47.2). Plutarch in his tour of the battlefield saw a temple (possibly that of Castor and Pollux) surrounded by corpses heaped as high as the roof (*Oth.* 14.2). Dio puts the casualties at 40,000 men from both sides, but it is unclear how many other battles are included in this total (64.10.3); and casualty figures can be notoriously unreliable, especially if they emanated from the victors (Carter (1993) 218). An enemy impeding its own flight through numbers is a *topos* (Oakley (1997) 466), but T.'s focus on corpses adds a nasty twist.   **neque . . . capti in praedam uertuntur:** the verb in the present tense makes this a *sententia*. Plutarch includes the detail while speculating about why there were so many corpses around the temple (*Oth.* 14.3). Difficulty in selling captives from a civil war features again, but the reason is the *consensus Italiae*, not lack of effort from the Flavian soldiers (3.34.2). Cf. Sallust on the citizens who died bravely during the final battle with Catiline: *neque . . . quisquam ciuis ingenuus captus est* (*Cat.* 61.5).   **Suetonius Paulinus et Licinius Proculus . . . castra uitauere:** the Othonian generals suddenly re-enter the narrative just when the battle is over, though T. damningly fails to name them during the fighting itself. Plutarch says that they feared the soldiers, who blamed them for the defeat (*Oth.* 13.1). That this sentence culminates in *uitauere* instead of (say) *petiuere* causes surprise (cf. *auersis itineribus urbem petiuere*, Liv. 22.7.2). So too does the pairing of Paulinus (23.4n.) and Proculus (33.1n.), always on opposite sides during debates about the campaign.   **Vedium Aquilam:** despite this dangerous encounter with his soldiers, Aquila still commands the *XIII Gemina* when it is mobilised for the Flavian cause (3.7.1), although he will ultimately defer to Antonius Primus (3.11.4).   **irae militum inconsultus pauor obtulit** 'a rash panic delivered [Aquila] to the angry soldiers'; abstract noun as subject (2.1n. *spes uicit*). For *inconsultus pauor* see Liv. 22.6.6, Curt. 6.2.4. *inconsultus* (from Plautus onwards) is in Livy (8×), but Sallust and Caesar avoid the adj. in favour of adverbial forms.   **multo adhuc die:** cf. *multo denique die* (Caes. *Gal.* 1.22.4). Mutinous conduct is often linked with darkness (1.80.2, *A.* 1.28.1; Ash (1999) 32–3): that these Othonians attack their general in daylight shows their desperation. It also demonstrates how swiftly the Othonian attack crumbled: by contrast, the second battle of Bedriacum lasts from 11am (3.16.1) until well into the night (*adulta nocte*, 3.23.3). On the gender of *dies*, see 22.1n. *uixdum orto die*.   **clamore seditiosorum et fugacium circumstrepitur** 'was surrounded by the shouts of mutinous deserters'. Some may be the praetorians who fled during the battle (Plut. *Oth.* 12.9–10). *fugax*, here a substantive (*TLL* s.v. *fugax* 1474.5–8), exemplifies T.'s point about soldiers accusing others of their own transgressions (*suum . . . obiectantes* 2.44.1). *circumstrepitur* is only here in the *H.* (also *A.* 3.36.4 with WM 313, 11.31.1, but in the active voice).   **non probris, non manibus:** anaphora of *non* (93.1n. *non principia noscere*) and asyndeton accentuate the escalating violence; cf. *probra, dein saxa, postremo ferrum sumpsere* (*A.* 14.17.1).   **desertorem proditoremque increpant:** sc. *eum*. The soldiers, themselves labelled *seditiosi* and *fugaces*, appear deeply hypocritical. The agent-nouns *desertor* + *proditor* are often paired (Caes. *Gal.* 6.23.8, Liv. 2.59.10, T. *H.* 1.72.1, *A.* 2.10.1). On such reproaches from soldiers, see Opelt (1965) 192–4.   **nullo proprio crimine eius** 'not because they had any particular charge against him'.   **suum . . . obiectantes:** T., always sensitive towards such hypocrisy (1.74.1), later has an even pithier denunciation: *factum esse scelus loquuntur faciuntque* (3.25.3). The singular distributive pronoun *quisque* goes with the pl. participle because the antecedent (the subject of *increpant*) is pl. (*quisque . . . extollentes* 2.70.3; *quisque . . . fulgentes* 2.89.2; GL §211), but T. often has pl. verbs agreeing with a singular collective noun or distributive pronoun (*quisque* 2.54.2, 2.66.3, 2.84.1, 2.84.2, 2.94.1), as does Livy (Kraus (1994) 106).

44.2 Titianum et Celsum: Plutarch's Celsus (23.4n.) is more active after the battle, delivering a speech to reconcile his fellow-officers to their defeat (*Oth.* 13.3–5) and almost getting killed by some Vitellian soldiers (*Oth.* 13.7–10). Plutarch's Titianus (23.5n.) urges that they send an embassy to the Vitellians (*Oth.* 13.6), but then changes his mind (*Oth.* 13.11). Yet T. ignores both men's actions after the battle, except for this brief, dishonourable mention.   **nox iuuit:** abstract noun as subject (2.1n. *spes uicit*). The combination, suggesting personification, recurs (*A.* 1.50.4, 2.82.4).   **Annius Gallus:** 11.2n.   **consilio precibus auctoritate:** the asyndetic trio accentuates Gallus' different techniques, but ideally a general should only have to use his *auctoritas*.   **flexerat:** the metaphor of bending recurs in contexts of soldiers' shifting moods (1.31.2, 1.66.1, *A.* 1.29.1, 1.41.3). These soldiers bend, but the resolve of the others will break (*remanentium fractus animus*, 2.33.3).   **ne super cladem . . . caedibus saeuirent:** 30.1n. *aduersa . . . pugna*; 8.1n. on *super* for *praeter* (here setting up chiastic and enclosing sound-effects). For the phrasing, cf. *inter semet ipsi seditionibus saeuiant* (Liv. 2.44.8). Where Plutarch's Gallus encourages the soldiers about their recent fighting (*Oth.* 13.2), T.'s Gallus grimly calls the battle a *clades* and acknowledges that the men still might slaughter one another.   **seu resumere arma mallent:** Gallus raises a possibility (resuming the fighting) which will gain momentum as T. moves towards the narrative of Otho's suicide. Suetonius suggests that Otho's troops were keen to obliterate their disgraceful defeat (*Oth.* 9.3).   **unicum uictis in consensu leuamentum:** sc. *esse. consensus* was also a political slogan used especially on Vitellius' coinage (*consensus exercituum*, Mattingly (1923) 81–5, 99–102, 110–12, with Damon (2003) 137–8), but the ex-Othonians' support for Vespasian will play a crucial role in his victory. 'T. prefers *leuamentum*, found in Cicero and other authors, to *leuamen*, found in Livy and poetry' (MW 119). He likes nouns with the weighty ending -*mentum* (38.1n. *temptamenta . . . bellorum*).

44.3 ceteris fractus animus: sc. *erat*. The phrase, recalling *remanentium fractus animus* (2.33.3), shows ring-composition. Yet their state of mind is not permanent: cf. *uictarum legionum haudquaquam fractus animus* (2.66.1).   **proditione:** 42.1n. *seu dolo seu forte*.   **fremebat:** 6.2n. *fremere miles*.   **ne Vitellianis quidem incruentam fuisse uictoriam:** 15.2n. for the phrase and litotes. T.'s Othonians evoke Sallust describing the battlefield after Catiline's defeat: *neque tamen exercitus populi Romani laetam aut incruentam uictoriam adeptus erat* (*Cat.* 61.7). Yet Sallust's *exercitus populi Romani* (suggesting loyalty to the state) is replaced by *Vitelliani* (suggesting loyalty to one man). **pulso equite, rapta legionis aquila:** in both abl. absolutes, the praetorians accentuate the positive. Yet although the Othonians did drive back the Vitellian cavalry (2.41.2), it was only a temporary success, and although the *Prima Adiutrix* did capture the eagle of the *Legio XXI Rapax* (2.43.1), they lost their legate and many standards.   **superesse . . . uenire . . . remansisse:** asyndeton reinforces their optimistic enumeration of the remaining strength, but they have no leader to mobilise it.

Normally a general, not his troops, would try to restore morale in this way. **cum ipso Othone:** the soldiers regard Otho almost as a talisman, whose mere presence will avert disaster. At the start of the imperial challenge, they had put him like an inanimate object among the standards on the platform (1.36.1). **fuerit:** 41.1n. *coeptauerint.* **Moesicas legiones:** 32.2n. *cum integris exercitibus.* **magnam exercitus partem:** this exaggerates (Chilver (1979) 209), but if Otho had opted to continue fighting 'he might still have had available over 50% of the force at Bedriacum' (Murison (1993) 136). **si ita ferret** 'if need be'. 'Such phraseology can be used with an expressed subject (e.g. *fors, res*) or impersonally' (WM 164). **honestius in acie perituros:** death in battle was seen as the most honourable distinction for a soldier. So, the soldiers trapped at the Caudine Forks lament that *se solos sine uolnere, sine ferro, sine acie uictos* (Liv. 9.5.10) and Catiline urges that his soldiers, *uirorum more pugnantes* (Sall. *Cat.* 58.21), should only allow a bloody victory for their enemies. The soldiers themselves will urge Otho that *ipsos extrema passuros ausurosque* (2.46.1). **his cogitationibus truces aut pauidi extrema desperatione ad iram saepius quam in formidinem stimulabantur** 'they were savage or anxious at these thoughts, but in their final despondency were more often goaded to anger than fear'; 7.2n. *stimulabat;* 27.1n. *in metum compulit* for *uariatio* of prepositions. Vespasian will soon seek to harness the Othonians' anger for his own cause (Ash (1999) 87). Some critics see *pauidi* as an odd label for the praetorians just after their indignant reflections, but thoughts of continuing the war naturally prompt anxiety.

45.1 At: transitional *at* (20.1n. *At*). **ad quintum . . . lapidem:** the Vitellians were five miles from the Othonians in their main camp. The temporary marching camp one mile away must have been abandoned. **consedit** is regular in military contexts (*TLL* s.v. *consido* 434.38–79, with 434.60–4 + *ad*). **non ausis ducibus:** the cohesion lent to the cause by the Vitellian generals emphasises the flawed (and absent) leaders of the Othonians. Victorious, over-confident armies could face difficulties: 'Often a previously routed army has recovered its strength and destroyed those in loose order and pursuing at random. Never does greater danger more frequently arise for the side that is celebrating than when over-confidence is suddenly turned to panic' (Veg. 3.25.8–9, cf. Onas. *Strat.* 36.3–6, Thuc. 2.11.4). Antonius Primus, trying to suppress his troops after the second battle of Bedriacum, argues: *duces prouidendo consultando cunctatione saepius quam temeritate prodesse* (3.20.1). **eadem die:** the Vitellians are tired after the battle and there is probably little daylight left. So the Romans refrain from attacking the Hernici *quia serum erat diei* (Liv. 7.8.5). To attack a camp at night is elsewhere presented as typically rash German strategy: *ausurosque nocturnam castrorum oppugnationem* (*A.* 2.12.1). On the gender of *dies*, see 22.1n. *uixdum orto die.* **oppugnationem castrorum:** descriptions of storming camps are a historiographical *topos* (Oakley (1997) 622–3), but this scene (anticipated here) is not delivered. Special equipment (not taken into battle by the Vitellians) was needed to storm a camp: cf. Curio's men *ad proelium egressi . . . iis rebus indigebant quae ad oppugnationem castrorum erant usui* (Caes. *Civ.* 2.35.4). The typical military camp on campaign was surrounded by a rampart and a defensive ditch with palisade stakes (*pila muralia*) planted on the upturned mound (Webster (1985) 169–75). The gate was given special defensive features (*Agr.* 26.2 with Ogilvie and

Richmond (1967) 243). Defending a military camp could generate spirited resistance, as *proprium esse militis decus in castris: illam patriam, illos penates* (3.84.2). **expeditis et tantum ad proelium egressis:** the lightly-armed Vitellians can neither storm the Othonian camp, nor construct one for themselves. **munimentum fuere arma et uictoria** 'as a defence they had their weapons and victory'. The syllepsis (3.2n. *precibus*), moving from physical *arma* to the abstract *uictoria*, abruptly undermines the praetorians' earlier speculation that the Othonian cause can be revived. The Vitellians now have their victory. T. similarly shifts from concrete to abstract in describing the Romans' euphoria after defeating Arminius: *nocte demum reuersae legiones, quamuis plus uulnerum, eadem ciborum egestas fatigaret, uim sanitatem copias, cuncta in uictoria habuere (A. 1.68.5).*

45.2 Postera die: 15 Apr. The Othonians' surrender after an intervening night recalls the Pompeians, who submit after Pharsalus *prima luce* on the next day (Caes. *Civ.* 3.98.1). On the gender of *dies*, see 22.1n. *uixdum orto die.* **ad paenitentiam inclinantibus:** the phrasing (and the present participle) casts the Othonians' *paenitentia* as temporary, allowing scope for the rekindling of the soldiers' fighting zeal before Otho (2.46). The combination is only here (*TLL* s.v. *inclino* 945.42). **missa legatio:** sc. *est.* In Plutarch Titianus proposes sending an embassy to the Vitellians, and Celsus and Gallus negotiate with Caecina and Valens (*Oth.* 13.6), but T., not specifying an agent, again leaves the ineffectual Othonian generals in the shadows. **nec . . . dubitatum** (sc. *est*) 'there was no hesitation'. The Vitellians hoped for a *uoluntaria deditio* (2.45.1), but are no doubt also worried that if fresh forces arrived from Moesia, the Othonians could renew the fighting. Their desire for speed is understandable. In Plutarch some Vitellian centurions have already been sent to the Othonians to urge surrender, and Celsus and Gallus meet them after setting out on their embassy (*Oth.* 13.7). **quominus:** the usual construction after (*non*) *dubito* when the doubt concerns the doubter's course of action is either a prolative infinitive or a *quin* clause (GL §555; 46.2n. *ut nemo dubitet*). **pacem concederent:** granting peace-terms was easy, but securing peace was much more difficult: cf. *interfecto Vitellio bellum magis desierat quam pax coeperat* (4.1.1). **legati paulisper retenti:** sc. *sunt.* In Plutarch the delay is dramatically caused by an impromptu attack on Celsus by some Vitellian cavalry (*Oth.* 13.9–10). **haesitationem attulit** 'caused disquiet'. This Ciceronian noun features again in the sense of 'irresolution' (1.39.2, *A.* 1.80.3), but it is stronger here, incorporating 'alarm' (*TLL* s.v. *haesitatio* 2511.66–72). **ignaris adhuc an impetrassent:** sc. *pacem.* The delegation only consists of Celsus, Gallus and a small escort, so *ignaris* (dat., the indirect object of *attulit*) indicates a large group, all the soldiers in the camp at Bedriacum. The anxiety of the Othonians is striking: generally, 'soldiers *en masse* had little to fear . . . from being on the losing side in a civil war, since their goodwill could be valuable to the victor and they might become recruits for his army' (Carter (1993) 217). **patuit uallum:** throwing open the camp formally indicates surrender (also at Plut. *Oth.* 13.12), but it also opens up a tragic panorama, almost in the manner of an *ekkyklema*. T. lavishes much more attention on the scene of fraternisation than Plutarch does (*Oth.* 13.13).

45.3 uicti uictoresque: 7.1n. *uictores uictosque.*   **in lacrimas effusi:** 29.2n.
silentio . . . lacrimis. Lucan's Pompeians and Caesarian soldiers shed tears after recognising each other *(arma rigant lacrimis, singultibus oscula rumpunt,* 4.180), leading to a
temporary armistice, but the civil war continues. The *locus classicus* for enemies crying
in each other's company involves Homer's Achilles and Priam in *Iliad* 24.   **misera
laetitia detestantes** 'found a melancholy satisfaction in cursing' (Irvine); appended
nominative present participle (27.2n. *omnem . . . iactantes*). *misera laetitia* is an especially
sharp, paradoxical oxymoron (Plass (1988) 45). Livy is more expansive: *mixta cum
dolore laetitia* (9.22.10, with Oakley (2005) 291). Cf. *mixtus gaudio dolor* (3.36.2). For most
Vitellians, gloom will turn to gloating within 40 days (2.70.3).   **alii fratrum, alii
propinquorum uolnera fouebant:** cf. Sallust describing the battlefield after Catiline's defeat: *uoluentes hostilia cadauera amicum alii, pars hospitem aut cognatum reperiebant (Cat.
61.8). uolnera fouebant* is Virgilian *(fouit ea uolnus lympha longaeuus Iapyx, A.* 12.420). T. uses
similar language for the aftermath of a collapsing amphitheatre: *hic fratrem, propinquum
ille, alius parentes lamentari (A.* 4.62.3).   **spes et praemia . . . funera et luctus:** the
chiasmus is sharpened by ellipse (sc. *erant*). The general incentives for fighting (material
rewards) devalue the tragic consequences (death and mourning).   **non aliquam
mortem maereret:** the alliteration creates an aptly sonorous finale to the sentence.   **honore solito crematur:** during campaign, cremation was a practical
measure, first instituted to prevent bodies being disinterred (Plin. *Nat.* 7.187). Ashes
were then placed in a glass or pottery vessel, to be buried or sent home (Webster
(1985) 280–1).   **necessarii ipsorum:** 20.1n. *ipsius.*   **ceterum uolgus super
humum relictum:** sc. *est. uolgus* (and the legate Orfidius' recent cremation) suggests
a direct correlation between social rank and proper observation of rites, with common
soldiers neglected unless relatives intervene. The lack of burial shockingly marks the
moral deterioration wrought by civil war and prepares for Vitellius' gruesome visit to
the battlefield almost 40 days later (2.70). Cf. Mezentius' plea: *corpus humo patiare tegi*
(Virg. *A.* 10.904). All Roman soldiers contributed to a burial fund with compulsory
deductions from their pay (Veg. 2.20.6, Onas. *Strat.* 36.1; Peretz (2005)), so normal
military rules are being ignored (Webster (1985) 279–81). Cf. Germanicus, who troubled to bury the remains of Varus and his men six years after Arminius' ambush
(*A.* 1.61–2; cf. Diod. Sic. 13.75.2, Paus. 10.21.6, Plb. 18.26.8, Liv. 26.25.13, Plut. *Flam.*
8). On unburied soldiers in Greek texts, see Pritchett (1985) IV 235–41.

46–51 FAREWELL TO OTHO: FINAL SPEECHES, SUICIDE, AND OBITUARY

Otho's death at Brixellum early in the morning of 17 Apr. 69 is a focal point in all
our accounts (Plut. *Oth.* 15–17, Suet. *Otho* 9.3–12.2, Dio 64.11–15). His extraordinary
suicide, moving and exemplary, but paradoxical and futile, neither stops the civil war
nor saves his soldiers from further suffering. Yet T. still ennobles and adds pathos to
the death-scene. So, Otho's calmness, first while waiting for news of the battle and
then while commiting suicide, imbues him with Stoic traits, further underscored by

the rising hysteria of those around him, especially the soldiers. He is altruistic towards his men and concerned for his friends and his nephew, conjuring up laudable models in the tradition (primarily the suicides of Cato the Younger and Seneca the Younger). We learn much about T.'s narrative concerns through his omission of a scene that is in all other accounts, namely the *exemplum* of a common soldier, who dramatically kills himself in front of Otho in order to validate his news about the defeat (Suet. *Otho* 10.1, Plut. *Oth.* 15.3, Dio 64.11). The soldier delivers some poignant final words (Dio, Plutarch), while *seeing* this incident makes a huge impact on Otho (Suetonius). It is very compelling, but T. transfers it to the aftermath of the second battle of Bedriacum, when the centurion Julius Agrestis kills himself in front of *Vitellius* to corroborate news of the defeat (3.54). All this is informative about T.'s historiographical concerns in depicting Otho's suicide. Narrating the soldier's suicide here could have upstaged Otho and diminished the sense of his bravery by showing him the way. The eloquent desperation of the soldier's death would also have diminished the fundamental tragedy of Otho, who killed himself when he did not have to do so (Murison (1993) 136–7).

    T. certainly ennobles Otho, but this exposes the historian to charges of inconsistency, as the emperor's noble, altruistic end abruptly reverses the pattern of his sordid life. Yet Otho's predisposition to suicide is foreshadowed before he even makes his bid for power: *mortem omnibus ex natura aequalem obliuione apud posteros uel gloria distingui; ac si nocentem innocentemque idem exitus maneat, acrioris uiri esse merito perire* (1.21.2). Other sources imply that his decision is spontaneous and histrionic: *ac statim moriendi impetum cepit* (Suet. *Otho* 9.3). There are also aesthetic reasons for T. to create a moving narrative of Otho's death: *obitae pro re publica mortes* (*A.* 16.16.1) can stir readers' emotions and 'the only *mors laudata* in the extant books of the *Histories* is Otho's' (Damon (2003) 96). Roman audiences enjoyed reading about death-scenes, especially in the years after the Julio-Claudian dynasty (Pliny *Ep.* 5.5.3, 8.12.5), and prior knowledge of Otho's end would raise readers' expectations of a purple passage. Another compelling reason for T.'s lavish treatment of Otho's suicide involves historical causation. Vespasian, shamelessly exploiting Otho's former soldiers, cast himself as an avenger of their dead hero, so T. needs to demonstrate the calibre of the man who could inspire such deep affection. The vivid and moving suicide shifts us into an intensely emotional register that prepares the way for this explanation. Finally, no doubt Otho himself could see the chance to shape his own posthumous reputation by a suicide that deliberately recalled the death of Cato the Younger (cf. Mart. 6.32). 'Every schoolboy, as the poet Persius reminds us (3.45), had to recite the speech of the dying Cato' (Griffin (1986) 195). Otho, one of T.'s most complex and intriguing characters in the *H.*, has prompted a lively critical debate (Drexler (1959), Harris (1962), Schunk (1964), Stolte (1973), Shochat (1981), Murison (1993) 131–42, Hutchinson (1993) 257–61, Perkins (1993), Ash (1999) 83–93).

   46.1 nequaquam trepidus et consilii certus 'utterly calm and resolved about his plan'. In T. Otho's calmness before his suicide is pervasive and he is (uniquely) *certus consilii* (Plut., Suet. and Dio do not reveal his plan at this point). T. implies that the rational Otho has already resolved on suicide, if the battle is lost; and his capacity for suicide is foreshadowed as early as 1.21.2. Reasoned rather than impulsive suicide brought greater *kudos:* 'It is common for many people to forestall death because of some impulse and urge (*impetu quodam et instinctu*), but it is the mark of a truly great mind to examine and weigh the reasons for death, and as reason advises, to accept or reject the idea of life or death' (Pliny *Ep.* 1.22.10). The ennobling potential of a calm suicide also reflects the Younger Seneca's distinctive brand of Stoicism (Rist (1969) 246–50; Long and Sedley (1987) 428–9). **maesta primum fama:** sc. *erat.* T. chooses the grander, more poetic *maesta* (1× *D.,* 11× *H.,* 16× *A.*) over the more prosaic *tristis* (2× *Agr.,* 1× *G.,* 2× *D.,* 11× *H.,* 23× *A.*), combining it with *fama* only here (though cf. *maestis . . . nuntiis* 3.64.2), an epic touch (*maesta . . . fama* Luc. 5.774–5, Stat. *Theb.* 4.346, 9.786–7). **profugi e proelio perditas res patefaciunt:** *perditas res* (also 3.73.1, 4.34.2) is a Livian favourite (13×), but extends the forceful alliteration that aptly suggests heightened emotion. Alliteration in T.'s narrative of Otho's death is especially marked (Harris (1962) 76). As often, rumour (here accurate) outstrips eye-witness testimony (*nam plerumque in nouitate rem fama antecedit,* Caes. *Civ.* 3.36.1). **non exspectauit . . . uocem imperatoris:** role reversal, as the general was usually the one to deliver an encouraging speech to his soldiers after defeat: e.g. Brutus to Cassius' troops after Philippi (Dio 47.47.2; cf. Onas. *Strat.* 36.3, Veg. 3.25.10). **bonum haberet animum iubebant:** sc. *ut.* This formulaic reassurance is stock Livian language (Oakley (1997) 667). There are five speeches on varying scales over only three chapters, but T. reserves direct discourse only for Otho (the Othonian soldiers: *bonum . . . ausurosque* 2.46.1, Plotius Firmus: *ne fidissimum . . . properare* 2.46.2, Otho: *hunc . . . uelit* 2.47, Otho: *irent . . . asperarent* 2.48.1, Otho: *an Vitellium . . . meminisset* 2.48.2). **superesse adhuc nouas uires:** 32.2n. *cum integris exercitibus;* 42.2n. *dispersi pauciores fessi.* **ipsos extrema passuros ausurosque** 'they were ready to suffer or dare the utmost'; *-que* = 'or' (*OLD* 7) in sentence terminal position (2.2n. *aduenasque*). The soldiers use a euphemism (*extrema passuros*) for their willingness to die for Otho, where Plutarch's soldiers are much more blunt (*Oth.* 15.2). The more pessimistic item is placed first (aptly enough after being defeated so recently): when other authors pair the verbs, the order is usually reversed (*ausi passique* Liv. 22.60.23, Sall. *Hist.* 3.86). **neque erat adulatio:** the gloss shows T. confident that his readers now know the warped dynamics of civil war, where protagonists flatter emperors rather than speak the truth. Galba warned Piso about this problem: *irrumpet adulatio, blanditiae et pessimum ueri affectus uenenum, sua cuique utilitas* (1.15.4). **furore quodam et instinctu** 'in some kind of furious enthusiasm'. Cf. *instinctam sacro mentem testata furore* (Luc. 5.150), describing the priestess Phemonoe's fake frenzy of inspiration. Yet the Othonian soldiers are genuinely agitated. **flagrabant:** the metaphor of fire for passion (cf. *militium ardor* 2.46.1) is standard, but some of these men burn with such ardour as to kill themselves beside Otho's funeral pyre (2.49.4). *flagro* + inf. (only here in T.) is a Statian construction (*Theb.* 3.118, 10.221).

46.2 qui procul adstiterant . . . proximi: T. elsewhere highlights different responses from sections of a crowd around a central speaker (e.g. 1.18.3), but here the soldiers unanimously supplicate the silent Otho in their midst. **tendere manus:**

stretching out one's hands to denote submission and respect features both in prayer
(Oakley (1997) 562) and supplication (3.10.2, 5.16.3, *A.* 1.11.3, 2.29.2, 12.65.3), but the
gesture implies that the soldiers are not carrying weapons after their recent ignomin-
ious flight (2.44.1). It also suggests that they know instinctively that Otho has resolved
to abandon the campaign, and reverses the start of the imperial challenge when we
saw him *protendens manus* to win over the troops (1.36.3). The reciprocal gesture captures the *peripeteia*.   **prensare genua:** clasping the knees is the archetypal gesture
of supplication (also 1.66.1). The *locus classicus* is Priam's approach to Achilles in a bid
to retrieve Hector's corpse (Hom. *Il.* 24.478); for added appeal one could also kiss
the knees (Hom *Il.* 8.371; Gould (1973)). T.'s soldiers here retain dignity absent from
Plutarch's frenzied Othonians (*Oth.* 15.2), allowing him to plot an emotional escala-
tion amongst the troops that reaches a climax after Otho's suicide.   **promptissimo
Plotio Firmo:** T. uniquely amongst our sources introduces a single named speaker,
whose robust name belies his current emotional state. Firmus was last seen trying
to calm the soldiers' passions after the praetorian mutiny (1.82.2), even though they
chose him directly as general, presumably thinking him compliant (1.46.1). Now a
passionate concern for Otho unites him with his soldiers.   **praetorii praefectus:**
specifying Firmus' rank enables T. to extend the alliteration that started with *proximi
prensare*. It is apt that this plea comes from an officer of the praetorians, a group that is
proprius Othonis miles (2.46.3).   **ne fidissimum exercitum, ne optime meritos
milites desereret:** the anaphora suggests heightened emotion. In Plutarch, the
soldiers themselves beg Otho not to abandon them (*Oth.* 15.2). Firmus casting the soldiers as *optime meritos* (cf. *tam . . . bene meritos* Suet. *Otho* 10.1) alludes directly to Caesar's
'altruistic' question about his troops (*cur uulnerari pateretur optimos de se meritos milites?*, *Civ.*
1.72.2), one of several references where Caesar prioritises (however disingenuously) a
minimally bloody victory. Otho concedes that his soldiers are loyal, but argues that
precisely this quality obliges him to abandon the campaign (2.47.1, 47.3). Cf. *genti
Numidarum optime meritae* (Sall. *Jug.* 62.1), also in an emotive context, as Bomilcar begs
Jugurtha to surrender. Commanders who abandon their men are pervasive in the
civil wars (3.31.1–2, 3.61.3, Caes. *Civ.* 1.20.2, Plut. *Ant.* 68.4–5), but at least Otho has
his soldiers' best interests at heart.   **maiore animo tolerari aduersa quam
relinqui** 'it showed greater spirit if troubles were tolerated rather than abandoned'.
Firmus' sententious style has a double meaning: *relinquo* = 'leave behind' (*OLD* 4),
but also 'leave behind at one's death' (*OLD* 8). Wittingly or not, Firmus already hints
at Otho escaping from his troubles by suicide. Suicide was sometimes seen as easier
than tolerating adversity (Caes. *Gal.* 7.77.5, Sen. *Phoen.* 190–2, *Ep.* 78.2 *aliquando enim et
uiuere fortiter facere est*, Mart. 1.8.5–6, 11.56.15–16). T. himself criticises those who court
fame *ambitiosa morte* without helping the state (*Agr.* 42.4).   **fortes et strenuos** is a
Livian combination (15×), usually in this order. Seneca the Younger describes a Stoic
as *uir fortis ac strenuus* (*Ep.* 77.6; also 9.19, 22.7), so Firmus in his terminology is perhaps
courting Otho's Stoic sensibilities.   **etiam contra fortunam:** Roman historical
narratives are rich in *exempla* of men who experience dramatic changes of fortune
and persevere (Marius is the archetype). Firmus here invites Otho to align himself

with one traditional model of bravery (perseverance in adversity), but the emperor favours his own unique alternative (altruistic suicide): *alii diutius imperium tenuerint: nemo tam fortiter reliquerit* (2.47.2).   **insistere spei** 'cling to hope'. The combination is only here (*TLL* s.v. *insisto* 1925.85).   **ad desperationem formidine properare:** Firmus' criticism hits home with partial success, as Otho insists to his nephew that he has decided to commit suicide *non . . . ultima desperatione* (2.48.2). Yet not everybody will read the suicide in this way: Mucianus claims that Otho was overcome *praepropera ipsius desperatione* (2.76.4).

   46.3 ut flexerat uultum uel indurauerat: 'the face anchors personal identity, dignity, and perceivable mood' (Lateiner (1995) 88).*flecto* (*OLD* 3c) + *oculos* 'avert one's gaze' is relatively common (cf. 70.4n. *at non . . . flexit oculos*), but *flecto* (*OLD* 10a) + *uultum* 'soften one's expression' is a Senecan innovation (*D.* 6.15.3), liked by T. (*non uultu aut sermone flecti A.* 4.54.1,with MW 219; cf. *flexo in maestitiam ore A.* 3.16.2, with WM 173). Livy has *ora . . . flectebant* (5.42.4), of physically turning the head. *induro*, first in Livy and Ovid, is only here in T.: cf. *non est quod frontem eius indures* (Sen. *Ben.* 7.28.3).   **clamor et gemitus:** sc. *erat. et* (*OLD* 13) = 'or'. Onlookers trying to 'read' emperors' faces to gauge their inner feelings feature elsewhere in T. (e.g. Gallus looking at Tiberius *uultu offensionem coniectauerat, A.* 1.12.3), but it reflects well on Otho that the soldiers are so candid about their own emotions.   **praemissi e Moesia:** 32.2n. *cum integris exercitibus*; 42.2n. *dispersi . . . fessi*.   **ut nemo dubitet:** by the present subjunctive T. relays the consensus of critics from his own time. The acc. + inf. after *dubito*, on the analogy of verbs of knowing and perceiving, features from Cornelius Nepos onwards (*NLS* §187b; cf. 45.2n. *quominus*).   **potuisse renouari bellum atrox lugubre incertum uictis et uictoribus:** 7.1n. *uictores uictosque*. An ascending trio in asyndeton modifies *bellum*. T. perhaps recalls Sallust on the war with Jugurtha as *atrox uariaque uictoria* (*Jug.* 5.1), justifying his subject-matter and suggesting the potential excitement of the narrative. Yet where Sallust strives to emphasise the war's *uniqueness*, T. pessimistically opens up the possibility of tedious and destructive *repetition* of the campaign between Otho and Vitellius. *lugubre* (only 1.40.1, *A.* 13.32.3) aptly alludes to Horace's ode to Asinius Pollio about his history of the civil wars under the republic (Woodman (2003) 196–213, Henderson (1998) 108–62), now in some sense being replayed: *qui gurges aut quae flumina lugubris | ignara belli?* (*Carm.* 2.1.33–4).

   47.1 inquit: Otho's speech to his soldiers is in the parallel tradition (Plut. *Oth.* 15.4–8, Dio 64.13). Parainetic themes and topoi from Otho's earlier speeches (1.21, 1.37–8, 1.83–4) recur here and underscore his changed position (Keitel (1987) 77–80).   **hunc . . . animum, hanc uirtutem uestram ultra periculis obicere** 'to expose this spirit, this courage of yours to further dangers'. In the parallel tradition Otho utters a similar sentiment after seeing a soldier commit suicide before him (*non amplius se in periculum talis tamque bene meritos coniecturum*, Suet. *Otho* 10.1). T.'s Otho, not goaded to speak by such a shocking stimulus, is cast as more reflective and measured. The focus on *animus* and *uirtus* recalls the opening of the speech to the mutinous praetorians (1.83.2; Keitel (1987) 78).   **nimis grande . . . pretium:** the prospect of victory at the cost of his soldiers' lives makes Caesar ill at ease (*Gal.* 7.19.4), a sentiment also associated with Pericles (Plut. *Per.* 27). **quanto . . . tanto:** ablatives of the measure of difference (GL §403). **si uiuere placeret:** there is no dat. clarifying the frame of reference, but we must understand *mihi*, especially as Otho later commands his soldiers *este superstites* (2.47.3). The imperfect subjunctive *placeret* is part of an unreal conditional, showing that Otho does not want to live. **tanto pulchrior mors erit** 'the more splendid death will be'. *pulchra mors* is a topos (normally situated in battle, Leigh (1997) 210–20). Otho visualises his death 'as a specimen of courage almost aesthetically attractive' (Hutchinson (1993) 260). Yet someone ready to exploit his soldiers' hopes for a renewed campaign to enhance the grandeur of his suicide could seem manipulative: just as he needed the soldiers to orchestrate his rise to power, he now requires them (like some tragic chorus) to enhance the impact of his death-scene. **experti in uicem sumus ego ac fortuna** 'we have put each other to the test, Fortune and I' (*OLD experior* 1, used in an absolute sense). Otho knows that he has been flirting with fortune (12.1n. *Blandiebatur . . . fortuna*), but she is fickle and now abandons him for her next favourite (1.1n. *struebat . . . imperio*, 7.1n. *fortuna*). This wry emphasis on *fortuna* is absent from his speech in Plutarch and Dio. Otho implicitly rejects Plotius' plea that he persist *etiam contra fortunam* (2.46.2; Keitel (1987) 77). For Pliny, prosperity (*secunda*) merely shows that men are lucky, but adversity (*aduersa*) makes them great (*Pan.* 31.1). **nec tempus computaueritis** 'Nor must you count up the length of my principate.' T. has *nec* for *ne* in a prohibition (*NLS* §128), as *nec speciem adulantis expaueris* (2.76.2). It also has a corrective function, adding emphasis and making a point elaborated by the following clause: Otho's principate may have been short, but his restraint is thus all the more impressive. **difficilius est temperare felicitati, qua te non putes diu usurum** 'it is more difficult to exercise moderation in good fortune that you do not think you will possess for long'. Plutarch substantiates: 'Vinius, seeing that Galba was a weak old man, took his fill of good fortune, on the grounds that it was virtually over as soon as it started' (*Galb.* 16.5). T.'s *sententia* invites readers to reflect on Otho's self-restraint during his principate, now rapidly approaching its end. In the previous narrative, T. emphasises Otho's restraint (*dilatae uoluptates, dissimulata luxuria et cuncta ad decorem imperii composita* 1.71.1; cf. 2.11.3) and clemency (1.71.2). Otho's comment about the corrosive potential of a meteoric rise recalls Galba's epigram: *miseriae tolerantur, felicitate corrumpimur* (1.15.3). Otho also casts himself as a realist who knew the likely duration of his principate (*non . . . diu*). The combination *felicitas + tempero* is only here (*TLL* s.v. *felicitas* 434.18), but the sentiment recalls Statius: *non parcit populis regnum breue* (*Theb.* 2.446).

47.2 ciuile bellum a Vitellio coepit: Otho's tone is confident, but T. has already said that *contra illi* (sc. Vitellius) *initium belli nemo imputabat* (2.31.1). In chronological terms Vitellius formally challenged Galba before Otho did: the German armies hailed Vitellius as emperor on 2–3 Jan. 69 (1.57.1), then the praetorians in Rome saluted Otho on 15 Jan. 69. (1.27–38). Yet Otho was already courting the soldiers on the march from Spain (1.23.1); and the geographical location of these events probably meant that many people heard about Otho's coup first. **ut . . . certaremus . . . fuit . . . ne . . . certemus . . . erit:** in a carefully balanced sentence, repetition of the same verb (*certo*) and a shift from perfect to future tenses (*fuit / erit*) shows Otho determined to claim credit for breaking the self-destructive cycle of civil war. *ut . . . certaremus* is a consecutive (result) clause indicating joint action triggered by Vitellius in the past (*fuit*), whereas *ne . . . certemus* is a final (purpose) clause indicating cessation of action to be triggered by Otho in the near future (*erit*).   **illic** = *a Vitellio*.   **penes me exemplum erit:** Plutarch's Otho (*Oth.* 15.4–8) acknowledges that the troops from Moesia are en route, but protests that as he is not fighting Hannibal, Pyrrhus or the Cimbri, but fellow-Romans, death is the only honourable choice. Dio's Otho (64.13) expresses his hatred for civil war, claiming that he would rather follow the models of the self-sacrificing Mucius Scaevola, Decius Mus, Marcus Curtius or Atilius Regulus, than evoke a power-hungry Marius, Cinna or Sulla, and urges his soldiers not to stop him from imitating his heroes. Thus, where the parallel tradition has Otho speak in terms of specific *exempla* from the past, T.'s Otho boldly visualises himself as an *exemplum* for the future. Yet despite Otho's confident tone, T. quickly reasserts authorial control over his exemplarity: *duobus facinoribus, altero flagitiosissimo, altero egregio, tantundem apud posteros meruit bonae famae quantum malae* (2.50.1).   **hinc Othonem posteritas aestimet:** abstract noun as subject (2.1n. *spes uicit*). Otho's self-dramatising and grandiloquent use of his name and a third-person verb suggests emotional detachment and pride (Hutchinson (1993) 260). This device (absent from the speech in Plutarch and Dio) recalls Lucretia (*nec ulla deinde impudica Lucretiae exemplo uiuet*, Liv. 1.58.10, with Oakley (1998) 743–4), Germanicus (*flebunt Germanicum etiam ignoti*, *A.* 2.71.3) and Turnus (*neque enim Turno mora libera mortis*, Virg. *A.* 12.74). It is associated with epic (Horsfall (2000) 276), and can have various nuances (Austin (1977) 174). T.'s Cremutius Cordus, also in a speech and facing imminent death, similarly considers his situation from posterity's viewpoint: *suum cuique decus posteritas rependit* (*A.* 4.35.3).   **fruetur . . . fratre coniuge liberis:** while emperor, Otho was fair to Vitellius' younger brother, Lucius Vitellius (1.88.1, Plut. *Oth.* 5.2), and ensured that his rival's children and mother were safe (Plut. *Oth.* 5.3). Lucius (suffect consul in 48) was active during his brother's principate, hosting a *famosissima . . . cena* in Rome with 2,000 fish and 7,000 birds for the guests (Suet. *Vit.* 13.2), meeting with senators (2.54.1), proposing a harsh sentence against the traitor Caecina (3.37.1), dramatically engineering Junius Blaesus' death (3.38), and leading troops to face the Flavian challenge (3.55.2, 3.58.1, 3.76–7). Lucius, *par uitiis fratris, in principatu eius uigilantior*, will finally be executed after surrendering to the Flavians (4.2.3). T. casts him as insidious, cruel and self-serving. As for the rest of the family, the *princeps* Vitellius had a son (Petronianus, now dead) by his first wife, Petronia (who remarried), and a son and a daughter by his second wife, Galeria Fundana (Suet. *Vit.* 6). In T. she is an *exemplum* of moderation (2.64.2, but Dio criticises her extravagant tastes, 65.4) and protects her relative, a former Othonian, Galerius Trachalus (2.60.2). The daughter (Vitellia?), of marriageable age when Vitellius seized power (*nubilis* 3.78.1), predictably became a political pawn. After being betrothed to D. Valerius Asiaticus (1.59.2), who died before the wedding, she was requested as a wife by Otho (Suet. *Oth.* 8.1), and offered in marriage to the Flavian general Antonius Primus (3.78.1). Vespasian later arranged her marriage, though the bridegroom is unknown (Suet. *Ves.* 14). The stuttering (Suet. *Vit.* 6) son Germanicus was *c.* six years old when Vitellius became *princeps* (2.59.3), but Mucianus executed him in 70 (4.80.1). Both children are on Vitellius' coinage (*RIC* I² Vitellius, no. 57 = Mattingly (1923) 119, *RIC* I² Vitellius, no.78 = Mattingly (1923) 12), exploited as symbols to criticise Otho's childlessness (Murison (1993) 150–5). **non ultione:** Otho eschews vengeance, but Vespasian, keen to woo the former Othonian soldiers, will claim that his predecessor requested it in a letter (possibly forged): *exemplar epistulae uerae siue falsae defuncti Othonis ad Vespasianum, extrema obtestatione ultionem mandantis* (Suet. *Ves.* 6.4). If the Flavian dynasty needed a forger, Titus claimed that he could imitate any handwriting (Suet. *Tit.* 3.2). **neque solaciis:** the friends and family of someone about to die were expected to offer the person comfort, but Otho himself calmly takes on this role, consoling his nephew Cocceianus (*solatus est* 2.48.2), just as Seneca the Younger comforts people before his suicide (*A.* 15.62.2) and Aeneas, facing death, *socios maestique metum solatur Iuli* (*A.* 12.110). Even Quintilian's nine-year-old son takes on this role (*Inst.* 6 pref. 11). **alii diutius . . . reliquerit:** it feels as if Otho writes his own epitaph (Hutchinson (1993) 261). The perfect subjunctive *tenuerint* is concessive, while *reliquerit* is future perfect indicative, suggesting the solidity of Otho's plans. It also replies to Plotius Firmus' *maiore animo tolerari aduersa quam relinqui* (2.46.2; Keitel (1987) 77).

47.3 ego: the self-effacing pronoun suggests a gulf between Otho and the worthy young Romans under his command. Yet his ability even to articulate such a thought paradoxically raises his standing, underscoring the calibre of the man about to be lost. **tantum Romanae pubis:** Otho opens up an emotional register, poignantly emphasising his soldiers' youth and encapsulating the senseless waste in sending them back to battle: cf. 'doomed youth' figures of Virgilian epic, such as Lausus (*A.* 7.649–50), Pallas (*A.* 8.587–91), and Euryalus (*A.* 9.179–80), where physical beauty and innocence are highlighted. Saving such figures is a reason to claim credit: so, Ovid's Medea, in helping the Argonauts, claims the *titulum seruatae pubis Achiuae* (*Met.* 7.56). T. uses *pubes* in an emotive context again, when denouncing the predatory Tiberius' rape of young men: *ut more regio pubem ingenuam stupris pollueret* (*A.* 6.1.2). Livy refers to the soldiers as *Romana pubes* (1.16.2) immediately after Romulus' mysterious death. **egregios exercitus** is a Livian combination (Oakley (1998) 342). **eat hic mecum animus, tamquam perituri pro me fueritis** 'let this thought accompany me, that you were ready to die for me'. Otho's *perituri* echoes the praetorians' *perituros* (2.44.3) and the soldiers' *extrema passuros ausurosque* (2.46.1; Keitel (1987) 77). **sed este superstites:** this is a crucial motivation for Otho to kill himself, but some of his soldiers will commit suicide beside his funeral pyre, while others will die fighting the Vitellians for Vespasian. Otho wryly reverses one traditional articulation of personal devotion to the emperor, namely the hope that the *princeps* will outlive the speaker (Versnel (1980) 568–72). Such hopes were also expressed by parents regarding their children (e.g. *qui totos dies precabantur et immolabant ut sibi sui liberi superstites essent*, Cic. *ND* 2.72), so Otho hints at an analogy where he is a father and the soldiers his children. **nec diu moremur, ego incolumitatem uestram, uos constantiam**

meam: 'this device elegantly underscores the change in his relationship with his men. Normally the commander uses the first person plural to stress his oneness with his troops . . . Through this device, Tacitus signals the end of the symbiotic relationship of Otho and his men' (Keitel (1987) 78). It also recalls the end of Plato's *Apology*, with similarly emphatic pronouns: 'For now it is time to go away, for me (ἐμοὶ μέν) to die, for you (ὑμῖν δέ) to live' (42a2–3); cf. *sed tempus est . . . iam hinc abire, me, ut moriar, uos, ut uitam agatis* (Cic. *Tusc.* 1.41.99). **pars ignauiae est:** Otho responds to Plotius' imputation of cowardice (*timidos et ignauos* 2.46.2; Keitel (1987) 77). **de nemine:** *OLD* s.v. *queror* 1c for the construction with *de*. **incusare deos uel homines eius est, qui uiuere uelit** 'blaming gods or men is the mark of someone who wishes to live'. Germanicus blames gods and men on his death-bed, but this parallel only endorses Otho's point, as Germanicus does not want to die (T. *A.* 2.71.1). The formulation also recalls Aeneas' desperate reaction to losing Creusa while escaping from Troy: *quem non incusaui amens hominumque deorumque?* (Virg. *A.* 2.745). The intertext raises a paradox: Aeneas (despite his instincts: *moriamur et in media arma ruamus*, *A.* 2.353) must live to secure his people's future, but Otho chooses to die for the good of the Roman state. *eius* = gen. of characteristic + copulative verb (*est*) and inf. (*incusare*); GL §422n.5.

48.1 ut cuique aetas aut dignitas 'according to each man's age and rank'. Otho's sensitivity to the social hierarchy around him emphasises his wasted potential. Lack of respect for aristocratic *dignitas* often characterises contenders for power during the civil wars of the late republic: *Pompeius . . . neminem dignitate secum exaequari uolebat* (Caes. *Civ.* 1.4.4; also Vell. 2.33.3, Luc. 1.125–6, Flor. 2.13.14). Cf. the violent sack of Cremona, where age and rank will offer no protection (*non dignitas, non aetas protegebat*, 3.33.1). **comiter appellatos:** the participle agrees with *iuuenes* and *senes* (objects of *mouebat*) later in the sentence. Mucianus (1.10.2), Titus (5.1.1), Germanicus (*A.* 1.33.2, 2.13.1, 2.72.2), the eastern prince Vonones (*A.* 2.2.4), the German prince Italicus (*A.* 11.16.2) and Gaius Piso (*A.* 15.48.3) all possess *comitas* 'affability' (or 'the friendly treatment of inferiors', Wallace-Hadrill (1982) 42). Otho's *comitas* (he administered Lusitania *comiter*, 1.13.4) is diametrically opposed to Galba's *seueritas*. Striking the right balance between these qualities was crucial (Liv. 4.10.8, Nep. *Att.* 15.1, Plin. *Ep.* 4.3.2). *appello* could simply mean 'address' (*OLD* 1), but 'address by name' (*OLD* 11), also possible, would have greater rhetorical impact (cf. *prope omnes nomine appellas*, Plin. *Pan.* 15.5, of Trajan). **irent** (for *abirent*) is a jussive subjunctive dependent on the subsequent *mouebat* with the usual introductory *ut* omitted (Heubner (1968) 195; cf. *peto* with dependent *ut* omitted, WM 130). **iram uictoris asperarent:** the verb depends on *mouebat*. T. always prefers the more striking *aspero* over the compound verb (cf. *sedari exasperatos Ligures*, Liv. 42.26.1). Cf. *sacras ita uocibus asperat iras* (Stat. *Theb.* 1.642). The metaphor is from sharpening weapons; and Junius Blaesus' demise illustrates the dangers of Vitellius *asperatus* (3.38.2). Suetonius presents Otho as generally concerned for his friends and family without the colourful language: the emperor urges *ut sibi quisque pro facultate consuleret* (*Otho* 10.2). **iuuenes auctoritate, senes precibus mouebat:** the ability to modify behaviour depending on one's audience is a valuable political skill. Catiline (*cum tristibus seuere, cum remissis iucunde, cum senibus*

grauiter, cum iuuentute comiter, cum facinerosis audaciter, cum libidinosis luxuriose uiuere, Cic. *Cael.*
13), Alcibiades (Plut. *Alc.* 23) and Jugurtha (Sall. *Jug.* 49.4) could all do it. On wielding
auctoritas, see Lendon (1997) 275. **intempestiuas suorum lacrimas coercens:**
Martial similarly contrasts the calm Festus, about to commit suicide, and his weeping
friends (*siccis ipse genis flentes hortatus amicos*, 1.78.3), as does T. for Seneca the Younger (*A.*
15.62.2). Socrates' friends also weep effusively, until Socrates himself checks their tears
(Plato *Phaedo* 117c5–e2). The phrase recalls a moment of heightened emotion between
a father and son from the declamation schools: *quid me intempestiuae proditis lacrimae?*
(Sen. *Con.* 2.3.4). **dari naues ac uehicula abeuntibus iubet:** the detail recalls
Cato the Younger, anxious about the impending journeys of his friends by land and
sea (Plut. *Cat. Mi.* 67.4, App. *BC* 2.98). Utica on the north African coast, where Cato
killed himself, was a more natural place to leave by boat than Brixellum, although
the Po could provide an escape route. **libellos epistulasque . . . abolet:** the
burning of incriminating documents is in the parallel tradition (Dio 64.15.1, Suet. *Otho*
10.2), though not in Plutarch. **studio . . . contumeliis:** the chiastic arrangement
(with internal *uariatio* of prepositions) aptly juxtaposes the two rivals for power, Otho
and Vitellius. **pecunias distribuit parce necat ut periturus:** the pithy *nec ut*
= *et non ut* 'quite unlike' (*OLD neque* 4a). Distributing money also features in the parallel tradition (Plut. *Oth.* 17.2, with Schmidt (1995), Suet. *Otho* 10.2). 'Proper frugality
neutralizes his own notorious profligacy' (Plass (1995) 82).

48.2 Saluium Cocceianum: Domitian will put him to death (in 81 or later;
Murison (1993) 140 n.25) for celebrating his uncle's birthday (Suet. *Dom.* 10.3), so
this tableau has potential for poignancy and tragic irony. Cocceianus has a similarly doomed counterpart on the other side, Vitellius' young son Germanicus (2.59.3,
3.67.2, 4.80.1). Cato the Younger before his suicide also comforts a pair of young men,
Demetrius and Apollonides (Plut. *Cat. Mi.* 69). **fratris:** 23.5n. *Titianum fratrem.*
Suetonius says that the brother was present (*Otho* 10.2), but as he lacks the emotional
leverage of his son, T. and Plutarch ignore him. **prima iuuenta:** the Virgilian
collocation (*A.* 7.51, 9.181) adds pathos and recurs in Cornelius Fuscus' character-
sketch (2.86.3). Plutarch just says that he was 'still a youth' (*Oth.* 16.2). **trepidum
et maerentem:** Cocceianus is both scared for his own safety and sad at his uncle's
impending suicide. Otho will argue that his suicide is necessary to guarantee Cocceianus' safety. *trepidus* contrasts pointedly with Otho as *intrepidus* (2.48.1). **ultro**
'unprompted'. **solatus est:** T. always prefers the simple *solor* over the compound
consolor. Suetonius says that Otho encouraged his nephew, but records no details (*Otho*
10.2), but Plutarch has a version of this consolatory speech (*Oth.* 16.2–4), including
the idea that Otho had planned to adopt Cocceianus (*Oth.* 16.3), which T. omits. This
dynastic issue perhaps struck T. as a distraction from the scene's emotional impact.
laudando . . . castigando: cf. *laudando promptos, castigando segnes* (*Agr.* 21.1; cf. Caes.
Civ. 1.3.1, Liv. 24.16.9, 27.8.19, 38.56.12). As this verbal combination is 'a cliché for
the good general's reactions (cf. Liv. 3.63.3–4)' (Ogilvie and Richmond (1967) 224),
T. again hints at wasted potential: Otho uses techniques associated with the ideal
commander to lay the ground for his own death. **pietatem:** *pietas*, associated

most often in the *H.* with brothers and armies, is often misdirected or undermined during the civil war (though not here). Salvius Titianus avoids trouble after Vitellius' victory because *pietas* obliged him to join his brother's cause (2.60.2), Vipstanus Messalla gains a reputation for *pietas* by interceding for his brother Aquilius Regulus, a notorious Neronian informer (4.42.1), while Vespasian praises Titus' *pietas* in defending his ambitious brother Domitian (4.52.2). Otho (1.83.2) and Vitellius (2.69.1, 3.36.2) problematically attribute *pietas* to their troops.   **an Vitellium tam immitis animi fore:** since Otho after victory is described as having an *immitem animum* (1.44.1), this question perhaps seems naïve, but the Flavians, not Vitellius, will execute Cocceianus, who is more useful to the victorious Vitellius alive than dead. Thus he can claim *clementia* (1.75.2; cf. *utilis clementiae fama* 4.63.1). In T. Vitellius' cruelty escalates over his principate (*aduentu fratris et irrepentibus dominationis magistris superbior et atrocior*, 2.63.1), but is ░░░ as ░░░eme as Suetonius' sensational catalogue of his *saeuitia* (*Vit.* 14).   **pro incoł░░░░ domo:** 47.2n. *fruetur . . . fratre coniuge liberis.* **mereri . . . clementiam uictoris:** the combination *mereor + clementia* does not feature before T. (*TLL* s.v. *clementia* 1337.19–20). Lucan's Caesar, frustrated by Pompey's murder, counts sparing the defeated as among the *unica belli praemia ciuilis* (9.1066–7), but Otho by killing himself denies this prize to Vitellius. *clementia* exercised during civil war can often be problematic. So Cato the Younger rejects Caesar's *insidiosa clementia* (Cic. *Att.* 8.16.2) since accepting it would involve recognising the legitimacy of the benefactor's authority (Plut. *Cat. Mi.* 66.2, Dio 43.10.3, Sen. *Con.* 10.3.5, *Suas.* 6.2; Leigh (1997) 54–68).   **festinato exitu** 'by his precipitated death'. Cf. *festinatae mortis graue solacium* (*Agr.* 44.5) for Agricola. His timely death spares him from seeing the worst excesses of Domitian's principate. Otho in death as in life (31.2n. *trahi . . . experiri*) is presented as almost addicted to speed.   **remisisse rei publicae nouissimum casum** 'that he had spared his country the last calamity' (Irvine). The perfect inf. casts the result as a *fait accompli*, but Otho's confidence is misplaced, as the Vitellians and Flavians will reactivate the civil war, nullifying his altruistic suicide.   **satis sibi nominis, satis posteris suis nobilitatis:** anaphora and asyndeton accentuate the same construction in each clause (partitive gen. enclosing a dat.), while alliterative vocabulary (*nominis / nobilitatis*) adds impact and weight.   **Iulios Claudios Seruios:** the asyndeton and homoioteleuton suggest the fleeting nature of dynastic power, especially the poetic pl. *Seruios* (Galba was the only member of his family to be *princeps*). The selection of *Seruios* (reflecting the *praenomen* Servius), rather than *Sulpicios* (reflecting the *nomen* or family-name Sulpicius) is striking, reflecting T.'s desire for *uariatio* (Irvine (1952) 165) or the carelessness of T.'s source (Chilver (1979) 213).   **in familiam nouam:** *nouus* (*OLD* 17) has the same sense as *nouus homo* (i.e. the first to attain the office of consul). Otho exaggerates the contrast between the three patrician families who held the principate before him, and his own family, which had risen to political prominence under Augustus, with the grandfather becoming a senator through Livia's influence (Suet. *Otho* 1.1). Even so Otho originated *familia uetere et honorata atque ex principibus Etruriae* (Suet. *Otho* 1.1). The real newcomers were the Flavians (Levick (1999) 4–13).   **erecto animo** 'in a confident mood' (also 3.65.1,

Livy 28.32.5). *erectus* for emotions is common (*OLD* 2a).   **capesseret uitam:** the
combination is here first (*TLL* s.v. *capesso* 311.52). *-esso*, a 'meditative' ending, indicating a verb that looks forward to an action (GL §191), is poignant, as Otho gives
this advice on the threshold of death and Cocceianus' own life will be cut short.
neu patruum . . . meminisset: Plutarch, regarding this as an especially touch-
ing moment, shifts from indirect to direct speech ('My boy, I entrust one final piece
of advice to you: do not completely forget nor remember too much that you had
a Caesar for your uncle' *Oth.* 16.4). T.'s word order intensifies the sting in the tail,
with *aut nimium meminisset* as a disturbingly prophetic coda. There is a powerful (and
relevant) *sententia* in Seneca: *optima ciuilis belli defensio obliuio est* (*Con.* 10.3.5). T.'s Otho
again refers to himself in the third person (cf. 47.2n. *hinc Othonem posteritas aestimet*).
This entreaty to a young relative to remember recalls Aeneas' plea to Ascanius: *tu
facito . . . | sis memor et te animo repetentem exempla tuorum| et pater Aeneas et auunculus excitet
Hector* (Virg. *A.* 12.438–40). Under the principate, commemoration and mourning of
dead relatives can be dangerous (e.g. Vitia, mother of Fufius Geminus, executed *quod
filii necem fleuisset, A.* 6.10.1; cf. *interdictum ne capite damnatos propinqui lugerent,* Suet. *Tib.*
61.2), unless you were emperor (Claudius commemorates Antony, Suet. *Cl.* 11.3).

   49.1 Post quae for *postea* is only here in the *H.*, but 6× in the *A.* (also Sil. 13.744).
paulum requieuit: this interlude of rest and reflection recalls Cato the Younger
preparing for suicide (Plut. *Cat. Mi.* 68.2, Flor. 2.13.71).   **atque** 'and thereupon'
(*OLD atque* 5c). Cf. 2.2.2.   **illum supremas iam curas animo uolutantem:**
the detail makes us admire Otho more, as his external calm and robust words appear to
mask with dignity some degree of inner turmoil. This is a far cry from Piso's damning
construction of Otho's inner life: *stupra nunc et comissationes et feminarum coetus uoluit
animo* (1.30.1). Cf. Aeneas, who *caecos . . . uolutat | euentus animo secum* (Virg. *A.* 6.157–
8).   **repens tumultus** is a Livian expression (3×; though cf. Caes. *Civ.* 2.25.2,
3.18.3, *Gal.* 5.26.1, 7.47.4, Ov. *Met.* 5.5). The intrusive outburst of the soldiers is also
in the parallel tradition (Dio 64.15 interrupting his distribution of money, Plut. *Oth.*
16.5, Suet. *Otho* 11.1 *tumultu . . . exorto*).   **consternatione . . . militum:** *consternatio*
is virtually a synonym for *seditio*. Otho used it for the praetorian mutiny (1.83.4).
abeuntibus: Plutarch says they were senators (*Oth.* 16.5; Dio 64.15, Suet. *Otho* 11.1 say
nothing about their identity).   **atrocissima in Verginium ui:** Verginius Rufus, 'a
cautious and somewhat calculating individual' (Murison (1993) 20), was born into an
equestrian family (1.52.4) from Mediolanum (Milan) in *c.* 14. After being made consul
in 63 (*A.* 15.23.1) and governor of Upper Germany in 67, Verginius defeated Vindex,
the rebellious governor of Gallia Lugdunensis, at Vesontio in mid-May 68 (even if
he claimed that he was negotiating with Vindex when his troops started the battle
without orders). His victorious soldiers even offered him the principate (1.8.2, Plut.
Galb. 6.3, Dio 63.25.1), but he refused it (proudly celebrated on his monument, Plin. *Ep.*
6.10.4, 9.19.1) and supported Galba, who promptly removed Verginius from his post
in Germany (1.8.2). After Galba's murder, Otho made Verginius suffect consul, partly
to soothe the soldiers in Upper Germany (1.77.2, Plut. *Oth.* 1.3). The soldiers' current
violence towards Verginius is a prelude to their impassioned approach to him after

Otho's death (2.51, Plut. *Oth.* 18.4–7; Levick (1985) 334–5. After the civil war, Verginius led a quiet life in his villa, the 'nest of his old age' (Plin. *Ep.* 6.10.1), at Alsium (on the coast 20 miles from Rome). Aged 83, Verginius became consul for the third time with Nerva in 97, but while preparing his speech of thanks, he fell and broke his hip (Plin. *Ep.* 2.1.5). T. himself delivered his funeral oration, a *memorabile . . . spectaculum* (Plin. *Ep.* 2.1.1). **clausa domo:** Verginius' house is also in Plutarch (*Oth.* 18.5). His family from Mediolanum must have had some property near Brixellum. **increpitis seditionis auctoribus:** Plutarch depicts Otho's grim expression and anger while dispersing the soldiers (*Oth.* 16.6). Yet T. avoids such physical details, allowing nothing to detract from Otho's calm exterior. *seditio*, as often, masks complexities. Since the soldiers later try either to make Verginius *princeps* or to get him to intercede on their behalf with Caecina and Valens (2.51), their current actions are probably motivated by fear for their own safety. This is not a straightforward mutiny. **uacauit abeuntium alloquiis** 'he made time for conversations with those who were leaving'. Otho remains affable to the end. **donec omnes inuiolati digrederentur** 'until such a time as they had all got away unhurt'; *donec* (*OLD* 2a) signifies intent.

49.2 Vesperascente die: the phrase (also *A.* 1.65.6 and 16.34.1) is in the *H.* only here. Emphasising the dwindling light (also Plut. *Oth.* 17.1; cf. *propinqua uespera*, *A.* 15.60.4) is metaphorically appropriate for an impending death (cf. Dylan Thomas: 'Do not go gentle into that good night | Old age should burn and rave at close of day; | Rage, rage against the dying of the light'). Yet Otho will kill himself at dawn, just as Cato the Younger does (Plut. *Cat. Mi.* 70.7). **sitim . . . sedauit:** Plutarch's Otho also drinks water (*Oth.* 17.1), but only T. and Suetonius (*sedata siti gelidae aquae potione, Otho* 11.2) specify its temperature. The restrained choice of water (not wine) pulls against Otho's image as a libertine. Even the austere Cato the Younger enjoys some wine after his last supper with his friends (Plut. *Cat. Mi.* 67.2). Otho is outdoing his model. **sedauit . . . subdidit . . . egit . . . incubuit:** each clipped sentence of the suicide narrative ends with a third-person perfect verb with Otho as the subject, suggesting the methodical fulfilment of a clear plan. Suetonius describes the event in two long sentences full of subordinate clauses and abl. absolutes (*Otho* 11.2). **allatis pugionibus duobus:** *duobus* (not in M) is in the other *codices* (and the parallel tradition), so editors generally retain it. T.'s Otho maintains imperial dignity as the daggers are brought to him. This detail is not in the parallel tradition, where the daggers are already conveniently nearby: cf. *arripuit duos pugiones* (Suet. *Otho* 11.2), δυεῖν ὄντων αὐτῶι ξιφῶν (Plut. *Oth.* 17.1). Nero also tests the blades of two daggers before his suicide, but then throws them away in fear (Suet. *Nero* 49.2). 'T. takes pains to show in Otho qualities of character absent from Nero' (Damon (2003) 257). A suicide weapon could be symbolic (Ash (1999) 88); and the *pugio* is especially apt for Otho, as it denoted emperors' powers of life and death over citizens (3.68.2, Suet. *Galb.* 11). Vitellius will later send this same *pugio* to Colonia Agrippinensis for dedication to Mars (Suet. *Vit.* 10.3). **utrumque pertemptasset:** the detail is in the parallel tradition (Suet. *Otho* 11.2, Plut. *Oth.* 17.1). Otho needs to find the sharper instrument to kill himself efficiently. Cato the Younger also tests his blade, but infamously botches the first suicide attempt, enabling a doctor to intervene ([Caes.] *Afr.* 88, Plut. *Cat. Mi.* 70.9, App. *BC* 2.99, Dio 43.11). Otho wants to avoid emulating his role model in this respect.   **alterum capiti subdidit** 'he put one under his pillow'. Otho had no need to do this, but the detail recalls Cato: before his suicide, he hid his sword under his pillow to stop his worried attendants from confiscating it (Dio 43.11). T. avoids *puluinus*, 'pillow', perhaps too lowly both for the grandeur of the suicide and for the genre of historiography (cf. *cum alterum puluino subdidisset*, Suet. *Otho* 11.2). Plutarch's Otho ostentatiously carries the sword under his arm while addressing his attendants (*Oth.* 17.1).   **explorato iam profectos amicos** 'after it had been established that his friends had already set out'. This altruistic concern for his friends develops his previous efforts to secure their escape (2.48.1). Cato also follows up an initial expression of concern about his friends' travel arrangements with a second inquiry (Plut. *Cat. Mi.* 67.4, 70.6).   **noctem quietam . . . non insomnem:** the litotes *non insomnem* emphasises Otho's feat in being able to sleep calmly on this of all nights (also *artissimo somno quieuit*, Suet. *Otho* 11.2). The appeal to an unnamed source (*ut affirmatur*) reveals T.'s concern that some readers will find the detail implausible. T. avoids the (possibly degrading) point in Plutarch (*Oth.* 17.3) that Otho slept so soundly that attendants outside the room heard him snoring (Hutchinson (1993) 260 n.5). Plutarch's Cato the Younger also slept well (and snored loudly) on the night before his suicide (Plut. *Cat. Mi.* 70.3).   **luce prima:** the focus on the dawn, just as Otho dies, encapsulates his rejection of life: cf. *circa lucem* (Suet. *Otho* 11.2) and ὄρθρου (Plut. *Oth.* 17.4). Virgil describes suicides in the underworld as *lucem . . . perosi* (*A.* 6.435). **in ferrum pectore incubuit** 'he fell with his chest upon the sword'. The phrasing is 'nobly restrained; there is only *pectore . . .* to make the physicality felt' (Hutchinson (1993) 258). Suetonius gives the exact location of the wound: *uno se traiecit ictu infra laeuam papillam* (*Otho* 11.2). All our accounts agree that Otho kills himself alone and unaided, unlike Nero, helped by his secretary Epaphroditus (Suet. *Nero* 49.3). The 'association of the good warrior with a wound in the breast' (Leigh (1997) 210) emphasises Otho's heroism and suggests wasted potential.

49.3 ad gemitum morientis: the subdued death-groan is in the parallel tradition (Suet. *Otho* 11.2, Plut. *Oth.* 17.5). Otho is more dignified than Cato, who knocks over a geometrical abacus as he falls (Plut. *Cat. Mi.* 70.8).   **unum uolnus inuenere:** in a suicide, the single wound indicates bravery (e.g. Brutus' suicide after Philippi, Plut. *Brut.* 52), which is shown by multiple wounds on the battlefield (Leigh (1997) 210–15). Otho achieves the efficient death sought by carefully selecting the sharper dagger. In Suetonius, Otho is seen *modo celans modo detegens plagam* (*Otho* 11.2), meaning that he is still alive when the attendants arrive.   **Funus maturatum:** sc. *est.*   **ambitiosis id precibus petierat** 'he had sought that with insistent prayers'. Suetonius' Otho is more peremptory: *nam ita praeceperat* (*Otho* 11.2). The request for a quick funeral is not in Plutarch or Dio, but other emperors left instructions about their funerals (Suet. *Aug.* 101.4).   **ne amputaretur caput ludibrio futurum:** Otho knew all about this potential humiliation from the fates of Galba, Piso and Vinius. Their severed heads, fixed on spears, were carried beside the standards of the victorious soldiers (1.44.2) and later put up for sale by the killers (1.47.2). Galba's head is *laceratum* (1.49.1; cf. Plut. *Galb.* 28.2–3), but T. avoids some gruesome details from the parallel tradition (Suet. *Galb.* 20.2). Severed heads often facilitated posthumous revenge and humiliation: Cyrus (Hdt. 1.214), Pompey (Luc. 8.688–91, Plut. *Pomp.* 80), and Cicero (Sen. *Suas.* 6.17, 6.19, *Con.* 7.2.1, Plut. *Cic.* 49, App. *BC* 4.20, Dio 47.8.3) were all victimised. Verbal insults can also occur: Nero, looking at Rubellius Plautus' severed head, allegedly says 'I didn't know that he had such a big nose' (Dio 62.14.1). **laudibus et lacrimis** is an alliterative but 'standard combination' (WM 103). **uolnus manusque eius exosculantes:** in Plutarch the soldiers kiss the wound and grasp Otho's hands (*Oth.* 17.9; cf. *manus ac pedes iacentis exosculati,* Suet. *Otho* 12.2). The emotive power of wounds is clear from Caesar's funeral, where a wax model of the corpse, with 23 wounds, was displayed before the angry people (App. *BC* 2.147; cf. Plut. *Caes.* 68.1). T. reserves *exosculor* (post-Augustan) for moments of heightened emotion (*A.* 1.34.2). The verb also suggests *peripeteia*: the jubilant people *exosculari Othonis manum* (1.45.1) just after his victory over Galba. Hand-kissing that was originally a proverbial sign of degradation (Henderson (2001) 158 with n.15) now expresses real affection.

49.4 iuxta rogum interfecere se: these suicides are also in the parallel tradition (Plut. *Oth.* 17.10, Suet. *Otho* 12.2, Dio 64.15). As Roman soldiers swore an oath to value their emperor's safety above everything (Epictetus 1.14.15), Otho's death creates a dilemma for the men. 'In this case the love for the leader and the grief for his death generate an epidemic destruction of one's own life' (Versnel (1980) 573). The soldiers are almost like ideal wives choosing to die with their husbands (Ash (1999) 35). **non noxa neque ob metum** 'not because they felt guilty or afraid'. Plutarch also rejects two explanations for the mass suicides, which took place 'not because they had experienced kindness from the dead man nor feared anything terrible from the victor' (*Oth.* 17.10). Romans sometimes commit suicide collectively (Luc. 4.529–81), but more often defeated barbarians kill themselves *en masse* ([Caes.] *Afr.* 91, Liv. 28.23.2–3, Plut. *Mar.* 27.2–3, *Sull.* 14.4, *Brut.* 31.2–4, T. *Agr.* 38.1). Such suicides can still happen in the modern era, as when 500 surviving Japanese soldiers on the island of Attu killed themselves with grenades in the small hours of 29 May 1943. **aemulatione decoris et caritate principis:** causal ablatives. *aemulatio decoris* is only here (*TLL* s.v. *aemulatio* 370.54; cf. 4.4n. *aemulatio*), but Livy has *aemulus . . . decoris sui* (7.26.12). *caritas principis* may evoke Livy's *caritas ducis* (10.17.3), describing the soldiers' affection for their general Decius Mus, who famously sacrificed his own life for his country by *deuotio.* **aliisque in castris:** the preposition is 'sandwiched' (3.2n. *tenuem in ambitum*). **celebratum** (sc. *est*) 'became common' (Fyfe / Levene). **Othoni sepulchrum exstructum:** sc. *est*; (34.2n. on *struo / exstruo*). Plutarch, while visiting the area (*Oth.* 14.2), saw the tomb at Brixellum. That it was built here, rather than in Ferentium in Etruria, Otho's ancestral home town, shows his anxiety about the fate of his body. Burial in the immediate locale was the best way to avoid humiliation. Cf. Galba, whose ashes were buried in his private garden near Rome on the Aurelian way (1.49.1, Suet. *Galb.* 20.2), and Vitellius, either thrown into the Tiber (Suet. *Vit.* 17.2) or buried in an unknown location by his wife (Dio 65.22.1). **modicum et**

mansurum 'modest and likely to survive'. The alliteration adds gravity. The simple inscription on the tomb read: Δαίμοσι Μάρκου Ὄθωνος 'To the departed spirits of Marcus Otho' (Plut. *Oth.* 18.2, following Lobeck's emendation of Δηλώσει Μάρκου Ὄθωνος, 'For the pointing out of Marcus Otho'). Vitellius, inspecting the inscription, claims that Otho deserved such a 'mausoleum' (Suet. *Vit.* 10.3). This term suggests a large, ornate tomb, but is not the way to describe Otho's modest memorial. Suetonius' Vitellius is being sarcastic (whatever the reality).   **hunc uitae finem habuit:** the formula recalls (with *uariatio*) T.'s transition from Galba's death to his obituary (*hunc exitum habuit Servius Galba*, 1.49.2). Similar formulae feature in Nep., Liv., Virg., Vell. and Curt. (MacL. Currie (1989), seeing the influence of Plato's obituary of Socrates at *Phaedo* 118, Oakley (1997) 567).   **septimo et tricensimo aetatis anno:** Otho, born 28 Apr. 32 (Suet. *Otho* 2.1), killed himself on the early morning of 17 Apr. 69, so he was 36 when he died (cf. Dio 64.15, Plut. *Oth.* 18.3, Suet. *Otho* 11.2). T. omits the contrast (in all the other sources) between the years Otho had lived and his short principate.

    50.1 e municipio Ferentio: the Etruscan town Ferentium, *c.* 40 miles north of Rome, had a prominent shrine to *Fortuna*. From here a dagger was taken to kill Nero during the abortive Pisonian conspiracy of 65 (*A.* 15.53.3). Vitruvius also calls the town a *municipium* (2.7.4). Suetonius opens his biography of Otho with his birthplace (*Otho* 1.1), but T. reserves it for the end.   **pater consularis:** Plutarch alludes to Otho's respectable lineage, but gives no details (*Galb.* 19.2). The father, L. Salvius Otho, a favourite of Tiberius, was (implausibly) alleged to be the emperor's son (Suet. *Otho* 1.2). He was suffect consul in 33 (Suet. *Galb.* 6.1), and served as proconsul of Africa and Dalmatia. Claudius awarded him patrician rank (Suet. *Otho* 1.3), perhaps during his censorship of 48 (*A.* 11.25).   **auus praetorius:** in Suetonius the grandfather, M. Salvius Otho, was born to an equestrian father and a lowly mother, possibly even a slave (though such allegations were common in invective), and was made senator by the influence of Augustus' wife Livia, in whose house he had been raised (*Otho* 1.1). His name appears on Augustus' coinage as one of the three officials of the mint in 7 BC (RIC I² Augustus, nos. 429–32).   **maternum genus impar nec tamen indecorum:** Otho's mother was Albia Terentia (Suet. *Otho* 1.3), perhaps from an equestrian family. The phrasing recalls Sallust on Jugurtha: *materno genere impar erat* (*Jug.* 11.3).   **pueritia ac iuuenta qualem monstrauimus:** sc. *fuit*. T. only says briefly and disapprovingly that Otho *pueritiam incuriose, adulescentiam petulanter egerat* (1.13.3), but Suetonius substantiates: Otho's father often had to beat him as a boy, and as a young man Otho used to go out at night searching for drunks to toss up in the air on his stretched-out cloak (*Otho* 2.1). T. avoids such sordid details and uses a grand 1st person plural verb (4.4n. *ut supra memorauimus*).   **altero flagitiosissimo, altero egregio:** i.e. first Otho seizing power by murdering Galba, then his altruistic suicide. Asyndeton sharpens the moralising antithesis between Otho's life and death (cf. *exitum, quo egregiam Otho famam, Vitellius flagitiosissimam meruere*, 2.31.1). A shameful life redeemed by a noble end (and vice versa) is a topos (Woodman (1983) 173), also evoked for Sempronius Gracchus: *constantia mortis haud indignus Sempronio nomine: uita degenerauerat* (*A.* 1.53.5).   **tantundem . . . bonae famae quantum malae** 'just as much renown as disgrace'. T. has the neuter substantive form of *tantusdem* (*OLD* s.v. *tantusdem* 2a) only here. *famae* = partitive gen. (cf. *tantundem noxae* Liv. 28.20.12, *tantundem auri atque argenti* Liv. 39.42.4).   **apud posteros:** T. as author asserts control over Otho's bid to shape his own exemplary status (*hinc Othonem posteritas aestimet* 2.47.2).

    50.2 conquirere fabulosa: the compound verb 'connotes going out of one's way to hunt out information, especially of a verbal or documentary nature' (Kraus (1994) 92). So, historians of Tiberius' principate did not accuse him of murdering Drusus, *cum omnia alia conquirerent* (*A.* 4.11.2; also *A.* 4.33.2, 14.44.1). Despite T.'s anxiety about incorporating the 'incredible' in the serious genre of history, he does so elsewhere: e.g. the phoenix in Egypt (*A.* 6.28), the serpents guarding the infant Nero (*A.* 11.11.3). At one level, historical narratives were supposed to deal with facts: so Quintilian refers to history, *in qua est gestae rei expositio* (2.4.2). Yet *innumerabiles fabulae* still feature, even in the *pater historiae* Herodotus (Cic. *Leg.* 1.5). T.'s introduction to the strange story of the bird is an insurance policy: by conceding that the episode is incredible, he aims to defuse criticism in advance (Oakley (1998) 101–2).   **fictis oblectare legentium animos:** readers were expected to approach historical narratives for entertainment (Cic. *Fam.* 5.12.4, *De or.* 2.59, Liv. *pref.* 4, Plin. *Ep.* 5.8.4, T. *A.* 4.32.2, 4.33.3), but historians had to judge carefully the balance between *dulce* and *utile* (Oakley (2005) 208), or risk a charge of infantalising their readers (cf. *id fabulas pueris est narrare, non historias scribere*, Sempronius Asellio fr. 2 Peter = Gell. 5.18.9). Lucian warns any historian tempted to include fiction in a historical narrative for entertainment that readers are quite discerning (*Hist.* 10).   **grauitate coepti operis** 'the solemnity of the work undertaken'.   **crediderim:** perfect potential subjunctive (37.2n. *concesserim*).   **uolgatis traditisque:** datives of disadvantage. T. signals (accurately or not) that this story comes from an oral source, suggesting his industrious research (cf. *A.* 3.16.1 with WM 168–70) without endorsing the truth of the anecdote. The episode is not in Plutarch or Suetonius, although Dio has a version (64.10.3). Pliny mentions 'new birds' that came over the Po during the civil war battles around Bedriacum, but his interest in them is culinary (*Nat.* 10.135).   **demere fidem non ausim** 'I should not go so far as to discredit' (*OLD audeo* 1c; *Agr.* 43.2, *D.* 8.1, *H.* 3.22.2, *A.* 1.81.1). *ausim* (the equivalent of *ausus sim*) is a potential perfect subjunctive. T. reports such portents elsewhere, often in the form of a list (1.3.2, 1.86 with Damon (2003) 273–5, 5.13.1, *A.* 12.43.1, 12.64.1, 13.58, 14.12.2, 15.47), but this one stands alone as a striking coda, adding a final note of grandeur and mystery to Otho's end.   **auem inuisitata specie:** descriptive abl.; T. has *inuisitatus* (also in Caes., Cic., Liv.) only here. This prodigy is part of a structuring diptych that picks up the earlier omen (1.62.3) of the eagle leading Fabius Valens' army south from Germany (Morgan (1993b)).   **Regium Lepidum**, founded originally by Aemilius Lepidus in 187 BC, was 24 miles south of Bedriacum on the Via Aemilia. T. mentions the small town only here.   **celebri luco** 'in a much-frequented grove'. That the grove was visited frequently may suggest that it was already regarded as sacred, as groves often were (cf. *A.* 3.61.1, Cic. *Diu.* 1.101, Virg. *A.* 7.81–91, 8.351–4, 9.86–7, Luc. 3.399–425).   **consedisse:** the verb recurs in omens involving birds (Liv. 7.26.3 with Oakley (1998) 241, 21.62.4) or bees (27.23.2,

35.9.4, Cic. *Diu.* 1.73, 1.78).   **incolae memorant:** simple form *memoro* for *commemoro*
(4.4n. *ut . . . memorauimus*). The present tense suggests that the incident was still a local
talking-point when T. was writing. The *oratio obliqua* throughout the account is perhaps
intended to 'invest the episode with the official tone and character of a public record'
(Morgan (1993b) 329). The inhabitants probably enjoyed a certain civic pride from
the fact that the portent happened in *their* town. Ovid similarly imagines local pride in
two metamorphosed trees (formerly Baucis and Philemon): *ostendit adhuc Thyneius illic |
incola de gemino uicinos corpore truncos (Met.* 8.719–20).   **nec deinde coetu hominum
aut circumuolitantium alitum territam pulsamue:** 'though *ales* can be used
as no more than a choice variant upon *auis*, it is also attested with some regularity
in augural contexts' (Oakley (1998) 243). The flock of birds around the portentous
auis behaves just like the human curiosity-seekers. This encourages readers to identify
the *auis* with a human; and Otho is the obvious candidate, especially as the bird's
unflustered behaviour recalls the calm emperor, *nequaquam trepidus* (2.46.1), who was
quickly surrounded by a crowd after becoming *princeps* (1.45.1; cf. 2.87.2). The engaging
picture of inquisitive normal birds marvelling at a special one recurs in the phoenix
episode: *multo ceterarum uolucrum comitatu nouam faciem mirantium (A.* 6.28.3). 'The idea
may perhaps originate from the "reverential escort" . . . that attended the *princeps*'
(Martin (2001) 160), a relevant notion here.   **ablatam ex oculis:** a portentous
bird in Livy also disappears straight after the event portended: *coruus ex conspectu elatus*
(7.26.5). The visual dimension reminds readers that there were original eye-witnesses
for the story, whose testimony was traditionally more reliable than hearsay evidence
(cf. *D.* 8.2 with Mayer (2001) 110, WM 169). *aufero* 'remove from sight' (*OLD aufero*
7) features in lofty genres such as epic and tragedy (Acc. *Trag.* 33, Lucr. 1.468, Ov.
Fast. 5.733, Sil. 12.647, Stat. *Theb.* 10.923; *TLL* s.v. *aufero* 1329.57–65).   **tempora
reputantibus** 'those calculating the times'. The present participle of this archaising
verb (16.2n. *reputabant*) is a dat. of the person judging (also 3.8.1, 4.17.3), a construction
liked by Livy (GL §353). Observers ready to make these calculations often appear
after such events (cf. *A.* 6.28.3, 15.41.2).   **initium finemque miraculi:** the bird's
unusual nature alone would have attracted attention, but the synchronism with an
important historical event makes it a portent (cf. the *miraculum* of the phoenix in Egypt,
A. 6.28.1).   **cum Othonis exitu competisse** 'coincided with the end of Otho's
life'. i.e. the bird appeared on the day of the battle (14 Apr.) and disappeared when
Otho killed himself (17 Apr.). Cf. Dio's bird, seen 'for many days' (64.10.3).

   51 nouata: sc. *est.* T. generally prefers the compound *renouo* for the simple form
here, a poeticism also in Livy (*nouato clamore* 8.39.5; Draeger (1882) §25). Separating
this *seditio* from the initial account of the funeral (2.49.3–4) is pointed. T. has several
closural devices in succession (the funeral, the obituary, the omen), but the feelings
of the soldiers, who express their grief through violence, spill over (an over-arching
trait of the civil war that defies neat compartmentalisation).   **ad Verginium uersi:**
Otho had successfully restrained his soldiers' strong feelings about Verginius (2.49.1).
modo ut reciperet imperium, nunc ut legatione . . . fungeretur: a similar
story about the troops offering the principate to Verginius or begging him to go on

an embassy for them is in Plutarch, but with extra details about Verginius' motives: he considers taking the principate from defeated troops foolish, after refusing it from a victorious army (*Oth.* 18.6). The *uariatio* of *modo . . . nunc* (also 3.85.1), 'found in the poets and Tacitus' (Oakley (1998) 723), emphasises the troops' fluctuation between two contradictory courses of action. Livy has *nunc . . . modo* (8.32.9).   **per auersam domus partem furtim degressus irrumpentes frustratus est:** Verginius also slips away from the soldiers by 'another door' in Plutarch (*Oth.* 18.6), but T.'s version of the chase is more dramatic. The narrow escape undercuts Verginius' dignified celebration of refusing the principate on his funeral monument (49.1n. *atrocissima . . . ui*). T. avoids by periphrasis the term *posticum* 'back-door', insufficiently grand for historiography (cf. *per auersam Palatii partem* 3.84.4).   **quae Brixelli egerant:** i.e. the praetorians who accompanied Otho to Brixellum before the battle (2.33.3). Their intense loyalty to Otho meant that they especially needed to obtain pardon from the victor.   **Rubrius Gallus:** 'a pliable character' (Shotter (1975) 70). Nero (perhaps unwisely) sent him with Petronius Turpilianus to confront Galba (Dio 63.27.1). Gallus promptly abandoned Nero for Galba, perhaps for personal reasons: 'the *nomen* Rubrius is not particularly common and Nero had violated a Vestal named Rubria (Suet. *Nero* 28.1)' (Murison (1993) 24 n.82). After switching his loyalty first to Otho and then to Vitellius, Gallus perhaps served as Flavius Sabinus' agent in securing Caecina's betrayal of Vitellius for Vespasian (2.99.2), but then disappears from T.'s extant narrative. Gallus was a smooth talker, fickle perhaps, but with a strong instinct for survival. He became governor of Moesia in 70 after Fonteius Agrippa died in battle and executed a punitive campaign against the Sarmatians (Jos. *BJ* 7.92). After serving on Vespasian's *consilium* (Levick (1999) 83), Gallus was also an *amicus* of Domitian, but 'guilty of an ancient offence which must not be mentioned' (Juv. 4.105). The scholiast suggests seduction of Domitia, later Domitian's wife, when she was a child (Braund (1996) 258).   **uenia statim impetrata:** sc. *est.* Yet the speedy pardon did not secure the praetorians' loyalty, soon the *robur Flauianarum partium* (2.67.1). Clemency in civil war is often problematic (48.2n. *mereri . . . uictoris*).   **ad uictorem:** in practical terms Sabinus must have surrendered his troops to Caecina and Valens, but the singular form reminds us of Vitellius' absence.   **Flauium Sabinum:** 36.2n.   **iis copiis:** i.e. Martius Macer's gladiators.

52–56 SPQR: THE SENATE AND PEOPLE REACT TO THE VITELLIAN VICTORY

Meanwhile, T. shifts his focus to the senate, waiting anxiously at Mutina in northern Italy. Their pointed absence from Rome emphasises the increasing decentralisation in what should ideally be a Romanocentric world. Lucan's Lentulus defiantly proposed to the senators in Epirus that the power invested in Rome was wherever the senate happened to be (*rerum nos summa sequetur* | *imperiumque comes*, 5.26–7), but T.'s senators are a sorry lot by comparison, emasculated and belatedly reacting to a shifting reality engineered by the soldiers. So later T. pointedly recasts the *SPQR* formula, with

an intrusive military component: *senatus milesque et populus* (*A.* 1.7.2). A vocabulary
of fear pervades these chapters, forcefully characterising the senate: *metus* (2.52.1),
trepidi, anxii, pauentium (2.52.2), *formidinem* (2.54.2). In the circumstances, they defend
themselves by using noncommittal language in an effort to avoid attracting attention.
The only exception is the gauche Licinius Caecina, a new man in the senate and as
yet unversed in its evasive ways. In an ironic twist, he attacks the Neronian informer
Eprius Marcellus for using ambiguous language (a charge to which the whole senate
is vulnerable), until the quarrel is cut short when *meliores* intervene (2.53.2). Yet is
this now all that being *melior* consists in? Caecina's charge may be accurate, but he
emerges as naïve and self-seeking, and T. uses language evocative of the republic
(*magnis inimicitiis claresceret,* 2.53.1) to mark how far short of the ideal such behaviour
falls. The senate's fears are only quelled when a soothing letter arrives from Fabius
Valens (2.54.2), but the fact that it is sent by a general, rather than the new emperor,
underscores where real power lies.

    Yet in contrast to the frightened senate, the people in Rome feel *nihil trepida-
tionis* (2.55.1), showing themselves to be (at best) complacent, or (at worst) callous.
After images from the battlefield of roads piled high with corpses (2.44.1), the people's unflustered celebration of the festival of Ceres, associated with productivity and
rebirth, seems alarmingly out of place. The fact that links between the goddess Ceres
and peace are especially strong only accentuates the irony: *pace Ceres laeta est* (Ov. *Fast.*
4.407 with Fantham (1998) 171), *Pax Cererem nutrit, Pacis alumna Ceres* (Ov. *Fast.* 1.704).
Ceres was also allocated a prominent position on the southeastern panel of the Ara
Pacis (Spaeth (1996) 125–51). Yet the people's current lack of fear marks a change in
the mood at Rome. After Otho's victory, the city had been *trepida* (1.50.1) and as his
campaign began, there was nobody at Rome *metu aut periculo uacuus* (1.88.2). However,
the war between Otho and Vitellius unfolded in the north, sparing people in Rome
from immediate destruction, so fears have subsided. Yet the imminent danger to the
city becomes clear as we see the rampaging Vitellian soldiers moving south through
Italy in the aftermath of their victory (2.56.1). These men, amoral and avaricious, are
like a barbarian horde, rather than Roman soldiers; and the jubilant atmosphere in
Rome will soon dissipate once they start to arrive (2.88.2).

    52.1 Posito ubique bello . . . extremum discrimen adiit: despite the reas-
suring abl. absolute, the 'finished' war will still bring much destruction (*Italia grauius
atque atrocius quam bello afflictabatur,* 2.56.1), but T. exaggerates to activate black humour
para prosdokian ('by violated expectation'), while the extremes suggested by *ubique* and
extremum enhance the effect. The war may be over everywhere else, but the senate in
'peacetime' now faces its own Waterloo. T. is sensitive to the peculiar disarray created
by civil war, where beginnings and endings are even messier than in foreign wars, and
fresh victors potentially become the 'enemy within' for those who have been obliged to
support the previous regime. The ecstatic response of the senate and people to Otho's
seizure of the principate shows the same dynamics at work (1.45.1).   **magna pars
senatus:** Otho ordered many magistrates and ex-consuls to accompany him when
he left Rome to confront the Vitellians (1.88.1), but there were still enough senators

left behind to convict Annius Faustus (2.10).   **profecta . . . ab urbe:** on 14 Mar.
69 (1.90.1).   **profecta . . . relicta:** the participles are explanatory. It was because
the senators left Rome and isolated themselves that they are in trouble.   **Mutinae:**
Mutina, a prosperous town on the Via Aemilia, was only *c.* 50 miles from the site of
the battle. The senators would not have forgotten its associations with a previous civil
war: in 43 BC Antony besieged Decimus Brutus here, only to be defeated by Hirtius,
Pansus and Octavian (App. *BC* 3.71–2).   **aduerso de proelio:** the monosyllabic
preposition is placed between the (emphasised) adj. and noun (3.2n. *tenuem in ambitum*). It is crucial to remember that the senators (and the soldiers) at Mutina for the
moment only know about Otho's defeat, but not about his suicide. This incomplete
picture helps to explain why the senators hedge their bets and the soldiers become
vindictive.   **allatum:** sc. *est.*   **milites:** these Othonian soldiers were 'in theory a
guard of honour, in fact gaolers' (Wellesley (2000) 87).   **ut falsum** 'as being false'
(*OLD ut* 10).   **infensum Othoni senatum:** after the praetorian mutiny in Rome
Otho tried to defuse his soldiers' hostility towards the senate (1.84.3–4; cf. 1.90.2), but
his success was only temporary. The soldiers wrongly assume that the senators feel
just as passionate as they do about their emperors. T. elsewhere shows the lukewarm
reaction of most senators to Galba's heir, Piso (*medii ac plurimi* 1.19.1), but this also
reflects the *ordo*'s feelings about emperors more generally. Survival is their priority.
custodire sermones 'kept watch on their conversations'. T. aptly has a military
metaphor for the soldiers' actions. The abstract object *sermones* is striking (*TLL* s.v.
custodio 1564.43–7; cf. *custodiri suspecta, Agr.* 18.2, where 'suspected districts' are being
watched, and the Ubii are on the Rhine *non ut custodirentur, G.* 28.5).   **uoltum habi-
tumque trahere in deterius** 'put the worst interpretation on their expressions and
demeanour' (20.1n. *in superbiam trahebant*). Sometimes soldiers genuinely try to read a
face to determine inner feelings (46.3n. *clamor et gemitus*), but these troops have already
cast the senators as disloyal. Policing facial expressions is symptomatic of oppressive
regimes (*A.* 16.5.2) with the result that people try to mask true feelings with insincere
facial expressions (App. *BC* 4.31; cf. 65.1n. *laetitiam . . . uoltu ferens*): 'He had set his features into the expression of quiet optimism which it was advisable to wear when facing
the telescreen' (Orwell (1949) 7). Yet it was not always easy to do so: cf. *quanto magis
occultare et abdere pauorem nitebantur, manifestius pauidi* (1.88.2). Cf. Alexander the Great's
friends, disapproving of his future father-in-law, but showing apparent approval *uultu,
qui maxime seruit* (Curt. 8.4.30). It was also a way to advance your career. So, Sallust
notices how *ambitio* prompts men *magis . . . uoltum quam ingenium bonum habere* (*Cat.* 10.5).
conuiciis . . . ac probris: the noisy, intimidating soldiers contrast with the quiet
senators, yet it is the latter who will pay.   **causam et initium caedis** 'an initial
pretext for massacre'.   **cum** 'just when'.   **alius insuper metus . . . instaret:**
abstract noun as subject (2.1n. *spes uicit*). The adj. *alius* and the adverb *insuper* (11.2n.
deforme insuper auxilium) point to two different kinds of fear for the senators. First there is
the immediate menace of the Othonian soldiery; second they fear that their greeting
of Vitellius' victory might be considered too sluggish. The combination *metus* + *insto*
is first in T. (*TLL* s.v. *insto* 2001.60; also at Justinian *Dig.* 4.2.1 pr. 3): cf. *ambigitur*

consumpseritne uocem eius instans metus (1.42). Silius has *instat . . . timor* (7.349–50). **praeualidis iam Vitelii partibus:** *praeualidus* is choice (28.1n. *cohortes . . . praeuali-das*). The abl. absolute, neatly enclosed by enveloping alliteration (4.1n. *pandi . . . pros-perum*), may have a conditional sense, since the senators are not totally sure that Vitellius' party has conclusively won.   **cunctanter . . . crederentur:** similarly, after Galba's murder, the senate and the people rush to insult the dead emperor and kiss Otho's hand (1.45.1). Yet the senators now have no obvious focus for their expres-sions of delight (however insincere), as Vitellius, en route from Germany, will not even reach the battlefield until almost 40 days later (2.70.1). The new emperor will even-tually grant an audience at Ticinum (2.69.1) to a senatorial deputation organised in Rome (2.55.2). The combination *excepisse uictoriam* is charged: all the senators can do is await military developments, like passive members of a theatre audience applauding a performance on stage, rather than drive the action themselves.

52.2 utrimque 'on two counts'. They fear reprisals either from Otho's or Vitellius' soldiers. As *utrimque* also has resonances of two sides in a battle (*OLD utrim* 2), it is an apt way to hint at impending violence.   **coeunt:** coming together momentarily implies a senate functioning well, but the motives for assembling are highly dubious, as the rest of the sentence makes clear.   **nemo priuatim expedito consilio** 'although nobody formulated a plan individually'. For the expression cf. *neque sua* (sc. *consilia*) *expedire* (3.73.1), *expediri . . . consilium* (Liv. 8.14.1).   **inter multos societate culpae tutior** 'since [each man] would be safer sharing the blame among many'. *culpa* suggests that the craven and powerless senators view the situation entirely from the soldiers' point of view: reacting cautiously to news of Otho's defeat and tardily welcoming Vitellius' victory are entirely reasonable if viewed objectively. The idea of 'safety in numbers' is a topos (1.1n. *senium . . . destinandi*). The notion of sharing the blame recurs in a senatorial context, but even more dubiously, when Paccius Africanus deflects an attack from Vibius Crispus by implicating him in the same charges: *societate culpae inuidiam declinauit* (4.41.3). The phrasing is Livian (*culpae societas*, 6.24.8).   **ordo Mutinensis:** i.e. *ordo decurionum*, the town-councillors of Mutina. **arma et pecuniam offerendo:** this is a deft way for the local dignitaries to play it safe. They could always claim afterwards that they were trying to help, but in the crisis itself, they left to the senators the difficult decision of picking the right side. The idea of senators themselves taking up arms is meant to seem incongruous: cf. *primores senatus aetate inualidi* (1.88.2).   **patres conscriptos** 'members of the senate' (lit. 'enrolled fathers'). T. refers elsewhere to the *obliterata iam nomina* (1.55.4) of the senate and Roman people which feature in a military oath. This honorific title is in the *H.* again only in Curtius Montanus' speech, deployed sarcastically at 4.42.5 (cf. Cic. *Phil.* 13.28) and as a collective rebuke at 4.42.6. It appears 14× in the *A.*, but only in direct speeches (Dickey (2002) 284–6 for its use as an address), and often in opening or closing statements (cf. Cic. *Red. Sen.* 1, *Phil.* 1.1, 2.1, 3.1, Plin. *Pan.* 1.1). Here it inappropriately implies a constitutional status which these senators lacked, as the rest of their number was in Rome (Wellesley (2000) 87). The term *patres conscripti* has generated considerable debate about the senate's original nature and whether it was exclusively patrician (Cornell (1995) 247; Ramsey (2003) 84). **intempestiuo honore:** this suggests another robust defence mechanism from the sly locals. By the respectful title, they publicly debase themselves, underscoring their low place in the hierarchy relative to the senators. Yet this allows the town councillors to use their superiors as a shield, directing potentially unwelcome attention away from themselves to the senators. The dignitaries of Mutina may initially seem gauche, but are actually quite shrewd.

53.1 Notabile iurgium: this neatly encapsulates the lack of dignity in senatorial proceedings, but it has special bite so soon after the honorific title used by the town councillors of Mutina. The last reference to *iurgia* involved the physical brawls between the Batavian cohorts and the legionaries (2.27.2). It suggests blurring of boundaries between soldiers (*conuiciis . . . ac probris*, 2.52.1) and senators. Suetonius uses *iurgium* for a dispute between a senator and an *eques*, which prompts Vespasian to pronounce that 'senators should not be insulted, but to return their insults is legal and proper for any citizen' (*Ves.* 9.2). **Licinius Caecina:** Pliny mentions a *uir praetorius* (*Nat.* 20.199) with this name, quite possibly the same man, whose father, worn down by illness, killed himself at Bavilum in Spain using opium. **Marcellum Eprium:** the inversion of names begins in the late republic, but becomes more common later (Adams (1978) 145–66): 'T. follows no clearly recognisable principle, though in certain places he is probably influenced by a desire for variety' (Goodyear (1972) 148). Eprius Marcellus, a *nouus homo* from Capua (*D.* 8.1), was *praetor* for one day in 48 under Claudius (*A.* 12.4.3, *CIL* x 3853), and legate of Lycia, but in 57 talked his way out of a corruption charge lodged by the Lycians (*A.* 13.33.3). Nero made him suffect consul in 62. An eloquent man, he became a notorious *delator*, most infamous for prosecuting Thrasea Paetus in 66, earning himself 5 million HS for his trouble (*A.* 16.33.2). Thrasea's son-in-law Helvidius Priscus, who was banished after the prosecution, returned under Galba to prosecute Eprius Marcellus, but he was obliged to desist (4.6). Tensions between the two men rose again at the same senatorial meeting that invested Vespasian with imperial power (4.7–8). Yet Eprius, 'skilfully navigating the surges of civil war' (Syme (1958a) 100), became one of Vespasian's closest friends, serving as procurator of Asia in 70–73 (*CIL* x 3853, xiv 2612, Syme (1958a) 594 n.5) and achieving a second suffect consulship in 74. Columella dedicated to him his *De cultura vinearum et arborum.* Just before Vespasian's death, Eprius was implicated in a plot with Vitellius' old general, Caecina (Suet. *Tit.* 6.2, Dio 66.16.3), and after being brought to trial before the senate, 'cut his throat with a razor, ending like Tigellinus' (Syme (1958a) 101). The date, purpose and nature of this plot remain controversial (Levick (1999) 192–5). **ut ambigua disserentem:** such 'political doublespeak' was a survival strategy (Bartsch (1994) 63–71). Phaedrus, the writer of fables, stresses the slave's vulnerability, 'because he dared not say what he wanted' (*Fabulae* 3 *prol.* 35), but under the principate the boundary between actual slavery and political subjugation is often blurred. **inuasit** 'attacked' (*OLD inuado* 3 for non-physical attacks, also 1.33.2, *A.* 6.4.2). T. uses it more often for physical attacks. The verb develops the metaphorical sense of brawling (cf. *iurgium, dirempti* 2.53.1) that underpins this abortive 'debate'.

nec ceteri sententias aperiebant 'not that the rest were speaking candidly'. Caecina could have accused anyone, but ambitiously picks the target most likely to enhance his career.   **inuisum . . . ad inuidiam:** what at first seems pleonasm is pointed repetition. Eprius (or his *nomen*) is regarded with ill will, but *inuidia* probably also preserves a sense of 'envy', suggesting the senators' jealousy of the rewards of an informer's career.   **Marcelli nomen** 'the notoriety of Marcellus'. The metonymy is particularly effective because it suggests that Caecina knows Eprius only by reputation, rather than by personal experience. If Caecina had attended the trial of Thrasea Paetus in 66 and heard Eprius speaking, *ut erat toruus ac minax, uoce uultu oculis ardesceret* (*A.* 16.29.1), he might have thought twice about attacking him.   **in senatum nuper ascitus:** this probably happened under Galba, which explains his naïvety about the dangers of attacking Eprius. After Claudius as censor in 47–8 enrolled new senators who had not previously held a magistracy, other emperors continued to replenish the senate by the process of adlection (*OCD³* 'adlection') both *ad hoc* (e.g. Vespasian's adlection of Plotius Grypus, 3.52.3) and systematically (Vespasian and Titus as censors conducted a major overhaul of the senate's personnel in 73–4, Levick (1999) 170–6).   **magnis inimicitiis** 'by attacking someone important' (cf. *magna adulteria*, 1.2.2). The adj. instead of a dependent noun in the gen. is lofty (2.1n. *iuuenilis animus*). It also suggests taking pride in one's *inimicitiae*, a republican idea (Epstein (1987)), but the grubby Caecina hardly lives up to that heritage.   **claresceret:** T. uses the striking simple form of the verb, not the compound, with the metaphorical tinge ('become famous', *OLD* 4; *TLL* s.v. *claresco* 1264.62–1265.10) first added by Statius (*Silu.* 3.3.120). A similarly ambitious prosecutor on the cusp of greatness, Domitius Afer, is *quoquo facinore properus clarescere* (*A.* 4.52.1; also *G.* 14.3, *A.* 11.16.2).   **moderatione meliorum** 'by the good sense of the moderate senators' (Wellesley; *OLD melior* 6). The (soothing?) alliteration aptly reflects the other senators' efforts to pour oil on troubled waters. Cf. *consensu meliorum compressi* (2.66.3).   **dirempti:** sc. *sunt*. The verb, with connotations of pulling apart two fighters, concludes the metaphor of a physical brawl for the 'debate' (53.1n. *inuadit*). Cf. *diremit consiliorum diuersitatem . . . Classicus* (4.76.4).

53.2 rediere omnes Bononiam 'they all turned back to Bononia'. Bononia (mod. Bologna), 25 miles from Mutina down the Via Aemilia, was even further from the battlefield (and potential news). Its location on the road system made *culta Bononia* (Mart. 3.59.1) a flourishing town. In 53 the young Nero spoke eloquently to secure 10 million HS from Claudius to rebuild it after a disastrous fire (*A.* 12.58.2. Suet. *Nero* 7.2). Perhaps the embarrassed senators want to extricate themselves from the town-councillors of Mutina, but the move will only cause them trouble (2.54.2).   **rursus consiliaturi** 'intending to discuss the situation further'. This verb (in Caes. and Cic., but not in Sall. or Liv.) is in T. only here. The quarrel between Caecina and Marcellus will be superseded by more important matters.   **medio temporis** 'in the meantime' (also at *A.* 13.28.2, 14.53.2).   **qui recentissimum quemque per-cunctarentur** 'to question every newcomer'. The verb = subjunctive because it is in a final (purpose) clause introduced by the relative pronoun. This haphazard way of acquiring fresh news shows how drastically civil war disrupts the normal network of communications.   **interrogatus Othonis libertus:** the anxious senators scramble to get information from a haughty freedman (perhaps Julius Secundus, Otho's secretary *ab epistulis*, Plut. *Oth.* 9.3), suggesting disintegration of the proper social hierarchy.   **suprema eius mandata:** these final instructions perhaps included a consolatory letter from Otho to his sister (Suet. *Otho* 10.2), letters to Vitellius interceding on behalf of his friends (Dio 64.15.1), and possibly his will, although in calmer times an emperor would deposit his will with the Vestal Virgins in Rome (*A.* 1.8.1, Suet. *Aug.* 101.1). Such *suprema mandata* could often be quite personal (cf. Sempronius Gracchus to his wife, *A.* 1.53.5). The Flavians claimed (perhaps falsely) that Otho also wrote to Vespasian, instructing him to avenge his death (Suet. *Ves.* 6.4). Such imperial 'instructions from the grave' were convenient for endorsing the actions of a new regime, e.g. the execution of Agrippa Postumus (*A.* 1.6.1).   **sola posteritatis cura:** the myth-making has already started. It is as if the freedman has heard Otho's speech: *hinc Othonem posteritas aestimet* (2.47.2).   **abruptis uitae blandimentis** 'he had broken off the pleasures of life'. The striking phrase, with its metaphor of breaking (cf. *abruptis uoluptatibus*, 4.64.3), recalls the more common *abrumpere uitam* (Virg. *A.* 8.579; cf. 4.631) and the opening of the Othonian campaign (12.1n. *blandiebatur*) to generate a sense of *peripeteia*. This abl. absolute and *sola posteritatis cura* encapsulate the two extremes of Otho's public image, hedonist and hero. Otho may have been working to improve his standing with posterity, but people will remember his fondness for the *blandimenta uitae*, as well as his abandonment of them. He outdoes Seneca the Younger's wife Paulina, who abandons suicide after being won over by *blandimentis uitae* (*A.* 15.64.2).   **hinc admiratio** 'at this there was admiration'. Despite this, the senators promptly acquiesce and favour Vitellius, the man of the moment.   **plura interrogandi pudor:** to have asked further questions could have seemed ghoulish, and in any case, the freedman has apparently resolved for them the crucial question of Otho's fate.   **atque** 'and what is more' (*OLD atque* 2).   **omnium animi in Vitellium inclinauere** 'their feelings unanimously turned to Vitellius' (*OLD animus* 9c, 10). T. emphasises the inner feelings of the senators: they must still express themselves cautiously, faced with the immediate threat of Otho's soldiers, but now know which way the wind is blowing. The chapter ends critically by showing the senators (without a single dissenter) passively following the prevailing political climate.

54.1 L. Vitellius: 47.2n. *fruetur . . . fratre coniuge liberis.*   **seque iam adulantibus offerebat** 'was making himself available to the senators who were already fawning'. Degrading senatorial *adulatio* before powerful individuals is now well entrenched. The senators similarly fawn on a relative of an absent emperor in the powers voted to Domitian after the Flavian victory (4.3.4). Family members are convenient substitutes when the new emperor himself is not available.   **cum** introduces an inverse *cum*-clause (36.1n. *cum intercursu*).   **Coenus** (only here in T.), like his unnamed colleague (2.53.2), is trying to get to Rome. His association with the disintegrating Othonian court reminds us that part of Otho's popularity derived from perceptions that he was similar to Nero (1.13.4). To surround himself with his predecessor's freedmen was one way to play on that popularity, but T. generally regards the prominence of freedmen in politics as symptomatic of *mala tempora* (1.76.3). Powerful

Neronian freedmen who outlived their emperor include Crescens, who held a dinner
in Otho's honour at Carthage (1.76.3), and Moschus, commander of the fleet (1.87.2).
atroci mendacio 'in an alarming lie'. Coenus' plausible lie is well chosen, as some
quartadecimani fought in the battle (2.43.2), which the full legion only just missed.
uniuersos perculit: again the senators' feelings and actions are influenced in an
unseemly way by a freedman: cf. the first (unnamed) freedman (2.53.2). *uniuersi* brutally elides the incipient distinction between Lucius Vitellius and the other senators
suddenly united again in vulnerability.   **affirmans:** appended nom. present participle (27.2n. *omnem . . . iactantes*).   **superuentu quartae decimae legionis:** the
famous *XIV Gemina*, intensely loyal to Otho (11.1n. *quattuor legiones* and *rebellione Britanniae compressa*). T. uses *superuentus* (coined by Pliny the Elder) only here.   **iunctis
a Brixello uiribus** 'after being united with the force from Brixellum'. These were
the loyal praetorians who accompanied Otho to Brixellum before the battle (2.33.3).
caesos uictores, uersam partium fortunam: to call the Vitellians victors at the
very moment of their (fictional) defeat pointedly accentuates the *peripeteia*, evoking the
motif of 'the conqueror conquered' (Kraus (1994) 241). Sudden reversal of fortune on
the battlefield triggered by fresh arrivals occurs elsewhere (*Agr.* 26), adding weight to
the plausible fiction.   **causa fingendi:** as ever, T. considers the motives behind the
actions. Cf. the second-century BC historian Sempronius Asellio on writing history:
'As for me, I consider that it is not just sufficient to proclaim what has been done, but
one should also show with what purpose and for what reason things have been done'
(Gell. *NA* 5.18.8).   **diplomata:** a *diploma* was a folding tablet bearing the emperor's
name and seal, entitling the carrier to use the administrative infrastructure (e.g. the
mansiones 'posting-stations', transport, provisions) of the imperial communication network (established by Augustus), including the postal system, in order to facilitate travel
around the empire. Someone with such a warrant could travel at least 50 miles in a
day (*OCD³* 'postal service'). It was very efficient, but was therefore subject to abuse.
When Pliny issued his wife with a *diploma* to accelerate her journey from Bithynia to
Italy after a bereavement, he wrote apologetically to Trajan (*Ep.* 10.120).   **laetiore
nuntio:** cf. 11.1n. *laeta*.   **reualescerent:** an Ovidian coinage (*Ep.* 21.231–2) used
again by T. in a boldly metaphorical sense (*A.* 14.27.1).

   54.2 raptim suggests that the ruse worked, with the Othonian *diploma* facilitating
a swift journey. T. always prefers the adverb *raptim* over *rapide*.   **paucos post dies
iussu Vitellii:** an alternative reading is *L. Vitellii* (Wellesley (1991) 1665–6). Even if
we reject this, it is certainly sensible (given an interval of only days) to take this as a
reference to the emperor's brother at Bononia (200 miles from Rome), rather than
to the emperor himself, perhaps now only at Andematunnum in Gallia Lugdunensis,
at least 600 miles from Rome (Murison (1993) 144); and in any case the emperor
is pointedly *uictoriae suae nescius* (2.57.1).   **poenas luit:** T. uses this lofty expression
(originally in Accius) only here in the *H.* (not in the minor works, 8× in *A.*). The
punishment is unspecified, but may well have been death. Freedmen of the previous
regime tended to fare badly with the next emperor: cf. Galba's Icelus (1.46.5), an
unnamed freedman of Vitellius (4.3.2), and Vitellius' Asiaticus (4.11.3), who were

all executed (Damon (2006) 246–50). T. proleptically finishes Coenus' story before explaining the immediate impact of his (ultimately self-destructive) lie. This envelops the subsequent account of the turmoil in a sense of pointlessness: all this trouble for the senators is for nothing. T.'s total silence about the purpose of Coenus' journey only adds to this effect. **periculum auctum:** sc. *est*. If the senators are afraid, their fear is caused by real danger: cf. *extremum discrimen* (2.52.1). **intendebat formidinem, quod** 'what was intensifying their fear was that'. T. is increasingly fond of using this verb metaphorically (derived from stringing a bow), which elsewhere governs emotions (G-G 662–3): e.g. *cupiditates* (1.12.3), *metus* (*A.* 1.28.4, 13.47.1, 14.23.1), *odium* (*A.* 13.15.3), *ardor* (*A.* 12.35.1). **publici consilii facie** 'apparently acting officially'. T. elsewhere refers to the senate house itself as *publicum consilium* (*A.* 6.15.3), but the phrase is still striking. The senators should, after all, be acting officially. Although they had left Mutina for their own personal safety, their move could still be taken as hostile to Otho, since Vitellius would need them to confer power on him in Rome, and their departure from the north could be seen as a prelude to that process. Moreover, Otho had been especially proud of senatorial involvement in his cause: *senatus nobiscum est* (1.84.3). **discessum:** sc. *esset*. **desertae . . . forent:** *forent* for *essent* (14.3n. *deletae . . . forent*). That T. refers to the Othonian *partes* is expressive: its leader is dead, but the Othonian soldiers still perceive it as existing. **in commune congressi:** the alliterative combination is only here (*TLL* s.v. *communis* 1977.4), but T. likes *in commune* (16×). **quisque consuluere:** the singular distributive pronoun with the pl. verb (44.1n. *suum obiectantes*) captures the body's rapid fragmentation after *publici consilii facie* above. **a Fabio Valente:** Valens was currently with the Vitellian troops near Bedriacum (2.45.1). The fact that he, rather than Caecina, contacts the senators suggests that the competition between the pair was already intensifying. Valens clearly saw letters as an important weapon: he had written to the praetorian and urban cohorts in Rome (1.74.3) and more recently, to the consuls in Rome (2.55.2). Caecina usually favours direct communication over such methods (though see 3.9.4): indeed, he trumps Valens' letter to his own troops by issuing instructions on the spot (2.100.2). **epistulae** often designates a single letter in T. (2.55.2, 2.64.2, 2.96.1), as in Vell. (Constans (1893) §17). **demerent metum:** this combination is in Terence (*Ad.* 736) and often in Livy, but the current context suggests that Valens' letter almost functions as a *deus ex machina*, benignly removing the senators' fears in one sweep: cf. *dempto iam tandem deum benignitate metu* (Liv. 29.15.1). The false *nuntius* Coenus first increases their terror, but now this letter dissipates it. **eo uelocius:** T. must prepare readers for the extraordinary speed with which the news of Otho's suicide (early on 17 Apr.) reached Rome on 18 Apr. (2.55.1 *Ceriales ludi*), covering a distance of 340 miles.

55.1 At Romae: (20.1n. *At*). This formula recurs (4.3.3, 4.68.1; and 9× in *A.*, but only once outside the first hexad). In the *A.* it normally signals a transition from foreign to domestic affairs, but typically in the *H.* (except for 4.68.1) the switch is only geographical, since it documents continued Roman activities in the sphere of civil war. It is only once in Sallust (*Cat.* 43.1) and absent from Livy (WM 210). **nihil trepidationis:** sc. *fuit*. *nihil* + the partitive gen. *trepidationis* forms the subject of the sentence (cf. 2.92.1 *nihil auctoritatis*). The absence of panic is a direct result of the absence of Vitellius and his soldiers, but the emotional *peripeteia* will come with their entry into the city: *in urbe tamen trepidatum praecurrentibus passim militibus* (2.88.3). The current lack of fear is meant to seem just as deplorable as Lucan's picture of the intense fear that grips Rome as Caesar and his troops move down from the north (1.486–522).   **Ceriales ludi:** these took place annually between 12–19 Apr. (Ov. *Fast.* 4.393–416 with Fantham (1998) 167–73), with the final day of the festival held in the Circus Maximus, when foxes were set on fire and released on to the track as an offering to Ceres (Ov. *Fast.* 4.681–2). A cult to Ceres (with strong plebeian associations) was introduced at Rome in 493 BC and a temple to her was dedicated at the foot of the Aventine by the popular leader Sp. Cassius in 486 BC (Dion. Hal. 6.17.2–4, Cornell (1995) 263–5), but it burned down in 31 BC (Dio 50.10.3) and was rebuilt by Augustus (*A.* 2.49.1). Plebeian aediles established the games to Ceres at some point before 202 BC. T. exploits Ceres' associations with peace and fruitfulness to contrast with the grim landscape of civil war, especially Otho's recent suicide. The polarity of holidays and warfare appealed to T., e.g. people enjoy the Saturnalia holiday (17 Dec.) while armed soldiers fight on the Capitol (*festis diebus* 3.83.3).   **ex more:** yet what follows (applause for Vitellius at news of Otho's death) is rather less traditional.   **cessisse:** *cedo* without *uita* to mean 'die' is unusual (*OLD cedo* 2e), but there is a precedent in the anonymous *Consolatio ad Liuiam* 75 (first century AD). The omission of *uita* may constitute a euphemism: cf. 'passed away'.   **a Flauio Sabino:** Vespasian's elder brother Flavius Sabinus (born *c.* AD 8), a mild man (3.65.2) who talked too much (3.75.1), becomes increasingly prominent in the narrative (Townend (1961), Gilmartin Wallace (1987), Jones (2000) 13–14, Damon (2003) 192–3). Sabinus, *domi militiaeque clarus* (3.75.1), took part in Claudius' invasion of Britain in 43 (Dio 60.20.3), became consul perhaps in 47 (Birley (1981) 225, Levick (1999) 22), served as legate of Moesia, the most important of the Danubian provinces, in *c.* 53–60 (*CIL* VI 31293), and was prefect of Rome under Nero, certainly from 62 and possibly for a period before that. He apparently served for 12 years, but the precise dates of his tenure have caused disagreement. Some prefer to emend *duodecim* (3.75.1), but others assume that T., or a scribe, made a mistake (Syme (1977) 89). Galba removed him from the city prefecture (1.14.1), but Otho (Plut. *Oth.* 5.4) or the soldiers (1.46.1) reinstated him. While Vitellius was trying to surrender to Sabinus as his brother Vespasian's representative, the soldiers had other ideas. After trapping Sabinus on the Capitol, they captured and killed him (3.70–4, Suet. *Vit.* 15.3, Jos. *BJ* 4.645, Dio 65.17.2–4). T. concedes that before Vespasian became *princeps*, Sabinus was far more prominent than his younger brother (3.75.1). In Suetonius, their formidable mother even taunts Vespasian as his brother's *anteambulo* i.e. the slave who cleared his master's way in the streets (*Ves.* 2.2), but the pair got on well enough in public (3.65.1). Domitian, trapped on the Capitol with his uncle and apparently fond of him, proposed that he should receive a state funeral (4.47).   **quod erat in urbe militum** 'such soldiers as were in the city'. There are parallels for the gen. expression (Cic. *Att.* 8.12a.4, Caes. *Gal.* 5.2.3, Liv. 7.23.3, 24.40.5, 40.19.8), used by T. again (4.15.3, 4.71.4, *A.* 4.24.2). Relatively few soldiers were left in

Rome, after Otho took with him *urbanas cohortes et plerosque e praetorianis* (1.87.1), and five praetorian cohorts accompanied Annius Gallus and Vestricius Spurinna (2.11.2), but the lead given by the remaining troops still bolsters public confidence. **sacramento Vitellii:** 6.1n. *sacramentum Othonis.* **adactum:** sc. *esse.* **certi auctores:** 1.3n. *certos nuntios.* **in theatrum:** announcing the news in the theatre was practical, since most people were there attending the festival of Ceres, but the setting also underscores the implictly surreal nature of this civil war and elides the distinction between dramatic representation and reality: cf. 'The Palatine . . . received four emperors, as [the soldiers] led one on and another off, as if through a stage-building' (Plut. *Galb.* 1.8 with Keitel (2006)). The *plebs* in Rome under Galba had previously demanded Otho's death *ut si in circo aut theatro ludicrum aliquod postularent* (1.32.1). Their wish has now been granted, although in a way that fulfils the conventions of Greek tragedy whereby death happens 'off-stage'. 'Perhaps already in the tradition . . . there was a tendency to see the brutal public assassinations of the year 69 as theatricalized death' (Bartsch (1994) 56). **Vitellio plausere:** 3.11. *ipsa . . . cessere.* Applause traditionally marked the end of a theatrical performance (Quint. 6.1.52), but any sense of closure here is illusory and short-lived, since the Flavian challenge is imminent. The theatre was a focal point for popular acclamation of a general, as in Pompey's dream, also tinged by a sense of imminent *peripeteia* (Luc. 7.7–24). **cum lauru:** laurel branches were displayed on festive occasions and during military triumphs. The laurel was perceived as a 'bringer of peace' and 'messenger of rejoicing and victories' (Plin. *Nat.* 15.133), but the optimistic symbolism is premature, since Rome herself will become a battleground in the final conflict between the Vitellians and Flavians. **Galbae imagines:** as Otho was responsible for Galba's murder, the people by taking up his *imagines* align themselves with Vitellius as Otho's challenger. Yet it should also recall their previous hypocritical happiness at his murder (*nouissimum malorum fuit laetitia*, 1.47.1) and implicitly raises questions about whether they are any more sincere now. Similarly, at Vitellius' murder, *uolgus eadem prauitate insectabatur interfectum, qua fouerat uiuentem* (3.85). **congestis in modum tumuli coronis** 'after piling up their garlands like a burial mound'. The alliterative enclosing word-order mirrors the concept being described, as the garlands and accompanying participle (combined only here: *TLL* s.v. *congero* 278.44) 'bury' the central prepositional phrase. If the *coronae* included laurel, then it was apt to leave them where Galba was murdered, as laurel was said to have powers of purification over blood (Plin. *Nat.* 15.135, 15.138). Garlands also served as an offering to the dead (Ov. *Fast.* 2.537). **iuxta lacum Curtium:** the *lacus Curtius* where Galba was murdered (1.41.2, Suet. *Galb.* 20.2, Plut. *Galb.* 27.1) was 'a small trapezoidal area of the forum measuring some 10.5 × 8.95 m.; by Livy's day it was dry and enclosed (Varr. *Ling.* v.150, Ov. *Fast.* vi.403–4), and people threw coins into it to express their hope for the safety of the *princeps* (Suet. *Aug.* 57.1)' (Oakley (1998) 96). Varro offers three aetiological explanations of how the place came by its name, but the best known (and most pointedly ironic in the context) was when a chasm opened up there, only closing again when M. Curtius, mounted on a horse and in full armour, altruistically hurled himself into the space in an act of *deuotio* (Liv. 7.6.1–6). There is pointed dissonance between Curtius' selfless sacrifice and the self-destructive murder of an elderly emperor on the same spot. **Galba moriens:** the present participle draws a discreet veil over the frenzied butchery of Galba (1.41.3). **sanguine infecerat:** there were altars at the site of the *lacus Curtius* (Ov. *Fast.* 6.403) so it was a sacred place. People remembered the desecration: Vitellius was forced at sword-point to look at the site of Galba's murder just before his own death (3.85). This combination of noun and verb recurs in T. in non-religious contexts (5.6.3, *A.* 1.42.4) and has associations with Augustan poetry (Hor. *Carm.* 3.6.34, Prop. 2.17.2, Virg. *A.* 5.413, Ov. *Met.* 11.396) and Sallust (*Jug.* 101.11).

55.2 cuncta longis aliorum principatibus composita statim decernun-tur 'all the powers accumulated over the long principates of other emperors were immediately decreed'. T. marks off the subject (*cuncta . . . composita*) by alliterative enclosing word order, hinting at future problems for Vitellius by suggesting a mis-match between the time needed for a *princeps* to establish personal *auctoritas* and the perfunctory haste of the senate's endorsement of his power (cf. Dio 59.3.1–2 on Augus-tus and Tiberius). This is the second of three notices of the senate officially endorsing a *princeps*, but only here is the new emperor's name not given. Each notice is cast in increasingly compact terms. Otho is first and has most detail: *decernitur Othoni tribunicia potestas et nomen Augusti et omnes principum honores* (1.47.1). Vespasian is last and his notice is most abridged: *senatus cuncta principibus solita Vespasiano decernit* (4.3.3). The senate acted quickly, voting Vitellius *imperium* on 19 Apr.: 'That date is attested by the Arval Acts, though the Brethren deferred the appropriate sacrifice until 1 May; at this time only one of their number (L. Maecius Postumus) was at Rome' (Brunt (1977) 100). *cunctus* = a synonym for *omnis* (1.3n. *cuncta . . . perlustrat*). **additae:** sc. *sunt*. **laudes gratesque:** this combination recurs in T. (4.39.1, *A.* 1.69.2, 12.37.4), who always applies it to humans, playing with a solemn and ancient formula common in Livy (7.36.7, 26.48.3, 27.13.2; also Plaut. *Mil.* 411–12, *Trin.* 821), where it is associated with gods (Oakley (1998) 349). There may be a hint that the senate is treating the German army like the gods. **missa legatio:** sc. *est*. The sending of a senatorial delega-tion from Rome to find Vitellius reminds us of the *arcanum imperii* that *posse principem alibi quam Romae fieri* (1.4.2). Members of these delegations were usually chosen by lot (e.g. Dio 59.23.2), but the duties could sometimes be dangerous. When Claudius was sent on an embassy to congratulate Caligula after a conspiracy was foiled, the emperor threw him into the Rhine (Suet. *Cl.* 9.1). **quae gaudio fungeretur** 'to convey their joy formally'. The hyperbolic language of this relative purpose clause is unprecedented (*TLL* s.v. *gaudium* 1712.18, 1715.81). *fungor* would normally be cou-pled with *officium* or *munus gratulandi*. Now *gaudium* is a matter of form and behaviour, not true feeling. **ad consules:** these were now Caelius Sabinus, later a successful jurist under Vespasian, and Vespasian's nephew Flavius Sabinus, who had replaced Verginius Rufus and Pompeius Vopiscus, consuls for March (*contra* 1.77.2). **haud immoderate** 'with considerable restraint'. The litotes momentarily suggests that T. compliments Valens, but the chapter's coda (*quod non scripsisset*) draws the irony into the open. More important than the letter's tone is the fact that Valens, a mere legate, has written at all, since this was the emperor's privilege. Mucianus raises eyebrows for similar reasons by writing to the senate after the Flavian victory (4.4.1). **quod non scripsisset:** in the morally debased world of the *H.*, even the absence of a shortcoming can be taken as a virtue. The subjunctive shows T. relaying the senators' reason (19.1n. *quod . . . legisset*), perhaps suggesting dark humour in the face of their own powerlessness.

56.1 Italia . . . afflictabatur: disease is naturally an expressive metaphor in *H.* 1–3 (cf. 2.67.1, 73, 86.4; Damon (2003) 100, Sontag (1978), Woodman (2006)). T. perhaps alludes to Cicero comparing the state plagued by the Catilinarian conspiracy to men in the grip of a persistent fever: *ut saepe homines aegri morbo graui . . . primo releuari uidentur, multo grauius uehementiusque afflictantur* (*Cat.* 1.31). The metaphor of disease is suggested anyway as '*grauis* is often used of illness or of persons seriously ill' (WM 255 citing *TLL* s.v. *grauis* 2282.79ff., 2295.23ff.), and *affligo* (*OLD affligo* 6) has particular associations with disease (cf. *ualetudo atrox, A.* 3.64.1, though WM 446 note that *atrox* is rather uncommon of illness). T.'s personification of (a diseased) Italy is poignant and recalls the prologue: *Italia nouis cladibus . . . afflicta* (1.2.2). **per municipia et colonias:** the combination recurs (2.20.1, 2.62.2, 3.57.1, 2× in *D.*, 4× in *A.*). 'T. sometimes uses *coloniae* without strict regard for colonial status, joining it with *municipia* to designate the Italian towns generally' (WM 86). **spoliare rapere ui et stupris polluere** 'pillaged, plundered, and perpetrated violent and vicious rapes'. The historic infinitives (5.1n. *anteire . . . obniti*) in asyndeton aptly mirror the Vitellian soldiers' hit-and-run activities. These verbs have no directly expressed object, also enhancing the sense of speed. The combination *polluo* + *stuprum* recurs in T. (3.41.1, *A.* 6.1.1, *A.* 13.17.2) and elsewhere (Cic. *Dom.* 105, *Mil.* 87, Hor. *Carm.* 4.5.21, Phaedr. 3.10.17), but the addition of *uis* intensifies the indignant tone. *stuprum*, initially 'disgrace in general . . . came to be specialised of a sexual disgrace, i.e. an illicit sexual act, whether an adulterous liaison or a forcible violation' (Adams (1987) 200–1). **in omne fas nefasque auidi aut uenales** 'mercenary and greedy for everything, whether it was permitted or not'. T. perhaps alludes to Horace on lusty Thracians over-indulging in drinking: *cum fas atque nefas exiguo fine libidinum | discernunt auidi* (*Carm.* 1.18.10–11). If so, this is apt, as the Vitellians are coming from the north and the Thracians are the archetypal 'northern barbarians'. Doublets combining *fas* + *nefas* were proverbial (Donatus on Ter. *Andr.* 214, *TLL* s.v. *fas* 295.54–60, Oakley (1997) 425, Wills (1996) 451), and T. has one in another emotionally heightened denunciation: *tantam uictoribus aduersus fas nefasque irreuerentiam fuisse* (3.51.1). Lucan uses such language to censure Caesar: *ipse per omne | fasque nefasque rues?* (5.312–13). T. normally follows *auidus* with a noun in the genitive, but *fas / nefas* are indeclinable, so he uses the preposition *in* (the only instance in T.'s extant work); *uenalis* + *in* occurs again (*A.* 12.46.2). **non sacro, non profano abstinebant** 'they did not hold back from attacking (*OLD abstineo* 9) anything, whether it was sacrosanct or not'. The asyndeton, anaphora and unexpected word-order emphasise the spectacular explosion of violence. Other authors describe escalation (from initial destruction of the non-sacred, *profanum*, to climactic devastation of the sacred, *sacrum*, as in *cum omnia profana spoliassent, ne sacris* *quidem abstinuerant*, Curt. 10.1.3, with a similar progression at Liv. 29.8.8–9). Yet T. avoids subordinate clauses and suggests simultaneous annihilation of the non-sacred and sacred. There is also an auditory climax, achieved by the increasing length and weight of the key words: – | – – | – | ͜– – | –͟– – (Kenney). **et fuere qui** 'indeed there were even those who'. *et* (*OLD et* 3) builds this panorama of violence to a minia-ture climax, tacitly acknowledging that what T. is about to say hardly seems credible. **inimicos suos . . . interficerent:** the notion of individuals exploiting civil war to settle private scores is a topos, but people actually dressing up as soldiers to kill their personal enemies themselves is an extraordinary escalation. Even when the triumvirs put private adversaries on the lists of the proscribed in 43–2 (App. *BC* 4.5), they relied on others to do the killing. **specie militum** 'disguised as soldiers'. **regionum gnari:** the combination (a choice variant for *gnari locorum*, 13.1n.) is first in T. (*TLL* s.v. *gnarus* 2122.67), but appealed to his imitator Ammianus Marcellinus (14.10.7, 19.9.4). **refertos agros, dites dominos:** T. reactivates a familiar motif, the destruction of agriculture as a hallmark of civil war, but suggests almost an excessive affluence, involving over-indulgence and hierarchy, not the wholesome innocence of the vulner-able farmers in Gallia Narbonensis (12.2n. *pleni agri, apertae domus*). *refertos*, only here in the *H.*, recalls Livy's description of the rich pickings found by Hannibal in the territory of Picenum, *refertum praeda* (22.9.3). The alliterative *dites dominos* (also 4.1.2) is Sallustian (*Hist.* 3.48.26, from the stirring speech of the tribune Licinius Macer to the people in 73 BC). The closer we move towards the centre, the richer the spoils, but the more destructive (potentially) they are for those who can be tempted by luxury: 'the center is no longer a refuge from danger but itself a source of peril' (Pomeroy (2003) 370). **in praedam . . . ad excidium:** 27.1n. *in metum compulit* for the *uariatio* of prepositions. **foret:** *foret* for *esset* (14.3n. *deletae . . . forent*). **ad excidium destinabant:** the expres-sion hints at the soldiers enacting their own latterday proscriptions. In any case, such decisions would normally be a general's responsibility (4.46.3). **obnoxiis ducibus et prohibere non ausis** 'while the generals were at their mercy and lacked the guts to intervene'; *et . . . non = neque* (32.1n.). T.'s wonderfully pregnant, pithy phrase (*obnoxiis ducibus*) reminds his readers that it was the common soldiers who could make and break emperors.

56.2 minus auaritiae in Caecina, plus ambitionis: sc. *erat*. The implicit point of comparison is Fabius Valens. For Sallust, *auaritia* (5.1n., 13.1n. *expleta auaritia*) is worse than *ambitio*, which can mark out good and bad men alike (*Cat.* 11.2). T. accentuates Caecina's *ambitio* again (2.99.2). **ob lucra et quaestus infamis** 'notorious because of his ill-gotten gains and profits'. The pl. forms are striking: cf. *ille . . . | attribuit uarios quaestus artemque lucrorum* (Manil. 4.165). Valens was infamously greedy (29.1n. *occultare*). **eoque:** 13.2n. **alienae etiam culpae dissimulator** 'was prepared to turn a blind eye to others' transgressions as well' (16.2n. *alieni . . . socia*). T. likes agent nouns ending in *–tor*: e.g. Nero as *incredibilium cupitor* (*A.* 15.42.2): 'Desire for vividness largely explains why T. affects *nomina agentis*, but it is not, I think, the whole explanation. Some of them may attract him simply because they are choice and unusual words' (Goodyear (1972) 221, with (1968) 30 for a table listing the frequency of distribution of *nomina agentis* in T.'s works). **iam pridem attritis Italiae rebus:**

the metaphor (favoured by T.: *Agr.* 9.4, *G.* 29.2, 1.10.1, 1.89.1, 3.50.3, 4.12.3, *A.* 15.16.1) in *attero* derives from grinding away a physical object: cf. *Hannibal . . . Italiae opes maxume attriuerat* (Sall. *Jug.* 5.4). This assertion conflicts with T.'s emphasis elsewhere on Italian prosperity (2.17.1). He may be exaggerating for emotional effect.   **iniuriae aegre tolerabantur:** T. perhaps imitates himself, after describing the Britons similarly: *has* [sc. *iniurias*] *aegre tolerant* (*Agr.* 13.1). The echo hints at the inverted world of civil war, as Romans now treat Italy like a foreign country.

57–73 THE VICTORIOUS VITELLIUS ADVANCES TOWARDS ROME

After the Vitellian victory, it is only a matter of time before the new emperor and his troops reach Rome, but T. pointedly decelerates the journey, splitting the narrative into two sections (2.57–73, 87–89), and interrupting it with disquieting digressions of murder in Mauretania (2.58–59.1), a Gallic pretender (2.61), the execution of Dolabella (2.63–4) and a runaway slave (2.72). T. builds up tension and even defers Vitellius' arrival in the city (2.89) until after the section on Vespasian's proclamation (2.74–86). This arrangement creates the impression that Vitellius' journey took time to complete, casting him as sluggish and lazy. Yet the relative chronology of these events is controversial (90.1n. *postera die*) and leaves T. open to charges of bias, perhaps reflecting pro-Flavian propaganda in his sources (Chilver (1979) 219). Vitellius probably learned of his victory on *c.* 20 Apr. at Andematunnum, 518 miles away from Cremona (Murison (1993) 144), which he reached on *c.* 23 May. However, the next part of his journey from Cremona to Rome is rather shorter (*c.* 373 miles) and does not involve crossing the Alps. The *terminus post quem non* for Vitellius' arrival in Rome is 18 Jul., but T. and all our other sources leave the precise date unclear, and herein lies the problem. Vespasian's proclamation in Alexandria took place on 1 Jul. (2.79), but if Vitellius arrived in Rome *before* that date, then T. misleadingly postpones this news (2.89) to suggest that his journey was unusually sluggish. Or Vitellius may indeed have arrived after 1 Jul., in which case T.'s arrangement accurately reflects the real chronology. Either way, T. depicts Vitellius' march as a 'triumphal progress' and 'as conforming increasingly to a kind of Bacchic rout' (Murison (1993) 145).

In this context, T.'s lavish and vivid description of Vitellius' grim visit to the battlefield at Cremona forty days after his victory (2.70) is calculated to generate disgust and disbelief (Keitel (1992), Morgan (1992), Manolaraki (2005)) despite all its stylistic flourishes (but McNeil (1990) 42 analyses the potential for aesthetic pleasure even in grotesque descriptions of battle). Its impact is heightened by a masterful array of creative narrative techniques, ranging from T.'s evocative vocabulary to diverging descriptions of the battlefield itself, first from T. as narrator and then from the internal protagonists, Caecina and Valens. This is a fine example of an 'aftermath narrative' (Pagán (2000)), a scene of a particular military event at a particular time, but having wider resonances with the past and the future. We can see that T. considers the visit emblematic because he imitates his description (2.70) in depicting Germanicus' earlier visit in 15 to the site of Varus' defeat by Arminius in 9 (*A.* 1.61–2). This suggests that

Germanicus is setting a pattern that will later be perverted by Vitellius (Woodman (1998) 70–85). Vitellius' visit to the battlefield also serves as a pivot between the description of the original battle (2.39–45) and the subsequent narrative of the Vitellian defeat at the second battle of Bedriacum on the same site (3.16–35). It raises central ethical questions about Vitellius' character and indeed about the whole war.

57.1 uictoriae suae nescius: Vitellius' ignorance is thematic (cf. *nihil . . . Vitellio anquirente*, 2.59.1; *tam propinquae sortis ignarus*, 2.70.4; *ignaro adhuc Vitellio*, 2.81.1) and shows his subordinates ignoring him.   **ut ad integrum bellum** 'as if the war had yet to be won' (16.3n. *ut*). This recalls Sallust's Metellus, who *rursus tamquam ad integrum bellum cuncta parat festinatque* (*Jug.* 73.1), but the difference between the dogged republican general and the 'unmilitary' Vitellius is pointed. Livy has *integrum bellum* (7×), also in his imitators Curtius (9.4.16) and Florus (2.13.64).   **trahebat** 'began to gather'. T. uses the simple form instead of the compound (*OLD contraho* 4a). It may imply a certain lethargy in these troops, which T. will elaborate as the victorious Vitellians advance to Rome (cf. *tota mole belli secuturus*, 1.61.2; *graui . . . agmine*, 2.87.1). Vitellius had *c.* 30,000 men (20.2n. *magno terrore*).   **pauci ueterum militum in hibernis relicti:** Vitellius presumably left veterans as they had the most experience, but the rebel leader Julius Civilis will scorn them: *nec aliud in hibernis quam praedam et senes* (4.14.4). Vitellius must have assumed that the winter-camps at Bonna, Mogontiacum, Vetera, Novaesium and Vindonissa were safe bases, but only Vindonissa and Mogontiacum will survive the rebellion. The three camps furthest to the north were destroyed (4.61.3).   **festinatis per Gallias dilectibus:** 16.2n. *dilectum agere*. This aggressive levy apparently extended as far north as the Batavians' territory. Their resentment at Roman recruiting techniques prompts them to join Civilis' rebellion (4.14.1–2). Troops hastily enrolled were not always reliable and the officers are later anxious about *subito dilectu suppletae legiones* (4.19.2).   **ut remanentium legionum nomina supplerentur** 'in order that the enlistments of the remaining legions could be raised to full strength'. *nomen* in this sense is only here in T. (G-G 953; *OLD nomen* 21b); *suppleo* (*OLD* 2b) is more often combined with *numerus* (cf. Suet. *Cal.* 43). The depleted legions left behind were the *I Germanica* (based in Bonna, led by Herennius Gallus; *RE* xii 1376–80), *IV Macedonica* (based in Mogontiacum, led by Alienus Caecina; *RE* xii 1550–6), *XV Primigenia* (based in Vetera, led by Munius Lupercus; *RE* xii 1758–60) and the *XVI Gallica* (based in Novaesium, led by Numisius Rufus; *RE* xii 1761–5), but they all sent *uexilla* south to Rome (2.100.1). All four pro-Vitellian legions were disbanded after the civil wars after failing to contain Civilis' rebellion (Chilver and Townend (1985) 14), although the rebel coalition had already massacred many of the *XV Primigenia* at Vetera (Levick (1999) 110).   **cura ripae:** the Roman military camps were on the left bank of the Rhine. Caesar initially saw this as the boundary between Gaul and Germany, but as a result of Domitian's war against the Chatti in 82–3, some military roads were later built in the territory across the river (Jones (1996) 53–5). The river was vulnerable as a defence in the winter when it froze, enabling people and even horses to cross it on foot (Herodian 6.7.7). A sudden and timely thaw in 89 stopped some German invaders from crossing (Suet. *Dom.* 6.2).   **Hordeonio Flacco:** the name will not impress readers, after his role in the narrative so far. Frail from old age and gout, this 'weather vane' of a man is *sine constantia, sine auctoritate* (1.9.1; cf. Plut. *Galb.* 18.8). Galba initially made him legate of Upper Germany to replace the dangerously popular Verginius Rufus (2.49.1n.), who had defeated Vindex's rebellion in Gaul. Yet Flaccus does not intervene when his soldiers smash Galba's statues (1.56.1). Vitellius' decision to keep him on as legate is unwise. Flaccus, worried about a looming war in Germany and inclined to support Vespasian (4.13.3; cf. 2.97.1), wavers in confronting Julius Civilis and his Batavians (4.18, 4.19.2–3) and delegates his responsibilities to others (4.24.1). The soldiers, intensely loyal to Vitellius, even suspect that Flaccus is in league with Civilis (4.25.4), who subsequently finds it useful to encourage this belief (5.26.3). After news of the Vitellian defeat arrives, Flaccus makes his troops swear an oath of loyalty to Vespasian (4.31.2) and distributes a donative to them in the new emperor's name (4.36.2), but in the exuberant celebrations that follow, the soldiers revive their long-standing hatred of Flaccus, pull him out of bed and kill him. Another general Petillius Cerialis later uses Flaccus as a negative *exemplum* in a speech to his mutinous soldiers (4.77.3). T. dismisses Flaccus as ineffectual, rather than malevolent, but as the German armies tend to generate pretenders, it is lucky that he was not more charismatic, or he could have made an imperial challenge himself.   **ipse:** sc. Vitellius.   **e Britannico exercitu delecta octo milia:** Vitellius may seem irresponsible to take these troops from a distant province, but he is still *uictoriae suae nescius*. The legions in Britain are *II Augusta*, *IX Hispana* and *XX Valeria* (each 5,000–6,000 strong, plus auxiliaries); Nero had already removed the *XIV Gemina* in 67 for his intended eastern campaign.

57.2 morte Othonis concidisse bellum 'that with Otho's death the war had collapsed'. The combination *concido* + *bellum* is only here (*TLL* s.v. *bellum* 1832.77), but the metaphor involves collapsing buildings or the fall of cities.   **uir-tutem . . . cumulat:** after a metaphor of collapse (*concidisse*), we get one of building up (*cumulat*). Vitellius tends to extol his soldiers indiscriminately (2.69.1, 3.36.2), which devalues his praise; and these troops have not even shown *uirtus* by fighting in the decisive battle. T. likes to use *cumulo* with abstract concepts such as words, titles and accusations (*Agr.* 40.1, *H.* 2.80.1, 3.36.2, *A.* 1.21.2, 4.21.2, 4.69.2, 13.2.3, 14.53.2), but when linked with praise, it always has negative connotations: so Mucianus tries to breed complacency in Antonius Primus *multis in senatu laudibus cumulatum* (4.39.4) and the senate disgraces itself as Pallas *antiquae parsimoniae laudibus cumulabatur* (*A.* 12.53.3). **postulante exercitu:** Suetonius does not specify that the request came from the soldiers: *rogantibus . . . cunctis* (*Vit.* 12).   **libertum suum Asiaticum:** Suetonius prefers the sensational, casting Asiaticus as the lover of Vitellius, who, annoyed at his slave's insolence and dishonesty, sold him to a travelling trainer of gladiators. Vitellius then retrieved Asiaticus and set him free (*Vit.* 12). T. emphasises his influential position in Rome (2.95.2) and documents with satisfaction his death by crucifixion (4.11.3).   **equestri dignitate:** freedmen being awarded equestrian status is a topos in T.'s narrative of the civil war. So, Galba's Icelus (1.13.1) and Vespasian's Hormus (4.39.1) are both honoured in this way. 'The growing influence of imperial freedmen

reflects (in Tacitus' view) a confusion in social values that did not begin to find a
remedy until the political turmoil died down' (Damon (2006) 250).   **inhonestam
adulationem compescit** 'he restrained this degrading flattery'. Suetonius' Vitellius uses strong language, deploring what would be a 'stain on the equestrian order'
(*Vit.* 12), but T. omits details of the new emperor's response. *inhonesta adulatio* has the
air of an authorial gloss, rather than Vitellius' own perception, and the adj. is broadly
expressive, not pleonastic: the flattery degrades both the soldiers making the request
and Vitellius himself.   **mobilitate ingenii:** Suetonius also says that Vitellius gave
Asiaticus equestrian rank after first rejecting such pleas, but does not cast it as a general character trait (*Vit.* 12), as T. does here. T. describes Vitellius in the same way
again at the end of his principate (3.84.4; cf. 1.7.2, the same phrase used of Galba).
palam . . . inter secreta conuiuii: T. likes *uariatio* of adverb + prepositional
clause with *palam* (also *A.* 1.49.1, 2.40.3, 4.71.4, 12.13.1). Suetonius also says that Vitellius changed his mind *super cenam* (*Vit.* 12). With this notice, T. activates a sympotic
theme that will dominate his account of Vitellius' journey to Rome (and indeed his
whole principate). Dio famously complains that writing imperial history is difficult
as decisions are made 'secretly and behind closed doors' (53.19.3) and T. especially
loathes such secretiveness, including 'trials' carried out *intra cubiculum* (*A.* 11.2.1). Moreover, although the *conuiuium* should ideally reinforce *amicitia* and facilitate accessibility
(under the republic sumptuary laws required citizens to dine with their doors open:
Macr. 3.17.1, Val. Max. 2.1.5), Vitellius cultivates the wrong friends in an atmosphere
of exclusion, isolation and self-indulgence.   **anulis:** slaves wore iron rings as symbols
of their captivity (Plin. *Nat.* 33.23), but the right to wear golden rings was the visible
public symbol of equestrian status. People resented individuals thought to have been
elevated too quickly (Petr. *Sat.* 71.9, Juv. 1.28, Mart. 11.37). In 22 a law was passed that
only a free-born man, with a free-born father and grandfather and the 400,000 HS
necessary for equestrian status, could wear gold equestrian rings (Plin. *Nat.* 33.32). Yet
in 48 under Claudius, 400 ex-slaves were still charged with illegally holding equestrian
status (Plin. *Nat.* 33.33). *anuli* is not a pl. for singular noun, but indicates a plurality of
rings (Nutting (1928)).   **foedum mancipium et malis artibus ambitiosum**
'a disgusting slave who was aiming for the top by his evil ways'. T. scornfully calls
the freedman a slave (also 3.47.1), denying his status, just as he does in recording his
death: *malam potentiam seruili supplicio expiauit* (4.11.3). *mancipium*, originally the process
of claiming property by laying hands on it, was later extended to refer to slaves. The
term already suggests degradation, but here T. modifies it with a pejorative adj. (the
only time that he does so in the surviving *corpus*).

58.1 Isdem diebus: T. often anchors digressions and tableaux of incidents
beyond Italy with impressionistic chronology (2.8.1 *sub idem tempus*). Events in Mauretania (not in the parallel tradition) could have featured elsewhere in the narrative, but their location here contributes to the elongation of Vitellius' journey to
Rome and underscores his complacent and unmilitary character.   **utramque
Mauretaniam:** this coastal area of north Africa facing Spain included the
western portion of the Atlas mountains and was inhabited by Moors. When their

king Bocchus died in 33 BC, he left his land to Octavian, who in 25 BC entrusted it to a client king Juba (ruled 25 BC–AD 23). Caligula executed Juba's son and successor Ptolemy (ruled 23–40) for unknown reasons, although Pliny attributes his intervention to *saeuitia* (*Nat.* 5.2). Mauretania rebelled, remaining unsettled for several years while trouble was mopped up by Hosidius Geta and Suetonius Paulinus, the first Roman *dux* to cross the Atlas mountains (Plin. *Nat.* 5.14). In *c.* 44, Claudius divided Mauretania into two provinces (Dio 60.9), Tingitana (to the west) and Caesariensis (to the east), assigning them to equestrian procurators. That arrangement lasted until 68, when Galba united the two provinces under a single governor (Levick (1990) 149–50), a practice which Vespasian continued (M-W 277–8). Trouble erupted again in Mauretania in 74–5 and 84–5 (Alföldy (1985) 99, Levick (1999) 122).   **Albino:** Lucceius Albinus (*RE* XIII 1559–61), only here in T., was an especially corrupt and disruptive governor of Judaea in 62–4 (Jos. *BJ* 2.272–6; cf. *Ant.* 20.117, 200–10), although Josephus concedes that he did confront the *sicarii* (*Ant.* 20.204). His son of the same name was a good friend of the younger Pliny (*Ep.* 3.9.7, 4.9.13).   **a Nerone . . . per Galbam:** *uariatio* of prepositions (Sörbom (1935) 46).   **addita . . . administratione:** the enclosing abl. absolute is marked off by assonance. Albinus (as procurator of Mauretania Caesariensis) supported Galba early. His additional assignment of Mauretania Tingitana, whose governor had perhaps opposed Galba (Murison (1993) 48), was a reward for his prompt co-operation.   **haud spernendis uiribus:** 11.1n. *haud spernenda manus*. This perhaps dramatises the scale of potential trouble. Albinus' troops are all auxiliaries. Only one legion (*III Augusta*) was normally stationed in Africa (4.48.1) at Ammaedara (until 75) to the east and away from Mauretania, although there was also the short-lived *I Macriana*, formed by Clodius Macer, disbanded by Galba, reformed by Vitellius and disbanded by the Flavians (2.97.2).   **decem nouem:** this form of *undeuiginti* is also in Caesar.   **cohortes . . . alae:** 4.4n. *auxilia . . . alarumque*. **ingens Maurorum numerus:** 4.2n. *ingens . . . fiducia*. The motif of the barbarian horde is archetypal (Hdt. 4.172, Xen. *An.* 1.7.4, 3.2.16, Cic. *Arch.* 9.21, *Marc.* 3.8, Liv. 5.34.2, 6.7.2, Vell. 2.106.1, T. *G.* 35.2–3, *A.* 2.21.1, 14.34.2, Dio 62.12.2; Kraus (1994) 131), but the multitude of Moorish auxiliaries will be cowed by the *magna . . . fama* of the German armies (2.58.2). Moors are seen again in T. participating in revolts in neighbouring Numidia (*A.* 2.52.2), serving as auxiliaries in the Roman army (*A.* 4.24.3), and acting as hired assassins in the murder of Piso, the proconsular governor of Africa (4.50.1).   **per latrocinia et raptus:** T. links these virtually synonymous nouns again (*G.* 35.3, 1.46.2). The pleonastic pairing is expressive and the pl. forms amplify the scale of the violence. The inclination to plunder was seen as an archetypal barbarian trait (WM 202–3, Oakley (1997) 634). T. associates it with the Moors again (*A.* 2.52.1, 4.23.1).   **apta bello manus** 'a band ready for war'. The nature of fighting appropriate for Africa involved furtive guerrilla tactics, traditionally the antithesis of Roman military methods. So Metellus realises that he must fight Jugurtha *non proeliis neque acie sed alio more* (Sall. *Jug.* 54.5).   **in Othonem pronus:** the locals probably did not share Albinus' personal inclination to support Otho, who had given certain Moorish towns as a gift to the province of Baetica in Spain (1.78.1).   **Hispaniae**

angusto freto diremptae: Livian phrasing (24.49.6; cf. 28.17.10). Trade between north Africa and southern Spain, separated at the closest point only by a narrow strait (Sall. *Jug.* 18.9) of 30 miles (Plin. *Nat.* 5.2), was easy. Spanish Baetica, 'one of the richest provinces in the Roman west, exporting metals, olive oil, and fish sauce' (*OCD³* 'Baetica'), offered tempting resources to Albinus, if he wanted to become a major political player in the civil wars.

58.2 inde Cluuio Rufo metus (sc. *fuit*) 'Cluvius Rufus was alarmed at this'. The possessive dat. *Cluuio Rufo* is to be taken with the predicate *metus* (as 2.67.1, 4.39.3, *A.* 1.60.1; cf. 2.85.1 without the dat.). His fear makes sense. In the 70s BC, Sertorius invaded southern Spain from north Africa (Plut. *Sert.* 11), and under the empire the Moors were still perceived as a threat to southern Spain (Calp. Sic. 4.37–42). Cluvius Rufus, a *uir facundus et pacis artibus, bellis inexpertus* (1.8.1), is a central political and historiographical figure of these civil wars. Under Vespasian he wrote a history (Syme (1958a) 179, 675) that perhaps began with Caligula, certainly covered Nero (*A.* 13.20.2, 14.2.1) and may have addressed the civil wars as well (Plut. *Oth.* 3.2), embracing antiquarian digression (Plut. *Mor.* 289c-d). Possibly he is even T.'s source for this segment on Mauretania. Rufus (consul probably in 39 or 40) was Nero's herald at the second Neronia and on the Greek tour (Suet. *Nero* 21.2, Dio 63.14.3), so critics posit a pro-Neronian history, but he may have helped the emperor unwillingly. Pliny recalls Cluvius Rufus requesting indulgence if Verginius Rufus (49.1n.) finds anything not to his liking in his writing (*Ep.* 9.19.5), but despite this claim to outspokenness, T. presents a defensive (2.65.1) and cautious (4.43.1) man. Galba (as governor of Hispania Tarraconensis, which he left in 68 to assume the principate in Rome) chose Rufus to govern the whole of Spain in his absence (Damon (2003) 114). Otho, after the coup, was nervous about Rufus and ostentatiously praised him by special edict, but news quickly followed that Spain had switched allegiance to Vitellius (1.76.1). Rufus himself may have been less decisive, but Vitellius allowed him to retain his post (2.65.2). Under Vespasian, he lived a quiet life writing history. **decimam legionem:** from 63–8 Nero relocated the X *Gemina* to Pannonia, but Galba returned it to Spain (to join the *VI Victrix*). **propinquare litori:** 18.1n. *si propinquaret.* **ut transmissurus** 'as if intending to send them across'. Both sides indulge in some posturing across the 30 mile wide strait. Caesar describes the preparations needed for a genuine offensive crossing of a *fretum* (*Gal.* 5.1). **qui . . . concilarent:** the subjunctive verb is in a final (purpose) clause introduced by the relative pronoun. **magna . . . fama:** the syntax aptly mirrors the contents, as the causal abl. of the subordinate clause overshadows the short main clause (13.2n. *quae* on 'appendix sentences'). The armies from Germany had a formidable reputation (1.70.1, 2.21.4, 3.9.4), but their calibre will deteriorate the closer they come to Rome, culminating in a dismal picture of their incompetence (2.93.1). **spargebatur** 'a rumour was being spread'. The metaphor involves sprinkling (also 1.26.1, 2.86.4, *Agr.* 38.2, *A.* 3.21.4), but the agents are left suitably vague. Val. Flac. 1.97 and Sil. 10.606–7 have the acc. + inf. construction after this verb, but more often it takes a direct subject or object such as *rumor* (Virg. *A.* 2.98, Quint. 7.2.12, 9.2.80, Fron. *Str.* 1.4.11, 1.9.1). Rumours are often a powerful weapon in the guerrilla wars that were common in Africa (*A.* 4.24.1).   **insuper:** 11.2n. *deforme insuper auxilium.*   **insigne regis et Iubae nomen** 'the distinction of a king and the name of Juba'. *insigne regis* = a diadem (*A.* 2.56.3, 6.42.4, 12.49.1, 15.29.1; *OCD³* 'diadem'). The chiastic word-order climactically builds up to Juba's illustrious name. This extraordinary figure (ruled 25 BC–AD 23), after being brought up in Italy and married to Antony and Cleopatra's daughter Cleopatra Selene, introduced Greco-Roman culture and some degree of urbanisation to Mauretania, including his beautiful capital, Caesarea. He was a cultured man and a prolific writer of lost works in Greek on history, ethnography, geography, zoology, painting and drama, including his book about a plant 'euphorbia', discovered by his doctor on Mount Atlas (Plin. *Nat.* 5.16; cf. *Nat.* 6.205 on two giant dogs brought back for him from the Canary Islands). The rumour that Albinus was fashioning himself as a new Juba helped Cluvius Rufus by casting the dangerous procurator as an arrogant (and unworthy) appropriator of an emotive historical figure, but the story was not necessarily made up by Vitellius' supporters.

   59.1 mutatis animis: T. has the phrase (2× in Liv.) again (4.78.1). It reminds us that any commander must ensure his soldiers' loyalty before embarking on a bold course of action.   **alae praefectus . . . cohortium praefecti:** specifying these officers' posts recalls the list of troops available to Albinus (2.58.1) and suggests the unfolding of a miniature civil war successfully engineered by Cluvius Rufus from afar, as the Moorish auxiliaries confront the *alae* and *cohortes.*   **opprimuntur . . . trucidatus . . . interfecta:** *uariatio* of verbs for killing, without the agents specified.   **Caesariensem . . . petit:** this detail suggests Albinus' cowardly character. As Cluvius Rufus purports to threaten Tingitana to the west, the procurator heads directly away from the danger.   **in appulsu litoris:** T. loftily uses an abl. noun *appulsu* + objective gen. *litoris* instead of a participle *appellens* + dat. *litori* (Damon (2003) 194). The scene recalls the murder of Pompey (whose wife is also present) as he lands in Egypt (cf. *terris appellere,* Luc. 8.567), even if Albinus himself is no second Pompey. It may also evoke the death of Protesilaus, the first Greek ashore at Troy and thus fated to die (Catul. 68.73–130, Ov. *Ep.* 13) or Priam, whose headless corpse is famously left to lie *litore* (Virg. *A.* 2.557).   **trucidatus:** sc. *est.* Pompey was likewise *trucidatus sub oculis uxoris suae* (Flor. 2.13.52, also Plut. *Pomp.* 79.3; Bell (1994) 831, citing a scholiast on Luc. 8.91 to show that Pompey's wife was also present in Livy's account), but Albinus' wife will be a victim rather than a witness.   **cum se percussoribus obtulisset:** Albinus' unnamed wife dies beside her husband in exemplary fashion. The 'wife willing to die with her husband or lover' is a topos (cf. Gibson (2003) 95 on Evadne as 'a byword for love and loyalty to a husband'; Sen. *Con.* 10.3.2). Arria (wife of Paetus) indignantly asks Scribonianus' wife, who had outlived him: *ego . . . te audiam, cuius in gremio Scribonianus occisus est, et uiuis?* (Plin. *Ep.* 3.16.9). Another wife (unnamed), after discovering that her husband is terminally ill, becomes his *comes . . . mortis* by tying herself to him and jumping into a lake (Plin. *Ep.* 6.24). Others in T. who boldly confront assassins include Galba (1.41.2), Sempronius Gracchus (*A.* 1.53.5), and Agrippina (*A.* 14.8.5).   **nihil . . . Vitellio anquirente:** *anquiro,* a Ciceronian favourite, is only here in the

H. (4× *A.*), further highlighting what Vitellius fails to do. The abl. absolute offers a moralising bridge back to the main narrative. T. denounces Vitellius' complacency over the entire Mauretanian affair, but adds impact by emotively juxtaposing the abl. absolute with the main clause about the murder of Albinus' helpless wife, an innocent and morally impressive victim. Yet Vitellius may not be as irresponsible as T. implies: the two Mauretanias were one of the procuratorial provinces whose loyalties tended to shift with the prevailing political wind (1.11.2) and they lacked their own legion. Vitellius' decision to allow Cluvius Rufus to remain as governor of Spain (2.65.2) perhaps suggests that he already had some information about these events.   **breui auditu quamuis magna transibat** 'with a cursory hearing he used to pass over reports, however important they were'. Generalising from one incident is a narrative technique more often associated with Suetonius.

   59.2 itinere terrestri: 14.1n. *in terrestre iter.*   **ipse Arare flumine deuehitur:** Vitellius is the antithesis of the ideal general, who marches at the head of his troops (5.1n. *anteire agmen*). The passive voice of the verb and the focus on the *Arar* (mod. Saône) suggests his laziness. This river is elsewhere characterised as especially sluggish (*incredibili lenitate*, Caes. *Gal.* 1.12.1; Sil. 3.452–3, Plin. *Nat.* 3.33) and so aptly reflects Vitellius' personality (at least for geographically well-informed readers). Cf. *uectus est per . . . flumina* (Suet. *Vit.* 10.2).   **nullo principali paratu** 'with no imperial trappings'. T. elsewhere likes this lofty adj. (post-Augustan when it means 'imperial') for 'entities whose importance is unduly inflated by a connection with the *princeps*' (Damon (2003) 132). Here T. hones a choice alliterative pairing by choosing *paratus* rather than *apparatus:* cf. *nullus apparatus arrogantiae principalis* (Plin. *Pan.* 76.7). In the parallel tradition Vitellius travels in the most exquisite boats garlanded with many different types of wreath (Suet. *Vit.* 10.2), evoking a mode of transport more usually associated with Cleopatra and the east (Pelling (1988) 187–8). T., avoiding the obvious, plays down this element to allow his account of Vitellius' decadent journey to build to a crescendo. **uetere egestate conspicuus:** Suetonius offers some scandalous substantiation, including the choice details of Vitellius moving his wife and children to an attic so that he can rent out his own house and pawning his mother's pearl earring (*Vit.* 7.2). Some of this smacks of invective (Plut. *Galb.* 22.7; cf. Dio 65.2.1).   **Iunius Blaesus:** Blaesus, 'an elegant but perhaps rather inert figure' (Murison (1993) 52), quickly supports Vitellius (1.59.2) and remains steadfastly loyal (3.39.2), but even so Vitellius' brother will callously play on the emperor's insecurities to secure Blaesus' death by poisoning (3.38–9, with Miller and Jones (1978)). The wealthy Blaesus, descended from Mark Antony (3.38.3), was considered capable of becoming *princeps*, even if he himself was unambitious; and Tiberius forced Blaesus' father and uncle to commit suicide (*A.* 6.40.2). All this made him vulnerable to attack. T.'s brief but positive obituary (3.39.2) reveals more about other men's capacity for treachery than about Blaesus himself. For Vitellius, Blaesus could play the same role as the wealthy Mucianus does for Vespasian, but where the Flavians set aside their differences, Vitellius' court is self-destructive.   **genere illustri:** 'his Antonian ancestry accrued from the Domitii Ahenobarbi through a marriage contracted by Blaesus' father: he was one of the *duo*

Blaesi (*A.* vi 40.2), either the consul of 28 or his brother' (Syme (1975) 62).   **largus animo et par opibus** 'generous-spirited but also having the money to match'. **circumdaret principi ministeria** 'surrounded the emperor with attendants'; *donec* + subjunctive (8.2n. *donec . . . aufugeret*). The word-order mirrors the concept being described. The abstract *ministerium* = *minister* (L-H-S 788 §23c). T. (also *Agr.* 40.2, *A.* 13.27.1) follows Seneca the Younger, Quintilian and Pliny the Elder in using *ministerium* for people (*OLD ministerium* 5a).   **comitaretur:** sc. *principem.*   **eo ipso ingratus** 'disagreeable for precisely that reason'. The dynamics of giving and receiving gifts in the ancient world are complex. If a gift exceeded the recipient's ability to reciprocate (as when Junius Blaesus helps Vitellius), then the recipient becomes a client, incurring humiliating gift-debt (Roller (2001) 198): *nam beneficia eo usque laeta sunt, dum uidentur exsolui posse: ubi multum anteuenere, pro gratia odium redditur* (*A.* 4.18.3). To accept gifts involves acknowledging weakness and inferiority, so Caligula is annoyed when the senators vote him honours, as this implies that they are his superiors (Dio 59.23.3). 'Whoever accepts a *beneficium* sells his liberty' (Publilius Syrus B5 (Friedrich), quoted by Lendon (1997) 69). Emperors loathe being reminded of debts or services that they cannot repay (4.80.3, *A.* 4.18.2). Seneca the Younger advises against bestowing a gift that will remind the recipient of his own weakness (*Ben.* 1.11.6).   **odium . . . uernilibus blanditiis uelaret:** cf. *uelare odium fallacibus blanditiis* (*A.* 14.56.3), for Nero's manipulative treatment of Seneca the Younger. Vitellius' servile flattery apparently shows self-debasement and acknowledges the gift-debt (which he cannot reciprocate), but like Otho, he does *omnia seruiliter pro dominatione* (1.36.3). A *uerna* (*OLD* 1) was a slave born in the master's household, typically treated leniently and often engagingly cheeky as a result (Tib. 1.5.25–6, Hor. *Sat.* 2.6.66, Sen. *Con. Sap.* 11.3), but Vitellius plays this role for deadly purposes. T. uses the adj. *uernilis* (his own coinage) very selectively (only again at 3.32.3) and avoids the noun altogether. In New Comedy, the flatterer was a standard unattractive figure, who wore a bald mask with a large nose and ears, and bulging eyes (Bieber (1961) 100).

    59.3 praesto fuere 'were at hand'.   **Lugduni:** Vitellius reaches Lugdunum on *c.* 1 May (Murison (1993) 154) after travelling 166 miles from Andematunnum. That the generals await Vitellius' arrival emphasises his slow progress, as they had farther to travel to Lugdunum (352 miles from Cremona, including a crossing of the Alps).   **uictricium uictarumque partium duces:** *uariatio* of the more standard pair *uictores uictique* (7.1n.). T. has *uictrices partes* (2.77.3) and *uictae partes* (2.63.1) again, but combines them alliteratively only here. Cf. *haec hodie ratis* | *Phlegethontis atri regias animas uehet,* | *uictamque uictricemque* (Sen. *Ag.* 752–4).   **laudatos:** Vitellius tends to praise people excessively (57.2n. *uirtutem . . . cumulat*).   **curuli suae circumposuit:** sc. *sellae* (Wanscher (1960)). The chair of state inlaid with ivory and used by high-ranking Roman officials was thought to have been introduced by the Etruscans (Liv. 1.8.3). The Trajanic writer Gavius Bassus suggests that the adj. derives from *currus,* as senators holding a curule magistracy rode to the senate in a chariot as a mark of honour (Gell. *NA* 3.18.4). In 19 BC Augustus was awarded the curule chair, and sat on it in the senate between the two consuls on a raised platform (Dio 54.10.5). Military men, not elected consuls, flank Vitellius, an arrangement that is eloquent about his power base. **infanti filio:** at this time Vitellius' son was six (Dio 65.1) and had been taken to Gaul from Italy by Vitellius' wife, Galeria. He apparently had such a bad stammer that he was almost dumb (Suet. *Vit.* 6). After surviving his father's principate, he was put to death by Mucianus (4.80.1). Vitellius' relationship with his family certainly serves to 'humanise the otherwise bleak picture which we have of this emperor' (Murison (1993) 155; Levene (1997) 142–3), but he is not beyond using his children for propaganda purposes. With *infans* (only here in the *H.*), T. suggests the boy's helplessness (Morgan (1991) 140). Vitellius cannot compete with the two grown-up sons of Vespasian (2.77.1). **paludamento opertum:** as the purple *paludamentum* (originally a general's cloak) was now worn exclusively by the emperor, this act 'was a unilateral act of investiture' (Morgan (1991) 140). Vitellius himself will enter Rome *paludatus* (2.89.1). Yet the incongruity between the small child and the symbolic cloak enveloping him is expressive. It is also inauspicious that in Rome, a son at his father's funeral traditionally covered himself over in a similar way (Plut. *Mor.* 267a). By having the army parade before the boy in the *paludamentum*, Vitellius was trying to inculcate affection for him in the soldiers, as with Caligula in his miniature army uniform (Suet. *Cal.* 9); but Caligula grew up amongst the troops and their fondness developed over time.   **sinu retinens:** this emotive detail (not in the epitome of Dio 65.1.2a) suggests a parent's role as protector (as at *A.* 1.40.4; cf. Sen. *Herc. Fur.* 1008), but Vitellius will be dead when his son really needs safeguarding.   **Germanicum:** Vitellius himself has already taken the title Germanicus (1.62.2, cf. Plut. *Galb.* 22.11, Suet. *Vit.* 8.2), misleadingly suggestive of military victory in Germany. This emotive and prestigious Julio-Claudian family *cognomen* was originally awarded to Tiberius' dead brother Drusus and his descendants by the senate (Suet. *Cl.* 1.3). The German armies were likely to be especially receptive to the powerful name, but this 'Germanicus' will not even reach adulthood. **cunctis fortunae principalis insignibus:** *cunctus* = a synonym for *omnis* (1.3n. *cuncta . . . perlustrat*). T. elsewhere proudly characterises Romans as people for whom *uis imperii ualet, inania tramittuntur* (*A.*15.31). Vitellius tries to exploit the trappings of power for his son, but only makes people more aware of the boy's vulnerability. *fortuna* + *principalis* (*TLL* s.v. *principalis* 1291.73–4), first combined here (also 2.81.3) appealed to T.'s emulator, Ammianus (31.12.10, 31.15.2). The *insignia* of imperial power included the *sella curulis*, the *paludamentum*, the laurel-wreath, the signet-ring, and the *pugio* symbolising an emperor's power over life and death (Weinstock (1971) 270–6).   **nimius honor inter secunda** '(this) excessive honour (conferred) in prosperity'. In a condensed expression, T. reveals what has so far only been implicit, that Vitellius (whose whole principate will be marked by excess) has honoured his son too lavishly. 'This was a world of mirrors, a mixture of sincerity, deception, and vanity, the whole mix a source of power to the emperor' (Lendon (1997) 173). Yet such power, inevitably fragile, depended on the soldiers' good-will.   **rebus aduersis in supplicium cessit** 'proved fatal in adversity'. Wellesley ((1989); (1991) 1666) emends M's *solacium* to *supplicium*, but Morgan (1991) 141 resists, proposing that T.'s *res aduersae* means the execution of the son, who felt *solacium* from his moment of past glory when facing death. Yet *supplicium* is more persuasive, as it plays up the *peripeteia* (cf. *laeta in praesens mox perniciem ipsis fecere*, 2.70.2) and coheres with the depiction of Vitellius' son as a passive victim of circumstances beyond his control. T. does not elaborate the boy's feelings elsewhere.

60.1 interfecti centuriones promptissimi Othonianorum: sc. *sunt*. These officers' loyalty reflects well on their dead *princeps*. The 'faithful and brave centurion' (Welch (1998) 90, Ash (1999) 8) unquestioningly giving his life for the cause is a stock Caesarian type in his civil war army.   **praecipua in Vitellium alienatio:** *alienatio* (only here in the *H.*) + *in* is unusual (cf. Cic. *Phil.* 2.1 with *ab*; *TLL* s.v. *alienatio* 1559.55–6). The legionaries of Illyricum felt a natural rivalry with their counterparts in Germany (Suet. *Ves.* 6.2), who had won the principate for their own candidate Vitellius, but their anger will be sharpened by the German troops' arrogant attitude towards them (2.74.1). So far they have no candidate, but T. proleptically suggests trouble brewing for Vitellius even in his moment of victory. The hostility of these Danubian legions is a driving factor in the emergence of the Flavian challenge (2.74.1, Suet. *Ves.* 6.3).   **per Illyricos exercitus:** under Augustus, Illyricum denoted Dalmatia, but at some (disputed) point Illyricum was divided into two provinces, Dalmatia and Pannonia (Wilkes (1969) 78–81, 95). In a looser sense, Illyricum could be used to denote neighbouring Noricum and Moesia as well. In 69, Moesia, Dalmatia and Pannonia were heavily stocked with troops (32.2n. *cum . . . exercitibus*, 42.2n. *dispersi . . . fessi*), who swiftly supported Otho (1.76.1). T. duly reports the speedy adherence of the enthusiastic legions in Illyricum to Vespasian's cause (2.85.1, 2.86.4).   **ceterae legiones . . . bellum meditabantur:** the precise reference point is disputed. Some suggest that T. means the legions of Syria and Judaea, but they have already been contemplating war (2.7.1). Others suggest more convincingly that T. refers to the spreading discontent within the troops of Illyricum, as legions that had gone to Italy to fight for Otho are sent back to their camps. So, the *XIV Gemina* (Dalmatia) is directly exposed to the arrogant German armies in Italy (2.66.1) before being sent to Britain, and the *XIII Gemina* (Pannonia) is given the unglamorous task of building amphitheatres in Italy (2.67.2) before returning home, while the *VII Galbiana* (Pannonia) and *XI Claudia* (Dalmatia) are swiftly sent back to their winter quarters (2.67.2). These men had been exposed to the arrogant troops from Germany and knew about the Othonian centurions' execution in Italy, so they could foster anti-Vitellian sentiment in Illyricum. Yet T.'s vagueness is deliberate, creating a looming air of menace from an unspecified number of troops hostile to Vitellius.   **contactu et aduersus Germanicos milites inuidia** 'after association with the German armies had bred hatred for them'. The combination *inuidia* + *aduersus* is Livian (28.40.8, 34.34.7, 40.12.10, 42.12.2).   **Suetonium Paulinum:** 23.4n.   **Licinium Proculum:** 33.1n.   **tenuit tristi mora squalidos** 'he [sc. Vitellius] kept them waiting miserably, dressed filthily in defendants' clothing'. Prompt attention, even in adverse circumstances, indicated respect (cf. *A.* 15.31). Defendants traditionally wore either black or filthy clothes (*sordes*) to elicit pity (Cic. *Mur.* 86, *Att.* 1.16.2, Liv. 6.20.2, 44.19.7, Dion. Hal. 9.54.4, Sen. *Con.* 10.1.4, Sen. *Dial.* 3.2.1 Quint. 6.1.30–3, T. *D.* 12.1, *A.* 2.29.1, 6.8.2, 12.59.2), as well as letting their hair and beards grow (Oakley (1997) 557). *sordidatus* is the more usual term for the phenomenon, but *squalidus* is in Ovid (*Met.* 15.38) and Quintilian (6.1.30). **donec auditi . . . uterentur:** 8.2n. *donec . . . aufugeret.* The defendant Cremutius Cordus (*A.* 4.34–5) enacts the archetypal *honesta defensio*, maintaining integrity and scoring points from his oppressor. T. may have in mind the technical *honesta causa*, where the nature of the case removes the need for a defence (*Rhet. Her.* 1.5, Cic. *Inu.* 1.20, Quint. 4.1.40): Proculus and Paulinus, defeated generals in a civil war, apparently have no tenable defence, but broken by the delay, they defend themselves in the most degrading way possible. *donec* (*OLD* 2 'until such a time as') shows Vitellius keeping them imprisoned until their resolve cracks. **proditionem ultro imputabant** 'they actually claimed credit for treachery'. This verb and noun are combined only here (*TLL* s.v. *imputo* 730.25); after the *H.* T. drops *imputo*. In the inverted moral climate of the civil wars, individuals claim credit for treachery (*imputare perfidiam*, 3.86.2; *Germanos . . . dolo a se flexos imputauit Ciuilis*, 5.24.1) and for killing (1.44.2, 3.51). Even Marius Celsus only claims credit for his loyalty to Galba (*exemplum ultro imputauit* 1.71.2) once Otho has already rescued him. Proculus and Paulinus can be contrasted with some impressively brave conspirators against Nero at their trial: *quidam ultro crimen faterentur, nonnulli etiam imputarent* (Suet. *Nero* 36.2). **spatium . . . fatigationem . . . permixtum . . . fortuita:** the Othonian generals rattle off points in their defence after the tense wait, in a manner perhaps ironically recalling the abrupt style of military dispatches. For the *longum iter* and the *fatigatio* (only here in T.), see 2.40; for the *permixtum uehiculis agmen*, see 2.41.3. **et Vitellius credidit de perfidia et fidem absoluit** 'In fact Vitellius believed their claims of treachery and acquitted them of loyalty'. The first *et* (*OLD* 3) may qualify *Vitellius* (cf. *et facilius de odio creditur* 1.34.1); or it could introduce a 'both . . . and' construction (*OLD* 9). The word order seems calculated to create ambiguity, but Vitellius comes out badly either way. This is an inverted world where values that should be positive (*fides*) become dangerous. Similar expressions with *para prosdokian* (52.1n. *Posito . . . bello*) feature elsewhere: *damnatos fidei crimine* (1.59.1), *fidei crimen confessus* (1.71.2). So T. can now afford to omit *crimen* for greater impact (*TLL* s.v. *absoluo* 173.35). 'Unprincipled shifts in political morality during the scramble for survival put language under stresses that could lead to strange dislocations' (Plass (1988) 51). The chiastic structure + *adnominatio* (17.2n. *capta . . . intercepti*) of *perfidia* and *fidem* sharpens T.'s point, as he filters one concept through the other, challenging us to contemplate the *mise en scène*'s warped values.

60.2 Saluius Titianus: 23.5n.   **pietate et ignauia excusatus:** T. jarringly juxtaposes two incongruous concepts, creating bathos by placing *ignauia* second. Even so, *pietas* is often a muted virtue in the *H.* (48.2n.) Vitellius ironically pardons Titianus for his *ignauia*, a characteristic that he himself has in abundance (1.50.1, 2.31.1, 2.94.2, 3.36.1, 3.86.1). His own brother will not be so lucky after Vespasian's victory (4.2.3). **Mario Celso:** 23.4n.   **creditum fama:** sc. *est.* The abl. *fama* is a remarkably compact alternative to a subordinate clause *cum fama uolgaretur* (Heubner (1968) 228). **obiectum:** sc. *est.* The agent is unspecified. Either T. does not know, or (more probably) he aims to recreate the shadowy world of senatorial activity at the time, when dangerous charges could seemingly come from nowhere. The passive voice, where 'the responsible party vanishes into the abyss of the passive' (Whitehead (1990) 3 n.5; Pauw (1980)) can be useful. **Caecilio Simplici:** Caecilius, proconsul of Sardinia in 67–8 (*CIL* x 7852 = *ILS* 5947) and consul with Quintius Atticus from Nov.-Dec. 69, pops up again when Vitellius tries to hand him his dagger (the symbol of his power) during his attempted abdication (3.68.2–3; cf. Dio 65.17.1). Caecilius refuses to accept it, perhaps from loyalty to Vitellius for intervening on his behalf now. **quod . . . uoluisset:** *obiecto* + *quod* features again (*A.* 16.7.2). With the subjunctive T. gives the accusers' reasons, without necessarily endorsing them himself (19.1n. *quod . . . legisset*). If Simplex is a 'suggestive name' (93.2n. *sane . . . uerterat*), it may suggest his inability to operate deviously in the murky world of politics, but as T., the only one to narrate this incident, holds back from pronouncing innocence or guilt, we must be cautious. **eum honorem pecunia mercari:** how far was the consulship really an honourable distinction in a year when so many men (16; Wellesley (1972) 205) held the position? T. later suggests that some foolish men did try to buy positions and favours from Vitellius, without naming names: *stultissimus quisque pecuniis* [sc. *beneficia*] *mercabatur* (3.55.2). **nec sine exitio Celsi:** T.'s litotes *non sine* 11× and *nec sine* 4× is an expressive stylistic trait liked by Suetonius (WM 263) and Livy (*non sine* 20×; *nec sine* 9×; *haud sine* 5×), but absent from Sallust. The syntax, where Celsus' murder is momentarily made to seem subsidiary to the main charge of buying a consulship, saves the sting for the tail. **innoxium et inemptum** 'which cost him neither murder nor money' (Wellesley). T. uses *inemptus* only here. The adjectives (not paired again in extant Latin literature) are arranged chiastically against the initial charges (involving *pecunia* and *exitium*). For similar alliteration in a judicial context, see *indefensum et inauditum* (2.10.2). **Trachalum:** the eminent and charismatic orator Galerius Trachalus from Ariminum in northern Italy (Syme (1958a) 609) had been consul in 68 with Silius Italicus. People thought that Trachalus was Otho's 'spin-doctor', advising him on politics in Rome and perhaps also writing the emperor's speech of departure (1.90.2). If so, Trachalus wisely avoided attacking Vitellius (*nulla Vitellii mentione* 1.90.2; cf. *contumeliosa in Vitellium* 2.65.1), which must have helped Galeria's bid to defend him. He was probably her relative. As well as having his *latum et sonans* 'copious and sonorous' (1.90.2; Damon (2003) 289) style, he was incredibly good-looking (Quint. 10.1.119) with an extraordinary speaking voice (Quint.12.5.5). After the civil wars he became proconsul of Africa under Vespasian (*CIL* v 5812). **Galeria:** 47.2n. *fruetur . . . coniuge liberis*.

61 pudendum dictu: 90.1n. *pudendus*. T. elsewhere expresses discomfort at narrating events which could detract from the dignity of historiography (*A.* 15.37.1), but his posture here is artful. Apparently this incident is 'shameful to relate' because of class structures (Mariccus is an upstart plebeian), but how far do the pretenders Vitellius and Mariccus differ from one another (apart from in their social rank)? The digression ends by focusing discreditably on the emperor (*spectante Vitellio* 2.61), as before (*nihil . . . Vitellio anquirente*, 2.59.1). **Mariccus quidam:** T. often names minor characters for effect (20.1n. *Saloninam*). Mariccus and his revolt do not feature in

the parallel tradition.   **e plebe Boiorum:** his plebeian identity contrasts pointedly
with the *magnorum uirorum discrimina*. The Boii, Celts who had migrated to northern Italy in *c.* 400 BC (their name survives in their former capital, Bononia), were
eventually defeated by the Romans in 191 BC (Liv. 36.39) when many were forced
back northwards (Strabo 5.1.6; cf. Williams (2001) 211–12, Rives (1999) 233). Their
movements fluctuate, but in *c.* 60 BC a large group settled amongst the Aedui in central Gaul (Caes. *Gal.* 1.28.5), while others migrated for a time to the upper Danube
(Plin. *Nat.* 3.146). Plautus (*Capt.* 888) puns on *Boius / boia* ('a yoke worn by criminals'), an infelicitous but proleptic resonance in the present context.   **simulatione
numinum** 'by pretending to have divine power'. Manipulating gullible barbarians
into thinking that their mortal leader is a god has precedents, above all Sertorius who
used a white doe to engender this belief (Plut. *Sert.* 11, 12.1). We can also compare
Vespasian's 'miracle cures' in the magical city of Alexandria making claim to divine
agency (4.81). Mariccus is only one of several impersonators in the book: (i) the false
Nero (2.8–9), (ii) Albinus, who is rumoured to have taken the title of Juba (2.58.2),
(iii) Geta, who impersonates Scribonianus (2.72) and ultimately (iv) Vitellius, who pretends to be a general and an emperor (2.89.1).   **inserere sese fortunae** 'to push
himself to prominence'. 19.1n. *inserentibus se*; 1.2n. *quantaecumque fortunae*.   **assertor
Galliarum** 'liberator of Gaul'. The terminology (originally indicating the prosecutor of someone wrongfully holding a free man as a slave) has an emotive history of
appropriation. The Roman people apparently demanded *assertores* to save them from
Caesar's tyranny (Suet. *Jul.* 80.1). Vindex, governor of Gallia Lugdunensis, himself
an *assertor libertatis* (Plin. *Nat.* 20.160), called on Galba to become *humano generi assertor*
(Suet. *Galb.* 9.2), while Vespasian claimed the accolade *assertor libertatis publicae* on a
sestertius of 71 (Mattingly (1923) no. 781). Mariccus foreshadows the Gallic rebel Julius
Civilis, who also exploits the freedom / slavery antithesis: *neque enim societatem, ut olim,
sed tamquam mancipia haberi* (4.14.2).   **nam id sibi indiderat** 'for he had bestowed
those titles upon himself'. The parenthesis (18.1n. *is enim*) from the authorial perspective sharpens the sense of outrage at Mariccus' audacity already articulated in *ausus
est*.   **proximos Aeduorum pagos trahebat:** it is unclear how best to translate
this. *trahebat* could mean 'was plundering' (*OLD* 5b), as T. extends the verb's sphere
of reference from people 'to non-personal *pagi*' (WM 486) and accentuates the gulf
between Mariccus' aspirational titles and the destruction of his Aeduan neighbours.
Or *trahebat* could mean 'was trying to win over' (*OLD* 10a). Perhaps the best solution is
to take it as a simple for compound form of the verb (*OLD attraho* 2) and translate 'was
coercing'. The Aedui certainly do not welcome his efforts, as their subsequent actions
show. The term *pagus* has led some to speculate that this revolt shows urban versus
rural fault-lines, but in T., the word 'denotes a "canton", not a "village"' (Morgan
(1993a) 771). Although the Aedui had participated in Julius Sacrovir's uprisings in
21 (*A.* 3.43–6) and in Vindex's revolt in 68, they had remained quiet so far during
the civil war, providing supplies to the Vitellians only out of fear (1.64.3), and they
appear not to have participated in Julius Civilis' subsequent rebellion. Their capital
was at Augustodunum (mod. Autun) in Gallia Lugdunensis.   **cum** introduces an

inverse *cum*-clause for dramatic effect (36.1n. *cum intercursu*). A similar device marks
the end of the disturbance (2.72.2; Morgan (1993a) 769). **grauissima ciuitas**
'that most responsible state'. *ciuitas* may indicate Augustodunum, the *caput gentis* (*A.*
3.43.1), but no doubt the whole state's resources were brought to bear against the
rebels. In T.'s account of the revolt of 21, the Roman general Gaius Silius scorns the
wealthy Aeduans' fighting ability: *quanto pecunia dites et uoluptatibus opulentos, tanto magis
imbelles Aeduos euincite* (*A.* 3.46.2). Yet Mariccus and his 8,000 men are a less formidable
enemy than Roman legionaries. **electa iuuentute:** *iuuentus* = 'men of military
age' (*OLD* 1b). During Sacrovir's revolt in 21, Augustodunum was full of young Gallic
noblemen being educated in the city (*A.* 3.43.1). **adiectis a Vitellio cohortibus:**
Vitellius shows responsibility in sending troops to help resolve this local disturbance,
but his route virtually ran through the trouble spot so it was relatively easy to intervene. The Aeduans seem to have appreciated the assistance: T. refers later to an
Aeduan tribune, Julius Calenus, a loyal supporter of Vitellius (3.35.2). **fanaticam
multitudinem:** T. uses this pejorative adj. again only of the revolt on Mona (mod.
Anglesey) inspired by the Druids (*A.* 14.30.2). **captus in eo proelio:** sc. *est.* The
image of Mariccus (captured alive) suffers when compared with the Aeduan leader,
Julius Sacrovir, who at least kills himself after his defeat (*A.* 3.46.4). T.'s decision to
pass over this battle without any detailed narration further vilifies Mariccus. **mox
feris obiectus:** *damnatio ad bestias* was usually a punishment reserved only for the
lowest classes, slaves and non-citizens. Executions of criminals during the *uenationes* in
the arena, usually during the middle of the day between the *uenatio* in the morning and
the *munus* in the afternoon (Sen. *Ep.* 7.3), could be staged as grotesque re-enactments of
mythological deaths. Sometimes the condemned men carried *tabellae* giving details of
their crime (Coleman (1990), Köhne and Ewigleben (2000) 73–4, Wiedemann (1992)
67–90). *mox*, 'in due course' (*OLD* 2a), suggests a delay between the capture and the
(attempted) execution, until Vitellius could watch Mariccus' death in person (Morgan (1993a) 775), probably in the amphitheatre at Lugdunum (Dio 65.1.3). **quia
non laniabatur:** Morgan (1993a) 774 n.24 compares the slave Androclus, thrown
to the beasts in Rome, and the benign lion who refuses to harm him (Gell. 5.14.5–30;
cf. Sen. *Ben.* 2.19.1). Animals in the arena could fail to attack condemned men for
more mundane reasons. If they had been brought from afar and kept in the *uiuarium*
for some time, their health could suffer (Epplett (2001) 219). Sometimes they were
just unpredictable, attacking whoever was closest (usually the handlers) instead of the
criminals (Wiedemann (1992) 89). **stolidum uolgus:** evidence suggests that spectators of such executions were likely to have been lower class, as the elite left after the
morning *uenatio* for their lunch and siesta before the afternoon's gladiatorial displays
(Wiedemann (1992) 67). So, Claudius' enthusiastic interest in the executions met with
special disapproval (Suet. *Cl.* 34.2, Dio 60.13.4). **inuiolabilem** 'indestructible'. T.
uses this choice (and largely poetic) adj. again only once, but in a different sense, about
the inviolable right to asylum at a temple of Diana (*A.* 3.62.1). **spectante Vitellio:**
the emperor's shameless, menacing gaze features elsewhere in the parallel tradition,
as when Vitellius orders a man to be executed before him, *uelle se dicens pascere oculos*

(Suet. *Vit.* 14.2; cf. T.'s *pauisse oculos* 3.39.1). It was allegedly a family trait: his brother
Lucius also watched the flogging and execution of Claudius Iulianus *in ore eius* (3.77.3).
Vitellius' gaze dominates again when he visits the battlefield at Bedriacum (*uestigia
recentis uictoriae lustrare oculis concupiuit* 2.70.1, *non Vitellius flexit oculos* 2.70.4). Yet there
will be *peripeteia* when Vitellius himself becomes a *foedum spectaculum* (3.84.5) shortly
before his death. Julius Caesar was especially adept at drawing the collective gaze to
himself (Bell (2004) 24–51).

    62.1 Nec ultra . . . saeuitum: sc. *est*. The expression is Livian (8.33.14). T.
favours the impersonal use of this biting verb in the perfect (*Agr.* 2.1, *H.* 1.2.3, *A.*
3.24.3, 3.55.3, 4.20.1), but here its application to *defectores* (T.'s striking coinage, used
here first) + *bona* together, as if they were equivalent, disturbingly equates destruction
of property and human life: cf. *neque in ipsos modo auctores, sed in libros quoque eorum saeuitum*
(*Agr.* 2.1).   **rata fuere . . . testamenta aut lex intestatis** 'the wills . . . were
ratified or the law of intestacy (was applied)'. *fuere* is the alternative third person pl.
perfect from *sum*, while the neuter pl. adj. *rata* (from *reor*) is the formal term for ratifying
a will or document (cf. *rata . . . pacta* 2.99.2, *amicitia societasque . . . rata* 4.64.2). There is a
mild zeugma here (Lausberg (1998) §692–708): *rata* suits documentary *testamenta* better
than the abstract *lex*. These wills presumably lack the often customary legacy to the
ruling *princeps* (*Agr.* 43.4), but Vitellius (or his advisers) allows them to stand anyway,
perhaps as the sums involved were not that great (cf. 1.48.4 on the annulment of the
wealthy Titus Vinius' will) or to acquire the reputation of a *ciuilis princeps* (cf. Tiberius
at *A.* 2.48.1).   **acie Othoniana** 'fighting for Otho'; 13.1n. *in acie.*   **lex intestatis:**
wealthy Roman citizens rarely failed to distribute property by a will (e.g. Aemilia Musa
at *A.* 2.48.1), but these relatively young Othonians had not anticipated dying, so reference to the law of intestacy (Crook (1973), Champlin (1991) 43–6) implicitly evokes
the poignant topos of wasted youth. The law for those who died intestate 'imposed a
standardized pattern of succession on all citizens' (Champlin (1991) 8). Drawing up a
will was time-consuming, but was also a social obligation for an aristocrat: cf. Cato the
Elder's remorse at having remained intestate for a single day (Plut. *Cat. Ma.* 9.9). The
subject also offered material for satire: cf. *subitae mortes atque intestata senectus* (Juv. 1.144),
for gluttons at the baths dying intestate, and the unwary fool rashly going out to dinner in Rome *intestatus* (Juv. 3.274).   **prorsus:** 5.1n.   **si luxuriae temperaret,
auaritiam non timeres** 'if he were to control his love of luxury, you should not
have feared his avarice'; 13.1n. *expleta auaritia.* The sentiment recalls the younger Pliny
urging moderation while entertaining friends: 'if you moderate your own gluttony
(*gulae temperares*), it is not a financial burden to share with others what you yourself eat'
(*Ep.* 2.6.5). T. 'uses the imaginary "you" singular to engage the reader's intellectual
participation and presume a commonality of experience, attitude, and values' (Sinclair
(1995) 53; cf. Gilmartin (1975), WM 83–4). This vivid device, also in Sallust and Livy
(and especially Ovid; Kenney (1990) 138), is used by T. proportionately more often
than any other historian except Velleius (WM 84). Here the imperfect subjunctive
forms the apodosis of an ideal conditional clause referring to past (GL §596.2). There
is an implicit contrast between Vitellius' greed for money (not all-encompassing) and

his gluttony (pervasive) in the next sentence.   **epularum foeda et inexplebilis libido:** cf. *libidinem foedam* (Sen. *Con.* 2.3.12), *libido inexplebilis* (Cic. *Tusc.* 4.21). This clause is in adversative asyndeton (supply 'but') with the previous sentence. Vitellius' gourmandising recurs in T. (1.62.2, 2.68.1, 2.71.1, and esp. *inexplebiles Vitellii libidines* 2.95.2) and elsewhere, suggesting the emperor's sluggishness (Ash (1999) 96–105). In one infamous dish, Minerva's Shield, Vitellius wastefully blended together an array of exotic ingredients (Suet. *Vit.* 13.2; cf. Dio 65.3, Plin. *Nat.* 35.163). He allegedly did not restrict himself to élite modes of consumption, but also guzzled food from road-side snack-bars (Suet. *Vit.* 13.3). Seneca the Younger has the archetypal scene where appetite for food is implictly aligned with lust for power (*Thy.* 970–1112).   **ex urbe atque Italia . . . strepentibus ab utroque mari itineribus** 'from Rome and Italy . . . while the routes from the Tuscan and Adriatic seas were bustling noisily'. T.'s blistering tone evokes satire, especially the indignant Eumolpus denouncing the plundering of luxury foods as symbolising Roman moral decline (Petronius 119.27–38 with Connors (1998) 109–14). An ascending trio of Rome, Italy and the whole empire (indicated by the polarised sea-routes: *mare superum*, the Adriatic, to the east of Italy, *OLD superus* 1c, and *mare inferum*, the Tuscan or Tyrrhenian, to the west of Italy, *OLD inferus* 1b) hyperbolically suggest the global scale of Vitellius' gluttony. The theme is also in the parallel tradition: delicacies are gathered for him *a Parthia usque fretoque Hispanico* (Suet. *Vit.* 13.2), while his appetite could even outstrip the limits of the empire (Jos. *BJ* 4.652). Centripetal consumption of luxury goods can succinctly demonstrate a tyrannical personality (Xen. *Ag.* 9.3, Sall. *Hist.* 2.70, Sen. *Helu.* 10.4, T. *A.* 15.37.2, Macr. *Sat.* 7.5.32). Under the self-consciously austere Flavians, the kaleidoscopic range of produce available in Rome was recast patriotically to reflect the notion of Rome at the heart of a huge empire (Plin. *Nat.* 3.54). T. pointedly redeploys the vivid verb *strepo* (also used of places at Virg. *A.* 6.709, Liv. 6.25.9 and elsewhere) for the provinces ringing with noise during the Flavian preparations for war (2.84.1).   **irritamenta gulae** 'stimulants for his gullet' is a choice Sallustian expression (*Jug.* 89.7, echoed by Plin. *Nat.* 16.31, Amm. 28.4.3, Augus. *CD* 22.24). The combination with *gula* is striking: the lofty *irritamentum* suggests culinary delicacies, while the prosaic *gula* (31.1n. *uentre et gula*) adds bathos and implies greed. 'Together, gluttony and gastronomy presented two deformed bodily images of decadent Rome, a stuffed and multiplied perversion of its original self' (Gowers (1993) 20). There are also Petronian associations (*ingeniosa gula est*, 119.33).   **gestabantur:** cf. *cibos . . . pugnantibus gestant* (*G.* 7.4), where mothers and wives of German tribesmen bring food to sustain them during battle. The echo suggests a sharp contrast between wholesome barbarians on the margins and corrupt Romans at the centre.   **exhausti** (sc. *sunt*) 'had their pockets drained'. Vitellius apparently chose a different host every day and each one spent no less than 400,000 HS on a single meal (Suet. *Vit.* 13.1). T. prefers an expressive metaphorical verb, rather than specifying sums of money spent, reserved for recording Vitellius' costs as emperor (2.95.3).   **conuiuiorum apparatibus** 'by providing feasts'. T. avoids the relatively humdrum verb *apparo* (Mankin (1995) 82; cf. *ornare et apparare conuiuium*, Cic. *Ver.* 4.44) for a grand, striking pl. noun, which recalls Horace: *Persicos odi, puer,*

apparatus (*Carm.* 1.38.1). The association does Vitellius no favours. T. redeploys his earlier description of incompetent *equites* in Rome, ineptly preparing for war by purchasing
luxuriosos apparatus conuiuiorum (1.88.3). Cf. *profusissimos obsoniorum apparatus* (Suet. *Vit.*
10.2).   **uastabantur:** this verb is used elsewhere for military devastation (1.61.1,
1.67.2, 2.12.2, *A.* 4.48.1, 15.8.1 and elsewhere), so it evokes in an inappropriate domestic context the idea of a Roman *imperator* campaigning against the enemy. 'Vitellius'
appetite is literally devastating' (Haynes (2003) 102).   **degenerabat a labore ac
uirtute:** cf. *ab . . . uirtute . . . degenerauerit* (Cic. *Flac.* 25), *degenerasse a suorum uirtutibus* (Suet
Nero 1.2). Such enervation of collective military strength is more often associated with
Asia and the east (4.4n. *segnitiam*), but Vitellius' soldiers are moving eastwards, at least
relative to their own permanent camps in Germany. *labor* could potentially benefit an
army (16.2n. *laborem insolitum*). The imperfect tense of *degenerabat* (also *gestabantur, uastabantur*) suggests a gradual attrition of the soldiers' powers on the journey over time (cf.
uires . . . corrumpebantur, 2.69.2) and is part of T.'s broad deceleration in his narrative
of Vitellius' journey.   **miles:** collective singular (6.2n. *fremere miles*).   **assuetudine uoluptatum et contemptu ducis:** 27.1n. *posito . . . contemptu.* A good general
occasionally lets his soldiers celebrate briefly, sometimes as a reward after battle,
but for the Vitellian troops, this extravaganza of self-indulgence becomes a (fatally)
permanent Saturnalia as they learn dangerous new behaviour patterns (2.69.2); the
'trickle-down' effect is accentuated again (2.68.1, 2.76.4). T. pointedly calls Vitellius
a *dux* just when his actions fail to match the proper conduct of a general. Suetonius
briefly mentions the Vitellian soldiers' worsening conduct (*Vit.* 10.2), but says nothing of their scorn for their general (in T. a crucial factor in explaining the Vitellian
defeat).

   **62.2 edictum quo uocabulum Augusti differret, Caesaris non
reciperet:** the subjunctives in the relative clause depend on the idea of Vitellius'
speech implicit in *edictum* (GL §628). Octavian originally took the name Caesar as
stipulated in his great-uncle's will and was awarded the title Augustus by the senate
(Suet. *Aug.* 7.2; Syme (1958b) 172–88), but Claudius adopted Caesar (the family name
of the Julian clan) as an imperial title on his accession and made it a prerogative of
the emperor and his heirs (Levick (1999) 66; Dio 43.44). Vitellius hesitates, perhaps
since he is seeking fresh and appealing names, ones not associated with the Julio-
Claudian dynasty. Yet he will adopt the name 'Augustus' in Rome, pressurised by the
people (2.90.2), and although he has already rejected 'Caesar' (1.62.2; cf. Plut. *Galb.*
22.11), an acceptance which would have antagonised the senate (Yavetz (1969) 564),
he will later wish to be called Caesar because of his 'superstitious respect for the name'
(3.58.3). This is a further erratic twist in the name-game for which Vitellius' spirited
mother Sextilia expresses such scorn (2.64.2; cf. Domitian at 4.2.1). Vespasian shows
no such hesitation when the soldiers give him the titles Caesar and Augustus (2.80.1),
although an emperor's deferral of honorary titles could meet with approval (Plin. *Pan.*
21.2). Suetonius gives the same detail about Vitellius' titles (*Vit.* 8.2), but locates it soon
after his initial proclamation in Germany when he accepted the name Germanicus.
cum de potestate nihil detraheret 'although he did not reduce his real power at

all' (*OLD detraho* 7b); cf. *nec quicquam de maiestate sua detractum* (Liv. 6.6.7). The subordinate
clause unmasks the hypocrisy of Vitellius' ostentatious and misleading edict, in a way
typical of T.: 'external evidence is the matter of the main clause, while interpretation,
usually of hidden causes, makes up the subordinate clauses' (O'Gorman (2000) 4).
pulsi Italia mathematici: sc. *sunt.* Vitellius' ultimatum that all astrologers should
leave Italy before 1 Oct. apparently met with a sharp response, as the *mathematici* put
up their own notice that 'a great good will have been done if Vitellius is no more by
the same date' (Suet. *Vit.* 14.4; cf. Dio 65.1.4). T. calls the astrologers 'treacherous for
the powerful, deceptive for the ambitious, and men who in our state will always be
proscribed, but kept close' (1.22.1 with Damon (2003) 150). Consulting them about
the duration of the emperor's life became a common charge under the principate as
a convenient indicator of treachery. They were expelled from the city in 139 BC by
praetor's edict (Val. Max. 1.3.3), in 33 BC by Agrippa (Dio 49.43), in AD 16 by the senate
under Tiberius (Suet. *Tib.* 36, T. *A.* 2.32.3) and in 52 by the senate under Claudius
(*A.* 12.52.3). The regularity of these expulsions suggests their futility: in 70 Vespasian
duly banished the astrologers, despite tending to consult them himself (2.78.1, Dio
66.9.2; Levick (1999) 69–70).   **ne equites Romani ludo et harena polluerentur** 'that Roman knights should not disgrace themselves by appearing in the games
and the arena'. Despite the stigma, high-ranking Romans could become gladiators
through poverty or a desire for excitement (Wiedemann (1992) 108–10). There is a
pointed inconsistency in Vitellius loftily addressing the problem of equestrians debasing themselves, while he himself as *princeps* engages in degenerate gluttony. Juvenal
sees aristocrats in the arena as the ultimate marker of collective disgrace: *res haut mira
tamen citharoedo principe mimus | nobilis. haec ultra quid erit nisi ludus?* (8.198–9).   **priores
id principes . . . perpulerant:** *id* = *eos ad id.* The forceful alliteration is apt
for the coercion being described. T. here stresses imperial compulsion of the upper
classes to perform in the arena, but Augustus introduced legislation to prevent such
appearances (Suet. *Aug.* 43.3, Dio 48.43.3, 56.25.7; cf. Suet. *Jul.* 39.1, Dio 43.23.5
for the first attested ban against senators fighting in the arena in 46 BC; Levick (1983)
105). We have one senatorial decree (found on a bronze tablet at Larinum) from AD
19 addressing the same problem (Levick (1983)). Under Tiberius, some senators and
knights even relinquished their status in order to appear as gladiators (Suet. *Tib.* 35.2).
Others were more reluctant: Caligula punished an equestrian by making him fight in
the arena (Dio 59.10.4), while Nero apparently paid *equites* to appear in the arena (*A.*
14.14.4; cf. Suet. *Nero* 12.1, Dio 61.9.1). In 63 even women and senators *per arenam foedati
sunt* (*A.* 15.32; also Stat. *Sil.* 1.6.53, Mart. *Sp.* 6, 6b, Juv. 1.22).   **aemulabantur corruptissimum quemque adulescentium pretio illicere:** aristocrats fighting in
the arena risked *infamia* and losing their rights as citizens (Wiedemann (1992) 28–9).
So, securing a scandalous performance in the arena from an aristocrat was an excellent way to stir interest in a gladiatorial show and to outshine the *ludi* of neighbouring
communities (21.2n. *a quibusdam ex uicinis coloniis* on such intense civic rivalries). T.'s
acc. + inf. construction after *aemulor* (instead of *certo*; cf. 3.61.1) is an innovation (but is
only here in his extant work).

63.1 aduentu fratris: Lucius Vitellius (47.2n. *fruetur . . . liberis*), previously at
Bononia (2.54.1), travelled north-west over the Alps to meet his triumphant brother
at Lugdunum.   **irrepentibus dominationis magistris:** 'T. mostly uses *inrepo*
intransitively and metaphorically, of gradual or clandestine insinuation' (WM 89).
The notion of *dominationis magistri* perhaps evokes the Platonic τυραννοδιδάσκαλος
(*Theages* 125a), used by Dio of Caligula (59.24.1) and Nero (61.10.2), inauspicious models (Heubner (1968) 231). Sinister entourages characterise both Galba (Titus Vinius,
Cornelius Laco, Icelus) and Otho (Ptolemy the astrologer, Licinius Proculus, Suetonius
Paulinus, Marius Celsus, Galerius Trachalus), but T.'s insinuation that Vitellius had
a similar band of political associates may exaggerate: in the following narrative, only
his brother Lucius and the freedman Asiaticus are in evidence. In Suetonius Vitellius
relies on the advice of 'the most worthless actors and charioteers' (*Vit.* 12). Vespasian is
not immune from such influence (*prauis magistris*, 2.84.2).   **superbior et atrocior:**
T. has not so far emphasised Vitellius' pride and ferocity, but the comparative adjectives artfully imply that the new emperor's pre-existing traits have now become more
extreme. T. often deploys vocabulary with interrelated and cumulative impact: so, the
man who is now *atrocior* will soon gaze at an *atrox spectaculum* (2.70.1). The technique
is more subtle than Suetonius' sensational catalogue of Vitellius' *saeuitia* (*Vit.* 13–14).
Dolabellam: the shadowy Cornelius (or possibly Publius) Dolabella, Galba's relative, only features twice in T. (also 1.88.1, his banishment to Aquinum by Otho despite
his innocence and nobility). Some courtiers wanted Galba to adopt him, but he was
unwilling to do so (Plut. *Galb.* 23.2), even disbanding a cohort of German soldiers
because they favoured him (Suet. *Galb.* 12.2). The banishment by Otho, apparently
under coercion from the praetorian guard, is also in Plutarch but the implication
is that it was for Dolabella's own protection (*Oth.* 5.1). Dolabella is portrayed with
broad and impressionistic strokes in all the sources, but this offers T. a perfect canvas
for depicting a stirring vignette of debased *amicitia* during civil war and the flawed
morality of Vitellius' short-lived principate.   **quem . . . rettulimus:** also 1.88.1;
4.4n. *ut supra memorauimus.*   **coloniam Aquinatem:** the adj. designates Aquinum,
a town in Latium on the Via Latina *c.* 75 miles south-east of Rome. Famous for its
purple dye (Hor. *Ep.* 1.10.27), it was perhaps Juvenal's birthplace (Braund (1996) 229).
sepositum: used of informal exile (*OLD sepono* 2b).   **audita morte Othonis:**
after the news came to Rome on 18 Apr. (2.55.1 *Ceriales ludi*), it would have reached
Aquinum quickly.   **urbem introierat:** Dolabella's move is not intrinsically foolish
(as his treatment from Otho could potentially even make the new regime favour him),
but Vitellius has a personal grudge against him (2.64.1).   **id ei . . . obiecit** 'laid
that against him as a charge'. The dat. pronoun *ei* refers to Dolabella, but T. reserves
the proper name for the more shocking context (*ex intimis Dolabellae amicis*).   **Plancius Varus:** this, his only appearance in T., does the upwardly mobile ex-praetor
and senator little credit, but M. Plancius Varus will be useful to the Flavians through
his extensive estates in Asia Minor and connections around his home city, Perge in
Pamphylia (Levick (1999) 62), where his Italian ancestors had settled. He served as
legate to the proconsuls in Asia and Achaea early in Vespasian's principate and was

then proconsul of Bithynia probably in the late 70s (Mitchell (1974) 29; cf. Houston (1972) 179). It is suggestive that a man from the east, an area traditionally associated by Roman authors with intrigue and double-dealing, here finds himself so outmatched by those at Rome.   **praetura . . . amicis:** Varus' public and private standing, both as a praetor with juridical reponsibilities and as a close friend to Dolabella, makes his treachery especially shocking. By modifying *amicis* with *intimis* (also 1.71.2, *A.* 4.29.1, 16.17.4, 16.34.1), T. implies that Varus is trampling over not just a formal bond of *amicitia*, but an emotional connection, accentuating the *volte-face*.   **Flauium Sabinum:** 55.1n. *a Flauio Sabino*.   **tamquam . . . ostentasset:** *tamquam* + subj. gives Varus' reasoning (21.1n. *tamquam . . . potuissent*). The idea that Dolabella, who had been banished by Otho, could then offer himself as a general for the defeated Othonians is highly implausible (and is meant to seem so); and anyway, most of Otho's troops are in the north, not in Rome.   **rupta custodia:** the metaphor of breaking associated with *custodia* is only here (*TLL* s.v. *custodia* 1560.38) and exaggeratedly suggests that Dolabella had been kept under close confinement: cf. *neque arta custodia* (1.88.1).   **addidit:** the verb hints that Flavius Sabinus is not impressed by the charges, as Varus tries to come up with something more convincing to flesh out his accusation.   **temptatam** (sc. *esse*) **cohortem quae Ostiae ageret:** trouble with the seventeenth cohort at Ostia triggered the praetorian mutiny (1.80.1), but it was not itself a big enough unit to facilitate an imperial challenge and may not even have been armed. Claudius had originally stationed an urban cohort at Ostia to fight fires (Suet. *Cl.* 25.2).   **nec ullis tantorum criminum probationibus** 'in the complete absence of any proofs for such serious charges'. The pl. *probationes* is rhetorically striking; the meaning 'proofs' is first at Sen. *Con.* 7 *praef.* 1 (WM 121) and it is only here in the *H.* (also *D.* 39.3, *A.* 3.7.1). Lack of evidence for grave charges does not necessarily stop successful convictions under the principate, but this abl. of attendant circumstances emphasises the injustice that will be done to Dolabella by Vitellius, who cares little about right and wrong.   **in paenitentiam uersus:** mercurial temperaments are often associated with women and easterners, inauspicious points of contact for Varus' characterisation. *paenitentia* (not in Sall., Caes., Cic.) features 3× in Livy, and then often in post-Augustan prose.   **seram ueniam post scelus quaerebat** 'he tried to obtain a belated pardon after the offence'. T. deliberately and provocatively leaves the nouns' precise points of reference ambiguous: *uenia* could indicate Varus seeking a formal pardon for <u>Dolabella</u> after the <u>apparent</u> *scelus* of Dolabella's 'treachery' (immediate context), or alternatively *uenia* could indicate Varus seeking a formal pardon for <u>himself</u> from Sabinus after the <u>real</u> *scelus* of his own treachery (wider context). These two interpretations are not mutually exclusive; or perhaps the first reading (immediate context) indicates what did happen, while the second reading (wider context) denotes what should have happened. The combination *sera* + *uenia* is only here in extant Latin literature.

63.2 cunctantem super tanta re: *super* = an archaising preposition (8.1n. *super exitu eius*). The combination *super tanta re* is in T. only once more, with *statuo* (4.9.2). Sabinus' hesitation is understandable: he has to balance justice (Dolabella is clearly innocent) with self-interest (he needs to show loyalty to Vitellius, at least until Vespasian makes his challenge). Yet the syntax, where this acc. clause precedes the main clause, has impact: our initial sense of Sabinus' measured dignity is swiftly undercut by an impression of his craven helplessness before a domineering woman. **Triaria uxor L. Vitellii ultra feminam ferox:** Lucius' wife first appears here. She coheres with the negative stereotypes of cruel and domineering women, common in narratives of civil war (especially if their husbands eventually lose), above all recalling Antony's wife, Fulvia, 'a grotesque caricature created by Octavian' (Welch (1995) 187): *nihil muliebre praeter corpus gerens* (Vell. 2.74.3; cf. Dio 47.8.2, Mart. 11.20.3–8). T.'s description recalls another figure who transgresses traditional gender lines, Maecenas, *otio ac mollitiis paene ultra feminam fluens* (Vell. 2.88.2). Triaria features again after the sack of Tarracina, wearing a sword and behaving arrogantly (3.77.3; cf. sword-girt Fulvia, Flor. 2.16.2).   **terruit:** T. chooses the simple form for the compound *deterreo* (also 3.42.2, Liv. 2.45.1 + *ne*), perhaps to exploit enclosing alliteration with *Triaria*.   **periculo principis** 'by endangering the emperor'. It is ironic that Triaria is so alarmist about Vitellius' safety before Sabinus, the brother of the man who poses the real danger. The theme of misplaced or misdirected Vitellian fears about phantom enemies culminates in the murder of Junius Blaesus (3.38–9).   **famam clementiae:** cf. *utilis clementiae fama* (4.63.1). Exercising clemency during civil war was problematic (48.2n. *mereri . . . clementiam uictoris*). New emperors often claimed *clementia* as an imperial virtue (Aug. *RG* 3.1–2, 34.2, Dio 53.7.2, 56.44.1–2) and Vitellius is no exception (1.75.2; cf. Otho at 1.71.1). Sabinus, who had spent so long at the heart of imperial power, would have known that Triaria was accusing him of appropriating a virtue ideally belonging to the new *princeps*.   **suopte ingenio mitis** 'lenient when left to his own devices'; cf. Sabinus as a *mitem uirum* (3.65.2). The weighty *suopte ingenio* (also 4.68.5, 5.14.2, *A.* 3.26.1) appears 6× in Livy and once in Sallust (but outside Latin historiography, only Plin. *Nat.* 7.130). T. tends to use the enclitic *–pte* only with the abl. singular of the possessive pronoun. For the implications of *suo ingenio* elsewhere in T., see Woodman (1989) 198–201.   **ubi formido incessisset:** *ubi* + subjunctive of repeated action (40n. *ubi . . . uincerentur*); abstract noun as subject (2.1n. *spes uicit*). There are precedents for applying *incedo* to fear, as *magnus . . . incesserat timor* (Caes. *Civ.* 3.44.6), but T. increasingly likes coupling this verb with abstract nouns (suggesting personification): after linking it with *fama* (4.54.3) and *cunctatio* (3.27.3) in the *H.*, such usage explodes in the *A.* (+ *rumor A.* 1.5.1, 2.55.6, 4.46.2, 6.23.2, 15.15.3; *nuntii A.* 11.32.1; *spes A.* 1.55.1; *certamen A.* 2.51.1; *ambitio* and *uis A.* 3.26.2; *religio A.* 3.71.1; *suspicio A.* 6.21.1; *licentia A.* 3.36.1).   **facilis mutatu:** T. also applies this striking phrase to the Armenians (*A.* 14.23.1).   **in alieno discrimine sibi pauens** 'alarmed for himself, although the danger threatened another man'; 16.2n. *alieni . . . socia*.   **ne alleuasse uideretur, impulit ruentem** 'he shoved someone who was already falling, lest he should appear to have lifted him up'. Strongly metaphorical language is degradingly suggestive of a physical fight between the pair, cast almost as gladiators or boxers, with Triaria as a warped female *lanista*. It also foreshadows the ugly murder of Dolabella *proiectum humi* (2.64.1) by his assassin.

64.1 Igitur: 2.2n.   **Petroniam uxorem eius:** Petronia is in Suetonius (*Vit.* 6),
though there is nothing about the tension between Vitellius and Dolabella. T. is always
alive to the suggestive possibilities of seeing one imperial dynasty through another:
so, Vitellius hates Dolabella just as Tiberius loathed Asinius Gallus, who married
the emperor's former wife, Vipsania (*A.* 1.12.4). This similarity may raise doubts
about the veracity of the story attached to Vitellius.   **uocatum per epistulas:**
this is a practical necessity, as Vitellius is still some distance away, but the detail
recalls Tiberius, another emperor who liked to communicate by letter: cf. *cruentas
epistulas* (*A.* 3.44.3) with Morello (2006).   **uitata Flaminiae uiae celebritate
deuertere Interamnium:** the phrasing recalls Cicero, *propter uiae celebritatem* (*Att.*
3.14.2). Vitellius is now en route to Cremona and Bononia (2.70–1) from Lugdunum
(2.59.3). Dolabella was presumably asked to head north from Rome to meet Vitellius,
for which the obvious route was the Via Flaminia (Ashby and Fell (1921)), clear again
now after the flooding that had blocked it for twenty miles at the start of Otho's
campaign (Suet. *Otho* 8.3). It is grimly appropriate for Dolabella's impending death
that the first part of the Via Flaminia was flanked with tombs (Juv. 1.170–1). Yet the
requirement that Dolabella should leave the main road to wait at Interamna (mod.
Terni) should have made him suspicious, since the Via Flaminia was notoriously busy
(and therefore safe). Vitellius wants to avoid the notoriety of judicially murdering an
aristocrat in a busy place, although the plan backfired. Dolabella would have left the
Via Flaminia for Interamna at Narnia, where Augustus had constructed a bridge
(Mart. 7.93.8).   **ibi interfici iussit** recalls *occidi . . . iussit* at the opening (2.63.1).
The repetition allows T. to attach two distinctive and discreditable explanations for
Vitellius' conduct, the influence of tyrannical advisers and a personal feud. *ibi* suggests
a distasteful level of involvement from the emperor, who even specifies the location
of the killing.   **uisum:** sc. *est*. The ellipse aptly mirrors the killer's desire for speed.
in itinere ac taberna proiectum humi iugulauit: the hendiadys ('a roadside
inn') helps emphasise the gulf between Dolabella's lofty social rank and the degrading
location of his death. Men of standing usually avoided staying in inns, and part of
the hostile tradition about Vitellius dwelt on his readiness to stay in such places (Suet.
Vit. 7.3). T. reserves *iugulo* for moments where its brutal physicality intensifies the
audience's awareness of shocking violence (3.77.3, 3.83.1, *A.* 1.18.3, 1.22.1). It is 5×
in Livy and 3× in Sallust, but absent from Caesar. Virgil has it twice in the context
of sacrifices (*A.* 11.199, 12.214), and Lucan once in the context of parricide on the
battlefield. *humi* is used with a sense of 'motion towards': cf. *proiectus humi* (Sil. 1.247).
It hints at a position indicative of (rejected) supplication (cf. 3.10.2), suggesting further
degradation.   **magna cum inuidia noui principatus cuius hoc primum
specimen noscebatur** 'causing great resentment for the new regime, since this
was taken as the first sign of its character'. An initial crime setting the tone for the rest
of a principate recurs in T.: the murder of Agrippa Postumus under Tiberius is the
primum facinus noui principatus (*A.* 1.6.1) and the murder of Junius Silanus under Nero
is the *prima nouo principatu mors* (*A.* 13.1.1). In these cases, it is unclear how far each
emperor was directly involved, but there are no doubts about Vitellius' participation.

There is also chronological telescoping: the principate of Vitellius (unlike Tiberius
and Nero) will be over almost as soon as it begins. Beginning a unit of narrative by
describing a death is pointedly ironic (Woodman (1998) 25). *specimen* (*OLD* 1) suggests
the visual register, deployed by T. in increasingly complex and judgemental ways with
Vitellius, who will both see and be seen in various degrading contexts. In the last four
words of the sentence, there is an elegant increase in the number of syllables from one
to four.

64.2 Triariae licentiam . . . onerabat 'made Triaria's outrageous behaviour
more burdensome'. T. is increasingly partial to using this verb metaphorically with
abstract qualities: *curas* (2.52.2, *A.* 1.19.2), *dilectum* (4.14.1), *haec* (*A.* 1.69.5), *pericula*
(*A.* 16.30.3).   **modestum . . . exemplum:** 13.2n. *praeclaro exemplo*. T. loftily uses
an adj. instead of a dependent noun in the gen. (2.1n. *iuuenilis animus*).   **e proximo** 'very close at hand' (also at 4.85.2). Polarised pairs of virtuous and villainous
women appear elsewhere for dramatic impact: e.g. Octavia and Poppaea (*A.* 14.59–
64).   **Galeria:** 47.2n. *fruetur . . . liberis*.   **non immixta tristibus** 'not mixed
up in grim affairs'.   **pari probitate:** T. later emphasises that *probitas* offers no
route to promotion in Vitellius' court (2.95.2). Elsewhere, it is associated with Nero's
wife, Octavia (*A.* 13.12.2), but not with male protagonists. For Juvenal *probitas* is an
upright, but obsolete characteristic: *probitas laudatur et alget* 'honesty is praised, and
shivers' (1.74). Sallust sees it as one of the *bonae artes* destroyed by avarice (*Cat.* 10.4).
Sextilia: Vitellius' mother is the archetypal Roman *matrona*, dignified and austere,
contrasting vividly with her dissolute son. She perhaps even recalls the exemplary
Cornelia, mother of the Gracchi, but she can hardly claim (as Cornelia did) that she
needed no adornment because her children were her jewels (Val. Max. 4.4 preface). In
Rome, Vitellius publicly uses Sextilia as a focus for his filial piety (2.89.2), but he out-
lives his mother, who only gains grief and a good reputation from her son's principate
(3.67.1). T. avoids Suetonius' story that Vitellius had a hand in his mother's death (*Vit.*
14.5), a rumour perhaps designed to evoke the matricidal Nero. Otho's kind treatment
of Sextilia reflects well on him (Plut. *Oth.* 5.3, 16.2).   **antiqui moris:** this gen. of
characteristic is also used for Galba's heir, Piso (1.14.2) and people from remote country towns shocked by Nero's performances (*A.* 16.5.1), while Galba himself manifests
antiquus rigor (1.18.3). A woman *antiqui moris* is manifestly a complete anachronism in
this shocking *nouus principatus:* mothers of the imperial household needed to be politically astute operators, such as Livia or Agrippina the Younger (although Antonia
is a closer model for Sextilia).   **quin etiam:** the anastrophe of these conjunctions
(17.2n. *quin etiam*) underscores Sextilia's swift and spirited response to the very first
letter she receives from her son as emperor.   **ad primas . . . epistulas:** 54.2n. on
epistulae for a single letter.   **non Germanicum a se, sed Vitellium genitum:**
letters in the ancient world, even to close family members, opened with standard formulae, which involved names: e.g. *C. PLINIVS CALPVRNIAE SVAE*, as Pliny writes to
his wife (*Ep.* 6.4.1). It is unclear whether Sextilia made her epigrammatic reply orally
or in writing. On the obverse of Vitellius' coins 'the title *Germanicus* (in full) gave way
to *German*, then to *Germa* or *Germ* and finally to *Ger*' and these last three abbreviations

'are found with *Imp Aug Tr P* i.e. after 18 Jul. when Vitellius, entering Rome, accepted the title *Augustus*, together with that of *Pontifex Maximus*' (Sutherland and Carson (1984) 262). **ambitu ciuitatis** 'the flattery of Rome'. *ciuitas* = the city of Rome (1.1n. *senium . . . destinandi*). **in gaudium euicta** 'moved to exultation' (Irvine). Combining this verb with a simple abl. of agent is relatively straightforward: *euicta dolore* (Virg. *A.* 4.474), *precibus uxoris euictus* (*A.* 4.57.3), *blandimentis uitae euictam* (*A.* 15.64.2). Yet T. also likes (as here) to couple it creatively with prepositional expressions indicating the (actual or potential) result: *euicta in lacrimas* (*A.* 1.57.4), *ad miserationem euicta* (*A.* 11.37.3). The gloomy but upright Sextilia is apparently the only one of Vitellius' entourage not sucked into the increasingly Saturnalian atmosphere of the decadent advance towards Rome. **domus suae tantum aduersa:** using *domus* to refer to the *familia* momentarily suggests the tragic stage; cf. *illustrium domuum aduersa* (*A.* 3.24.1). Sextilia has potential for adding tragic *color* to Vitellius' downfall (Levene (1997) 142).

65.1 Digressum a Lugduno: a precise date is elusive, but Vitellius probably left in early May (Murison (1993) 146–7). **Cluvius Rufus:** 58.2n. *inde . . . metus.* **assequitur omissa Hispania** 'caught up with him after relinquishing his responsibilities in Spain' (*OLD assequor* 2; *OLD omitto* 4). The anxious Cluvius Rufus does not presume that the governorship is still his, despite having intervened in Mauretania on Vitellius' behalf (2.58.2). **laetitiam et gratulationem uoltu ferens:** 52.1n. *uoltum . . . in deterius.* By choosing the simple form of the verb, having only one noun in the abl. and dispensing with *prae*, T. condenses Livy's *prae se ferens in uoltu habituque insignem memoriam ignominiae acceptae* (27.34.5), Valerius Maximus' *fauorabilem prae se ferens uultum* (4.5 preface), and Velleius' *ardorem animi uultu oculisque praeferens* (2.118.2). Poets prefer the simple form *ferens* in such expressions (Ov. *Met.* 11.271–2, Sil. 2.208). **animo anxius:** 1.3n. *anxius animo.* Both the phrasing and the nature of Cluvius Rufus' mission recall Titus' aborted assignment to congratulate Galba (2.1.1). Yet where Titus was protected by his relative youth and powerful father, Cluvius Rufus, holder of an official government post, cannot turn back. **petitum:** sc. *esse.* Personal enemies could always exploit the political situation to pursue private vendettas (cf. *priuata uulnera rei publicae malis operire* 1.53.2), but Cluvius Rufus fell victim remarkably quickly, especially given his pro-Vitellian activities in the province. **Hilarus:** this 'suggestive name' (93.2n. *sane . . . uerterat*), not necessarily T.'s invention, is cited here for irony, as a man called 'Cheerful' forces smiles from an anxious Cluvius Rufus. Here the notion of *nomen omen* breaks down, as Vitellius will punish this freedman (cf. Plin. *Nat.* 7.284–5, name play involving the serene death of another Hilarus). **Caesaris libertus:** Hilarus may have been one of Cluvius Rufus' own staff, perhaps procurator of Hispania Tarraconensis, responsible for financial administration (Heubner (1968) 235). He could also be a member of (or sympathetic to) the pro-Othonian group in Mauretania, seeking revenge for Albinus' death, engineered by Rufus. **detulerat, tamquam . . . temptasset** 'had denounced him because he had allegedly tried to attain' (*OLD defero* 9b; *OLD tempto* 8). *tamquam* + subj. gives Hilarus' reason (21.1n. *tamquam . . . potuissent*). **Vitellii et Othonis:** this sequence of names probably reflects the order in which Cluvius Rufus in Spain heard about the

rival principates (Vitellius being declared emperor on 2–3 Jan. 69 in Germany and
Otho in Rome on 15 Jan. 69). **principatu . . . possessionem:** the alliteration
(8.1n. *credentibus . . . contextu*) adds bite to the accusation. If Hilarus was part of Albinus'
entourage, his allegation that Rufus tried to seize Spain as a power-base is pointed,
as an identical rumour had circulated about Albinus (2.58.2). Vitellius could easily
have believed the charge, especially after Galba's imperial challenge originating from
this very province. **eoque:** 13.2n. The 'evidence' sounds unconvincing. In the circumstances, it was practical to leave the *diplomata* blank until the situation was calmer.
diplomatibus: 54.1n. **interpretabatur** 'he construed'. **quaedam ex orationibus eius contumeliosa in Vitellium:** Otho's spin-doctor Trachalus sensibly
held back from insulting Vitellius in a speech for Otho (*contumeliis in Vitellium abstinuit*,
1.90.2), while the Othonian generals were also restrained (*quamuis uberrima conuiciorum
in Vitellium materia abstinerent*, 2.30.3). Written evidence was clearly more dangerous
than speeches. So Otho himself tried to safeguard his associates by burning any documents insulting Vitellius (2.48.1). Vitellius' general Caecina learns from experience:
initial letters marked by *probra* against Otho (2.30.3) are replaced by more restrained
letters after he decides to abandon Vitellius (*nulla in Vespasianum contumelia*, 3.9.4).

65.2 auctoritas 'has an even stronger positive force than *dignitas*, stressing not
merely the right to receive by virtue of honour, but the right to command' (Lendon
(1997) 275); abstract noun as subject (2.1n. *spes uicit*). T. often comments on insufficient or insecure *auctoritas:* Hordeonius Flaccus (1.9.1), Galba (1.21.2), Otho (1.45.2; cf.
2.48.1), Antonius Novellus (2.12.1), and Vitellius (2.92.1) are all found lacking. Those
that do possess it are Suetonius Paulinus (1.87.2), Annius Gallus (2.44.2), Lucius Vestinus (4.53.1), Veleda (4.61.2) and above all Antonius Primus (3.10.3, 3.20.1, 3.80.2).
ultro 'actually' (*OLD* 4). The implicit contrast is with Vitellius' generous treatment
of his freedman Asiaticus (2.57.2). **comitatui principis adiectus:** sc. *est*. The
impression is of Vitellius acquiring a new toy. His *comitatus* will become increasingly
ungainly as he approaches Rome (*tot legatorum amicorumque comitatus, inhabilis ad parendum* 2.87.1). **non adempta Hispania:** the abl. absolute is in ring-composition
(*omissa Hispania*, 2.65.1) and signals the end of the episode. Vitellius' arrangement
was predictably ephemeral: by Jan. 70, Mucianus regards the province as vacant,
discessu Cluuii Rufi (4.39.4). **exemplo L. Arruntii:** the ex-consul Arruntius (*OCD³*
'Arruntius (2) (*RE* 8), Lucius') famously thought *capax imperii* by Augustus (*A.* 1.13.3–4),
was appointed governor of Hispania Tarraconensis, but Tiberius then kept him in
Rome for ten years (*A.* 6.27.3). After Arruntius had provoked Sejanus' hostility, the
new prefect of the praetorian guard, Macro, accused him of *maiestas* and adultery. He
killed himself shortly before Tiberius' death. T. puts in his mouth hard-hitting and
prophetic words about the likely calibre of Caligula as *princeps* (*A.* 6.48.1–3; Levick
(1976) 128–9). His adopted son, Arruntius Camillus Scribonianus, governor of Dalmatia, led a short-lived rebellion in 42 under Claudius, but was killed (Levick (1990)
59–60). As an *exemplum*, the candid Arruntius contrasts sharply with Cluvius Rufus,
cast by T. as fearful (2.58.2, 2.65.1). Helvidius Priscus praises Cluvius Rufus for never
endangering anyone under Nero's principate (4.43.1), hardly a ringing endorsement

(even if it was not meant sarcastically).   **Arruntium T. Caesar . . . Vitellius Cluvium:** the chiastic arrangement of names places the unadorned 'Vitellius' close to 'Tiberius Caesar' so that the title 'Caesar' contrasts Tiberius, the legitimate *princeps*, with Vitellius, who seized power illegitimately by military force. T. refers to Tiberius 9× in the *H*., but only once more with the title 'Caesar' (2.95.1) added, again in a context which sharply distinguishes between Vitellius and Tiberius (himself hardly a model *princeps* by T.s standards). T.'s word order also neatly places the absentee governors next to the respective emperors who kept them close at hand.   **ob metum . . . nulla formidine:** *uariatio* of prepositional clause + abl. of manner. The notion that Tiberius feared Arruntius does not cohere with T.'s version at *A.* 6.27.3. The discrepancy has troubled critics (Chilver (1979) 227), but T. is quite capable of presenting the same event differently in separate works to suit his immediate narrative needs: cf. the diverging versions of the Nero-Otho-Poppaea love triangle (1.13.3, *A.* 13.45–6).   **non idem . . . honos:** sc. *fuit*. This transitional device is richly ironic. *honos* means Vitellius not taking away Cluvius Rufus' province and including him in his entourage, but in the next case, the soldiers, not the emperor, call the shots.   **Trebellio Maximo:** Trebellius Maximus, son of a legionary commander (*A.* 6.41.1), suffect consul with Seneca the Younger in 56, and Nero's appointee as governor of Britain from 63, was allowed to stay on by Galba, only to be replaced in 69. T., evidently not a fan, characterises his tenure as avaricious and disrupted by quarrels with the ambitious commander of the *Legio XX Valeria Victrix*, Roscius Coelius, whose activities split the soldiers into two factions: as a result *Trebellius ad Vitellium perfugerit* (1.60). T.'s father-in-law Agricola later managed to tame the unruly legion after Roscius Coelius (referred to only as the *decessor*, *Agr.* 7.3) departed in 70. T.'s version of these events at *Agr.* 16.3–4 is different, but equally humiliating for Trebellius Maximus: (i) the soldiers' mutiny is attributed to their frustration at the lack of military action, (ii) Roscius Coelius is not mentioned, and (iii) the soldiers do not drive out Trebellius Maximus, but let him govern on sufferance. Yet there is some archaeological evidence for the success of Trebellius Maximus' policy of Romanisation (Ogilvie and Richmond (1967) 202). Trebellius resurfaces safely after the civil wars as one of the Arval Brethren in 72 (*CIL* VI 2053).   **ob iracundiam militum:** *ira* is the emotion and *iracundia* the character trait (Cic. *Tusc.* 4.27, Sen. *Dial.* 3.4.1; Hurley (2001) 217). Claudius apparently issued edicts apologising both for his *ira* and *iracundia* (Suet. *Cl.* 38.1 with Harris (2001)). T. consistently uses the resonant *iracundia* more sparingly than *ira* (*Agr.* 7 : 1, *G.* 1 : 0, *D.* 2 : 0, *H.* 36 : 8, *A.* 62 : 2), perhaps striving for literary impact. His earlier assertion that in the civil wars, *in Britannico exercitu nihil irarum* and that no other soldiers acted *innocentius* (1.9.2) may seem inconsistent with the current reference to *iracundia*. Yet T. meant previously that these soldiers did not promote their own imperial candidate and that there was no fighting in the province. These same troops join the Vitellian cause without hesitation (1.59.2) and send detachments (2.57.1, 2.100.1; cf. 4.46.2).   **in locum eius** 'to replace him' (also 3.36.2). *in* + acc. + gen. to expresses purpose (20.1n. *in . . . iniuriam*). The phrase evokes Livy (who often has *in locum eius . . . suffectus / inauguratus*; cf. *D.* 17.2) and times when appointments were made differently.

Vettius Bolanus e praesentibus: after serving as a legionary legate under Corbulo in Armenia (*A.* 15.3.1), he was suffect consul in 66 and administered Britain from 69–71 (Birley (1981) 62–5). His style apparently was not to impose discipline on the soldiers, so he was more popular than his predecessor (*Agr.* 16.5). Statius (*Sil.* 5.2.143–9) is more positive about his military achievements, but the context is a poem for Bolanus' son, Crispinus. As Agricola had served under Bolanus in Britain, T. probably asked him about the governor. *e praesentibus* shows how little effort Vitellius made to resolve the governorship of Britain; and his subsequent observation that Vettius Bolanus never had the province under complete control and that his loyalty was questionable (2.97.1) raises further questions about the manner of the appointment. He flourished under Vespasian, becoming proconsul of Asia in 76.

    66.1 Angebat: 24.1n. *angebant.*   **uictarum legionum:** *I Adiutrix, VII Galbiana, XI Claudia, XIII Gemina, XIV Gemina.* With five angry and demoralised ex-Othonian legions in Italy, Vitellius' concern is understandable, but his own troops are equally volatile.   **haudquaquam fractus animus:** Livy 'is the only author to use *haudquaquam* at all frequently' (Oakley (1997) 674). T. uses *haudquaquam* selectively and powerfully (again 3.65.1, *A.* 11.11.3, 12.2.1, 14.55.4; not in the minor works). These Othonians have perked up since their defeat (cf. *remanentium fractus animus* 2.33.3; *ceteris fractus animus* 2.44.3).   **hostilia:** the neuter pl. substantive (*OLD* 2) is Sallustian (*Hist.* 4.69.17 Reynolds, *Jug.* 3.2, 107.2), and also appealed to Livy (13×). T. uses it 6× in the *H.* (only 3× in *A.*).   **praecipua quartadecimanorum ferocia** 'the men of the fourteenth legion being particularly aggressive'; the deeply pro-Othonian *legio XIV Gemina* (11.1n. *rebellione Britanniae compressa* and *quattuor legiones*). The combination *praecipuus* (11.1n. *praecipui fama*) + *ferocia* is only here in extant Latin. In an appended abl. of manner T. focuses on those defeated Othonians with the most lively story to illustrate the dangers of legions dislocated from their normal bases during a civil war.   **qui se uictos abnuebant:** this initially sounds exaggerated, but the men have a point. They are indignant at the manner of their defeat, since through an accident of war, the battle took place *before* the Othonian generals had intended (2.39–45 intro.). It is psychologically easier to accept defeat if a decisive final battle has exhausted all other possibilities (e.g. the Carthaginian defeat at Zama in 202 BC). **quippe:** explanatory (10.3n. *quippe . . . meminerant*).   **Bedriacensi acie** 'at the battle of Bedriacum' (13.1n. *in acie*).   **uexillariis tantum pulsis:** 2.43.2 (and 32.2n. *paucis diebus*).   **remitti eos in Britanniam . . . placuit:** we can question the wisdom of this decision in light of the current *iracundia* (2.65.2) amongst the military and a new governor in the province. The person or group responsible for the decision is not named.   **placuit atque interim Batauorum cohortes una tendere** 'and it was decided that meanwhile the Batavian cohorts should encamp together with them'; 27.2n. *cohortes Batauos.*   **ob ueterem aduersus quartedecimanos discordiam:** the idea must be for the Batavians to monitor the legionaries. Yet the causal preposition draws attention to a questionable decision. Although the Batavians were originally auxiliaries for the *XIV Gemina*, the two groups had fought on opposite sides at the battle of Bedriacum, so feelings were likely to run high. As these

Batavian auxiliaries have already shown an inflammatory rivalry, even with men from another legion (1.64.2), trouble seems inevitable. Indeed, it was perhaps even a calculated provocation, giving the restive legion an opportunity to add to its disgrace and thereby justifying its transfer. *discordia* + *aduersus* (instead of *inter*), only in T., features here first (*A.* 12.44.5, 15.2.4; *A.* 4.32.1 has *aduersum*). It implies that the focal point is the hostility of the Batavians towards the legionaries (rather than their mutual enmity, as suggested by *inter*).

66.2 in tantis armatorum odiis 'when there was such hatred between armed men' (Irvine). **Augusta Taurinorum** (mod. Turin) was an Augustan colony founded in *c.* 25 BC (*CIL* v 7047) in northern Italy at the confluence of the Dora and Po rivers (Plin. *Nat.* 3.123). It was probably the capital of the Ligurian Taurini, captured by Hannibal in 218 BC (Plb. 3.60, Liv. 21.39, App. *Hann.* 5), but figures surprisingly rarely in Classical literature given its important location. Its accidental conflagration in 69 is its most prominent moment. The case here is locative. **Batauus . . . insectatur, legionarius . . . tuetur:** the asyndeton and lack of *uariatio* in the word-order (itself a form of *uariatio* in T.; 22.2n. *subruit . . . portas*) neatly and simply pits the two opponents against one another. Although in such contexts we might expect T. to show off his industrious research by naming minor characters, the status of the two men (*Batauus* vs *legionarius*) is thematically more important that their names, so T. does not clutter his account with unnecessary detail. Batavian auxiliaries, intentionally or otherwise, often appear in situations disruptive of military discipline (cf. 1.64.2, 2.27.2, 4.19). **fraudatorem:** *fraudator* (first in Cic., only here in T.) was brought into historiography by Livy (4.50.1, only here), again in a context of military strife, the memorable clash between the harsh commander M. Postumius and his rebellious soldiers, who stoned him to death. Its redeployment by T. in a petty squabble between an auxiliary and a workman suggests bathos. *fraudator* (once in Phaed., Sen. the Younger, Quint., Mart.) appears 21× in Justinian as a technical term. T. likes agent nouns ending in *-tor* (56.2n. *alienae . . . dissimulator*). **ut hospitem** 'as his host' (*OLD hospes* 1b). Soldiers were often billeted with civilians, but wealthy communities sometimes paid to avoid this duty (Cic. *Att.* 5.21.7). Germanicus issued an edict before his visit to Egypt in 19 forbidding the seizing by force of billets for lodging and the terrorising of private citizens (EJ 320; Campbell (1984) 246–54). In this case, the legionary tries to protect his temporary host. **sui cuique commilitones aggregati** 'each man was joined by his respective comrades'. *commilitones* often feature in speeches (7× in the *H.*), as speakers try (not always justifiably) to stir camaraderie with the soldiers (Campbell (1984) 32–9). Julius Caesar habitually addressed his men with this *blandius nomen* (Suet. *Jul.* 67.2). When the term appears in T.'s narrative, the emotive context is underscored by alliteration (as here, with *cuique*): *caedem commilitonum* (1.31.2), *cladem commilitoni* (4.72.4). T. uses *aggrego* (+ dat., instead of + *ad*) in an earlier escalating quarrel between Batavian auxiliaries and legionaries (*dum his aut illis studia militum aggregantur*, 1.64.2). **a conuiciis ad caedem:** enveloping alliteration (4.1n. *pandi . . . prosperum*) marking a deterioration (cf. 27.2n. *e petulantia etiam perfidiam*). **transiere:** 3.1n. *ipsa . . . cessere*; the alternative third person pl. perfect is an apt form for a swift

outbreak of disorder.   **proelium atrox:** this fine Livian expression (12×, incl. once
+ *atrocissimum*, 3× + *atrocius*) jars harshly with the sordid context of the squabble. T.
also uses it for a real battle (3.22.3; also *Agr.* 26.2).   **arsisset:** the verb *ardeo*, used
metaphorically for the near-miss of a battle, anticipates the real fires that will break
out in Augusta Taurinorum on the night of the soldiers' departure.   **ni:** the sense of
closure is misleading. There will be more trouble between legionaries and auxiliaries
(2.88). *ni* (14.3n.) is a dramatic device in battle-descriptions, clearly ironic here, as
these troops are not on the battlefield.   **duae praetoriae cohortes:** predictable
supporters of the pro-Othonian legionaries, given the praetorians' famous loyalty to
Otho (8.2n. *dextras . . . ferentem*).   **his fiduciam et metum Batauis:** the chiastic
structure elegantly 'separates' the fighting factions.

   66.3 quos: sc. *Batauos.*   **ut fidos:** T.'s Vitellius (as often) jumps to conclusions (cf. 2.59.1 *nihil . . . Vitellio anquirente*). The fact that the Batavians quarrel with
the pro-Othonian legionaries does not therefore make them loyal to Vitellius.   **eo
flexu itineris ire iubet, quo Viennam uitarent** 'he ordered them to travel by
a roundabout route chosen so that they could avoid Vienne'. This abl. of means is
the antecedent of *quo* in the next clause. The combination *flexu* + the gen. *itineris* (only
here) is a choice variant of *flexu uiae* and similar expressions (Liv. 22.12.7, 29.34.9,
Lucr. 3.587, Manil. 4.394,), though Lucretius has *per iter flexum* (4.93). After crossing
the Graian Alps, the usual route into Gaul would be via Cularo (mod. Grenoble)
to Vienne, but these troops are to divert northwards and pass through Lugdunum.
et Viennenses timebantur: bitter civic rivalry had prompted Lugdunum to stir
the Vitellian soldiers against neighbouring Vienne. Her citizens realised the danger
and supplicated the troops, soothed by a financial handout from their general Fabius
Valens, possibly provided by the Viennese themselves (1.65–6). For their efforts, the
citizens had their weapons confiscated and had to provide the troops with provisions.
This all meant that the town was potentially hostile to the Vitellians, so exposing
it to a disillusioned and defeated Othonian legion could have triggered a dangerous alliance. The episode demonstrates how easily in civil wars short-term selfish
strategies from an individual general can cause problems for the whole party in the
future.   **relictis passim ignibus:** the soldiers were careless rather than malicious.
ambusta: sc. *est.* At the best of times, fires were a common hazard for towns in the
ancient world (e.g. *A.* 3.72.2, 4.64.1, 6.45.1, 15.38–40, Sen. *Ep.* 91.1, Fron. *Aq.* 1, 18.2,
Suet. *Vit.* 8.2, *Ves.* 8.5, Juv. 3.197–222 with Mayor (1872) 172) and people tried to avert
danger by writing spells on their walls (Plin. *Nat.* 28.20). Rome faced special risks from
the pressure on space (Plut. *Cras.* 2.4). In AD 6, Augustus organised *uigiles* in Rome as a
fire brigade (Suet. *Aug.* 30.1; *OCD³* '*uigiles*') and likewise Claudius at Puteoli and Ostia
(Suet. *Cl.* 25.2), but in a society dependent on fire for warmth and cooking, accidents
were inevitable. One man, seeing a block of flats on fire, said that if only some remedy could prevent houses in Rome from catching fire, then he would sell his country
property and move to the city (Gell. 15.1.3). Yet the vagaries of civil war heightened
the risks: Placentia's amphitheatre (2.21.1–2), buildings outside Cremona (3.30.2) and
the temple of Capitoline Jupiter (3.71–2) are all destroyed by fire. Cicero even boasted

that he had freed Rome from the threat of fires triggered by civil disturbances: *urbem incendiis . . . liberassem* (*Cat.* 3.15; cf. *Phil.* 1.30). **quod damnum:** reparation of fire damage could allow the *princeps* (or another wealthy citizen) to show public munificence, as when Tiberius donated 100 million HS after the fire in Rome in 36 (*A.* 6.45.1). Yet the damage done across Italy during the civil wars stretched resources, and priorities lay elsewhere, above all in Rome (4.53). This was unfortunate for the towns of northern Italy, which had suffered most in the fighting: 'The resurgence of Rome, which escaped damage until struck in its heart by the fire on the Capitol, was vital to Vespasian's own position' (Levick (1999) 124) whereas the town of Augusta Taurinorum was not. **ut pleraque belli mala** 'like many catastrophes of the war'. T.'s *sententia* recalls his earlier point about the destruction of Placentia's amphitheatre, first played down during the war and then exaggerated afterwards (2.21.2). Yet this conflagration of Augusta Taurinorum will simply be effaced by greater disasters, so T. records it for posterity. **obliteratum:** sc. *est.* T. simultaneously rescues the disaster from oblivion and deplores that it was outstripped by even greater catastrophes. **seditiosissimus quisque:** this sonorous and unusual superlative (Cic. 3×, Val. Max. 3×, Suet. and SHA once each) features again in T., each time with *quisque* (4.34.4, *A.* 1.44.2), following Livy's *seditiosissimum quemque* (4.2.7). It is absent from Sallust and Caesar (though it is in [Caes.] *Afr.* 28.2). **signa Viennam ferebant** 'tried to march to Vienne'; singular distributive pronoun with pl. verb (44.1n. *suum obiectantes*). The imperfect of endeavour denotes attempted or desired action (GL §233). T. uses the composite expression *signa ferre* innovatively, as it usually means 'to break up camp' (but cf. *ferte signa in hostem*, 'attack the enemy', Liv. 9.23.13). *signa proferre* would be normal for 'to advance' (e.g. Liv. 4.32.10). The expression and word order sustain the alliteration after *seditiosissimus quisque*. **consensu meliorum compressi:** sc. *sunt.* Cf. *moderatione meliorum dirempti* (2.53.2). **transuecta:** sc. *est.*

67.1 separati: the praetorians were presumably separated from the other troops (and perhaps also from each other), although two cohorts had recently defused trouble at Augusta Taurinorum (2.66.2). One cogent reason for isolating the praetorians was to stop the other troops getting jealous about the financial handout. **addito honestae missionis lenimento:** *honestae missionis* = defining gen. In Suetonius, Vitellius simply dismisses the praetorians for disgracefully abandoning Galba for Otho (*Vit.* 10.1). T.'s *honesta missio* (5× in Justinian as a technical term) conflicts with this (indicating a dispute in the sources over the praetorians' dismissal). The 'solace' could have been as much as 20,000 HS, so it was tempting (Dio 55.23). The striking medical metaphor in *lenimentum* (first in Val. Max. 4.6 ext. 2) perhaps casts the praetorians as 'diseased'. Vitellius later accuses these same men of spreading false rumours about Vespasian's challenge (2.96.2), which suggests his lack of confidence in the current measures. **arma ad tribunos suos deferebant:** the detail is in Suetonius, but in a more dubious context (*iussas tribunis tradere arma, Vit.* 10.1). When these praetorians, now Flavians, are fighting in the second battle of Bedriacum, Antonius Primus trenchantly points out to them their own equipment, now in the Vitellian soldiers' hands: *illic signa armaque uestra sunt* (3.24.3). **donec motum a Vespasiano bellum crebresceret**

'until the news spread that war had been set in motion by Vespasian'. The subjunctive
here does not signal the expected result of an action or an intention, but the actual
result (*NLS* §224 n.ii), a 'silver' usage. It seems better to take *motum* (sc.*esse*) . . . *bellum* as
an indirect statement after *crebresceret* (used impersonally, as at *A.* 2.39.3, a peculiarly
Tacitean construction), although it could also be the nom. subject of the verb ('until
the war set in motion by Vespasian became widespread'). The familiar combination
motum . . . bellum is 11× in Livy (also in Sall., Cic.), but *crebresco* is conspicuously non-
Livian: amongst poets, it is first in Virgil (*A.* 3.530, 12.222, 12.407), then in Statius
(*Theb.* 4.30) and Valerius Flaccus (3.210). Prose authors (Asconius, Pliny the Younger,
Quintilian) use it sparingly, except T. who has it 6×, more than any other author.
crebresco appears to be a simple for compound form, *increbresco* or *percrebresco* (Goodyear
(1981) 310). T. may allude to Virgil: *et saeuus campis magis ac magis horror | crebrescit* (*A.*
12.406–7).   **resumpta militia:** cf. 2.82.3 for the Flavians re-enlisting these men.
robur Flauianarum partium: Chilver (1979) 229 suspects exaggeration, especially
as the *praetorianum uexillum* (3.21.2) seems paltry when compared with the five legions
fighting for Vespasian at the second battle of Bedriacum. Yet depth of feeling, not just
numbers, can determine strength, and later references to the dismissed praetorians
(2.82.3, 2.96.2) suggest their strategic importance in undermining Vitellian morale.

    67.2 prima . . . legio: the *prima Adiutrix* (11.2n. *cum legione prima*; 11.3n. *classico-
rum . . . numerus*).   **pace et otio mitesceret:** 18.2n. *si . . . mitesceret*. Soldiers often
slacken amidst *otium* (34.1n. *ne . . . otium tereret*), as Vitellius will be reminded when
his men reach Rome.   **undecima et septima . . . redditae:** the Dalmatian
legion *XI Claudia* was based at Burnum, while the Pannonian legion *VII Galbiana* was
based perhaps at Carnutum. Sending them back did the Vitellians no good: *haud cunctanter Vespasiano accessere* (2.86.1).   **tertiadecimani struere amphitheatra iussi:**
34.2n. on *struo / exstruo*. The price for humiliating the Othonian *legio XIII Gemina* (11.1n.
quattuor legiones; 26.2n. *Vitellianus miles*) is that after the second battle of Bedriacum, the
men are especially keen to destroy Cremona, whose citizens unwisely mock them
during the building (3.32.2). The amphitheatres were probably made of wood (21.2n.
nulla . . . tam capax foret).   **Caecina Cremonae, Valens Bononiae spectaculum . . . parabant:** pl. verb with two singular subjects (24.3n. *Paulinus . . . Celsus
sumpsere*); 53.2n. *rediere . . . Bononiam* on Bononia. The word order mirrors the sequence
of the shows (2.70.1 Caecina; 2.71.1 Valens), with asyndeton emphasising the two generals' rivalry. Neighbouring towns often expressed civic rivalry through gladiatorial
displays, caring little about the sponsors. Martial scorns the low-class organisers (a
cobbler and a fuller) of another pair of shows: *sutor Cerdo dedit tibi, culta Bononia, munus
| fullo dedit Mutinae: nunc ubi copo dabit?* (3.59). Caecina and Valens are not so lowly,
but by organising these shows they still seek popularity and aim to outdo each other.
numquam . . . ut obliuisceretur: after a stylistically spartan summary of the
defeated Othonians' dispersal, the chapter ends with a flourish as T. snubs Vitellius
in an appended abl. absolute clause (*numquam . . . Vitellio*; cf. *nihil . . . Vitellio anquirente*
2.59.1), which introduces a damning final clause (*ut . . . obliuisceretur*; an abl. abs. +
result clause similarly end a chapter with innuendo at *A.* 4.2.3). T. redeploys this witty

syntax to discredit Vitellius: *ceterum non ita ducibus indulsit . . . ut non plus militi liceret* (2.94.1). Again, the sting is in the final clause. In a different context (and with a term other than *uoluptates*, so nicely alliterative with *Vitellio*), this coda could even have been positive: elsewhere the ability to balance *otium* and *negotium* is seen as an asset in upper-class Romans (e.g. *iam uero tempora curarum remissionumque diuisa, Agr.* 9.3). *intentus* + dat. is more common in T. than *intentus* + *ad* (G-G 663), combined pejoratively with *curas* again: *Domitianus . . . nondum ad curas intentus, sed stupris et adulteriis filium principis agebat* (4.2.1); *Tiberius . . . quanto intentus olim publicas ad curas, tanto occultiores in luxus et malum otium resolutus* (*A.* 4.67.3)

68.1 uictas quidem . . . apud uictores: Haase (1855) added *uictas* (now gener-ally accepted). After *quidem* (a 'contrasting *quidem*', WM 191; Solodow (1978) 67–74), one might expect *sed* introducing the second clause, but asyndeton creates an even stronger contrast (Morgan (1995b) 578 n.1).   **modeste distraxerat** 'had dispersed them in a controlled way'. Vitellius handles this problem more competently than the Flavians do (cf. 4.1.1, 4.46.3 *huc illuc distrahi coepere*). Some of his own defeated legions will even join Civilis' rebellion in Germany rather than obey Vespasian (4.54.1).   **orta** (sc. *est*) **seditio, ludicro initio** 'a riot began; it started off as fun'. The playfulness extends to sound-effects, with homoioteleuton and internal rhyming (Fletcher (1940) 184–7, Woodman (1998) 218–29 on such 'jingles'). T. likes pleonasm (Lausberg (1998) §502) with 'beginning' words, above all in the *H.* (1.39.2, 1.76.3, 2.72.1, 2.79, 3.14, 3.44, 3.58.4), but the habit then tails off (*A.* 1.31.3, 2.1.1, 14.17.1, 15.38.1). Other authors also indulged: e.g. Enn. *Scaen.* 248–9 (= *Rhet. Her.* 2.34) *inchoandi exordium | coepisset* (Heubner (1963) 91; L-H-S 793–4 §39). T. here imitates himself at the opening of the praetorian mutiny in Rome under Otho: *paruo . . . initio . . . orta seditio* (1.80.1). This parallelism should prompt readers to compare the two scenes (1.80–5; 2.68–9): both focus on a banquet (1.81.1, 2.68.1) and drunken soldiers (1.80.1, 2.68.1). Where T. reports a long speech from Otho (1.83.2–84), he does not give Vitellius' words (2.69.1), but both *principes* play to their soldiers in different ways.   **ni** (14.3n.) is not in M, but editors generally accept the emendation.   **inuidiam †bello† auxisset:** editors question M's *bello* on the basis of its relevance in this context. Doerderlein (1841) suggests *Vitellio*, but the appearance of the same name so early in the next sen-tence cast doubts on this emendation as pleonastic, and in any case the combination *inuidiam augere* + dat. is problematic. Athetising *bello* (Morgan (1996b) 578) seems best. **discubuerat** 'was at dinner' (Irvine). Vitellius' journey to Rome is punctuated by feasting, a theme initiated at 2.62.1. '*discumbere* with a singular subject is first in Nepos at Suet. *Vit. Ter.* 3 (if the citation is genuine)' (WM 157). Its prominent position here at the start of the sentence (4.3n. *profligauerat*) suggests that Vitellius' priority is eating; even his honoured guest is relegated to an abl. absolute clause.   **Ticini:** 17.2n. **adhibito ad epulas Verginio:** 49.1n. *atrocissima . . . ui.* Given the soldiers' passions, Vitellius is wise to keep Verginius nearby. T. conspicuously fragments the narrative, as the notice of this banquet would most naturally fall at 2.68.4, when the soldiers first break into the feast. Yet by placing the report here, T. hints at a causal link between Vitellius' gourmandising and his soldiers' lack of discipline. The convivial atmosphere sits uncomfortably with the *numerus caesorum* in the previous sentence, but reflects a broad fascination in ancient literature with juxtaposing dining and death: e.g. *destrictus ensis cui super impia | ceruice pendet, non Siculae dapes | dulcem elaborabunt saporem* (Hor. *Carm.* 3.1.17–19). It is disturbing that the fracas breaks out while the commander-in-chief is indulging himself.   **legati . . . gaudent . . . agit:** T.'s *sententia* directs readers in advance how to read the violence (2.68.2), bolstering his earlier message about the 'trickle-down' effect from Vitellius (*degenerabat . . . contemptu ducis* 2.62.1). This generalisation about intermediate officers passing on models of behaviour from the emperor to the soldiers gains credibility from the recent picture of Caecina and Valens busily preparing gladiatorial shows (2.67.2). These two Vitellian officers increasingly vie with one another destructively (92.1n. *olim . . . dissimulata*) through warped *aemulatio* (4.4n. *aemulatio*).   **seueritatem:** only Galba in the *H.* is regularly associated with *seueritas* (1.5.2, 1.18.3, 1.37.4; cf. Otho, 1.85.1), but his officers did not emulate him in this.   **tempestiuis conuiuiis** 'prolonged banquets'. *tempestiuus* (often 'ready at the right time' or 'ripe') appears in a set phrase, coined by Cicero (5×), indicating a dinner party starting early, which is thus elaborate (*OLD tempestiuus* 3e; also in Curt., the Younger Sen., Quint., Suet., Flor.). T. has it again in a striking context (*A.* 11.37.2).   **omnia:** sc. *erant.*   **indisposita** 'chaotic' is apparently coined by T. (only here in extant Latin), but the younger Seneca has the adverb *indisposite* (*Ep.* 124.19, twice).   **peruigiliis ac bacchanalibus** 'all-night orgies' is probably best taken as a hendiadys, as *peruigilium* (unlike the verb *peruigilo*; cf. Ov. *Fast.* 6.326, Curt. 6.2.2) generally has a positive sense (cf. *sellisternia ac peruigilia celebrauere feminae, A.* 15.44.1). The pl. forms of the pentasyllabic pair add to the sense of excess. Suetonius has *in Appennini quidem iugis etiam peruigilium egit* (*Vit.* 10.3), indicating some sort of thanksgiving ritual for Vitellius' victory. T. was perhaps playing with something in the common source (especially if he added the eye-catching *bacchanalibus*, only here in T.).

    68.2 igitur: 2.2n.   **duobus . . . interfectae:** the syntax is elaborate and sprawling, with most of the action packed into the four complex subordinate clauses. The scene-setter is a long abl. absolute (*duobus . . . accensis*), whose protagonists reappear in the successive subordinate clauses. Then there is a *postquam* clause and two further abl. absolutes (*insultante Gallo; iis . . . deductis*), the second of which envelops (*a*) a relative pronoun construction (*qui . . . conuenerant*) developing the antecedent *iis* and (*b*) *ad* + a gerundive of purpose. All this dwarfs the two short main clauses (*erupere legionarii; duae cohortes interfectae*), further condensed by an alternative third person perfect and ellipse of *sunt.* The effect is to immerse readers in the chaotic and syntactically messy build-up of the fight, then to shock them with the stark and brutal result laid out in the simple main clauses. The violent escalation is illustrated by ring-composition: a fight between *duo milites* ultimately causes the slaughter of *duae cohortes.*
    duobus militibus, altero legionis quintae, altero e Gallis auxiliaribus: the adversative pronouns *alter* ∼ *alter* in asyndeton (as usual with this construction; *TLL* s.v. *alter* 1739.3–1741.54) are in apposition to *duobus militibus. alter* ∼ *alter* is useful for contrasting two sides in martial contexts (Liv. 3.62.6, 9.40.2). T. uses it again, usually contrasting two people (1.6.1, 2.7.1, 3.75.2), but also contrasting two deeds

of one man (2.50.1). Single combat has an epic or republican flavour (Oakley (1985) 392–410), albeit here bathetic. In describing the fight, T. recalls the famous clash between Manlius Torquatus and the Gaul, narrated by Claudius Quadrigarius (Gell. 9.13) and Livy (7.9.6–10.14, with Oakley (1998) 113–48; Ash (1999) 115). That shining republican example of Roman valour triumphing over barbarity is here tarnished: unlike Torquatus and the Gaul, both T.'s combatants are on the same side, and this time the Gallic auxiliary (rather than the Roman) wins. For the *Legio V Alaudae*, see 43.2n. *impetu quintanorum*.   **per lasciuiam** 'by way of amusement' (also 3.33.2, 3.62.2, *A.* 12.7.3, 14.20.4; 4× in Livy). Playfulness in this work usually foreshadows or generates destruction (cf. 2.88.2, involving these same troops). T. comments on the tendency for young soldiers to lark about (*more iuuenum qui militiam in lasciuiam uertunt*, *Agr.* 5.1); predictably Agricola does not.   **ad certamen luctandi:** in Greek culture, wrestling was seen as good training for soldiers, and the heroic Heracles excelled in it, as in his wrestling-contest with the god Achelous (Soph. *Trach.* 18–25, 517–18, Ov. *Met.* 9.1–92, Apoll. 2.7.5). It also features in epic (Virg. *A.* 6.642–3, Stat. *Theb.* 6.834–910). Yet Romans associated wrestling (Poliakoff (1987) 23–53) with decadent nations (Luc. 7.271, Sil. 14.136–9) and believed that good soldiers should not wrestle (Plut. *Phil.* 3.3–5). This may reflect badly on the Vitellians here.   **accensis:** *accendo*, often metaphorically applied to battles (*OLD* 4b, 5b), is apt for a play fight that will soon turn real.   **prociderat:** the legionary takes a tumble with remarkable speed.   **insultante Gallo** 'As the Gaul was scoffing'. In the story about Manlius Torquatus, the Gaul memorably sticks his tongue out (Gell. 9.13.12, Liv. 7.10.5), so this boastful Gaulish auxiliary broadly evokes the earlier fight. The behaviour coheres with sterotypical images of Gallic arrogance in the literary tradition, but 'ritualised boasting' was also central to single combat (Rawlings (1998) 189 n.36; Oakley (1998) 139).   **in studia diductis** 'having taken opposite sides'. Spectators at the fight between Torquatus and the Gaul were equally caught up in the spectacle (Liv. 7.10.9). Enthusiasm unleashed by arena sports is the obvious analogy here: cf. *quatitur certamine circus | spectantum* (Sil. 16.322–3); *studiisque fauentum* (Virg. *A.* 5.148); one supporter of the Reds in the circus was so devoted that he even threw himself into his favourite driver's funeral pyre (Plin. *Nat.* 7.186; Cameron (1976) 56). Such enthusiasm easily escalates into physical violence (*A.* 14.17).   **erupere legionarii:** 3.1n. *ipsa . . . cessere*. In military narratives *erumpo* is regularly applied to troops making a sortie (*OLD* 1b; cf. 2.26.1), but these soldiers are not (supposed to be) in a battle. In the Torquatus story, the spectators also get involved, but only after the fight is over and to congratulate their hero (Liv. 7.10.12). A closer Livian analogy is the fight between Valerius Corvus and a Gaul (7.26.1–10), where those watching initiate a fierce battle in the aftermath.   **in perniciem auxiliorum:** *in* + acc. + gen. expresses purpose (20.1n. *in nullius iniuriam*).   **duae cohortes interfectae:** sc. *sunt*. i.e. auxiliary cohorts. The units could vary in size, but an auxiliary cohort's theoretical strength was *c.* 480 men (Goldsworthy (1996) 21–3). The high death-toll endorses T.'s opening comment about the *numerus caesorum* (2.68.1) and ring-composition (68.2n. *duobus . . . interfectae*) shows disastrous escalating violence.

68.3 Remedium tumultus fuit alius tumultus: the polyptoton (i.e. repetition of a word with a morphological variation in the same clause), as so often in T., simultaneously amuses and shocks (and the pithy sentence gains impact from contrast with its enormous predecessor). This is an instance of *para prosdokian*, 'violated expectation' (Plass (1988) 59), where the recurrence of *tumultus* at the end creates surprise. One might have expected *labor* (*vel sim.*; 19.1n. *is labor*). Caesar has a similar formulation (*praesenti malo aliis malis remedia dabantur, Civ.* 1.81.4), but T. conspicuously substitutes *tumultus* for *malum*. Although *tumultus* is common in the *H.*, it is particularly apt for trouble that started with a Gaul, since it is virtually a technical term for Gallic uprisings (WM 337). **puluis procul et arma:** this is often a pivot in formal battle narratives, as in a conflict between Romans and Samnites when a *puluis uelut ingentis agminis incessu motus* appeared on the horizon, thickened by the ruse of dragging leafy branches behind some mules (Liv. 10.41.5; cf. 9.43.12, 21.46.4, 42.58.3, Fron. *Str.* 2.4.1, 4.7.20). One cloud of dust suggesting that Caesar's army was approaching proved so terrifying that a siege was abandoned (Polyaen. 8.23.6). Cassius famously killed himself after the first battle of Philippi in 42 BC as he could not see the whole battlefield through the dust and wrongly assumed that the situation was hopeless (App. *BC* 4.113; Plut. *Brut.* 43 blames his bad eyesight; cf. Dio 47.46.5). Here T. adds to the episode's almost parodic character, as the Vitellians again fall short of the traditional Roman military ideal. **conclamatum** 'a shout went up'; sc. *est.* In general, T. studiously avoids the simple form *clamo* (favouring *clamito* instead), but four times he has the resonant compound *conclamo*. The impersonal passive form is perfect for swift action sequences (15.1n. *trepidatum*). Here it also adds to the chaos by masking the agent: nobody afterwards could have said who raised this false alarm. **quartam decimam legionem:** this pro-Othonian legion (11.1n. *rebellione Britanniae compressa* and *quattuor legiones*) was being sent back to Britain (2.66.3). The fluster of the Vitellian soldiers may seem irrational, but we should remember that the first battle of Bedriacum started in a similarly random way (2.41.1) and individual legions did not have access to the strategic overview of the campaign (cf. 1.83.3). As often, the absence of a senior office exacerbates the situation. Fabius Valens, who had brought the legion from Germany (1.61.1), was busy preparing a gladiatorial show (2.67.2). **coactores agminis** 'the rearguard of the(ir own) column'. The rearguard's tardiness suggests complacency, as troops on the march were meant to avoid the column getting thinned out or severed (Veg. 3.6). T. colourfully combines an agent-noun + gen. *agminis* for the more usual verb + acc. *agmen* (e.g. Cic. *Att.*15.13.1, Liv. 22.2.4, Curt. 3.3.25; *OLD cogo* 2b). T. likes to vary standard terms, especially legal, military and administrative ones (Goodyear (1972) 342–5). **dempsere:** 3.1n. *ipsa . . . cessere.*

68.4 Verginii seruus forte obuius ut percussor Vitellii insimulatur 'a slave of Verginius, encountered by chance, was accused of being Vitellius' assassin'. The construction *insimulo* + *ut*, first here, appealed to T.'s imitator Ammianus Marcellinus (*ut procacem insimulat* 16.7.2). To kill someone by the sword at a public banquet was difficult with so many people present, but Sertorius was assassinated in this way in 72 BC (Plut. *Sert.* 26). Poison was more practical (e.g. *A.* 13.16), but a guest's slave would still find it difficult to contaminate the food. Either way, the chance encounter with the slave suggests a totally opportunistic accusation.   **et** joins two main clauses, the first expressing the circumstances of the second with the force of an inverted *cum* clause (*OLD et* 17; again at 2.95.2 *nondum . . . et*). Cf. Virg. *G.* 2.80, Ov. *Fast.* 6.384, Luc. 1.231.   **miles:** collective singular (6.2n. *fremere miles*).   **mortem Verginii exposcens:** 49.1n. on Verginius Rufus; 27.2n. *omnem . . . iactantes* on the appended nom. present participle. T. generally prefers the simple *posco* to the compound *exposco* (absent from the minor works; 10× in the *H.*; 6× in the *A.*).   **ne Vitellius quidem** temporarily realigns the emperor with a general group (everybody else) to which he would not normally belong, deftly suggesting that aberrant conduct usually defines him (also 1.69.1, 1.77.2, 3.64.2).   **quamquam . . . pauidus:** *quamquam* lacks a finite verb (3.2n. *quamquam in aperto*). References to Vitellius' fearfulness accumulate (*metu* 2.64.1, *angebat* 2.66.1, *proximus . . . metus* 2.67.1), but he increasingly fears the wrong things (3.39.1) or suppresses legitimate fears for misguided reasons (2.96.2). Here T. by remarkable sleight of hand introduces a general character-trait of Vitellius just when it is not manifested. He may hint at the stereotypical tyrant, beset by fears (*A.* 6.6, Eur. *Ion* 621–8, Xen. *Hier.* 2.8–10, Sen. *Con.* 1.7.2, 4.7).   **ad** 'in response to' (*OLD* 33a).   **de innocentia eius:** the only other appearance of *innocentia* in the *H.* is to note its absence (from Antonius Primus, 3.49.1).   **exitium . . . flagitabant:** *uariatio* after *mortem . . . exposcens*. The combination is only here (*TLL* s.v. *exitium* 1528.64). Cf. *eo usque flagitatus est, donec ad exitium dederetur* (*A.* 1.32.2).   **consularis et quondam ducis sui:** by this periphrasis (*pronominatio* or *antonomasia*; 33.2n. *idem . . . auctores*) T. sharpens his indignant tone. Verginius Rufus' consular rank should normally have earned the troops' respect. So, the senatorial generals under whom a soldier had served were often listed on his tombstone followed by the letters *c.v.* (*clarissimus uir*), indicating pride in aristocratic commanders (*ILS* 2311); and when Claudius' freed-man Narcissus addresses the troops, he is greeted with shouts of 'Io Saturnalia!', indicating their scorn for his social status (Dio 60.19.3; Lendon (1997) 242). Yet these troops also have a personal relationship with Verginius Rufus, after serving with him in suppressing Vindex's rebellion, so the betrayal is even more bitter. That is why the murder of Pompey, killed by his own former soldier, is so shocking (Plut. *Pomp.* 78, Luc. 8.606–8, Dio 42.3); Appian emphasises this, poignantly making Pompey say 'Do I know you, fellow-soldier?' (*BC* 2.85).   **omnis seditio infestauit** 'did every mutinous act harass'. *infesto* is a hapax legomenon in T., influenced perhaps by Ovid, who has the verb twice, both times with Scylla and Charybdis as the subject (a fitting echo given that turbulent *seditio* is the subject here): *quas Scylla infestet quasue Charybdis aquas* (*Am.* 2.11.18), *Scylla latus dextrum, laeuum inrequieta Charybdis | infestat* (*Met.* 13.730–1). T. perhaps also thought this an apt formulation as the cognate adj. *infestus* with *signa* indicates a military attack (*OLD infestus* 3b).   **manebat admiratio uiri et fama, sed oderant ut fastiditi** 'admiration and esteem for the man remained, but they hated him because he had scorned them'; 49.1n. for Verginius rejecting the soldiers' attempts to make him emperor. The frenzied troops perhaps behave with the mercurial passions of a rejected lover: cf. *odi et amo . . .* (Catul. 85).

69.1 Postero die: a precise date is elusive, but it was probably in May, as Vitellius visits the battlefield at Cremona on *c.* 23 May. By clarifying that this is the next day, T. discredits Vitellius for his needless sycophancy towards the soldiers, now that the immediate crisis is over. It also evokes the pattern of the praetorian mutiny under Otho (*postera die* 1.82.2). On the gender of *dies*, see 22.1n. *uixdum . . . die.*   **senatus lega-tione . . . audita . . . collaudauit . . . frementibus . . . accessisse:** the syntax reinforces the prevailing power structure. The senators are relegated to an abl. abso-lute (with no indication of their words to the emperor), while the main clause quickly switches to Vitellius courting the soldiers. The next abl. absolute reports the auxiliaries' words (implicitly more important than those of the senators). For the subordination of the senate to the soldiery in a different way, cf. 1.17.2 (discussion of where Piso's adoption should be announced).   **ibi:** at Ticinum (2.68.1), after the senators had left Bononia (2.53.2), a journey of *c.* 130 miles.   **opperiri iusserat:** to make people wait could indicate disdain (Petr. 31.8, Juv. 1.109, 5.15–16, 10.161–2), as when Caesar leaves the senate dangling on the morning of the Ides of March (*iam dudum opperientis*, Suet. *Jul.* 81.4). So, the Parthian Vologeses asks that his brother Tiridates when visiting Rome should not be kept waiting at people's doors (*A.* 15.31). The haughty Vitellius has done this before: 60.1n. *tenuit tristi mora squalidos.* If this practice is associated with east-ern regimes, then it is apt for Vitellius' increasingly decadent Bacchanalian progress towards Rome.   **ultro pietatem militum collaudauit** 'he actually praised the soldiers' upright conduct'(*OLD ultro* 3). This does not solve anything (cf. 2.88.1). *pietas* is problematic in the *H.* (48.2n. *pietatem*). The compound *collaudo* (a Livian favourite) is only here in T. (cf. *laudo* 90×), drawing attention to Vitellius' devalued praise, lavished on undeserving soldiers, who have just demanded Verginius Rufus' life. Cf. *militum deinde uirtutem collaudauit* (Liv. 26.48.4), where Publius Scipio rightly praises his soldiers after their successful assault on New Carthage.   **frementibus auxiliis:** 6.2n. *fremere miles.* The participle is concessive (GL §609).   **tantum impunitatis atque arro-gantiae legionariis accessisse** 'that the legionaries had been allowed so much leeway and arrogant behaviour'. *accedo* (*OLD* 15c) 'to be given to', often with abstract qualities as the subject (*tantum impunitatis atque arrogantiae*), takes the dat. (*legionariis*). Cf. *plus socordiae quam fiduciae accessisse uictoribus* (3.2.1). *tantum* + the partitive genitives *impuni-tatis* and *arrogantiae* focalise the legionaries through the indignant auxiliaries: first, the riot goes unpunished, now the arrogant legionaries smugly enjoy their immunity, after Vitellius' undeserved praise. The sophisticated language of the whole clause is belied by the bestial undercurrents of *frementibus* (previous n.). No doubt the auxiliaries' actual words were much coarser.   **in Germaniam remissae:** sc. *sunt.* The original plan was to send them to Britain with the *Legio XIV Gemina*, but it must have seemed more sensible to separate them after the fighting at Augusta Taurinorum. The Batavians are in Germany at 4.15.1.   **principium interno simul externoque bello fatis parantibus:** i.e. the murky Batavian revolt (4.12–37, 4.54–79, 5.14–26), 'almost com-pletely unsupported by other evidence' (Murison (1991) 1707), seen variously as a con-tinuation of the civil war or (in pro-Flavian sources) as a foreign conflict (Walser (1951) 86–128, Brunt (1960), Bessone (1972), Urban (1985)). T.'s description here (also

plerumque permixta, 1.2.1; *mixta belli ciuilis externique facie*, 4.22.2) asserts his independence from these pro-Flavian versions (Levick (1999) 108). *internum bellum* is here first
(4.75.1, *A.* 11.16.1), a variant for the familiar *bellum ciuile*, and then in Augustine (*in
Psalm.* 143.5). The prevalence of internal strife in the Roman state is made clear by
the efforts to find creative alternative expressions: e.g. *bellum interneciuum* (Cic. *Dom.* 61,
Phil. 14.7, Liv. 9.25.9, 22.58.3) or the Ciceronian and Livian favourite *bellum intestinum*
(not in T.). With the appended abl. absolute *parantibus fatis*, T. dramatically juxtaposes
a mundane notice of a troop-movement in the main clause (*cohortes . . . remissae*) and a
dramatic prolepsis of the next conflict prepared by personifed fates (1.1n *struebat . . .
imperio* for *fatum*). As often in T., the main clause is trumped by a subordinate one.
reddita: sc. *sunt.*   **ciuitatibus Gallorum auxilia:** the people of Cologne and
the Treveri and Lingones eagerly contributed resources, including *auxilia*, to Vitellius,
who accepted their help (1.57.2). The more cautious Flavians turn down an offer
of some Sarmatian auxiliaries, considering them vulnerable to bribes and desertion
(3.5.1).   **ingens numerus** evokes the 'barbarian horde' motif (58.1n. *ingens Maurorum numerus*). See 4.2n. *ingens . . . fiducia* for *ingens*.   **prima statim defectione:** i.e.
Vitellius' revolt from Galba. Placing *statim* between *primus* (*uel sim.*) and a dependent
noun is a Livian flourish avoided by Cicero and Caesar (Kraus (1994) 293). Cf. *primo
statim . . . ortu* (*Agr.* 3.1), *primo statim introitu* (1.31.2), *primus statim aspectus* (4.46.3). In the
A., T. abandons it.   **inter inania belli** 'as a form of military window-dressing'
(Wellesley). Cf. *inani auxilio* (2.16.1) to describe Corsican assistance for Vitellius. T. uses
inania as a substantive (also 3.19.2) increasingly in the *A.* (7×). The preposition *inter*
suggests the existence of other empty resources for the war, the most obvious perhaps
being the figurehead of Vitellius himself.

    69.2 largitionibus . . . sufficerent: Vitellius' handout to the praetorians
is his most recent act of largesse (2.67.1), but financial problems still loom (*deesse
pecuniam*, 2.94.2). Cf. Vespasian *egregie firmus aduersus militarem largitionem eoque exercitu
meliore* (2.82.2). The pl. *largitiones* (where a collective singular could have served) suggests excess.   **affectae iam imperii opes** 'the already depleted resources of the
empire'. The empire's financial problems persisted after the civil wars (5.1n. *auaritia*).   **amputari** 'to be reduced' (*OLD amputo* 3b). This verb features most often
for amputating body-parts (2.49.3, 3.84.5, *A.* 1.74.3, 14.64.2, 15.67.4). Its application
here awakens the metaphor of the army as a body (28.2n. *non abrumpendos . . . artus*),
hinting at Vitellius as the deficient 'head' self-destructively cutting off his own 'limbs'.
numeros 'numerical strength' (*OLD numerus* 5).   **uetitis supplementis** 'recruiting was banned'.   **promiscae** 'without distinction'. There were various degrees of
military discharge, full and conditional (Goodyear (1972) 266 on *A.* 1.36.3), through
whose controlled application Vitellius could have staggered payments and selected
the most suitable men for retirement. The current random procedure defeats the
purpose of the exercise.   **exitiabile:** sc. *erat.* Chilver (1979) 230, uncertain about
how this move harmed the whole empire, suspects exaggeration, but T. perhaps thinks
of long-term financial damage, which obliged Vespasian to run his economy tightly
(5.1n. *auaritia*). Dismissing soldiers on a large scale could cause problems (as it did

notoriously after the republican civil wars), especially. as these troops included auxiliaries, mostly recruited in the provinces (Campbell (1984) 12) and perhaps apt to
cause trouble in unfamiliar terrain. The dispersal of retired legionaries could also
cause concern: when Tiberius contemplates touring the provinces, one of his reasons
is to supervise the discharge of the veterans (*A.* 4.4.2 with MW 98). T. uses *exitiabilis*
(again 3.22.3; 5× in the *A.*) more selectively than the virtual synonym *exitiosus* (19×
in total).   **ingratum** (sc. *erat*) 'was unpopular'.   **inter paucos:** the prepositional
phrase economically does the job of a causal subordinate clause, *cum pauciores essent*
(as *inter infensos uel obnoxios*, 1.1.1; *inter gaudentes et incuriosos*, 1.34.2; *inter discordes*, 2.92.1).
periculaque et labor: this combination (favoured by Caes., Sall.) was especially
unwelcome to the Vitellian troops, who relished beating Vindex *sine labore ac periculo*
(1.51.1). Cf. *exercitus . . . neque periculi neque laboris patiens* (Sall. *Jug.* 44.1). The idealised
Agricola especially liked *labor et periculum* (*Agr.* 18.5).   **luxu:** 11.3n. *nec . . . luxu iter.*
Vitellius' soldiers progressively deteriorate after the victory (62.1n. *assuetudine uoluptatum*).   **contra ueterem disciplinam:** T. likes to evoke 'traditional discipline'
as a standard which soldiers explicitly fail to meet (1.5.2, *A.* 1.35.1). This Ciceronian expression (e.g. *Verr.* 2.2.7, 2.3.137) is also in Livy (9.31.9; cf. *antiqua disciplina*,
45.35.6, 45.37.2) and Velleius Paterculus (*uetus disciplina deserta*, 2.1.1).   **et instituta
maiorum:** ancestral practices feature as a yardstick again (*A.* 2.2.3, 14.43.1, 16.28.2),
typical in Roman historiography (Ginsburg (1993)). Sallust has a whole survey of *instituta maiorum* and how modern standards have declined from that acme of excellence
(*Cat.* 5.9).   **apud quos uirtute quam pecunia res Romana melius stetit:**
T. musters the moralising weight of Ennius as a finale (*moribus antiquis stat res Romana
uirisque, A.* 156 Sk.; quoted at Cic. *Rep.* 5.1, SHA *Auidius* 5.7), as others had done before
(e.g. *disciplinam militarem, qua stetit ad hanc diem Romana res*, Liv. 8.7.16, and *mores . . . uiros,
pref.* 9 with Ogilvie (1970) 27; cf. Ov. *Met.* 14.808–9). Cicero quotes the line from Ennius
in a context where (again) contemporary practice falls short of ancestral standards,
evoking a time when *ueterem morem ac maiorum instituta retinebant excellentes uiri* (*Rep.* 5.1). T.
probably alludes both to Ennius and to Cicero (cf. *res Romanas diutius stare non posse, Att.*
1.18.2), but the primacy of money at Rome is also a theme in Sallust's *Jugurtha* (*Romae
omnia uenalia, Jug.* 8.2; cf. 20.1, 31.25, 35.10). By changing Ennius' present tense *stat*
to the perfect *stetit*, T. reinforces the distinction between the debased contemporary
world and the higher standards of the early republic. Ennius' quote was probably
in the elder Manlius' speech while delivering his son, Torquatus, to the lictor to be
condemned to death: he had killed the Gaul, but broken a military order (Skutsch
(1985) 317–18). If so, T. again alludes to Torquatus and the Gaul (as at 2.68.2).

   70.1 Inde: from Ticinum.   **Cremonam flexit** 'turned off to Cremona'. If
flecto = 'change direction' (*OLD* 5), T. always uses the verb intransitively. There are
precedents in Livy (3.8.6, 27.43.12), who generally uses it transitively (with *uia, iter*
etc.).   **spectato munere Caecinae:** the epitomised Dio also says that Vitellius
watched his officers' gladiatorial shows, but the original text probably made more
explicit the horror of viewing a show amidst bodies lying unburied on the battlefield
(65.1.3). T. allows the point to emerge more simply and powerfully, by juxtaposition

(Keitel (1992) 344). This chapter is packed with references to watching (*lustrare oculis, spectaculum, intueri, non Vitellius flexit oculos*); perhaps we too are meant to feel uneasy as voyeurs of such a shameful scene (35.2n. *in oculis* on warped spectatorship; 61n. *spectante Vitellio* on Vitellius' menacing gaze).   **insistere Bedriacensibus campis** 'to set foot on the plain of Bedriacum'. Victorious generals survey battlefields elsewhere (Caesar at Pharsalus, Luc. 7.786–96; Hannibal at Cannae, Liv. 22.51.5–9, Sil. 10.449– 53), but with negative connotations; and at least Caesar and Hannibal participated in the action, unlike Vitellius, seeing this carnage for the first time. T.'s Vitellius is a man 'who, as a spectator of his own life, is most noted for his absence from its major events' (McGillicuddy (1991) 170). The parallel tradition has a similar scene (Suet. *Vit.* 10.3, Dio 65.1.3), so the common source probably featured the visit. It suggests closure, albeit illusory as the Vitellians will fight the next battle against the Flavians on the same site (3.15–31). The next battlefield tour will pointedly be by Julius Agrestis, who peruses the site of the Flavian victory as he tries to persuade Vitellius that he has really lost (3.54.2). 'An aftermath narrative affords an author the opportunity to explore the intertwining nexus of past, present, and future' (Pagán (2000) 425). For other such scenes, see Sall. *Cat.* 61, *Jug.* 101.11, Stat. *Theb.* 12.1–59.   **uestigia recentis uictoriae:** echoes of passages where *uestigia* refer to literary predecessors (Hor. *Ars* 286–7, Stat. *Theb* 12.816–17) suggest that we should filter T.'s account through his original depiction of the battle and other passages about visits to battlefields in the literary tradition (Manolaraki (2005) 260). It also points forward to Antonius Primus taunting those wanting to delay the Flavian campaign: *iuuabit sequi et uestigiis uincentis insistere* (3.2.4).   **lustrare oculis** alludes to Lucan's Caesar's warped gaze in viewing the battlefield at Pharsalus (*iuuat . . . | . . . lustrare oculis campos sub clade latentes*, 7.794–5), although T. may mute the sensationalism by placing it at the start of his description before Vitellius has visited the battlefield (Manolaraki (2005) 259). Where Vitellius only plays Caesar after the battle, his lieutenants had taken on that role during the campaign (Morgan (1994a)).   **concupiuit:** the concept of 'desire' jars in the context, as the subsequent description will show, but perhaps Vitellius has no idea what he is about to see; indeed, a man who was *uictoriae suae nescius* (2.57.1) may essentially want to verify through autopsy (more reliable than talk, *D.* 8.2) that he really has won. In the passage where T. imitates this one, Germanicus' *cupido* (more respectable) is to pay his last respects to Varus and his legions (*A.* 1.61.1; cf. *A.* 2.54.1 and 2.2n. *illum cupido*), not to view a macabre battlefield. T.'s Germanicus, as often, sets a pattern, to be perverted later by more dubious characters. Vitellius' men will soon mirror his behaviour, as they ghoulishly rush to the forum, seized *cupidine uisendi locum, in quo Galba iacuisset* (2.88.3).   **foedum et atrox spectaculum:** cf. *spectaculum horribile* (Sall. *Jug.* 101.11), *dulcia . . . trucibus spectacula Poenis* (Sil. 10.453), *ad . . . foedam . . . etiam hostibus spectandam stragem* (Liv. 22.51.5). Vocabulary accentuating the visual is central to all 'aftermath narratives' (Pagán (2000) 432–3), but T. pointedly trumps Vitellius' gaze with his own damning view of the scene, sharpened by two censorious adjectives (Manolaraki (2005) 249). He also inverts his own jaunty description of Agricola's clash with the Britons at Mons Graupius: *grande et atrox spectaculum* (*Agr.* 37.2). Yet death can lead to uplifting spectacles, as with the *insigne atque etiam memorabile . . . spectaculum* of Verginius Rufus' funeral (Plin. *Ep.* 2.1.1). See especially Keitel (1992). **intra quadragensimum pugnae diem** 'less than 40 days had elapsed since the engagement' (Wellesley); *c.* 23 May. T.'s formulation indicates that the carnage is still pretty fresh, although old enough for putrefaction to have set in. In most other instances, such tours happen soon after the fighting, explicitly (*postero die* Liv. 22.51.5, *tum* Sall. *Jug.* 101.11, *postquam clara dies* Luc. 7.787, *reduci . . . Phoebo* Stat. *Theb.* 12.4) or by implication (Sall. *Cat.* 61.1, Sil. 10.450). Even six years after a battle, there can be gruesome remnants, as in the site of Varus' disaster (*sextum post cladis annum, A.* 1.62.1). **lacera . . . uastitas:** the asyndeton (effective in such contexts: cf. *sequi, fugere, occidi, capi,* Sall. *Jug.* 101.11) juxtaposes six brutal clauses where the adj. or complement always precedes the noun(s) with which it agrees (itself a form of *uariatio* in T.; 22.2n. *subruit . . . portas*). Combining syntactical tautness and visual crescendo, T. moves from a trio of references to bodies (*corpora, artus, formae*), to two allusions to the terrain (*humus, arboribus ac frugibus*), to a single term summarising the whole scene (*uastitas*). **lacera corpora:** these corpses, now left unburied (45.3n. *ceterum . . . relictum*), impeded the Othonian retreat (*obstructae strage corporum uiae,* 2.44.1). In Statius there is a pitiful competition for the *informes trunci* (*Theb.* 12.33) among grieving relatives, but even more grimly in T., nobody bothers to compete for these soldiers' remains. The combination *corpus* + the verbal form *laceratum* is common from Ennius onwards (and T. has it at 3.74.2), but Livy (1.28.10) and Sallust (*Hist.* 3.98) prefer *corpus* + the adj. *lacerum* (also in Ov., Luc., Plin. the Elder, Stat.). **trunci artus:** such body-parts are a grimly common feature of aftermath narratives: *laceri artus* (*Agr.* 37.3), *recisae . . . manus* (Stat. *Theb.* 12.29–30). The 'rhetoric of dismemberment' (associated especially with Senecan tragedy, Lucan and Flavian epic) is ubiquitous in post-Augustan poetics (Most (1992)). Since the body and its parts can also supply a vocabulary for the style of ancient texts (e.g. Quint. 8.5.27), it is apt that T. describes the mutilated remains in such clipped, truncated language. **putres uirorum equorumque formae:** the long syllables and triple assonance of *-or-* enhances the sense of desolation (cf. Ferri (2003) 126–7). Dead horses often feature in aftermath narratives (*A.* 1.61.3, Sall. *Jug.* 101.11) and living ones can add poignancy (Hom. *Il.* 17.426–7, Sil. 10.458–71; *uiduis . . . equis,* Stat. *Theb.* 12.26–7, Virg. *A.* 11.89–90). The time elapsed since the battle means that identifying these men would be impossible, as *putres* reminds us (cf. *confusaeque ingentem caedis aceruum,* Virg. *A.* 11.207). **infecta tabo humus:** T. trumps his earlier description of a battlefield's *cruenta humus* (*Agr.* 37.3) with an expressive phrase that he will recall after the next battle of Bedriacum (*noxia tabo humus* 3.35.1). He also alludes to Sallust on the site of one of Marius' victories over Jugurtha (*humus infecta sanguine, Jug.* 101.11), but substitutes *tabum,* perhaps because *sanguis* (inappropriately) implies fresh blood rather than putrid matter. The substitution also echoes Virgil's cataclysmic vision of the cattle-plague, where Tisiphone piles up *turpi dilapsa cadauera tabo* (*G.* 3.557). There is a grim topos elsewhere that former battlefields (such as Philippi, Virg. *G.* 1.493–7) will often become fertile (Parker (1992); 'The blood of England shall manure the ground | And future ages groan for this foul act', Shakespeare, *Richard II* IV.1.137–8), but *infecta* points instead to pollution (cf. *quae seges infecta surget non decolor herba?*, Luc. 7.851). **protritis arboribus ac frugibus:** the detail reinforces the motif that the destruction of agriculture is a hallmark of civil war (56.1n. *refertos agros*). Yet some trees survive to offer Antonius Primus a tactical advantage in the next battle (*densis arbustis*, 3.21.2).

70.2 nec minus inhumana pars uiae: sc. *erat*. With the *nec minus* (or *haud minus*) transitional formula (without *quam*), T. switches between episodes or components of a scene, taking an element from the first and identifying it in the next (*nec minus saeuum spectaculum*, 2.88.3; also *A.* 1.68.1, 2.34.2, 4.1.3, 14.14.1, 15.67.3, 16.10.1). This often allows caustic or witty links. Here T. transfers the people's lack of humanity to the physical landscape marred by them, with the paradox that items as diverse as rotting corpses and flowers can indicate identical callousness. *inhumanus* (also 3.83.3, of indifference to slaughter), a Ciceronian favourite (also in Liv., but not in Sall. or Caes.), only features in the *H*. **Cremonenses . . . construauerant:** this verb only appears once more in T. in an equally grim context: *constrata equorum uirorumque corporibus litora* (*A.* 2.25.3). The compound rather than the simple *sterno* enables the enveloping alliteration (4.1n. *pandi . . . prosperum*). **lauru rosaque:** these are incongruous symbols of peace and celebration against such a bloody backdrop (55.1n. *cum lauru*). *rosa* is a collective singular (cf. *multa . . . in rosa*, Hor. *Carm.* 1.5.1, with Nisbet and Hubbard (1970) 74). Scattering roses was a way to express happiness (Lucr. 2.626, Hor. *Carm.* 3.19.21–2, Ov. *Am.* 1.2.40, *Fast.* 5.336, 5.360, Stat. *Silu.* 1.2.19, Suet. *Nero* 25.2), but here the flash of colour recalls the blood that stains the battlefield. **exstructis altaribus:** 34.2n. on *struo / exstruo.* **caesisque uictimis:** the context is sacrifice (probably of cattle), but the formulation makes us think of the human victims from the battle; and 'slaughtering like cattle' is a motif of historiographical battle-descriptions since Sallust (Woodman (1977) 202). With similar irony, Sabinus cries that *has Seiano uictimas cadere* (*A.* 4.70.1). For a more subdued battlefield sacrifice, see Virg. *A.* 11.197–9. **regium in morem** 'in the manner appropriate for a king'. Although the impetus is from the locals, the association of Vitellius with monarchy damningly evokes foreign dynasts and the regal period at Rome: cf. *Vrbem Romam a principio reges habuere* (*A.* 1.1.1). T. also recalls Nero (*regiae amicitiae*, *A.* 13.42.4; *oblectamenta regia*, *A.* 14.16.2). With this choice expression (again only at Flor. 2.7.10), T. varies the more familiar *more regio* (*A.* 6.1.1). The 'sandwiching' of the preposition emphasises the adj. (3.2n. *tenuem in ambitum*). **laeta in presens:** the *peripeteia* of ephemeral joy becoming misery is a motif from tragedy and historiography. The *locus classicus* is Solon advising the tyrant Croesus that no man should be called happy until he is dead (Hdt. 1.32). The short-lived happiness of the Cremonese recalls the joyful mood at Rome (2.55.1), soon to be shattered. These general hints of trouble ahead are becoming more insistent (the death of Vitellius' son, 2.59.3; the Batavian revolt, 2.69.1). **mox perniciem ipsis fecere** 'soon proved devastating to themselves', i.e. the destruction of Cremona by Flavian troops (3.33), angry at the citizens' pro-Vitellian stance (3.32.2). The oracular tone recalls T. on Arrius Varus' ill-gotten promotion, *laeta ad praesens . . . mox in perniciem uertere* (3.6.1). The periphrastic construction *facio* + acc. of the internal object (GL §332–3, *NLS*

§13), instead of a single verb (e.g. *perdo*), adds grandeur (cf. *idque ipsis perniciem adferret*, *A.* 1.79.1). Cf. *perniciem . . . facit* (Sen. *Ben.* 5.12.6).

70.3 Aderant . . . monstrabant: pl. verbs with two singular subjects (24.3n. *Paulinus . . . Celsus sumpsere*). The macabre device of buoyant tour-guides of the battlefield (not in Suet. or Dio) also features at Cannae (*praebebat . . . spectacula*, Sil. 10.453), while Statius has *dolor* and *luctus* serve as bloody battlefield guides (*Theb.* 12.23–4). T. has *cladis eius superstites* (*A.* 1.61.4) recreate Varus' disaster, but otherwise the narrator himself serves as a guide to the (unmediated) scene (Luc. 7.786–96, Liv. 22.51.5–9, Sall. *Cat.* 61, *Jug.* 101.11). T. creatively moves from an authorial tour (2.70.1–2) to one guided by internal protagonists (2.70.3). Their unified front here belies fragmentation at the start of the battle (2.41.2).   **hinc . . . hinc . . . inde:** similar demonstrative devices, conducive to *enargeia*, feature in the visit to the site of Varus' disaster (*hic . . . illic . . . ubi . . . ubi . . . quo . . . quot . . . quae . . . ut*, *A.* 1.61.4) and when Virgil's Trojans explore the deserted Greek camp (*hic . . . hic . . . hic . . . hic*, *A.* 2.29–30; Woodman (1998) 74). Here the device hints at accompanying gestures from the excited generals (Manolaraki (2005) 250).   **irrupisse legionum agmen . . . equites coortos:** the generals pointedly reverse the order of events laid down by T. as narrator, suggesting that the start of fighting was more organised than it was and drawing a veil over the disobedience of the cavalry, which nearly ended in disaster: *equites prorupere . . . disposita Vitellianarum legionum acies* (2.41.2; cf. *pulso equite* 2.44.3).   **circumfusas auxiliorum manus** 'the auxiliaries had overwhelmed (the enemy)'. *circumfundo* is used reflexively here (*OLD* 3b). The generals refer to the charge of the Batavians at the end of the battle (*latus hostium inuecti*, 2.43.2). Their edited highlights and selective concentration on the start and finish of the fighting is misleading, lulling Vitellius (but not us) into thinking that victory was easy.   **iam** at the start of a sentence (or clause) 'brings one into the centre of the action, an epic technique developed in prose by Livy' (Kraus (1994) 114); cf. 1.2.2, 1.37.5, 1.39.1, 3.2.4, 3.31.1, 3.60.2.   **tribuni praefectique:** yet T. says nothing about their activities in his narrative of the battle itself.   **sua quisque facta extollentes:** singular distributive pronoun with the pl. participle (44.1n. *suum obiectantes*). *sua* and *quisque* appear in the usual prose order (*OLD quisque* 2).   **falsa uera aut maiora uero miscebant** 'were blending lies with truth (or with an exaggeration of the truth)'. With *aut*, T. ostentatiously corrects himself (*OLD aut* 6b), pushing truth from the picture as the fictionalised account of the battle supplants what really happened. The self-aggrandising may not have been entirely wilful: it was (and is) notoriously difficult for an individual to assess the impact of his own deeds on the whole battle (Plut. *Oth.* 14.1).   **clamore et gaudio** 'with joyful shouting'. The hendiadys (also *gaudio clamoribusque*, 4.49.3) makes us linger on an emotional outburst that seems peculiarly incongruous with the grim scene.   **deflectere . . . recognoscere . . . armorum . . . corporum intueri mirari:** the asyndeton and homoioteleuton of paired words allows an acceleration through the sentence that reflects the soldiers' increasing excitement at their surroundings (Chausserie-Laprée (1969) 476). So too does T.'s use of historic infinitives (5.1n. *anteire . . . obniti*).   **recognoscere:** the compound (again only at *Agr.* 6.5) is much less common in T. than the simple *cognosco*. The prefix reminds us that although the common soldiers had been present, Vitellius was there for the first time.   **aggerem armorum:** commentators compare *A*. 2.18.2, the *agger* constructed by legionaries after defeating the Germans and piled with arms *in modum tropaeorum*. If it is such a monument, it is disturbing that the Vitellians celebrate victory over fellow-citizens in this way. Yet this pile of weapons is probably just left over from the battle, especially as the soldiers look at it with wonder (less plausible if they themselves had built it as a monument to victory); and elsewhere T. normally identifies such structures as celebratory (*A*. 2.22.1). If the pile of weapons is random, it suggests Vitellian carelessness in leaving such a valuable resource for the enemy.   **strues corporum:** Plutarch's friend Mestrius Florus after the battle saw corpses implausibly heaped up around a temple, an arrangement regarded as *mirabile* and requiring explanation (*Oth*. 14.2). **erant quos uaria sors rerum lacrimaeque et misericordia subiret** 'there were some who were moved to tears by the mutability of human life'. T. allows a singular verb (*subiret*) to attach to the last of a number of preceding subjects (Goodyear (1981) 77–8 on *A*. 1.56.2; also *manebat*, 1.76.2; *sit*, 1.84.2; *uidebatur*, 2.78.2; *sperabatur*, 3.60.1). *erant quos* implies that the emotional response came from only some of those present. T.'s account of burying Varus and his men suggests the appropriate response: *permoto ad miserationem omni qui aderat exercitu ob propinquos, amicos, denique ob casus bellorum et sortem hominum* (*A*. 1.61.1). After the original battle, everyone had cried (*uicti uictoresque in lacrimas effusi, sortem ciuilium armorum misera laetitia detestantes*, 2.45.3), but the time elapsed has apparently hampered the soldiers' ability to respond appropriately. T. also alludes to Virgil's Aeneas, whose cathartic tears after gazing on images of the Trojan war on Dido's temple reflect his bitter-sweet joy that even Carthaginians can empathise with their fate: *hic etiam . . . sunt lacrimae rerum* (*A*. 1.461–2). The Carthaginians' humanity contrasts sharply with some of the Roman voyeurs, who fail to empathise with dead fellow-citizens.

   70.4 at: transitional *at* (20.1n. *At*).   **non Vitellius flexit oculos:** wry ring-composition with *flexit* (2.70.1) at the start, as Vitellius compounds his initial error of judgement (diverting his route to Cremona) by now failing to avert his gaze. The formulation in terms of what Vitellius fails to do implicitly shows the proper response to such carnage. Looking away could alleviate shame and guilt (always intensified by being watched): cf. the legionaries surrendering after the Caudine Forks, whose humiliation is exacerbated *per hostium oculos* (Liv. 9.6.3). The motif of the bloodthirsty gaze is also part of the stereotypical tyrant. So Sulla has the severed heads of the proscribed brought to him *ut oculis illa, quia ore nefas erat, manderet* (Val. Max. 9.2.1; cf. 3.39.1, Suet. *Vit*. 14.2, Cic. *Verr*. 5.65, *Phil*. 11.8).   **tot milia insepultorum ciuium:** even Hannibal at Cannae buried the Roman dead (Liv. 22.52.6, Sil. 10.558–75). T.'s *ciues* is emotive, but more restrained than Suetonius, whose Vitellius distastefully asserts that *optime olere occisum hostem et melius ciuem* (*Vit*. 10.3). T. wanted to horrify, but not to disgust (Morgan (1992) 28). This combination of number (*milia*), moving detail (*insepultorum*) and status of the dead (*ciuium*) recurs in Galba's entry to Rome: *trucidatis tot milibus inermium militum* (1.6.2). Cf. *iacebant tot Romanorum milia* at Cannae (Liv. 2.51.6).

T., like most Roman authors, can alter his tone depending on the identity of the dead (*magnam uictoriam tot milibus hostium caesis . . . celebrari, Agr.* 39.1; *caesi hostes decem milia passuum cadaueribus . . . oppleuere, A.* 2.18.1).   **laetus:** a grossly inappropriate response to the sight; cf. Caesar at Pharsalus (*iuuat,* Luc. 7.794). The spectacle of the carnage at Cannae is *foedam . . . etiam hostibus* (Liv. 22.51.5) and the soldiers at Pharsalus have terrible nightmares (*uaesana quies,* Luc. 7.764).   **tam propinquae sortis ignarus . . . dis loci:** T.'s description of Vitellius' sacrifice inauspiciously recalls Galba, who shortly before his fall, *ignarus . . . et sacris intentus fatigabat alieni iam imperii deos* (1.29.1).   **instaurabat sacrum** 'offered a sacrifice'. *instauro* (common in Livy) appears only once more in T., again in the context of death (Tiberius' imminent demise, *A.* 6.50.3).

71.1 Exim: T. always prefers this compact form (here first) to the unsyncopated *exinde* (also 4.25.4, 34× in the *A.*, never in the minor works). Livy has it once (27.5.6: cf. *exinde* 10×), but it is not in Sall. or Caes.; WM 152.   **gladiatorum spectaculum editur:** see 2.67.2 for the preparations. This notice of the show so soon after the warped spectatorship on the battlefield distastefully blurs the distinction between entertainment and warfare, but T. has no need to comment directly. It is the 'bookend' to the earlier notice of Caecina's show (*spectato munere,* 2.70.1).   **aduecto ex urbe cultu** 'after equipment was brought from Rome'. The striking *cultus* (*OLD* 6b; Curt. 10.2.24) also suggests the splendour of the gladiatorial gear. Specialised equipment was crucial for distinguishing different kinds of fighters, but also 'precious metals and intricate craftsmanship broadcast the liberality of the *editor*' (Wiedemann (1992) 119). The most substantial find of (unambiguously) gladiatorial equipment was in the barracks at Pompeii in 1766–7. Many items are lavishly embossed and decorated, so some identify them as parade equipment, but this has recently been questioned (Köhne and Ewigleben (2000) 38–45).   **propinquabat:** sc. *urbi.*; simple for compound form of verb (18.1n. *si propinquaret*). The destination (Rome) has to be understood from the previous sentence (*ex urbe*), while the subject (Vitellius and his entourage) becomes clear from the pejorative description that follows.   **quanto . . . tanto:** ablatives of the measure of difference (GL §403).   **corruptius iter:** sc. *erat.* The idea that vice gravitates towards Rome is a topos, especially after the acquisition of empire (Sall. *Cat.* 37.5, Prop. 2.23.21, Luc. 9.429–30, T. *A.* 15.44.3, Juv. 3.62, 6.295–7), but the corrupting influences are cast as foreign more often than domestic.   **immixtis histrionibus et spadonum gregibus et cetero Neronianae aulae ingenio:** 'since it was joined by actors, gangs of eunuchs and everything else that was typical of Nero's court'. For T., troops being mixed with other elements is symptomatic of civil war (Damon (2003) 180). The abstract noun *ingenium* (*OLD* 2) indicates the inherent nature of something, leaving the audience to supply colourful details from the imagination (Sörbom (1935) 75–6 for *uariatio* of abstract + concrete nouns). With the three ablatives in a tricolon crescendo, T.'s syntax mirrors the burgeoning scale of the procession (and overwhelms the main clause); and the number of disreputable hangers-on will continue to rise as Vitellius approaches Rome (*scurrae histriones aurigae* 2.87.2; these sorts of people allegedly even influence Vitellius' political decisions, Suet. *Vit.* 12).

With *spadonum gregibus* (a choice combination also at Curt. 6.6.8, Suet. *Tit.* 7.1), T. alludes to Horace's scornful description of Cleopatra's entourage of eunuchs (*contaminato cum grege turpium,* | *morbo uirorum, Carm.* 1.37.9–10), also echoed in his description of Nero's associates (*illo contaminatorum grege, A.* 15.37.4, with Woodman (1998) 181). **Neronem ipsum Vitellius admiratione celebrabat** 'Vitellius had always been an admirer of Nero himself'. The idea that Vitellius and Nero shared character-traits is pervasive in the literary tradition (Ash (1999) 104–5), no doubt reflecting Flavian orthodoxy after Vespasian's victory. So Philostratus' Euphrates simply calls Vitellius Nero's image (*VA* 5.33). Vitellius tried to cash in on Nero's popularity, especially after reaching Rome (2.95.1, Suet. *Vit.* 11.2, Dio 65.7.3). T. could have placed this flashback about Vitellius' admiration for Nero anywhere, but here it prompts us to read his whole principate as filtered through Neronian ideology.   **sectari cantantem solitus** 'having habitually accompanied him on his singing tours'. T. uses *sector,* the frequentative form of *sequor,* pejoratively again for satellites courting the powerful (*A.* 4.1.2, 15.33.3).   **necessitate, qua honestissimus quisque:** sc. *sectari eum solitus est.* The implicit point of comparison is Vespasian, who apparently once fell asleep while Nero was singing (cf. Suet. *Nero* 23.2 for the extreme measures people took to escape the theatre during such perfomances). T. and Suetonius both have the story, but place it at different times and places (Rome in 65, *A.* 16.5.3; Greece in 66, *Ves.* 4.4. Cf. Dio 63.10.1a, 66.11). T. omits Vespasian's name in favour of the generalising *honestissimus quisque,* no doubt keen to avoid a charge of uncritically accepting pro-Flavian propaganda. Vespasian cannot have upset Nero unduly, despite his undiplomatic napping, as in 67 he was sent to repress the Judaean revolt (Levick (1999) 25).   **luxu et saginae mancipatus emptusque** '(because he was) enslaved and bound to luxury and gluttony'; sentence-terminal *-que* (2.2n. *aduenasque*). The two participles mask a causal connection with what precedes, showing *uariatio* after the abl. *necessitate* (giving the rejected reason). For *luxus* (here dat.), see 11.3n. *nec . . . luxu iter.* The gladiatorial associations of *sagina* (3× in T., all applied to Vitellius or his men: 1.62.2, 2.88.1) are pointed. Gladiators traditionally ate barley porridge (Plin. *Nat.* 18.72) 'to build up the body fat in order to give them the maximum possible protection against sword-cuts, and maximum weight for combat' (Wiedemann (1992) 116). Using this diction selectively, T. shows the degradation of the troops at their emperor's hands (Keitel (1992) 346).

71.2 Vt Valenti et Caecinae uacuos honoris menses aperiret 'to open up a few months of office (free) for Valens and Caecina'. The predicative adj. (GL §325) *uacuos* (*OLD* 6) agreeing with *menses* is slightly pleonastic after *aperio* (*OLD* 9). There might seem to be a hint of a critical reading, with *uacuos* (*OLD* 2) as 'a few illusory months of office' (i.e. a damning gloss from T.). That possibility is eliminated when we realise from the main clause that this subordinate clause indicates purpose (Vitellius would not deliberately allocate illusory honours), not result.   **coartati aliorum consulatus:** sc. *sunt.* Valerius Maximus used *coarto* in the novel sense of restricting time (4.1.3, Suet. *Aug.* 34.2). Here it creates enveloping alliteration (4.1n. *pandi . . . prosperum*) with *consulatus.* Otho, behaving 'as if the time were one of profound peace', similarly made consular arrangements (1.77.2), which Vitellius now alters to disperse patronage. The situation was that Otho and his brother Titianus were consuls to the end of February, Verginius Rufus and Pompeius Vopiscus for March, Caelius Sabinus and Flavius Sabinus until the end of June, and Arrius Antoninus and Marius Celsus until the end of August. It was this last pair whose consulships were reduced, as Otho had originally chosen them to serve from Jul.–Sept. 69. The end of the year was where Vitellius intervened most heavily. For Oct.–Dec., Galba had chosen Valerius Marinus and Pedanius Costa, but Otho relegated them to serve one month (Oct.) in favour of his own nominees, Martius Macer and Quinctius Atticus (to serve from Nov.–Dec.). Vitellius' interventions thus secured Sept.–Dec. for his two generals (Townend (1962b) 113–29, Chilver (1979) 140–1 on the consuls of 69). That he did this in a party atmosphere after the pair has put on shows to honour him does him little credit. **dissimulatus** 'was ignored' (*OLD dissimulo* 3). **tamquam** 'on the ground of being' (*OLD tamquam* 7b). Causal *tamquam* without a finite verb is a Livian innovation. **Marti Macri:** 23.3n. *Martio Macro*. **Valerium Marinum:** *RE* VIII 54–5. Although Marinus (only here in T.) was designated consul by Galba, he was on good terms with Otho, as he was one of the Arval brethren from 30 Jan. to 14 Mar. (*CIL* VI 2051). Pliny the Elder, celebrating the utility of flaxen sails, says that Marinus, one of the praetorian senators, sailed from Puteoli to Alexandria in 9 days in the summer of 69, despite a very gentle breeze (*Nat.* 19.3). He was presumably joining Vespasian after Vitellius had snubbed him. **nulla offensa** 'not for any offence'; causal abl. **mitem et iniuriam segniter laturum** 'because he was a mild man and would accept the snub without resentment'. The syntax succinctly avoids a long subordinate clause introduced by a conjunction; a causal sense must be supplied to the adj. and future participle from *nulla offensa*. Vitellius assumes wrongly, judging from Marinus' swift trip to Egypt (Pliny, *Nat.* 19.3). **Pedanius Costa omittitur:** all our surviving sources pass over Costa (only here in T.). Vitellius' festering dislike of him recalls his *odium* towards Junius Blaesus (2.59.2), except that the emperor (bolder now) will deprive Blaesus of his life, rather than a consulship (3.38–9). **aduersus Neronem ausus:** the third reference to Nero in one chapter continues to associate Vitellius with his dubious predecessor. *audeo* (*OLD* 3), used absolutely without an acc. or an inf. since Ennius, is usually combined with *contra* or *in* (even in T.; *A.* 4.59.3, cf. 14.7.4): *aduersus* adds assonance, helping the clause to cohere. **exstimulator** this colourful agent noun is only in T. (*A.* 3.40.1; WM 329), but Cicero has *instimulator* (*Dom.* 11), another hapax. **alias protulit causas:** T. does not bother to give them. The gulf between words and real motives epitomises T.'s vision of the principate (especially in the *A.*), where people rarely say what they mean (unless death is imminent). The emperor Tiberius, the worst offender, is the most difficult for characters in the text (and outside it) to read (*A.* 4.71.3). **actaeque:** sc. *sunt*. **insuper:** 11.2n. *deforme insuper auxilium*. **gratiae:** the senate has already carefully thanked the German army (2.55.2; cf. 4.39.1 where the Flavian troops are thanked). People giving thanks to *principes* for situations foisted on them against their will (a survival technique) recurs in T. and elsewhere (*Agr.* 42.2, *A.* 6.25.3, 12.26.1, 14.56.3, Sen. *De ira* 2.33.2, *De tranq.*

14.4). In one outburst, T. claims that the gods are habitually thanked whenever Nero orders an exile or execution (*A.* 14.64.3; cf. 15.71.1).

72.1 Non ultra paucos dies . . . mendacium: T. undercuts the importance of the event, anticipating its failure right from the start. The impostor's story (Morgan (1993a) 776–81), told retroactively when Vitellius puts him to death at Bononia, could have appeared earlier. Locating it here prompts unflattering comparisons between Vitellius (the upstart emperor) and Geta (the runaway slave) and raises fundamental questions about Roman identity during civil war. T. deliberately evokes the genre of Roman comedy in relating the incident, uncomfortably blurring the boundaries between reality and pretence in both inner and outer frames. If Geta is an implausible servile impostor, what is Vitellius? He is not a lowly slave, but he shares many of the same servile and play-acting traits (and he is now surrounded by actors himself, 2.71.1). Farcical elements of the inner frame spill over into the serious outer frame. **quamquam acribus initiis coeptum:** *quamquam* lacks finite verb (3.2n. *quamquam in aperto*) and the clause shows pleonasm (68.1n. *orta . . . initio*). T. ends another digression on debt similarly (*acribus . . . initiis, incurioso fine, A.* 6.17.4), a 'typically Tacitean coda' (Martin (2001) 139). Here, a summarising device at the start of the episode recalls Roman comedy, where the *argumentum* anticipates the main action of the plot.   **mendacium ualuit:** abstract noun as subject (2.1n. *spes uicit*). Not all servile impersonators are as shifty as this one: cf. *egregio mendacio* (4.50.2), contrived by a slave masquerading as his master to save him. There is a (bathetic) parallel in Petronius (*ut duraret . . . tutum mendacium*, 117.5), when Eumolpus and his friends self-consciously concoct a *mimus* (117.4) to enable them to enter the wealthy city of Croton (cf. *seruiliter ficti*, 117.6). **extiterat:** 4.3n. *profligauerat.*   **quidam:** not naming the pretender builds up to the dramatic recognition (*anagnorisis*) at the finale when the impostor is unmasked (Arist. *Po.* 1452a29, 1454b19). In the other two cases of pretenders, the man is either named immediately (2.61) or all available information appears up front (2.8.1).   **Scribonianum se Camerinum ferens:** hyperbaton accentuates the name, but his identity is contentious. Nero executed a father and son named Sulpicius Camerinus in 67 for refusing to relinquish the ancestral *cognomen* Pythicus, now reserved for the emperor's victories (Dio 63.18.2; the notorious prosecutor Aquilius Regulus was instrumental, Plin. *Ep.* 1.5.3). One of these is possible (if the name Scribonianus came through the mother). Yet commentators prefer to identify the man as a son of M. Licinius Crassus Frugi (consul in 64). The father had also been prosecuted by Regulus in 67 and executed (1.48.1, Plin. *Ep.* 1.5.3), and his wife, Sulpicia Praetextata, and four sons resurface later, seeking revenge against the Neronian *delator* (4.42.1). If this identification is correct, the son's name Camerinus comes from a marriage alliance with the Sulpicii. Most significantly, this man was the nephew of Galba's adopted heir Piso Licinianus (Chilver (1979) 232). He thus came from an illustrious family which was related to Pompey the Great (as the *cognomen* Scribonianus indicates; Syme (1960) 18) and whose members had, at different stages, aspired to the principate or attracted the aspirations of those wishing to challenge the emperor (O'Gorman (2006)).   **Neronianorum temporum metu** 'during the Neronian reign of terror'. The homoioteleuton adds

lugubrious resonance to a phrase (coined, as far as we can tell, by Pliny the Younger) uniquely modified by an adj.: cf. *metus temporum*, 1.49.3, Plin. *Ep.* 5.1.7, 7.19.6, 9.13.3.
in Histria: (*OCD³* 'Istria') this peninsula, at the north-eastern head of the Adriatic sea, was a hotbed of pirates under the republic and then backed Pompey in the civil wars. It was incorporated into Italy under Augustus and was relatively near to Vitellius' current location in Bononia (especially by sea). It is only here in T., but was worryingly close to the legions of Pannonia, Dalmatia and Moesia, which would form the backbone of the Flavian forces. Pliny describes the region (*Nat.* 16.66; cf. 3.129).
occultatum . . . quod . . . manebat: *quod* + the indicative gives T.'s explanation (not the impostor's) for Istria as a hiding-place. *occultatum* ('having hidden himself') can either be T.'s viewpoint (identifying Camerinus for his readers) or the impostor's (explaining himself to potential supporters). A (longer) relative clause would have been clearer, but wasted words. It is perhaps best to read both clauses as T.'s comment. T. increasingly prefers *occulto* over *occulo* (13.2n. *occuleret*). **clientelae . . . fauor:** chiastic phrasing binds together the concrete and abstract reasons for choosing Istria as a hiding-place. The family (Syme (1960)) owed much of its wealth to M. Licinius Crassus, consul in 70 BC and *triumuir*, who gained financially from Sulla's proscriptions (Plut. *Cras.* 2 and 6.6). The family, already prominent, won further prestige from marriages, including the union of Crassus Frugi (consul in 27) and Pompey the Great's descendant, Scribonia.

72.2 igitur: 2.2n. **deterrimo quoque in argumentum fabulae assumpto** 'after every scoundrel was assembled for the plot of his play'. The metaphor, 'truly remarkable phraseology for a work such as this' (Morgan (1993a) 778), prompts us to read the episode metatheatrically. From earliest times, Roman history had inspired the *fabula praetexta*, serious drama on historical subjects (Hor. *Ars* 285–8; Flower (1995), Wiseman (1998)), but drama could in turn influence historical narratives. Particular scenes and episodes lent themselves especially well to this mode of presentation. So, Livy uses a theatrical metaphor for Tarquinius' ascent to power (*sceleris tragici exemplum*, 1.46.3), as does T. for the 'drama' of Agrippina the Younger's murder (*scaenam ultro criminis parat*, *A.* 14.7.6) and for Blaesus' downfall (*datae L. Vitellio delationis partes*, 3.38.2). The *argumentum fabulae* is the technical term for the plot of a play (Quint. 5.10.9, Gell. 6.5.5). It was a familiar idea that actors (traditionally lower-class) and satellites of the theatre were adept at inciting trouble, e.g. the mutinous soldier Percennius, *dux olim theatralium operarum* (*A.* 1.16.3; Nippel (1995) 93–4, Horsfall (2003a) 39–42). Yet T. adds novelty as the *deterrimi* 'become' actors precisely in order to instigate violence. **uolgus . . . militum:** the rebels are lower class, as are those who support the other two pretenders: *inopia uagos* (2.8.1), *fanaticam multitudinem* (2.61). **errore ueri seu turbarum studio** 'misled, or looking for trouble' (Irvine). *siue / seu* is omitted from the first explanation (37.1n. *seu*). The second chiasmus in quick succession is peculiarly apt in a chapter whose finale is crucifixion. **aggregabantur:** T. favours this uncomplimentary verb for lower classes or soldiers flocking (without discernment) to a cause (1.27.2, 1.60, 1.64.2, 2.87.2, 3.12.1), but it also applies to more

respectable types jumping on the bandwagon (2.96.1).   **cum:** an inverse *cum*-clause for dramatic effect (36.1n. *cum intercursu*), the same closural device as in the story of the pretender Mariccus (2.61).   **pertractus:** sc. *est.*   **interrogatus:** sc. *est.*   **quis-nam mortalium esset:** *mortales* = grandly archaic (20.1n. *insita mortalibus natura*). The direct question's lofty register, 'Who, pray, might you be?', suggests deliberate mockery. T. uses the emphatic *quisnam* only in indirect questions. Majestic formulae for asking people their identity is an epic motif (Hom. *Od.* 1.170, 10.325, 14.187, 15.264, 19.105, 24.298, *Il.* 21.150, Virg. *A.* 1.326–9, 8.112–14), but was also useful in comic scenes, as when Hercules quotes from Homer to ask Claudius for his identity at the gates of heaven (Sen. *Apoc.* 5.4).   **postquam . . . fides:** sc. *erat* (as at 1.22.2).
noscebatur: this inverts the classic dramatic motif where a protagonist (usually an aristocrat) is recognised by some token which allows resumption of former status (Lowe (2000) 72, 193–4).   **condicione** 'in status' (*OLD* 7).   **fugitiuus:** this slave is a runaway, but the 'running slave' is a motif from Roman comedy. One 'appears in every other play of Plautus' (Gratwick (1987) 242; Brothers (1988) 164–5).   **Geta:** the generic name is an ethnic marker, whatever the slave's origins. The Getae were a Thracian tribe on the lower Danube, often cast by Roman authors as wild warmongerers (cf. *dura pharetrato bella mouente Geta*, Ov. *Pont.* 1.8.6), an apt association here; and in one tradition, the Getae believed themselves to be immortal (Hdt. 4.93), an ironic twist, given Geta's imminent demise (Haynes (2003) 198 n.32). The name also designates slaves in Terence's *Phormio* and *Adelphi*, but these characters are conspicuously loyal, unlike this pretender (Morgan 1993a 779). *astuti . . . Getae* were stock figures in comedy (Prop. 4.5.44).   **sumptum de eo supplicium in seruilem modum** scans as an iambic senarius, ending the episode in a manner 'recalling the metre commonly used in comedies of imposture and recognition' (Morgan (1993a) 780). *in seruilem modum* is a delicate way to indicate crucifixion, the standard method of execution for slaves (Cic. *Clu.* 187, Liv. 22.33.2, Val. Max. 8.4.2, Suet. *Dom.* 10.1, SHA *Pert.* 9.10; Garnsey (1970) 126–9, Watson (1987) 129–33). T. can be more explicit (cf. *patibulo affixus*, 4.3.2; *crucibus affixi, A.* 15.44.4), but perhaps wants to avoid stirring pity for Geta (which could happen; cf. Sen. *De ira* 3.40.1–3). The specification *in seruilem modum* is striking (Geta, as a slave, would normally face crucifixion), but not redundant. The death-notice promptly dispels the playful conceit of a Roman comedy in miniature, as 'the presiding Saturnalian spirit' of that genre always ensures that violence to slaves is postponed (Fitzgerald (2000) 33).

73 Vix credibile memoratu est 'it is scarcely believable to relate'. This pointed emphasis of the boundary between reality and fiction apparently signals a return to the main narrative after the digression. Yet it also suggests a spilling over of the pretender's fictionalised world into the primary account. The Geta episode should, after all, have taught Vitellius to be wary, but he is incredibly complacent. *uix credibile* + *memoratu* are not combined elsewhere in extant Latin (not even by T, though he does have *uix credibile dictu, A.* 1.35.5). Sallustian influence is likely: *incredibile memoratu* (*Cat.* 6.2, 7.3, *Jug.* 40.3). Apuleius has the paradoxical *infandam memoratu . . . gulam* (*Met.* 10.15).   **quantum**

superbiae socordiaeque Vitellio adoleuerit: abstract nouns as subject (2.1n. *spes uicit*) of *adolesco* since Cic. (*Leg.* 1.22, *Fin.* 5.55, *Tusc.* 3.2; *OLD* 3); *Vitellio* = possessive dat. The alliterative partitive genitives highlight a dangerous pair of traits. Arrogance makes Vitellius unpopular, while indolence leaves him vulnerable when threatened. **speculatores e Syria Iudaeaque:** there is no evidence that Vitellius had sent these (probably military) couriers (*OLD speculator* 1; Austin and Rankov (1995) 150) to ascertain the situation in the east, and they are more likely to have come from Vespasian and Mucianus. Unsolicited good news arriving so soon should make Vitellius wary.   **nuntiauere:** 3.1n. *ipsa...cessere.* This raises questions about the timing of the announcement (and Vitellius' attitude). It is now some time between the battlefield visit (*c.* 23 May) and Vitellius' arrival in Rome (on or before 18 Jul.). After Otho's suicide on 17 Apr., time was required for news (even by sea) of Vitellius' victory to reach Syria and Judaea, for the provinces to react, and for agents to make the return journey to notify the emperor about the oaths. These *speculatores* arrive suspiciously quickly, and Vitellius himself should know that an imperial challenge was always possible, even if oaths had been sworn. Caution, not complacency, is advisable.   **etsi uagis . . . auctoribus:** *etsi* + an abl. absolute followed by a *tamen* attached to the main clause is striking and only here in T. (though examples of *etsi . . . tamen* prefacing two contrasting abl. absolutes are in Cic., Caes., Liv.).   **erat tamen in ore famaque Vespasianus** 'there was nevertheless widespread talk about Vespasian'. Various omens apparently heralded Vespasian's principate, including *praesagia* in Rome (Suet. *Ves.* 5.7); and without naming Vespasian, T. describes Julius Caesar's statue which turned from west to east, just before Otho left Rome (1.86.1, Plut. *Oth.* 4.6). In unsettled times, people naturally seized on such 'signs' (whatever their veracity) in a bid for clarity. Similar excited talk followed Basilides' pronouncement to Vespasian when he visited the altar of Carmel: *nec quidquam magis in ore uolgi* (2.78.4). The idea of someone constantly being on people's lips (*OLD os¹* 3) perhaps recalls Ennius' epitaph (*uolito uiuos per ora uirum*, Cic. *Tusc.* 1.34; cf. *ore legar populi perque omnia saecula fama . . . uiuam*, Ov. *Met.* 15.878–9) and Livy's *Postumius in ore erat* (9.10.3, with Oakley (2005) 131). The hendiadys *in ore famaque* is unprecedented.   **plerumque ad nomen eius Vitellius excitabatur** 'Vitellius was generally agitated at any mention of his name'.   **ipse exercitusque:** the juxtaposition of pronoun and noun (facilitated by the enclitic *-que*) evokes the motif of Vitellius' vices trickling down to corrupt his army (2.62.1, 68.1, 69.2, 76.4), a powerful theme to be resumed graphically at 2.87.1.   **ut nullo aemulo** 'as though without a rival' (16.3n. *ut*); abl. of attendant circumstances.   **saeuitia libidine raptu:** a stark trio of ablatives (combined uniquely here), made starker by asyndeton.   **in externos mores proruperant:** 'instantaneous' pluperfect (1.1n. *dispersat*). T. adds novelty to the idea of *metus hostilis* (i.e. productive fear of a foreign enemy keeping Rome's citizens morally upright). The Vitellians illustrate the theory by degenerating in the absence of an enemy, but in fact there is a *hostis* to be feared (and a Roman one at that). At the same time, Vespasian's chances improve, as he now has a 'foreign' enemy to sharpen his own conduct in response to *metus hostilis*. There is some rôle reversal, as the east, usually the place to prompt degeneration, produces an alert and robust

Flavian army, whereas the Vitellian troops in Italy (traditionally a healthier environment) deteriorate rapidly. T. especially favours the metaphorical use of *prorumpo* (cf. 1.60.1, *A.* 4.71.3, 5.3.1, 6.51.3, 11.2.1, 13.12.2 with people as the subject) for a powerful force (so far held back) bursting forth. It may suggest disease (Cic. *Mur.* 39.85, Nep. *Att.* 21.3). The idea that the Vitellians have so far shown restraint on their journey is shocking; and the 'cliffhanger' stirs curiosity that T. will satisfy when the narrative of the march resumes (2.87).

74–86 VESPASIAN IN THE EAST BEGINS HIS IMPERIAL CHALLENGE

T. now suspends his account of Vitellius' decadent journey to Rome and returns to the Flavian challenge, last considered extensively at 2.1–7. There, Vespasian and Mucianus agreed that war was appropriate, but only at the right time (*arma in occasionem distulere*, 2.7.2), after *fortuna* had made Otho or Vitellius the victor (2.7.1). That moment is now here and T. marks its significance by having Vespasian ponder his military resources and the possible dangers (cf. Otho at 1.21), even considering the case against military intervention (2.74.2–75). His reflections recall the model of Caesar as he contemplates crossing the Rubicon (Plut. *Caes.* 32), a moment which raises some similar narrative issues. The deliberation also evokes the *suasoria*, the speech of advice to a historical character (*D.* 35.4, Quint. 2.1.2–3, Juv. 1.15–16; Sussman (1978) 11), considering (e.g.) whether Alexander should cross the Ocean (Sen. *Suas.* 1) or enter Babylon (Sen. *Suas.* 4), except that here Vespasian is advising himself. Yet he is never seriously going to change his mind about challenging Vitellius. So why include the scene? As well as dignifying Vespasian, the whole sequence (2.74–7) undercuts pro-Flavian accounts, which cast Vespasian's rising as spontaneous (Morgan (1994b) 119 n.6). By stressing the would-be emperor's hesitation, T. implies that Vespasian has been contemplating the challenge for some time (ever since 2.1–7). At the same time, T. indicates why Vespasian is more likely to survive than his predecessors: he is prepared to analyse danger in advance, even if some factors, such as a possible assassination (2.75), are beyond his control (and T.'s audience would no doubt think of Domitian's fate here). Vitellius' escapist persona (*ut nullo aemulo*, 2.73) is the immediate point of comparison, but so too is Titus, whose own hopes are buoyant (2.4.2) and who could still have put himself forward as emperor instead of his father. This alternative is still live even now, with Mucianus being *in Titum pronior* (2.74.1) and prepared to call him *capax . . . imperii* (2.77.1) in public.

The other reason why T. dwells on Vespasian's hesitation is to decelerate the narrative and to split Vitellius' journey to Rome into two sections (2.57–73, 87–89), thereby portraying the new emperor as lethargic and lazy immediately after his victory. One invaluable device for fleshing out this section is Mucianus' colourful speech of encouragement to the wavering Vespasian (2.76–77; cf. Jos. *BJ* 4.592–600, where the soldiers use some similar material while persuading *themselves* to intervene for Vespasian). His speech recalls (but trumps) Fabius Valens' self-interested address to

Vitellius to persuade him to become an imperial challenger (1.52.3–4; cf. speeches to the wavering Flavius Sabinus, 3.64, and to Gnaeus Piso, *A.* 15.59.1–2). Such hortatory orations reflect T.'s familiarity with the declamation schools, especially the deliberative *suasoriae*. Yet Mucianus' speech, much more than just a rhetorical exercise, is well integrated with the surrounding narrative. It introduces in his own voice a silver-tongued character central to the future Flavian dynasty, who has so far only been focalised externally by T. as narrator (1.10.1–2, 2.5.1). As the relationship between an imperial challenger and his advisers is crucial in resolving crises (Damon (2003) 139), Mucianus now needs to be put under the spotlight: *ipse qui suadet considerandus est* (2.76.1). That is perhaps the whole *raison d'être* of this speech, which, after all, sets out to persuade Vespasian about something that he has already committed himself to do (2.7.2). Mucianus' words are as much about his own character and standing as they are about Vespasian's apparent reluctance to enter the fray. 'To give advice for or against something seems to me to be a job for the weightiest character (*grauissimae . . . personae*)' (Cic. *De or.* 2.333; cf. Quint. 3.8.12–13). As a counsellor, Mucianus needs to show that he is serious. He needs to be seen to break the pattern of self-interested advisers insincerely saying whatever the situation requires to get a weak-willed man to do what they want. Achilles had famously said that he hates a man who says one thing and means another as much as the gates of Hades (Hom. *Il.* 9.312–13). We (and Vespasian) need to judge the depth of Mucianus' commitment to the Flavian cause; and this speech serves as his 'manifesto'. See Aubrion (1985) 384–90 on the speech; Lausberg (1998) §224–38 and Levene (1999) on deliberative oratory; Marincola (1997) 128–33 on the role of character in persuasion; Roisman (2005) especially 23 on the wise adviser, whose character can be more telling than his advice.

After the speech, T. memorably says that Mucianus plays the role of a *socius imperii* more than a *magister* (2.83.1), partly endorsing Mucianus' own description of himself as a *socius* for Vespasian (2.77.1), even if the language from the theatre (83.1n. *agens*) raises questions about his motives; and we are inevitably reminded of another emperor, Tiberius, and his infamous *socius laborum* (*A.* 4.2.3) and *adiutor imperii* (*A.* 4.7.1), Sejanus. Yet where Tiberius is an established *princeps*, Vespasian is only an imperial challenger. Mucianus thus runs substantial risks in supporting him, although if the bid succeeds, the rewards will be great, as T. cynically reminds us (2.84.2). Vespasian certainly needs Mucianus' talents (and wealth). He himself is a competent soldier, but lacks the political and rhetorical skills of his elegant *socius imperii*. Could Vespasian have stirred up civilians and soldiers in the theatre at Antioch with the brazen, but well-judged lie that Vitellius planned to interchange the legions based in Germany and Syria (2.80.3)? It seems doubtful. The ability to lie convincingly will render Mucianus invaluable after the Flavian victory in Rome, when he will do many dirty jobs that Vespasian conveniently avoids by absence (e.g. executing Calpurnius Galerianus, 4.11.2, and Vitellius' son, 4.80.1; defusing Antonius Primus' power, 4.39). This current section shows off Mucianus' talents. Yet it ends by zooming in on Antonius Primus, the rogue Flavian general who will supersede Mucianus' honied words with lightning military action (2.86). As so often in life, planning is superseded by the unexpected.

74.1 At Vespasianus: the transitional *at* (20.1n. *At*) deftly switches from the barbarised Vitellius in Italy to the more traditional paradigm of *Romanitas*, Vespasian on the margins of the empire.   **bellum . . . circumspectabat:** the choice compound for simple verb varies Livy's *arma et bellum spectare* (3.69.2, 9.10.5) and *arma spectare* (10.11.7, 10.18.5; also Curt. 9.7.2). The prefix *circum-* aptly suggests the wide vista of opportunities available. Vespasian's analytical gaze is pointedly more constructive than Vitellius' warped ogling of the battlefield (2.70); but his soldiers have already cast their eyes over the potential resources (*uires suas circumspicere*, 2.6.2).   **procul uel iuxta sitas uires:** T. evokes *socios amicos procul iuxta sitos* (Sall. *Hist.* 4.69.17 Reynolds), from King Mithridates' letter to the wealthy Parthian ruler Phraates III during the third Mithridatic war (74–66 BC). Mithridates is trying to address the Roman threat to the eastern kings and to enlist allies; and the context for the phrase is a description of the victims of Roman imperialism. This skilful piece of Sallustian deliberative oratory (Aldheid (1988)) also has verbal and thematic echoes in Mucianus' speech. **miles . . . irridebant:** the largely positive factors which Vespasian might be considering (2.74.1) are filtered through T. as narrator (though see notes on *transisset* and *sperabantur* below), whereas the risks are vividly presented from Vespasian's own perspective in indirect speech (2.74.2–75).   **miles . . . audierint:** collective singular subject with a pl. verb (22.2n. *pars . . . obruti*).   **ipsi adeo paratus** 'were so attached to him', sc. *erat*. The adj. *paratus* + the dat. (*ipsi:* sc. *Vespasiano*) is not in Cic. or Caes. **praeeuntem . . . precantem:** sc. *Vespasianum*. The enveloping alliteration (4.1n. *pandi . . . prosperum*) and chiasmus marks off Vespasian's insincere efforts to adhere to normal military routine. The half-hearted oath swearing reminds us that this whole section is a flashback from when Vitellius in Italy hears that *adactum in uerba eius Orientem* (2.73). This is that moment, clarifying how badly Vitellius misjudges the news. **per silentium:** the mood has obviously deteriorated since the soldiers swore their last oath (6.1n. *sacramentum Othonis*). The image of troops responding to oaths with menacing or petulant silence recurs (Vitellians / oath to Galba 1.55.1; Vitellians / oath to Vespasian, 4.31.2).   **Muciani:** 5.1n.   **nec alienus:** 22.2n. *Caecinae haud alienus.*   **et in Titum pronior** 'but he was quite well-disposed to Titus', sc. *erat. et* has a slight adversative force (*OLD et* 14) and suggests Mucianus' flexibility; he can support father or son, depending on how events develop. The comparative *pronior* is ambivalent, meaning either 'more sympathetic' or 'quite well-disposed'. Mucianus demonstrates his enthusiasm for Titus, potentially problematic for Vespasian (5.1n. *etiam Muciani moribus*), in his speech (2.77.1).   **praefectus Aegypti:** Egypt was the only major province run by an equestrian governor. It was considered too dangerous for senators to visit without the emperor's permission, because of the province's resources, above all grain (*prouincia . . . annonae fecunda*, 1.11.1), which could potentially be used to starve Rome into submission (Jos. *BJ* 4.605). The two legions based there, the *III Cyrenaica* and the *XXII Deiotariana*, did not participate in the fighting, but their support of Vespasian was strategically important.   **<Ti.> Alexander:** imperial pretenders, including Vespasian (Jos. *BJ* 4.605), predictably courted the equestrian prefect of Egypt, Tiberius Julius Alexander (*PIR²* I 139, Pflaum (1960) 46–9, *OCD³* 'Iulius Alexander, Tiberius'). In Josephus Vespasian makes the first approach to the prefect (*BJ* 4.616–19), but T. leaves this open. He was certainly the first military governor to declare for Vespasian on 1 Jul. 69. Alexander came from a prominent and wealthy Jewish family of Alexandria: his father Alexander had been chief customs officer, the Alabarch (Jos. *AJ* 20.100), his uncle Philo was a prominent philosopher (*OCD³* 'Philon (4)'), and his brother Marcus in 41 had married Berenice (daughter of King Agrippa I of Judaea, Jos. *AJ* 19.277, and Titus' current love-interest, 2.2.1). This made Berenice's brother, Agrippa II, Alexander's former brother-in-law. Alexander himself, a renegade Jew, had been procurator of Judaea (46–8) and an administrator for Corbulo's war in Armenia (T. calls him an *illustris eques, A.* 15.28.3), before becoming prefect of Egypt in May 66 (Jos. *BJ* 2.309, Turner (1954) 59). Trouble soon erupted with the Jews in Alexandria, which Alexander suppressed by military force after failed attempts at mediation. After Nero's suicide, he issued a proclamation on 6 Jul. 68 calling Galba the 'benefactor of all races of humankind' (the Greek text is in Evelyn-White and Oliver (1938) 23–44, discussed by Chalon (1964) and translated by Sherk (1988) 118–23). Despite the tone, this is probably a pragmatic response to the *status quo*, not real enthusiasm (even if Alexander had come to an earlier understanding with Galba; Turner (1954) 60). Vespasian may have been different: Alexander's early support is pivotal (2.79) and the adoption of 1 Jul. as Vespasian's *dies imperii* acknowledges his contribution (Levick (1999) 54). Alexander also helped Titus in the final reduction of Judaea (Jos. *BJ* 5.46, 6.237). Evidence for his career after the war is thin, although Juvenal's scornful reference to 'some Egyptian Arabarch' having a triumphal statue (1.129–31) has often been taken to refer to Alexander.   **consilia sociauerat** 'had made common cause'. Valerius Flaccus coined this phrase (5.281), also in the post-Hadrianic Granius Licinianus (35.33, Criniti's edition), a leaner version of the alliterative *consilia consociare* (Cic. *Red. Sen.* 16, Liv. 28.27.13, 42.29.5). T. uses it again in a conspiratorial context (*qui consilia sociarent*, 4.15.1). The pluperfect implies that Flavians had been planning for some time (*contra* pro-Flavian propaganda).   **tertiam legionem:** the *legio III Gallica* (4.4n. *quattuor*).   **quod . . . transisset:** the subjunctive shows that T. gives Vespasian's reason, not his own (19.1n. *quod . . . legisset*). Moesia is some way from Judaea, so Vespasian would not normally expect to have a personal connection with a legion located there, but he does, thanks to its previous base in neighbouring Syria. The dead Nero has effectively planted a pro-Flavian 'seed' in fertile military terrain.   **ceterae Illyrici legiones securae sperabantur:** sc. *esse.* i.e. the *XIII Gemina* and *VII Galbiana* in Pannonia, the *XI Claudia* in Dalmatia (after the *XIV Gemina* had been sent to Britain), and the *VII Claudia* and *VIII Augusta* in Moesia. Mucianus is still unsure of their status when setting out against Vitellius. He considers attacking Dyrrachium in northern Greece and blockading the Adriatic instead of marching through Moesia (2.83.2). The passive of *spero* + the nom. (*OLD* 2), an extension of the personal construction with verbs of saying and thinking (GL §528), features in Latin here first. The implied agents are Vespasian and his supporters.

omnis exercitus flammauerat arrogantia uenientium a Vitellio militum 'the arrogance of the soldiers coming from Vitellius had incensed all the legions'; abstract noun as subject (2.1n. *spes uicit*). The simple verb for the compound *inflammo* is a poeticism featuring again only once in T. (if *A.* 15.44.4 is excised, as some editors propose): *instinctos flammauere* (4.24.3). The pl. *exercitus* is an alternative for the recently deployed *legiones* (Goodyear (1972) 323). The focus on the Vitellian troops' *arrogantia* so soon after highlighting Vitellius' *superbia* (2.73) (and the appearance of his name here) reinforces the idea of the emperor's flaws trickling down to his troops (62.1n. *degenerabat*).   **truces corpore** '(despite being) savage in appearance'. A concessive sense is suggested by what follows: although the Vitellians deride other Roman soldiers as their inferiors, they themselves so clearly fall short of the ideal.   **horridi sermone** 'talking raucously'. The adj. *horridus*, more usual for soldiers' appearance (11.3n. *horridus*) than their voices, is common in the vocabulary of literary criticism (not always pejoratively e.g. Liv. 2.32.8) for uncouth speech and writing (*OLD* 4b). The metaphor in *horridus*, 'derived from the analogy between speech and grooming' (Fantham (1972) 172), here follows naturally from the description of the soldiers' physical appearance. The combination *horridus* + abl. of respect is choice (cf. *horridum sermonem*, Quint. 9.4.3). The notion of speech indicating inner character is pervasive in ancient literature (e.g. *ut uita sic oratione durus incultus horridus*, Cic. *Brut.* 117), and simple soldierly speech elsewhere can indicate honesty (4.73.1), but here T. probably has in mind the harsh sound-effects of the northern Vitellians' language. This topic has a long pedigree in ancient historiography: cf. the troglodyte Ethiopians, whose speech sounds like squeaking bats (Hdt. 4.183.4).

    74.2 in tanta mole belli: 6.1n. *tarda mole ciuilis belli*.   **plerumque cunctatio [*est*]; et Vespasianus** 'men generally hesitate; and Vespasian (was no exception)', sc. *erat*. What sounds like a pithy generalisation is one of many references countering pro-Flavian suggestions that the challenge was spontaneous.   **modo . . . aliquando** 'now . . . at other times'. This typically innovative *uariatio* of adverbs (*TLL* s.v. *modo* 1314.15) recurs in T. to describe fluctuating conduct (*A.* 1.81.2, 6.35.1, 11.34.1, 16.10.4, with Sörbom (1935) 43).   **aduersa reputabat:** the verb is archaising (16.2n. *reputabant*). Vespasian's measured reasons for hesitating before his challenge pointedly differ from Vitellius' *cunctatio*, deriving from his natural sluggishness (*segne ingenium*, 1.52.4). The imaginative reconstruction of Vespasian's inner thoughts recalls T.'s internal focalisation of Titus (2.1.3).   **quis ille dies foret** 'what would that day mean?'; *foret* for *esset* (14.3n. *deletae . . . forent*). The day in question will be 1 Jul. (2.79). Vespasian's language is self-dramatising, as the notion of a pivotal day recalls epic (33.3n. *is primus dies*). The *quis dies* formula, used elsewhere to express horror after inauspicious or violent events (Cic. *Mur.* 46, *Luc.* 69, Ov. *Am.* 3.12.1, Luc. 2.99, Sen. *Her. O.* 1268, Quint. *Decl. min.* 316.8, 328.5, Stat. *Theb.* 1.166, 12.698), adds pessimistic undercurrents. It is applied here unusually to an event in the future.   **sexaginta aetatis annos et duos filios iuuenes bello permitteret?** Vespasian, born on 17 Nov. 9, will be 60 next birthday (Suet *Ves.* 2.1), while Titus (born 30 Dec. 39; Mooney (1930) 504–5) is 29 and Domitian (born 24 Oct. 51) is 17. By syllepsis (3.2n.

precibus), *permitto* (*OLD* 3b 'commit') takes as objects a concrete (*filios*) and an abstract (*annos*) noun, thanks to the unusual cardinal number *sexaginta* + acc., instead of the ordinal equivalent in the abl. (*sexagesimo aetatis anno*) modifying an acc. pronoun (*se*). By describing himself periphrastically in terms of years lived, Vespasian emphasises his accumulated experience. By coupling himself with his sons, he thinks in dynastic terms from the start (but he is also aware of the risks to his family, showing a softer side). The phrasing (*sexaginta . . . iuuenes*) shows a syllabic diminuendo and crescendo centring on *et*.   **esse priuatis cogitationibus progressum** 'in private deliberations, a steady advance is possible'. The noun *progressus* (*OLD* 1) has a pregnant sense, without an adj. to clarify its meaning. This is elucidated subsequently by contrast with the extremes of success and failure facing would-be emperors: *imperium cupientibus* (cf. *priuatis cogitationibus*) *nihil medium inter summa aut praecipitia* (cf. *esse . . . progressum*).   **et prout uelint, plus minusue sumi ex fortuna** 'and just as people wish, they can advance more boldly or cautiously, depending on how they fare' (lit. 'more or less of the way can be taken, according to fortune'). What this compact generalisation means precisely is difficult to tease out, but the metaphor of advancing along a specific route (from *progressum*) still seems to be active, with the simple form *sumo* used for *assumo* ('take on in addition').   **nihil medium:** sc. *esse*. The dramatic notion of 'no halfway measure' recurs elsewhere (Cic. *Phil.* 8.4, Liv. 7.39.14 with Oakley (1998) 375, 30.33.11, Sen. *Con.* 3.2.1, Quint. 6.1.45).   **inter summa aut praecipitia** 'between the summit and the abyss' (Wellesley). Latin authors often describe extremes on a vertical plane, but the standard terminology involves *summa* and *ima* (e.g. *summa montium et maris ima*, Plin. *Nat* 32.64; cf. Lucr. 1.1056, 2.488, Liv. 37.45.18, Ov. *Fast.* 6.279, Sen. *Nat.* 2.4.1, Plin *Nat.* 14.63, Stat. *Theb.* 9.263–4). With typical *uariatio*, T.'s *praecipitia*, a substantive adj. expressing the notion of toppling from on high, replaces *ima* (suggesting that there is no future after the fall).

75 uersabatur ante oculos Germanici exercitus robur 'there danced before his eyes the strength of the German army'. T. gives similar language to the orator Aper, with *Vlixes et Nestor* (*D.* 16.5) and *isti* (*D.* 23.2) as the subject, not an abstract noun (2.1n. *spes uicit*). The combination *uersor* + *ante oculos* (once at Lucr. 2.113) is above all Ciceronian (19×), but then is scantily attested (Quint. *Decl. min.* 337.7, Sil. 13.394), perhaps because Cicero used it too much. The German armies also make the Flavian council of war hesitate (58.2n. *magna . . . fama*), but in reality their strength is ebbing away during the undisciplined march towards Rome.   **notum uiro militari:** Vespasian was a legionary legate in Germany during Claudius' principate and commanded the *legio II Augusta* in the invasion of Britain (Suet. *Ves.* 4.1). Then he was proconsul of Africa (Suet. *Ves.* 4.3) before being appointed to suppress the Judaean revolt (Levick (1999) 14–39). The epithet *uir militaris* is Livian (10.24.4, 30.15.13, 30.37.9, 35.26.10). In T. (3.73.2, *A.* 4.42.2, 15.26.3, 15.67.3) it often features where a soldier's professional experience endorses an argument or adds emotional power (Syme (1957) 134–5; cf. Campbell (1975) 11–12).   **ciuili bello inexpertas:** Vespasian is perhaps being unduly pessimistic, as his own legions are *exercitae bello* (2.4.4) from the Jewish revolt (cf. *inexperti belli ardor* for Mucianus' troops, 2.4.4). Yet civil war requires peculiar ruthlessness (now possessed by the Vitellian

troops), not just battle-hardened soldiers.   **Vitellii uictrices:** sc. *legiones*.   **plus
querimoniarum quam uirium:** T. documents the Othonians' complaints
(2.66.1), but also their crucial contribution to the Flavian cause (2.67.1).   **fluxam ...
fidem:** the enveloping alliteration (4.1n. *pandi ... prosperum*) involves language applied
normally to non-Romans (Morgan (1994b) 121): Plaut. *Capt.* 439 (Greeks), Sall. *Jug.*
111.2 (Mauretanians), Liv. 28.6.11 (Greeks) and 40 50.5 (Celtiberians), T. 3.48.2 (*barbari*
of Pontus). Mercurial military *fides* in civil war (exacerbated by financial donatives) is
all part of the erosion of traditional Roman identity. Appian, analysing the Perusine
war (41–40 BC), comments on the fluctuating loyalty of the soldiers 'who felt that they
were not so much serving in the army as lending assistance from personal goodwill
and by their own choice' (*BC* 5.17). In Plutarch the soldiers 'flocked to the highest
bidder' (*Brut.* 23.1).   **periculum ex singulis . . . enim:** the potential danger
from these soldiers, initially undefined, is clarified by the question in the *enim* clause.
Pro-Flavian accounts present Vespasian forced at sword-point to make an imperial
challenge (*BJ* 4.603), but the budding emperor slowly formulates a different kind of
threat.   **profuturas:** sc. *esse*.   **si unus alterue praesenti facinore paratum
ex diuerso praemium petat?** 'if one or two men should seek by a timely crime the
reward offered from the other side?'. Yet the complacent Vitellius has not encouraged
this (2.73). The unprecedented pair *praesens facinus*, a circumlocution for assassination,
contributes to the alliteration of this clause. Vespasian apparently believed that Galba
sent assassins from Spain to Judaea to kill him (Suet. *Galb.* 23), but this is not in T., who
instead relays Vespasian's fears more generally. T.'s Otho also considered the possibility of his own assassination (*occidi Othonem posse*, 1.21.1), but as a protreptic device to
spur himself to action and thereby prevent it. Here the thought of assassination is a
deterrent (Morgan (1994b)). We can compare Tiberius' lapidary sentiment, *principes
mortales, rem publicam aeternam* (*A.* 3.6.3 with WM 109), subordinating the individual
to the state, but Vespasian, not yet *princeps*, lacks the usual defences of an emperor.
sic . . . sic: the anaphora and asyndeton nicely capture Vespasian's heightened
emotions.   **Scribonianum . . . interfectum:** sc. *esse*. Vespasian, like any good
orator (Quint. 5.11.1), adds an *exemplum* to make his argument more cogent. Mucianus
will try to trump Vespasian's *exemplum* with one of his own, Corbulo (2.76.3). Under
Claudius, Arruntius Camillus Scribonianus, governor of Dalmatia, led a short-lived
rebellion (*simul audita et coercita*,1.89.2) with his two legions in 42 (Levick (1990) 59–60).
T.'s version in the *A.* is not extant, so details are scanty (Suet. *Cl.* 13.2, 35.2 with
Hurley (2001) 113–14, *Otho* 1.2, Dio 60.15.1–3, *Epit. de Caes.* 4.4, Orosius 7.6.6–7, Plin.
Ep. 3.16.7).   **percussorem eius Volaginium:** this detail, crucially validating the
whole *exemplum*, is controversial, as Dio says that Scribonianus fled to the island of Issa
in the Adriatic, where he killed himself (60.15). Whether the assassin really existed or
not, Vespasian believes that one of his own soldiers killed Scribonianus; and naming a
minor character adds verisimilitude.   **e gregario ad summa militiae prouectum** 'was promoted from a common soldier to the highest rank'; sc. *esse*. No external
evidence for this promotion exists. Volaginius perhaps became a centurion (Chilver (1979) 234), but the conveniently vague *summa* (a neuter pl. substantive + defining
gen. *militiae*; cf 74.2n. *inter summa*) is Vespasian's exaggeration and dispenses with detail.

Assassins of emperors could not always expect rewards, as Caligula's killers found to their cost (Suet. *Cl.* 11.1). *gregarius* is a substantive only here (elsewhere in T., and in other authors, it modifies *miles*). It may be intended to mirror the linguistic register of a military man (cf. *militariter locutus*, 2.80.2). **facilius uniuersos impelli quam singulos uitari:** Vespasian tries to boost his confidence with a final aphorism, much pithier than the Livian *sententia* about acquiring empire: *parari singula acquirendo facilius potuisse quam uniuersa teneri posse* (37.35.6).

   76.1 His pauoribus nutantem . . . firmabant 'were heartening Vespasian as he faltered because of these anxieties'. *firmo* is often used figuratively of a person or his mind (*OLD* 7a), but the combination with *nuto* may activate the metaphor of Vespasian as a tottering building (*OLD firmo* 1; *OLD nuto* 4b). Elsewhere this architectural metaphor is applied to Vespasian himself shoring up the tottering state: *nihil habuit* [sc. *Vespasianus*] *antiquius quam prope afflictam nutantemque rem publicam stabilire* (Suet. *Ves.* 8.1; cf. *imperium . . . firmauit, Ves.* 1.1). T. perhaps inverts a theme that was originally in pro-Flavian sources.   **et . . . et** 'both . . . and' (*OLD et* 9).   **iam et = iam etiam** (as at *G.* 15.3, 42.2, *H.* 1.22.3, *A.* 3.33.4). Livy introduced the abbreviated form to prose, possibly from desire for euphony (Goodyear (1972) 200).   **coram:** Mucianus addresses Vespasian publicly (*OLD coram* 2b), both to show his commitment to the Flavian cause and to clarify that he was supporting Vespasian, not Titus, as an imperial candidate.   **locutus:** sc. *est.*   **omnes . . . adquiratur:** deliberative oratory does not always need a formal *prooemium*, but still should not begin abruptly (Quint. 3.8.6); and there is always scope for *captatio beneuolentiae* (Quint. 3.8.7). Mucianus' calm and reflective opening allows the anxious Vespasian to settle down and ponder some general 'rules' useful for anybody in this situation. That broad perspective is enhanced by some historical underpinning through a double allusion to Sallust. T. first evokes the opening of King Mithridates' letter (combining elements of a *suasoria* and deliberative oratory) to the wealthy Parthian ruler Phraates III (74.1n. *procul uel iuxta*): *omnes qui secundis rebus suis ad belli societatem orantur considerare debent liceatne tum pacem agere; dein quod quaeritur satisne pium, tutum, gloriosum an indecorum sit* (*Hist.* 4.69.1 Reynolds). In this apt model, two easterners contemplate an alliance against a corrupt and greedy Roman enemy (led by the republican general Lucullus, whose later reputation as a notorious hedonist also coheres with the decadent Vitellius). The second (less insistent) allusion is to the opening of Caesar's speech about the fate of a domestic enemy, the Catilinarian conspirators: *omnes homines, patres conscripti, qui de rebus dubiis consultant, ab odio amicitia ira atque misericordia uacuos esse decet* (*Cat.* 51.1). Through this allusive language, Mucianus casts himself as Mithridates and Caesar, authoritative figures both likely to appeal to the military man Vespasian.   **qui magnarum rerum consilia suscipiunt** 'who plan some great exploit'. Mucianus indicates rebellion in euphemistic language and insinuates the idea that the endeavour's 'greatness' is clear. The sense of magnitude picks up *in tanta mole belli* (2.74.2).   **quod inchoatur:** euphemistic periphrasis again. **rei publicae utile . . . gloriosum . . . non arduum:** Cicero stresses (*Inu.* 2.156) that in deliberative oratory the central arguments are based on two factors, 'honour' (*honestas*) and 'expediency' (*utilitas*), with 'glory' (*gloriosum*) as a subdivision of *honestas*

(*Inu.* 2.166; also 2.54, 2.12) and 'safety' (*incolumitas*) as a subdivision of *utilitas* (*Inu.* 2.169). Quintilian (3.8.23, 25) agrees that *honestum* and *utile* are fundamental (Levene (1999) 200–2). In the *prooemium*, Mucianus follows rhetorical handbooks by raising questions of (public) expediency (*rei publicae utile*), (personal) honour (*ipsis gloriosum*), and also practicality (*promptum effectu*), albeit modified (*certe non arduum* 'certainly not too difficult'). Mucianus seems to put more emphasis on *utilitas* than *honestas* (though cf. *magnarum rerum* above), but this may be deliberate; Vespasian is a practical man, after all, and was pondering whether he could realistically do the job with the available resources (2.74.2–75). **ipse qui suadet:** the *auctoritas* of a *prudentissimus* and *optimus* speaker is the best way to enhance the credibility of deliberative oratory (Quint. 3.8.12–13). Cf. Menander's line about the speaker's nature, not his speech, that persuades (cited at Plut. *Mor.* 801c, with the proviso that both speech and character are important). Mucianus must establish himself as a *uir bonus* who advises Vespasian for the sake of patriotism, not selfish motives (Quint. 4.1.7; Lausberg (1998) §275). Cf. Mardonius, who advises Xerxes to invade Greece for entirely selfish reasons (Hdt. 7.7). **adiciatne consilio periculum suum:** Mucianus' clever indirect question about an (apparently general) factor will be personalised and answered directly in the body of the speech (*discrimen ac pericula ex aequo patiemur*, 2.77.2). By careful preparation he enhances his credibility and *auctoritas* as a *suasor*. **si fortuna coeptis adfuerit:** abstract noun as subject (2.1n. *spes uicit*). This perhaps inauspiciously echoes the start of Otho's campaign (*blandiebatur coeptis fortuna*, 2.12.1), but Mucianus' conditional clause shows him to be sensibly cautious; and *fortuna* does favour the Flavians (1.1n. *struebat . . . imperio*). **cui summum decus adquiratur** 'who gains the highest glory' (another hint of *honestas*). Again, Mucianus will answer his own general question later in the speech (*ceterum inter nos non idem prosperarum aduersarumque rerum ordo erit*, 2.77.2).

76.2 ego te . . . positum est: the juxtaposed pronouns suggest a close bond between the pair and abruptly move the speech from *prooemium* (*omnes . . . adquiratur*) to *narratio* (*ego . . . est*) stating the specific situation related to the general questions of the prologue (Quint. 3.8.10). Mucianus' self-assigned role in summoning Vespasian to *imperium* haughtily disregards official bodies such as the senate (a foretaste of his attitude after victory, 4.4.1). **Vespasiane:** the simple address by *cognomen* (Dickey (2002) 56–63) may be intended to appeal to Vespasian's down-to-earth personality: in T., neither Galba, Otho or Vitellius are addressed so modestly by their supporters. **tam salutare rei publicae, quam tibi magnificum. iuxta deos in tua manu positum est:** the text and punctuation are problematic. Editors correct M's *tamquam salutare* either to *quam* (construing it as the first of two indirect questions forming the subject of *positum est* and punctuating with a comma after *magnificum*) or *tam* (construing it as a *tam . . . quam* correlative clause dependent on *imperium* and punctuating with a full stop after *magnificum*). Neither is ideal, but at least the *tam* reading leads more smoothly to Mucianus' protest that he is not flattering Vespasian (*nec . . . expaueris*). The adj. *salutare* implicitly casts Vespasian as a saviour, an image live in pro-Flavian propaganda: *Vespasianus Augustus fessis rebus subueniens* (Plin. *Nat.* 2.18). Mucianus empowers Vespasian (albeit with a passing nod to possible divine influence), recalling Piso's words to the soldiers that the impact of his adoption *in uestra manu positum est* (1.29.2; 27.2n. *in ipsorum manu sitam*). Yet where Piso genuinely subordinates himself to powerful soldiers, Mucianus defers to Vespasian only superficially. His real attitude emerges later in his boastful letter to the senate: *in manu sua fuisse imperium donatumque Vespasiano* (4.4.1). The senate sees this as arrogant towards the state and insulting to the new emperor, but conceals its unease.   **Nec speciem adulantis expaueris** 'don't fear what might seem to be mere flattery' (Wellesley); 47.1n. *nec . . . computaueritis*. The compound *expauesco* (Liv. 6.34.6, Hor. *Carm.* 1.37.23 and often in 'silver' writers) is only here in T. (cf. Syme (1958a) 719–20 for words only in speeches in *A.*, including many compound verbs). In moving to the speech's main *argumentatio*, Mucianus disclaims flattery just after flattering Vespasian by calling him to the principate. Galba in his adoption speech had warned Piso of *adulatio*'s dangers for an established *princeps* (*irrumpet adulatio*, 1.15.4), but the peril is just as great for a would-be emperor, as Fabius Valens' fawning speech to Vitellius shows (1.52.3–4). Plutarch, in his essay on how to tell a friend from a flatterer (*Mor.* 48e–74e), acknowledges the power of flatterers to overturn regimes (*Mor.* 49e) and sees the most dangerous variety as the man who seems not to flatter (*Mor.* 50e). For T., the *exemplar . . . adulatorii dedecoris* (*A.* 6.32.4) is the emperor's father, Lucius Vitellius. Suetonius gives engaging examples of his technique (*Vit.* 2.5).   **a contumelia quam a laude propius fuerit post Vitellium eligi** 'it is perhaps closer to an insult than a compliment to be chosen to succeed Vitellius'. *propius* + *ab* 'closer' (*OLD prope* 5; cf. *prope ab*, 1.10.1); *fuerit* is a perfect potential subjunctive (37.2n. *concesserim*), or (by a useful ambiguity) a future perfect (conveying confidence about the outcome of the challenge). Yet no official body had chosen Vespasian as *princeps*. The passive *eligi* (diplomatically leaving the agent unspecified) recalls Galba enthusiastically endorsing adoption as the best way to choose a successor (*loco libertatis erit quod eligi coepimus*, 1.16.1), an option not open to Vitellius. Succeeding Vitellius is deemed virtually an insult as his tenure has debased the office of *princeps*, even if there is scope for earning credit by contrast. The reverse can also apply, as in the story that Augustus deliberately chose Tiberius as his successor to enhance his posthumous reputation through the latter's failings (*A.* 1.10.7, Suet. *Tib.* 21.3, Dio 56.45.3).   **non aduersus . . . domum:** although deliberative oratory is primarily concerned with the future, it also considers the past (Quint. 3.8.6). Mucianus thus contrasts the proposed (relatively easy) challenge against Vitellius with hypothetical (and implicitly more difficult) campaigns against all the past Julio-Claudian emperors. The more elaborate phrasing for Augustus and Tiberius, both given a separate prepositional clause (as opposed to Caligula, Claudius and Nero, who are lumped together) shows which *principes* T.'s Mucianus considers the most challenging.   **diui Augusti acerrimam mentem** 'the very sharp intellect of the divine Augustus'. For argument's sake, Mucianus conveniently draws a veil over Augustus' questionable military qualities, made up for by capable associates such as Agrippa. By contrast, Vespasian is *acer militiae* (2.5.1). Suetonius lists the insurrections against Augustus (*Aug.* 19).   **cautissimam Tiberii senectutem** 'the supremely wary old age of Tiberius'. The adj. and noun are combined only here (*TLL* s.v. *cautus* 642.70–1). Mucianus may allude to Sejanus' machinations, in the end handled deftly by Tiberius, but for obvious reasons would not want to raise the topic of a disloyal right hand man too directly. Both Augustus' shrewdness and Tiberius' wariness are conspicuously lacking in Vitellius, the point of contrast. **uel** 'or even'. **fundatam longo imperio domum** 'a dynasty put on a firm basis through long rule'. Mucianus simultaneously belittles Caligula, Claudius and Nero (only deemed formidable for continuing the dynasty) and Vitellius (whose dynasty is fledgling in comparison). The metaphor of a real house is active here (also Plin. *Ep.* 4.21.3, Quint. *Decl. mai.* 9.10), although Mucianus' argument (ease of toppling Vitellius as opposed to the Julio-Claudians) is undermined by the violent fates of Caligula and Nero. **exsurgimus:** the first person plural diplomatically depicts the solidarity of a shared venture, if Vespasian chooses to act. Mucianus uses this form sparingly but effectively in his speech to suggest a firm bond between them (*sumus*, 2.76.3, *uincimus* + *patiemur* 2.77.2, *habemus*, 2.77.3). *exsurgo* is used metaphorically by Livy (3.41.5), and by T. only here; its association elsewhere with the rising sun (*Agr.* 12.4) and Rome's physical growth (Liv. 6.4.6) subtly imparts grandeur to what could have been seen as a sordid rebellion against the current *princeps*. **cessisti etiam Galbae imaginibus:** Mucianus flatteringly implies that Vespasian was a realistic contender for the principate from the start, pipped only by Galba's prestigious family, to which he graciously gave way. In fact, T. suggests that Vespasian bore Galba no ill will (*nec Vespasiano aduersus Galbam uotum aut animus*, 1.10.3). Galba boasts of his lofty lineage in the adoption speech to Piso (1.15.1); and T. also comments on it in his obituary (1.49.2). *imagines*, wax portrait-masks of prominent family members, were proudly displayed in the halls of aristocratic homes and carried in procession at family funerals (Plb. 6.53, Plin. *Nat.* 35.6–8; Flower (1996)). Galba's own *imago*, if it was ever made, would have borne signs of the abuse inflicted on his severed head after his death (1.49.1). **torpere ultra:** after a compliment, Mucianus now stings Vespasian with a pejorative term placed prominently and applied elsewhere to the sluggish Vitellius (1.62.2, 3.36.1). *ultra*, 'any longer', hints at the powerful notion of καιρός, doing something at the right time (Cic. *Inu.* 1.40, Quint. 3.6.26, 5.10.43), which has now almost passed (cf. *abiit . . . tempus*, 2.76.3, *hodie*, 2.77.2; Lausberg (1998) §385, §388). **polluendam perdendamque rem publicam:** the alliteration and homoioteleuton add force as Mucianus damningly glosses Vitellius' principate to galvanise Vespasian (cf. *Vitelliani . . . polluere*, 2.56.1). Detailed invective about Vitellius is saved for later in the speech. There are precedents for *perdere rem publicam* (Cic. *Dom.* 48, *Sest.* 31, Sall. *Cat.* 31.7, 46.2), but the resonant combination with *polluere* is unique. Philostratus' Vespasian also vividly casts Vitellius (a drunkard who takes perfume-baths and seduces married women) as the 'final straw' in a colourful speech (*VA* 5.29.26). **sopor et ignauia uideretur** 'would seem slothful and cowardly'. Mucianus above all must persuade Vespasian that he has to intervene, so piles on provocative terms. Quintilian questions the role of *necessitas* in deliberative oratory, arguing that there is *always* a choice, even if doing nothing leads to death (3.8.23; similarly Cic. *Inu.* 2.170–3). That is no doubt valid, but Mucianus here uses language likely to get results. **etiam si tibi quam inhonesta, tam tuta seruitus esset** 'even if such slavery were as safe for you as it would be dishonourable'. *seruitus* is almost entirely confined to speeches in T. (6.2n. *seruitii necessitas*). Mucianus adds a clever twist to the familiar choice between safety and honour: often a safe course of action brings with it dishonour (Cic. *Att.* 7.22.2, Sen. *Suas.* 2.11, Sen. *Ben.* 3.12.2, Curt. 8.2.28), but if Vespasian does nothing, he will not even be safe. To increase the pressure, Mucianus emotively glosses 'doing nothing' as *seruitus*. Vespasian's safety is an important theme in Mucianus' speech (also *trucidatus Corbulo*, 2.76.3): he concedes that the challenge has dangers, but he will share in them (*discrimen ac pericula ex aequo patiemur*, 2.77.2). If Vespasian does nothing, he will be on his own (*tibi*).

76.3 abiit iam et transuectum est tempus: *geminatio* ('reduplication') can add force to a concept by using synonyms (Quint. 9.3.45–7; also Cic. *De orat.* 3.206), which 'appear to contain more meaning since they strike both the ears and the mind more frequently' (Gell. 13.25.11 quoting Favorinus). The combination *tempus abire* has precedents (Cic. *Mur.* 7, *Cael.* 74, Ov. *Pont.* 4.2.42, Quint. *Decl. min.* 250.2), but *transuectum* (for *exactum* or *transactum*) + *tempus* features only here. The more common notion *tempus adest* would have been the predictable device in this kind of hortatory speech. **quo posses uideri concupisse** 'when you could have seemed to covet power'. Various editors emend M's reading to *posses uideri non cupisse*, 'you could have seemed not to desire power', corrupted by dittography from *confugiendum* that follows. The emendation suggests that Vespasian successfully dissembled his ambitions for as long as possible, but that the pretence is now unsustainable, given Vitellius' obvious flaws. The manuscript reading implies that if Vespasian had moved earlier, it would have given the impression that he desired power, but now he is simply responding to a situation that leaves him no choice, as he seeks power as a refuge and defence. M's reading makes sense and seems preferable. **confugiendum est ad imperium:** invoking the need to save oneself by swift action recurs in similar deliberative speeches (*perniciosior sit quies quam temeritas*, 1.21 2; *tres patris consulatus . . . iam pridem . . . auferre priuati securitatem*, 1.52.4; *ubi imperium Vespasianus inuaserit . . . non ipsi . . . securitatem nisi exstincto aemulo*, 3.66.2), but the notion of the principate as a 'safe haven' is paradoxical. Very few emperors died peacefully in their beds. Activities such as philosophy traditionally offered a safer refuge (*ad philosophiam ergo confugiendum est*, Sen. *Ep.* 14.11). **excidit** 'slipped your mind?'. **trucidatus Corbulo:** Mucianus, like any good orator, reinforces his point with a powerful *exemplum*. Nero's famous commander, Cn. Domitius Corbulo (*OCD³* '*Domitius Corbulo, Cn.*'; Ash (2006)), was forced to kill himself late in 66 or early in 67 (Dio 63.17) after a mysterious conspiracy (only reported at Suet. *Nero* 36.1), but apparently led by Corbulo's son-in-law, Annius Vinicianus. His daughter, Domitia Longina, married Domitian, perhaps as early as 70. With the demise of the obvious military man to send to Judaea, Vespasian's career was helped (Levick (1999) 25), but his own military talents must have made him identify with Corbulo. Mucianus himself, who served under Corbulo in 58, no doubt saw the precedent in a different light when marginalising the competent Flavian general Antonius Primus after the civil war (4.39). **splendidior origine quam nos sumus:** Corbulo was linked to many prominent families through his mother Vistilia's six marriages (Plin. *Nat.* 7.39;

Syme (1970)). His father, who had a strong sense of his place in society (*A.* 3.31.3), probably became consul under Caligula (Dio 59.15.3). With the first person plural, Mucianus artfully suggests solidarity with Vespasian through their undistinguished family backgrounds. This may be valid, but we know little of Mucianus' origins (*PIR*² L 216). Vespasian's pedigree was certainly not lofty (his father had been a tax-collector, though his mother was better born; Suet. *Ves.* 1.3). He was the first of his family (with his brother) to reach the senate (Levick (1999) 4–8).   **fateor:** the good orator anticipates an objection and addresses it in advance.   **sed et Nero nobilitate natalium Vitellium anteibat:** Mucianus' point (enhanced by alliteration) is that although he and Vespasian may not have worried the high-born Nero, Vitellius, not coming from such a lofty background, is more likely to feel threatened. In fact, Vitellius has good aristocratic credentials: his father was consul three times and Valens played on this family pride to persuade Vitellius to make an imperial challenge (1.52.4). This rather artificial argument tries to get around an inconvenient point for Mucianus in stimulating Vespasian's fears, namely that his relatively humble background makes him a very unlikely potential *princeps*.   **satis clarus est apud timentem quisquis timetur** 'Any man who is feared has a sufficiently high pedigree for the one who fears him'. Aphorisms about fearing and being feared are common (*cum timeret Otho, timebatur*, 1.81.1, *necesse est multos timeat quem multi timent*, Sen. *De ira* 2.11.3, *adice nunc quod qui timetur timet*, Sen. *Ep.* 105.4), but introducing the notion of social class is novel. The combination *clarus* + *apud* (also 2.77.1) only features twice in extant Latin (*TLL* s.v. *clarus* 1275.5), both in this speech, suggesting a linguistic affectation peculiar to Mucianus.

   76.4 posse . . . principem fieri: after an aphorism, Mucianus develops the point that Vespasian needs to act swiftly, as Vitellius only has to consider his own elevation to know that an army can create an emperor and that Vespasian is a serious threat. Cf. the *arcanum imperii* (hardly a secret now) that *posse principem alibi quam Romae fieri* (1.4.2).   **sibi ipse Vitellius documento** 'Vitellius' own case proves to him'; sc. *est.*   **nullis stipendiis, nulla militari fama, Galbae odio prouectus** 'with no record of army service, no military reputation, elevated only by Galba's unpopularity'. Two descriptive abl. phrases marked by anaphora are followed by a nom. participle phrase for *uariatio*, with asyndeton throughout. The implicit point of comparison is Vespasian, who trumps Vitellius by his military record and reputation. The negative formulation is useful for indirect adulation. Vitellius, declared emperor on 2–3 Jan. 69 in Germany, originally thought that he was challenging Galba, not Otho (declared emperor in Rome on 15 Jan. 69).   **ne Othonem quidem ducis arte aut exercitus ui . . . uictum** 'Otho, not conquered either by skilful generalship or a mighty army'. Vitellius was absent, and in the battle-narrative (2.39–45), Caecina and Valens have conspicuously low profiles. In belittling the Vitellian army, Mucianus directly addresses Vespasian's earlier concerns about the formidable *Germanici exercitus robur* (2.75), introducing an important theme of his speech (*si quid . . . deteritur*, 2.76.4; *illi . . . bellum ipsum*, 2.77.3).   **praepropera ipsius desperatione:** 20.1n. *ipsius.* The striking adj. *praeproperus* (28.1n. *cohortes . . . praeualidas* for the prefix) features only here in

T., but Livy has *praepropera celeritas* (31.42.1; cf. *nimis celeri desperatione*, 21.1.5) and Cicero *praepropera festinatio* (*Fam.* 7.8.1, 10.26.2; also + *prensatio*, *Att.* 1.1.1). Valerius Maximus has it, then Pliny the Elder, Silius Italicus and Fronto, but it seems recherché. Mucianus echoes the view that Otho could have won had he continued fighting (2.48.2, 2.66.1), indicating that the Flavians have an effective information network suggestive of early preparations for an imperial challenge. Otho himself says that he dies *festinato exitu* (2.48.2), rather than too hastily.   **iam desiderabilem et magnum principem:** the idea that a destructive successor retroactively renders desirable a ruler originally regarded as neutral (or worse) features elsewhere (Sall. *Hist.* 1.31 Maurenbrecher, Liv. 24.5.2, Suet. *Tib.* 21.2, SHA *Antoninus Geta* 7.6; 76.2n. *a contumelia*). The Flavians in their propaganda will cynically cast themselves as Otho's avengers to win his former soldiers' support (Suet. *Ves.* 6.4), but Mucianus seems ambivalent about Otho, implying that he was neither *desiderabilis* nor *magnus*.   **fecit:** sc. *Vitellius*.   **cum interim:** *cum* + the present indicative introduces a circumstantial clause, connecting the events of the subordinate clause with a time or circumstance articulated in the main clause (1.60; Sall. *Jug.* 12.5, 49.4, Virg. *A.* 10.665; L-H-S 623 §333c).   **spargit legiones, exarmat cohortes, noua cotidie bello semina ministrat:** Mucianus means Vitellius indiscriminately disbanding legionary and auxiliary units (*promiscae missiones*, 2.69.2) and disarming the praetorian cohorts (2.67.1), but his language (marked by asyndeton) is colourful and metaphorical. The pregnant *spargo* suggests the metaphor of sprinkling (58.2n. *spargebatur*), anticipating the agricultural metaphor of *bello semina* in the final colon (cf. WM 207 on *bellum spargere*), and showing epic tinges (*sparsas . . . cohortes*, Luc. 1.394). Velleius Paterculus coined *exarmo* (twice in T.; also 1.31.3), which was then ignored until the Neronian era (Calp. Sic., Col., Sen. the Younger, Luc., Petr.), so it is an apt word for the ostentatious Mucianus, whose hedonistic lifestyle (5.1n. *magnificentia*) evokes the ethos of that principate. It then appealed to the Flavian epicists and Frontinus, Pliny the Younger, and Suetonius. The 'seeds of war' metaphor is in Livy (*semina . . . belli*, 40.16.3; cf. *semina discordiarum*, 3.19.5), Lucan (1.158–9, 3.150), Silius Italicus (1.654) and Statius (*Theb.* 1.243; cf. *semina pugnae*, 3.235, 7.563). The Augustan poets like *ministro* (*OLD* 3) for *praebeo*, but it is also in Cicero and Livy. With *cotidie*, Mucianus maintains pressure on Vespasian to act: every day counts.   **popinis et comissationibus** 'amidst cookshops and carousals'. T. uses both words only once more: *comissationes* features pejoratively again in a speech (1.30.1), and *popinae* in the narrative, for the 'normal' leisure activities continuing despite the fighting in Rome (3.83.2).   **principis imitatione:** debilitation of the troops through imitation of Vitellius is a theme of the narrative (2.62.1, 68.1, 69.2).   **tibi . . . nouem legiones:** sc. *sunt*. Talking up one's own military strength naturally features in similar deliberative speeches (*adfore Britanniam, secutura Germanorum auxilia*, 1.52.3, *esse illi proprium militem . . . omnia prona uictoribus*, 3.64.1), usually as a prelude to denigrating one's opponent. Mucianus, with Vespasian (2.74.1), already counts the *III Gallica* in Moesia (4.4n. *quattuor*) as Flavian. The others are Mucianus' *IV Scythica*, *VI Ferrata* and *XII Fulminata* in Syria, Vespasian's *X Fretensis*, *V Macedonica* and *XV Apollinaris* in Judaea, and Tiberius Alexander's *III Cyrenaica* and *XXII Deiotariana* in Egypt.   **nulla acie**

exhaustae, non discordia corruptae 'not sapped by any battle, not infected by mutiny'; (13.1n. *in acie*). The point of comparison is Vitellius' army after the battle of Bedriacum. Mucianus has his cake and eats it, simultaneously suggesting that Otho did not fall *exercitus ui* (2.76.4) and that the Vitellian army is exhausted after the battle. T.'s recent account of the Vitellian *seditio* (2.68) endorses his strategic point about *discordia*.   **firmatus usu:** this expression appealed to Ammianus Marcellinus (16.10.21), though the more familiar combination refers to an army *cibo firmatus* (Liv. 9.32.4, 27.13.13, 28.15.3, Curt. 7.5.14, Fron. *Str.* 2.2.8; cf. *proeliis exercitati*, Caes. *Gal.* 2.20.3). The contrast with the Vitellian soldiers (*miles . . . neque labore firmari*, 2.93.1) is clear.   **belli domitor externi:** the combination is unique, but the agent-noun (only in the *H.*: 5.5.5, 5.16.3) recurs elsewhere in rousing expressions suggesting conquest on a grand scale (cf. *terrarum domitor*, Luc. 9.1014; *Lycurgi domitor et rubri maris*, Sen. *Her. F.* 903; *domitor tumidi . . . maris*, Sil. 9.291, *domitor telluris Hiberae*, Sil. 15.642; *orbis domitor*, Man. *Astr.* 1.793*)*. Mucianus employs licence (as only some of the troops have been involved in the Jewish war and the war itself is not yet finished). The postponed adj. adds impact and also suggests a moral hierarchy of experience in foreign, not civil war.   **classium . . . robora:** three fleets are available to the Flavians, in Pontus, Syria and Egypt. The Vitellians could counter with fleets at Ravenna and Misenum (3.2.2), although these will turn traitor under Lucilius Bassus (2.100.3). Naval resources would no doubt have been more central to Flavian strategy, if Antonius Primus had not hijacked the campaign (and a grain-blockade was always an option, 3.8.2, 4.38.2, 4.52.2). So, Mucianus moves the fleet from the Black Sea to Byzantium to secure Greece and Asia (2.83.2), but that plan was overtaken by the second battle of Bedriacum.   **fidissimi reges:** e.g. the wealthy Antiochus IV, king of Commagene, Sohaemus, king of Emesa, and Agrippa II, who ruled in eastern Palestine with Berenice (81.1nn.).   **tua ante omnis experientia** 'your own experience, in which you excel all others'; *OLD ante* 8c. Experience in a martial context appears again as a virtue (*A.* 14.36.3, Vell. 2.78.2, 2.110.6, Stat. *Theb.* 6.775). Despite Mucianus' flattery, Vespasian has military experience, but has never taken part in a civil war.

77.1 Nobis nihil ultra arrogabo 'For myself, I shall claim nothing beyond'. T. has the verb only once more, in Piso's speech, again in a play of false modesty (*nihil arrogabo mihi nobilitatis aut modestiae*, 1.30.1). For the shift from pl. to singular cf. *nobis . . . ausim, Agr.* 43.2, *dignitatem nostrum . . . non abnuerim* (1.1.3).   **numeremur:** *OLD numero* 8 'class'. Mucianus reverts to the first-person plural, paradoxically hinting that despite being only one man, he is a more valuable associate than the pair of generals Caecina and Valens.   **Mucianum:** the third person adds grandeur (47.2n. *hinc Othonem*). **antepono te mihi:** Mucianus (more ready to make an emperor than become one himself, 1.10.2) disingenuously turns a personal preference into a flattering judgement of quality.   **tuae domui triumphale nomen:** sc. *est*. Vespasian won triumphal insignia for his military activities in Britain during Claudius' invasion (3.44, *Agr.* 13.3, Suet. *Ves.* 4.2, Dio 60.20.3) as commander of the *Legio II Augusta*. His brother Sabinus was also involved, leading the *Legio XX Valeria Victrix*, although later sources concentrate almost exclusively on the emperor's achievements (celebrated at Jos. *BJ*

3.5, Val. Flac. 1.7–11, Sil. 3.597–8). T.'s *domus* tacitly acknowledges the contribution of both brothers. After L. Cornelius Balbus in 19 BC, no senator outside the imperial family was allowed to celebrate a triumph. Successful commanders were awarded *insignia* or *ornamenta* (e.g. the *toga picta*, an ivory sceptre, a triumphal statue): *OCD³* 'ornamenta', 'triumph'.   **duo iuuenes:** Titus (born 30 Dec. 39) is 29 and Domitian (born 24 Oct. 51) is 17.   **capax iam imperii alter:** this remark indicates the close friendship between Mucianus and Titus (2.5.2, 2.74.1), an asset to the Flavians, provided that it does not diminish Vespasian's support by raising the prospect of Titus as *princeps*. Part of Mucianus' rationale in the speech is to dispel this possibility by publicly pledging allegiance to Vespasian (even if there may still be a veiled threat: if Vespasian fails to act, then another competent candidate exists in Titus). *iam* ('already') + *alter* ('one of the pair') is deft and diplomatic, in that it hints that young Domitian may become as accomplished as his brother, without being overtly fawning. Mucianus' real feelings about Domitian may be revealed by his eloquent silence about him in the rest of the speech (cf. 4.85.2 for subsequent tensions between the pair). Being considered *capax imperii* did not always result in a great emperor (1.49.4). Both Augustus (*A.* 1.13.2) and Hadrian (Dio 69.17.3) made lists of *capaces imperii*, but the distinction of being named was naturally precarious. For a much earlier 'prediction' of Titus' principate by metoposcopy, see Suet. *Tit.* 2.   **apud Germanicos quoque exercitus clarus:** 76.3n. on *clarus* + *apud*. Titus, currently legionary legate of the *XV Apollinaris* in Judaea, apparently earned distinction as military tribune in Germany and then Britain (Suet. *Tit.* 4.1), but this stage of his career has attracted some creative fiction: the epitomised Dio says that Titus accompanied Vespasian to Britain in 43 and saved his father's life in 47 (60.30.1), but (born in 39) he would have been only eight at the time. T. perhaps omits Titus' service in Britain (at some point between 61 and 63?) because it was undistinguished (Jones (1984) 15), but a cogent reason for Mucianus to emphasise Titus' standing amongst the German armies is that Vespasian was especially worried about them (2.75). Pliny the Elder talks fondly of serving with Titus in the army (*nobis quidem qualis* [sc. *tu*] *in castrensi contubernio!, Nat. Praef.* 3), probably in Germany, but there are no details about Titus' *claritas* at a time 'when the Rhine frontier was abnormally peaceful' (Chilver (1979) 236).   **fuerit:** perfect potential subjunctive (37.2n. *concesserim*).   **non cedere imperio ei** 'not to yield power to him' sc. *Vespasiano*; *imperio* = abl. of respect.   **cuius filium adoptaturus essem:** the rumour was that Galba planned to adopt Titus (1.1n. *accitum in adoptionem*). T.'s readers had seen Nerva narrowly avert civil war by adopting Trajan, so such speculation about the succession held special relevance, as Trajan had no children (and indeed would die childless; Dio 69.1.2). Mucianus also seems to have been childless, or so his speculation here implies. In Josephus Vespasian's soldiers present the father's experience and the son's vigour as an ideal combination (*BJ* 4.597).

77.2 prosperarum aduersarumque rerum ordo: T. uses these polarised adjectives (17× in total) especially in speeches (1.65.2, 3.13.3, 3.66.2, 4.52.1). Before T., only Cicero juxtaposes them with an enclitic form (*ad prosperam aduersamue fortunam, ND* 3.89). The standard pairing in Latin involves *aduersus* + *secundus*.   **erit:** the indicative suggests that the result is only a matter of time (also *habebo* and *patiemur*). **si uincimus:** the present indicative in the protasis, rather than the future, implies that the decision to revolt has already been taken: cf. *si uincimus, omnia nobis tuta erunt* (Sall. *Cat.* 58.9; Heubner (1968) 271). **honorem quem dederis habebo:** despite appearing indebted to Vespasian and dependent on him for future honour, Mucianus knew that his timely support was an invaluable personal insurance policy for the future and financially advantageous (2.84.2): 'Mucianus, so vital to Vespasian's victory, was able to presume upon the emperor's gratitude to treat him impudently thereafter' (Lendon (1997) 127). Vespasian never felt able to admonish Mucianus, who considered himself secure *meritorum fiducia* (Suet. *Ves.* 13), and rewarded him with suffect consulships in 70 and 72, but the credit did not last indefinitely. Mucianus gradually found himself eclipsed in the 70s (Levick (1999) 194).   **discrimen et pericula:** these emphatic synonyms are common in Cicero (*Off.* 1.154, *Man.* 12, *Balb.* 25, *Lig.* 15, *Phil.* 7.1), but only in the singular apart from *discriminum et periculorum comites* (*ND* 2.166). T.'s combination (sing. + pl.) freshens the expression. Mucianus fleshes out the theoretical skeleton from the start of his speech when he urged Vespasian to consider whether the adviser adds *periculum suum* to his advice (2.76.1).   **immo:** with one exception (*G.* 14.5), T. always uses *immo* in speeches, usually in the closing stages. An arresting particle, it corrects or modifies the preceding statement, often for rhetorical effect (Liv. 26×, Sall. 4×; not in Caes.).   **tu . . . rege, mihi . . . trade:** this emerges as the broad Flavian plan after the meeting at Beirut (2.81.3): Vespasian is to remain in Egypt, while *dux Mucianus et Vespasiani nomen* (2.82.3) will proceed against Vitellius in Italy. Yet the later meeting at Poetovio, not attended by Vespasian or Mucianus, sees the general Antonius Primus usurp control by opting to invade Italy ahead of Mucianus and against Vespasian's orders (3.8.2). So Mucianus, despite his apparent readiness here, does not face the *proeliorum incerta*, except perhaps one contentious battle against the Dacians after Antonius Primus' defeat of the Vitellian forces (3.46.2–3, Wellesley (1972) 208–15). The division of labour recalls a motif from spirited battle-speeches in Livy, where responsibility for infantry and cavalry is divided between two commanders (*mihi legiones peditumque pugna curae erunt; penes te equestre sit decus*, 8.38.16, with Oakley (1998) 768), but Mucianus' partition here is rather different.   **tuos exercitus:** Černjak reads *omnes* for *tuos* (endorsed by Wellesley (1991) 1668), but *tuos* can stand, provided that we understand it to mean the whole army, not just the specific legions commanded by Vespasian so far. The pronominal adj. emphasises that the troops are controlled by Vespasian, not Mucianus; and the pl. alluringly suggests expansive resources.   **proeliorum incerta:** cf. *incerta belli* (*A.* 4.23.2, Liv. 30.2.6, 39.54.7). T. is devoted to the neuter substantive adj. + defining gen. (2.2n. *laeua maris*).

   77.3 acriore hodie disciplina . . . desciuerunt: T. uses *hodie* only in speeches (10×) for vividness and immediacy. Its unusual and emphatic position between the comparative adj. and noun creates a jerky effect suggesting excitement (cf. *has alteras hodie litteras* Cic. *Att.* 13.37.1), as do Mucianus' short sentences, lively metaphor, asyndeton, polarisation and parataxis as he moves towards the end of the speech. Traditionally, the peroration has two objectives, to refresh the memory and to influence the emotions (Lausberg (1998) §431): *at hic, si usquam, totos eloquentiae aperire fontes licet* (Quint. 6.1.52). Mucianus does not disappoint. **uicti:** again Mucianus makes a point work in diametrically opposed ways. These are the same conquered troops depicted as causing trouble in Italy earlier in the speech (*exarmat cohortes*, 2.76.4). **agunt** 'conduct themselves' (*OLD ago* 36). **hos** [sc. *uictos*] . . . **accendit: illi** [sc. *uictores*] . . . **hebescunt:** the peroration is dominated by a pair of polarised portraits, first collective (defeated Othonians / victorious Vitellians), then individual (Vespasian / Vitellius), each shaped by arguments drawn from personality and economically designed to appeal both to the emotions and to *utilitas:* as Vitellius and his supporters are morally defective, they are easy to defeat. The simple paratactic arrangement of clauses, with both verbs at the end, sharpens the contrast between *hos* and *illi*, but there is *uariatio* in switching from abstract nouns as subject (2.1n. *spes uicit*) with a singular verb, to the pronoun *illi* as subject with a pl. verb. **ira odium ultionis cupiditas . . . accendit:** the asyndeton and tricolon crescendo reinforce the intense feelings of the defeated Othonians as projected by Mucianus. The point is endorsed by T.'s observations in the main narrative (2.60.1, 2.66.1), and Vespasian will shamelessly exploit Otho's former soldiers by casting himself as an avenger of their dead hero (Suet. *Ves.* 6.4). Yet Mucianus also hints at the need for speed: an emotion such as *ira* can be considered 'temporary' (Quint. 5.10.28) and so must be exploited quickly. So too does the fire metaphor of *accendo*, common enough, but indicating that the Othonians' emotions can be extinguished at any point. **per fastidium et contumacia hebescunt** 'are dulled by their arrogance and indiscipline'. Mucianus implies that the debilitated state of the Vitellians is constant (again belittling them as a potential enemy), in contrast with the temporary window offered by the Othonians' emotions. The *uariatio* of a prepositional phrase with *per* + an abl. of means (Sörbom (1935) 84–5) draws attention to the mechanisms of the Vitellian deterioration. T. also uses *hebesco* of men at *A.* 3.69.2 (WM 469): the metaphor (if active) suggests a blunt knife or sword. **aperiet et recludet contecta et tumescentia uictricium partium uolnera bellum ipsum** 'the war itself will open up and expose the hidden, but swelling wounds of the victorious side'; abstract noun as subject (2.1n. *spes uicit*). Mucianus' *bellum ipsum* presupposes that the Flavian challenge will happen. The relatively simple figurative use of a wound for emotional pain is common in Latin (*OLD uulnus* 3) and features in T. (*Agr.* 7.1, 29.1, 45.5), but there is an unusually elaborate and sustained metaphor through the repellent imagery of the carefully chosen pairs of verbs and participles. *uulnus* + *aperio* is technical (Cels. 7.5.1), but T. innovates in linking *uulnus* + *recludo* (76.3n. *abiit . . . tempus* for the reduplication in *aperiet et recludet*). He uses the simple form *tumesco* for the compound *intumesco*, apparently the technical term (20× in Cels.). A similarly elaborate image of a subcutaneous ulcer for an army is used by the general Plancus, who says that he cannot help shuddering *si quid intra cutem subest uulneris, quod prius nocere potest quam sciri curarique possit* (Cic. *Fam.* 10.18.3). T.'s imagery recalls Demosthenes (an apt allusion from Mucianus, *satis decorus etiam Graeca facundia*, 2.80.2): 'O Athenians, the war itself will reveal the unsound parts (τὰ σαθρά) of Philip's affairs' (*Phil.* 1.44). **nec mihi maior in . . . fiducia est**

quam in 'I rely less on . . . than on'. Mucianus incorporates a final compliment and insult through the affectation of comparing how Vespasian's positive attributes and Vitellius' flaws will influence the war's progress.   **in tua uigilantia parsimonia sapientia:** Plutarch advises recipients of praise to be sceptical (*Mor.* 57a), but Mucianus extols Vespasian selectively, balancing praise with condemnation of Vitellius in a *syncrisis*. Idealised types were often praised for *uigilantia* (Woodman (1983) 319; Cic. *Fam.* 7.30.1, Plin. *Ep.* 3.5.8, 8.23.5, *Pan.* 10.3), a military virtue, but *parsimonia* is striking, especially as a positive spin on what is elsewhere called Vespasian's *auaritia* (5.1n.). Orators, especially in the peroration, should mitigate negative characteristics by using euphemisms, so that (e.g.) *auaritia* becomes *parsimonia* (Quint. 4.2.77). Vespasian's *auaritia* is not under the spotlight in this speech (unlike Vitellius' excesses), but Mucianus' appropriation of the positive term *parsimonia* shows how deft he is at flattery.   **in Vitellii torpore inscitia saeuitia:** Mucianus has dropped insinuations about Vitellius (*a contumelia . . . eligi*, 2.76.2; *nullis stipendiis . . . prouectus*, 2.76.4; *ne . . . quidem ducis arte*, 2.76.4), but reserves overt invective for the climax of the speech. It was especially desirable to stir *indignatio* against an opponent in the peroration (Cic. *Inu.* 1.100; Lausberg (1998) §438). Yet Mucianus' trio of negative characteristics is relatively restrained, particularly compared with T.'s censure of Vitellius in the narrative (e.g. 2.62.1). Mucianus pays more attention to the debilitated Vitellian army than their emperor, but that only mirrors Vespasian's own concerns (2.74.2–75) and itself is a snub.   **meliorem in bello causam quam in pace:** Mucianus ends on a practical note by appealing to Vespasian's desire for safety (as the following *nam* clause indicates), but the broad category *melior . . . causa* shows the Flavians seizing the moral high ground by fighting.   **nam qui deliberant, desciuerunt:** a powerful gnomic end to the speech ('a masterpiece of compression and epigrammatic logic', Plass (1988) 45), 'not uncommon in deliberative oratory' (McGushin (1994) 199). An *epiphonema* (a *sententia* in the final position of a proof or a statement) often has an emotive summarising effect (Quint. 8.5.11). This one recalls Titus Vinius' words to Galba: 'Asking whether we should remain loyal to Nero amounts to disloyalty' (Plut. *Galb.* 4.4). It is also Senecan (*Ben.* 5.14.2, *Cons. Sap.* 7.4, *De ira* 1.3.1).

    78.1 audentius: *legati amicique* encouraged Vespasian before (2.76.1), but Mucianus' speech has bolstered the whole entourage, not just the would-be emperor. **circumsistere hortari . . . referre:** the historic infinitives (5.1n. *anteire . . . obniti*) in asyndeton reflect the swift and enthusiastic encouragement of those present. **responsa uatum et siderum motus:** the chiasmus highlights a factor (often seen by T. as dangerous) which the ambitious cynically exploit to gain influence with powerful men. So *mathematici* (1.22.1) encourage Otho before he challenges Galba, although Vitellius is more wary (62.2n. *pulsi . . . mathematici*). Suitable omens always cluster around founders of a dynasty, as with Augustus (Suet. *Aug.* 94); if nothing plausible was circulating at the time, it could always be made up later (1.10.3).   **nec erat intactus tali superstitione:** the emphatic litotes shows how wary T. is about this trait. Whatever T.'s own views about haruspicy and astrology, Vespasian's undue faith in such practices makes him vulnerable to manipulation (Aubrion (1985) 106, Ash

(1999) 129–31; cf. Davies (2004) 165–70, *OCD³* '*superstitio*'). Cf. Libo Drusus, ensnared by his friend Firmius Catus pointing to the astrologers' alluring predictions (*A.* 2.27.2). Alexander the Great (*non intactae a superstitione mentis*, Curt. 4.6.12) consults a sooth-sayer about a prodigy during the siege of Gaza, but unlike Vespasian, he responds to a specific sign and is not manipulated by subordinates. Livy is more positive about an unnamed *uir haud intacti religione animi* (5.15.6).   **ut qui . . . habuerit** 'for he was the sort of man to retain'. The relative pronoun + subjunctive indicate the general char-acter of the antecedent, Vespasian (25.2n. *cui . . . placerent*). Here the relative clause also has a causal sense, emphasised by *ut* (a construction rare until Livy; Oakley (1998) 95).

mox rerum dominus: this evokes Virgil's Jupiter referring to *Romanos, rerum dominos gentemque togatam* (*A.* 1.282), quoted by Augustus (Suet. *Aug.* 40.5) and applied flatter-ingly by Martial to Domitian (14.124.2). The expression is concessive and bathetic, sharply distinguishing between Vespasian's lofty imperial position and his addictive retention of an astrologer. It occurs in another grand context, when the priest of Jupiter at Clunia predicts that *oriturum quandoque ex Hispania principem dominumque rerum* (Suet. *Galb.* 9.2). Galba took this to refer to himself.   **Seleucum:** Suetonius gives this name to Otho's astrologer (*Otho* 4.1), Ptolemaeus elsewhere (1.22.2, Plut. *Galb.* 23.7). T. probably rightly identifies him as Vespasian's *mathematicus*.   **rectorem et praescium** 'as his guide and seer'. Ironically *rector* often indicates a more rational sort of adviser (e.g. Plin. *Ep.* 4.17.6) and can even designate an emperor (Suet. *Cl.* 10.4), specifically Vespasian himself (Plin. *Nat.* 2.18).   **palam:** Tiberius was the first *princeps* to keep an astrologer openly at court (*A.* 6.21). *palam* implies that this prac-tice is potentially shameful, but the covert presence of such figures in the imperial *domus* is arguably more pernicious (cf. the *mathematici* of Poppaea's boudoir, 1.22.2). Even Augustus (in whose principate Manilius wrote the first surviving Latin poem on astrology, the *Astronomica*) consulted an astrologer, Theogenes. Yet significantly, he did this during his youth *in secessu Apolloniae* (Suet. *Aug.* 94.12). Emperors were often inconsistent regarding astrology (Barton (1994b) 41–9): Tiberius, personally *addictus mathematicae* (Suet. *Tib.* 69.1), still banished the astrologers (Suet. *Tib.* 36.1).

78.2 recursabant animo: T. has this verb, poetic in flavour, only here. *animo . . . recursat* (Virg. *A.* 4.3) is used of Dido's burgeoning passion for Aeneas. The focalisation of the portent through Vespasian is a vivid device for his characterisation and indicates his growing confidence after Mucianus' speech.   **uetera omina:** T. is selective, passing over other early omens from the tradition: (*a*) the oak-tree that produced a huge shoot at Vespasian's birth (only Suet. *Ves.* 5.2), (*b*) Vespasian covered in mud as a punishment during his aedileship in 38, but interpreted as a positive metaphor (Suet. *Ves.* 5.3, Dio 59.12), (*c*) the dog who brought Vespasian a human hand (Suet. *Ves.* 5.4, Dio 66.1), (*d*) the ox who knelt before Vespasian (Suet. *Ves.* 5.4, Dio 66.1), (*e*) Vespasian's dream about the extraction of Nero's tooth (Suet. *Ves.* 5.5, Dio 66.1). One reason for T.'s choice may be the psychological impact that the cypress omen made on Vespasian (Morgan (1996c) 44). Some critics are struck by T.'s pl. form to describe a single omen (Morgan (1996c) 49 n.30), but Vespasian may be contemplating a range of omens, even if T. elaborates only one.   **cupressus arbor:** the story (also Suet.

Ves. 5.4 and Dio 66.1) was probably in the common source. No doubt T. would have narrated the withering of this same tree shortly before Domitian's assassination in 96 (Suet. *Dom.* 15.2; Morgan (1996c) 47). For fallen trees to take root again was (and is) not unknown (Plin. *Nat.* 16.131), but this instance is extraordinary for the speed of the recovery. There was a similar portent involving an elm in the grove of Juno during the Cimbrian wars at the end of the second century BC (Plin. *Nat.* 16.132). Incidents (or dreams) involving trees were often interpreted as signifying future events (e.g. *A.* 13.58, Hdt. 1.108, Ov. *Fast.* 3.31–8, Sil. 16.586–91, Suet. *Aug.* 94.11, *Galb.* 1.1, Soph. *El.* 417–23, Dio 41.61, 43.41, 48.43, Quint. Smyrn. 12.517).   **in agris eius:** T. 'tidies up' Suetonius, who says that the remarkable tree was on Vespasian's grandmother's land at Cosa (*in agro auito*, *Ves.* 5.4). In the omen being 'remembered' by Vespasian, all the attention is naturally on himself.   **conspicua altitudine** 'remarkably tall'. This combination is only here in extant Latin (*TLL* s.v. *altitudo* 1765.23).   **repente prociderat:** the expression deftly removes a contradiction in the other sources. Suetonius said that the tree had toppled although there was no storm (*Ves.* 5.4), but Dio blames a violent wind (66.1).   **postera die:** cf. *insequenti die* (Suet. *Ves.* 5.4). On the gender of *dies*, see 22.1n. *uixdum orto die*. The speedy regrowth is especially impressive as cypress trees were notoriously difficult to rear (*difficillime nascentium*, Plin *Nat.* 16.139), except in Crete (Plin. *Nat.* 16.142).   **eodem uestigio** 'on the same spot'. T. adds a detail not in Suetonius (*Ves.* 5.4) to increase the portent's significance.   **procera et latior** 'just as tall and broader'. Some editors emend *latior* to *laetior* since cypress trees are normally tall (e.g. *rectos . . . cupressos*, Ennius *A.* 511 Sk. cited at Gell. 13.21.13), rather than broad, but this is unnecessary: the 'abnormal' is required in a portent (and omens involving trees often stress breadth to suggest wide rule from a small start). Others argue that T. is thinking of the 'male' cypress, with branches that spread more broadly than the tapered 'female' cypress (Plin. *Nat.* 16.141). **grande id prosperumque consensu haruspicum:** sc. *auspicium* and *ducebatur.* Such agreement amongst *haruspices* is unusual, but Vespasian is no doubt idealising the moment in retrospect. Flavius Sabinus was much more prominent than his brother around the time of the portent (Suet. *Ves.* 2.2).   **summa claritudo:** the archaising *claritudo* (for the Ciceronian synonym *claritas*) is a Sallustian favourite (MW 108), which makes its debut in *H.* (1.85.1, 3.86.1). *claritas* appears once in *Agr.* and *G.*, 3× in *H.*, and 2× in the *A.*, where it is almost entirely ousted by the more striking *claritudo* (31×). As often in T., the more recherché term becomes standard. 'The words with the root *clar-* are, in essence, more descriptive than laudatory – that is until they are elevated by the Augustan poets, especially Vergil' (Habinek (2000) 270).   **iuueni admodum Vespasiano:** comparison with the same phrase at *D.* 1.2 suggests that T. means 'a man of young pre-quaestorian age' and that Vespasian was aged about 18 (Chilver (1979) 238).   **promissa:** sc. *est.*   **triumphalia et consulatus et Iudaicae uictoriae decus:** Vespasian won triumphal ornaments between 44 and 47 (77.1n. *triumphale nomen*), his consulship came in the last two months of 51 (Suet. *Ves.* 4.2, *Dom.* 1.1), and he won a significant victory in the Jewish campaign by June 68 when Jerusalem was encircled (5.10.1, Jos. *BJ* 4.490; Levick (1999) 38), even though the war was not complete (4.3n. *bellum Iudaicum*). The paratactic arrangement of these items glosses over the gap of almost 40 years between the last item and the original occurrence of the portent. Vespasian has a long memory. **implesse fidem ominis** 'to have provided confirmation of the omen'. **uidebatur:** 70.3n. *erant quos.* **portendi sibi imperium credebat:** Vespasian's readiness to believe this omen's significance contrasts with his jokes as an old man about the portents allegedly signifying his imminent death (Suet. *Ves.* 23.4). By emphasising the long-standing psychological significance of the portent for Vespasian, T. further undermines Flavian propaganda that the imperial challenge was spontaneous.

78.3 Est . . . Carmelus: the ecphrastic topographical opening of the section (Lausberg (1998) §819) abruptly shifts the narrative to a more recent portent (again, carefully selected), but details are postponed by a short digression on the rites of Carmelus, the eponymous god of a mountain (once belonging to Galilee and now to Tyre, Jos. *BJ* 3.35) near the coast on the borders of Syria and Judaea *c.* 20 miles north of Caesarea. This place had long been associated with divine activity. Here in the ninth century BC the prophet Elijah successfully overwhelmed followers of the rival Canaanite god Baal by prompting the god of Israel to light a fire where Baal had failed to do so (1 Kings 18). If, through the mountain site, Carmelus can still be associated with Baal at this point (Levick (1999) 46), then Vespasian's consultation of the god's priest is suggestive; for Baal was a non-Jewish god, whose help and advice was being sought in the struggle against the Jews (cf. Jos. *BJ* 4.370 for divine help for Vespasian in fighting the Jews). The inspection of the entrails (*inspectis . . . extis,* 2.78.3) certainly suggests that Carmelus is non-Jewish. The area was also associated with Zeus (Scylax, *Periplus* 104), who was no doubt 'grafted' on to the pre-existing cult. More prosaically, traders accidentally discovered how to make glass near this mountain (Plin. *Nat.* 36.191). Vespasian's consultation of Carmel's oracle is in Suetonius, but the story is much less vivid and detailed (*Ves.* 5.6). **Iudaeam inter Syriamque:** anastrophe involving co-ordinated substantives is rare even in T. before the *A.* (Morgan (1996c) 49 n.31). Here the position of the preposition mirrors the concept being described. **ita uocant montem deumque:** sentence terminal -*que* (2.2n. *aduenasque*). The '*uocant*-formula' is common in ethnographical contexts (WM 340). Mountains, wild and isolated places, were often associated with gods: Zeus was said to be born on mount Ida and Hermes on mount Cyllene. The identification of particular mountains as gods started early: e.g. Atlas, both a divine Titan and a physical mountain (Hes. *Th.* 517–20, Hdt. 4.184, Virg. *A.* 4.246–51). Greeks and Romans were happy to use pre-existing place-names for new gods outside the traditional pantheon, whether derived from cities, rivers or mountains (a reflection of spirituality, but also a way to engender civic and local pride, and a useful device for poets). **nec simulacrum deo aut templum:** Carmelus is thus more 'alien' than Paphian Venus (2.3), who at least has a temple and a cone-shaped image. Romans were naturally struck by the absence of temples and images of gods in other cultures, and T. himself comments on the Jews: *igitur nulla simulacra urbibus suis, nedum templa sistunt* (5.5.4); similar statements are made about the Persians (Hdt. 1.131, Cic. *Rep.* 3.14, *Leg.* 2.26), the Gauls (Diod. Sic. 22.9.4) and the Germans

(*G.* 9.3 with Rives (1999) 162–3), suggesting an ethnographical commonplace. Yet the Roman king, Numa, inspired by Pythagoras, forbade cult-images of the gods, deeming it impious to compare higher entities with lower forms and judging that divine spirit should be grasped with the mind alone (Plut. *Num.* 8.7–8; also Varro at August. *CD* 4.27). The first such image was allegedly a statue of Ceres made at Rome in 485 BC (Pliny *Nat.* 34.15). Vesta is the one Roman divinity who, for special reasons, continued not to have statues (Ov. *Fast.* 6.295–8; also Statius' *clementia, Theb.* 12.493–4). Lucilius in the second century BC satirised those who confused representations of gods with the gods themselves (fr. 484–9, Marx; cited by Feeney (1998) 93 with discussion, 92–7). **sic tradidere maiores:** the parenthesis (18.1n. *is enim*) gently diminishes the sense of 'otherness' for the Roman reader. There may be no image of the god or temple, but at least these locals respect their own *mos maiorum* (held dear in Roman culture, at least ideally).   **ara tantum et reuerentia:** punchy adversative asyndeton (3.2n. *simulacrum . . . exsurgens*). What could have been presented as a cultic oddity endows the locals with a simple piety, free from garish display (cf. the Arcadians, unquestioningly respectful of the gods, Ov. *Met.* 1.220–1). It evokes ethnographical descriptions (*G.* 9.3) and idealised images of early Rome, as when Evander tells Aeneas that the leafy Capitoline hill is the home of a god, believed by his simple Arcadians to be Jupiter (Virg. *A.* 8.351–3): the sanctity of the area (not an elaborate temple) generates religious awe.   **illic sacrificanti Vespasiano:** T. now turns to the portent itself. Suetonius gives other recent portents (*Ves.* 5.6–7): (*a*) the captive Josephus' prediction, (*b*) Nero's dream, (*c*) Julius Caesar's statue turning eastwards (also in T., 1.86.1), (*d*) eagles at Bedriacum (a version is at 2.50.2). T. selects the prediction of Basilides for its contemporary influence in the east. The dat. clause at first seems to set a devout Vespasian in an environment that reflects his straightforward and austere character (cf. *antiquo ipse cultu uictuque, A.* 3.55.4), but appearances can be deceptive.   **spes occultas uersaret animo:** Roman deviousness intrudes on the simple setting of the pious mountain sanctuary, but Vespasian's hidden hopes are not elaborated. The context hints at imperial ambitions, but much depends on the timing of this visit to Carmelus (78.4n. *et statim . . . et tunc*): a swift end to the Jewish war could easily have been Vespasian's main hope. Unsubstantiated barbs such as this one leave T. open to accusations of bias; but he is at pains to confront the prevailing trends of pro-Flavian historiography (Briessmann (1955), Nicols (1978), Ramage (1983); 2.101.1) and to demonstrate that his *auctoritas* as a historian is not compromised by Vespasian's patronage (1.1.3).   **Basilides sacerdos:** the priest's identity is controversial, as the subject of a subsequent miracle in Alexandria has the same name. This is the apparition of an Egyptian nobleman (or freedman, Suet. *Ves.* 7.1), who appears to Vespasian in the temple of Serapis (4.82). Some suggest that these references are to the same man (Scott (1934) 138–40, Nicols (1978) 125–6, Rajak (1983) 189, Le Bonniec and Hellegouarc'h (1989) 223 n.11), but this seems unlikely, especially since this incident predates the one at Alexandria, where Basilides is a local (Morgan (1996c) 44 n.12).   **quidquid . . . hominum:** the direct speech in T. vividly contrasts with Suetonius' indirect speech, where the *sortes* ('lots') promise Vespasian (blandly) that *quidquid cogitaret uolueretque animo, quamlibet magnum, id esse prouenturum* (*Ves.* 5.6). Instead, T. has an elegantly constructed pronouncement from the colluding priest. An expansive *seu . . . seu . . . siue* tricolon in the subordinate clause precedes a main clause marked by a trio of climactic subjects in asyndeton, each responding in order to the items in the subordinate clause (*domum exstruere* ∼ *magna sedes*; *prolatare agros* ∼ *ingentes termini*; *ampliare seruitia* ∼ *multum hominum*). The priest's potentially allegorical but ambiguous language of estate management brilliantly tantalises and intrigues readers (and the contemporary audience), without the 'code' being immediately obvious. The whole scene recalls the soothsayer's pronouncement to the ambitious Marius (Sall. *Jug.* 63.1; cf. Plut. *Mar.* 8.6). **Vespasiane:** the simple vocative (76.2n. *Vespasiane*) belies the grandeur of the moment. **domum exstruere:** 34.2n. on *struo / exstruo. domus* sets up the fundamental ambiguity, as the surface meaning involves the physical structure of a house (*OLD* 1; *domum . . . exstruere*, Sall. *Rep.* 8.1; *quae sunt exstructa domorum*, Lucr. 6.561; *in exstruendis et decorandis domibus*, Sen. *Con.* 2.1.12), but it also permits a metaphorical sense, the members of a household (*OLD* 6), here with dynastic connotations (cf. *Augustus in domo successorem quaesiuit, ego in re publica*, 1.15.2). There is a similar ambiguity when Otho, en route to his imperial challenge, leaves Galba with the excuse that he is going to buy a dilapidated property (*emi sibi praedia uetustate suspecta*, 1.27.2). Double meanings that are only clear after the event are the building-blocks of portents and oracular pronouncements: e.g. Apollo's oracle at Delphi warns Nero to beware of the 73rd year. This reassures him, but the reference is to Galba (Suet. *Nero.* 40.3). On oracular wordplay, see Plass (1988) 71–8: 'The equivocation on which they [omens or oracles] hinge is rooted in language itself' (78). **prolatare agros** 'enlarging your estate'. Vespasian probably inherited his paternal grandmother's estate at Cosa in Etruria (Suet. *Ves.* 2.1), but the family also had property near Rome (Suet. *Ves.* 5.2; Levick (1999) 6–7). There were advantages and disadvantages in extending one's estate (Plin. *Ep.* 3.19); it was sometimes safer (given the possibility of natural disasters) to invest in several scattered properties, rather than one big holding (Plin. *Ep.* 4.6, 8.17.3). **ampliare seruitia:** *amplio* (for *augeo, uel sim.*) is in T. only here. The (more elevated) abstract noun *seruitium*, used metonymically for *serui* (*OLD* s.v. *seruitium* 3b), is favoured by T. (following Cic., Liv.; Woodman (1983) 178, Kraus (1994) 162). If read with the 'hidden' meaning of the pronouncement in mind, it cynically casts Roman citizens as slaves, with Vespasian as a potential *dominus* (*rerum dominus*, 2.78.1; cf. Mucianus on Vespasian's own imminent *seruitus* if he does not challenge Vitellius, 2.76.2). We can compare Galba's indignant contrast between 'egalitarian' Rome and nations ruled by kings, where one *domus* dominates a realm of slaves (*neque enim hic, ut gentibus quae regnantur, certa dominorum domus et ceteri serui*, 1.16.4). **magna sedes, ingentes termini:** 4.2n. *ingens rerum fiducia* for *ingens*. The most relevant imperial subtext is Nero's Golden House in Rome (*A.* 15.42.1, Suet. *Nero* 31, Elsner (1994) 117–18, 120–2), ostentatiously rejected by Vespasian (Dio 66.10.4) and reappropriated for the public as the Flavian amphitheatre and the baths of Titus. It was certainly a big project, perceived either as coterminous with the city, as in a popular couplet of invective (*Roma domus fiet: Veios migrate, Quirites | si non et Veios occupat ista domus*, Suet.

Nero 39.2; also *unaque iam tota stabat in urbe domus*, Mart. *Spect.* 2.4) or even as encircling Rome (*bis uidimus urbem totam cingi domibus principum Gai et Neronis, huius quidem, ne quid deesset, aurea*, Plin. *Nat.* 36.111).

78.4 et statim . . . et tunc: this raises the question of chronology. Basilides' original pronouncement may have been as early as the summer of 68, after the encirclement of Judaea and the death of Nero, while Vespasian awaited confirmation of his current appointment. Its significance was only becoming clear by June 69 with the imminent imperial challenge (Morgan (1996c) 49, Levick (1999) 38, 68). **fama exceperat** 'rumour had pounced on'; abstract noun as subject (2.1n. *spes uicit*). T. says nothing about how the priest's pronouncement became known to others (cf. the priest Sostratus, careful to speak to Titus in private *petito secreto*, 2.4.2). Perhaps Vespasian and his entourage deliberately circulated it as Roman propaganda during the Jewish war. **aperiebat** 'was starting to reveal the meaning' (*OLD* s.v. *aperio* 12). Vespasian has not yet been declared emperor, but his intentions must have been an open secret by June 69. **nec quidquam:** sc. *erat*. **in ore uolgi:** whereas the first omen (the cypress tree) has a psychological impact on Vepasian, the second portent (Basilides), not focalised through Vespasian, influences other people (Morgan (1996c) 44). The prevailing talk about Vespasian in the east will soon be matched by the gossip in Italy (*erat tamen in ore famaque Vespasianus*, 2.73). **crebriores apud ipsum sermones** (sc. *tanto*) 'there were more frequent discussions in his company'. The omission of *tanto* briefly (and wryly) suggests that the point of comparison for *crebriores sermones* is the unprecedented popular talk of the previous sentence, now outdone by Vespasian's impressively loquacious entourage (or even by Vespasian himself: *apud* is ambiguous), but *quanto* clarifies that the correlation is with the next clause. If the talk is before Vespasian, it smacks of *adulatio*, and in a neat ring-composition reverts to the theme at the start of the chapter (*ceteri audentius . . . referre*, 2.78.1). **quanto sperantibus plura dicuntur** 'to the extent that optimism always prompts more grandiose talk'. There is further ambiguity, as *sperantibus* can indicate things said 'to' or 'by' the hopeful. T. apparently does not want to exclude either possibility. *plura* indicates not just the volume of speech, but its ambitious subject matter, as in the elliptical *ergo Epicharis plura* [sc. *dixit*] (*A.* 15.51.3), where Epicharis tries to enlist Volusius in the Pisonian conspiracy, gets an initially encouraging response, and then goes further (*plura*), elaborating all the *princeps*' crimes. **haud dubia destinatione discessere** 'with their resolve strong, they departed'. Apart from one appearance in Livy (32.35.12), *destinatio* is a 'silver' word. The forceful alliteration aptly conveys the Flavians' common resolve after all this talk. The current meeting between Vespasian and Mucianus perhaps took place at Carmel, triggering memories of Basilides' prediction (Morgan (1996c) 53). **Antiochiam:** Antioch (mod. Antakya; *OCD*³ 'Antioch (1)'; Kondoleon (2000), Ball (2000) 56–60) on the river Orontes *c.* 15 miles from the coast, was founded in 300 BC by Alexander the Great's associate, Seleucus I. Pompey annexed the city in 64 BC (Freeman (1994)) and made it the provincial capital of Syria thanks to 'its situation, at the bottle-neck of a fertile though swampy inland plain, with a mild Mediterranean climate and a navigable passage along the Orontes to the sea' (Butcher (2003) 108).

It was a centre of learning (*urbi . . . eruditissimis hominibus liberalissimisque studiis affluenti*, Cic. *Arch.* 4) and had a magnificent golden temple of Capitoline Jupiter (Liv. 41.20.9), as well as an honorific cenotaph for Germanicus after he was cremated in the city (*A.* 2.83.2). Antioch also had a mint (2.82.1), which struck coins for Galba and Otho, but not Vitellius (Levick (1999) 46). T.'s admirer Ammianus, a native of the city, proudly calls it *orientis apex pulcher* (22.9.14) and talks of its wealth of commodities (14.8.8). The stylish, hedonistic governor Mucianus would certainly have enjoyed life there, in the imperial palace on an island between two branches of the Orontes (Grainger (1990) 124–5).   **Caesaream:** Strato, king of the Phoenician city Sidon, founded Caesarea (*OCD³* 'Caesarea (2) in Palestine'; Holum *et al.* (1988) 55–154, Millar (1990) 26–8) on the coast of Judaea in the fourth century BC. It was originally called Strato's Tower. Pompey annexed it in 63 BC, and in 30 BC Octavian presented it to Herod the Great, who embarked on a huge rebuilding project (22–10 BC), including a palace, amphitheatre and harbour (Jos. *BJ* 1.408–15, *AJ* 15.331–41). He renamed the city after his benefactor Caesar Augustus. Its new population, ethnically and socially diverse, was largely brought in from other areas, and in 6, the city became Judaea's provincial capital. Massive violence erupted in 66, when the city's non-Jews killed 20,000 Jewish fellow citizens, part of the prelude to the Jewish war. Vespasian made Caesarea his base of operations during the Jewish war, and later promoted it to a Roman colony (Levick (1999) 139).   **illa . . . hoc Iudaeae caput est:** as one would expect, the pronoun *illa* is feminine, by attraction to its antecedent *Antiochia*, even though its complement *caput* is neuter (cf. Goodyear (1972) 313 for T. failing to incorporate attraction in other cases involving pronouns). The chapter's monosyllabic ending creates a natural pause before T. resumes the narrative proper and (with *Iudaeae*) sets up ring-composition with the digression's opening (*est Iudaeam*, 2.78.3).

    79 Initium . . . coeptum: sc. *est*. The pleonasm (68.1n. *orta . . . initio*) aptly mirrors the halting, drawn-out start to the Flavian challenge.   **ferendi . . . imperii:** the simple form *fero* (*TLL* s.v. *fero* 547.12; *OLD fero* 23) for the compound *transfero* may hint that *imperium* was not yet securely in anyone's grip to be transferred *from*. **Alexandriae:** in 331 BC Alexander the Great founded Alexandria (*OCD³* 'Alexandria (1)'), Egypt's main Mediterranean port, famous for its libraries and lighthouse. Octavian, after making Egypt a province, appointed Cornelius Gallus as the first (equestrian) prefect (74.1n. *praefectus Aegypti*). After a strategy meeting at Berytus (2.81.3), the plan is for Vespasian to safeguard the grain supply by travelling to Egypt (2.82.3), but en route to Alexandria he hears news of his victory at Bedriacum (3.48.3). The citizens welcome Vespasian enthusiastically once he arrives (Phil. *VA* 5.27) and he spends the autumn and winter of 69 there engaging in miracle cures and sight-seeing (4.81–4).   **Tiberio Alexandro:** 74.1n.   **kalendis Iuliis:** this is the first of only three precise dates in the book (cf. nine in *H.* 1, and two each in *H.* 3 and 4). Suetonius supports *1 Jul.* 69 for the initial proclamation in Alexandria (*Ves.* 6.3), but contradicts T. (and himself!) in saying that the first move to make Vespasian emperor came from detachments of the Danube legions in *August* 69 (*octauo imperii mense, Vit.* 15.1, *Ves.* 6.2). Yet T. certainly implies that the actions of the Danube legions *followed* the proclamation in Alexandria (2.85–6). In another contentious account, Josephus claims that the soldiers of *Judaea* (not Alexandria) were the first to proclaim Vespasian emperor (*BJ* 4.603–4), after which he wrote to Tiberius Alexander for help (*BJ* 4.616–17), but this version reflects pro-Flavian propaganda, at pains to cast the revolt as unplanned. Such conflicting accounts show how difficult it was to establish the correct sequence of events, so vulnerable to subsequent distortion (wilful or otherwise). Participants sought self-preservation after supporting the wrong side and some historians were naturally predisposed to favour the winners under the new regime.   **sacramento:** 6.1n. *sacramentum Othonis*.   **legiones eius:** the *III Cyrenaica* and *XXII Deiotariana*. Their camp, where the oath was administered, was at Nicopolis (Levick (1999) 47). **isque primus principatus dies in posterum celebratus:** sc. *est*. Suetonius also makes this proleptic point, which was perhaps in the common source: *qui principatus dies in posterum obseruatus est* (*Ves.* 6.3). In reality, the start of Vespasian's principate was much messier (4.1.1). The senate did not endorse him as emperor until 21 Dec. 69 (4.3.3), but pointedly he gave constitutional weight to the soldiers' intervention in retrospect by selecting 1 Jul. 69 as his *dies imperii* (although Vitellius was killed on 20 Dec. 69). We are lucky to have the bronze tablet preserving the *Lex de imperio Vespasiani*, the controversial bill legitimising Vespasian's powers. Its final clause, validating Vespasian's actions before the bill was passed, further marginalised the senate and set a dangerous precedent to the soldiers (Brunt (1977), Crawford (1996) 1, 549–54, Levick (1999) 86 and 233 n.21).   **quamuis . . . nuntius:** the apparently authoritative main clause (7 words) is dwarfed by a series of subordinate clauses (26 words), each complicating the simple statement that 1 Jul. was later celebrated as Vespasian's *dies imperii* (13.2n. *quae* on 'appendix sentences'). T. questions the convenient façade of that date: if the soldiers' actions were to be given such constitutional weight, why not pick 3 Jul., when Vespasian's own troops endorsed him (*quamuis . . . iurasset*)? What about the delicate diplomacy of Titus, who laid the groundwork for the imperial challenge well before 1 Jul. (*ne Titus . . . nuntius*)?   **Iudaicus exercitus:** *V Macedonica, X Fretensis* and *XV Apollinaris*.   **quinto nonas Iulias:** 3 Jul. is generally accepted as correct. Some critics favour Suetonius' 11 Jul. (*Ves.* 6.3), which allows time for news of the proclamation to reach Caesarea from Alexandria, but if events were as carefully orchestrated as T. implies, the 'news' would not need to travel between the two cities (Jones (2000) 49–50).   **eo ardore:** T. recognises the troops' enthusiasm (a keynote of pro-Flavian accounts), but only after clearly signalling that Vespasian and his entourage planned the challenge in advance (2.74–8). Their avid proclamation contrasts with the German troops' declaration for Vitellius, hesitant at first (including a hiatus of a specious oath to the SPQR: 1.55.4), although later their enthusiasm grows (Damon (2003) 213).   **ut ne Titus quidem filius exspectaretur** 'that they would not even wait for his son Titus'. This implies that the original plan was for Titus to be present at the proclamation. He had set off on a final mission to Syria on *c.* 25 Jun. (Nicols (1978) 71, Flaig (1992) 365 n.36, Levick (1999) 47).   **Syria remeans:** T. generally favours *remeo* + the abl. without a preposition for countries 'from which' (Furneaux (1896) 47; *A.* 1.3.3, *A.* 2.69.1 with Goodyear (1981) 405–6;

but cf. *ex Campania remeauerat, A.* 15.60.4). Until the end of Augustan era, *remeo* (only 5× in prose authors: Liv., Cic., Varro) was mainly poetic, but Columella, Seneca the Younger and (especially) Pliny the Elder adopt it for prose texts (Oakley (2005) 70–1). **consiliorum . . . nuntius:** this is a further sign of careful Flavian planning as the main protagonists make final preparations. Even if the soldiers accelerate the plan by acting before Titus' return, it does not unduly upset the strategy: Mucianus is ready (cf. *id ipsum opperiens,* 2.80.2).   **Cuncta** = synonymous for *omnia* (1.3n. *cuncta . . . perlustrat*).   **impetu militum acta:** sc. *sunt.* T. echoes *omnia deinde arbitrio militum acta* (1.46.1) after Otho's proclamation, implying that this is simply the way things now happen, for better or worse. This is a more muted version than in Josephus, where soldiers surround the reluctant Vespasian with drawn swords (T. transfers this instead to Otho; 1.27.2) and threaten to kill him if he does not accept the principate (*BJ* 4.603). T. resists pro-Flavian accounts of the acclamation.   **non parata contione, non coniunctis legionibus** 'although no assembly had been prepared and the legions had not been marshalled'. Speeches were originally made at a *contio* (*OLD* 1b), a mil-itary assembly, after successful battles (Plb. 6.39.2–3, Caes. *Gal.* 5.52.4; Goldsworthy (1996) 276–7) and often feature in traditional historiography (Oakley (1998) 148). In T., they become political vehicles for winning military support in advance (e.g. Galba announces his adoption of Piso at a *contio,* 1.18.2) or extending it (e.g. Vitellius praises his soldiers for their victory at Bedriacum, 2.57.2). The anaphora and asyndeton of the two appended abl. absolutes aptly convey the Flavian troops' haste.

   80.1 dum . . . salutauere: the elaborate syntax reflects the confusion and excite-ment of the proclamation. Two subordinate clauses introduced by *dum* in asyndeton, with their verbs and nouns arranged chiastically (*quaeritur tempus . . . casus obseruantur*), are followed by two nom. participle clauses (*adsistentes . . . salutaturi*), with the sen-tence culminating in a short, powerful main clause (*imperatorem salutauere*). Vespasian is 'buried' at the heart of the subordinate clauses (*Vespasianum*), reflecting how the action and emotions pile up around him. Suetonius' version is much less dramatic and adorned (*Iudaicus deinde exercitus V Idus Iul. apud ipsum iurauit, Ves.* 6.3).   **prima uox** 'the man to speak first' (Irvine). T.'s use of abstract for concrete by synecdoche is choice. Whoever publicly proclaimed Vespasian as emperor would irreversibly com-mit himself to the cause and if the proposal misfired, could face danger. Yet if the challenge succeeded, the rewards were potentially great. Anyone with a sharp instinct for self-preservation would naturally hesitate before taking on this role; and neither of Vespasian's closest supporters, Titus and Mucianus, was present in Judaea. Fabius Valens played this part for Vitellius (1.57.1), a reflection of his remarkable loyalty to his *princeps,* despite his other flaws (3.62.2).   **dum animo spes timor, ratio casus obuersantur** 'while hope and trepidation, reason and chance passed before their minds'. There are precedents for *obuersor* (*OLD* 2) + *animo / animis* (Cic. *Tusc.* 2.52, Liv. 1.25.3, 35.11.3, Val. Max. 1.7.7, 5.3.5, Sen. *Ben.* 4.20.3), but it is more often combined with forms of *oculi* (cf. 5.17.1). The juxtaposition of polarised abstract concepts in asyndeton vividly marks the sharp emotional fluctuations of Vespasian's supporters. **egressum cubiculo Vespasianum:** this detail is not in Josephus or Suetonius, but such a mundane part of the daily routine triggers bathos after the grand practical and emotional concerns outlined in the two previous *dum* clauses. All this detailed and extensive discussion amongst the Flavian generals will be promptly undercut by ordinary, practical soldiers, who simply want to put the coup in motion: Vespasian leaves his quarters and they finally have access to him.   **pauci milites:** the capacity of relatively few soldiers to drive events recalls T.'s scornful comment about the *duo manipulares* (1.25.1), who undertook to hand over the empire, and the paltry *tres et uiginti speculatores* (1.27.2; cf. 1.30.3), who proclaimed Otho emperor. Such mirroring of earlier events suggests that this is apparently the way that these things happen now, regardless of the candidate. The detail undercuts pro-Flavian accounts, which imply that many soldiers proclaimed Vespasian emperor (Jos. *BJ* 4.601–4).   **solito . . . ordine** 'as a matter of routine' (Irvine).   **salutaturi . . . salutauere:** the verbal polyptoton (68.3n. *remedium . . . tumultus*) pointedly marks the abrupt shift in the soldiers' salutation of Vespasian, not as their *legatus*, but as *imperator*. Future participles are rarely repeated by finite verbs (Wills (1996) 303 cites *A.* 3.16.4, Hor. *Epod.* 1.9–11, Ov. *Ep.* 5.59), so T.'s syntax vividly underscores their U-turn. The polyptoton shows *uariatio* after the *adnominatio* (17.2n. *capta . . . intercepti*) that marked Otho's proclamation: *consalutatum imperatorem ac paucitate salutantium trepidum* (1.27.2).   **ceteri adcurrere . . . cumulare:** 57.2n. *uirtutem . . . cumulat* on *cumulo*. Historic infinitives (5.1n. *anteire . . . obniti*) in asyndeton aptly convey the speed of those who jump on the bandwagon. The notion of large numbers promptly following the lead of a decisive few has an Othonian precedent (1.45.1) and offers material for a gnomic statement: *insita mortalibus natura propere sequi quae piget inchoare* (1.55.1).   **Caesarem . . . uocabula:** 62.2n. *edictum . . . reciperet.*   **mens a metu ad fortunam transierat:** 'instantaneous' pluperfect (1.1n. *disperserat*). For *mens* as the seat of emotions, see *OLD* 6; *fortuna* here has specific resonances of imperial power (1.2n. *quantaecumque fortunae*). There is striking brachylogy, as the focus moves from an emotion experienced (fear) to (a sense of) following good fortune. Critics disagree about whether T. refers to Vespasian or his followers. Advocates of the followers point to a contrast with *in ipso* in the next clause, but the other camp argues that Vespasian was earlier described as *pauoribus nutans* (2.76.1). It is perhaps best to take *mens* as the collective state of mind amongst the Flavians, including Vespasian.   **nihil tumidum, arrogans aut in rebus nouis nouum:** Vespasian apparently maintained his affability during his principate, supposedly 'grounded' temperamentally by his own relatively lowly origins (Suet. *Ves.* 12, Dio 66.11). Juxtaposing *in rebus nouis* (*OLD nouus* 10) + *nouum* (*OLD nouus* 9b) shows *paronomasia*, generated by two different senses of the adj. Adjectival polyptoton can be witty (Wills (1996) 229; cf. Plutarch's quip that he inhabits a μικρὰν πόλιν 'small city', where he prefers to stay to stop it getting μικροτέρα, 'even smaller', *Dem.* 2.2), but T.'s linguistic playfulness also embraces a serious point, that Vespasian did not allow imperial power to go to his head.

80.2 ut primum tantae altitudinis obfusam oculis caliginem disiecit 'as soon as the dizziness that had blurred his vision after such a great elevation had cleared'. *caligo* is only here in T.; its metaphor suggests fog, mist, or any natural

phenomenon, which hampers sight and disorientates (e.g. the ash-cloud from the eruption of Vesuvius, Plin. *Ep.* 6.20.13). It indicates temporary blindness, as when Nero experiences such a thick *caligo* in the temple of Vesta that he cannot see (Suet. *Nero* 19.1; cf. Celsus, where *oculorum caligo* is a technical term for blurred vision coinciding with the onset of a particular illness, 2.7.30, 2.8.18, 4.2.2). The elevated language recalls epic, as when Jupiter *nubila disiecit* (Ov. *Met.* 1.328). Metaphors involving blindness and sight often serve to characterise emperors (e.g. Domitian's *tam caeca et corrupta mens assiduis adulationibus*, *Agr.* 43.4; or Tiberius *quasi aspiciens undantem per domos sanguinem*, *A.* 6.39.2); and Vespasian will eventually move from restoring his own 'sight' to curing a real blind man in Alexandria (4.81). Triller (1742) emended M's *multitudinis* to *altitudinis* (generally accepted), on the analogy of Livy: *cum altitudo caliginem oculis offudisset* (26.45.3). This describes men on tall ladders during the siege of New Carthage.
militariter locutus: 5.1n. *aptior sermone* for the gruff, simple speech of military men. Livy coined the adverb *militariter*, only here in T., but Apuleius, the writers of the *Historia Augusta*, and Justinian took it up.   **laeta omnia et adfluentia excepit** 'he received a whole torrent of congratulations'.   **namque** 'for in addition'.   **id ipsum opperiens:** T. elsewhere associates the *id ipsum* formula with the foresight associated with the ideal general (*id ipsum ueritus, Agr.* 37.1, *id ipsum metuens,* 3.15.1; 19.1n. *prouidentia ducis*). Here we have another reminder that Vespasian's proclamation was carefully stage-managed.   **alacrem militem:** the *IV Scythica, VI Ferrata* and *XII Fulminata*.   **Antiochensium theatrum:** in 47 BC Julius Caesar built (or refurbished) the theatre at Antioch (John Malalas *Chronographia* 217.3–4 (Schenk), a late source, but the author came from Antioch; Segal (1995) 64 n.109), but it has not been located. Such theatres served both for entertainment and for expressing collective approval (or disapproval) of provincial governors hoping to win popular acclamation. It was the perfect setting for the 'showman' Mucianus.   **ubi . . . mos est:** an ethnographic formula (22.1n. *more patrio*). Other Roman authors comment on the theatre as a location for debates and exchanging information in cities dominated by Greek culture (Cic. *Flac.* 16, Liv. 24.39.1, Nep. *Timol.* 4.2, Val. Max. 2.2.5, Sen. *Con.* 9.4.19, Fron. *Str.* 3.2.6, Apul. *Met.* 3.2.6–9, Juv. 10.128 with Mayor (1872) 116).   **concurrentes et in adulationem effusos:** Latin authors often associate such quick-footed sycophancy with stereotypical easterners, especially Greeks (*adulandi gens prudentissima* Juv. 3.86; Plaut. *Miles* 55–71, Ter. *Eun.* 248–53, Mart. 12.82), but T. has repeatedly shown that the Romans are now tainted with similar traits (e.g. *libido assentandi,* 1.1.1; *irrumpet adulatio,* 1.15.4; *ne tum quidem obliti adulationis,* 1.29.1; *certant adulationibus ceteri magistratus, accurrunt patres* 1.47.1; *obuii ex urbe senatores equitesque, quidam metu, multi per adulationem,* 2.87.2).   **satis decorus etiam Graeca facundia:** the Romans had a history of ambivalence towards Greek *paideia* (Whitmarsh (2001) 9–15), but competent bilingualism (particularly in their compatriots) could still impress, especially if it served a practical purpose (*eruditissimus et Graecis litteris et Latinis,* Cic. *Brut.* 205; *lingua doctus utraque,* Mart. 10.76.6; Cic. *De or.* 2.2, Hor. *Carm.* 3.8.5, Plin. *Ep.* 3.1.7, 7.25.4, Suet. *Gram.* 7.1, *Tib.* 70.1–2, 71, *Cal.* 3.1–2, *Cl.* 42.2, *Nero* 7.2; Biville (2002) 77–102). Learning Latin and Greek at the same time could damage facility for idiomatic expression

in both languages (Quint. 1.1.13), but living where the language was spoken helped fluency: Crassus, while governor of Asia, was so competent in five Greek dialects that he gave judgement in whatever language was used in the case (Quint. 11.2.50; cf. Gell. 17.17). T.'s description inverts Sallust's Marius (*non Graeca facundia neque urbanis munditiis sese exercuit, Jug.* 63.3), stressing the bifurcation between the 'military man' Vespasian and the 'rhetorician' Mucianus (2.5.1).   **omnium . . . ostentator:** the agent-noun *ostentator* (once in Plaut., Cic., Liv., Gell.) features again in T., but in a different sense (*A.* 1.24.2). The description condenses Livy on Scipio Africanus: *non ueris tantum uirtutibus mirabilis, sed arte quoque quadam ab iuuenta in ostentationem earum compositus* (26.19.3). A memorable case of his showmanship is when he tells his soldiers that normal tidal movements are in fact Neptune's divine intervention during an attack on New Carthage (Liv. 26.45.9). We have just seen Mucianus' ostentatious speech to Vespasian (2.76–7), and there are fragments of his flamboyant written legacy about natural curiosities in Pliny the Elder's *Nat.* (Ash forthcoming). The best example of Mucianus' ostentation is his banquet in a hollow plane-tree (Plin. *Nat.* 12.9).

80.3 nihil aeque . . . accendit quam quod: these burning passions aptly contrast with chilly Germany (*Germanica hiberna*), where Mucianus falsely claims the troops in Syria will be sent. Livy has *accendo* (*OLD* 6c) + a *quod* clause: *illa etiam res accendit quod* (37.49.6). A comparative clause can also be the subject: *ut nihil aeque amorem incitet et accendat quam carendi metus* (Plin. *Ep.* 5.19.5; also Sen. *Suas.* 7.1).   **asseuerabat:** the imperfect tense suggests that Mucianus did not restrict his fiction to his address in the theatre, but repeated it elsewhere (Chilver (1979) 241).   **Germanicas legiones in Syriam** . . . **Syriacis legionibus Germanica hiberna . . . mutarentur:** the chiasmus and the asyndeton of the two subordinate clauses mirror the geographically extreme swap. This strategic propaganda is in the parallel tradition without being attributed to Mucianus, but only the German legionaries are earmarked for transfer to the east (Suet. *Ves.* 6.4). Vitellius' dispersal of defeated Othonian troops around the empire (2.66.1) would only have enhanced the plausibility of Mucianus' story. So too would his own status as governor, responsible for liaising with the emperor and maintaining detailed records about the troops (Austin and Rankov (1995) 155–61). T.'s mutinous Percennius complains that even upon discharge, soldiers could be dragged *adhuc diuersas in terras* (*A.* 1.17.3) by an unwelcome grant of substandard land in another country. Some soldiers clearly wanted to stay put.   **ad militiam opulentam quietamque:** this activates the traditional image of easy and profitable service in the east (4.4n. *segnitiam*), although T. had previously bucked the stereotype by emphasising the unusual *uigor* of Mucianus' tough eastern legions, despite the *integra quies* (2.4.4). The combination *militia* + *opulenta* is unique, but T. plays with words, since *opulentus* can mean both 'profitable' (*OLD* 1), as here, and 'well supplied with military resources' (*OLD* 2; Oakley (1998) 409), as in *ipsis omnia opulenta et fida* (2.32.2).   **Syriacis legionibus Germanica hiberna caelo et laboribus dura mutarentur** 'that their winter-camp in Germany, harsh due to the cold weather and hard work, was to be taken in exchange by the Syrian legions'. Horace has *muto* in this sense: *quid terras alio calentis | Sole mutamus?, Carm.* 2.16.18–19, in an ode

celebrating simple *otium* at home; Nisbet and Hubbard (1978) 263). *Syriacis legionibus*
= dat. of agent, often used boldly by T. as a poeticism: earlier prose authors restrict
it to the gerundive or passive participle or adj. in *-bilis* (GL §354; Furneaux (1896)
46, Goodyear (1981) 346). Pliny describes the miserable damp lifestyle endured in
Germany by the locals, with bodies frozen by the north wind (*Nat.* 16.3–4); also there
is *perpetua . . . hiems, triste caelum* and the *durata glacie stagna* (Sen. *Prou.* 4.14). T. thinks
that the country's inhabitants must be indigenous, as nobody sane would abandon
temperate Asia, Africa or Italy for *Germaniam . . . informem terris, asperam caelo, tristem
cultu aspectuque* (*Germ* 2.2, with Rives (1999) 108). Even in Gaul, storms from the north
were apparently so severe that they tore off your clothing (Diod. Sic. 5.26.1); Britain
is not considered much better (*Agr.* 12.3). **quippe:** explanatory (10.3n. *quippe . . .
meminerant*). **plerique necessitudinibus et propinquitatibus mixti** 'many
had formed ties of intimacy and kinship' (Irvine). Although formal marriages between
soldiers and local women were not legal until the principate of Septimius Severus,
soldiers often had relationships and fathered children, especially when wars were
few and far between (Campbell (1978), Phang (2001)). In practice, discharge *diplomata*
formally recognised such links by granting citizenship to wives and children, and
emperors were usually lenient (Dio 60.24.3; Campbell (1984) 439–45). Julius Sabinus
is proud that Julius Caesar had allegedly slept with his great-grandmother while
campaigning in Gaul (4.55.2); and T. also says that the general Petillius Cerialis only
escaped capture in an attack as he was spending the night with a local woman, Claudia
Sacrata (5.22.3). The story of the widow of Ephesus, seduced by a soldier, offers a
fictional version of such fraternisation (Petr. 111–12). **uetustate stipendiorum:**
the *VI Ferrata* and *XII Fulminata* had been posted in Syria since the time of Augustus,
while the *IV Scythica* arrived under Nero. At the second battle of Bedriacum the *III
Gallica*, transferred to Moesia from Syria shortly before Nero's death, even salutes the
rising sun (*ita in Syria mos est*, 3.24.3), showing its soldiers' acculturation. After victory
Vespasian respected these links by keeping the *VI Ferrata, XII Fulminata* and *IV Scythica*
in the area, and re-establishing there the temporarily displaced *III Gallica* (Keppie
(1986)). **in modum penatium** 'like a home'. The idea recurs when the Flavian
soldiers attack the praetorian camp in Rome, shouting that *proprium esse militis decus
in castris: illam patriam, illos penates* (3.84.2). Livy also depicts the camp as the soldier's
home (in a speech): *patria altera militaris est haec sedes, uallumque pro moenibus et tentorium
suum cuique militi domus ac penates sunt* (44.39.5). The emotional resonance of the *castra* for
soldiers is an added reason why Roman colonies were so often founded on the former
sites of military camps (Keppie (2000) 302–6); and attempts to transplant soldiers
from the area of their provincial service could fail, even if relocation was to Italy (*A.*
14.27.2).

81.1 Ante idus Iulias: 15 Jul. 69. We should remember parallel events in
Italy. Vitellius arrived in Rome on or before 18 Jul. (2.91.1), so his principate was
seriously undermined even in its earliest stages by events in Syria. **in eodem
sacramento fuit:** 6.1n. *sacramentum Othonis*. The expression is unprecedented, but
T. strives for *uariatio* after multiple instances of oath-swearing. **accessere cum**

regno Sohaemus . . . Antiochus: the brisk syntax, an alternative third person plural (3.1n. *ipsa . . . cessere*) of *accedo* ('join', *OLD* 7b) and two singular subjects in asyndeton (24.3n. *Paulinus . . . Celsus sumpsere*), mirrors the rapid spread of support for the Flavian cause. The singular noun in *cum regno* is collective, as both rulers have kingdoms.　**Sohaemus** (*RE* III A 796–8; Barrett (1977), Sullivan (1977a) 216–18) became king of Emesa on the Syrian river Orontes in northern Syria (Ball (2000) 33–47) in 54 after his older brother Azizus died (Jos. *AJ* 20.158–9). The latest member of an influential eastern dynasty, he supplied the Romans with 4,000 troops in 66 when Cestius Gallus, then governor of Syria, was marching on Jerusalem to confront the insurrection (Jos. *BJ* 2.500; 3.68), and when Titus was left to run the Jewish war after the conference at Beirut, Sohaemus even went with him on campaign (5.1.2, Jos. *BJ* 3.68). He also helped Vespasian (in dubious circumstances) to oust his fellow-client king Antiochus IV from Commagene (Jos. *BJ* 7.226). Sohaemus consistently assisted the Romans, especially the Flavians. An inscription from Heliopolis (*ILS* 8958) calls him both *Philocaesar* and *Philo[r]ohmaeus* (for *Philorhomaeus*), and shows that he was awarded honorific *ornamenta consularia* (at an unknown date: Braund (1984a) 29). We do not know when he died, but his dynasty lasted at least until Domitian's principate, when Emesa was made part of Syria; and in 187, Julia Domna, one of his descendants, married the emperor Septimius Severus (Birley (1988) 72). In 54 Nero gave the kingdom of Sophene to a Sohaemus (*A.* 13.7), but it is unclear if he is the same man (Barrett (1977) and Sullivan (1977a) 216 think so).　**haud spernendis uiribus:** sc. *uir.* The abl. of quality (rather than the gen.) in apposition is a poetic touch. The litotes is Livian (11.2n. *haud spernenda manus*).　**Antiochus** IV (*OCD³* 'Antiochus (9)', Sullivan (1977b) 785–94) was made king of Commagene by Caligula in 38 (Dio 59.8.2), quickly deposed, and reinstated by Claudius in 41 (Jos. *AJ* 19.276, Dio 60.8.1). He ably protected Cilicia against the Cietae in 52 (using *blandimenta* and *fraus, A.* 12.55.2) and helped Corbulo against the Parthians (*A.* 13.7.1, 13.37.3), receiving some Armenian territory in return (*A.* 14.26.2). Yet despite promptly helping Vespasian both in the civil war (25.2n. *rex Epiphanes*) and in the Jewish war (5.1.2, Jos. *BJ* 5.460–3), the emperor annexed his kingdom in 72 after Caesennius Paetus, governor of Syria, accused him and his son of planning an alliance with Parthia (Levick (1999) 165, Braund (1984a) 171). After a short *bellum Commagenicum* (*ILS* 9198), he was captured at Tarsus and sent in chains to Rome (Jos. *BJ* 7.238; cf. *ILS* 9200), a callous return for his help. Josephus (*BJ* 5.461) sees Antiochus as exemplifying Solon's maxim that no man should be called happy until he is dead (Hdt. 1.32). Yet Vespasian apparently relented to some extent, allowing Antiochus and his family to live 'honourably' in Rome (Jos. *BJ* 7.243). Commagene was then joined to Syria.　**uetustis opibus ingens et inseruientium regum ditissimus** 'mighty in ancestral wealth and the richest of the kings offering their services'. T. likes elevated combinations of *ingens* (4.2n. *ingens . . . fiducia*) + the abl. (*corpore ingens*, 1.53.1; *ingens uiribus opibusque*, 1.61.1;), evocative of epic poetry (*cornibus ingens*, Virg. *A.* 7.483; also 3.462, 8.258, 11.641, *G.* 3.14); and *uetustis opibus* recurs (*A.* 16.7.1), modelled perhaps on Livy: *regnum . . . nullis uetustis fundatum opibus* (45.19.10). Not all editors retain the compound *inseruio*, considering *inseruientium regum* an odd way to express 'subject princes' (generally assumed to be the meaning here), so some read *seruientium*. Yet *seruio* is too pejorative in the context (cf. 4.32.2, 5.8.2), and T. may have chosen *inseruio* (*OLD* 1, 'serve the interests of') not as a general label, but to reflect the immediate context (Antiochus as the richest of the three kings now offering their services to the Flavians). The compound should stand (*TLL* s.v. *inseruio* 1882.3).   **mox per occultos suorum nuntios excitus ab urbe:** when Titus made his abortive trip to congratulate Galba (2.1–2), Agrippa went with him (Jos. *BJ* 4.498) and completed the journey to Rome. Titus turned back, perhaps at the end of January. Agrippa was no doubt on a fact-finding mission: he could travel to Rome more safely, and unlike members of the Flavian family could also leave the city quickly without attracting attention. The chronology of Agrippa's movements is elusive (*mox* = 'after that'? 'soon'?), but the need for *occulti nuntii* (recalling Vespasian's *spes occultae*, 2.78.3) suggests that he was summoned back before the proclamation, 'another example of careful Flavian planning' (Chilver (1979) 242).   **Agrippa** (*OCD*[3] 'Iulius Agrippa (2) II, Marcus', Sullivan (1977c) 329–45, Millar (1993) 61–79, 91–2), only 17 when his father Agrippa I died in Caesarea in 44 (Jos. *AJ* 19.354–9), was brought up in Rome (Jos. *AJ* 19.360), but Claudius thought him too young to rule Judaea and sent out a Roman procurator instead (Jos. *AJ* 19.360–6). That could have been that, but after his uncle Herod died in 48, Claudius allowed Agrippa, now 21, to inherit his territory of Chalcis in Syria (Jos. *AJ* 20.138), only to exchange it for a different (bigger) area in eastern Palestine in 53 (Jos. *BJ* 2.247). Nero granted him more land (Jos. *BJ* 2.252, *AJ* 20.159), proof that Rome trusted Agrippa to control a religiously diverse and potentially explosive area. Yet the procurator of Judaea, Gessius Florus, exacerbated tensions so much that in 66 the Jews expelled Agrippa from Jerusalem (Jos. *BJ* 2.406–7), after unsuccessfully trying to dissuade them from war (Jos. *BJ* 2.345–401; Levick (1999) 27). When Vespasian took control of the war, Agrippa promptly offered him troops (Jos. *BJ* 3.29) and generous hospitality at his palace in Caesarea over the summer of 67 (Jos. *BJ* 3.443–4). This was probably when Titus' affair with Agrippa's sister Berenice began. Agrippa's consistent support for the Flavians (both in the civil and Jewish wars) was no doubt motivated by self-interest, but he seems to have enjoyed genuinely good relations with them. Vespasian increased the size of his kingdom (Jos. *BJ* 7.97, Levick (1999) 119) and in 75 awarded him *ornamenta praetoria*, when Titus was living with his sister Berenice in Rome (Dio 66.15.3). Even after his sister had fallen from favour, Agrippa apparently did not suffer. Josephus consulted him as a source for the *BJ*, but he may have been dead before the *AJ* was published in 93. His nephew Antonius Agrippa was killed in the eruption of Vesuvius in 79 (Jos. *AJ* 20.144). Agrippa's kingdom was absorbed into the Roman provinces of Judaea and Syria after his death (Sullivan (1977c) 344).   **ignaro adhuc Vitellio:** Vitellius' ignorance of events around him is thematic (57.1n. *uictoriae suae nescius*), but his culpability in this case is diminished by Agrippa's long-standing connections with Rome from childhood and the chaotic movement of people in and out of the city during the civil war; and *adhuc* ('so far'; *OLD* 1) suggests that Vitellius will soon find out about the Flavian challenge (cf. 2.73).   **celeri nauigatione properauerat** 'had made a quick passage' (Irvine). The pleonasm (Lausberg (1998) §502) involving the vocabulary of speed (paradoxically slowing down the narrative) is striking, especially compared with *nauigatione celeri . . . assequitur* (*A.* 2.55.3; cf. *celeriore . . . nauigatione rex est usus*, [Caes.] *Alex.* 28.2). Other authors like it: *eloquere propere celeriter* (Plaut. *Rud.* 1323); *usque adeo properanter . . . | exitium celeri celeratur origine* (Lucr. 5.300–1); *seu matura dies celerem properat mihi mortem* (Tib. 3.7.205); *nisi celeriter . . . properabit motus* (Sen. *Nat.* 6.21.2); *delubra occulta celeritate properantur* (Plin. *Pan.* 51.3).

81.2 regina Berenice: 2.1n.   **florens aetate . . . magnificentia munerum grata:** the chiasmus postpones and sharpens T.'s wry joke about the old man Vespasian's prosaic and practical reason for finding Berenice charming: her money (cf. 5.1n. *auaritia*). The implicit point of comparison for *quoque* is the amorous Titus, popularly thought to be *accensus desiderio* for Berenice (2.2.1). The combination *florens aetate for-maque* (Liv. 26.49.13; cf. 30.12.17, Val. Max. 4.3.3) reflects traditional ancient concepts of idealised female beauty. Berenice was in her early forties. Sniping sources cast her as jealous of her younger sister's looks (Jos. *AJ* 20.143).   **quidquid prouinciarum alluitur mari** 'every province located on the seaboard' (*OLD* 1b for *alluo* indicating geographical position). The language involves ring-composition within the book; cf. *quidquid castrorum* (2.6.2), also in a catalogue of (then only potential) Flavian support. T. means the coastal provinces north of Syria, namely Cilicia, and Lycia and Pamphylia (cf. 9.1n.), but the periphrasis (aesthetically more agreeable than a simple enumeration) sounds more expansive than simply naming the provinces and suggests the Flavian campaign's irrepressible momentum as it heads westwards.   **Asia atque Achaia tenus:** anastrophe of prepositions is a distinctive aspect of T.'s style (Goodyear (1972) 93–4, WM 80, Lausberg (1998) §714.4), but in Latin *tenus* always follows its object. **quantumque introrsus in Pontum et Armenios patescit** 'all the territory that extends inland towards Pontus and the Armenians'; *patesco* (*OLD* 4) features again in this sense (*G.* 30.1, *A.* 2.61.2). T. means areas such as Mesopotamia, Galatia and Cappadocia, Commagene, Lycaonia, and Pisidia.   **sed inermes legati regebant:** T. adds bathos after the ebullient catalogue of fresh support for the Flavian cause. Goodwill never goes amiss, but soldiers are what counts, and Vespasian must still fight his campaign. When the Flavian soldiers list potential support in the east (*septem legiones . . . ipsum mare*, 2.6.2), they focus above all on the military potential of different areas.   **nondum additis Cappadociae legionibus:** Vespasian will soon change the military arrangements in Cappadocia (6.2n. *Cappadocia*).

81.3 Consilium . . . habitum: sc. *est*. The extended *consilium* scene, standard in ancient historiography, has been recurrent in the narrative so far (1.32.2–34.1 with Damon (2003) 166, 2.32–3). Yet T. avoids recreating the Flavians' detailed discussion, partly so as not to slow the momentum of his account, which has moved on now from words (2.76–7) to action, but also because the *consilium*'s decisions will be superseded by the decisive actions of Antonius Primus. The meeting probably took place during the second half of July (Levick (1999) 47).   **Beryti:** the Hellenised Phoenician city Berytus (mod. Beirut; *OCD³* 'Berytus', Millar (1990) 10–23) became a Roman colony in 15 BC, when Agrippa settled legionary veterans there (Strabo *Geog.* 16.2.19).

Its military heritage made it an apt place for a campaign meeting, but it was also
conveniently located half-way between Caesarea and Antioch, the respective bases
of Vespasian and Mucianus. Herod the Great had provided a significant building
programme for Berytus (Jos. *BJ* 1.422; 78.4n. *Caesaream*), as did his grandson Agrippa
I (responsible for an amphitheatre and a show involving 1,400 condemned criminals,
Jos. *AJ* 19.335) and his son Agrippa II (81.1n.), who adorned the city with statues
and a theatre (Jos. *AJ* 20.211). It was a cultured place: local boy Valerius Probus, a
grammarian who flourished under the Flavians, had access to certain *ueteres libelli* no
longer available (or popular) in Rome (Suet. *Gram.* 24.1–2), and at the start of the third
century AD, Septimius Severus founded a law school there. The local wine was good,
and the city produced exceptionally sweet grapes (Plin. *Nat.* 15.66).   **cum legatis
tribunisque et splendidissimo quoque centurionum ac militum:** legates
and military tribunes would naturally attend a *consilium* called by their commanding
officer (4.19.2, Liv. 8.6.12, 9.2.15, 25.14.2, 34.35.1), as would the centurions (Caes.
Gal. 5.28.3, 6.7.8; Oakley (2005) 64), but common soldiers, even distinguished ones,
being present is unusual (and only recently *cuncta impetu militum acta*, 2.79). Then as
now, soldiers were ideally supposed to follow orders, not to think for themselves. This
perhaps suggests that the most public part of the meeting was intended for show,
and as a way to boost collective morale, while the detailed planning was reserved for
a smaller group (including Mucianus). Common soldiers are also present at another
Flavian *consilium*, prompting comment from T. on the unusual practice (3.3; cf. 3.13.1).
The special circumstances of civil war allowed (or necessitated) normal military procedure to be altered, but set difficult and dangerous precedents for the future (1.83.3;
Wellesley (1972) 80; 19.2n. *rationem ostendens*). The superlative *splendidissimus* (common
in Cic., only once in Liv., absent from Sall., Caes.) clusters in the *H.* (4×; also *G.*
41.1, *D.* 6.2, *A.* 3.54.1, with WM 390). Its metaphorical association with shining (as
with many Latin words denoting honour, Lendon (1997) 274) is especially apt here,
as it evokes the gleaming armour associated with well-turned-out soldiers (22.1n. *fulgentes*).   **et e Iudaico exercitu lecta decora** 'as well as the pick of the crop from
the Jewish army'. The lofty *lecta decora* is only here (*TLL* s.v. *decus* 245.9), but creatively
combines expressions such as *decora omnium prouinciarum* (1.84.3) and *speculatorum lecta
corpora* (2.11.3). Cf. *lecta robora uirorum* (Liv. 7.7.4). Virgil's use of *decus* for the beauty
emanating from warriors such as Aeneas and Turnus (*A.* 4.150, 7.473, with Horsfall
(2000) 319) may also resonate here.   **tantum . . . peditum equitumque . . .
aemulantium . . . regum:** this tricolon crescendo marked by homoioteleuton is
a resonant finale to the Flavian *consilium* (ostentatious at last after all the secrecy).
aemulantium inter se regum: in Josephus, Vespasian's main task at this meeting
is to receive congratulatory embassies from Syria and other provinces amidst pomp
and ceremony: there is no sign that planning a military campaign was on the agenda
(*BJ* 4.620–1).   **paratus** 'spectacle'. The pl. (G-G 1053) accentuates our sense of
scale; cf. the impoverished Vitellius sailing down the Arar, *nullo principali paratu* (2.59.2).
speciem fortunae principalis effecerant 'immediately created the impression
of imperial grandeur'. T. uses an 'instantaneous' pluperfect (1.1n. *disperserat*) and lofty

adj. for a dependent noun in the gen. (2.1n. *iuuenilis animus*). *fortuna principalis* is innovative (59.3n. *cunctis . . . insignibus*). The overall pageantry of a meeting can sometimes
be more significant than the gathering's minutiae (cf. Henry VIII and Francis I at the
Field of the Cloth of Gold in 1520).

82.1 Prima belli cura . . . ueteranos: sc. *erat*. The ellipse of *erat* and the
asyndeton syntactically reflects the brisk pace of activity. Livy likes *cura belli* (14×;
Woodman (1977) 112), but T. uses it only here. **agere dilectus:** 16.2n. *dilectum
agere*. **reuocare ueteranos** is a technical military term (Woodman (1977) 160;
ILS 2034, 2312, Cic. *Verr.* 6.80, Liv. 33.3.4, Vell. 2.111.1, Flor. 2.15.4) for reservists,
experienced soldiers still available for active service (normally for five years), but no
longer obliged to live in camp. A *praefectus* or *centurio ueteranorum* usually organised them
(Goldsworthy (1996) 16) and they could be extremely useful (*A.* 3.21.2 records a victory
of 500 veterans against Tacfarinas). Keeping veterans available for service also meant
postponing the expenses associated with their discharge (Suet. *Tib.* 48.2, *Cal.* 44.1).
exercendis armorum officinis 'for operating workshops for weapons'. T. only
connects manufacturing arms with the Flavians (again 2.84.1; Chilver (1979) 243), suggesting their systematic and practical attitude to seizing power conspicuously absent
from the other campaigns (cf. 1.38.3, the Othonian troops chaotically seizing arms in
Rome). Horace is the only poet to use *officina* (*Carm.* 1.4.8, *Epod.* 17.35), which does not
scan in dactylic hexameters, leaving it predominantly to prose writers. The phrase
armorum officinae recurs (Cic. *Phil.* 7.13, *Pis.* 87, [Caes.] *Alex.* 2.2, Caes. *Civ.* 1.34.5, Nep.
Ag. 3.2, Flor. 1.31.10). Good generals often took responsibility for overseeing the manufacture of weapons (e.g. Publius Cornelius Scipio at New Carthage, Liv. 26.51.8), an
increasingly elaborate process as technical developments were integrated in Roman
fighting techniques and crucial for success: 'The legion was accustomed to be victorious not only on account of the number of soldiers, but the type of its tools also'
(Veg. 2.25.1). So too *fabri* (craftsmen) were an essential part of a legionary's personnel,
but the scale of operations envisaged by T. here is altogether larger. In the second
battle of Bedriacum, the Vitellians will deploy a particularly vicious *ballista* against the
enemy until two brave Flavian soldiers disable it (3.23.2). **apud Antiochenses
aurum argentumque:** alliteration of *aurum* + *argentum* is common in Latin from
Plautus onwards, but T. extends the sound effect through the prepositional phrase.
signatur 'was coined' (cf. *signatum argentum, A.* 6.17.1). For the earliest Vespasianic
coinage struck at Antioch, see *RIC* II.4 and 56 (with Downey (1961) 202–4). The
systematic minting of coins indicates a highly organised campaign: cf. the Vitellian
soldiers haphazardly offering their belts and medals to finance the challenge (1.57.2).
cuncta . . . festinabantur: *cunctus* = a synonym for *omnis* (1.3n. *cuncta . . . perlustrat*). The phrase recurs in T. (*A.* 6.50.4), modelled perhaps on *Metellus . . . cuncta . . .
festinat* (Sall. *Jug.* 73.1). **per idoneos ministros:** the combination (here first) was
not taken up by other authors (*TLL* s.v. *idoneus* 230.21). Again, the detail suggests the
Flavians' careful advance planning, as the production of arms and money naturally
needed trustworthy individuals to oversee the process. **suis quaeque locis** 'each
in the proper place'. *quaeque* is a (generally accepted) correction of M's *quoque*, added

to the manuscript by a later scribe.   **ipse Vespasianus:** the would-be Flavian emperor, vigorously and personally involved in the preparations, contrasts sharply with Vitellius' sluggishness at the same stage (1.62.2). The climactic and idealising *ipse* casts Vespasian as the central cog in the machine, as does the shift within the whole chapter from passive verbs with multiple agents implied (*destinantur, signatur, festinabantur*, 82.1), to active third-person verbs in the central section with Vespasian and Mucianus as subjects (*percoluit, ostenderat, obtulit*, 82.2), back to passive and impersonal forms at the end (*missi, prouisum, placuit, scriptae, praeceptum*, 82.3). The sandwiching of Vespasian's role as a morale-booster between multiple practical activities also suggests a well-balanced campaign. Yet after this promising opening, there is a deterioration in the image of the Flavians presented by T.: the picture is initially favourable (2.82), but cracks appear in the façade (2.83), culminating in a damning portrayal of an increasingly money-grubbing campaign (2.84; Morgan (1994c) 175).   **adire hortari . . . incitare . . . coercere:** cf. *simul suas legiones adire, hortari* (*A.* 15.12.3). The historic infinitives (5.1n. *anteire . . . obniti*) in asyndeton syntactically reflect Vespasian's dynamism.   **bonos laude, segnes exemplo incitare saepius quam coercere:** T. apparently condenses a more prolix sentence in Caesar: *laudat promptos Pompeius atque in posterum confirmat, segniores castigat atque incitat* (*Civ.* 1.3.1). The formulation recalls the idealised Agricola, who proceeds *laudando promptos castigando segnes* (*Agr.* 21.1), but Vespasian can afford his gentle and non-interventionist leadership techniques only because he has not yet had to confront his followers in a truly recalcitrant mood. For *coerceo* ('coerce', *OLD* 6), cf. *uerberare seruum ac uinculis et opere coercere rarum* (*G.* 25.1).   **uitia magis amicorum quam uirtutes dissimulans** 'more ready to see his friends' merits than their faults'. Vespasian is pragmatic, as *uitia erunt, donec homines* (4.74.2). Such conduct sounds gracious, but is worrying, after we have seen previous emperors unable to confront the *uitia* of their exploitative *amici*. The most telling case is Otho, denounced by Piso for ruining the empire *etiam cum amicum imperatoris ageret* (1.30.1). Yet one secret of Flavian success is having competent and reliable imperial *amici* such as Mucianus.

82.2 praefecturis et procurationibus . . . plerosque . . . percoluit: *praefecturae* are military commands, while *procurationes* can denote financial posts in the imperial administration (or the non-senatorial governorships of minor provinces, less likely here, given the numbers involved). The forceful alliteration highlights an activity suggestive of *hybris*, especially the senatorial appointments: Vespasian, not yet emperor, confidently distributes imperial favours anyway (cf. Caesar, scornfully denouncing Pompey's premature distribution of posts, *Civ.* 3.82.3–4). Two cases of newly enrolled senators (53.1n. *in senatum . . . ascitus*) from 69 are Tiberius Julius Celsus Polemaenus of Sardes, military tribune of the *legio III Cyrenaica* (M-W 316) and Plotius Grypus, who was also made legate of the *legio II Augusta* (3.52.3, 4.39.1). The inventive compound verb *percolo* (also *A.* 4.68.1 and *Agr.* 10.1; Constans (1893) §3) for *ualde colere* 'seems not to be found between Plautus and T.' (MW 248; *TLL* s.v. *percolo* 1216.5–6), but appealed to Apuleius.   **egregios uiros et mox summa adeptos:** promotion based on merit rather than cronyism also marks Agrippa's idealised methods of leadership (*ascire ... optimum quemque fidissimum*, *Agr.* 19.2). After the civil war, Vespasian promoted his friends, including Antistius Rusticus (M-W 464) and Caristanius Fronto (M-W 315), but in reshaping the senate he also introduced new men from both Italy and the provinces (including the Greek-speaking provinces). This has earned him praise (Levick (1999) 170–83). **quibusdam fortuna pro uirtutibus fuit** 'but in some cases, luck took the place of virtue'. T.'s (so far) upbeat depiction of Vespasian's promotions still has a sting in the tail: 'the immediate juxtaposition of a criticism is typical of T.' (WM 188). He perhaps thinks of disreputable types being advanced e.g. Baebius Massa, a notorious prosecutor under Domitian (4.50.2, *Agr.* 45.1, Juv. 1.35, Plin. *Ep.* 3.4.4, 7.33.4–8), or Lucilius Bassus, commander of the fleet, who notoriously deserted Vitellius (2.100.3, 3.12; Levick (1999) 171). **donatiuum . . . neque . . . nisi modice ostenderat** 'had only conjured up the prospect of a moderate donative'. *ostendo* (*OLD* 13) + *donatiuum* is only here in Latin (*TLL* s.v. *donatiuum* 1991.6). Promising money to the soldiers could engender loyalty, but sometimes backfired, if the donative was repeatedly postponed (1.30.3; cf. *donatiuo, quod uobis numquam datur et cotidie exprobratur*, 1.37.5). **neque . . . ne . . . quidem:** the co-ordination of *neque* (without its concluding *et*; *OLD neque* 8) and *ne . . . quidem* is unusual (cf. *D.* 26.2), but it serves to emphasise the *ne . . . quidem* clause, as does T.'s more common co-ordination of three clauses with *neque* + *neque* + *ne . . . quidem* (*G.* 7.2, 44.4, *A.* 1.66.2, 3.14.1, 3.50.1). **alii in pace:** Germanicus (*A.* 1.36), Tiberius (Suet. *Tib.* 48.2) and Caligula (Dio 59.2.1) all sweetened the army with money, but after Claudius gave 15,000 HS to each praetorian upon becoming emperor (Suet. *Cl.* 10.4; Hurley (2001) 100–1) and Nero followed suit (Dio 61.3.1; cf. *A.* 12.69.2), the soldiers had particularly high expectations at accession time. The praetorian prefect Nymphidius Sabinus promised a huge sum to the troops in Galba's name (30,000 HS to each praetorian and 5,000 HS per legionary, Plut. *Galb.* 2.2), but it was never paid, with Galba stubbornly saying that *legi a se militem, non emi* (1.5.2; Plut. *Galb.* 18.4, Suet. *Galb.* 16.1, Dio 64.3.3). Otho also used money (and promises of it) to buy the soldiers' good-will (1.24, 1.25.1, 1.82.3), as did the Vitellians (1.66.1, 2.94.2, 4.36.1). The Flavians' firm stance is undermined somewhat when Hordeonius Flaccus distributes money in Germany in Vespasian's name (4.36.2, 4.58.3), but generally, the party is fairly austere. Mucianus eventually paid 100 HS per soldier after entering Rome (Dio 65.22), a relatively modest sum, given that the annual salary at this time was 3,000 HS for a praetorian soldier and 900 HS for a legionary (Alston (1994)). **egregie firmus:** *egregie* + an adj. (also *egregie concordes*, *A.* 2.43.6) has an archaic tinge. T. is apparently the first to use it for about a century (Cic *Q. fr.* 1.1.17, Liv. 44.20.7; Goodyear (1981) 329). The adj. *firmus* (6× in *H.*; 2× each in *Agr.*, *D.*, *A.*) is frequent in Cicero and Caesar, who both prefer it to the synonym *ualidus* (Adams (1974) 59–60, MW 188). T. aptly uses language evocative of the republic to describe Vespasian conducting himself in the manner of an idealised republican general. **militarem largitionem:** with an adj. instead of a dependent noun in the genitive, which here would be objective (2.1n. *iuuenilis animus*. Cf. *largitione militum*, Caes. *Civ.* 1.39.4), T. uses lofty language for a sordid practice. **eoque exercitu meliore:** 13.2n. *eoque*. The brachylogical abl. of quality not attached to a noun or adj. (Furneaux (1896) 48–9; Goodyear (1972) 210 and (1981) 421) shows *uariatio* after the preceding nom. adj. phrase (cf. *uir facundus et pacis artibus*, 1.8.1); *eo* = abl. of the measure of difference. The implicit point of comparison for *exercitus melior* (Cic. *Fam.* 10.18.3, Var. *L.* 5.87.5, Liv. 36.17.5) is Vitellius' army, flawed through bribery, and although the primary sense of *melior* is 'more efficient', it also has a moral tone.

82.3 missi ad Parthum Armeniumque legati: sc. *sunt*. The singular adjectives may refer collectively to the two peoples by synecdoche (*Rhet. Her.* 4.45, Quint. 8.6.20, 9.3.20; Lausberg (1998) §573.3) or perhaps simply to their respective rulers, Vologeses and Tiridates. The collective singular *Parthus* is used in this way again (*A.* 2.56.1, 6.35.1, 6.42.2, 15.4.3, 15.10.1), but not *Armenius*, so perhaps the rulers are meant. The Parthian King Vologeses I (ruled 51–78) had tried to make his brother Tiridates king of Armenia, but Nero's general Corbulo curbed him and arranged a diplomatic settlement. Vologeses apparently helped the Flavians (Suet. *Ves.* 6.4), while after Vespasian's victory, Parthian envoys arrived from the king belatedly offering the services of 40,000 cavalry (4.51). Vologeses also sent a golden crown to Titus after the fall of Jerusalem (Jos. *BJ* 7.105), but all these efforts (whether sincere or not) did not stop Vespasian refusing his request for Roman help in his war against the Alani (Suet. *Dom.* 2.2, Dio 66.15). The idea of a Roman requesting help from Parthia (the traditional enemy of the empire) is meant to be shocking: cf. overtures to the Parthians from Pompey (Luc. 8.218–38) and Quintus Labienus 'Parthicus' (Vell. 2.78.1, Dio 48.24.5).

prouisumque 'precautions were taken'; sc. *est*. By denuding the eastern provinces of troops, Vespasian was potentially leaving the empire vulnerable to Parthia (a concern in previous civil wars, Caes. *Civ.* 3.31.4). This foresight evokes the ideal general and is also shown by the Flavian leaders in Illyricum (3.5.1), but diplomacy was not foolproof, and the Rhoxolani have already exploited the civil war by invading Moesia (1.79). The Flavians do not have an unblemished record: trouble will erupt in Germany when Julius Civilis takes advantage of the civil wars (3.46.1), after being instructed by the Flavian general Antonius Primus to create a diversion *tumultus Germanici specie* (4.13.2).

uersis ad ciuile bellum legionibus: the abl. absolute recalls Livy on the salutary shock inflicted on the Romans, fighting seditiously amongst themselves, when the people of Praeneste attack and force them to engage in external war (*ab seditione ad bellum uersi*, 6.28.3). Such are the benefits of *metus hostilis*, but in T. the soldiers turn, not to foreign campaigning, but to civil conflict, as they are drawn centripetally towards Rome.   **terga nudarentur:** the graphic expression personalises and accentuates the sense of Roman vulnerability with resonances from epic (*terga fuga nudant*, Virg. *A.* 5.586; *nudataque foeda | terga fuga*, Luc. 4.713–4; *nudantis . . . | terga fuga*, Sil. 17.444–5), a lofty genre incongruous with the degrading concept described here.   **Titum instare Iudaeae:** although *insto* suggests immediacy, the Jewish campaign is actually suspended for the rest of the year. Vespasian hands over to Titus the *ualidissima exercitus pars* (4.51.2), but only after the Flavian victory at Bedriacum and Vitellius' death on 20 Dec. 69. 'From 1 July until Titus resumed operations after the Flavian victory there is nothing to record from Judaea but road-building and reorganization . . . The agony of Jerusalem dragged on' (Levick (1999) 39).   **claustra Aegypti** 'the keys of Egypt'. *claustrum* = 'bolt' or 'bar', but its metaphorical designation of a key point is Ciceronian (*OLD claustrum* 3). T. means the coastal area of Egypt, possibly the two cities Alexandria (offering defence of the sea) and Pelusium (defending the land routes from the east): *tota Aegyptus maritimo accessu Pharo, pedestri Pelusio, uelut claustris munita existimatur* ([Caes.] *Alex.* 26.2). T.'s omission of a qualifying *uelut* suggests that the term is generally recognised (also Suet. *Ves.* 7.1), even if its precise frame of reference is not. It previously designated Pelusium (Liv. 45.11.5; cf. *claustra . . . Pelusi*, Prop. 3.9.55, corr. Palmier) or Philae (Luc. 10.313) alone, and T. could mean just Alexandria (Vespasian's destination, 3.48.3). He uses the metaphor again of Egypt, the *claustra annonae* (3.8.2; cf. *claustra . . . terrae ac maris, A.* 2.59.3) and applies it to other places (the Caspian gates, 1.6.2; the Alps, 3.2.2; Forum Iulii, 3.43.1).   **sufficere . . . aduersus Vitellium pars copiarum:** this crushingly belittles the enemy, but in fact the Flavian invasion force will be quite substantial. Mucianus leads an advance column, followed by the *Legio VI Ferrata* (5,000 men) and 13,000 men drafted from the other five eastern legions, the *IV Scythica, XII Fulminata, X Fretensis, V Macedonica,* and *XV Apollinaris* (2.83.1). There will be scope too for reinforcements from the Danube legions (*III Gallica, VII Claudia, VIII Augusta, VII Galbiana, XI Claudia* and *XIII Gemina*). Eventually at least 40,000 Flavian troops are at the second battle of Bedriacum (3.33.1).   **ac nihil arduum fatis** 'the irresistible force of destiny' (Fyfe / Levene). It almost sounds like a motto. By brachylogy, T. substitutes a nom. neuter singular pronoun + adj. phrase for *quod nihil arduum esset fatis:* cf. *et omnia prona uictoribus* (3.64.1), *et celebritate loci nihil occultum* (*A.* 3.9.3; Furneaux (1896) 59). It extends the punchy idiom of Livy, who likes the substantivised nom. neuter singular of the past participle (compact and efficient): *diu non perlitatum* ('the fact that a favourable omen had not been obtained for a long time') *tenuerat dictatorem* (7.8.5; Oakley (1998) 109). T.'s grand language may reflect upbeat Flavian jargon of the time, but also recalls the Othonian council of war (an inauspicious echo): Titianus and Proculus evoke *fortunam et deos et numen Othonis* as intrinsic to their challenge (2.33.1).   **scriptae:** sc. *sunt.*   **praeceptumque:** sc. *est.* **ut praetorianos . . . reciperandae militiae praemio inuitarent** 'that they should seek to win over the praetorians with the incentive of renewing their military service' (*OLD inuito* 5b). After Flavian overtures (8.2n. *dextras . . . ad praetorianos*), some praetorians duly fight for Vespasian at the decisive battle (3.21.2).

83.1 Mucianus . . . sinebat: journeys have great potential for exploring character (cf. Odysseus, Aeneas). Where Vitellius progresses slowly and with increasing hedonism (2.57–73, 87–9), Mucianus is devious and self-aware. Yet the chronology and itinerary of his expedition from the east to Rome (of which this is the first leg) are controversial (Wellesley (1972) 208–15, Syme (1977), Morgan (1994c)) and expose T. to charges of hostility towards Mucianus (Wellesley (1972) 15, 209). In Josephus Mucianus sets out from his capital Antioch, not from the meeting-place at Beirut (*BJ* 4.630–2), probably within the first two weeks of August (Nicols (1978) 73–4). The original plan was apparently to march from Antioch through Asia Minor to Byzantium (765 miles), where the Pontic fleet was sent in advance; then he would proceed (by whatever route; Heubner (1968) 260) through the Danube provinces to Aquileia and down into northern Italy (to add pressure to Vespasian's blockade, depriving Italy of grain). That strategy was compromised by the decision of Antonius Primus (after the council of war at Poetovio) to pre-empt him by invading northern Italy. Fortunately for the Flavians, this led to the Vitellian defeat at the second battle of Bedriacum (24–25 Oct. 69), but also allowed the opportunistic Dacian tribes to invade Roman territory across the Danube before that final battle (3.46.2). So Mucianus stopped (perhaps at Viminacium, Wellesley (1972) 211, or at Naissus, Syme (1977) 83) to confront this trouble, though he delegated it to a subordinate and did not necessarily remain for long (Syme (1977) 82). He reached Rome only a few days after the city's capture i.e. *c.* 25 Dec. (4.4.1, 4.11.1). Such is the broad picture. T. does not report these events in great detail as Mucianus and his army did not determine the outcome of the civil war (Syme (1977) 90); and it is clear from the narrative that if anyone is to blame for leaving Rome vulnerable to invasion across the Danube, it is Antonius Primus. **cum expedita manu:** without a baggage train (40.1n. *expeditus*). Curtius Rufus likes the term (8×), which is only in prose authors (3.61.2, *A.* 1.60.3, 2.7.1, [Caes.] *Afr.* 9.1, Flor. 1.45.22), but not Livy, who combines *expeditus* instead with other nouns: e.g. *exercitus* (6.3.5), *equitatus* (8.33.5), *agmen* (10.12.7), *cohortes* (10.34.11), *miles* (21.36.1), *legiones* (9.31.8, 9.44.10). T. perhaps sought a fresher combination.   **socium . . . agens:** *agere* aptly suggests the theatre (*OLD* 26; Morgan (1994c) 167 n.5), raising questions about Mucianus' sincerity and reliability; cf. *cum amicum imperatoris ageret* (1.30.1), *filium principis agebat* (4.2.1), *agere senatorem* (*A.* 16.28.2). Mucianus has already claimed to be Vespasian's *socius* (2.77.1). The term is Livian, especially in military contexts: Camillus calls Publius Valerius to be his *socius imperii* (6.6.12, 6.6.16; Oakley (1997) 452), and Fabius Maximus (less harmoniously) asks Publius Decius to do the same (10.22.3, 10.24.6, 10.26.2). Such 'helpers' can have positive connotations, at least on the surface. So, Trajan is praised for having been the elderly Nerva's *socius imperii* (Plin. *Pan.* 9.1) and Augustus claims credit for having selected successive men as his *potestatis collega* (*RG* 6.2), though T. (more cynically) sees Agrippa, *socius potestatis* (*A.* 3.56.2), as a convenient veil for the emperor's absolute power. Yet the notion of a partner in power is problematic after Tiberius' infamous *socius laborum* (*A.* 4.2.3) and *adiutor imperii* (*A.* 4.7.1), Sejanus. Will the devious Mucianus follow the same path? He is certainly no *minister*, a role involving subordination (*OLD* 3); cf. Claudius amidst his wives and freedmen: *non principem sed ministrum egit* (Suet. *Cl.* 29.1).   **non lento itinere, ne cunctari uideretur, neque tamen properans** 'not advancing so slowly that they would look as though they were dawdling, but still not hurrying'. T. depicts another general, Corbulo, artfully failing to hurry to the rescue of his subordinate Paetus: *nec a Corbulone properatum, quo gliscentibus periculis etiam subsidii laus augeretur* (*A.* 15.10.4). A more positive precedent is Agricola in Scotland: *ipse peditem atque equites lento itinere, quo nouarum gentium animi ipsa transitus mora terrerentur, in hibernis locauit* (*Agr.* 38.3).   **gliscere famam ipso spatio sinebat** 'he allowed [his army's] reputation to grow by mere distance'; 8.2n. *gliscentem . . . famam*. An army's reputation can have huge impact, whatever the reality, as with Vitellius' German troops (58.2n. *magna . . . fama*). Mucianus' strategy is primarily designed to intimidate the people of Asia Minor (although they have already sworn an oath of support, 2.81.2), serving as a way to get them to contribute money to the Flavian cause (Morgan (1994c) 168). This same army will later generate a useful rumour during the second battle of Bedriacum, when the Flavians' morale is boosted by (false) news of Mucianus' arrival (3.25.1).   **gnarus:** 13.1n. *gnari locorum.*   **modicas uires sibi:** sc. *esse.* T. innovates by uniquely pairing *modicae + uires* (to designate soldiers) for *modicae + copiae* (Liv. 2.11.7, 34.30.6; *TLL* s.v. *modicus* 1230.59).   **maiora credi de absentibus:** tending to exaggerate what is unknown or far away, resulting in greater fear, is a topos (4.68.1, *Agr.* 25.3, 30.3, *A.* 2.24.1, 2.82.1, 3.44.1 with WM 341–2; Thuc. 6.34.7, Liv. 21.32.7, 28.44.3, 37.58.7, Caes. *Gal.* 7.84.5; Marincola (1997) 94).   **sed legio sexta et tredecim uexillariorum milia . . . sequebantur:** whatever the impact of Mucianus' calculated marching-speed, he is followed by substantial numbers of soldiers with real clout (82.3n. *sufficere . . . copiarum*). T.'s simple syntax cuts through all of Mucianus' elaborate posturing (*Mucianus . . . absentibus*). No auxiliaries are explicitly mentioned, but T. perhaps counted them within the 13,000 (Chilver (1979) 244). 'It was no small feat to conduct some 18,000 legionaries across Anatolia and through the Balkans' (Syme (1977) 81).   **ingenti agmine:** 4.2n. *ingens . . . fiducia.*

83.2 classem e Ponto Byzantium adigi iusserat: 6.2n. *Cappadocia Pontusque.* The Pontic fleet (Starr (1975) 125–9), with 40 fast Liburnian ships (3.47.3, Jos. *BJ* 2.367, though this is a speech) and a larger trireme (Arr. *Periplus* 4.4), was normally based at Trapezus on the Black Sea's south-east coast. It provided supplies for Roman troops campaigning against the Parthians (*A.* 13.39.1) so its removal totally undermines earlier Flavian concerns about exposing the empire to Parthian attacks (2.82.3). The redeployment to Byzantium was a calculated gamble (perhaps prompted by the difficulties of sailing any distance after mid-September, Veg. 4.39), in case the fleet was required to blockade the Adriatic from Dyrrachium; but the move's undesirable consequences will be a rebellion in Pontus, led by a freedman Anicetus (Woods (2006)), who has a free run *quia lectissimas Liburnicarum omnemque militem Mucianus Byzantium adegerat* (3.47.3). The pluperfect *iusserat* suggests that Mucianus had sent the fleet on its way to Byzantium (presumably with Vespasian's approval) before leaving Antioch in the first half of August. Even if his alternative plan came to nothing, the fleet could usefully assemble provisions for his troops before they reached Byzantium (Goldsworthy (1996) 111).   **ambiguus consilii num** 'in two minds about the strategy, (pondering) whether'. *ambiguus* is followed by an indirect question (also *A.* 3.15.1, 6.1.1, 11.10.4, 14.4.4, 14.33.1; WM 164, *TLL* s.v. *ambiguus* 1844.21–7); and the novel phrasing (again 4.21.1) appealed to T.'s admirer, Ammianus Marcellinus (*ambiguus consiliorum*, 21.13.2). Yet if the plan was ditched, why mention it? Not only does it help characterise Mucianus' relationship with Vespasian, which must have been based on trust if the would-be emperor's *socius* has this much leeway, but it also reminds us of an ugly 'alternative' historical narrative of the civil war, where the Flavians win by shutting off the sea-routes and starving Italy into submission.   **omissa Moesia Dyrrachium pedite atque equite simul longis nauibus uersum in Italiam mare clauderet** 'after avoiding Moesia, to take Dyrrachium with his infantry and cavalry, and shut off the sea facing Italy with his warships'. The chiastic arrangement is made more striking by zeugma (62.1n. *rata*), since *clauderet* suits *mare* better than *Dyrrachium*. The periphrasis *uersum in Italiam mare* (*OLD uerto* 10b; cf. *oramque maris in occidentem uersi*, Liv. 42.37.3) may be because T. wants potentially to designate both the Adriatic (east of Italy) and the Ionian (south of Italy) seas as the focus of Mucianus' strategy. His alternative plan is to take the army along the Via Egnatia (built *c.* 130 BC and running from Byzantium to the Adriatic coast) across Thrace and Macedonia towards the port of Dyrrachium (a march requiring *c.* 46 days, Morgan (1994c) 170 n.19), while the fleet travels there via the Aegean. Dyrrachium (*OCD³* 'Dyrrhachium', *RE* v 1882–7), a focal point in a previous civil war, is a resonant name here: it was Pompey's main base on the Adriatic in 48 BC, which prompted attacks (ultimately unsuccessful) from Caesar (Caes. *Civ.* 3.41–72). Mucianus probably concocted his strategy during the meeting in Beirut, while the status of the Danube legions was still uncertain and an alternative route to Italy was needed in case the soldiers in Pannonia, Moesia and Dalmatia did not firmly support Vespasian. As the pro-Vitellian fleets at Misenum and Ravenna were larger than the Pontic fleet, and sailing would become more difficult in the autumn and winter (a factor which influenced Mucianus, Jos. *BJ* 4.632), the alternative plan was not ideal. **tuta . . . Asiaque . . . peterentur:** Mucianus moves from the practicalities of the alternative plan to its potential results. It is striking that T. shows him more concerned for the safety of defenceless Asia and Achaea than for the wellbeing of Italy, especially the south (Morgan (1994c) 171).   **pone tergum** 'might count as a formula' (Goodyear (1981) 230). T. only uses the striking preposition *pone* + acc. selectively, once with *fores* (*A.* 4.69.1), but 5× with *tergum* (3.60.1, 3.84.5, 4.82.1, *A.* 2.16.1), following Seneca the Younger (*Marc. Cons.* 6.9.3) and Quintilian (*Decl. mai.* 6.18). It is a self-consciously archaic touch (Quint. 8.3.25, Fest. p. 292 L). After T., Apuleius, himself a stylistic virtuoso, was inspired to use the phrase 6× in his *Metamorphoses*.   **quas inermes exponi Vitellio** 'and as unarmed provinces, they were vulnerable to Vitellius'. T. uses the relative pronoun *quas* (antecedent *Achaia Asiaque*) in a subordinate clause instead of adding a main clause in *oratio obliqua* introduced by *et has*. This is why what is technically a subordinate clause in *oratio obliqua* (where we might expect a verb in the subjunctive) is expressed by an acc. + inf. as if it were reporting a main clause. This usage is first in Cicero (GL §635, K-S II §239.3a).   **atque ipsum Vitellium in incerto fore, quam partem Italiae protegeret:** *atque* (*OLD* 1 'and what is more') adds a final emphatic argument for the alternative plan. Yet it is intensely ironic that Mucianus pictures a pensive Vitellius concerned with the strategy of war and anxious to protect Italy, when we last saw him behaving 'like a foreigner' and hedonistically enjoying the fruits of power as if he had no rival (2.73). Far from offering protection, Vitellius and his men will persistently treat Italy as a foreign conquest (*ut hostile solum*, 2.87.2; *ut captam urbem*, 2.89.1; *tamquam apud alterius ciuitatis senatum populumque*, 2.90.1). T. likes *in incerto* (*OLD incertus* 10b) + an indirect question as an alternative to *dubito an* or *de*.   **sibi:** sc. *Vitellio* (dat. of disadvantage).   **Brundisium . . . litora:** T. could have described the region more generally, but he stresses the potential damage inflicted on Italy through the alternative Flavian plan by naming places in the south (all featuring only here in the narrative) in a tricolon crescendo. This is a form of *enumeratio*, making the 'whole' more graphic by listing its parts (Lausberg (1998) §669). Tarentum, with its *laudatus portus* (Sen. *Tranq.* 9.2.13), choice local oysters (Gell. 6.16.5), agreeable wines (Plin. *Nat.* 14.69), and colossal statue by Lysippus (Plin. *Nat.* 34.40), was especially pleasant.   **infestis classibus peterentur:** Mucianus either allows himself some comforting hyperbole with the pl. *classibus* (technically the Flavians only have one fleet from Pontus), or he indulges in a poeticism (with *classibus* for *nauibus*, a Virgilian figure; Pease (1967) 287). All examples of *peto* + *classis* elsewhere have the singular (Liv. 21.50.11, 27.30.7, Val. Max. 3.2.13, Ov. *Ep.* 1.5, Plin *Nat.* 7.111), except one (*Troia per undosum peteretur classibus aequor?*, Virg. *A.* 4.313), so T. probably alludes specifically to Virgil. Emphatically adding *infestis* and changing Virgil's *peto* 'head for' (*OLD* 1) to 'attack' (*OLD* 2) brings home the idea that Mucianus legitimately views Italy as hostile terrain as it harbours Vitellius.

84.1 Igitur: some see chapters 83 and 84 as wrongly transposed in the manuscripts (Wellesley (1991) 1668). Morgan (1994c) 175 argues plausibly that the order is correct, as (*a*) *igitur* (2.2n.) is not resumptive, but introduces the logical consequences of Mucianus' behaviour in the previous chapter and (*b*) *nauium* picks up on *classibus* at end of previous chapter.   **nauium militum armorum paratu strepere:** 62.1n. *strepentibus.* The asyndeton and homoioteleuton of the three nouns and verb in the historic infinitive briskly depict the east as a hive of industry; and the chapter apparently opens on an upbeat note. Yet sandwiching *milites* between two nouns denoting objects bizarrely dehumanises and reifies the soldiers (a kind of anthropomorphism in reverse). The verb is associated elsewhere with diligent preparations for war, but features with the compound *apparatus* rather than the simple noun: *urbs ipsa strepebat apparatu belli* (Liv. 26.51.7), *omnia belli apparatu strepunt* (Curt. 4.2.12). T. was perhaps thinking of Sallust: *paratu militum et armorum* (*Hist.* 1.88 Reynolds).   **sed nihil aeque fatigabat quam:** sc. *prouincias.* This marks a sharp shift in mood, as the tough reality of preparing for war begins to bite (cf. *nihil aeque prouinciam exercitumque accendit*, 2.80.3). It undercuts the sentence's initially buoyant opening by clarifying that preparing ships, men and weapons exhausted these provinces just as much as raising funds. We remember too that in this area are *inermes prouinciae* (2.83.2), not used to such military activities. **pecuniarum conquisitio:** the rare noun *conquisitio* is used only by T. (2×; also *Agr.* 6.5), Cicero (2×) and Livy (9×), but usually for levying soldiers, rather than raising funds. Expressions using the cognate verb *conquiro* are much more common (e.g. *pecuniis . . . conquirendis*, 3.76.2; *quae [pecunia] conquiritur undique*, Cic. *Fam.* 12.30.4). A similar pinch has already been felt in Rome (*populus sentire paulatim belli mala, conuersa in militum usum omni pecunia*, 1.89.1).   **eos esse belli ciuilis neruos:** financial pressures on the Flavians persisted after the war ended (5.1n. *auaritia*). The primary meaning of *neruus* is 'muscle' or 'sinew' (*OLD* 1), but metaphorically (*OLD* 5) it could indicate anything, such as money, that gives strength or vitality to a cause or an institution: *uectigalia neruos esse rei publicae semper duximus* (Cic. *Man.* 17), *neruos belli, pecuniam infinitam* (Cic. *Phil.* 5.5), *emptio frumenti ipsos rei publicae neruos exhauriebat, aerarium* (Flor. 2.1.7). There is a similar maxim in the parallel tradition, but located after the Flavian victory when

Mucianus repeatedly says that money forms the νεῦρα . . . τῆς ἡγεμονίας, 'sinews of government' (Dio 66.2.5; cf. Aeschines *Ctes.* 166.6, Cic. *Man.* 17, App. *BC* 4.99, Dion. Hal. *Dem.* 57.7, Plut. *Agis* 27.1). Morgan (1994c) 172 calls T.'s formulation a cliché, but associating it with civil war is still novel. The expression is more striking than the Othonian general Suetonius Paulinus' observation about *pecuniam, inter ciuiles discordias ferro ualidiorem* (2.32.2).   **dictitans:** historians and biographers like this frequentative form (also 4.68.2, 4.72.3, *A.* 20×, but not in the minor works) for introducing vivid aphorisms revealing a person's character. T. and Livy both favour the nom. singular present participle.   **Mucianus non ius aut uerum in cognitionibus, sed solam magnitudinem opum spectabat** 'in judicial inquiries, Mucianus had no regard for the principles of law or truth, but only the size of a man's bank balance' (*OLD specto* 9). The disjunctive particle *aut* after a negative (an alternative for *nec . . . nec*) is already in Plautus (*Poen.* 219–20; K-S II §168.6). The combination with *non* is in Sall., Caes., and Liv., but T. esp. likes it (27×: G-G 126). Participating in jurisdiction was an increasingly important part of a Roman provincial governor's duties, but he had to be present in person to intervene (Lintott (1993) 55–6). So T. refers here to Mucianus' preparatory activities as governor in Syria before setting off with his army in the first half of August, even if this early acquisitiveness is programmatic for Vespasian's whole principate (cf. Suet. *Ves.* 16.2 for his fiscally motivated prosecutions). In light of Mucianus' predatory activities, it is ironic that after the Flavian victory, the zealous senators in Rome will formulate an oath that they derived no profit (*praemium*) from the downfall of citizens (4.41.1).   **passim delationes:** sc. *erant.* Informers who target rich people trying to hide their assets also feature in narratives of previous civil wars (App. *BC* 1.95, 4.32). This was not a new phenomenon (cf. 10.2n. *prout potens* for some powerful Neronian *delatores,* 2.53.1, 4.41.2), but emphasising their dominance is a convenient way for T. to condemn the prevailing social conditions (cf. 1.2.3). **locupletissimus quisque in praedam correpti:** sc. *sunt.* T. often uses *corripio* to depict the *delatores* seizing their victims (WM 260, G-G 230). The pl. verb with *quisque* + a superlative (without designating by a gen. or prepositional phrase the broad group from which *quisque* comes; cf. *missi . . . honoratissimus quisque ex patribus,* Liv. 2.15.1) is also in Livy (*cum et leuissimus quisque nouas res . . . mallent,* 24.1.7) and Suetonius (*magisteria sacerdotii ditissimus quisque . . . comparabant, Cal.* 22.3), but is still striking and restricted to the *H.*: *eo suffragio turbidissimus quisque delecti* (3.49.2), *spendidissimus quisque in Vespasianum proni* (4.27.3). Extraordinary measures for fleecing the wealthy were symptomatic of civil war, as with the brutal triumviral proscriptions (App. *BC* 4.31; cf. spontaneous betrayal of the wealthy after the Flavian victory: *egentissimus quisque . . . prodere* <u>ultro</u> *dites dominos,* 4.1.2). The legal system was just as open to abuse in peacetime (*A.* 4.20.1, 6.16.1, 11.1.1, 12.59.1), but some defendants may have been able to purchase immunity: *quid faciunt leges, ubi sola pecunia regnat . . .?* (Petr. 14.2).

84.2 quae grauia . . . aususque est: the main clause (*quae . . . mansere*), outlining the essential problem, is dwarfed by a complex subordinate clause (an abl. absolute, supplemented by two prepositional phrases and extended by a *donec* clause with Vespasian as the subject), which explains not so much how the ruthless money-seizing measures evolved as how they could continue after the civil war. The subordinate clause, highlighting deterioration in Vespasian's principate, fostered in part by *praui magistri*, also prepares us for more sombre things to come (13.2n. *quae* on 'appendix sentences'). **quae grauia atque intoleranda:** the thundering language eloquently expresses T.'s exasperation: cf. *o magnum atque intolerandum dolorem! o grauem acerbamque fortunam!* (Cic. *Verr.* 2.5.119). In such expressions, if the gerundive is paired with another adj., it usually takes the final climactic position in crescendo, often after the conjunction *atque* (cf. *illa foeda atque intoleranda*, Sall. *Cat.* 58.14; *misera atque miseranda*, Cic. *Cat.* 4.12; *dura atque intoleranda*, Sen. *Ep.* 71.23; *uana atque intoleranda*, Gell. 10.12.1). **necessitate armorum:** *arma = bellum* by synecdoche (6.1n. *ualidissima . . . arma*), an especially apt figure here, as an important reason for the grave financial impositions is the manufacture of arms (*armorum paratu*, 2.84.1). Cf. *bellorum necessitas* (Sen. *Ep.* 67.4). **excusata** 'excusable'. This use of the perfect participle from *excuso* (6× elsewhere in T.), though not common, does occur elsewhere in Silver Latin (Sen. *Con.* 7.1.20, Sen. *Ep.* 95.8, Quint. 11.1.14; Goodyear (1972) 307, *TLL* s.v. *excuso* 1307.56–65, *OLD excusatus*). **etiam in pace:** the expressive idea that war and peace are virtually indistinguishable from one another recurs in T. (*opus aggredior . . . atrox proeliis, discors seditionibus, ipsa etiam pace saeuum*, 1.2.1; *bellum magis desierat quam pax coeperat*, 4.1.1), especially in the *A.*, as various *principes* 'make war' on their own state (*A.* 6.39.2; Keitel (1984) 312–17), suggesting that 'the Julio-Claudian era already displayed many of the symptoms of internecine strife long before the civil war actually broke out' (Woodman (1998) 136). **mansere:** 3.1n. *ipsa . . . cessere*. **ipso Vespasiano inter initia imperii ad obtinendas iniquitates haud perinde obstinante donec indulgentia fortunae et prauis magistribus didicit aususque est** 'since Vespasian himself over the early stages of his principate was not exactly determined to maintain unjust practices until he learned the knack from indulgent fortune and wicked advisers, and became daring'. T.'s pregnant *haud perinde* (*OLD perinde* 1c) has led to conflicting interpretations (Vespasian was . . . (*a*) 'not as determined as Mucianus'? (*b*) 'not as determined as other rulers were'?, (*c*) 'not as determined as he himself was later'?). The temporal reading (*c*) is most prominent through the contrast between *inter initia imperii* and *donec*, but *haud perinde* also has a sardonic tone, especially combined with *obstino*, which paradoxically implies that later Vespasian was indeed 'determined' to maintain unjust practices. The sarcasm is 'launched' through *ad obtinendas iniquitates*, a parody of the legal term *ius* (*suum*) *obtinere*, 'to hold on to one's legal rights' (*OLD obtineo* 8; Morgan (1994c) 172). With an elliptical phrase like *haud perinde*, it is necessary to supply different shades of meaning according to context (Goodyear (1981) 449). **inter initia imperii:** Suetonius has the identical phrase (*Nero* 22.1). The (post-Augustan) combination *inter + initia* seems chronologically broad, suggesting a period of time (*OLD inter* 6), rather than a specific moment (cf. *initio statim principatus*, Suet. *Ves.* 16.3; *imperii initio*, Suet. *Dom.* 20.1). The formulation perhaps explains why the unjust practices were allowed to persist. Although Vespasian's *dies imperii* was 1 Jul. 69, he did not reach Rome until more than a year later, at the end of Sept. 70 (Levick (1999) 91). During this time, Mucianus *initia principatus ac statum urbis . . . regebat* (*Agr.* 7.2), so the new emperor's

presence was felt only indirectly.   **indulgentia fortunae et prauis magistris:**
the combination of an abstract noun + dependent gen. and an abl. noun + adj. in
agreement shows *uariatio*. Livy coined *indulgentia fortunae* (23.2.1), favoured especially
by Seneca the Younger (*De ira* 16.6, *Vit. beat.* 16.3, *Ep.* 66.44, *Nat.* 3.29.9, 5.18.12,) and
used by T. again (2.99.2; also Vell. 2.1.4, 2.80.1, 2.121.3, Plin. *Pan.* 82.6, Apul. *Apol.* 19).
The phrase *praui magistri* is only here in Latin, but perhaps plays on Cicero's *magistri*
uirtutis (*Rep.* 3.4, *Mur.* 65, *Tusc.* 2.28.1). T. probably has in mind Eprius Marcellus and
Licinius Mucianus (paired disparagingly at 2.95.3), but the phrase links Vespasian
inauspiciously with his predecessor Vitellius (63.1n. *irrepentibus dominationis magistris*).
didicit aususque est: T.'s critical tone strikes some critics as contradicting his earlier positive analysis that Vespasian *solus . . . omnium ante se principum in melius mutatus est*
(1.50.4). Yet the context of that assessment is still ambivalent (*ambigua de Vespasiano fama*,
1.50.4; Morgan (1994c) 173) and the point at which Vespasian changes is unspecified;
it could be late in his principate, after the financial ruthlessness T. criticises here.
propriis quoque opibus: Mucianus had spectacular wealth (5.1n. *magnificentia*),
which prompts comparisons with Maecenas, Augustus' right-hand man, who also
contributed some of his personal fortune to the civil war, and got even richer as a
result (*ampla quidem, sed pro ingentibus meritis praemia, A.* 14.53.3). No doubt Mucianus'
personal financial assistance (an insurance policy for the future) prompts his later
boast that *in manu sua fuisse imperium donatumque* (4.4.1). T.'s *propriis . . . opibus* (inspired
perhaps by Ovid: *ne proprias attenuarat opes, Pont.* 4.5.38) is a choice variant for the
ubiquitous *suis opibus*.   **largus priuatim quo auidius de re publica sumeret:**
this appended adjectival clause ruthlessly undercuts Mucianius' apparent generosity
presented in the main clause. M's reading is *quod*, which troubles editors: if taken as a
relative pronoun, it lacks an antecedent (and the adj. *largus* is not the equivalent of the
verb *largiens*). So they generally accept Muret's correction (1789), *quo*, introducing a
final clause with a comparative adj. Morgan (1994c) 174 defends *quod* as introducing a
causal clause with the subjunctive verb indicating Mucianus' thoughts (cf. *A.* 2.37.1 for
a similar contested *quo / quod* reading), but *quo* is more acidic (and Tacitean), damning
Mucianus for cynically using his own money in the short-term to secure long-term
profits from the state. The unusual combination of the intransitive *sumo* (*OLD* 6) +
de (cf. *multum . . . de nocte sumitur*, Plin. *Ep.* 9.40.2) further emphasises his exploitative conduct.   **conferendarum pecuniarum exemplum:** when other authors
combine *confero* + *pecunia*, the singular form of the noun is standard (Cic. *Verr.* 2.145,
Liv. 22.1.19, 45.29.1, [Caes.] *Afr.* 88.1, Nep. *Att.* 8.6, Sen. *Suas.* 1.7, Phaedr. 4.5.17, Sen.
Ben. 2.21.5, Plin. *Nat.* 33.138, Plin. *Ep.* 10.39.5). T.'s plural conveys giving on a lavish
scale and generates homoioteleuton, making the phrase stand out and neatly establishing ring-composition with the start of the chapter (cf. homoioteleuton of *nauium*
militum armorum and the repetition of *pecuniarum*).   **secuti:** sc. *sunt*.   **rarissimus**
quisque . . . habuerunt: singular distributive pronoun with pl. verb (44.1n. *suum*
obiectantes). T.'s sarcastic coda sits asyndetically and paratactically with what precedes,
so we must supply its concessive relationship with *ceteri . . . secuti*. The superlative
rarissimus (only in the minor works apart from here; once in Cic., not in Sall., Caes.,

Liv.) + the pronoun *quisque* is choicer than an alternative such as *paucissimi*. If *reciperando* prompts thoughts of the *reciperatores*, judges who adjudicated over cases involving the recovery of property (Mooney (1930) 384), then there is further irony in its application to such illegal profiteering.

85.1 Accelerata [sc. *sunt*] . . . **coepta Illyrici exercitus studio transgressi in partes:** T. says that Vespasian's undertakings were not triggered, just accelerated by the enthusiastic Illyrian army. This undercuts pro-Flavian accounts that the soldiers rather than Vespasian provided the initial impetus for the imperial challenge (Suet. *Ves.* 6.3). The point is made more emphatic by *accelero* + *coepta*, combined only here (*TLL* s.v. *accelero* 272.76, s.v. *coeptum* 1430.38–9).   **tertia legio exemplum . . . praebuit:** the *legio III Gallica* (4.4n. *quattuor*). We know that the armies of Illyricum are unhappy after Vitellius' victory at Bedriacum (2.60.1), but when did the revolt itself occur? It is crucial to acknowledge that this movement developed over time, making precise chronology difficult to reconstruct. Suetonius gives different versions, saying first that the armies of Pannonia and Moesia revolted in *August* 69 (*Vit.* 15.1) and then that the *III Gallica* (*Ves.* 6.3) initially prompted the legions to inscribe Vespasian's name on their standards *before 1. Jul.*, but that revolt was then deliberately suppressed for a while (*parumper, Ves.* 6.3). T. does not give exact dates, but also implies an initial incident at Aquileia involving the three Moesian legions *III Gallica, VII Claudia* and *VIII Augusta*, followed by their sending letters to solicit the Pannonian legions (which must have taken some time); and it was therefore only in August that all the Danube legions officially came over to Vespasian. Before 1 Jul., T.'s Vespasian is optimistic that these legions will support him, but not yet sure (*ceterae Illyrici legiones secuturae sperabantur*, 2.74.1). In Josephus the Moesian and Pannonian legions declare for Vespasian after 1. Jul., but before the strategy meeting at Beirut in the second half of July (*BJ* 4.619). **octaua** [sc. *legio Augusta*]   **erat ac septima Claudiana, imbutae fauore Othonis** 'namely the Eighth Augustan and Seventh Claudian legions, deeply devoted to Otho'. The copula *erat* is a thoughtful gloss, in case we have forgotten the relevant legions (cf. 18.1n. *is enim*). T. then reverts to the pl. with *imbutae*, the common predicate of two singular subjects (GL §285). The metaphor of *imbuo* (not in Caes. or Sall.; 11× in Liv.) suggests dipping or staining: it appears 5× in the *D.* for giving someone a basic grounding in e.g. *eloquentia*, but in the *H.* T. uses it especially for the attributes of soldiers (almost always pejoratively): 1.5.1, 1.83.4, 3,15.2, 3.49.2, 4.72.2, also 4.7.2 (Vespasian as *imperator*), 4.42.4 (Regulus), and 5.5.2 (Jews). T's nomenclature (*Claudiana*) for the *VII Claudia* (the usual name) is quirky, but consistent.   **quamuis proelio non interfuissent:** 32.2n. *cum integris exercitibus*.   **Aquileiam progressae . . . hostiliter egerant:** *hostiliter* (once in Cic., Sall., Pomp. Trog.; 2× in Ov., Suet.) is a Livian adverb (23×; 4× in T.). The mention of Aquileia in north-east Italy and the verb's pluperfect tense indicates a 'flashback'. The pro-Othonian Moesian legions had reached Aquileia shortly before Otho's suicide on 17 Apr. (2.46.3), so they must have heard the news soon afterwards and rioted. In Suetonius the troops hear about both the defeat and suicide on the march, but still carry on to Aquileia (*Ves.* 6.2). T.'s syntax is drily witty: the long trio of abl. absolutes ruthlessly elaborating the violence (*proturbatis . . . diuisa*) lands with a bump in a simple main clause (*hostiliter egerant*, combined here first; *TLL* s.v. *hostiliter* 3054.6), apparently stating the obvious by this point. In contrast, Suetonius does not describe the trouble in detail (*omni rapinarum genere grassati, Ves.* 6.2).   **qui de Othone nuntiabat:** *de morte* (+ gen.) + *nuntio* is more usual (Cic. *Mur.* 34, *Scaur.* 12, *Mil.* 48, Vell. 2.59.5). Omitting *mors* hints at unlucky messengers trying diplomatically to avoid traumatic words, but still facing violence from the distraught soldiers: cf. Suetonius' more explicit version of this announcement that Otho *uim uitae suae attulisse* (*Ves.* 6.2).   **laceratis uexillis nomen Vitellii praeferentibus:** yet Suetonius explicitly says that the soldiers inscribed Vespasian's name on the standards (*Ves.* 6.3). Applying the violent verb *lacero* to *uexillum* (only here) shows an expressive destructiveness: military standards were normally a highly emotive object for troops (18.2n. *correptis . . . uexillisque*) so they must hate Vitellius bitterly. **rapta . . . diuisa:** this is a grubby and opportunistic outbreak, certainly no idealistic swelling of support for Vespasian.   **unde metus et ex metu consilium:** sc. *erat*. The polyptoton (cf. 68.3n. *remedium . . . tumultus*) apparently marks the time elapsed between the initial revolt at Aquileia in April and the soldiers' later plan (perhaps in July) to recast it as an expression of support for Vespasian. Suetonius also stresses that the soldiers feared retribution (*cum timerent ne sibi reuersis reddenda ratio ac subeunda poena esset, Ves.* 6.2), but implies that the *consilium . . . eligendi . . . imperatoris* (*Ves.* 6.2) immediately followed the riot (without Vespasian in mind).   **posse imputari Vespasiano quae apud Vitellium excusanda erant** 'that credit could be claimed with Vespasian for conduct which would require an apology before Vitellius'. The acc. + inf. construction after *consilium* features again (3.8.2, 3.78.2, *A.* 1.1.3); and the financial metaphor of *imputo* (*OLD* 3) is darkly humorous, so soon after the rapacious soldiers dividing the money from the legionary chest between themselves. The language also taps into a central theme, namely the inextricable links between soldiers, money and (routes to) imperial power.   **Pannonicum exercitum:** the *VII Galbiana* and *XIII Gemina* (and presumably also the one remaining Dalmatian legion *XI Claudia*, based at Burnum).   **aut . . . uim parabant:** this alarming coda momentarily conjures up an 'alternative history' of a grim civil war on the Danube (vulnerable to the hostile foreign tribes to the north) involving the pro-Flavian legions of Moesia and the Pannonian legions still loyal to Vitellius. The Moesian soldiers' uncertainty about their Pannonian colleagues casts light both on why Vespasian's hopes about winning over the Danube legions were tentative (2.74.1) and why Mucianus contemplated a southerly march, avoiding the Danube area in favour of Dyrrachium (2.83.2). Even if these Pannonian soldiers shrewdly played up their 'early' support for the new emperor later, they only supported Vespasian unambiguously once the campaign was safely under way (3.1–3).   **abnuenti:** a dat. participle economically stands for a conditional clause.

85.2 In eo motu: T., a consummate narrator, knows the power of zooming in on individuals to personalise a sweeping narrative (cf. the Ligurian woman, 2.13.2), especially as the prevailing focus of 2.82–85.1 has been the bustling preparations for civil war and the initial movements of the troops. The chronological marker is broad.

Aponius Saturninus . . . pessimum facinus audet: this damning story may be a surprise, as Aponius (Milns (1973), *PIR²* A 938) was first seen being awarded a triumphal statue by Otho after successfully suppressing an incursion by the Rhoxolani (1.79). Yet T. always revels in such tensions between upright character implied by such official honours and the more corrupt reality. Aponius, a member of the Arval brethren since 57 (*CIL* vi 2039) and suffect consul under Nero (year unknown), was cautious during the civil war. After trying to play it safe by giving Vitellius some (but not all) information about the desertion of the *III Gallica*, he transfers his allegiance to Vespasian (2.96.1). Men lower in the military hierarchy (Antonius Primus, Cornelius Fuscus) order him (despite being a consular legate) to march his troops swiftly from Moesia to northern Italy (*celeraret*, 3.5.1). The biddable Aponius, not unduly disturbed by lack of endorsement from Vespasian, brings up the *VII Claudia*, now commanded by the tribune Vipstanus Messalla instead of the unlucky Tettius Iulianus (3.9.3). He apparently left the day-to-day tasks to Messalla: when his angry soldiers revolt, they find him in a pleasant country villa (*hortos, in quibus deuertebatur*, 3.11.3), but he escapes by hiding in the furnace of a bath-house (practical, if degrading). This evidently spoiled his appetite for civil war, and he fled to Padua. T. finds Aponius utterly unimpressive (prompted perhaps by his source Vipstanus Messalla, cast as a hero in comparison). The current epsiode does Aponius no long-term harm under the Flavians, since he became proconsul of Asia after 73 (*ILS* 8817 = M-W 270; Syme (1958a) 594). In Caligula's principate, a man of the same name nodded in his sleep at an auction and unwittingly bought 13 gladiators for 90,000HS (Suet. *Cal.* 38.4; Milns (1973) 293 proposes our Aponius for the dupe, or it was perhaps his father, Nicols (1978) 134).

misso centurione: the incident, itself witnessed by very few, is only in T., who is thus free to tell the story with whatever emphasis he wanted. Vipstanus Messalla is perhaps the most likely source.   **Tettium Iulianum:** Iulianus (*RE* v A 1107–10), legate of the *VII Claudia*, received *consularia ornamenta* from Otho after taking part in the successful campaign against the Rhoxolani (1.79.5), and was also designated as praetor for 70. Yet on 1 Jan. 70, the senate deprived him of the post for abandoning his legion when it went over to the Flavians (4.39.1), but reinstated him on 3 Jan. once his flight to Vespasian became known (4.40.2). He became suffect consul in 83 and won an important victory at Tapae in Domitian's Dacian war in 88 (Dio 67.10.1). If he went on to become governor of Moesia (Nicols (1978) 135), it was poetic justice after his undignified treatment by the post-holder in 69, Aponius Saturninus. He appears to have been a competent military man: his innovation of inscribing soldiers' names on their shields, facilitating praise or punishment of individuals, improved his troops' performance (Dio 67.10.1).   **ob simultates:** the disreputable practice of pursuing private quarrels under the pretext of politics (especially on the imperial margins) recurs. So, in Africa the legionary commander Valerius Festus arrests the camp prefect Caetronius Pisanus *proprias ob simultates* (4.50.3) and in Britain Julius Classicanus, hating Suetonius Paulinus, *bonum publicum priuatis simultatibus impediebat* (*A.* 14.38.3). T.'s moralism in this episode is reasonably clear-cut, partly to condemn the deterioration of Roman national character through civil war. Yet the relationship between public and private disputes could often be complex. In Livy people protest that they have no personal quarrel in taking a particular course of action, presumably anticipating a familiar criticism (26.27.11, 28.18.3), and it was certainly possible to gain long-standing private enemies while genuinely serving the public interest (33.46.8); and general knowledge of private feuds can sometimes destroy the credibility of proposals, even sensible ones (Liv. 23.13.6). Pretending subsequently that private quarrels had really been undertaken for the public good could facilitate reconciliation (Cic. *Att.* 14.13a.3).   **quibus causam partium praetendebat** 'which he dressed up as serving the interests of the party'. The combination *causa + praetendo* (1.65.2) features only in T. (*TLL* s.v. *causa* 689.8). Cf. Julius Civilis, who *Vespasiani amicitiam studiumque partium praetendit* (4.13.2).   **gnaris locorum:** 13.1n. *gnari locorum.*   **per auia Moesiae:** T. uses the neuter pl. *auia* as a substantive (predominantly a poetic usage) again, either alone (*in auia, A.* 1.63.1, 14.23.2), coupled with other adjectives (*in remota et auia, Agr.* 19.4; similar expressions at *Agr.* 37.5, *A.* 4.45.1, *A.* 6.21.1, *A.*15.11.2), or with a defining gen. (*auia Belgarum, H.* 4.70.1; similar expressions at *A.* 2.15.2, *A.* 2.68.1, *A.* 13.37.3; 2.2n. *laeua maris*). Livy has *auia loca* (9.19.16; Oakley (2005) 260), but Virgil first uses the adj. as a substantive (*A.* 2.736, 9.58, followed by Ov., Vell., Luc., Val. Flac., Sil., Stat., and also Apul. and Flor.). In T., such terrain is associated with barbarians or (as here) with Romans behaving (or forced to behave) in a non-Roman way.   **ultra . . . Haemum:** the mountain (*praematura montis Haemi et saeua hiems, A.* 4.51.3; *opertum nubibus Haemum, Ov. Pont.* 4.5.5) stands for a formidable mountain-range (mod. Stara Planina, Bulgaria; Liv. 40.22.1–8, Amm. 21.10.3) separating Moesia from Thrace, and reflects Tettius' extreme measures to escape from Aponius. In myth, Haemus lived incestuously with his sister Rhodope, and the pair called themselves Zeus and Hera (*nunc gelidos montes, mortalia corpora quondam, Ov. Met.* 6.88). Apuleius aptly names a big fierce Thracian robber Haemus (*Met.* 7.5).   **deinde** 'from then on' (*OLD* 4).   **susceptum ad Vespasianum iter trahens:** Vespasian himself was heading from Antioch to Alexandria (eventually reaching it at some point after the second battle of Bedriacum on 24–25 Oct. 69), but he only set out in the middle of October (Dio 65.9.2 with Halfmann (1986) 179). It helped Tettius to hedge his bets when Vespasian extended the distance for him to cover by setting off for Egypt. *traho* (*OLD* 16) + *iter* (cf. *retardet iter,* Ov. *Tr.* 3.9.32; *iter repressit,* Enn. *var.* 11 (Vahlen) = Macr. *Sat.* 6.2.26) on the analogy of *traho + bellum* (31.2n.) is innovative.   **ex nuntiis cunctabundus aut properans:** *uariatio* of adj. + present participle (19.2n. *minus turbidos . . . accipientes*). T.'s choice *cunctabundus* (again only at *A.* 1.7.5) revives a Livian usage (6.7.2, 33.8.2; Oakley (1997) 459), perhaps originally in Claudius Quadrigarius (fr. 10b Peter: the reading may be *cantabundus*) and later appealing to Apuleius and Aulus Gellius. Resonant and rare *-abundus* adjectives (usually imperfective), a Livian favourite, lend themselves particularly well to historiography, though some are more vivid than others (Goodyear (1972) 201). Tettius' mode of travelling recalls the devious Mucianus moving *non lento itinere, ne cunctari uideretur, neque tamen properans* (2.83.1), except that the fugitive has no troops or means of defence.

86.1 At: transitional (20.1n. *At*). Shifting to introductory character-sketches of prominent Flavians in the section's last chapter (2.74–86) seems paradoxical, but shows T.'s narrative artistry in whetting our appetites for these protagonists, who will reappear at the start of book 3.   **tertia decima legio:** the Othonian *legio XIII Gemina* (11.1n. *quattuor legiones*, 26.2n. *Vitellianus miles*).   **septima Galbiana:** the full title of this Pannonian legion is given to avoid confusion with the *VII Claudia* based in Moesia (2.85.1). It was last seen building amphitheatres in northern Italy, but had returned to base since then (2.67.2).   **Bedriacensis pugnae:** only the *XIII Gemina* had definitely arrived in time for the first battle of Bedriacum.   **haud cunctanter:** the litotes emphasises their swift support of Vespasian.   **ui praecipua Primi Antonii:** 53.1n. *Marcellum Eprium* on the inverted names. T. obliquely introduces arguably the most influential protagonist on the outcome of the whole civil war in an appended abl. of manner, a playful touch. Antonius Primus (born *c.* 20), crucial both as the catalyst for Vespasian's victory and as a test-case for the calibre of T.'s historical methods, came from Tolosa in Gaul (Mart. 9.99.3, Suet. *Vit.* 18, who also records his nickname *Beccus*, 'Beaky'). The ambivalent character-sketch offered here has been criticised as incompatible with the allegedly more positive portrait in book 3, cast as uncritically drawn from pro-Flavian sources (Wellesley (1972) 4). Yet there is logical coherence in showing Primus to be a competent, but disreputable general: nothing in T.'s narrative of his subsequent actions will detract from the opening assessment, which acknowledges Primus' talents, but warns of a dangerously amoral personality (Ash (1999) 147–65, especially 148–9; Treu (1948), Dorey (1958), Shotter (1977), *OCD³* 'Antonius (*RE* 89) Primus'). Galba was murdered before he could make full use of Primus, and Otho also ignored him. After dramatically seizing the initiative at the conference at Poetovio in late August, Primus swept into northern Italy and won the second battle of Bedriacum (24–25 Oct.), oversaw the destruction of Cremona, and then advanced to Rome, but not quickly enough to save the Capitoline temple from destruction. After Mucianus edged him from power in 70 and Vespasian resisted his pleas (4.80.2–3), he apparently returned home to Tolosa, but he becomes almost invisible in our sources. At some point between 95 and 98, Martial wrote *felix Antonius* a warm tribute on his 75th birthday (10.23), defiantly suggesting that he had nothing to be ashamed of in his previous life (though the epigram could well have been published after the last of the Flavian dynasty had died).   **legibus nocens** 'found guilty before the laws'. The unusual addition of *legibus* to *nocens* emphasises the due process of the law, thus enhancing indignation that such a man should be restored to the senate.   **tempore Neronis:** the unusual singular form (cf. *temporibus Neronis*, 2.10.1) follows the analogy of similar phrases involving *aetas* (cf. *diui Augusti aetate*, Plin. *Nat.* 35.116).   **falsi damnatus** 'convicted of fraud'. The relevant statute is the *lex Cornelia de falsis* (originated by Sulla in 81 BC), covering crimes such as forgery, bribery of judges or witnesses, and false testimony. Such cases were usually tried in the urban prefect's court, although sometimes they were brought before the senate (Garnsey (1970) 27–30, WM 211). Cases could often be sensational, such as the trial of Aemilia Lepida, who claimed to have had a son by the rich and (hitherto) childless

Sulpicius Quirinus, a story concocted to inherit his money (*A.* 3.22–3). Penalties for *falsum* could be harsh: the philosopher Flavius Archippus was condemned to work in the mines in Domitian's principate (Plin. *Ep.* 10.58.3). The penalty imposed on Antonius Primus was exile (3.13.3, Dio 65.9.3), and his crime, committed in 61, involved witnessing a false will drawn up by the predatory Valerius Fabianus, who coveted the money of his rich old relative, Domitius Balbus (*A.* 14.40). **inter alia belli mala:** the prepositional formula allows T. to make a general point (that civil war affords upward mobility to unscrupulous men unlikely to have risen so high during peacetime), while addressing a specific case, thus broadening the scope and relevance of his historical narrative (cf. *inter alia dominationis arcana, A.* 2.59.3; 66.3n. *ut pleraque . . . mala*). The idiom of substantive neuter pl. (*mala*) + a defining gen. (2.2n. *laeua maris*) recalls Livy's special liking for the construction with *belli* (Oakley (1997) 638–9 on *subita belli*). **senatorium ordinem reciperauerat:** further dubious *reciperatio* in civil war (cf. *in reciperando*, 2.84.2). There were many routes out of the senate, including impoverishment, death, crime or *infamia*, but restoration of status was more elusive (Talbert (1984) 27–9). Each year a senatorial whiteboard (*album senatorium, A.* 4.42.3) on public display listed senators' names in order of seniority, and disgraced senators would either be discreetly removed from the list or else given a black mark (*nota*, Suet. *Cl.* 16.2), sometimes with the reason appended (Gell. 17.21.39). Money could secure restoration (Suet. *Otho* 2.2), or the emperor (or other powerful men, *A.* 14.48.1) could intervene (1.77.3, *A.* 13.11.2,), even if such decisions were easily reversible (4.44.2). The senate itself could also take the initiative (*A.* 13.32.2, perhaps).

86.2 septimae legioni: *VII Galbiana.* Galba's appointment of Primus created a remarkably passionate bond between the general and his men (*flagrantissimus in Antonium amor*, 4.39.4), who cared more about his competence than his morals. **scriptitasse Othoni credebatur:** T. uses the unusual frequentative verb *scriptito* (not in Sall., Caes., Liv., but 8× in Cic.) only once more (3.52.2). It suits Primus' energetic personality. He was presumably offering his services to Otho against Vitellius, not betraying Galba, who reinstated him as a senator and promoted him to a military command. **a quo neglectus:** Otho must have thought the services of Suetonius Paulinus (*nemo illa tempestate militaris rei callidior habebatur*, 2.32.1) sufficient, together with his other generals Marius Celsus, Annius Gallus and Licinius Proculus. Yet we may wonder whether Paulinus, a *cunctator natura* (2.25.2), would have been compatible with the dynamic Primus. **in nullo Othoniani belli usu fuit** 'his services were not used in the Othonian war'. This applies specifically to Primus as a potential adviser to Otho, as he and his legion, the *VII Galbiana*, did march from Pannonia to northern Italy (despite arriving too late for the final battle). **labantibus Vitellii rebus:** the verb *labo* (*OLD* 5), suggesting the metaphor of a tottering building, is applied elsewhere to cities and states (cf. *ingentibus bellis labaret res publica, A.* 3.73.2 with WM 483–4; *labentem et prope cadentem rem publicam*, Cic. *Phil.* 2.51; *rei publicae partis aegras et labantis*, Cic. *Mil.* 68; *cum res Troiana labaret*, Ov. *Met.* 15.437; *cadentis imperi moles labat*, Sen. *Oed.* 84). **grande momentum addidit** 'he added tremendous force'. After the building metaphor (prev. n.), Primus is almost cast as a demolition machine. T.

likes *grande momentum* (1.59.1, 1.76.2), a variant for the more familiar *magnum momentum* (favoured by Cic., Liv., Caes.; cf. *magni momenti locum obtinuit*, 3.8.1).   **strenuus . . . spernendus:** the rapid-fire syntax mirrors the man's dynamism, as asyndeton and (apart from the opening *strenuus manu*) nominative adjectives concluding the clauses propel readers through the sentence.   **strenuus manu, sermone promptus** 'physically energetic and a ready talker'. Other authors have *manu strenuus* (Curt. 6.11.1, 7.2.33, Gell. 4.8.2), but T. may have been inspired by Velleius Paterculus: *impetu strenuus, manu promptus* (2.73.1, of Sextus Pompeius). T.'s chiasmus sets up a formidable nexus of physical and mental attributes for Primus, a variant of the broad *corpus / animus* pairing (93.1n. *corpus . . . imminuebant*). Generals were not always eloquent (5.1n. *aptior sermone*), but the articulate Primus will use his talents dramatically to hijack the Flavian campaign (3.2).   **serendae in alios inuidiae artifex:** yet in this, Primus is outdone after the victory by Mucianus, who elicits from his friends letters criticising Primus, which he then promptly sends to Vespasian (3.52.3); cf. *inde graues simultates, quas Antonius simplicius, Mucianus callide . . . nutriebat* (3.53.3). The combination *inuidia + sero* (*OLD* 4) is unique, although T. often likes agricultural metaphors in the incongruous context of civil war (cf. *seditio mitesceret*, 2.18.2; *uberioribus . . . probris*, 2.21.4; *uberrima conuiciorum . . . materia*, 2.30.3; *bello semina*, 2.76.4). T. softens the homoioteleuton of *artifex + gen.* gerundive (cf. *faciendarum amicitiarum artifex*, Sen. *Ep.* 9.6; *tractandorum animorum artifex*, Quint. 11.1.85) by inserting *in alios*. Ammianus (as often) imitates T.: *transferendae . . . in alios inuidiae artifex* (27.9.2).   **discordiis et seditionibus potens:** T. echoes Virgil on Drances, *seditione potens* (*A.* 11.340, with Horsfall (2003b) 218, citing νείκει ἄριστε, Hom. *Il.* 23.483), except that unlike Primus, Turnus' enemy is *senior* (*A.* 11.122), with a *frigida bello | dextera* (*A.* 11.338–9); and of course Drances (however acerbically) argues for peace, whereas Primus ardently pursues civil war. T. trumps Virgil's one abl. noun in the singular with two nouns in the pl., perhaps suggesting the huge scale of the violence triggered by Primus (whereas Drances is restricted to Italy). *potens* (*OLD* 3b) + the abl. of respect is ambiguous: is Primus capable with respect to repressing (cf. 3.10.4) or promoting (3.15.2) riots and mutinies? He can potentially do both.   **raptor largitor** 'light-fingered and free-handed' (Fyfe / Levene). T. likes agent nouns (56.2n. *alienae . . . dissimulator*), but uses *largitor* again only once (*A.* 3.27.2), and *raptor* twice (*Agr.* 30.4, *A.* 1.58.2). Cicero, Sallust and Livy first have *largitor* (not always pejorative, Oakley (1997) 537–8), which is then largely appropriated by the poets (Pers., Sil., Stat.); *raptor* (since Plautus) is predominantly poetic, until Seneca the Elder and Velleius Paterculus begin to use it in prose. The combination of concepts recalls Sallust on Catiline (*alieni appetens, sui profusus, Cat.* 5.4).   **pace pessimus, bello non spernendus** 'a scoundrel in peacetime, but a force to be reckoned with in war'. Primus' problematic peace-time rôle emerges later, when his arrogance (4.80.2–3), resentment of the suave Mucianus (3.53.1), and continuing influence with the soldiers (4.39.3), obliges Mucianus to curb his power swiftly to secure peace, partly by dispersing his partisan soldiers around the empire (4.39.4). The language evokes Velleius' portrait of another talented general (but dangerous demagogue), Marius, *quantum bello optimus, tantum pace pessimus* (2.11.1; cf. *neque bello fortes neque pace boni*,

[Caes.] *Afr.* 54.5). T. adds *uariatio* by using a gerundive in litotes, instead of a second superlative adj.

86.3 Iuncti: i.e. they were united in spirit: the Moesian legions under Aponius Saturninus do not physically move from their base until later (3.5.1). **Dalmaticum militem:** the collective singular *miles* (6.2n.) is standard, but reminds us that (in contrast with the multiple legions in Moesia and Pannonia) there is now only one legion (*VII Claudia*) in Dalmatia, as the *XIV Gemina* has been transferred to Britain. **quamquam consularibus legatis nihil turbantibus** 'although their consular legates were by no means actively rebellious'. *quamquam* lacks a finite verb (3.2n. *quamquam in aperto*). T. presumably means three men, Aponius Saturninus, the legate of Moesia (2.85.2), as well as the pair about to be mentioned, Tampius Flauianus (Pannonia) and Pompeius Siluanus (Dalmatia). **Tampius Flauianus:** after a suffect consulship perhaps in 45 or 46, Tampius became proconsul of Africa, probably under Nero (Plin. *Nat.* 9.26 records him smearing a playful dolphin with unguent). The *princeps* probably considered this *natura ac senecta cunctator* (3.4.1) a safe pair of hands for Pannonia and its legions. As consular legate, Tampius won *ornamenta triumphalia* at an unknown date for his achievements beyond the frontier (*ILS* 985 = M-W 274), but his enthusiastically pro-Othonian troops apparently disliked him, since he was related to Vitellius by marriage (3.4.1), a factor which prompted the *VII Galbiana* to attack him (3.10.2). He was only saved by the guile of Antonius Primus, who 'arrested' him (3.10.3). It had not helped that Tampius fled to Italy when the troops first rebelled against Vitellius in the late summer (although the fact that Otho co-opted him on 26 Feb. 69 to join the *Aruales Fratres* suggests that he at least trusted him). His contribution to the civil war was arguably to add respectablility at an early stage (*consulare nomen*, 3.4.2) and to stir the troops, who responded enthusiastically to Antonius Primus partly through his contrast with the placid elderly legate. No doubt the Flavians also appreciated his money. Tampius was apparently rewarded by Vespasian, who made him *curator aquarum* in 74–5 (Fron. *Aq.* 102) and gave him a second suffect consulship, perhaps in 76 (*CIL* IV 2560, *CIL* X 6225 = *ILS* 985; Levick (1999) 177, Milns (1973) 285–6). **Pompeius Siluanus:** his career (*PIR*[1] P 495, Milns (1973) 286–7) follows a similar trajectory to that of Tampius Flavianus, but he was perhaps a little older. He was suffect consul in 45 (Jos. *AJ* 20.14), then proconsul of Africa (perhaps 53/4–55/6), which prompted charges of extortion, but Nero acquitted him in 58 (*A.* 13.52). As legate of Dalmatia (*ILS* 5951 = M-W 451), Silvanus was not directly threatened by his troops, as Tampius had been, and he marched south through Italy with Antonius Primus. T. pours scorn on his skills as a general: this man, *socors bello*, apparently wasted any chance for action by his endless talk (3.50.2), so that he had to be diplomatically 'managed' by the legionary commander Annius Bassus, who had real control. After the civil war, he held two curatorships, the first in 70, an abortive commission to raise a public loan of 60 million HS (4.47), and the second as *curator aquarum* from 71–3 (Fron. *Aq.* 102). His second consulship was held with Tampius, perhaps in 76 (*CIL* IV 2560). **diuites senes:** character-sketches (or lack of them) can usefully bring home a protagonist's historical significance. Compared with the extensive introductions of the Flavian fire-brands Antonius Primus and Cornelius Priscus, these two governors are dismissed with a single label. Silvanus' wealth prompts comment from T. again (*pecuniosa orbitate et senecta*, *A.* 13.52.2). **tenebant:** pl. verb with two singular subjects (24.3n. *Paulinus . . . Celsus sumpsere*). **Cornelius Fuscus:** although Fuscus (Syme (1937b), (1958a) 683–4, Pflaum (1960) 77–60, *OCD*[3] 'Cornelius (*RE* 158) Fuscus'), made procurator of Illyricum by Galba in 68 and probably known to T. personally (Syme (1958a) 684), did not play an extensive role in the Flavian campaign, he has the air of a potentially useful general, if anything untoward had happened to Antonius Primus or Licinius Mucianus. His appearance at Ravenna (*propere accucurrit*, 3.12.3) just after a pro-Flavian rebellion organised by the treacherous Lucilius Bassus (whereupon the men promptly chose him as their commander) hardly seems coincidental. Since these sailors, mostly drawn from Dalmatia and Pannonia (3.12.1), must have known Fuscus personally, it is plausible that Antonius Primus sent him there to wait in the wings. Fuscus then used the fleet to take Ariminum on the Adriatic coast (3.42.1), securing the food supply (Levick (1999) 51), and after the Flavian victory, he was awarded praetorian insignia for his services (4.4.2). His activities in the 70s are unknown, but as early as 83, Domitian chose him as his praetorian prefect, so he would have featured prominently in the *H.*'s lost books. Juvenal, including him as one of Domitian's advisers, dismisses him as an armchair general contemplating battles from his marble villa (4.111–12), but he was killed on active service while fighting the Dacians in 86 or 87 (Dio 67.6, Eutrop. 7.23, Oros. 7.10.4). His death marked a devastating low point for Domitian's campaign (*Agr.* 41.2, Suet. *Dom.* 6.1, Dio 68.9), but his appointment shows that the emperor trusted him: 'it was the first time outside Egypt that a knight had borne such responsibility in the field' (Levick (1999) 180); Martial wrote an upbeat epigram purporting to be the gravestone of his *uictrix umbra* in Dacia (6.76). **uigens aetate, claris natalibus:** his relative youth, in contrast with the elderly procurators, is attractive to the soldiers and opens a less damning character-sketch than the one for Antonius Primus (against which it is actively set). T.'s *uariatio* of a participle clause + abl. of quality is enhanced by the pl. *natales* for *origo*, a usage of the Younger Seneca (cf. *splendidis natalibus ortam*, *Agr.* 6.1). **prima iuuenta quietis cupidine senatorium ordinem exuerat:** T. recalls Antonius Primus, but describes a diametrically opposed action (cf. *senatorium ordinem reciperauerat*, 2.86.1). The rejection of senatorial status was perhaps not done from dislike of a busy official career, or temperamental incompatability, as with the young Ovid (cf. *curia restabat: claui mensura coacta est*, *Tr.* 4.10.35). It may instead show healthy survival instincts under a difficult *princeps*, or expresses frustration at an ineffectual institution; *prima iuuenta* (48.2n.) adds allure, and *quies* is virtually a political term (37.2n. *quietem . . . expetitum*). Even so, apparent modesty may mask artfulness, as equestrians could be much more powerful than senators: e.g. Lucius Vestinus (4.53.1), Sallustius Crispus (*A.* 3.30.2), Annaeus Mela (*A.* 16.17.3), and above all, Augustus' Maecenas (*A.* 3.30.2), famous for remaining within the equestrian order (Woodman (1983) 239–40). **dux coloniae suae:** there are many suggestions for the *colonia*, whose declaration for Galba was important enough to win Fuscus his procuratorship: Pompeii, Vienne,

Corduba, Aquileia, or Forum Iulii (Chilver (1979) 248–9). The question, still open, was probably resolved in T.'s obituary, which doubtless would have featured in the lost books of the *H*. **acerrimam bello facem praetulit** 'he applied the strongest torch to the war' (*OLD* 10b for *acer* to describe fire); *bello* = adnominal dat., a usage much liked by T. (Goodyear (1972) 216). A familiar metaphor (*cui . . . adulescentulo . . . non . . . facem praetulisti?* Cic. *Cat.* 1.13; Oakley (1998) 726) is given a novel twist by adding a (superlative) adj. (cf. *acriores ad studia dicendi faces subdidisse*, Quint. 1.2.25). This time T. does not soften the metaphor with *uelut* (cf. *flagrantibus iam militum animis uelut faces addiderat Maeuius Pudens*, 1.24.1). It is wryly incongruous that a man called Fuscus ('dark') is a fire-starter. **non tam praemiis periculorum quam ipsis periculis:** the paradoxical idea that Fuscus was not greedy (what we normally expect by now), so much as drawn to danger, is bound together by alliteration. Yet how can we square this with the man who gave up the senate *quietis cupidine?* It suggests either that Fuscus' personality changed, or (more likely) that he rejected a senatorial career for complex reasons, above all a desire for a stimulating life (Aubrion (1985) 445). Where Fuscus seeks dangers, the acquisitive Antonius Primus petulantly complains by letter to Vespasian that all his labours would be pointless *si praemia periculorum soli assequantur qui periculis non adfuerint* (3.53.3). So, *praemia*, not *pericula*, motivate Primus, who guards his reward closely. That is a familiar consideration for a soldier, who usually desires *maiora periculis praemia* (Curt. 3.8.21, 9.2.27; cf. Liv. 33.39.6, Cic. *Balb.* 6). **pro certis et olim partis** 'rather than what was certain and long established' (Fyfe / Levene). Likewise Catiline's young and hedonistic supporters *incerta pro certis, bellum quam pacem malebant* (Sall. *Cat.* 17.6; cf. 20.3), but T. avoids the obvious *certa / incerta* polarity (Sall. *Jug.* 83.1, Liv. 39.54.7, Cic. *Sen.* 68, Sen. *Suas.* 1.10.). **noua ambigua ancipitia:** the asyndeton, elision and syllabic crescendo convey energy and excitement. The trio of adjectives used as substantives is unprecedented (cf. *noua et ancipitia*, *A*. 14.22.2), though Virgil has *matres*, who are *ancipites* and *ambiguae* (*A*. 5.654–5) and Valerius Maximus has *nouae atque ancipitis rei exitum* (4.7 ext. 1). The formulation nicely captures Fuscus' devil-may-care attitude.

   86.4 igitur: 2.2n. **mouere et quatere . . . aggrediuntur:** sc. Cornelius Fuscus and Antonius Primus, although the lack of clarity about the verb's subject raises questions about the main driving force for the Flavian party's actions (cf. *scriptae* below). *aggredior* (*OLD* 5 'proceed') + inf. is in Lucr., Sall., Cic., and Caes. (6× in T.; G-G 35). The infinitives suggest forces of nature being unleashed. Seneca uses similar language for an earthquake (*cum terra quatitur et sursum ac deorsum mouetur*, *Nat.* 6.21.2) and a violent storm (*Eurus orientem mouet | Nabataea quatiens regna et Eoos sinus*, *Ag.* 482–3). It seems an excessive way to describe a letter-writing campaign; but real violence will follow. **quidquid usquam aegrum:** cf. *quid aegrum fuerit* (1.4.1). The metaphor of disease is especially expressive in the context of civil war (56.1n. *Italia . . . afflictabatur*). The reference is to sections of the imperial army whose loyalty to Vitellius wavers, but soon we will see real sickness permeating the Vitellian soldiers in Rome (2.93.1). *aeger* here designates what is 'sick' for Vitellius, and by implication 'healthy' for Vespasian, but the state's interests are nowhere in the foreground. **foret:** *foret* for *esset*

(14.3n. *deletae . . . forent*).   **scriptae:** sc. *sunt*. The agents are not specified, which prompts us to ask how much Primus and Fuscus co-operated with the main Flavian group, even now. The letters to the legions in Britain and Spain have a rationale behind them, but the other letters are speculative, showing a less clearly defined recruitment campaign than the one after the planning meeting at Beirut (2.82.3). **quartadecimanos:** the deeply pro-Othonian *legio XIV Gemina* (11.1n. *rebellione Britanniae compressa* and *quattuor legiones*).   **ad primanos:** the *prima Adiutrix* (11.2n. *cum legione prima*, 11.3n. *classicorum . . . numerus*).   **pro Othone, aduersa Vitellio:** *uariatio* of preposition + adj. (Sörbom (1935) 92–3, WM 471).   **sparguntur per Gallias litterae:** while the legions in Britain and Spain, known to hate Vitellius, were biddable targets, the Flavians approach the Gallic states indiscriminately, aptly reflected in the verb's 'sprinkling' metaphor (58.2n. *spargebatur*). There was no need now for secrecy, but the strategy brought other risks in soliciting untested strangers for support. So, the Batavian auxiliary leader Julius Civilis, in touch with Primus by letter (4.13.2, 4.32.1, 5.26.3) and perhaps initially contacted during this current recruitment drive, advances his plans for widespread rebellion, while apparently backing the Flavian cause. More positively, Agricola, while dealing with the aftermath of his mother's murder, must have received or heard about one of these letters: *statim in partis transgressus est* (*Agr.* 7.2). Some of the bearers will be killed by Vitellius (2.98.1). The pl. *litterae* for plural letters is striking (7× in T.: G-G 776), apparently a Ciceronian flourish (*OLD littera* 7a; *TLL* s.v. *littera* 1526.1–8).   **momentoque temporis** 'in an instant' (*OLD momentum* 5; Oakley (2005) 174). The expression (also 4.82.2; 15× in Livy) is almost exclusively associated with prose authors, except for [Virg.] *Catalepton* 3.10, on Fortune's power to implement a lightning *peripeteia* (an especially relevant intertext here). **flagrabat:** the metaphor elegantly develops *acerrimam bello facem* above (2.86.3). It recurs for this phase of the civil war (*flagrare Italiam bello*, 3.46.2), and later finds all too literal expression in the burning of Cremona (*iam flagrabat*, 3.32.3) and the Capitol (*sic Capitolium . . . conflagrauit*, 3.71.4).   **ingens bellum:** 4.2n. *ingens . . . fiducia* for *ingens*. The phrase, common in Livy and the poets, appears only once more in T. (*A.* 3.73.2 with WM 483–4).   **fortunam secuturis:** future participle in an abl. absolute (32.1n. *irrupturis . . . nationibus*). The end of this section (2.73–86) on the start of the Flavian challenge is in ring-composition with the opening section about its planning (2.1–7): *Struebat iam fortuna* (2.1.1). A good soldier should make fortune follow him by deploying *uirtus* in battle (Liv. 4.37.7), but these troops hold back and hedge their bets.

87–101 THE ARRIVAL OF VITELLIUS IN ROME AND HIS FIRST STEPS AS EMPEROR

After elaborating all the energetic Flavian preparations in the east (2.74–86), T. returns to the pleasure-seeking Vitellius and his men, still en route to Rome. The fragmented narrative of the journey actually makes the pace of the Vitellians seem to decelerate, but meanwhile, the hedonism has reached new heights. Darkly parodying the standard 'catalogue of troops' before a battle (2.87.1), T. describes in detail the menacing, chaotic force bearing down on the unsuspecting city. The citizens will soon discover for themselves how ruthless these soldiers are: only seven miles outside Rome, these men kill innocent civilians without a single Vitellian officer intervening (let alone Vitellius himself). It feels like a grim repeat of Galba's *tardum . . . iter et cruentum* (1.6.1). Yet despite the bloodshed, Vitellius goes through the motions of entering Rome in a palatable way, on foot, in civilian dress, and leading a meticulously regimented military procession (2.89). T. plays deftly and expressively with the illusion of a 'professional' army under the 'control' of its superiors, a hollow pretence so soon after the massacre of unarmed citizens. Far from being a proper *princeps*, Vitellius seems like a charlatan and a hypocrite, leading gangs of murderers into the city. T. enhances that impression by describing the first Vitellian arrivals in barbarised terms (2.88.3) and evoking an intensely bleak moment from republican history, Livy's Gauls on the rampage in Rome after their victory at the river Allia in 390 BC. At least then the invaders were foreign enemies; now these are legionaries led by a Roman citizen.

   The gloomy atmosphere of the *aduentus* becomes even darker once Vitellius is in Rome. Taking up office as chief priest on 18 Jul., the anniversary of two republican disasters (including the Allia), Vitellius quickly surrounds himself with selfish freedmen and brutal soldiers, pandering to the masses by putting on gladiatorial shows (2.95.1) and spending money lavishly (2.95.3). When news of Vespasian's challenge begins to filter through, Vitellius first suppresses it by intimidation (2.96). When he finally does mobilise his two generals, Caecina and Valens (now disastrously at odds with one another), his soldiers have been utterly debilitated by urban delights. Their departure from Rome shows a complete transformation from the proud and extravagant *aduentus* (2.99). The book ends with Caecina's betrayal of Vitellius, later 'rebranded' by pro-Flavian writers as 'concern for peace' and 'patriotism' (2.101). A victory for Vespasian and his army now seems inevitable, but beating the dismal, fragmented Vitellians hardly seems much of an achievement, however much patriotic historians lauded it afterwards as a timely triumph over dangerous forces.

   87.1 ad omnes municipiorum uillarumque amoenitates resistens 'stopping to enjoy all the delightful towns and country houses'. An expressive pl., *amoenitates* (all seven other instances in T. are singular; cf. especially *A.* 14.52.2, 15.52.1) and the compound *resisto* (*OLD* 1a) for the simple *sisto* offer expansive vocabulary, aptly mirroring the leisurely pace of the journey. Vitellius apparently allowed the state to pay for his banquets en route (Suet. *Vit.* 10.2), but no doubt the burden fell on individuals too.   **graui . . . agmine:** adj. + noun 'surround' the city that they will soon take. This Livian combination (3×), which also appealed to Curtius Rufus, appears again in T. (*graue legionum agmen*, 1.70.3; and twice with the comparative adj., *A.* 1.64.4, 4.73.1). *graue* primarily means 'heavily armed' (*OLD* 2c), but in the hedonistic context, it also implies slow, unfit soldiers, putting on weight, and the clogging presence of all the extraneous hangers-on. In Josephus there is also a huge column, made especially vast by the camp followers as Vitellius travels to Rome 'dragging after his army a great crowd besides' (*BJ* 4.586).   **sexaginta . . . regeretur:** for each group in the Vitellian *agmen* (the soldiers, camp followers, and retinue of generals and friends, all subjects of *sequebantur*), T. first uses a descriptive nom. + dependent gen. phrase emphasising numbers (*sexaginta . . . armatorum / calonum . . . amplior / tot . . . comitatus*), but then adds a damning abl. or adj. clause criticising the potential for insubordination (*licentia corrupta / procacissimis . . . ingeniis / inhabilis . . . regeretur*). The list's paratactic format darkly parodies the serious literary device of the pre-war 'catalogue of troops' seen earlier (cf. 1.61, 2.11).   **sexaginta milia armatorum:** T. gives numbers of troops for dramatic effect again (*quadraginta armatorum milia irrupere*, 3.33.1). The separate groups under Vitellius, Caecina and Valens (20.2n. *magno terrore*) have now been amalgamated. The combined figure could have featured before now, but giving it here concentrates our minds again on the scale of the Vitellian menace after the 'Flavian interlude' (2.74–86). It also prepares for a hyperbolic tally of camp followers (*numerus amplior*, 2.87.1).   **licentia corrupta** 'ruined by loose discipline'. T. saves the most important detail for the subordinate clause. Suetonius also notes the lack of discipline on the march (*nulla familiae aut militis disciplina*, *Vit.* 10.2), but does not elaborate its effect on the soldiers.   **calonum numerus amplior:** these soldiers' attendants are only in the *H.*, often in dubious contexts (1.49.1, 3.33.1). Their practical duties include carrying provisions (3.20.3, Fron. *Str.* 4.1.6), doing subsidiary jobs during battles (Liv. 9.37.8, 10.41.6), sometimes even fighting (Liv. 27.18.12); and they could end up as booty themselves (4.60.2, Liv. 41.3.4). Their swollen numbers here (apparently more than 60,000) only add to the burdensome *agmen*.   **procacissimis etiam inter seruos lixarum ingeniis** 'together with the camp followers, particularly undisciplined, even by slave standards'; 41.3n. *lixae*. In military descriptions, troops on the move can be listed with an attendant abl. (cf. *Albani . . . ingenti exercitu . . . impetum fecere*, Liv. 1.23.3, GL §392). That association may enhance bathos here. So too does the grand *lixarum ingeniis*, combined for the first time with *procacissimis* (cf. *procacia urbanae plebis ingenia*, 3.32.2). As often, T. is at his most lofty and creative when describing sordid people or concepts. As *lixae* are generally free men, the pregnant use of *inter* (*gloriosissimum inter maiores* 5.17.2, *tumulum altiorem inter ceteros*, Liv. 33.10.1) to express comparison with slaves is an extra slur (*TLL* s.v. *inter* 2136.3–5).   **tot . . . comitatus:** in an imperial context, *amicus* can designate a 'counsellor'. Vitellius' closest *amici* are Lucius Vitellius, Caecina Alienus, Fabius Valens, Publilius Sabinus, Alfenus Varus and Julius Priscus, and he inherited as *amici* Cluvius Rufus, Flavius Sabinus (*praefectus urbi*), Flavius Sabinus (*consul*), Marius Celsus, Silius Italicus and Vibius Crispus (Wellesley (1972) 206, Crook (1955) 21–30, Millar (1977) 110–22).   **inhabilis ad parendum** 'not cut out for obedience'. Livy apparently coined *inhabilis* (4×), whose scansion (⌣⌣⌣) restricts it to prose writers. The retinue of *legati* and *amici* is perhaps the 'odd one out' as a potentially disobedient force (at least compared with the huge groups of soldiers and camp followers), so T. puts it third in the list, condemning the *comitatus* by association. Yet the *amici* will advise Vitellius sensibly about entering the city (2.89.1). **etiam si summa modestia regeretur** 'even if it were being controlled with the strictest discipline'. In a furtive, but effective censure, T. admits that anyone would

have trouble restraining this retinue (an apparently generous concession), but Vitellius
was not even trying.

87.2 onerabant multitudinem: in other combinations of this noun and verb,
multitudo (as subject of *onero*) oppresses something not already overladen (*corpus*, Cels.
3.22.4; *pons*, Curt. 4.16.16; *pudor*, Liv. 31.15.2; *urbs*, Liv. 39.3.6). T.'s hyperbole is innovative, as the swollen *multitudo* is itself swamped by further numbers. As can happen
(Quint. 8.6.74), the trope has a touch of dark humour, enhanced by the word order:
what could possibly make this gargantuan *agmen* any bigger?   **obuii . . . senatores
equitesque:** that members of the elite travel to meet Vitellius, rather than awaiting
him in Rome, compromises their dignity and undermines their power (1.45.1, 2.52.1,
2.69.1, 4.6.3).   **quidam . . . multi . . . omnes . . . ne . . . remanerent:** T. offers
uariatio in listing the aristocracy's motives (causal abl., prepositional phrase, negative
final clause) and presents the three groups (increasing in size) in a tricolon crescendo,
a lofty stylistic touch despite the degrading picture being portrayed.   **ceteri ac
paulatim omnes:** 1.111. *senium . . . destinandi* for the topos of 'safety in numbers'.
They behave like sheep. We remember that Tiberius habitually called the senators
'men primed for slavery' (*A.* 3.65.3).   **aggregabantur:** 72.2n.   **flagitiosa per
obsequia Vitellio cogniti** 'known to Vitellius through their degrading services'.
The context is probably Vitellius' support for Nero at his performances (Suet. *Vit.* 4),
when he would naturally have met such low-ranking entertainers. The monosyllabic
preposition is placed between the (emphasised) adj. and noun (3.2n. *tenuem in ambitum*).
scurrae histriones aurigae: this striking trio of declassé types in asyndeton is not
combined elsewhere in Latin, but reinforces the carnivalesque nature of Vitellius' journey (71.1n. *immixtis . . . ingenio*). The *scurra*, only once again in T. (*A.* 12.49.1), was a type
of urbane parasite, a man about town, who used his wit to personal advantage (Plaut.
Trin. 199–202; Ramage (1973) 30–1, Corbett (1986)). It crops up most often in texts
from the republic (though not in historiography), especially in Horace (Mayer (1994)
216, Lejay (1911) 551–3), but *scurrae* became established figures in the imperial household, e.g. Augustus' Gabba (Braund (1996) 277), a witty man (Plut. *Mor.* 759F–760A).
They also feature at élite dinner parties (Plin. *Ep.* 9.17).   **amicitiarum dehonestamentis** 'in the shameful services provided by these friendships'. T. uses grandiose
language for the undignified, shunning an abl. adj. + noun (*dehonestis amicitiis*) for
an abstract noun + defining gen. Sallust coined *dehonestamentum* for the republican
general Sertorius' scars and gouged-out eye, a badge of honour for his bravery (*Hist.*
1.88 Reynolds, Gell. 2.27.2–3), but only the younger Seneca took it up (once) before
T. revived it, in places displaying a decline from the original Sallustian context (4.13.2,
A. 12.14.3, 14.21.4). The pl. is only here and Sen. *Con. sap.* 19.3. Pluralising abstract
nouns often makes them concrete, designating multiple instances of a phenomenon
(GL §204.5, K-S I §22.2).   **mire gaudebat:** a rare combination (Liv. 22.40.7, Plin.
Nat. 9.12, 37.78). Vitellius takes the wrong sort of pleasure from these lowly types, who
are meant to entertain the élite, not offer them friendship. Reputations could suffer
from keeping socially inferior company, as with Claudius (Suet. *Cl.* 5); and it was a
common focus for invective (e.g. Cicero *Mil.* 55 on Clodius' dubious circle of

'prostitutes, perverts and call-girls'). **nec coloniae modo . . . sed ipsi cultores aruaque:** consuming the resources of the colonies and country towns is bad enough, but the Vitellians also squander the very heart of agricultural production (hence the climactic *ipsi*), creating long-term problems. *aruum* (7× in T.) originally meant 'ploughed land', but poets extended the sense in various ways, which appealed to the historians (Sall. *Hist.* 1.14 Reynolds, *Jug.* 90.1, Liv. 2.14.3, 9.36.11, followed selectively by Val. Max., the younger Sen., the elder Plin., Quint.). **congestu copiarum** 'to furnish supplies'. An alliterative pair, combined only here (*TLL* s.v. *congestus* 281.15–16; the word, first in Cic. and Lucr., appealed to Sen. and Luc.). **maturis iam frugibus:** this is a conveniently broad chronological marker. The last date indicated was *c.* 23 May (70.4n. *intra . . . diem*); and Vitellius will arrive in Rome on or before 18 Jul. (2.91.1). It also reactivates the 'destruction of agriculture' motif, a hallmark of civil war (12.2n. *pleni agri, apertae domus*). **ut hostile solum:** 16.3n. *ut.* This combination (*A.* 11.16.3, 11.20.1, Val. Max. 6.9.9, Stat. *Theb.* 9.180–1) is an unusual variant for the more common *hostilis terra.* The Vitellians persistently treat Italy like a foreign conquest (83.2n. *atque . . . protegeret*).

88.1 Multae . . . caedes (sc. *erant*) 'there were many vicious fights' (15.2n. *atrox ibi caedes*). **post seditionem Ticini coeptam:** T. repeats the pejorative label (*seditio,* 2.68.1, 4) from the original narrative (2.68–69.1). This unusual combination, *seditio + coepta* (3.11.4, *A.* 1.20.1, inspired by Liv. 28.29.12), reminds us that this is unfinished business, inexcusably left unresolved by the supreme commander Vitellius; and the intermediate generals, Caecina and Valens, are conspicuously absent from this section. **manente . . . discordia:** the normal construction after *discordia* has the preposition *inter.* T. innovates by introducing two genitives (also at 4.50.4, 4.72.3). **ubi aduersus paganos certandum foret** 'although when they had to fight civilians' (40n. *ubi . . . uincerentur* on the subjunctive; 14.3n. *deletae . . . forent* on *foret* for *esset*). **consensus** (sc. *erat*) 'they managed to co-operate'. Schöntag (1872) suggested this for M's *consensu* (perhaps created by haplography with the *sed* that follows). The expression succinctly points up irony, as a fierce foe, not a vulnerable one, is supposed to engender co-operation, but these soldiers are predators. **ad septimum . . . lapidem:** after leaving Bononia (2.71), Vitellius had crossed the Apennines (Suet. *Vit.* 10.3) and travelled to Rome, presumably by the Via Cassia. Galba's entry to Rome also saw similarly inauspicious killings just outside the city at the Mulvian bridge (1.6.2, Plut. *Galb.* 15.6–8). **singulis ibi militibus** 'between the individual soldiers there'. If there were 60,000 soldiers, this would have taken some time, but Vitellius was not dishing up the food himself. **gladiatoriam saginam:** for T., Vitellius plays the *lanista,* fattening up his barbaric 'gladiators' (71.1n. *luxu et saginae*; Goldsworthy (1996) 291–3 on normal military rations). Yet although the soldiers have apparently not been stinting on the march, it was sensible to feed them before they entered Rome to reduce the immediate burden on the city's resources. **totis se castris miscuerat:** the interlaced word order mirrors the concept described. By metonymy, *castra* stands for *milites* (the container for the thing contained: 20.1n. *municipia et coloniae*). For T., the mixing of troops with other (inappropriate) elements is symptomatic of civil war (Damon

(2003) 180). Amazingly, the enthusiastic *plebs* visits the Vitellian military camp as if on a day trip, suggesting a curious innocence. Yet these soldiers, unlike real gladiators, are not constrained by an arena, so the 'spectators' are vulnerable.

88.2 incuriosos milites . . . quidam spoliauere 'some disarmed the oblivious soldiers'; 3.1n. *ipsa . . . cessere*. T. often uses the Sallustian *incuriosus* of soldiers who have abandoned their normal routine (Damon (2003) 130). The practical jokers were clearly trying to get the soldiers' attention, rather like tourists outside Buckingham Palace, baiting the sentries, who are not supposed to respond. That level of self-control reflects military discipline, but the indolent Vitellian soldiers are simply not paying attention. **uernacula utebantur urbanitate** 'what passed with the like of them for wit'. The parenthesis (18.1n. *is enim*) seems to apologise in advance for a moment potentially at odds with the genre's dignity. The (slightly oxymoronic) notion of *uernacula urbanitas* (also at Petr. 24.2) derives from the *uerna*, originally a slave born in his master's household, but then meaning 'home-bred' more generally, and in the context of humour, 'down-to-earth' or 'childish'. The other common application of this adj. is military, a *legio uernacula* (Caes. *Civ.* 2.20.4; cf. *A.* 1.31.4), designating soldiers levied in the province where they will serve. That association sets up a contrast: these Vitellian troops from the north are foreigners, who will have little in common with these practical jokers from Rome. Their humour, hardly malicious, recalls the good-natured atmosphere of Anna Perenna's festival (Ov. *Fast.* 3.523–42). **abscisis furtim balteis:** cutting through these substantial leather belts without being detected was no mean feat. Worn over the shoulder (Quint. 11.3.140), they supported a scabbard for the sword and could stop spears (Caes. *Gal.* 5.44.8). **an accincti forent** 'whether they were wearing their swords'; *forent* for *essent* (14.3n. *deletae . . . forent*). For a Roman soldier, the loss of his sword was the ultimate disgrace (Apul. *Met.* 9.41; Lendon (1997) 247). The lofty *accinctus* applied to soldiers is T.'s innovation (WM 303), imitated by the younger Pliny and Ammianus (*TLL* s.v. *accingo* 302.75–303.2): no doubt the jokers themselves used coarser language. **rogitantes:** appended nom. present participle (27.2n. *omnem . . . iactantes*). The frequentative form nicely suggests the increasing irritation at the repeated gibe, which the soldiers did not enjoy even the first time. **insolens contumeliarum animus:** the collective singular *animus* is substituted for the soldiers themselves (*OLD animus* 2a); cf. *Parthi contumeliarum insolentes* (*A.* 6.34.1). T. only ever has *insolens* in the sense 'unused to' + gen. (*OLD* 1). **inermem populum gladiis inuasere:** 3.1n. *ipsa . . . cessere*. T. uses relatively simple language for the violent attack; the event speaks for itself, a brutal answer to a facetious question. With dark humour, he avoids the ubiquitous *adnominatio* of *inermis / armatus* (cf. *A.* 15.67.1), so that he can pointedly refer to *gladii*, the focus of the people's original joke. **caesus** (sc. *est*) **. . . pater militis:** T. personalises the violence by focusing on a specific case, aptly involving a family relationship between an unnamed father and son. A related instance expresses the futility and cost of civil war after the battle of Bedriacum (45.3n. *alii . . . fouebant*); and T. later uses a fraternal connection flouted by a callous soldier (who does the killing himself) to demonstrate the moral bankruptcy of the times (3.51). Names are not given, but such universalising devices are still powerful.

agnitus: sc. *est.*   **uolgata caede:** T. has ring-composition with the opening of the episode (*multae . . . caedes*, 2.88.1).   **temperatum** (sc. *est*) **ab innoxiis** 'they held back from attacking innocent people'. The impersonal construction masks agency. The worrying implication is that the soldiers apparently restrain themselves, without the generals intervening: cf. *precibus ducis mitigati ab excidio ciuitatis temperauere* (1.63.1).

88.3 trepidatum: 15.1n. A 'syntactical bridge' (shored up by alliteration) moves from one impersonal passive verb (*temperatum*) in the previous sentence to a second one. The Vitellian soldiers finally exert self-control, but not in time to check people's fear in Rome.   **praecurrentibus passim militibus** 'as the first soldiers to arrive were dashing about everywhere'.   **forum:** the detail aligns the Vitellians with Livy's Gauls in Rome after their infamous victory at the Allia: *in forum perueniunt, circumferentes oculos ad templa deum arcemque* (Liv. 5.41.4).   **cupidine uisendi locum:** Josephus also stresses the visual aspect, but his Vitellians greedily gaze at the glittering city's gold and silver before plundering it (*BJ* 4.587). Barbarians are often cast as wide-eyed tourists: e.g. the Frisian leaders Verritus and Malorix visit Pompey's theatre, *inter ea quae barbaris ostentantur* (*A.* 13.54.3).   **in quo Galba iacuisset:** T. means the *lacus Curtius* (55.1n.). The euphemistic periphrasis makes the aftermath of Galba's death sound more peaceful than it was: his body was abused under cover of darkness and his severed head was only found the next day (1.49.1). The Vitellians may be trying to orientate themselves morally as much as anything: Galba was the emperor they initially challenged, even if it was Otho whom they fought.   **nec minus saeuus spectaculum:** 70.2n. on the *nec minus* formula. Men who have been likened to gladiators (2.88.1) are now a *spectaculum* in their own right (cf. 70.1n. *foedum . . . spectaculum*). **tergis ferarum et ingentibus telis horrentes** 'bristling with their animal hides and huge weapons' (*OLD tergum* 7; 4.2n. *ingens . . . fiducia* for *ingens*). The descriptive abl. clauses show chiastic alliteration, but with inner *uariatio* of gen. noun (*ferarum*) and abl. adj. (*ingentibus*). That the soldiers still wear this stifling gear in the heat of summer reminds us that they are Germans unfamiliar with Rome. In Roman historiography, animal pelts and massive weapons are stereotypical for barbarians (Ash (1999) 183 n.37), but there may be a specific echo of the Allia Gauls, conspicuous for their *formas . . . inuisitatas* and *genus armorum* (5.34.4); also perhaps a dash of Virgil's Sicilian king, Acestes, *horridus in iaculis et pelle Libystidis ursae* (*A.* 5.37).   **cum . . . transirent:** rather an unwieldy way to say that the careless soldiers slipped, collided with locals and started to brawl and fight. The elaborate syntax mirrors the confusion of the crowded urban streets.   **ubi . . . procidissent:** 40n. *ubi . . . uincerentur* on the subjunctive.   **lubrico uiae uel occursu alicuius** 'because of a slippery street or someone getting in the way'. Neuter substantive adj. *lubrico* + defining gen. noun *uiae* (2.2n. *laeua maris*). T. favours such combinations elsewhere: *lubrico itinerum* (1.79.2), *lubrica uiarum* (3.82.3), *lubrico paludum* (*A.* 1.65.5), and even the metaphorical *lubricum iuuentae* (*A.* 6.49.2). Lofty language explains a series of ungainly (even comic) tumbles; and the bathos is accentuated by Livy's *uia . . . lubrica* (21.35.12), referring to Hannibal's formidable way down from the icy Alps. Juvenal offers a vivid picture of the crowded, muddy streets of Rome, including getting your feet trodden on by a soldier in hobnailed boots (3.243–8; cf. Hor. *Ep.* 2.2.75, Mart. 3.36.3–4, 12.26.8, Sen. *De ira* 3.12.4 for the mud).   **quin et** 'and furthermore'. The adverb (strengthened by *et*) amplifies what precedes (*OLD* 3b; G-G 399, 1326), a nice rhetorical flourish to end the chapter.   **tribuni praefectique:** here (at last) is some mention of the military hierarchy, but these officers cause just as much terror as their men.   **cum terrore et armatorum cateruis** 'with terrifying squadrons of armed men'. The striking hendiadys elaborates the armed victors' emotional impact on the unarmed people of the city; *armatorum cateruae* is a Livian phrase (25.39.5), liked by T. (*Agr.* 37.3, *A.* 12.33). **uolitabant:** this verb is applied especially to soldiers flitting about (*OLD uolito* 3b), often in menacing contexts. Here it may suggest that these cavalcades had no military purpose, as the soldiers just canter about to show off. It appealed to Virgil (Horsfall (2003b) 321), and T. has it again for the terrifying atmosphere in Rome after Nero discovers the Pisonian conspiracy (*uolitabantque per fora, per domos . . . pedites equitesque, A.* 15.58.2).

89.1 a ponte Mului 'after crossing the Mulvian bridge'. By this bridge (the inauspicious site of Galba's massacre of the marines), the Via Flaminia crossed the Tiber, two miles north of Rome (technically *urbem extra, A.* 13.47.2). From there, the route would take Vitellius to his formal entrance into the city via one of the gates (perhaps the *Porta Flaminia* and then the *Porta Fontinalis* near the Capitol).   **paludatus:** if Vitellius had crossed the *pomerium* wearing a *paludamentum* (59.3n. *paludamento opertum*), he would have entered the city as a conqueror, hardly ideal for winning over the people (Marshall (1984) 122). Yet in Suetonius, this is just what he does (*Vit.* 11.1). A similar aspersion was cast against Antony, who went around Rome wearing a general's cloak and accompanied by bodyguards (Dio 42.27.2, 45.29.2, 46.16.5, App. *BC* 3.45). In 193, the new emperor Alexander Severus judiciously changed from military to civilian garb to enter the city, concerned about the impression he would make (Dio 74.1). Vitellius' coinage shows him both in military dress (*RIC I*² Vitellius, no. 131) and in the *toga praetexta* (*RIC I*² Vitellius, no. 147).   **accinctus:** 88.2n.   **senatum et populum ante se agens:** at the traditional *aduentus* of the successful general, citizens flock out enthusiastically to welcome him (Cic. *Pis.* 51, Vell. 2.59.6, [Caes.] *Gal.* 8.51.1–3, Liv. 24.16.16, 27.45.6, 35.43.9, Plin. *Pan.* 23.2, *Pan. Lat.* 2.37.4, 4.32.5, 5.8.1, 7.8.7, 11.10.5, 11.3). Here Vitellius seems to be herding the sycophantic senate and people like sheep. The *aduentus* topos (Weinstock (1971) 289–90, 295–6, 299–300, 329–39, Pearce (1970) 313–16, Woodman (1977) 130–6, Oakley (2005) 100–3) also provided inspiration for poets (Hor. *Carm.* 4.2.33–60). In 107, the first *ADVENTVS* coins were issued, portraying Trajan's triumphant return from the second Dacian war (Halfmann (1986) 145). These were in circulation before the *H.* was published, offering a damning point of comparison with Vitellius for T.'s first readers.   **quo minus . . . ingrederetur:** we expect a main verb after *agens*, but instead T. gives us a *quo minus* clause, an artful arrangement which emphasises the change of plan.   **ut captam urbem:** 16.3n. *ut.* The miserable fate of the *urbs capta* was a traditional historiographical motif (Paul (1982), Purcell (1995)), except that here it is activated for Rome. Vitellius is thereby cast as foreign (83.2n. *atque . . . protegeret*), despite his last-minute change of costume.

deterritus: sc. *est*.   **praetexta:** i.e. the purple-bordered toga worn by magis-trates. Vitellius' symbolic transition from the military to civilian sphere by changing his clothes seems shallow, thanks to the soldiers who have preceded him (2.88.3); and much blood will be spilled in the city before his principate is over.   **composito agmine** 'in a carefully arranged column'. This label can also apply in a metaliter-ary sense to T.'s painstaking description of the procession (see below).   **incessit:** walking on foot is meant to indicate Vitellius' modesty and accessibility. Despite the decadent triumphal progress through Italy, Vitellius follows the advice of his *amici* and avoids entering Rome in the same spirit. Riding on a horse would have made him seem too much like a triumphant general.   **quattuor . . . splendebant:** T. describes the procession in two carefully constructed sentences. The first is domi-nated by linear progression (*mox / dein*), from eagles at the front to auxiliaries at the back, and by meticulous enumeration (*quattuor / totidem / duodecim / quattuor et triginta*), creating the impression of an inventory of military resources. The second sentence adds *uariatio*, as T. abandons linear progression and moves around the *agmen*, piling up words suggestive of its dazzling visual impact (*candida ueste / fulgentes / splendebant*).   **quattuor legionum aquilae:** the eagles (43.1n. *aquilam*) belong to the *I Italica*, *V Alaudae*, *XXI Rapax*, and *XXII Primigenia*.   **per frontem** 'formed the front'; sc. *fuerunt*. This is a novel way to express the concept for a procession (*TLL* s.v. *frons* 1361.1–2), although (inauspiciously) *frons* is common for the front line of an army in battle order (*OLD frons* 6). These eagles are actually preceded by the senior officers, notice of whom is postponed until later in the description (2.89.2). Suetonius also focuses on the standards, but is much less precise about their location (*inter signa atque uexilla*, *Vit.* 11.1).   **totidemque . . . uexilla:** 18.2n. *correptis . . . uexillisque*. These colours belong to the *I Germanica, IV Macedonica, XV Primigenia* and *XVI Gallica*.   **circa** 'on either side' (*OLD circa¹* 4).   **post peditum ordines eques:** for *uariatio*, T. switches from the pl. *pedites* to the collective singular *eques*. The presence of cavalry underscores Vitellius' more deferential position on foot.   **ut nomina gentium aut species armorum forent discretae** 'arranged according to their nationality or the nature of their weapons'; *foret* for *esset* (14.3n. *deletae . . . forent*). As often (G-G 1712–13), T. prefers the snappier *ut* (*OLD ut* 17) for *prout*, but here chooses to follow it with a gener-alising subjunctive (also *ut . . . attulisset*, 1.85.2). The meticulous attention paid to the variety of weapons in arranging the procession contrasts with the soldiers' own recent neglect of their arms outside the city (*incuriosos milites*, 2.88.2) and subsequently (*fluxa arma*, 2.99.1). Suetonius also focuses on weapons in the procession, but as a mark of intimidation rather than organisation (*detectis commilitonum armis*, *Vit.* 11.1).

89.2 praefecti . . . tribunique: the disciplined display of these officers so soon after their colleagues have been terrifying people in Rome brings home the shallow nature of the procession.   **quisque . . . armis donisque fulgentes:** singular distributive pronoun with pl. participle (44.1n. *suum obiectantes*); *armis + fulgentes* is Virgilian (22.1n. *fulgentes . . . campi*). The soldiers have now cleaned the civilian blood from their weapons, after killings which make more impact than the bravado of this parade. The *dona militaria*, which evolved under the republic, included torques, *phalerae* (next n.), ceremonial lances and an elaborate system of military crowns, distributed according to a soldier's rank. These rewards, a symbolic recognition of an individual's bravery, were partly intended to replace actual booty (Feugère (2002) 52–7). The rebel leader Arminius mocks them as *uilia seruitii pretia* (*A.* 2.9.3).   **phalerae torquesque:** i.e. the most common rewards for soldiers below the rank of centurion: *phalerae* = decorative discs, often made of precious metals and worn on a harness, and *torques* = twisted metal collars of Gallic origin (Liv. 24.42.8). They are often proudly depicted on soldiers' tombs. Some lavish examples have survived (Feugère (2002) 54).   **decora facies** has good historiographical credentials. Sallust uses it for Jugurtha (*Jug.* 6.1) and Asinius Pollio for Cicero (Sen. *Suas.* 6.24); T. has it only once more for the conspirator Gaius Piso (*A.* 15.48.3).   **et non Vitellio principe dignus exercitus** 'and an army worthy of an emperor other than Vitellius'. This concluding notice reminds us that T. has omitted a description of the visual impact made by Vitellius himself (cf. Otho on the march, 2.11.3). This criticism is especially barbed (strained even), as T. has just used the dissolute conduct of this same army on the march to condemn Vitellius by association (2.87–8). The *non* emphatically negates Vitellius alone (*TLL* s.v. *et* 905.65–906.7; GL §270, 442n.1, K-S I §149.5, L-H-S 452 §241 for *non* negating substantives). For the idea, cf. *nec quicquam ad iusti exercitus formam praeter ducem deerat* (Liv. 7.39.8).   **Capitolium ingressus:** Vitellius studiously tries to avoid looking like an *imperator triumphans*, but the Capitol was the final destination of the triumphant general (Liv. 10.7.10, Plut. *Rom.* 25.7). Vitellius then took up residence on the Palatine in the *domus Tiberiana* (Suet. *Vit.* 15.3).   **ibi matrem complexus:** 64.2n. *Sextilia*. This is a curiously domestic moment after all the public display of the parade, but T. is interested in Vitellius' family relationships (Levene (1997) 142–3). By showing Vitellius' deference to his mother so soon after entering Rome, T. hints at Tiberius and Nero (both thought to be under their mothers' thumbs).   **Augustae . . . honorauit:** Tiberius was the first to award this title to his mother Livia, as stipulated by Augustus' will (*A.* 1.8.1). Claudius did the same for his mother Antonia posthumously (Suet. *Cl.* 11.2). Later, Trajan's wife and sister refuse the senate's offer of the title *Augusta*, an acceptable display of feminine modesty (Plin. *Pan.* 84.6). Sextilia disdains empty titles (2.64.2), but has little choice in the matter.

90.1 Postera die: 22.1n. *uixdum orto die* on the gender of *dies*. When did Vitellius reach Rome? The *terminus post quem non* is 18 Jul. when Vitellius was already *pontifex maximus* (2.91.1). This post could only be taken up in Rome (Mommsen (1887–8) 1106–7). So Vitellius must have arrived on or before that day, perhaps by 4 Jun. (Coale (1971) 49–58) or the end of June, if not later (Murison (1979) 194–7). Whatever the date, Vitellius' delivery of his speech after a night's rest makes its self-congratulatory tone more distasteful: it is premeditated.   **tamquam . . . populumque:** behaving or treating others like foreigners (1.45.1, 2.12.2) is a motif applied particularly to the Vitellians (2.87.2, 2.88.3, 2.89.1, 3.72.1). T. often links the *urbs capta* theme with tyrannical conduct (Keitel (1984) 306–25).   **magnificam orationem:** a Livian combination (6.20.8, 38.50.11). Here *magnificus* 'boastful' (*OLD* 4), especially of speech (*OLD* 4b), is pejorative. This style typifies Vitellius: cf. 3.37.1 for his speech to the senate *composita in magnificentiam*, 'carefully put together in a boastful style'. In Roman culture, where excessive self-praise was problematic (Gibson (2003); cf. Mart. 1.64 on the boastful Fabulla), eulogy from a third party was far preferable (e.g. Pliny on Trajan in the *Panegyricus*). Yet Vitellius, lacking his own silver-tongued Mucianus, must act as his own fraudulent spin-doctor. Although Caecina is <*s*>*cito sermone* (1.53.1, cf. Plut. *Oth.* 6.6), his appearance (trousers and a multi-coloured cloak, 2.20.1) alienates people. T. consistently avoids direct speech for Vitellius, suggesting his passivity (cf. Laird (1999) 116–52). Even his utterances in indirect speech are rare, effectively marginalising him (Keitel (1991) 2786, Scott (1998) 8–18).   **de semet ipso:** the personal pronoun intensified by the enclitic *-met* and combined with the determinative pronoun *ipso* is emphatic (cf. 4.20.4). It points up the awkwardness of self-praise and T.'s disapproval. **industriam temperantiamque suam:** yet Vitellius consistently displays lethargy (1.52.4, 1.62.2, 2.77.3, 3.86.1) and self-indulgence (1.62.2, 2.62.1, 2.95.2, 3.36.1, 3.56.2). T. elsewhere links *industria + labor* (*D.* 2.2), *uigor* (*Agr.* 42.4), *uigilantia* (*A.* 4.1.3) and *probitas* (2.95.2), so this pair is unusual, but pointed. As *temperantia* can also designate control of bodily appetites (Sen. *Ep.* 14.15, Plin. *Nat.* 28.56, Livy 30.14.5, Cic. *De or.* 2.247, *Rhet. Her.* 3.14), Vitellius' boast is especially unfitting after all his gluttony and drunkenness (1.62.2, 3.56.2, Suet. *Vit.* 10, 13 and 17). It also undermines his *Romanitas*, as Germans stereotypically lack *temperantia* (*G.* 23.1) regarding alcohol. Ideal generals or statesmen often show *industria* (*Rhet. Her.* 4.13, Cic. *Phil.* 13.24, *Cael.* 73, *Man.* 29, Liv. 23.14.1, 38.23.11, Vell. 2.43.4, Sall. *Jug.* 95.4, Nep. *Ag.* 3.2, Tac. *A.* 12.12.1), a trait that Vitellius patently lacks. Marius notes how often 'hard-working' politicians change after their election: *primo* <u>*industrios*</u> *supplicis modicos esse, dein per* <u>*ignauiam et superbiam*</u> *aetatem agere* (Sall. *Jug.* 85.1). Vitellius is not even *industriosus* before becoming *princeps*.   **laudibus attollens:** cf. *laudibus attollebatur* (3.9.4). Otho leaves Rome more public-spiritedly, *maiestatem urbis et consensum populi ac senatus pro se* <u>*attollens*</u> (1.90.2). Vitellius' praise is indiscriminate, and so devalued (57.2n. *uirtutem . . . cumulat*).   **consciis . . . Italia:** the appended abl. of attendant circumstances has a concessive function. It totally undermines the boastful speech; and the swift move from the immediate circle of listeners to *omnis Italia* as witnesses lays bare the absurdity of Vitellius' self-promotion. Shifting from one locale to the whole country is an effective device: *captam . . . urbem, uastitatem Italiae* (1.50.2), *mala primum in urbe nata, mox per Italiam fusa* (*D.* 28.2), *statim curia, deinde Italia exactus* (*A.* 6.3.3).   **somno et luxu** 'in sloth and luxury' (*OLD somnus* 3); both are abl. of manner to be taken with the verb *incesserat*; 11.3n. *nec . . . luxu iter* on *luxus*. The stinging and colourful pair is combined only here in Latin: cf. the conspirator Scaevinus, with a *dissoluta luxu mens et proinde uita somno languida* (*A.* 15.49.4). Vitellius will not awake from this languor until 3.55.1 (*ut e somno excitus*).   **pudendus** is used by T. selectively (*D.* once; *H.* 3×; *A.* 3×). Vitellius, now a source of shame to everyone but himself, will finally try to escape danger by creeping into *pudenda latebra* (3.84.4), either a dog-kennel (Dio 65.20) or a porter's room (Suet. *Vit.* 16), a pointed *peripeteia*.

90.2 uolgus tamen uacuum curis et sine falsi uerique discrimine 'however, the carefree people, unable to distinguish between what was false and true'; cf.

nullo militum aut populi discrimine (4.1.1), 'without distinguishing between soldiers and civilians'. In Livian language (*sine recti prauique discrimine*, 9.30.2; cf. 1.33.8, 6.14.11, 24.16.12 with Oakley (1997) 526), T. offers a *sententia* about the people's mindless adulation of the *princeps*. The crowd's enthusiasm for Vitellius recurs (3.58.1, 3.68.3, 3.69.1, 3.79.1, 3.80.1), although it dissipates at the end (3.83.1; Yavetz (1987) 135–86). **solitas adulationes edoctum** 'thoroughly versed in the customary flatteries'. Long experience of the imperial system has shown the people how to behave. Such flatteries are *solitae*, both to the protagonists in the narrative and to T.'s audience (cf. *praeter suetam adulationem*, *A.* 13.8.1). The adulation is also likely to be ephemeral: cf. *uolgus mutabile* (1.69). Juvenal condemns the fickle Roman people, so ready to abandon anyone who has lost power: *sequitur fortunam, ut semper, et odit | damnatos* (10.73–4). On the link between mindless adulation and lack of political insight, see Aubrion (1985) 230.   **astrepebat:** T.'s first use of a colourful compound verb (4.49.3, *A.* 1.18.1 with Goodyear (1972) 205–6, 2.12.3, 11.17.3, 12.34), which he reserves for mechanical support from crowds (only 3× elsewhere: Calp. *Ecl.* 4.2, Sen. *Phaed.* 1026, Plin. *Pan.* 26.2).   **nomen Augusti:** 62.2n. *quo uocabulum Augusti*. His abortive attempt to reject the title shows an inconsistent personality, especially after awarding the title *Augusta* to his mother (2.89.2).   **expressere ut adsumeret** 'they forced him to take up'. The construction with *ut* (only here in T.) is first in Cicero and Livy (*TLL* s.v. *exprimo* 1786.73–83, *OLD* 4b).   **tam frustra quam recusauerat** 'as pointlessly as he had refused it'. T. often highlights futile or sham elements through nicely placed modifiers or negatives (Plass (1988) 123–4); cf. *non ita . . . ut non*, 2.94.1. Vitellius held the title *Augustus* for less than six months, before his unceremonious death on 20 Dec. 69.

91.1 ciuitatem: 1.1n. *senium destinandi.*   **cuncta interpretantem** 'putting an interpretation on everything'; *cuncta* = a synonym for *omnia* (1.3n. *cuncta . . . perlustrat*). Both groups (1.52.2, 2.39.1, 5.13.2) and individuals (1.27.1, 4.82.2, 4.86.2) make a habit of this. During a civil war (or any crisis), when first impressions count, popular interpretation of events is often more important than the 'truth'.   **funesti ominis loco:** *funestum omen* is a poetic combination (Var. *L.* 7.95 = Matius *C.* fr. 2, Prop. 2.28.38). Cicero uses it at a heightened emotional moment (*Clu.* 15, quoted approvingly at Quint. 4.2.121). T. reserves *funestus* for dramatic points in the narrative (*A.* 1.65.7, 6.24.2, 6.27.1). The *omen* itself is striking as it is self-inflicted; and prominent too, since T. reports fewer omens and prodigies for Vitellius than for previous emperors (Morgan (2000) 35).   **maximum pontificatum . . . edixisset:** although under the republic the priestly college selected the *pontifex maximus* as its spokesman in the senate, Augustus took on this role himself in 12 BC, fusing it with his imperial duties (Suet. *Aug.* 31, Aug. *RG* 10.2; Beard (1990) 34–48, Watson (1992) 12), and his successors followed suit. T. joined the priestly quindecimviral college in 88 (*A.* 11.11.1), so is naturally sensitive towards such matters.   **antiquitus infausto die Cremerensi Alliensique cladibus:** by avoiding the more obvious arrangement *die antiquitus infausto*, T. emphasises the adverb *antiquitus*, denouncing Vitellius' insensitivity towards Rome's past. Suetonius has the same fact, but without explaining the day's status (*Vit.* 11.2). T.'s clarification is superfluous in one way, as the anniversary of the Gaulish defeat of the Romans at the Allia on 18 Jul. 390 BC was infamous (cf. Livy 6.1.11, 6.28.6, Cic. *Att.* 9.5.2, Gell. 5.17.2, Macr. 1.16.23, *CIL* IX 4192, *TLL* s.v. *Alliensis* 1676.27–48; Grafton and Swerdlow (1988) 14–42, Scullard (1981) 166), but the detail sharpens his indignant tone. The other anniversary is the defeat of the Fabii at the river Cremera in 477 BC by Etruscan soldiers from Veii. Ovid says it was on 13 Feb., not 18 Jul. (*Fast.* 2.193–242), but Livy (6.1.11 with Kraus (1994) 93–4, Oakley (1997) 396) has 18 Jul. for both disasters. Such days were *religiosi*, when 'one must refrain from offering sacrifice or beginning any new business whatsoever' (Gell. 4.9.5). Vitellius (however sceptical) could not afford to ignore public opinion: cf. Otho, who carried out a lustration of the city (1.87.1) partly to calm the people when an ominous flood blocked the route from the city (1.86.3). **adeo omnis humani diuinique iuris expers** 'so ignorant was he about all civil and religious precedent'. The formula *humanum diuinumque ius* is pervasive (from Cic., Caes. onwards), and a complimentary adj. applied to an individual almost always takes the gen. (*sciens, A.* 6.26.1; *peritus*, Sen. *Ben.* 7.2.4, Gell. 11.18.2; *consultissimus*, Liv. 1.18.1; *prudentissimi*, Liv. 39.16.9; *auctor celeberrimus*, Vell. 2.26.2). Perhaps the common source had a similar expression: cf. *omni diuino humanoque iure neglecto* (Suet. *Vit.* 11.2). T. has an analogous observation about the Germans (*non diuini, non humani iuris memores, A.* 2.14.3), but *expers* here (suggesting Vitellius' lack of knowledge rather than forgetfulness) is more damning. **pari libertorum amicorum socordia** 'his friends and freedmen were just as complacent'. Vitellius relies especially on Asiaticus (57.2n.); as the Flavian threat intensifies, his freedmen are cast as more loyal than his friends (3.58.2; 87.1n. *tot . . . comitatus*). **uelut inter temulentos agebat** 'he used to transact business as if surrounded by drunkards'; cf. *ut inter uinolentos* (*G.* 22.2). Vitellius, dubbed *temulentus* himself (1.62.2, 3.56.2), has led drunken soldiers to Rome (2.68.1), and now conducts business with complete freedom, as if his drunken entourage is incapable of intervening. Other accounts stress Vitellius' drinking even more than T. does (Jos. *BJ* 4.651, Plut. *Galb.* 22.11, Suet. *Vit.* 17.2, Dio 65.20, Philostr. *VA* 5.29).

91.2 sed comitia consulum cum candidatis ciuiliter celebrans 'canvassing with his candidates like a common citizen' (Fyfe). *ciuiliter* (*OLD* 4) implies acting modestly like any other citizen, but the ostentatious alliteration (8.1n. *credentibus . . . contextu*), unparalleled within T., eschews the low-key, drawing attention to the phrase and marking it off from what follows, where Vitellius' idea of behaving as a *ciuis* is to play to the mob. These consular elections cover the remaining months of 69, for which Vitellius has already chosen his consuls, Caecina and Valens (71.2n. *coartati . . . consulatus*), who are now formally elected. The process probably also involved designating consuls for 70. At 3.55.2 Vitellius brashly selects consuls for many years ahead (Suet. *Vit.* 11.2 specifies ten years). **omnem infimae plebis rumorem . . . affectauit** 'he courted constant talk from the dregs of the people'. **fautor** (56.2n. *alienae . . . dissimulator*) designates an admirer or supporter (especially at the games or the theatre, *OLD* 2). Vitellius famously followed the Blues (Suet. *Vit.* 7.1), one of the four standard teams, allegedly once driving a chariot for them (Dio 65.5.1) and even executing people for not supporting them (Suet. *Vit.* 14.3); and apparently he was made governor of Lower Germany through the influence of Titus Vinius, a fellow fan of the Blues (Suet. *Vit.* 7.1). The Blues (Vitellius, Caracalla) or the Greens (Gaius, Nero, Domitian, Verus, Commodus Elagabalus) were special favourites of the emperors (Cameron (1976) 54). **quae grata sane et popularia, si a uirtutibus proficiscerentur** 'this behaviour, which would indeed (*sane*) have been graceful and democratic, had it been prompted by virtuous impulses . . .'; *quae . . . popularia* (sc. *fuissent*) functions as the apodosis of a conditional clause (Greek would use a participle + ἄν in such constructions) and *proficiscerentur* is an imperfect subjunctive used in a pluperfect sense (*NLS* §198–9). With *sane* (31.1n.) and the ellipse of a verb, T. seems to concede momentarily that Vitellius' actions were well received, but the protasis corrects this impression. Augustus set the precedent for emperors enjoying popular entertainment (whether sincerely or not), since *ciuile rebatur misceri uoluptatibus uolgi* (*A.* 1.54.2, cf. Suet. *Aug.* 45.1–2), but Vitellius' excessive craving for popular approval recalls Nero (Bartsch (1994) 1–35). **memoria uitae prioris:** this causal abl. is in adversative asyndeton (supply 'but') with the previous clause. Our sources generally cast Vitellius' pre-imperial life as disreputable: he allegedly spent time on Capri with Tiberius' prostitutes (Suet. *Vit.* 3.2, Dio 64.4.2) and supported Nero's performances (Suet. *Vit.* 4). **indecora et uilia accipiebantur:** these adjectives are paired only here in Latin. T.'s passive verb without an agent specified (cf. *acceptum est*, 2.91.1) suggests that this was the universal response to Vitellius' shallow attempts to court popular appeal (Sage (1990) 937). **Ventitabat in senatum:** the frequentative verb *uentito* (only here in *H.*; once in the *Agr.*, 8× in *A.*), used by prose authors (only Catull. 8.4 in the poets), is placed emphatically at the start of the sentence and shows Vitellius going through the motions by attending the senate. **paruis de rebus:** the monosyllabic preposition is placed between the (emphasised) adj. and noun (3.2n. *tenuem in ambitum*).

91.3 ac forte Priscus Heluidius: the names are inverted (53.1n. *Marcellum Eprium*). Helvidius Priscus (*OCD³*, Brunt (1975), Syme (1958a) 211–12, Levick (1999) 82–9, especially 234 n.30) first appears here, but his formal character sketch only comes later (4.5–6). This famous Stoic (like his father-in-law, Thrasea Paetus) came from Cluviae in Southern Italy. He was tribune of the *plebs* in 56, and after Nero condemned Thrasea Paetus in 66, he was exiled, but returned under Galba, whose body he rescued (Plut. *Galb.* 28.4). Under Vespasian, his great enemy in the senate was Eprius Marcellus (53.1n.), an architect of Thrasea Paetus' condemnation. T. portrays Priscus as outspoken, and always willing to disagree with others (see 4.6–9, 4.43). Hence, *forte* here is faintly ironic, as it introduces habitual behaviour. Although Priscus as praetor took part in the ceremony to purify the Capitol (4.53; Wardle (1996) 208–22), his relationship with Vespasian gradually deteriorated, resulting first in exile and finally execution in 74–5 (Suet. *Ves.* 15, Dio 66.12.2). This would inevitably have featured in the missing books of the *H.* (where Priscus will be mentioned *saepius*, 4.5.1). Under Domitian, Herennius Senecio wrote a panegyric about him (*Agr.* 2.1, Plin. *Ep.* 7.19.5, Dio 67.13): T. probably used it as a source. **contra studium eius:** T. does not explain what led to this disagreement, but implies that it was not important (cf. *paruis de rebus* 2.91.2), thereby belittling Vitellius. The concern instead is to explore the *princeps'* short-lived relationship with the senate.   **non tamen ultra quam tribunos plebis in auxilium spretae potestatis aduocauit** 'but he did nothing more than summon the tribunes of the people to come to the aid of his scorned authority'. Under the republic, tribunes of the *plebs* protected plebeian rights, but as emperor Vitellius had his own tribunician power, so the appeal was unnecessary. Instead he puts on a show of restraint by deputising the decision rather than using his own authority. Emperors could use these powers to enhance their own standing: cf. a court case of 62 (*A.* 14.48.2), allegedly concocted to allow Nero to promote his reputation for clemency by using his imperial tribunician power (not wielded in the event). T. uses *ultra* (*OLD ultra¹* 1c; with *quam*, Liv. 5.12.9, Cic. *Inu.* 1.26, 1.91) adverbially in a rather compressed construction. *in* + acc. + gen. expresses purpose (20.1n. *in nullius iniuriam*).   **mitigantibus amicis . . . uerebantur:** 65.2n. *ob iracundiam militum* on *iracundia*. The malleable, lethargic Vitellius rarely shows anger, despite his friends' fears; and his short-lived moods (including anger, 3.38.2) can easily be manipulated by others.   **Thraseae:** Thrasea Paetus (*OCD³* 'Clodius Thrasea Paetus, Publius', Geiger (1979), Griffin (1984) 165–6, 176–7), another famous Stoic, was consul in 56 under Nero. Yet, increasingly uncomfortable with the senate's servility, Paetus clashed with other senators and the emperor himself (*A.* 13.49, 14.48–49, 15.20, 15.23). After withdrawing from public life in 63–4, he was prosecuted for *maiestas* by Eprius Marcellus and Cossutianus Capito in 66 (*A.* 16.33.2). This prompted his suicide, modelled on the younger Cato's death (Plut. *Cat. Mi.* 37.1 for Paetus' biography of him) and carried out in front of his son-in-law Helvidius Priscus and the Cynic philosopher Demetrius (*A.* 16.35, where the narrative breaks off). Vespasian and Paetus had apparently been friends (4.7.2), no doubt a link later played up by the Flavians to associate the new regime with Nero's victims.   **solitum . . . dicere:** since Nero deeply disliked Paetus, Vitellius' opposition to this senator in the past is obsequious rather than an expression of independence (whatever he now claims). In 62, Vitellius voted against Paetus, after a debate about punishing the praetor Antistius (unfairly charged with treason); T. denounces Vitellius, 'most eager in his sycophancy', as a coward for 'attacking every decent man and keeping quiet when someone answered back' (*A.* 14.49.1). So, Vitellius' current boast is deeply hypocritical. **irrisere . . . aemulationis:** T. casts bitter amusement from the powerless as part of the political reality under the empire (3.37.2, *A.* 1.8.6), but these observers do not even bother to hide their derision, suggesting their scorn for Vitellius.

92.1 Praeposuerat . . . centurionem: 4.3n. *profligauerat* on the verb and 33.1n. *praefectus praetorii* on the post. Alliteration (8.1n. *credentibus . . . contextu*) emphasises some dubious appointments. Vitellius eventually imprisons Sabinus because of his friendship with the treacherous Caecina (3.36.2); *a praefectura cohortis* designates the office he held previously (*TLL* s.v. *ab* 37.71–38.38). Promotion from commanding a mere auxiliary cohort to praetorian prefect is a meteoric rise: the Flavians gave the job to the prominent Arrecinus Clemens, a senator and Vespasian's relative by marriage (4.68.2). Vitellius sends the other prefect, the centurion Julius Priscus, to hold the Apennines (3.55.1), but he quickly returns (3.61.3), finally committing suicide *pudore magis quam necessitate* (4.11.3). The fates and careers of the pair are closely linked with the destinies of their powerful sponsors, Caecina and Valens. They are also bound up with the later betrayal of Vitellius. For the appointments angered Lucilius Bassus, commander of the fleets at Misenum and Ravenna, who thought (without justification, according to T.) that he deserved the praetorian post (2.100.3). Frustrated, he betrays Vitellius and joins Caecina.   **Priscus . . . pollebant:** pl. verb with two singular subjects (24.3n. *Paulinus . . . Celsus sumpsere*).   **inter discordes:** 69.2n. *inter paucos*.   **Caecina ac Valens:** T. arranges this and the previous names chiastically: (*a*) *Publilium Sabinum* ∼ *Iulium Priscum* ∼ *Priscus* ∼ *Sabinus*, (*b*) *Valentis* ∼ *Caecinae* ∼ *Caecina ac Valens*. The generals have been virtually ignored since their rival gladiatorial shows in northern Italy (2.70–1).   **nihil auctoritatis** 'no authority' (55.1n. *nihil trepidationis*).   **olim . . . dissimulata:** hatred of Galba initially united the pair (1.52.3, 1.53.1), who invaded Italy by separate routes (Caecina brought the Upper German army over the St. Bernard pass; Valens led the Lower German army via Lugdunum and Mount Genèvre). Once in Italy, mutual contact is unavoidable, and taxing: they exchange insults (2.30.3) and organise rival gladiatorial shows (2.70–1). Their strained relationship establishes a pattern where unlikely bonds formed during an imperial challenge rapidly unravel in victory. After the Flavian victory, Mucianus' anger towards Antonius Primus and Arrius Varus is *male dissimulata* (4.11.1). **prauitas amicorum et fecunda gignendis inimicitiis ciuitas** 'the dishonesty of friends and a city prolific in generating quarrels'; *ciuitas* = the city of Rome (1.1n. *senium destinandi*). T. chiastically combines abstract (*prauitas*) + concrete (*ciuitas*) nouns, adding *uariatio* in the dependent elements (gen. ∼ adj. clause). The abl. pl. gerundive *gignendis* (agreeing with *inimicitiis*) depends on the adj. *fecunda* (cf. *A.* 13.57.1 *flumen gignendo sale fecundum*), which elsewhere T. marginally prefers to construct with the gen. (only in poetry or post-Augustan prose), rather than the abl. He probably avoids the dependent gen. here for *uariatio* after *amicorum* (itself used to avoid the less colourful *praui amici*). The choice combination *fecunda* + *gignendis* paints Rome as a fertile mother, but one whose (abstract) offspring is destructive.   **ambitu comitatu et immensis salutantium agminibus contendunt comparanturque** 'they competed and courted comparison by their ostentatious retinues and the huge columns attending their morning receptions' (*OLD contendo* 8b 'compete', with the focus of competion in the abl.; 30.2n. *uigore . . . fauore* for *et* introducing one or more items after asyndeton). The abstract noun *ambitus* (*OLD* 10) can be taken as a hendiadys with *comitatus*, a unique combination of nouns in Latin. T., scornful of judging a man's social standing by the size of his retinue (*Agr.* 40.4), counts the *salutatio* (the morning call when a great man's clients greeted him in his house) amongst the *inania* of power. The alliterative pair of verbs with a shift from active to passive and linked by *–que* is pointedly ostentatious (also *confluunt celebranturque*, *A.* 15.44.3).   **uariis . . . inclinationibus:** the victorious Vitellius tried to honour Caecina and Valens equally by placing both men beside his curule chair (2.59.3), but his private vacillation undermines the public display. The appended abl. absolute (typical of T.) subordinates the mercurial Vitellius to his powerful generals, who should be courting him. The noun *inclinatio* (+ *uaria*) appeared previously for rocking boats (*uariis trepidantium inclinationibus*, 2.35.2), perhaps hinting that Vitellius too is all adrift.   **nec umquam satis fida potentia, ubi nimia est** 'for power is never completely sure of itself, even when it is excessive'. Herodotus expresses the idea (less pithily) that the powerful are often insecure: 'Absolute power ought, by rights, to preclude envy on the principle that the man who possesses it has at his command everything he could wish for; but in fact it is not so, as the behaviour of kings to their subjects proves' (3.80). *nimia* in the subordinate clause is deliberately paradoxical, to give the aphorism more impact: if the power is not just great but excessive, its holder might – wrongly – be expected to be especially confident. The apparently gnomic statement also criticises Vitellius, who still fluctuates dangerously, despite his excessive power.

92.2 subitis offensis aut intempestiuis blanditiis mutabilem 'as he alternated between suddenly taking offence and untimely flatteries'; *subita* + *offensa* (in *D.*, *H.*) are combined only here in Latin (*TLL* s.v. *offensa* 494.45–6), as are *intempestiuae* + *blanditiae*, a pair which implicitly asks when *is* the right time for a *princeps* to flatter. Such fickleness is elsewhere linked with crowds (1.69, Liv. 2.7.5, Val. Flac. 1.761) and women (*uarium et mutabile semper femina*, Virg. *A.* 4.569–70; cf. Hor. *Carm.* 1.5.5–12, Tib. 4.3.61, Calp. *Ecl.* 3.10), both inauspicious parallels for an emperor.   **contemnebant metuebantque:** 2.2n. *aduenasque* on sentence terminal *–que*. This is a dangerous combination for Vitellius. Fear amongst subjects was often perceived as protecting rulers: 'fear preserves kingdoms' (Sen. *Oed.* 704; cf. 31.1n. *terrorem atque odium*). Yet Caecina is so scornful of Vitellius that he betrays him.   **nec eo segnius inuaserant** 'yet they had not for that reason been any slower to seize . . .'. *nec eo segnius* (liked by Livy as a bridging device) recurs once more in T. (3.25.3), again pulling against an assertion in the previous sentence. The generals' acquisitiveness here contrasts with their lethargy in all other respects (*Valentem . . . infirmitas tardabat* 2.99.1, *Caecinae . . . torpor recens* 2.99.2). Valens especially is cast as sluggish in a military context (*lento deinde agmine* 1.66.3; *sinistrum lenti itineris rumorem* 2.93.2; *segnius quam ad bellum incedens* 3.40.1).   **domos hortos opesque imperii:** the indignant Vitellian soldiers who denounce the treacherous Caecina and Bassus echo the phrase: *id Basso, id Caecinae uisum, postquam domos hortos opes principi abstulerint, etiam militibus principem auferre* (3.13.3). Caecina reverts to old habits: Galba put him on trial after he was caught embezzling public funds (1.53.1). Valens was apparently susceptible to such temptations after his poverty-stricken youth: *inopi iuuenta senex prodigus* (1.66.2). Yet (unlike Caecina) he stayed loyal to Vitellius.   **flebilis . . . turba:** often applied disparagingly to the masses (1.35.1, 1.40.1, 2.16.2, 2.88.3, 3.16.2, 3.74.1, 4.67.1), *turba* here prompts sympathy for the nobles' plight, as does *flebilis* (a Senecan favourite, particularly in the tragedies; 5× in T.), 'lamentable', used in the passive sense (also *A.* 16.13.2). All proper distinctions are blurred: nobles are not usually described as lamentable, needy or a crowd. **ipsos liberosque . . . reddiderat:** where Nero had apparently executed people and exiled their children to alleviate his financial problems (Dio 63.11.3), Galba recalled them as a publicity coup, including an exiled *puer nobilis* as an emotive prop at his proclamation (Suet. *Galb.* 10.1), but only Otho gave them real help (1.77.3, 1.90.1). The focus on the nobles' offspring enhances the emotional impact of this section (children could often stir sympathy: Cic. *De or.* 1.228, *Orat.* 131, *Flac.* 106, *Font.* 46, *Brut.* 90, *Sul.* 89, Quint. 6.1.30). Yet Vitellius is unmoved, despite having used his own son to appeal to audiences (2.59.3, 3.68.2).   **nulla principis misericordia:** the abstract noun stands for *liberalitas* (*TLL* s.v. *misericordia* 1125.31–61), highlighting a quality conspicuously lacking in Vitellius (cf. 2.70.4), who ironically will soon be an object of pity himself (3.58.3, 3.66.2, 3.68.1), even if at the end *deformitas exitus misericordiam abstulerat* (3.84.5). Even Nero could show pity, opening up the Campus Martius, Agrippa's buildings and his own gardens to the homeless after the fire of Rome in 64 (*A.* 15.39.2), while the otherwise dour Tiberius gave money to senators suffering amidst *honesta innocentium paupertas* (*A.* 2.48.3).   **iuuarentur:** 'nouns of multitude' (*turba*) often take a pl. verb in Latin (4.57.3, 5.13.2, *A.* 2.24.2, 15.44.4; GL §211, L-H-S 436–7 §233a), here an imperfect subjunctive in the passive voice after *cum*, 'while' (GL §585).

92.3 gratum primoribus ciuitatis etiam plebs approbauit quod 'a measure welcome to the leading men of the state, and also endorsed by the people, was that . . .'. T. gives the reaction before elaborating the measure itself (cf. *laetum . . . quod*, 2.95.1). *primores ciuitatis* is borrowed from Livy (15×; Oakley (1997) 514–15 and WM 456). T. has it 11× himself (not in the minor works).   **iura libertorum** 'rights over their freedmen' (Watson (1987) 35–45 (esp. 40) on such *iura*); *libertorum* = objective gen. As the former masters of these freedmen had been exiled, they lost the right to claim support (financial or otherwise) from their ex-slaves. This they need after their return, as the *princeps* will not help them. Vitellius, in reinstating these rights, passes on to the ex-slaves an obligation which he might otherwise have borne himself. No doubt the *plebs* liked to see the haughty *liberti* cut down to size again, even temporarily. **quamquam . . . corrumpebant:** unlike Livy and Cicero, T. generally prefers the subjunctive after *quamquam* (cf. 2.20.1 *ueheretur*), although there are about twenty places (as here) where he uses the (more Ciceronian) indicative instead: e.g. 1.68.1, *A.* 2.35.1, 12.11.1 (Wellesley (1972) 90).   **seruilia ingenia** 'these wily creatures' (Wellesley). The singular, *seruili ingenio* is in Sallust (*Hist.* 3.98c, Reynolds; also T. *H.* 5.9.3), but Livy coined the pl. *seruilia ingenia* (35.49.8; also T. *A.* 2.12.3). The abstract for concrete noun is lofty language for a sordid phenomenon, as rich freedmen deviously avoid helping their impoverished former masters in a topsy-turvy society. The point may also be that a leopard cannot change his spots: such conduct is only natural for freedmen born as slaves.   **abditis pecuniis per occultos aut ambitiosos sinus** 'with money concealed in the toga-folds of obscure or ambitious men'. T. regularly substitutes an adj. for a noun in the gen. (2.1n. *iuuenilis animus*), and *vice versa* (Goodyear (1972) 118 on *bella ciuium* for *bella ciuilia* at *A.* 1.3.7); *abdo* + *per* is only in T. and Ammianus (*TLL* s.v. *abdo* 57.83–4). The freedmen chose obscure men as unlikely to attract investigation and ambitious ones since colluding with them now was an investment for the future, once they had become more powerful. Money was usually carried in the fold of a toga, as *aurum in sinu eius inuenerunt* (Quint. 7.1.30; cf. Tib. 2.6.46 *occulto . . . sinu*).

quidam . . . potentiores: T. wryly calls these imperial freedmen's former masters *domini* just when the gulf between the two groups is at its greatest.

93.1 redundante multitudine: *redundo* 'overflow' is used metaphorically (32.1n. *Hispanias . . . redundare*). In metaphors and similes, the notion of water or the sea for crowds is common (Hom. *Il.* 1.144–6, Dem. 19.136, Plb. 11.29.9 and 21.31.9, Cic. *Clu.* 138, Liv. 28.27.11, 38.10.5, Virg. *A.* 1.148–53, 2.496–9, 7.528–30, Sil. 13.24–9), but T. adds novelty by an image of a human sea spilling out of the barracks and flooding into the city.   **plenis castris . . . uagus:** *uariatio* of (*a*) two abl. absolutes (*plenis . . . multitudine*) functioning as temporal / causal subordinate clauses and (*b*) a nom. adj. *uagus*, agreeing with the collective singular *miles* (6.2n.), which contrasts with the numbers implied by *multitudo*. Josephus also describes Vitellius transforming the whole of Rome into a military camp, but emphasises the soldiers' greed in a city glittering with silver and gold (*BJ* 4.585–7).   **urbe tota uagus:** barbarians are often described in such nomadic terms (*OLD* 1b), as with the Rhoxolani (1.79.1), tribes on the Pontus (3.48.1), Numidians (*A.* 2.52.1), Gaetulians and Libyans (Sall. *Jug.* 18.2, 19.5), Gauls (Livy 5.44.5), Nomads (Mela 2.11, 3.107), Numidians (Luc. 4.677) and Sarmatians (Stat. *Silu.* 3.3.170). The detail reinforces the Vitellian solders' foreign identity and suggests degeneration of their military skills. If troops are *uagi* (*OLD* 4), it is often pejorative, especially for Romans (4.35.2, *A.* 1.21.1, Liv. 2.50.6, Suet. *Tib.* 37.1; cf. Sall. *Jug.* 44.5).   **non principia noscere . . . firmari:** *noscere . . . seruare . . . firmari* are historic infinitives (5.1n. *anteire . . . obniti*). The only other instance of *non . . . non . . . neque* (*A.* 2.37.3) in T. is in a speech: anaphora of *non* is much more common (G-G 963–4). Vitellius later mirrors his soldiers' collective apathy in what he is *not* doing: *non parare arma, non adloquio exercitioque militem firmare, non in ore uolgi agere* (3.36.1).   **per illecebras urbis:** T. likes the resonant pl. *illecebrae* (10×), coined by Plautus, but taken up by Cicero and the Augustan poets (also 4× in Liv., once in Sall.). Cities and the east were the traditional places for such allurements. So Capua inclines to luxury *illecebris omnis amoenitatis maritimae terrestrisque* (Liv. 23.4.4) and Greece and Asia are *omnibus libidinum illecebris repletas* (Liv. 34.4.3). T. uses a similar formulation in a military context, where Sejanus wants to move the praetorian camp *procul urbis illecebris* (*A.* 4.2.1). Vices tend to gravitate towards Rome (71.1n. *corruptius iter*).   **inhonesta dictu** 'things better left undescribed'. By not giving details, T. allows his readers to imagine for themselves how the dissolute soldiers spent their time in the city (cf. Livy's list of distractions for soldiers: *uinum et epulae et scorta balineaque et otium*, 23.18.12). On terms inconsistent with the dignity of history, see Goodyear (1972) appendix 4, 342–3; cf. 3.2n. *continuus . . . exsurgens.*   **corpus otio, animum libidinibus imminuebant** 'they were ruining their bodies through idleness and their morale through lusts'. This evokes Livy on Hannibal's troops, ruined by exposure to luxuries in Capua: *eneruauerunt corpora animosque* (23.18.12). The combination *animus + imminuo* (*OLD* 3 'impair') is certainly Livian (3.38.1, 28.33.7, 35.26.10). This *corpus / animus* pair recurs in T. (including *H.* 1.22.1, 1.31.3, 2.30.2, 2.99.1), most notably in Sejanus' character-sketch (*A.* 4.1.3), which itself recalls Sallust's Catiline (*Cat.* 5.3–4; cf. Vell. 2.127.3 with Woodman (1977) 252–3). Sallust elsewhere argues that the ephemeral *corpus* is vulnerable to temptations, but that the *animus* is (or should be) immune (*Jug.* 2.3). Yet the Vitellian soldiers' *animi* are susceptible. Sulla's soldiers suffer similar damage in Asia (*loca amoena, uoluptaria facile in otio ferocis militum animos molliuerant,* Sall *Cat.* 11.5), but the Vitellians are in Rome, not Asia, the traditional place for triggering moral decline. Whereas under the republic, temptations abroad (especially in the east) made Romans decadent, now Rome, at the heart of a huge empire, can provide her own debilitating enticements (Juv. 2.159–70 with Braund (1996) 164–7, Courtney (1980) 148–50: 'very Tacitean in content'), even if the imperfect tense (*imminuebant*) suggests gradual deterioration over the summer. The Vitellians were in Rome between *c.* the end of June (90.1n. *postera die*) and mid-September. Caecina will leave Rome on *c.* 17 Sept. (2.99–100) and Valens on *c.* 25 Sept. (3.36.1). For the dates, see Wellesley (1972) 195.   **salutis** 'life itself' (*OLD* 2).   **infamibus Vaticani locis:** the Vatican district of Rome was probably malarial (Vitr. 1.4.12, Cic. *De or.* 2.290, Strabo 5.3.4, Sil. 8.378), so the Vitellians from the north, lacking natural resistance to the disease, were vulnerable, especially compared with indigenous southerners (Sallares (1991) 238). So Caesar's troops fall ill in southern Italy after living in the 'healthy districts of Gaul and Spain' (*Civ.* 3.2) and the Holy Roman Emperor Otto III died of malaria in January 1002 after travelling from Germany to Rome (Görich (1993) 134).   **unde crebrae in uolgus mortes** 'as a result of which deaths frequently fell upon the crowd'. T. adds vividness by suggesting that death descends on its prey, but to call the Vitellians *uolgus* diminishes their status as soldiers: two-fifths of the references to *uolgus* in the *H.* designate soldiers (Newbold (1976) 85). T. boldly omits a main verb or participle, substituting the preposition *in* + the acc. for a simple gen. or dat. to create a striking phrase: cf. *asperrima in Sardianos lues* (*A.* 2.47.2, with Goodyear (1981) 309, 337), *in ceteros metus* (*A.* 4.2.1).   **fluminis auiditas** 'eagerness for the river'; *fluminis* = objective gen. T. probably means jumping into the Tiber to cool down, rather than drinking the water. Whereas before these Vitellian troops vigorously swim across the Po to fight some Othonian gladiators (2.35), now they plunge into the Tiber to relieve heat and disease (ironic, as Germans, especially Batavians, were famously good swimmers: 17.2n, 4.12.3). That life in the city impairs a soldier's ability to fight is a *topos* (2.19.1, *A.* 4.2.1, Liv. 27.3.2, Sil. 11.410–39).   **aestus impatientia:** inability to bear heat is traditionally associated with displaced northerners (32.1n. *fluxis corporibus*). Yet it also suggests the Gauls who invaded Rome after their victory at the Allia (390 BC), distressed by a debilitating plague and stifling heat (Ash (1999) 47; Liv. 5.48.3, cf. Plut. *Cam.* 28.2).

   93.2 insuper: 11.2n. *deforme insuper auxilium.*   **prauitate uel ambitu** 'by means of perversity or corruption'.   **sedecim . . . scribebantur:** *scribo* (*OLD* 7b) = 'enrol soldiers'. Under Tiberius, there were nine praetorian cohorts (*A.* 4.5.3), of 500 or 1,000 men each, but Sejanus added a further three cohorts (*AE* (1978) 286). Under Vitellius, the total number of praetorian cohorts was raised to sixteen, of 1,000 men each. This suggests an increase from either 6,000 or 12,000 to 16,000 men (Chilver (1979) 16–22, 254–5), even if the imperfect, *scribebantur*, suggests that the modifications took time. The passive voice leaves it unclear whether Vitellius authorised the expansion; this

was an important decision, as the praetorian cohorts could make or break emperors (e.g. Claudius). In due course, Vitellius will send 14 praetorian cohorts to hold the Apennines (3.55.1): some of these remain at Narnia, while others return to Rome (3.58.1). When their camp is stormed, the praetorians in Rome fight bravely for Vitellius (3.84.1–3), while the rest surrender to Vespasian only reluctantly (4.2.2–3). The *praefectus urbi* Flavius Sabinus had initially made the soldiers in Rome swear an oath to support Vitellius (2.55.1).   **urbanae cohortes:** 21.4n. *urbanae militiae.*
quis singula milia inessent 'each to consist of a thousand men'; *quis*, the shortened form of *quibus*, is a dat. pl. relative pronoun after *insum* (G-G 658), although T. generally uses *quis* more often as an abl. (Martin (1968) 146). *inessent* = subjunctive in a final (purpose) clause introduced by a relative pronoun.   **tamquam ipsum Caecinam periculo exemisset** 'on the grounds that he had rescued Caecina himself from danger'. *tamquam* (*OLD* 7a) + the subjunctive (21.2n. *tamquam . . . potuissent*) gives Valens' alleged reason for being bolder in enlisting troops, hinting that his claim to have saved Caecina is inflated. We get a different impression of this 'rescue' earlier (2.24–27.1), when Valens' soldiers almost renew their mutiny *tamquam fraude et cunctationibus Valentis proelio defuissent* (2.30.1).   **sane . . . uerterat:** here *sane* has an affirmative sense (cf. 2.91.2 above), but although T. broadly confirms Valens' contribution in assisting Caecina, he uses more critical language (*sinistrum . . . rumorem*) than Valens himself. With *conualuerant* (*OLD conualesco* 1b 'gain in power'), T. perhaps puns on the name of Valens, 'powerful' (43.1n. *rapuit*).   **Valentem adsectabatur:** the army of Lower Germany was not always so enthusiastic about Valens (2.30.1), but its current support should not have unsettled Caecina unduly: Valens was after all general of this force from the start of the campaign.   **creditur:** there were different theories about when and why Caecina changed his allegiance: cf. *credidere plerique* (2.99.2). T. often depicts Caecina through other protagonists in the text (external focalisation) rather than revealing what he is thinking (internal focalisation), so his precise motives for treachery remain elusive.   **unde . . . fides fluitasse:** *unde*, 'as a result of which', is causal (*OLD* 11). Alliteration of *c* and *f* closes the chapter forcefully (8.1n. *credentibus . . . contextu*). The frequentative *fluito* (*OLD* 4) is mostly poetical (Lucr. 3.1052, Stat. *Theb.* 5.378, Hor. *Sat.* 2.3.269, *Ep.* 1.18.110). T. drops it after the *H.*, where it features in military contexts (2.34.2, 3.27.3, 5.18.1). Claudian has a strong echo (*fluitante fide*, Gild. 1.247).

94.1 Ceterum non ita . . . liceret: the syntax, with its deftly deployed negatives in both halves (90.2n. *tam . . . recusauerat*), dryly implies at first that Vitellius will set a limit to indulging his generals (*non ita . . . indulsit*), only to reveal that he treats the soldiers even more lavishly (*ut non plus militi liceret*). A comparison with Livy brings out T.'s wit: *quod adeo indulsisset militibus, ut . . . pateretur* (45.28.10).   **sibi quisque militiam sumpsere** 'each man chose his division of service for himself'; singular distributive pronoun + pl. verb (44.1n. *suum obiectantes*). T. means that the soldiers could continue serving as legionaries or auxiliaries, or alternatively decide to join the urban or praetorian cohorts.   **quamuis indignus:** T. primarily means 'unde-serving', as military service in Rome (better paid and seen as easier than service in the provinces, *A.* 1.17.6) was highly sought after. Yet there are also undertones of 'unsuitable', whether because these auxiliaries had patchy Latin, or were a threat after having already launched a usurper to power.   **urbanae militiae:** i.e. both praetorian and urban cohorts, though the term can mean just the latter (21.4n. *urbanae militiae*).   **rursus** 'on the other hand' (*OLD* 6).   **bonis . . . uolentibus:** the participle masks a conditional clause (*si uellent*), but shows *uariatio* after *si ita maluerat* above. It is surprising that T. concedes the presence of any good Vitellian soldiers, given their prominence so far as an unruly 'chorus' for the decadent emperor, but here he emphasises the hopeless management of the military machine: rowdy soldiers are allowed to serve in the city, although a spell in the provinces could have improved them, while the most competent troops, whose talents are badly needed in turbulent Rome, are retained elsewhere.   **alares** 'auxiliary cavalry units'. Only Frontinus uses this adj. as a substantive (*Str.* 2.4.1) before T. (also *A.* 15.10.3, 15.11.1). The more familiar term (Cic., Caes., Liv.) is *alarii* (5× in T.).   **permissum:** sc. *est*. The passive voice veils agency, though presumably Vitellius is meant. Not naming him further diminishes his standing, distancing him from the tedious reality of dealing with soldiers' requests (one of the emperor's responsibilities as supreme commander of the army; Campbell (1984) 267–73).   **nec deerant:** the litotes suggests that large numbers found the prospect of service in Rome unattractive.   **fessi morbis et intemperiem caeli incusantes:** the chiasmus shows *uariatio* in both inner and outer frames: adj. (*fessi*) + present participle (*incusantes*) envelop a causal abl. in the pl. (*morbis*) and lofty acc. + gen. expression (*intemperiem caeli*; again at *A.* 16.13.1), coined by Livy (5.13.4, 8.18.1; taken up by Col., Sen. the Younger, Plin. the Elder, Quint., Curt.).   **robora tamen legionibus alisque subtracta** 'yet the legions and the auxiliary cavalry units had lost their backbone'. Despite some *boni* remaining, many men were still transferred to the urban units: *robora* suggests brute force, rather than moral calibre. **conuolsum castrorum decus** 'the prestige of the urban units was shattered'; *castra* (combined alliteratively with *conuolsum*) indicates by metonymy (20.1n. *municipia et colonia*) the urban and praetorian cohorts, whose élite status evaporated with the influx of so many undistinguished recruits.   **uiginti milibus:** T. recaps his earlier point (93.2n. *sedecim . . . scribebantur*), although the figure of 20,000 is problematic, as it implies that the whole praetorian and urban force was replaced by new soldiers, which seems unlikely. Either T. exaggerates to convey the chaos, or after a short-lived arrangement, some of the 20,000 rejoined their original units.   **permixtis magis quam electis:** mixing up the proper military hierarchy is symptomatic of civil war (41.3n. *mixta*).

94.2 Contionante Vitellio: the present participle suggests that the troops do not even wait for Vitellius to finish speaking before making their demands. His words matter little to them (nor does T. bother to report them).   **postulantur ad supplicium:** the expression is not found before T. (also 1.82.3), but gives novelty to the more common *deposco ad supplicium* (Cic., Liv., [Caes.], Curt.).   **Asiaticus . . . Galliarum:** the trio is otherwise unknown, but naming them attests to T.'s diligent research.   **quod . . . bellassent:** the verb is subjunctive because T. gives the soldiers' reason, not his own (19.1n. *quod . . . legisset*). Their grievances date from the time when Verginius Rufus, governor of Upper Germany, led a combined force of legionaries from his own province and Lower Germany to defeat the rebel C. Julius Vindex, governor of Gallia Lugdunensis, at Vesontio in mid-May, 68 (Murison (1993) 26). Yet after that campaign, T. casts these soldiers as greedy and malicious (1.51.1), not idealistic, and their malice towards these Gallic leaders recalls their undiscerning bullishness towards Gauls in general after their victory (*nec socios, ut olim, sed hostes et uictos uocabant*, 1.51.3). Their demand seems ill-timed and mercurial.   **nec coerce-bat . . . Vitellius:** as often, by indicating what Vitellius does not do, T. reveals what he should have done. There is no indication that Vitellius put the trio of Gauls to death, but the fact that these troops freely make such requests shows how little respect they have for their emperor; and his complete failure to restrain them further undermines his crumbling authority. The pl. + defining gen. (*eius modi uoces*) sees T. generalising from one instance, a technique which he favours especially in pejorative contexts (cf. Tigellinus' banquet *quas . . . ut exemplum referam, ne saepius eadem prodigentia narranda sit, A.* 15.37.1), although it falls short of accepted standards in modern histo-riography.   **super insitam animo ignauiam:** *super* = *praeter* (8.1n. *super . . . oris*); 7.1n. *discordiam . . . periturum* for Vitellius' *ignauia*. M has *mortem* before *animo*, but most editors simply excise it, perhaps as a misplaced gloss for *supplicium* above (Heraeus). **conscius sibi instare donatiuum et deesse pecuniam** 'aware that the dona-tive was almost upon him and that he had no money'; 82.2n. *alii in pace* for such handouts to the soldiers. The acc. + inf. after *conscius* dates from Terence (*Ad.* 348, *Hec.* 392; then Cic., Liv., Ov., the elder Plin., *TLL* s.v. *conscius* 371.45–7, 372.61–70), but it is not pervasive (and only here in T.). His combination *instare* + *donatiuum* is unique (*TLL* s.v. *donatiuum* 1991.7; *OLD insto* 7e), almost personifying the *donatiuum* as a hunter and Vitellius as prey. Vitellius, notoriously short of money as a private citizen (59.2n. *uetere egestate*), is beset by financial problems on an even bigger scale as *princeps*.

94.3 liberti principum: Vitellius inherited the imperial household of his pre-decessors, including their rich and powerful freedmen (Millar (1977) 69–83), who could fare badly when regimes changed (54.2n. *poenas luit*). The Roman aristocracy often resented their influence (*scis enim praecipuum indicium non magni principis magnos libertos*, Plin. *Pan.* 88.2) and Trajan publicly distances himself from such figures (Plin. *Ep.* 6.31.9), but freedmen's lowly origins meant that emperors found them less threatening than aristocrats (who could challenge them for imperial power). Their wealth could be considerable (Plin. *Nat.* 33.134): Claudius' freedman Pallas was allegedly worth 400 million HS at his death (Dio 62.14.3), including contributions from the senate (Plin. *Ep.* 7.29.2, 8.6.10). Vitellius' decision to tap this resource was potentially a shrewd public relations gambit, but it was undermined both by the nature of his spending (2.95.2) and by reliance on his own freedmen (2.95.2).   **conferre:** sc. *pecuniam*.   **pro numero mancipiorum** 'proportionate to the number of their slaves'. Wealthy imperial freedmen, with villas and estates to maintain, would naturally own slaves. Even Domitian's old nurse Phyllis maintained a suburban villa of her own (Suet. *Dom.* 17.3).   **ut tributum** 'a kind of tax'(*OCD*³ '*tributum*'; Brunt (1990)

COMMENTARY: 95.1

324–53). Under the empire, inhabitants of Rome and Italy were exempt from *tributum* (denoting direct land and poll-taxes paid in the provinces, a process aided by Augustus' provincial census), but they paid various indirect taxes (*uectigalia*).   **iussi:** T. masks the agent (presumably Vitellius) of the one measure designed to raise money, lavishing attention instead on the emperor's extravagant spending, with the agent emphasised (*ipse . . . illudere*).   **ipse . . . exstruere . . . opplere . . . illudere:** 34.2n. on *struo / exstruo*. A trio of historic infinitives in asyndeton syntactically mirrors the busy haste of Vitellius spending money. Putting on shows in the circus could have been cast as a sensible *captatio beneuolentiae* after Vitellius' arrival in Rome, but T. sees such activities as a dubious continuation of the hedonistic journey to Rome and a damning reflection of the emperor's weak personality. On Vitellius' fondness for chariot-racing, see 91.2n. *in theatro . . . fautor.*   **sola perdendi cura** 'concerned only with wasting money' (*cura* = abl. of attendant circumstances). Piso indicted Otho on similar grounds (*perdere iste sciet, donare nesciet*, 1.30.1), but Vitellius is more generous than his predecessor in putting on shows, usually one of the *princeps'* obligations to his people (Millar (1977) 368–75, Veyne (1990) 398–403). Emperors who failed to sponsor and attend *munera*, such as Tiberius (Suet. *Tib.* 47; cf. Dio 57.11.5), were regarded as odd. T.'s pre-emptive gloss colours our reaction to the details of Vitellius' activities that follow.   **tamquam in summa abundantia** 'as if it were a boom time'. Vespasian faced a financial crisis on his accession (5.1n. *auaritia*).   **pecuniae illudere** 'he frittered away his money'. *illudo* + dat. in this sense (*OLD* 3) is a peculiarly Tacitean usage (also for Severus and Celer, architects of Nero's Golden House and predisposed *uiribus principis illudere*, *A.* 15.42.1).

   95.1 quin et: 88.3n.   **natalem Vitellii diem:** either 7 or 24 Sept., AD 15 (Suet. *Vit.* 3.2), so he is now 54 years old, although there is a notable discrepancy with the age given at his death, 56 (*H.* 3.86.1, Suet. *Vit.* 18; Dio 65.22 has 54).   **editis tota urbe uicatim gladiatoribus:** *gladiator* (pl.) = gladiatorial show (*OLD* 1b). The adverb *uicatim* (21× in extant Latin), only here in T., is pointed. In 73, Rome had as many as 265 separate *uici*, designating the subdivisions of the city's 14 Augustan *regiones* (Plin. *Nat.* 3.66). The stunning visual impression created (accurately or not) is that gladiators fight on every street corner, as activities normally restricted to a special space (the amphitheatre) spill over indiscriminately into the urban landscape. Dio has nothing similar, saying only that 'many men and beasts were slaughtered' (65.4.3) over a two-day celebration.   **celebrauere:** the annual celebration of birthdays, especially amongst the Roman elite, usefully reinforces normal social hierarchies through exchanging gifts, dedicating offerings, making prayers and vows, and laying on banquets (Hor. *Carm.* 4.11). The emperor's birthday above all (particularly his inaugural one as *princeps*) was celebrated lavishly and included gladiatorial shows (Suet. *Aug.* 57.1, *Tib.* 26.1, Dio 54.8.5, 54.26.2, 56.25.3, 69.8.2; Weinstock (1971) 206–11). Simpler acknowledgement was also possible: e.g. the younger Pliny's birthday letter to Trajan (*Ep.* 10.88 and 10.89, Trajan's thanks).   **ingenti paratu . . . insolito:** 4.2n. *ingens . . . fiducia* for *ingens*. T. marks out the disapproving appended abl. clause (attendant circumstances) with enveloping assonance.   **ante illum diem insolito**

'unfamiliar before that day'. T.'s contemporary audience, used to the huge shows produced in the Flavian amphitheatre, inaugurated in 80 with a festival lasting 100 days (Suet. *Tit.* 7.3, Dio 66.25), needs context for the Vitellian displays. They may seem modest compared with Trajan's celebration of his second Dacian triumph as recently as 107, when 10,000 gladiators fought (Dio 68.15), but they were lavish at the time.   **Laetum . . . quod:** cf. *gratum . . . quod* (2.92.3). T. has already surveyed in detail collective attitudes towards Nero's death, cast as sharply polarised along social lines, from *patres laeti* at the top to the *plebs sordida* and *deterrimi seruorum*, who are *maesti et rumorum auidi* (1.4.3). The Neronian 'revival' symbolised by Vitellius' funeral service stirs similar contrasting reactions, except that the categories are moral *(foedissimi* and *boni)*, rather than social.   **exstructis . . . aris:** 34.2n. on *struo / exstruo*. Suetonius also locates the ceremony here *(medio Martio campo, Vit.* 11.2). From the Campus Martius, one could look up to the tomb of the Domitii, where Nero's ashes had been placed by his two nurses and mistress Acte, who lavished 200,000 HS on the funeral after his suicide on 9 or (possibly) 11 Jun. 68 (Suet. *Nero.* 50).   **inferias Neroni fecisset** 'he had made ritual funeral offerings to Nero'; 71.1n. *Neronem . . . celebrabat* on Vitellius' admiration for Nero. The parallel tradition also relates Vitellius' ceremony for Nero, but with more details about a lyre performance at the subsequent feast (Suet. *Vit.* 11.2) and an explicit statement that Nero is Vitellius' model (Suet. *Vit.* 11.2, Dio 65.7). **caesae publice uictimae cremataeque:** although *caedere uictimas* is a standard expression, T. in the *H.* reserves it for scenes of unseemly public sacrifice (2.70.2). Animals form the offering, but we are perhaps also meant to think about the human victims of this war: cf. *has Seiano uictimas cadere (A.* 4.70.1; *uictimae* = people). There will be killing in the Campus Martius soon enough (3.82.3).   **Augustales:** Tiberius established the *Sodales Augustales* in 14 to run the cults of Augustus and the *gens Iulia.* The priests were 21 leading citizens chosen by lot and four members of the imperial household *(A.* 1.54.1, Suet. *Cl.* 6.2; Scheid (1978), *OCD³* 'Augustales'). Suetonius also mentions the presence of official priests, but without giving their designation *(adhibita publicorum sacerdotum frequentia, Vit.* 11.2), but T., a former priest himself (91.1n. *maximum pontificatum),* was interested in such details.   **quod sacerdotium** 'a priesthood, which'. Apparently a 'gloss' to flesh out the identity of the Augustales, this appended subordinate clause (in apposition to the main clause) points to the debasement of this once respectable priesthood, now honouring an unworthy descendant of Augustus. **ut Romulus Tatio regi:** T. later corrects himself, saying that Tatius (not Romulus) had instituted the Titian priesthood *(sodales Titios)* to preserve Sabine rituals *(A.* 1.54.1). Tatius ('a mysterious and colourless figure', Ogilvie (1970) 72; Liv. 1.10–14) was a Sabine king, supposed to have ruled jointly with Romulus for a time. He was eventually murdered (with good reason) on a visit to Lavinium and features in a famous fragment of Ennius, possibly spoken by Romulus condemning the dead man: *O Tite, tute, Tati, tibi tanta, tyranne, tulisti (Annales* 104 Sk.). Romulus also acquitted Tatius' murderers (Dion. Hal. 2.53), which suggests that T.'s explanation of the priesthood in the *A.* seems more plausible. Mention of Romulus here contributes to the sense of decline in the Augustales honouring Nero.

95.2 nondum . . . et: 68.4n. *et.*   **Asiaticus:** 57.2n. *Asiaticum.*   **Polyclitos, Patrobios et uetera odiorum nomina:** 'men like Polyclitus, Polybius and the detested names of the past'; 30.2n. *uigore . . . fauore* for *et* introducing one or more items after asyndeton. T. likes using a pl. for singular proper names (a form of synecdoche; Lausberg (1998) §573.3) to express scorn (1.37.5, 2.95.3, *A.* 12.60.4) or to magnify (*A.* 15.14.2); it features in oratory (Cic. *Phil.* 8.9), but also in everyday speech (Quint. 8.6.20). Galba executed Nero's freedman, Polyclitus (Plut. *Galb.* 17.2). Sent to Britain in 61 to report to Nero on the aftermath of the revolt (*A.* 14.39.1–2), in 67 he ransacked Rome during Nero's absence, together with another freedman Helius (Dio 63.12.3), and became a byword for the archetypal powerful imperial freedman (Plin. *Ep.* 6.31.9). Galba also executed Nero's *libertus* Patrobius (1.49.1, Suet. *Galb.* 20.2, Dio 64.3), but not much is known about him beyond this. T. uses *odium* (*OLD* 4) in the sense of *homo odiosus* by metonymy. This has precedents (Plut., Ter., Cic., the younger Sen.), but the pl. is choice (*duobus acerrimis odiis latera sua cingere ausa est*, Val. Max. 3.7.5).   **probitate aut industria . . . prodigis epulis et sumptu ganeaque:** in condemning the ethos of Vitellius' court, T. powerfully echoes Sallust (*quis est omnium his moribus, quin diuitiis et sumptibus, non probitate neque industria cum maioribus suis contendat?*, *Jug.* 4.7). Yet there is a twist: now lavish expenditure alone is not the means of competition, but money directed towards gastronomic feats. The prosaic *ganea* (a 'cheap eating-house') stands by metonymy for 'gluttony' (*A.* 3.52.1 with WM 380, 6.4.4; once each in Cic., Sall., Liv., Col., the younger Plin., though his uncle has it 4×). It is perhaps even bathetic in the immediate context, aptly reminding us that Vitellius' 'egalitarian' appetite also extends to everyday foods (Suet. *Vit.* 13.3).   **unum . . . iter:** this is apparently a variant of the more familiar formula involving *una uia* (Cic., Sall., Liv., the younger Sen., Quint.), recalling but inverting *sententiae* such as *ad uirtutem una ardua uia est*, (Sall. *Rep.* 2.7.9).   **satiare inexplebiles Vitellii libidines:** cf. 62.1n. *epularum . . . libido.* T. plays with ideas (if not words), as it is impossible to sate the insatiable, but avoids the adj. *insatiabiles* as too unsubtle (cf. *quomodo . . . insatiabilia satiabuntur*, Sen. *Ben.* 4.37.2).

95.3 abunde ratus: sc. *esse.* The adverb (only here in T.) serves as a predicate; cf. *abunde libertatem rati* (sc. *esse*) (Sall. *Hist.* 3.48.26 Reynolds).   **praesentibus frueretur:** T. parodies Epicurean philosophy, with its invocations to enjoy the present (Cic. *Fin.* 1.62, *Tusc.* 3.38). The spirit of *carpe diem* (Hor. *Carm.* 1.11.8) permeated banquets and was fostered there by symbols of death (e.g. model skeletons) to encourage guests to enjoy themselves (Dunbabin (1986)). Yet the sympotic excesses of Vitellius, who lives for the moment, really are a prelude to his death, as T.'s readers know (WM 128). Such escapism before dying also marks out Messalina's lover, Silius, who ignores the dangers of the future and decides *praesentibus frui* (*A.* 11.12.2).   **nec in longius consultans** 'without considering the longer term'. The expression is only here in Latin (*TLL* s.v. *consulto* 592.51).   **nouiens milliens sestertium** '900 million sesterces' (GL appendix 493). The numerical adverbs *nouiens milliens* (9,000×) combine with *sestertium* (100,000 HS), which is treated as a neuter singular, although it was originally a gen. pl. in the phrase *centena milia* (100,000) *sestertium* (= *sestertiorum*); but ellipse of *centena milia* became standard and *sestertium* on its own came to indicate 100,000 HS.

Multiplying this by 9,000 produces our figure of 900 million. Whether it is at all accurate is unclear (Scheidel (1996) discusses the stylisation of financial figures in ancient authors).   **interuertisse creditur:** *interuerto* (*OLD* 2b, *TLL* s.v. *interuerto* 2303.58) in the sense of 'waste' features here first. T. likes to quantify financial wastage with figures, as with Nero's squandered 2,200 million HS (1.20.1), but he carefully avoids committing himself to the sum's accuracy to maintain a stance of impartiality. Dio confirms the figure, though adds the detail that the money was spent on dinners (65.3.2). Its magnitude may be down to pro-Flavian sources, but T. remains commendably critical of his facts regarding the victors' finances. So, he reports that the Flavians arranged for a loan of 60 million HS from private sources, either from real need or to make it seem that way (*uerane pauperie an uti uideretur*, 4.47), i.e. to cast aspersions on the dead Vitellius. T. is nobody's fool.   **magna et misera ciuitas . . . passa:** the city of Rome (wretched, but resilient) is emotively personified (like some suffering Ovidian heroine). T. suggests a more robust character for the state than we see in a fragment attributed to the elder Seneca, whose elderly Rome uses the emperors as a walking-stick and is too weak to stand on her own (Lact. *Inst. div.* 7.15.14).   **inter Vinios Fabios, Icelos Asicaticos:** in generalising pairs of plurals (95.2n. *Polyclitos*) in asyndeton, T. first lists typical examples of high-ranking, but dubious members of the imperial entourage, then similarly undesirable freedmen. Otho's principate conspicuously does not supply him with an example (despite *Othonem . . . passa*, above) and the four *exempla* chosen were all safely dead when T. was writing. Galba's close associate, the senator Titus Vinius (initially consul for 69), had been killed in the forum (T. gives an obituary, 1.48.2–4), whereas Vitellius' general Fabius Valens is still alive (for now). Galba's freedman Icelus had been put to death (1.46.5), while Vitellius' freedman Asiaticus (57.2n.) will soon meet the same end (4.11.3).   **uaria et pudenda sorte agebat** 'suffered humiliation of every kind'.   **donec successere . . . mores:** T. beautifully undercuts the 'climax' of his sentence; for a moment, it looks as if Mucianus and Marcellus will herald a change, but instead we see depressing continuity with the calibre and methods of their predecessors.   **Marcellus:** Eprius Marcellus (53.1n.).   **Mucianus:** 5.1n.   **et:** epexegetic (*OLD* 11).   **alii homines quam alii mores** 'a change of personnel, not practices'.

    96.1 tertiae legionis: the *legio III Gallica* in Moesia (4.4n. *quattuor*).   **nuntiatur:** the timing of this announcement is as elusive as the initial revolt (85.2n. *tertia . . . praebuit*), although *nondum quartus a uictoria mensis* (2.95.2), if taken literally, points to mid-August. Yet that notice is preceded by mention of Vitellius' birthday (2.95.1; 7 or 24 Sept.) out of sequence. T.'s main interest lies not in chronology, but in Vitellius' psychological response to the news.   **missis . . . epistulis:** *epistulae* = pl. for singular (54.2n. *epistulae*). Saturninus' letter to Vitellius causes trouble later when a copy falls into the hands of the Moesian legions (3.11.1), who take it as indicating their commander's treachery. After being hunted down to a country villa, Saturninus (85.2n.) has a narrow but degrading escape and resigns his post (3.11.3–4).   **is quoque Vespasiani partibus aggregaretur:** *aggrego* (72.2n. *aggregebantur*) + the dat. *partibus* is only in T. (also 3.12.1; *TLL* s.v. *aggrego* 1321.65). Adding *quoque* suggests that Saturninus is jumping

on a bandwagon, set in motion by others; and it generates surprise that Vitellius is only
now hearing about these disloyal soldiers.   **neque . . . cuncta . . . perscripserat**
'he had not given a full account of everything'; *cuncta* = a synonym for *omnia* (1.3n.
cuncta . . . perlustrat). Saturninus' letter exemplifies a broad pattern in civil war of people
communicating non-committally, to facilitate safe relations with the next *princeps*.
Written documents were especially susceptible to prevaricating language and half-
truths. A conspicuous exception is the procurator Pompeius Propinquus' candid letter
from Belgica, informing Galba that the legions of Upper Germany have broken their
oath of allegiance (1.12.1), but predictably he is swiftly executed by Vitellius (1.58.1).
Such precedents help to explain Saturninus' caution.   **ut trepidans re subita**
'since he was wavering at this sudden development'; *res subita* (4.49.3, *A.* 11.20.1,
14.5.2) is Livian (9×), but the phrase especially recalls *Poenus in re subita . . . trepidauit*
(Liv. 28.30.7).   **amici adulantes:** the reference must mask some sort of council
meeting, the proper response to such news, but T., aiming to demonstrate Vitellius'
complacency, does not elaborate.   **mollius interpretabantur:** this combination
of verb + (comp.) adverb is innovative and unique. Saturninus' selective, misleading
letter is now compounded by Vitellius' flattering advisers (46.1n. on the prevailing
flattery of emperors during this civil war).   **unius legionis eam seditionem:** sc.
esse. The flattering tone of the *amici* is reflected in the fact that *seditio* is a less extreme
term than *defectio* above (Liv. 28.26.2), as is their (unfounded) assumption that the
trouble is restricted to a single legion.   **ceteris exercitibus constare fidem:** the
amici use upbeat, alliterative language, evoking Vitellius' own coinage (*RIC I*² Vitellius,
nos. 27–30, 47, 52–4 *FIDES EXERCITVVM, RIC I*² Vitellius, nos. 4, 20–6, 40, 48–51
CONSENSVS EXERCITVVM) and Livy (2.13.9, 37.32.14; *OLD consto* 6).

96.2 Vitellius apud milites disseruit: swiftly addressing the soldiers about
the *seditio*, in words that parrot those of his *amici*, is a dubious strategy. In denying an
incident about which the troops may not even have heard, Vitellius will only stir their
suspicions, or as Otho says pithily: *tam nescire quaedam milites quam scire oportet* (1.83.3).
praetorianos nuper exauctoratos: 67.1n. *addito . . . lenimento* on the discharge of
these praetorians. *exauctoro* is a technical term for military discharge (*TLL* s.v. 1188.55–
1189.10), restricted to prose authors (6× in Liv., not in Sall., Caes.).   **nec ullum
ciuilis belli metum asseuerabat** 'he emphatically asserted that there was no
reason to fear civil war' (*OLD metus* 5). The combination *asseuero* + *metus* is only here in
Latin (*TLL* s.v. *asseuero* 875.45–6). From what we have seen recently of these soldiers,
distracted by the delights of the city (2.93.1), civil war was probably the last thing on
their minds.   **suppresso . . . coercerent:** the robust and apparently absolute main
clause (*nec . . . asseuerabat*), as so often in T., is undermined by the contents and length
of the two appended abl. clauses.   **suppresso Vespasiani nomine:** T. resumes
an earlier theme (2.73).   **qui sermones populi coercerent** 'to stop the people
from gossiping'. T. is adamant that external censorship by any means is futile (1.17.2,
3.54.1, *A.* 4.35.5, 14.50.2).   **id praecipuum alimentum famae erat:** *uariatio* of
fama after *sermones* (Sörbom (1935) 20). T. uses the food metaphor of *alimentum* (*OLD*
4) + gen. only in *H.* (4.36.2, 4.76.3; 21.2n. *ignis alimenta*). Cf. *addidit alimenta rumoribus*

aduentus Attali (Liv. 35.23.10) and *iterum dantur malignis alimenta sermonibus* (Quint. *Decl. mai.* 18.13).

97.1 Auxilia ... exciuit 'summoned reinforcements'. The Flavian general Antonius Primus, arguing for a speedy campaign, later lists the Vitellians' useful resources in Germany, Britain, Gaul (omitted here) and Spain (3.2.2). The threat of such reinforcements explicitly accelerates his attack on the enemy (3.15.1). If Vitellius had acted more quickly, then the outcome could have been different (an instance of 'side-shadowing', Pagán (2006), as T. hints at alternative outcomes). Yet Vitellius would arguably have done better to drill the soldiers already in the vicinity. After all, he had at his disposal 60,000 men at least (2.87.1), so quality rather than quantity is the issue. In any case, Antonius Primus artfully siphons off the *accita a Vitellio auxilia* (4.13.2) in Germany by setting up the 'diversionary' uprising of Julius Civilis.   **segniter et necessitatem dissimulans** 'although he did so sluggishly and pretending that there was no need for urgency'; *uariatio* of co-ordinated adverb + participle phrase (*dissimulo* + *necessitas* are combined in Latin only here; *TLL* s.v. *dissimulo* 1482.17). This concealment shows inconsistency with the previous chapter, where Vitellius is apparently genuinely ignorant about the looming crisis, thanks to Saturninus' obfuscation and the misleading reassurances of his *amici*.   **perinde ... cunctabantur** 'were equally lethargic'. The two legates mirror Vitellius' behaviour on the surface, but T. makes it much easier for us to understand their slowness than the emperor's. Both men have pressing local reasons not to relinquish any more of their (already depleted) troops, whereas Vitellius has every reason to act quickly.   **Hordeonius ... Vettius Bolanus ... Britannia:** the syntax is typically economical, leaving us to supply the relationships between different parts of the sentence. To explain the legates' delay, we have two hidden causal clauses (*Hordeonius ... bello, Vettius ... Britannia*). Both are in apposition to the main clause (*perinde ... cunctabantur*), and are marked by asyndeton and *uariatio* in relation to one another. So in the first subordinate clause, there is a nom. adj. clause (*anxius proprio bello*), but in the second, we have a causal abl. absolute (*numquam ... Britannia*). **Hordeonius Flaccus:** 57.1n.   **suspectis iam Batauis:** 27.2n. *cohortes Batauos.*   **anxius proprio bello** '[because he was] alarmed at a possible war of his own'; *proprium bellum* is Livian (7.11.5, 8.4.3, 27.38.7; also Cic. *ND* 2.70). Flaccus' concerns about (what will become) the murky Batavian revolt (4.12–37, 4.54–79, 5.14–26) are entirely justified, but still he does not act to pre-empt trouble.   **Vettius Bolanus:** 65.2n.   **numquam ... Britannia:** Vettius Bolanus had only been in the province since April or May, hardly long enough to establish his authority. Maintaining order was not made any easier by Vitellius' removal of 8,000 men from *II Augusta, IX Hispana* and *XX Valeria* in Britain (2.57.1). Even though the emperor did later send back the *XIV Gemina* (2.66.1), Antonius Primus had already sent letters trying to win over this legion (2.86.4); and the *II Augusta*, led by Vespasian during the invasion of Britain (Suet. *Ves.* 4.1), was unlikely to co-operate enthusiastically with Vitellius. T. comments on its pro-Flavian stance, especially compared with the *IX Hispana* and *XX Valeria* (3.44).   **uterque ambigui** 'and each man's loyalty was in doubt'. The authorial gloss raises a more sinister reason for the legates' tardy reponse. Synesis (*constructio* *ad sensum*) with *uterque* is already in Plautus (*uterque insaniunt, Curc.* 187; also Caes. *Civ.* 3.30.3, Sall. *Cat.* 49.2, Liv. 9.43.4 with Oakley (2005) 562, Vell. 2.66.1; K-S I §9.2) and again in T. (G-G 1728).   **nullo . . . consulari:** sc. *legato.* Cluvius Rufus (58.2n.) had left to join Vitellius and now commanded Spain *in absentia* (2.65.2).   **trium legionum:** the *I Adiutrix* (11.2n.), *X Gemina* (58.2n.) and the *VI Victrix.* This last legion (the first to hail Galba emperor) quickly followed the *I Adiutrix* in switching its loyalty to Vespasian after the capture of Fabius Valens (3.44.1). It left Spain as part of the force to confront Civilis' revolt (4.68.4) and duly took part in the fighting in Germany (5.16.3).   **pares iure** 'held equal authority'. Britain offers a precedent for this *ad hoc* arrangement: there the legionary legates, *pares iure* (1.60), controlled the province between them after the flight of Trebellius Maximus, and successfully maintained order. Velleius apparently coined the phrase (2.29.4).   **prosperis . . . rebus:** this appended abl. masks the protasis ('if' clause) of an unreal condition. Vitellius' affairs did not prosper, but even if they had, T. says that the emperor was *ne prosperis quidem parem* (3.64.2).   **certaturi ad obsequium** 'would have bent over backwards to please him'. This non-Ciceronian use of the future active participle, as if it were the apodosis of an unreal conditional sentence, features first in Livy (*nihil relicturis, si auiditati indulgeretur,* 45.35.6; L-H-S 390 §208); cf. *si liceret, uere narraturi* (3.54.1). *ad* (*OLD* 42) has a sense of purpose (more common for *ad* + adj.). T. uses it with *certo* again (*ad supplenda exercitus damna certauere, A.* 1.71.2; also Cic. *Fam.* 10.8.6, Sen. *Ep.* 82.16, Sil. 6.591–2). Livy combines it with the abl.: *obsequio . . . certasse* (1.35.5).   **aduersam eius fortunam ex aequo detrectabant** 'they all kept their distance from his misfortunes'. *detrecto + aduersa fortuna* is unique in Latin (*TLL* s.v. *detrecto* 835.54–5). 'Safety in numbers' is a topos (1.1n. *senium . . . destinandi*).

97.2 legio: i.e. the short-lived but controversial *I Macriana,* which the Flavians will soon disband (58.1n. *haud spernendis uiribus,* Chilver (1979) 65). Clodius Macer designated it *liberatrix* on the reverse of his coinage, with various figures (Africa, a lion's head, *Libertas*) on the obverse (*RIC* I² L. Clodius Macer, nos. 5–6, 12, 19–20). **Clodio Macro:** the story of Clodius Macer (*OCD³* 'Clodius Macer (*RE* 38), Lucius', Murison (1993) 48), Nero's legionary legate of the *III Augusta,* shows why Africa (with its corn-supply) was such a significant region in the empire and sometimes necessitated unusual arrangements (4.48). Despite Galba's being proclaimed emperor in Spain, Macer in *c.* Apr. 68 decided to rebel against Nero in his own right, designating himself *propraetor* of Africa. From his base in Numidia, he seized Carthage (with its naval resources) and allegedly planned a famine in Rome, with the help of Nero's wardrobe mistress, Calvia Crispinilla (1.73). He also issued coins bearing his own name and image (*RIC* I² L. Clodius Macer, nos. 1–29, 32–42), even if the legends (*S(enatus) C(onsulto)*) claim adherence to the senate. In Plutarch, Macer's violence and rapacity prompt his rebellion (an attempt to escape justice, *G.* 6.2), but this smacks of invective. T. disparages Macer as a petty tyrant (*dominus minor,* 1.11.2), but acknowledges his real potential for causing disruption (1.7.1). Macer was put to death in the late summer or early autumn of 68 by the procurator of Africa, Trebonius Garutianus, on Galba's orders (1.7.1, Suet. *Galb.* 11, Plut. *Galb.* 15.3). That did not signal the end of troubles: Macer's successor, Valerius Festus, even killed the governor of the province, Lucius Piso (4.48–50). **militiam cepere:** a striking combination, only here in Latin (*TLL* s.v. *capio* 328.25–6, *TLL* s.v. *militia* 960.54–5). **cetera iuuentus:** a lofty expression from historiography (Liv. 1.59.5) and epic (Virg. *A.* 5.134, Stat. *Theb.* 10.223–4). **dabat impigre nomina:** *nomen dare* (also 3.58.2) is a technical term for military enrolment (*TLL* s.v. *do* 1675.5–10). The eagerness of these young men to enlist contrasts with the prevailing sluggishness of Vitellius, Hordeonius Flaccus, Vettius Bolanus and the legates in Spain (2.97.1). **quippe:** explanatory (10.3n. *quippe*). **integrum illic ac fauorabilem . . . famosum inuisumque:** *fauorabilis* (*OLD* 1) = 'popular' and *famosus* (*OLD* 2) = 'notorious'. Enveloping (4.1n. *pandi . . . prosperum*) and chiastic alliteration and assonance set up a polarity between the tenures of the two men, now compared (4.4n. *nomen . . . celebre* on *syncrisis*). Suetonius likewise depicts Vitellius' proconsulship of Africa in 60–1 as commendable, saying that he showed a *singularis innocentia* (*Vit.* 5). Vitellius' good conduct explains why the young men now keenly enlist. Yet Suetonius depicts Vespasian's proconsulship very differently from T., stressing instead his integrity and honesty, despite once getting pelted with turnips during a riot (*Ves.* 4.3); Silius is equally positive about Vespasian: *reget impiger Afros* (3.599). Who is right? To vindicate T.'s negative portrait, critics point to Vespasian's lasting unpopularity in Africa (4.49.1), but this is problematic (as the detail comes from T. himself). More compelling is the fact that T. swims against the tide of pro-Flavian propaganda in criticising Vespasian and that his tenure as proconsul in 62 coincided with a food crisis in Rome. This may have required unusually heavy grain levies in Africa (*A.* 15.18.2; Levick (1999) 23) suggests that turnips were all that the hungry locals had to eat). **experimentum contra fuit** 'experience proved them wrong'. The adverb *contra* (*OLD* 10) serves as a predicate (as *fortuna contra fuit*, 3.18.1). This laconic but eloquent final observation reinforces the generalisation that Vespasian *solus . . . omnium ante se principum in melius mutatus est* (1.50.4), but it may strain the truth for rhetorical effect. The provincials in Africa suffered less during eight months under Vitellius as emperor (the 'good' proconsul) than they did during the long principate of Vespasian (the 'bad' proconsul), when natives 'lost land, freedom, and transhumance rights' (Levick (1999) 156).

98.1 primo nicely signals that Africa's loyalty will soon turn. **Valerius Festus** (*OCD³* 'Valerius Festus (*RE* 2), Gaius Calpetanus Rantius'), legate of the *III Augusta*, was a new man from Arretium. Despite being Vitellius' relative, probably by marriage, he secretly switched his loyalty to Vespasian and concocted a sound scheme to prove his allegiance, though one that raises questions about his scruples. When a plan to assassinate the governor of Africa, Lucius Piso (the brother-in-law of the Piso adopted by Galba), misfired, Festus intervened to make sure that the killing took place (4.49–50) and won gratitude from the Flavians as a result. He was then granted *ornamenta triumphalia* after defeating the Garamantes, became suffect consul in 71 with Domitian, and served as curator of the Tiber in 72–3 (M-W 443), legate of Pannonia (73), and legate of Hispania Tarraconensis (?78–81). Festus is probably the same man who, after a painful illness, killed himself early in the principate of Domitian, whose *amicus* he had been (Mart. 1.78). His career is recorded on an inscription found at Trieste (M-W 266).   **studia prouincialium cum fide iuuit** 'he faithfully backed up the enthusiastic provincials'. The combination *studia* + *iuuo* (*OLD* 2) is apparently an innovative and unique variant on the more familiar *studia* + *foueo* (a verb which T. uses later in the sentence).   **mox . . . inualuissent:** the simple main clause (*mox nutabat*) is dwarfed by a lengthy subordinate clause stemming from two nom. participles (*fouens*; *defensurus*), a typical 'appendix sentence' (13.2n. *quae*). Festus' wavering loyalty is already dangerous, but the subordinate clauses complicate T.'s reading of his behaviour, in that although the legate communicates secretly with Vespasian, while pretending to support Vitellius (*palam . . . fouens*), even this is not necessarily his final stance (*haec . . . inualuissent*). Men like Festus are potentially dangerous for both Vitellius and Vespasian, an unexpected twist, even if things appear to be going the challenger's way.   **palam . . . occultis:** 23.4n. *palam . . . occultis*.   **fouens** 'supporting' (*OLD foueo* 6).   **haec illaue defensurus, prout inualuissent** 'intending to use in his defence one set of exchanges or the other, depending on which strengthened his position'. Most critics take *haec illaue* to refer loosely to the cause of Vitellius or Vespasian, with T. changing construction in mid-sentence (anacoluthon), but the neuter pl. pronouns could indicate the communications (*epistulis edictisque* ∼ *nuntiis*) as the antecedent. The rare verb *inualesco* (only here in T.), first used by technical authors (Cels., Col.), then appropriated by Quintilian, is also in the younger Pliny and Suetonius.   **deprehensi . . . per Raetiam et Gallias . . . quidam:** these soldiers are involved in the Flavians' far-reaching letter campaign (2.86.4). That Vitellius' men fail to capture them in significant numbers is culpable, as such unfamiliar figures stuck out in regions where the soldiers knew one other (cf. 1.75.1).   **necantur:** killing these captives continues the motif of Vitellius' denial of the Flavian challenge (2.73, 2.96.2). The intelligence gleaned from their documents is not elaborated.   **plures fefellere** 'most escaped capture' (*OLD fallo* 6c).   **occultati:** T. increasingly prefers *occulto* over *occulo* (13.2n. *occuleret*).

98.2 ita . . . noscebantur . . . ignota: T. is being sardonic. Vitellius' preparations are generally known (*sc.* as not, in any meaningful sense, to exist), whereas Vespasian's plans (which did exist) are mostly unknown, since so few of his messengers were caught. Asyndeton between the two parts of the main clause, and *Vitellii* ∼ *Vespasiani* prominent at the head of each clause sharpens the *syncrisis*.   **primum socordia . . . dein . . . retinebant:** *uariatio* of causal abl. + a paratactic indicative clause, functioning as if it were a subordinate causal clause (similarly *non partium studio, sed erat grande momentum*, 1.76.2).   **Pannonicae Alpes praesidiis insessae nuntios retinebant** 'garrisons occupying the Pannonian Alps detained all messengers'. The Alps towards Pannonia, also known as the Julian Alps, could be crossed by a road leading from Aquileia in north east Italy to Poetovio (the base of the *XIII Gemina*, 3.1.1) in Pannonia. The implication is that the Flavian garrisons have now seized this route, and that the messengers in question are Vitellian. The verb *insido* (*OLD* 2) in military contexts is a staple of ancient historiography, but by making *Alpes* (not *praesidia* with an abl. absolute *insessis Pannonicis Alpibus*) the subject of *retinebant*, T. reactivates and strengthens the motif of personified natural elements collaborating with the Flavian cause (6.2n. *secundum . . . mare*). **mare . . . secundum . . . aduersum:** further collusion with the Flavians from nature. **etesiarum flatu:** the Etesian winds (Gk ἔτος = 'summer') blow in the Mediterranean during July and August from a north-westerly direction, making it quicker and easier to travel from west to east than vice versa (Martin (2001) 171 on *flatibus etesiarum, A.* 6.33.3). Their name was old (Hdt. 2.20) and they could notoriously disrupt travel (Caes. *Civ.* 3.107, though Cic. *Fam.* 12.25.3 personifies them as *boni ciues*). The winds prompted much discussion e.g. at the philosopher Favorinus' dinner-party (Gell. 2.22).

99.1 Tandem: this modifies *iubet*. T.'s survey of responses in the provinces (2.97–8), placed between the initial summoning of reinforcements (2.97.1) and the mobilisation of Caecina and Valens, suggests delay and sharpens the sense of Vitellius' lethargy, as does the condemnatory *tandem*, used surprisingly sparingly by T. (only 3× in *H.*, 2× referring to Vitellius). **irruptione hostium** 'at the prospect of an enemy invasion'. Although the Flavians have taken control of the Pannonian Alps, they have not yet invaded northern Italy, but that will soon come (*occupata Aquileia*, 3.6.2). **atrocibus undique nuntiis:** 15.2n. *atrox*. This abl. of attendant circumstances (or possibly an abl. of agency after *exterritus*) shows that despite the Flavian blockade (2.98.2), the reports did eventually get through. **exterritus:** 8.1n. *Achaia . . . exterritae.* **praemissus Caecina:** Josephus confirms that Caecina was sent on ahead, although unlike T., he stresses Vitellius' supreme confidence in his general, suggesting *hybris* before the inevitable *peripeteia* (*BJ* 4.634). It is now probably mid-September. Valens will set off in a few days' time (3.36.1), although T. expressively and proleptically inserts his entire account of the Vitellian defeat at the second battle of Bedriacum (24–5 Oct. 69; 3.16–35) between the departures of Caecina and Valens, relating the Vitellian preparations in flashback and thereby showing their futility. **Valentem . . . tardabat:** abstract noun as subject (2.1n. *spes uicit*). Applying *infirmitas* to convalescence (*TLL* s.v. *infirmitas* 1433.23–4), rather than to the illness itself, is unusual. T. always prefers the simple verb *tardo* to the compound *retardo* (cf. *corporis infirmitas non retardauit*, Cic. *Phil.* 7.12). The impressionistic syntax in this clause, set paratactically after *praemissus Caecina*, means that we must supply a temporal or causal relationship with what precedes. Valens' sickness mirrors his ill soldiers (2.93.1, 2.94.1); and Vitellius himself will soon succumb (3.38.1). **e graui corporis morbo:** pleonastically adding the defining gen. *corporis* to *morbus* (without any parallel gen. *animi*) was a stylistic quirk in Lucretius and Cicero. It later appealed to Pliny the Elder, T. (3.38.1, *A.* 3.54.1, 4.53.1) and Apuleius. **longe alia . . . species:** the point of comparison is the army's exemplary entry into the city as a finely tuned military machine (2.89). Dio also emphasises the Vitellians' debilitation after revelling in the luxuries of Rome, but refrains from comment until Caecina reaches Cremona (65.10.2). By making the comparison now, T. may (again, 2.93.1) have in mind the woeful transformation of Hannibal's troops after their winter in Capua: *itaque hercule, uelut si cum alio exercitu a Capua exiret, nihil usquam pristinae disciplinae tenuit* (23.18.14). Another (implicit) point of contrast is the Othonian army's departure from Rome, led by the emperor himself

and sent off enthusiastically (if insincerely) by the crowd (1.90.3).   **non . . . non
ardor animis:** the rapid-fire syntax (asyndeton, anaphora, ellipse of verb), normally suggesting speed and efficiency, is a sharp mismatch for these listless troops.
The combination *ardor + animus* is only in prose authors (Cic., Liv., the elder Sen.,
Val. Max., Curt.), apart from one instance in Ovid (*Met.* 8.469). It recalls Mucianus'
earlier prediction about the Vitellians' *ardor* being worn down *popinis et comissationibus
et principis imitatione* (2.76.4).   **lentum et rarum agmen** 'the column was slow
and straggling'. This is symptomatic of inadequate or non-existent leadership. The
Vitellians' discipline does not improve even in the final battle: *rariore iam Vitellianorum acie, ut quos nullo rectore suus quemque impetus uel pauor contraheret diduceretue* (3.25.1).
fluxa arma 'their weapons were being carried any old how' (*OLD fluxus* 2). The
noun + adj. are combined nowhere else in Latin (*TLL* s.v. *fluxus* 983.33–4). Roman
soldiers entering or leaving a city should march at attention for display, but now every
man carries his weapon(s) as he sees fit. One criterion for arranging the procession
entering Rome was the *species armorum* (89.1n.), so these carelessly carried weapons
show the soldiers' decline. Josephus lists the impressive range of arms carried by the
Roman army on the march (*BJ* 3.93–7). Elaborate carvings on tombs show that soldiers normally retained pride in their weapons even in death (Feugère (2002) 34).
impatiens solis pulueris tempestatum: the syllabic crescendo in the three
defining genitives is a flourish, while the focus on the heat and dust again recalls the
Gauls suffering in Rome after Allia (Liv. 5.48.2, Plut. *Cam.* 28.2; 93.1n. *aestus impatientia*). The allusion to the love-struck Sybaris, previously *patiens pulueris atque solis* (Hor.
Carm. 1.8.4 with Nisbet and Hubbard (1970) 111–12), but now avoiding the Campus
Martius, further diminishes the status of these Vitellian soldiers.   **quantumque
hebes . . . tanto . . . promptior:** T. likes combining *quanto / quantum* + a positive
adj. (not the expected comparative *hebetior*) and *tanto* + a comparative adj. (*A.* 1.57.1,
with Goodyear (1981) 78–9, *A.* 1.68.4, 12.11.2). Livy can also show such irregularities
in comparative sentences (*quantum . . . augebatur militum numerus, tanto maiore pecunia in
stipendium opus erat*, 5.10.5), but the construction is not in Cicero. T. also omits the
connecting *tanto* or *eo magis* for an even pithier comparison (e.g. *A.* 4.69.2). This adj.
hebes is only here in the *H.* (twice in *A.*). Although it designates 'sluggish' (*OLD hebes* 4)
soldiers, it was originally applied to blunt weapons (*OLD hebes* 1), so it is an apt label
for soldiers who have neglected their arms (*fluxa arma*). *labor* could potentially benefit
an army (16.2n. *laborem insolitum*).

99.2 Accedebat huc 'in addition to these problems'. This useful bridging device
for prose authors here marks the shift to the problematic Caecina, but T. uses it
only once (also in Sall., Caes., Petr., the younger Sen., the younger Plin.).   **Caecinae . . . soluti in luxum:** this gen. participle, in apposition to *Caecinae*, with which
it agrees, is co-ordinated with the whole *seu . . . erat* clause (just as *Galbam . . . con-
temptorem . . . seu . . . uitantur*, 1.18.1). Livy also has *soluo* (*OLD* 8c) + *in* (*in spem pacis
solutis animis*, 6.11.5), but generally the expression has *animi* as the complement of the
verb, rather than the actual person.   **nimia indulgentia fortunae:** this causal
abl. links Caecina with Vespasian, for whom the *indulgentia fortunae* (2.84.2) was also

detrimental. The expression is Livian (23.2.1), but appealed later to Velleius Paterculus (2.1.4, 2.80.1, 2.121.3), Seneca the Younger (*Ep.* 66.44, *Nat.* 3.29.9, 5.18.12, *Ira.* 16.6) and Pliny the Younger (*Pan.* 82.6). **seu** (37.1n.) sets up an alternative (even more damning) reading of Caecina's conduct: for a general to slide into decadence was bad enough, but to do this with malice aforethought (weakening the army to prepare for treachery) is far worse. **infringere . . . uirtutem:** T. often uses *infringo* with abstract nouns, though only here with *uirtus* (G-G 633; *uirtus infracta . . . est*, Stat. *Ach.* 1.888), apparently varying the more common *infringo + uires* (*TLL* s.v. *infringo* 1493.70– 3). The theory that Caecina deliberately engineered the army's debilitation in Rome is impossible to substantiate, even if he did set his men a bad example by indulging in luxury (2.92.2). Yet Fabius Valens and Vitellius are just as culpable. Such speculation distinguishes ancient historiography from its modern counterpart, but the technique is normal in the genre, even if it earns T. criticism (Ryberg (1942), Sullivan (1975/6), Whitehead (1979), Develin (1983)). T. may not even intend it as a 'serious' explanation: it again posits the causal connection between the debilitated army and Vitellius' defeat. **inter artes erat** 'was one of his tricks'. The prepositional formula neatly suggests further trickery to come. **credidere plerique:** 93.2n. *creditur* for the different theories about Caecina's treachery. T. himself does not vouch for the story (not in the parallel tradition), but reports it for thoroughness (2.3n. *fuerunt qui . . . crederent*) and because it was believed at the time. It reinforces his picture of the general collapse of morale and loyalties. Sabinus, Caecina and Gallus are all dead, so no witness could prove or disprove the details. **Flauii Sabini:** 55.1n. Since Sabinus' *inualidus senecta* (3.65.1) is the keynote elsewhere, his enterprising solicitation of Caecina seems implausible, especially as such candour (even via a third party) was very dangerous, if the general rejected the offer and reported him to Vitellius (cf. Volusius Proculus, who informed Nero about the Pisonian conspiracy after contact with Epicharis, *A.* 15.51.4). **concussam Caecinae mentem** 'Caecina's loyalty was undermined' (*OLD concutio* 3b; *TLL* s.v. *mens* 730.57–8 for this striking use of *mens* for *fides*; cf. *concussa . . . fide*, 5.25.1). T. is influenced by Lucan, where Petreius' speech *omnis | concussit mentes* (4.235–6). **Rubrio Gallo:** 51n. **rata apud Vespasianum fore pacta transitionis** 'any conditions agreed for changing sides would be validated with Vespasian'. The price for Caecina's betrayal was no doubt high, starting with a cast-iron guarantee of his own safety, but the Flavians' conditions perhaps included an edict in due course from Caecina as consul publicly supporting Vespasian (4.31.1). Caecina is seen arranging *pacta perfidiae* (3.9.2) shortly before the final battle. T.'s pejorative label *perfidia* (cf. *perfidiam meditanti* above) underscores Flavius Sabinus' euphemistic language here (also used by the Flavian generals to Caecina at 3.9.5): *transitio* (*OLD* 2; 3× in *H.*) casting treachery more positively is first used by Cassius Parmensis (Cic. *Fam.* 12.13.3). **odiorum inuidiaeque:** 92.1n. *olim . . . dissimulata* on the dysfunctional relationship between the Vitellian generals. *admonebatur* governs the genitives. **impar apud Vitellium . . . apud nouum principem:** Caecina belittles Vitellius with a simple name, whereas Vespasian is already the *nouus princeps*, even though he does not yet hold office. The combination *impar + apud* is only here in Latin (*TLL* s.v. *impar* 519.57).

100.1 multo cum honore: the monosyllabic preposition is placed between the (emphasised) adj. and noun (3.2n. *tenuem in ambitum*). Such warmth and respect for Caecina is poignant after T.'s analysis of the general's treachery (2.99.2), but also suggests Vitellius' lack of insight.   **digressus:** when precisely Caecina departed is uncertain, but it was perhaps *c.* 17 Sept. 69 (Wellesley (1972) 195). Caecina's attempted coup at Hostilia (3.13–14) was on 18 Oct. (a lunar eclipse mentioned by Dio 65.11.1 allows precision). Troops would normally march the 345 miles between Rome and Hostilia in 18–20 days, but extra time should be allowed for Caecina's meeting with Lucilius Bassus at Ravenna; and the soldiers were not in good condition.   **partem equitum ad occupandam Cremonam:** there must have been a council of war, but T. sharpens the impression of chaos amongst the Vitellians by not reporting it. Caecina apparently also sent to Cremona the *I Italica* and the *XXI Rapax* (3.14), but T. does not report that detail here.   **uexilla primae, quartae, quintae decimae, sextae decimae legionum:** the *prima Germanica, IV Macedonica, XV Primigenia* and *XVI Gallica* (57.1n. *ut . . . supplerentur*). The bulk of these four legions had remained at their bases in Germany. M here is corrupt (*in quattuor decum xuj legionum*), but Ferlet's restoration (1801), based on the legions identified at 3.22.2, is generally accepted.   **quinta et duoetuicensima:** the *V Alaudae* (43.2n. *impetu quintanorum*). The *XXII Primigenia* (*RE* xii 1797–1820), created by Caligula, was normally based at Mogontiacum, and indeed some of its personnel had remained there (4.24.1, 4.37.2) with their legate Dillius Vocula. While Galba governed Upper Germany in 40, the legion directly experienced his strict discipline (Suet. *Galb.* 6.2–3), which perhaps made it hesitant at first to rebel against him (1.55.1). Its legionaries fought for Vitellius on the left wing at the second battle of Bedriacum (3.22.2).   **secutae:** sc. *sunt.* **postremo agmine:** this Livian expression (6×; also Sil. 16.496) will feature again in an inauspicious context (*A.* 2.8.3). The catalogue's businesslike military language belies the shabby state of the army being described.   **unaetuicensima Rapax et prima Italica:** 18.1n. *ueterano exercitui* on the *XXI Rapax*; 41.2n. *Italicae legionis* on the *I Italica.*   **trium Britannicarum legionum:** the *II Augusta, IX Hispana,* and *XX Valeria Victrix* (32.1n. *Britannicum . . . distineri,* 97.1n. *numquam . . . Britannia*).   **electis auxiliis:** this combination (only here; *TLL* s.v. *eligo* 386.41) varies the more familiar *delecta auxilia* (3× in T.) of Livy.

100.2 quem ipse ductauerat: this striking Sallustian expression (*Cat.* 11.5, 17.7, 19.3, *Jug.* 38.1, 70.2) is especially conspicuous as T. has *ducto* only here. The verb, associated with the genre of comedy and colloquial speech, originally meant to take home a prostitute (*OLD ducto* 1b), but Sallust boldly appropriates it in combination with *exercitus* to indicate commanding an army. The phrase did not catch on (and T. is the only later author to use it, apart from those quoting Sall.). Quintilian cites it as an example of κατέμφατον, language which has an obscene meaning, thanks to daily usage, and he condemns people in his own day for still smirking at Sallust's *ductare exercitum* (8.3.44). Given Valens' propensity for sexual misdemeanours (30.3n. *foedum et maculosum*), T.'s unique selection of a Sallustian expression, riddled with *double entendre,* does not seem entirely innocent (and indeed Valens will march north *multo ac molli* *concubinarum spadonumque agmine*, 3.40.1).   **sic sibi cum Caecina conuenisse** '[he wrote that] this was his agreement with Caecina'. That Valens explicitly made this point in his instructions to his soldiers is odd (it should not even need saying), but suggests that he does not trust Caecina an inch, and perhaps even anticipated trouble from him. The forceful alliteration stresses its importance.   **qui praesens eoque ualidior** 'but he was on the spot and so had more influence'; 13.2n. *eoque*. The *qui* (Caecina in the previous sentence = the antecedent) is an adversative connecting relative pronoun (*OLD qui* 14).   **mutatum id consilium:** sc. *esse.* Caecina resorts to this lie as he desperately wants to keep Valens apart from his loyal soldiers from Lower Germany (2.93.2). Valens duly sets out in a few days without a proper military column (3.40.1), so that he is forced to summon (insufficient) reinforcements from Rome when news of Caecina's treachery breaks (3.41.1).   **ut ingruenti bello tota mole occurreretur** 'so that they could confront the impending war with their full strength'; 6.1n. *tarda mole . . . belli.* The figurative and choice verb *ingruo* (28× in T., but only in Plaut., Liv. and Virg. before Sen. the Younger; Oakley (1997) 413–14) + *bellum* features again (3.58.1, *A.* 1.60.2 with Goodyear (1981) 91–2). Here Caecina deploys resonant Livian (*ubi quid bellici terroris ingruat,* 6.6.6) and Virgilian language (*si bellum ingrueret, A.* 8.535) for the imminent 'epic' struggle. Yet despite his grandiose rhetoric, the strategy seems sensible. After all, why should a large portion of the army stay behind waiting for the sickly Valens to recover when the Flavian threat is so pressing?

100.3 ita accelerare legiones, <pars> Cremonam pars Hostiliam petere iussae 'so the legions made haste, some with orders to head for Cremona, others for Hostilia'. The syntax (and therefore whether to punctuate with a comma after *legiones* or *Cremonam*) is controversial. It seems best (with Heubner (1968) 321) to take *legiones* as designating the whole force and *accelerare* as absolute, and to add another *pars* before *Cremonam* as the correlative of *pars Hostiliam*. The alternative is to add an *aliae* after *Hostiliam.* Yet at least the strategy is clear. The Vitellian force was divided into two (unequal) groups for despatch to Cremona (*I Italica, XXI Rapax*) and Hostilia (units from *I Germanica, IV Macedonica, XV Primigenia, XVI Gallica, II Augusta, IX Hispana, XX Valeria Victrix,* plus the full legions *V Alaudae, XXII Primigenia*). These were both strategic towns north of the river Po, which was to be used as a natural line of defence in confronting the Flavians. In the event, Caecina will take up position with the main force slightly north of Hostilia, behind the marshes of the river Tartarus (an ominous name; 3.9.1), although this group will abandon the camp and rejoin their colleagues at Cremona, after Caecina's attempted betrayal of Vitellius (3.14).   **Rauennam:** the Etruscans probably founded Ravenna (*RE* IIA 300–5, *OCD³*, Wellesley (1972) 235–6), an ancient city on the Adriatic. After Actium, it underwent much expansion after Augustus chose it as his naval base (Suet. *Aug.* 49.1; the port itself was called *Classis*), including a canal running from the Po to the city (Plin. *Nat.* 3.119). Its location between the Po delta and the sea made it liable to flooding and shortages of good drinking water (Mart. 3.56–7 with Watson and Watson (2003) 303–4).   **praetexto classem alloquendi:** with so many military forces pushing northwards through Italy by land, the fleet at Ravenna potentially played an invaluable defensive role, so

the pretext is convincing.   **mox patuit:** many editions corrected M's *patui* to *Pataui*,
but this is unsatisfactory, as Patavium was 100 miles north of Ravenna and right in the
line of the advancing enemy. Martin (1951) elegantly resolves the problem by reading
patuit, contrasting (typical for T.) appearance (*praetexto*) and reality (*patuit*).   **secretum componendae proditionis quaesitum** (sc. *esse*) 'that a secret interview for
arranging treachery had been sought'.   **Lucilius Bassus:** this is the first appearance of Sextus Lucilius Bassus (*RE* XIII 1640–2, Pflaum (1960) 92–4), the shifty former
cavalry commander, who held that post presumably on the Rhine. There he became
known to Vitellius, who promoted him to prefect of the fleets at Ravenna and Misenum
(an unprecedented dual command). His betrayal of the emperor at least has a tangi-
ble and familiar reason (bitterness at lack of promotion). This distinguishes him from
Caecina, whose motives are much harder to pin down. T. perhaps found Bassus less
intriguing than Caecina: his characterisation is certainly less developed. Although his
desertion of Vitellius was not in itself pivotal, especially since the campaign unfolded
on land, it crucially gave Caecina confidence to change his allegiance. Bassus, after
overseeing the fleet's desertion of Vitellius, was put under honourable arrest by the
Flavian supporter Cornelius Fuscus and sent (possibly by prior agreement) to Atria,
where he was then set free (3.12.3). He reappears later, mopping up trouble in Campania for the Flavians (4.3.1). For his services, he was adlected to the senate and
made governor of Judaea in 71, where he took the strongholds of Herodium (Jos. *BJ*
7.163) and Machaereus (Jos. *BJ* 7.164–209); he died in 72 or 73 (Jos. *BJ* 7.252, Levick
(1999) 120).   **non statim:** *statim* underscores T.'s disapproval. It implies that Vitellius
probably planned to make Bassus his praetorian prefect and that the prestigious joint
command of the fleets was an interim appointment. Thus, Bassus' impatience is cast
as entirely unreasonable.   **praefecturam praetorii:** instead Vitellius appointed
Publilius Sabinus and Julius Priscus (92.1n.) to satisfy Caecina and Valens.   **foret:**
foret for *esset* (14.3n. *deletae . . . forent*).   **iracundiam:** 65.2n. *ob iracundiam militum.*
flagitiosa perfidia 'by his scandalous betrayal'. The expressive combination (only
here in Latin; *TLL* s.v. *flagitiosus* 838.22–3) might seem pleonastic, as *perfidia* is surely
pejorative on its own, but T., anticipating his digression on the perversion of language,
where terms like 'betrayal' can be positively recast (2.101.1), emphasises Caecina's disgraceful conduct by the damning adj. *flagitiosa* (a great Ciceronian favourite: 51×, plus
cognates).   **nec sciri potest:** T. is often frank about the limits of his knowledge
(3.2n. *ratio in obscuro*), a concession designed to reinforce his authorial *auctoritas*. Here it
also serves as a transitional device.   **quod euenit inter malos ut et similes sint**
'since it often happens that bad men resemble each other', 'since evil minds think alike'
(Wellesley); *OLD euenio* 3 + *ut* (*TLL* s.v. *euenio* 1014.20–39) introducing a result clause.
The neuter relative pronoun *quod* (*OLD qui* 13) sets up a parenthesis, which 'glosses'
in advance as a general rule (*euenit* = present tense) T.'s alternative explanation of
the relationship between Caecina and Bassus in the *an* clause (*eadem . . . impulerit*). The
sentence would be grammatically complete without the parenthesis, but it shifts our
focus from the particular to the general, investing the narrative with a timeless relevance and satisfying the moralising agenda of ancient historiography. T. apparently

modifies a Homeric proverb ('See now how one bad man brings along another; for the god always guides one man towards a similar type', *Od.* 17.217–18). Yet where Homer observes that similar types often gravitate towards one another (cf. our 'Birds of a feather'), T. stresses that similar personalities can exist independently in two men. **eadem illos prauitas impulit:** abstract noun as subject (2.1n. *spes uicit*).

101.1 Scriptores temporum: the phrase has a unique precedent in Livy from a digression about Publius Scipio's personal qualities (*temporum illorum scriptoribus*, 29.14.9). Livy claims that he omits a character sketch, after failing to find one in contemporary accounts, and justifies himself by arguing that he is not prepared to introduce his own conjectures about a matter now long buried in the past. T. here alludes to this passage to assert his independence as a historian: unlike the defensive Livy, T. will give his own opinions and is not dependent on what the *scriptores temporum* hand down to posterity. The phrase is conveniently all-encompassing (again at *A.* 2.88.1, 12.67.1, 13.17.2). Many authors wrote about these civil wars (Jos. *BJ* 4.496), although T. himself directly cites only Pliny the Elder (3.28) and Vipstanus Messalla (3.25.2, 3.28 with Morgan (2006) 282–3; Marincola (1997) 250–1). This digressive close to the book develops T.'s opening discussion (1.1.1–2) about the pitfalls of imperial historiography, especially his point that authors who flatter expose themselves to the degrading charge of slavishness (*adulationi foedum crimen seruitutis*, 1.1.2). **potiente rerum Flauia domo:** the unique combination *Flauia domo* (rather than *gente*) designates the whole period 69–96 (the principates of Vespasian, Titus and Domitian). T. thereby creates the impression of a monolithic and depressingly uniform historiographical response to the civil wars, only now being reversed by his own astutely critical narrative (composed between *c.* 100–109). No doubt the realities of the historiographical scene were more nuanced (even Josephus calls Caecina a traitor: *BJ* 4.644), but T. (typically in this genre) needs to promote himself at the expense of his rivals' narratives (Marincola (1997) 115–16, 241–57). **monimenta huiusce belli:** an intensely ironic periphrasis designates the rival historical accounts of the civil wars. Above all, the architectural metaphor (*OLD monumentum* 5b; *TLL* s.v. *monumentum* 1464.28–1465.23) calls to mind the 'monumental(ising)' historiography of Livy (*incorruptis rerum gestarum monumentis, pref.* 6; Kraus and Woodman (1997) 57–8), so physically huge, as Martial jokes, that his library cannot hold it all (14.190), but also morally uplifting and entertaining on a grand scale. By contrast, any 'edifice' constructed from the grim subject matter of these current civil wars is likely to be tarnished, deformed and embarrassing, although these *scriptores temporum* arguably leave an even more depressing legacy, as their accounts are also tainted by *adulatio*. **curam pacis et amorem rei publicae:** the warping of language during civil war is a Thucydidean motif (3.82.4 with Hornblower (1991) 483). Plutarch observes how flatterers habitually use the wrong words to describe particular phenomena (*Mor.* 56c) and cites an example from Plato (*Rep.* 474a; cf. 560e-61a, Arist. *Pol.* 1261b16, Sall. *Cat.* 38.3, 52.11). The (biased) choice of synonyms, which intensify or lessen the *res*, is a useful rhetorical strategy (Quint. 4.2.77, 5.13.26, 8.4.1; Lausberg (1998) §402), and could also be a way to salvage pride (*Agr.* 21.2). We have already seen it when Otho appeals to his riotous soldiers to check their *fortitudo*, a euphemistic gloss for an insurrection (1.83.2). **corruptas in adulationem causas** (sc. *perfidiae*) 'discreditably slanting their explanations [for this betrayal] so as to flatter [the new regime]'. This taut clause is in apposition to *curam . . . publicae* after *trado* (*OLD* 10c), as T. damningly glosses the sycophantic historians' grotesque euphemisms for the treachery of Caecina and Bassus. He feels so strongly that in Vitellius' obituary he again condemns people who claim credit for betraying him, especially after they did the same to Galba: *sed imputare perfidiam non possunt qui Vitellium Vespasiano prodidere, cum a Galba desciuissent* (3.86.2). Caecina and Bassus are (again) the obvious reference points.   **nobis**, placed prominently, is dat. after *uidentur* at the end of the sentence. Livy resorts to the self-reference in the first person plural (Nisbet and Hubbard (1970) 85, Woodman (1977) 198, Sinclair (1995) 52, Lausberg (1998) §573.3 with Quint. 9.3.20) most often amongst extant Roman historians (Marincola (1997) 11–12). Historians were expected to improve existing accounts of the same period, but this could allow self-promotion, as here. T. likes to set himself up (by adversative asyndeton) as a 'lone voice' against a large body of writers, most famously when warning his readers not to compare his own depressing *annales* with the exciting republican historians (which he then does): *nobis in arto et inglorious labor* (*A.* 4.32.2; also *A.* 6.7.5).   **super insitam leuitatem et prodito Galba uilem mox fidem** 'apart from their innate fickleness and the low regard in which their loyalty was held after they had betrayed Galba'; *super* = *praeter* (8.1n. *super . . . oris*). This damning *praeteritio* is designed to show why the explanations of the *scriptores temporum* for the conduct of Caecina and Bassus are so wildly wrong. Romans placed greater weight than we do on a person's innate character in determining responsibility and capacity for an action (partly why the decadent Otho's exemplary suicide is so troubling for ancient authors): so, the logic goes, naturally fickle people such as Caecina and Bassus will always embrace treachery.   **aemulatione etiam inuidiaque:** these causal ablatives explain *peruertisse . . . Vitellium*. Postponing *etiam* (G-G 404) creates an emphatic position for *aemulatione* (+ *inuidia* elsewhere in T., always linked by *et*, 1.65.1, 2.21.2, 3.65.1).   **ab . . . anteirentur:** assonance marks off this syntactic unit.   **peruertisse ipsum Vitellium:** repeating the emperor's name with the emphatic *ipse* sharpens their paradoxical, self-destructive conduct. They choose to destroy Vitellius, rather than be outstripped by anyone else in receiving his favours.

101.2 animos obstinatos pro Vitellio: the combination *animi obstinati* (only here in T.) is in grand genres, tragedy (Acc. *Trag.* 84) and historiography (Sall. *Cat.* 36.4; Liv. has it 6×, Kraus (1994) 107–8; it is also in Apul. and Curt.). These same soldiers and centurions will demonstrate their consistently strong resolve when Caecina tries to make them desert Vitellius (3.13–14; cf. Dio 65.10.3–4, who casts the men as utterly mercurial). He first approaches the *primores centurionum et paucos militum* (3.13.1) while most men are on duty away from the camp, but then meets stubborn resistance once they all return.   **subruebat** 'set about undermining'. For the general's attempts to destabilise his soldiers, T. wryly chooses a verb with a conspicuous military metaphor (*OLD subruo* 2). It was usually associated with undermining walls or ramparts during a siege (used thus by T. 5×, G-G 1559, including 2.22.2). T. has the metaphorical usage only here (perhaps inspired by *animum . . . subruit*, Hor. *Ep.* 2.1.179–80).   **minor difficultas:** T. duly describes the fleet's change of allegiance, but during the process, Bassus is afraid about the outcome (3.12). Still, unlike Caecina (3.13–14), he does secure the men for the Flavian cause.   **lubrica ad mutandam fidem classe** 'since the fleet was ready at the least impulse to change its allegiance'. The adj. *lubricus*, used elsewhere of streams (*OLD* 3) and slippery reptiles and fish (*OLD* 2b), suits the aquatic noun to which it is applied (uniquely; *TLL* s.v. *classis* 1292.40), but it hardly sounds complimentary. The combination with *ad* + the gerundive (here first) is very rare (*TLL* s.v. *lubricus* 1690.26–30). T. was perhaps struck by Silius on the lovestruck water nymph Agylle, where *lubrica* is used in the same sense (*OLD* 7): *flore capi iuuenem primaeuo lubrica mentem | nympha* (5.18–9).   **ob memoriam . . . militiae:** under Otho the fleet was *partibus fida* (1.87.1), especially after Galba's massacre of marines on entering Rome (11.3n. *classicorum*), and had recently seen service for Otho off the coast of Gallia Narbonensis (2.14.1). A book which began by looking to the near future (2.1.1) ends by glancing back to the recent past.

SELECT BIBLIOGRAPHY

TACITUS: EDITIONS, TRANSLATIONS AND COMMENTARIES

Chilver, G. E. F. (1979) *A historical commentary on Tacitus' Histories I and II*. Oxford

Chilver, G. E. F. and Townend, G. B. (1985) *A historical commentary on Tacitus' Histories IV and V*. Oxford

Furneaux, H. (1896) ed. *The Annals of Tacitus I*. Oxford

Goodyear, F. R. D. (1972) ed. *The Annals of Tacitus Books 1–6: Annals 1.1–54*. Cambridge

  (1981) ed. *The Annals of Tacitus Books 1–6: Annals 1.55–81 and Annals 2*. Cambridge

Heubner, H. (1963) ed. *P. Cornelius Tacitus die Historien*, vol. I. Heidelberg

  (1968) ed. *P. Cornelius Tacitus die Historien*, vol. II. Heidelberg

  (1978) ed. *P. Cornelius Tacitus: Historiarum Libri*. Stuttgart

  (1994) ed. *P. Cornelius Tacitus: Annales*. Stuttgart and Leipzig

Irvine, A. L. (1952) ed. *Tacitus: Histories Books I and II*. London

Le Bonniec, H., and Hellegouarc'h, J. (1989) eds. *Tacite Histoires Livres II et III*. Paris

Martin, R. H. and Woodman, A. J. (1989) eds. *Tacitus Annals Book IV*. Cambridge

Wellesley, K. (1972) ed. *Cornelius Tacitus: the Histories Book III*. Sydney

  (1989) *Cornelii Taciti Historiarum Libri*. Leipzig

Woodman, A. J. and Martin, R. H. (1996) eds. *The Annals of Tacitus Book 3*. Cambridge

OTHER WORKS

Adams, J. N. (1972) 'The language of the later books of the *Annals*', *CQ* 22: 350–73

  (1973) 'The vocabulary of the speeches in Tacitus' historical works', *BICS* 20: 124–44

  (1974) 'The vocabulary of the later decades of Livy', *Antichthon* 8: 54–62

  (1978) 'Conventions of naming in Cicero', *CQ* 28: 145–66

  (1987) *The Latin sexual vocabulary*. London

  (1992) 'Iteration of compound verb with simplex in Latin prose', *Eikasmos* 3: 295–8

Ahl, F. (1984) 'The rider and the horse: politics and power in Roman poetry from Horace to Statius', *ANRW* II 32.1: 40–110

Aldheid, F. (1988) 'Oratorical strategy in Sallust's letter of Mithridates', *Mnemosyne* 41: 67–92

Alföldy, G. (1985) '*Bellum Mauricum*', *Chiron* 15: 91–109

  (1995) 'Bricht der Schweigsame sein Schweigen? Eine Grabinschrift aus Rom', *MDAI(R)* 102: 251–68

Alston, R. (1994) 'Roman military pay from Caesar to Diocletian', *JRS* 84: 113–23

Asali, K. J. (1997) *Jerusalem in history*. London

Ash, R. (1997) 'Warped intertextualities: Naevius and Sallust at Tacitus *Histories* 2.12.2', *Histos* 1

  (1999) *Ordering anarchy: armies and leaders in Tacitus' Histories*. London and Michigan

(2002) 'Epic encounters? Battle narratives and the epic tradition', in D. S. Levene and D. P. Nelis, eds. *Clio and the poets: Augustan poetry and the traditions of ancient historiography* (Leiden) 253–73

(2006) 'Following in the footsteps of Lucullus? Tacitus' characterisation of Corbulo', *Arethusa* 39: 355–75

(forthcoming) 'The wonderful world of Mucianus', in E. Bispham and G. Rowe, eds. *Vita uigilia est: Festschrift for Barbara Levick. BICS*

Ashby, T. and Fell, R. A. L. (1921) 'The Via Flaminia', *JRS* 11: 125–90

Aubrion, E. (1985) *Rhétorique et histoire chez Tacite.* Metz

Austin, N. J. E. and Rankov, B. (1995) *Exploratio. Military and political intelligence in the Roman world from the second Punic war to the battle of Adrianople.* New York

Austin, R. G. (1971) ed. *P. Vergili Maronis Aeneidos Liber Primus.* Oxford
(1977) ed. *P. Vergili Maronis Aeneidos Liber Sextus.* Oxford

Ball, W. (2000) *Rome in the east: the transformation of an empire.* London

Bannon, C. J. (1997) *The brothers of Romulus: fraternal pietas in Roman law, literature and society.* Princeton, New Jersey

Barchiesi, A. (2001) 'The crossing', in S. J. Harrison, ed., *Texts, ideas and the classics: scholarship, theory and classical literature* (Oxford) 142–63

Barrett, A. A. (1977) 'Sohaemus, King of Emesa and Sophene', *AJP* 98: 152–9

Barton, T. (1994a) 'The *inuentio* of Nero: Suetonius', in J. Elsner and J. Masters, eds. *Reflections of Nero* (London) 48–63
(1994b) *Ancient astrology.* London

Bartsch, S. (1994) *Actors in the audience: theatricality and doublespeak from Nero to Hadrian.* Cambridge, Mass. and London

Batstone, W. W. (1988) 'The antithesis of virtue: Sallust's *synkrisis* and the crisis of the late Republic', *CA* 7: 1–29

Beard, M. and North, J. (1990) *Pagan priests: religion and power in the ancient world.* London

Beard, M. (1990) 'Priesthood in the Roman republic', in M. Beard and J. North, eds. *Pagan priests: religion and power in the ancient world* (London) 19–48
(2003) 'The triumph of Flavius Josephus', in A. J. Boyle and W. J. Dominik, eds. *Flavian Rome: culture, image, text* (Leiden and Boston) 343–58

Bell, A. A. (1994) 'Fact and *exemplum* in the accounts of the deaths of Pompey and Caesar', *Latomus* 53: 824–36
(2004) *Spectacular power in the Greek and Roman city.* Oxford

Berry, C. (1994) *The idea of luxury: a conceptual and historical investigation.* Cambridge

Bessone, L. (1972) *La rivolta Batavica e la crisi del 69 d.c.* Turin

Bieber, M. (1961) *Greek and Roman theatre.* Princeton, New Jersey

Birley, A. R. (1981) *The Fasti of Roman Britain.* Oxford
(1988) *Septimius Severus: the African emperor.* London
(2000) 'The life and death of Cornelius Tacitus', *Historia* 49: 230–47

Birley, E. (1977) 'The aftermath of an incident in A.D.69', *Chiron* 7: 279–81

Bishop, M. C. and Coulston, J. C. N. (1993) *Roman military equipment from the Punic wars to the fall of Rome.* London

Biville, F. (2002) 'The Graeco-Romans and Greco-Latin: a terminological framework for cases of bilingualism', in J. N. Adams, M. Janse and S. Swain, eds. *Bilingualism in ancient society: language contact and the written word* (Oxford) 77–102

Bloch, R. S. (2002) *Antike Vorstellungen vom Judentum: der Judenexkurs des Tacitus im Rahmen der griechisch-römischen Ethnographie* (Historia Einzelschriften 160). Stuttgart

Le Bohec, Y. (1994) *The imperial Roman army*. London

Bömer, F. (1969) *P. Ovidius Naso Metamorphosen I–III*. Heidelberg

(1976) *P. Ovidius Naso Metamorphosen IV–V*. Heidelberg

(1982) *P. Ovidius Naso Metamorphosen XII–XIII*. Heidelberg

Bosworth, A. B. (1973) 'Vespasian and the provinces: some problems of the early 70s AD', *Athenaeum* 51: 49–78

(1976) 'Vespasian's reorganisation of the north-east frontier', *Antichthon* 10: 63–78

Bowersock, G. W. (1993) 'Tacitus and the province of Asia', in T. J. Luce and A. J. Woodman, eds. *Tacitus and the Tacitean tradition* (Princeton) 3–10

Braund, D. (1984a) *Rome and the friendly king: the character of the client kingship*. London, Canberra and New York

(1984b) 'Berenice in Rome', *Historia* 33: 120–3

(1996) 'River frontiers in the environmental psychology of the Roman world', in D. L. Kennedy, ed. *The Roman army in the east* (Ann Arbor, Michigan) 43–7

Braund, S. Morton (1996) ed. *Juvenal Satires Book I*. Cambridge

Briessmann, A. (1955) *Tacitus und das Flavische Geschichtsbild* (Hermes Einzelschriften 10). Wiesbaden

Brink, K. O. (1944) 'A forgotten figure of style in Tacitus', *CR* 58: 43–5

Brothers, A. J. (1988) ed. *Terence: the self-tormentor*. Warminster

Brunt, P. (1960) 'Tacitus on the Batavian revolt', *Latomus* 19: 494–517

(1975) 'Stoicism and the principate', *PBSR* 43: 7–35

(1977) '*Lex de imperio Vespasiani*', *JRS* 67: 95–116

(1990) *Roman imperial themes*. Oxford

Büchner, K. (1964) *Tacitus und Ausklang*. Wiesbaden

Butcher, K. (2003) *Roman Syria and the near east*. London

Cadbury, D. (2002) *The lost king of France: a true story of revolution, revenge and DNA*. New York

Cameron, A. (1976) *Circus factions: Blues and Greens at Rome and Byzantium*. Oxford

Campbell, J. B. (1975) 'Who were the *uiri militares*?', *JRS* 65: 11–31

(1978) 'The marriage of soldiers under the empire', *JRS* 68: 153–66

(1984) *The emperor and the Roman army*. Oxford

(1993) 'War and diplomacy: Rome and Parthia, 31 BC–AD 235', in J. Rich and G. Shipley, eds. *War and society in the Roman world* (London and New York) 213–40

Carter, J. (1993) ed. *Julius Caesar. The civil war book iii*. Warminster

Casson, L. (1971) *Ships and seamanship in the ancient world*. Princeton, New Jersey

Cernjak, A. B. (1976) 'Quelques problèmes de critique textuelle chez Tacite (*A.* XI.18.1, *Hist.* II.6.1 et II.77.2)', *Quaderni dell'istituto di filologia latina* 4: 99–111

Chalon, G. (1964) *L'Édit de Tiberius Iulius Alexander*. Lausanne

Champlin, E. (1991) *Final judgments: duty and emotion in Roman wills 200 B.C.–A.D. 250.* Berkeley, Los Angeles, Oxford

Chaplin, J. D. (2000) *Livy's exemplary history.* Oxford

Chausserie-Laprée, J. P. (1969) *L'expression narrative chez les historiens latins: histoire d'un style.* Paris

Chevallier, R. (1976) *Roman roads*, trans. N. H. Field. Berkeley and Los Angeles

Chilver, G. E. F. (1970–1) 'The war between Otho and Vitellius and the North Italian towns', *CSDIR* 3: 101–14

Christes, J. (1993) '*Modestia* und *moderatio* bei Tacitus', *Gymnasium* 100: 514–29
   (1995) 'Das persönliche Vorwort des Tacitus zu den Historien', *Philologus* 139: 133–46

Clausewitz, K. von (1832) *Vom Kriege* = A. Rapoport (ed.) and J. J. Graham (trans.) (1968) *On war.* London

Coale A. J., Jr. (1971) '*Dies Alliensis*', *TAPA* 102: 49–58

Coleman, K. (1988) ed. *Statius Siluae IV.* Oxford
   (1990) 'Fatal charades: Roman executions staged as mythological enactments', *JRS* 80: 44–73
   (1993) 'Launching into history: aquatic displays in the early empire', *JRS* 83: 48–74

Coleman, R. G. G. (1999) 'Poetic diction, poetic discourse and the poetic register', in J. N. Adams and R. G. Mayer, eds. *Aspects of the language of Latin poetry*, *PBA* 93: 21–93

Connors (1998) *Petronius the poet: verse and literary tradition in the Satyricon.* Cambridge

Constans, L. (1893) *Étude sur la langue de Tacite.* Paris

Conte, G. B. (1994) *Genres and readers.* Baltimore

Corbeill, A. (1996) *Political humor in the late Roman republic.* Princeton, New Jersey

Corbett, P. (1986) *The scurra.* Edinburgh

Cornell, T. J. (1995) *The beginnings of Rome: Italy and Rome from the bronze age to the Punic wars (c. 1000–264BC).* London

Courbaud, E. (1918) *Les procédés d'art de Tacite dans les Histoires.* Paris

Courtney, E. (1980) *A commentary on the satires of Juvenal.* London

Crawford, M. (1996) ed. *Roman statutes.* London

Crook, J. (1951) 'Titus and Berenice', *AJP* 72: 162–75
   (1955) *Consilium principis.* Cambridge
   (1973) 'Intestacy in Roman Society', *PCPS* 199: 38–44

Currie, H. MacL. (1989) 'An obituary formula in the historians (with a Platonic connection?)', *Latomus* 48: 346–53

Damon, C. (1997) *The brothers of Romulus: fraternal pietas in Roman law, literature and society.* Princeton, New Jersey
   (2003) ed. *Tacitus Histories I.* Cambridge
   (2006) '*Potior utroque Vespasianus*: Vespasian and his predecessors in Tacitus' *Histories*', *Arethusa* 39: 245–80

Davidson, J. (1991) 'The gaze in Polybius' *Histories*', *JRS* 81: 10–24

Davies, J. (2004) *Rome's religious history: Livy, Tacitus and Ammianus on their gods.* Cambridge

Develin, R. (1983) 'Tacitus and the techniques of insidious suggestion', *Antichthon* 17: 64–95

Dickey, E. (2002) *Latin forms of address from Plautus to Apuleius*. Oxford

Dobson, B. (1974) 'The significance of the centurion and *primipilaris* in the Roman army and administration', *ANRW* II 1: 392–434

Doerdelein, L. (1841) *Emendationes Historiarum Taciti*. Erlangen

Dorey, T. A. (1958) 'Tacitus' treatment of Antonius Primus', *CP* 53: 244

Downey, G. (1961) *A history of Antioch in Syria*. Princeton

Draeger, A. A. (1882) *Über Syntax und Stil des Tacitus*. 3rd edn. Leipzig

Drexler, H. (1959) 'Zur Geschichte Kaiser Othos bei Tacitus und Plutarch', *Klio* 37: 153–78

Dunbabin, K. M. D. (1986) '*Sic erimus cuncti* . . . The skeleton in the Graeco-Roman world', *JDAI* 101: 185–255

Edwards, C. (1993) *The politics of immorality in ancient Rome*. Cambridge

Elsner, J. (1994) 'Constructing decadence: the representation of Nero as imperial builder', in J. Elsner and J. Masters, eds. *Reflections of Nero* (London) 112–27

Emmett, A. (1981) 'Introductions and conclusions to digressions in Ammianus Marcellinus', *Museum Philologum Londiniense* 5: 15–33

Epplett, C. (2001) 'The capture of animals by the Roman military', *G&R* 48: 210–22

Epstein, D. (1987) *Personal enmity in Roman politics, 218–43 BC*. Beckenham, Kent

Evelyn-White, H. G., and J. H. Oliver (1938) *The temple of Hibis in the El-Khargeh oasis. Part 2: Greek inscriptions*. New York

Eyben, E. (1992) *Restless youth in ancient Rome*, trans. P. Daly. London

Fanetti, D. (1983) 'Esame statistico e interpretazione del tricolon in T.', *Annali della Facoltà di Lettere e Filosofia dell'Università di Siena* 4: 1–39

Fantham, E. (1972) *Comparative studies in republican Latin imagery*. Toronto
(1998) ed. *Ovid Fasti Book IV*. Cambridge

Farnell, L. R. (1977) *The cults of the Greek states*, vol. II. New Rochelle, New York

Feeney, D. (1998) *Literature and religion at Rome: cultures, contexts, and beliefs*. Cambridge

Feldherr, A. (1997) '*Caeci avaritia*: avarice, history and vision in Livy V', in C. Deroux, ed. *Studies in Latin literature and Roman history VIII* (Brussels) 268–77

Feldman, L. (1993) *Jew and gentile in the ancient world*. Princeton, New Jersey

Fenno, J. (2005) '"A great wave against the stream": water imagery in Iliadic battle scenes', *AJP* 126: 475–504

Ferlet, E. (1801) *Observations littéraires, critiques, politiques, militaires, géographiques sur les Histoires de Tacite*. Paris

Ferri, R. (2003) ed. *Octavia: a play attributed to Seneca*. Cambridge

Feugère, M. (2002) *Weapons of the Romans*, trans. D. G. Smith. Charleston, South Carolina

Fitzgerald, W. (2000) *Slavery and the Roman literary imagination*. Cambridge

Flaig, E. (1992) *Den Kaiser herausfordern: die Usurpation im römischen Reich*. Frankfurt am Main

Fletcher, G. B. A. (1940) 'Assonances or plays on words in Tacitus', *CR* 54: 184–7

Flower, H. (1995) '*Fabulae praetextae* in context. When were plays on contemporary subjects performed in republican Rome?', *CQ* 45: 170–90

(1996) *Ancestor masks and aristocratic power in Roman culture.* Oxford

Flower, M. and Marincola, J. (2002) eds. *Herodotus Book IX.* Cambridge

Freeman, P. M. W. (1994) 'Pompey's eastern settlement: a matter of presentation?', in C. Deroux, ed. *Studies in Latin literature and Roman history VII* (Brussels) 143–79

Freis, H. (1967) *Die cohortes urbanae* (Epigraphische Studien 2. Beihefte der Bonner Jahrbucher, 21). Cologne

Fuhrmann, M. (1960) 'Das Vierkaiserjahr bei Tacitus: über den Aufbau der Historien Buch I–III', *Philologus* 104: 250–77

Gallivan, P. A. (1973) 'The false Neros: a re-examination', *Historia* 22: 364–5

Gargola, D. J. (1990) 'The colonial commissioners of 218 BC and the foundation of Cremona and Placentia', *Athenaeum* 68: 465–73

Garnsey, P. (1970) *Social status and legal privilege in the Roman empire.* Oxford

Geiger, J. (1979) 'Munatius Rufus and Thrasea Paetus on Cato the Younger', *Athenaeum* 57: 48–72

Gibson, B. J. (1998) 'Rumours as causes of events in Tacitus', *MD* 40: 111–29

Gibson, R. (2002) 'Pliny and the art of (in)offensive self-praise', *Arethusa* 36: 235–54

(2003) ed. *Ovid Ars Amatoria Book 3.* Cambridge

Gilmartin, K. (1973) 'Corbulo's campaigns in the east: an analysis of Tacitus' account', *Historia* 22: 583–626

(1975) 'A rhetorical figure in Latin historical style: the imaginary second person singular', *TAPA* 105: 99–121

Gilmartin Wallace, K. (1987) 'The Flavii Sabini in Tacitus', *Historia* 36: 343–58

Ginsburg, J. (1981) *Tradition and theme in the Annals of Tacitus.* Salem, New Hampshire

(1993) '*In maiores certamina*: past and present in the *Annals* of Tacitus', 86–103 in T. Luce and A. J. Woodman, *Tacitus and the Tacitean tradition.* Princeton, New Jersey

Godolphin, F. R. B. (1935) 'The source of Plutarch's thesis in the Lives of Galba and Otho', *AJP* 56: 324–8

Goldsworthy, A. K. (1996) *The Roman army at war 100 BC–AD 200.* Oxford

Golvin, J.-C. (1988) *L'amphithéâtre romain.* Paris

Goodyear, F. R. D. (1968) 'Development of language and style in the *Annals* of Tacitus', *JRS* 58: 22–31

Görich, K. (1993) *Otto III. Romanus Saxonicus et Italicus.* Sigmaringen

Gould, J. (1973) 'Hiketeia', *JHS* 93: 74–103

Gowers, E. (1993) *The loaded table: representations of food in Roman literature.* Oxford

Grafton, A. T. and Swerdlow, N. M. (1988) 'Calendar dates and ominous days in ancient historiography', *JWI* 51: 14–42

Grainger, J. D. (1990) *The cities of Seleukid Syria.* Oxford

(2003) *Nerva and the Roman succession crisis of AD 96–99.* London

Gratwick, A. S. (1987) ed. *Terence: the brothers.* Warminster

Griffin, M. (1984) *Nero: the end of a dynasty*. London

(1986) 'Philosophy, Cato and Roman suicide II', *G&R* 38: 192–202

Guerrini, R. (1986) 'Tito al santuario Pafio e il ricordo di Enea (Tac. *Hist.* II, 4)', *Atene e Roma* 31: 28–34

Habinek, T. (2000) 'Seneca's renown: *gloria, claritudo*, and the replication of the Roman elite', *CA* 19: 264–303

Hadley, W. S. (1899) 'On Tac. *Hist.* ii.28. *fin.*', *CR* 13: 368

Hahn, E. (1933) *Die Excurse in den Annalen des Tacitus*. Leipzig

Halfmann, H. (1986) *Itinera principum: Geschichte und Typologie der Kaiserreisen im römischen Reich*. Stuttgart

Hansen, W. (2000) 'Foam-born Aphrodite and the mythology of transformation', *AJP* 121: 1–19

Hardie, P. R. (1986) *Virgil's Aeneid: cosmos and imperium*. Oxford

Hardy, E. G. (1890) *Plutarch's lives of Galba and Otho*. London

Harmand, J. (1967) *L'armée et le soldat à Rome de 107 à 50 avant nôtre ère*. Paris

Harris, B. F. (1962) 'Tacitus on the Death of Otho', *CJ* 58: 73–7

Harris, W. V. (2001) *Restraining anger: the ideology of anger control in classical antiquity*. Cambridge, Mass

Harrison, S. J. (1991) *Vergil Aeneid 10*. Oxford

Hassall, M. (1970) 'Batavians and the conquest of Roman Britain', *Britannia* 1: 131–6

Hayes, K. J. (2000) *Edgar Allan Poe and the printed word*. Cambridge

Haynes, H. (2003) *The history of make-believe: Tacitus on imperial Rome*. Berkeley, Los Angeles, London

Heilig, K. J. (1935) 'Ein Beitrag zur Geschichte des Mediceus II', *Wiener Studien* 53: 95–110

Henderson, J. (1998) *Fighting for Rome: poets, Caesars and civil war*. Cambridge

(2001) *Telling tales on Caesar: Roman stories from Phaedrus*. Oxford

Herzog, P. H. (1996) *Die Funktion des militärischen Planens bei Tacitus*. Frankfurt am Main

Heubner, H. (1955) 'Tacitea I', *Gymnasium* 62: 100–108

Hill, G. F. (1904) *Catalogue of the Greek coins of Cyprus*. London

Holum, K. G., Hohlfelder, R. L., Bull, R. J., and Raban, A. (1988) *King Herod's dream: Caesarea on the sea*. New York and London

Hornblower, S. (1991) *A commentary on Thucydides*, vol. 1. Oxford

Horsfall, N. (2000) ed. *Virgil Aeneid 7: a commentary*. Leiden

(2003a) *The culture of the Roman plebs*. London

(2003b) ed. *Virgil Aeneid 11: a commentary*. Leiden

Houston, G. W. (1972) 'M. Plancius Varus and the events of AD 69–70', *TAPA* 103: 167–80

Hurley, D. W. (2001) ed. *Suetonius Diuus Claudius*. Cambridge

Hutchinson, G. O. (1993) *Latin literature from Seneca to Juvenal*. Oxford

Hyland, A. (1990) *Equus: the horse in the Roman world*. New Haven and London

Ihm, M. (1978) ed. *Suetonius: De vita Caesarum libri*. Stuttgart

Jones, B. W. (1984) *The emperor Titus*. London and Sydney

(1992) 'The reckless Titus', in C. Deroux, ed. *Studies in Latin literature and Roman history VI* (Brussels) 408–20

(1996) *Domitian*. Bristol

(2000) *Suetonius Vespasian*. Bristol

Kahn, R. (1999) *A flame of pure fire: Jack Dempsey and the roaring '20s*. New York, San Diego, London

Keaveney, A. and Madden, J. (2003) 'Berenice at Rome', *Museum Helveticum* 60: 39–43

Keitel, E. (1984) 'Principate and civil war in the *Annals* of Tacitus', *AJP* 105: 306–25

(1987) 'Otho's exhortations in Tacitus' *Histories*', *G&R* 34: 73–82

(1991) 'The structure and function of speeches in Tacitus' *Histories* I–III', *ANRW* II 33.4: 2772–94

(1992) '*Foedum Spectaculum* and related motifs in *Histories* 2–3', *Rheinisches Museum* 135: 342–51

(1995) 'Plutarch's tragedy tyrants: Galba and Otho', *PLLS* 8: 275–88

(2006) '*Sententia* and structure in Tacitus *Histories* 1.12–49', *Arethusa* 39: 219–44

Keith, A. L. (1923–4) 'The taunt in Homer and Virgil', *CJ* 19: 554–60

Kenney, E. J. (1990) ed. *Apuleius: Cupid and Psyche*. Cambridge

Keppie, L. (1984) *The making of the Roman army*. London

(1986) 'Legions in the east from Augustus to Trajan', in P. Freeman and D. Kennedy, eds. *The defence of the Roman and Byzantine east* (Oxford) 411–29 (= 182–200 in L. Keppie, *Legions and veterans: Roman army papers*. Stuttgart)

(2000) *Legions and veterans: Roman army papers 1971–2000*. Stuttgart

Kern, P. B. (1999) *Ancient siege warfare*. Bloomington and Indianopolis

Kirchner, R. (2001) *Sentenzen im Werk des Tacitus*. Stuttgart

Klingner, F. (1940) 'Die Geschichte Kaiser Othos bei Tacitus', *Sächsische Sitzungsberichte*. Leipzig

Koestermann, E. (1961) 'Die erste Schlacht bei Bedriacum 69 n. Chr.', *RCCM* 3: 16–29

Köhne, E. and Ewigleben, C. (2000) *The power of spectacle in Rome: gladiators and Caesars*. London

Kondoleon, C. (2000) *Antioch: the lost city*. Princeton, New Jersey

Konstan, D. (1985) 'Narrative and ideology in Livy Book 1', *CA* 5: 199–215

Kraus, C. S. (1992) 'How (not?) to end a sentence? The problem of *-que*', *HSCP* 94: 321–9

(1994) ed. *Livy Ab Vrbe Condita VI*. Cambridge

Kraus, C. S. and Woodman, A. J. (1997) *Latin historians*. Oxford

Kremer, B. (1994) *Das Bild der Kelten bis in augusteische Zeit* (Historia Einzelschriften 88). Stuttgart

Kroll, W. (1927) 'Die Sprache des Sallust', *Glotta* 15: 280–305

Kuntz, F. (1962) *Die Sprache des Tacitus und die Tradition der lateinischen Historikersprache*. Diss. Heidelberg

Laird, A. (1999) *Powers of expression, expressions of power: speech presentation in Latin literature.* Oxford

Lateiner, D. (1995) *Sardonic smile: nonverbal behavior in Homeric epic.* Ann Arbor, Michigan

Lattimore, R. (1939) 'The wise advisor in Herodotus', *CP* 34: 24–35

Laurence, R. (1994) 'Rumour and communication in Roman politics', *G&R* 41: 62–74

Lausberg, H. (1998) *A handbook of literary rhetoric: a foundation for literary study*, trans. M. T. Bliss, A. Jansen, D. E. Orton. Leiden, Boston, Cologne

Lebreton, J. (1901) *Études sur la langue et la grammaire de Cicéron.* Paris

Leigh, M. (1997) *Lucan: spectacle and engagement.* Oxford

Lejay, P. (1911) *Oeuvres d'Horace: Satires.* Paris

Lendon, J. E. (1997) *Empire of honour: the art of government in the Roman world.* Oxford

Levene, D. S. (1993) *Religion in Livy.* Leiden
  (1997) 'Pity, fear and the historical audience: Tacitus on the fall of Vitellius', in S. Morton Braund and C. Gill, eds. *The passions in Roman thought and literature* (Cambridge) 128–49
  (1999) 'Tacitus' *Histories* and the theory of deliberative oratory', in C. S. Kraus, ed. *The limits of historiography: genre and narrative in ancient historical texts* (Leiden) 197–216

Levick, B. (1976) *Tiberius.* London, Sydney, and Dover, New Hampshire
  (1983) 'The *senatus consultum* from Larinum', *JRS* 73: 97–115
  (1985) 'L. Verginius Rufus and the year of the four emperors', *Rh. Mus.* 128: 318–46
  (1990) *Claudius.* London and New Haven
  (1999) *Vespasian.* London and New York

Lintott, A. (1993) *Imperium Romanum: politics and administration.* London

Long, A. A. and Sedley, D. N. (1987) *The Hellenistic Philosophers: Volume One.* Cambridge

Lowe, E. A. (1929) *The unique MS of Tacitus' Histories (Florence Laur. 68.2).* Montecassino
  (1980) *The Beneventan script: a history of the south Italian minuscule.* Rome. Second edition revised by V. Brown

Lowe, N. J. (2000) *The classical plot and the invention of western narrative.* Cambridge

Madvig, J. N. (1884) *Aduersaria critica ad scriptores Graecos et Latinos III.* Copenhagen

Malcovati, H. (1953) *Oratorum Romanorum fragmenta.* Turin

Mankin, D. (1995) ed. *Horace: Epodes.* Cambridge

Manolaraki, E. (2005) 'A picture worth a thousand words: revisiting Bedriacum (Tacitus *Histories* 2.70)', *CP* 100: 243–67

Marincola, J. (1997) *Authority and tradition in ancient historiography.* Cambridge
  (1999) 'Tacitus' prefaces and the decline of imperial historiography', *Latomus* 58: 391–404

Marsden, E. W. (1969) *Greek and Roman artillery: historical development.* Oxford
  (1971) *Greek and Roman artillery: technical treatises.* Oxford

Marshall, A. J. (1984) 'Symbols and showmanship in Roman public life: the *fasces*', *Phoenix* 30:120–41

Martin, R. H. (1946) '*-ere* and *–erunt* in Tacitus', *CR* 60: 17–19
  (1951) 'Caecina's meeting with Bassus', *Eranos* 49: 174–6

(1953) '*Variatio* and the development of Tacitus' style', *Eranos* 51: 89–96

(1968) '*Quibus* and *Quis* in Tacitus', *CR* 82: 144–6

(1981) *Tacitus*. London

(2001) ed. *Tacitus Annals V and VI*. Warminster

Matthews, V. J. (1996) *Antimachus of Colophon: text and commentary*. Leiden

Mattingly, H. (1923) *Coins of the Roman empire in the British Museum*. Volume One. London

Mayer, R. (1991) 'Roman historical *exempla* in Seneca', in *Sénèque et la prose latine* (Fondation Hardt pour l'étude de l'antiquité classique. Entretiens 36, Geneva) 141–76

(1994) ed. *Horace Epistles Book I*. Cambridge

(2001) ed. *Tacitus Dialogus de Oratoribus*. Cambridge

Mayor, J. E. B. (1872) ed. *Thirteen Satires of Juvenal with a commentary*. London

McGillicuddy, S. P. (1991) 'Self and other in the *Histories* of Tacitus'. Doctoral thesis, Ohio State University

McGushin, P. (1992) ed. *Sallust: The Histories*, vol. I. Oxford

(1994) ed. *Sallust: The Histories*, vol. II. Oxford

McNeil, D. (1990) *The grotesque depiction of war and the military in eighteenth century English fiction*. London and Toronto

Meer, L. B. van der (1987) *The bronze liver of Piacenza*. Amsterdam

Millar, F. (1977) *The emperor in the Roman world (31 BC–AD 337)*. London

(1990) 'The Roman *coloniae* of the near east: a study of cultural relations', in H. Solin and M. Kajava, eds. *Roman eastern policy and other studies in Roman history* (Helsinki) 7–58

(1993) *The Roman Near East: 31 BC to AD 337*. London

Miller, N. P. and Jones, P. V. (1978) 'Critical appreciations III: Tacitus *Histories* 3.38–9', *G&R* 25: 70–80

Milns, R. D. (1973) 'The career of M. Aponius Saturninus', *Historia* 22:284–94

Mitchell, S. (1974) 'The Plancii in Asia Minor', *JRS*: 27–39

Mitford, T. B. (1980a) 'Roman Cyprus', *ANRW* II 7.2: 1285–1384

(1980b) 'Cappadocia and Armenia Minor: historical setting of the *limes*' *ANRW* II 7.2: 1169–1228

(1990) 'The cults of Roman Cyprus', *ANRW* II 18.3: 2176–211

Moles, J. L. (1988) ed. *Plutarch: the life of Cicero*. Warminster, Wiltshire

Mommsen, T. (1871) 'Die zwei schlachten von Betriacum i. J. 69 n. Chr.', *Hermes* 5: 161–73

(1887–8) *Römische Staatsrecht II*, 3rd edn. Leipzig

Mooney, G. W. (1930) ed. *C. Suetoni Tranquilli de vita Caesarum libri VII–VIII*. London, New York, Toronto

Morello, R. (2006) 'A correspondence course in tyranny: the *cruentae litterae* of Tiberius', *Arethusa* 39: 331–54

Morgan, M. Gwyn (1991) 'An heir of tragedy: Tacitus *Histories* 2.59.3', *CP* 86: 138–43

(1992) 'The smell of victory: Vitellius at Bedriacum (Tac. *Hist.* 2.70)', *CP* 87: 14–29

(1993a) 'The three minor pretenders in Tacitus *Histories* II', *Latomus* 52: 769–96

(1993b) 'Two omens in Tacitus' *Histories* (2.50.2 and 1.62.2–3)', *Rh. Mus.* 136: 321–9

(1994a) 'Rogues' march: Caecina and Valens in Tacitus, *Histories* 1.61–70', *MH* 51: 103–25

(1994b) 'Vespasian's fears of assassination: Tacitus *Histories* 2.74–75', *Philologus* 138: 118–28

(1994c) 'Tacitus *Histories* 2.83–4: content and positioning', *CP* 89: 166–75

(1994–5) 'Tacitus *Histories* 2.14.2', *Würzburger Jahrbücher für Altertumswissenschaft* 20: 225–31

(1995a) 'Tacitus, *Histories* 2.7.1', *Hermes* 123: 335–40

(1995b) 'Tacitus, *Histories* 2.68.1', *Mnemosyne* 48: 576–9

(1996a) 'Cremona in AD 69. Two notes on Tacitus' narrative techniques', *Athenaeum* 84: 381–403

(1996b) 'Recriminations after *Ad Castores*: Tacitus, *Histories* 2.30', *CP* 91: 359–64

(1996c) 'Vespasian and the omens in Tacitus *Histories* 2.78', *Phoenix* 50: 41–55

(1997) 'Caecina's assault on Placentia: Tacitus *Histories* 2.20.2–22.3', *Philologus* 141: 338–61

(2000) 'Omens in Tacitus' *Histories* 1–3', in R. L. Wildfang and J. Isager, *Divination and portents in the Roman world* (Odense) 25–42

(2004) 'Tacitus *Histories* 2.4.4 and Mucianus' legion in 69', *MH* 61: 129–38

(2005) 'Martius Macer's raid and its consequences: Tacitus, *Histories* 2.23', *CQ* 55: 572–81

(2006) *69 AD. The year of the four emperors*. Oxford

Most, G. (1992) '*Disiecti membra poetae*: the rhetoric of dismemberment in Neronian poetry', in D. Hexter and R. Selden, eds. *Innovations of antiquity* (New York and London) 391–419

Murison, C. L. (1979) 'Some Vitellian dates: an exercise in methodology', *TAPA* 109: 187–97

(1991) 'The historical value of Tacitus' *Histories*', *ANRW* II 33.3: 1686–1713

(1993) *Galba, Otho and Vitellius: careers and controversies*. Zurich and New York

Nerandeau, J.-P. (1979) *La jeunesse dans la littérature et les institutions de la Rome Républicaine.* Paris

Newbold, R. F. (1976) 'The *uulgus* in Tacitus', *RhM* 119: 85–92

Newlands, C. (2002) *Statius' Siluae and the poetics of empire*. Cambridge

Nicolet, C. (1991) *Space, geography, and politics in the early Roman empire*. Ann Arbor

Nicols, J. (1978) *Vespasian and the Partes Flauianae* (Historia Einzelschriften 28). Wiesbaden

Nippel, W. (1995) *Public order in ancient Rome*. Cambridge

Nisbet, R. G. M. (1991) 'How textual conjectures are made', *MD* 26: 65–91

Nisbet, R. G. M. and Hubbard, M. (1970) *A commentary on Horace Odes book 1*. Oxford

(1978) *A commentary on Horace Odes book II*. Oxford

North, J. (1990) 'Diviners and divination at Rome', in M. Beard and J. North eds. *Pagan priests: religion and power in the ancient world* (London) 51–71

(2000) *Roman religion. Greece and Rome New Surveys in the Classics* 30. Oxford

Nutting, H. C. (1928) 'Tacitus, *Histories* I. 13', *CQ* 22: 172–5

Oakley, S. P. (1985) 'Single combat in the Roman republic', *CQ* 35: 392–410

(1997) *A commentary on Livy books VI–X*, vol. I. Oxford

(1998) *A commentary on Livy books VI–X*, vol. II. Oxford

(2005) *A commentary on Livy books VI–X*, vol. III. Oxford

Ogilvie, R. M. and Richmond, I. A. R. (1967) *Cornelii Taciti de uita Agricolae.* Oxford

Ogilvie, R. M. (1970) *A commentary on Livy books 1–5*, rev. edn. Oxford

O'Gorman, E. (2000) *Irony and misreading in the Annals of Tacitus.* Cambridge

(2006) 'Alternative empires: Tacitus' virtual history of the Pisonian principate', *Arethusa* 39: 281–302

Oliver, R. P. (1976) 'The second Medicean MS', *ICS* 1: 190–225

Opelt, I. (1965) *Die lateinischen Schimpfwörter und verwandte sprachliche Erscheinungen.* Heidelberg

Orwell, G. (1949) *Nineteen eighty-four.* London

Pagán, V. (2000) 'The mourning after: Statius *Thebaid* 12', *AJP* 121: 423–52

(2006) 'Shadows and assassinations: forms of time in Tacitus and Appian', *Arethusa* 39: 193–218

Pagliani, M. L. (1991) *Piacenza.* Rome

Panciera, S. (1956) '*Liburna*: rassegna delle fonti, caratteristiche della naue, accezioni del termine', *Epigraphica* (Rome) 18: 130–56

Parker, H. N. (1992) 'The fertile fields of Umbria: Propertius 1.22.10', *Mnemosyne* 45: 88–92

Passerini (1940) 'Le due battiglie presso Betriacum', in *Studi di antichità offerti a Emmanuele Ciaceri* (Genoa, Rome and Naples) 178–248

Paul, G. M. (1982) '*Urbs capta*: sketch of an ancient literary motif', *Phoenix* 36: 144–55

(1984) *A historical commentary on Sallust's Bellum Jugurthinum.* Trowbridge, Wiltshire

(1993) 'The presentation of Titus in the *Jewish War* of Josephus. Two aspects', *Phoenix* 47: 56–66

Pauw, D. A. (1980) 'Impersonal expressions and unidentified spokesmen in Greek and Roman historiography', *Acta Classica* 23: 83–95

Pearce, T. E. V. (1970) 'Notes on Cicero *in Pisonem*', *CQ* 20: 309–21

Pease, A. S. (1967) ed. *Publi Vergili Maronis Aeneidos Liber Quartus.* Darmstadt

Pelling, C. B. R. (1988) ed. *Plutarch: Life of Antony.* Cambridge

Peretz, D. (2005) 'Military burial and the identification of the Roman fallen soldiers', *Klio* 87: 123–38

Perkins, C. A. (1993) 'Tacitus on Otho', *Latomus* 52: 848–55

Petzke, P. (1888) *Dicendi genus Tacitinum quatenus differat a Liviano.* Berlin

Phang, S. E. (2001) *The marriage of Roman soldiers (13 BC–AD 235): law and family in the imperial army.* Leiden

Pflaum, H.-G. (1960) *Les carrières procuratoriennes équestres sous le haut-empire romain*, vol. I. Paris

Pinkster, H. (1992) 'The Latin impersonal passive', *Mnemosyne* 45: 159–77

Pirenne-Delforge, V. (1994) *L'Aphrodite grecque*, *Kernos* supplement 4. Athens and Liége

Plass, P. (1988) *Wit and the writing of history*. Madison, Wisconsin

(1992) 'Variatio in Tacitus', in C. Deroux, ed. *Studies in Latin literature and Roman history VI* (Brussels) 421–34

(1995) *The game of death in ancient Rome: arena sport and political suicide*. Madison, Wisconsin

Poliakoff, M. (1987) *Combat sports in the ancient world: competition, violence and culture*. Yale

Pomeroy, A. (1991) *The appropriate comment: death notices in the ancient historians* (Studien zur klassischen Philologie 58). Frankfurt am Main, Bern, New York, Paris

(2003) 'Center and periphery in Tacitus' *Histories*', *Arethusa* 36: 361–74

Powell, A. (1972) '*Deum ira, hominum rabies*', *Latomus* 31: 833–48

(1998) 'Julius Caesar and the presentation of massacre', in K. Welch and A. Powell, eds. *Julius Caesar as artful reporter: the war commentaries as political instruments* (London and Swansea) 111–37

Powell, J. G. F. (1988) ed. *Cicero: Cato Maior de senectute*. Cambridge

Pritchett, W.K. (1971–). *The Greek state at war*, 5 vols. Berkeley

Purcell, N. (1995) 'On the sacking of Carthage and Corinth', in D. Innes, H. Hine and C. B. R. Pelling, eds. *Ethics and rhetoric: Classical essays for Donald Russell on his seventy-fifth birthday* (Oxford) 133–48

Rajak, T. (1983) *Josephus: the historian and his society*. London

Ramage, E. S. (1973) *Urbanitas: ancient sophistication and refinement*. Norman, Oklahoma

(1983), 'Denigration of predecessor under Claudius, Galba and Vespasian', *Historia* 32: 201–14

Ramsey, J. T. (2003) ed. *Cicero: Philippics I–II*. Cambridge

Rawlings, L. (1998) 'Caesar's portrayal of Gauls as warriors', in K. Welch and A. Powell, eds. *Julius Caesar as artful reporter: The war commentaries as political instruments* (London and Swansea) 171–92

Reynolds, L. D., and Wilson, N. G. (1991) *Scribes and scholars: a guide to the transmission of Greek and Latin literature*, 3rd edn. Oxford

Ribichini, S. (1981) *Adonis: Aspetti orientali di un mito greco*. Rome

Rist, J. M. (1969) *Stoic philosophy*. Cambridge

Rives, J. B. (1999) *Tacitus Germania*. Oxford

Rivet, A. L. F. (1988) *Gallia Narbonensis*. London

Roby, H. J. (1879) *A grammar of the Latin language*, 2 vols. London

Rogers, P. M. (1980) 'Titus, Berenice and Mucianus', *Historia* 29: 86–95

Roisman, H. (2005) 'Nestor the good counsellor', *CQ* 55: 17–38

Roller, M. (2001) *Constructing autocracy: aristocrats and emperors in Julio-Claudian Rome*. Princeton, New Jersey

Rougé, J. (1952) 'La navigation hivernale sous l'Empire romain', *REA* 54: 316–25

(1981) *Ships and fleets of the ancient Mediterranean*. Middletown, Connecticut

Rowland, A. J. (1974) 'Sardinians in the Roman empire', *AS* 5: 223–9

Ryberg, I. S. (1942) 'Tacitus' art of innuendo', *TAPA* 73: 383–404

Saddington, D. B. (1982) *The development of Roman auxiliary forces from Caesar to Vespasian.* Harare

Sage, M. (1990) 'Tacitus' historical works: a survey and appraisal', *ANRW* II 33.2: 851–1030

Sallares, R. (1991) *The ecology of the ancient Greek world.* London

Schäfer, P. (1997) *Judeophobia. Attitudes towards the Jews in the Ancient World.* Cambridge Mass. and London

Scheid, J. (1978) 'Les prêtres officiels sous les empereurs julio-claudiens', *ANRW* II 16.1: 610–54

Scheidel, W. (1996) 'Finances, figures and fiction', *CQ* 46: 222–38

Schmidt, M. G. (1995) 'Othos letztes Geldgeschenk', *Philologus* 139: 163–6

Schunk, P. (1964) 'Studien zur Darstellung des Endes von Galba, Otho und Vitellius in den Historien des Tacitus', *SO* 39: 38–82

Schwinge, E.-R. (1970) 'Die Schlacht bei Bedriacum', in M. von Albrecht and E. Heck, eds. *Silvae* (Tübingen) 217–32

Scott, J. M. (1998) 'The rhetoric of suppressed speech: Tacitus' omission of direct discourse in his *Annals* as a technique of character denigration', *AHB* 12: 8–18

Scott, K. (1933) 'The political propaganda of 44–30 BC', *MAAR* 11: 7–49
   (1934) 'The role of Basilides in the events of AD 69', *JRS* 34: 138–40

Scott, R. T. (1968) *Religion and philosophy in the Histories of Tacitus.* Rome

Scullard, H. H. (1981) *Festivals and ceremonies of the Roman republic.* London

Seaford, R. A. S. (1984) 'The last bath of Agamemnon', *CQ* 34: 247–54

Segal, A. (1995) *Theatres in Roman Palestine and Prouincia Arabia.* Leiden

Shatzman, I. (1974) 'Tacitean Rumours', *Latomus* 33: 549–78

Sherk, R. (1980) 'Roman Galatia: the governors from 25 BC to AD 114', *ANRW* II 7.2: 954–1052
   (1988) *Translated documents of Greece and Rome, vol. 6. The Roman Empire, Augustus to Hadrian.* Cambridge

Shochat, Y. (1981) 'Tacitus' attitude to Otho', *Latomus* 40: 365–77

Shotter, D. C. A. (1968) 'A note on Tacitus *Hist.* 2.7.1', *CP* 63: 287
   (1975) 'A time-table for the *bellum Neronis*', *Historia* 24: 59–74
   (1977) 'Tacitus and Antonius Primus', *LCM* 2: 23–7
   (1993) *Suetonius: The lives of Galba, Otho, Vitellius.* Warminster

Shumate, N. (1997) 'Compulsory pretense and the "theatricalisation of experience" in Tacitus', in C. Deroux, ed. *Studies in Latin literature and Roman history VIII* (Brussels) 364–403

Sinclair, P. (1995) *Tacitus the sententious historian.* University Park, Pennsylvania

Skutsch, O. (1985) ed. *The Annals of Q. Ennius.* Oxford

Solodow, J. (1978) *The Latin particle quidem.* University Park, Pennsylvania

Sontag, S. (1978) *Illness as metaphor.* Harmondsworth

Sörbom, G. (1935) *Variatio sermonis Tacitei aliaeque apud eundem quaestiones selectae.* Uppsala

Spaeth, B. S. (1996) *The Roman goddess Ceres.* Austin, Texas

Speidel, M. P. (1984) *Roman army studies: Volume One.* Amsterdam

(1991) 'Swimming the Danube under Hadrian's eyes: a feat of the emperor's Bata-
   vian horseguard', *AS* 22: 277–82
Starr, C. G. (1975) *The Roman imperial navy 31 BC–AD 324*. Westport, Connecticut
Starr, R. J. (1981) 'Cross-references in Roman prose', *AJP* 102: 431–7
Stegner, K. (2004) *Die Verwendung der Sentenz in den Historien des Tacitus*. Stuttgart
Stolte, B. H. (1973) 'Tacitus on Nero and Otho', *AS* 4: 177–90
Sullivan, D. (1975/6) 'Innuendo and the "weighted alternative" in Tacitus', *CJ* 71:
   312–26
Sullivan, R. D. (1977a) 'The dynasty of Emesa', *ANRW* II 8: 198–219
   (1977b) 'The dynasty of Commagene', *ANRW* II 8: 732–98
   (1977c) 'The dynasty of Judaea in the first century', *ANRW* II 8: 296–354
Sussman, L. (1978) *The elder Seneca*. Leiden
Sutherland, C. H. V. (1987) *Roman history and coinage 44 BC–AD 69*. Oxford
Sutherland, C. H. V. and Carson, R. A. G. (1984) *The Roman imperial coinage*, vol. I, rev.
   edn. London
Syme, R. (1937a) 'Pamphylia from Augustus to Vespasian', *Klio* 30: 227–31 (= E.
   Badian ed. *Roman Papers I*, 42–6. Oxford)
   (1937b) 'The colony of Cornelius Fuscus: an episode in the *bellum Neronis*', *AJP* 58:
      7–18
   (1957) 'The friend of Tacitus', *JRS* 47: 131–5
   (1958a) *Tacitus*. Oxford
   (1958b) '*Imperator Caesar*: a study in nomenclature', *Historia* 7: 172–88
   (1960) 'Piso Frugi and Crassus Frugi', *JRS* 50: 12–20
   (1970) 'Domitius Corbulo', *JRS* 60: 27–39
   (1975) 'Notes on Tacitus, *Histories* iii', *Antichthon* 9: 61–7
   (1977) 'The march of Mucianus', *Antichthon* 9: 78–92 (= A. R. Birley (1984) ed.
      Roman Papers III, 998–1013. Oxford)
   (1991a) 'Vestricius Spurinna', 541–50 (= A. R. Birley (ed.), *Roman Papers VII*, 541–50.
      Oxford)
   (1991b) 'Ministers of the Caesars', 521–40 in *Roman Papers VII*. Oxford
Talbert, R. J. A. (1984) *The senate of imperial Rome*. Princeton, New Jersey
Tarrant, R. J. (1983) 'Tacitus', in L. D. Reynolds, ed. *Texts and transmissions: a survey of
   the Latin classics* (Oxford) 407–9
Thulin, C. O. (1906–9) *Die etruskische Disciplin*. Göteborg
Townend, G. B. (1961) 'Some Flavian connections', *JRS* 51: 54–62
   (1962a) 'Claudius and the digressions in Tacitus', *RhM* 105: 358–68
   (1962b) 'The consuls of AD 69/70', *AJP* 83: 113–29
   (1964) 'Cluvius Rufus and the *Histories* of Tacitus', *AJP* 85: 337–77
Treu, M. (1948) 'M. Antonius Primus in der taciteischen Darstellung', *WJA* 3: 241–
   62
Tuplin, C. J. (1989) 'The false Neros of the first century AD', in C. Deroux, ed. *Studies
   in Latin literature and Roman history V* (Brussels) 364–404
Turner, E. G. (1954) 'Tiberius Iulius Alexander', *JRS* 44: 54–64

Urban, R. (1971) *Historische Untersuchungen zum Domitianbild des Tacitus*. Munich

(1985) *Der 'Bataveraufstand' und die Erhebung des Iulius Classicus*. Trier

Versnel, H. S. (1980) 'Destruction, *deuotio* and despair in a situation of anomy: the mourning for Germanicus in triple perspective', in *Perennitas: studi in onore di Angelo Brelich* (Rome) 541–818

Veyne, P. (1990) *Bread and circuses: historical sociology and political pluralism*, trans. B. Pearce. London

Vout, C. (1996) 'The myth of the toga: understanding the history of Roman dress', *G&R* 43: 204–20

Walker, A. D. (1993) '*Enargeia* and the spectator in Greek historiography', *TAPA* 123: 353–77

Wallace-Hadrill, A. (1982) '*Ciuilis princeps*: between citizen and king', *JRS* 72: 32–48

Walser, G. (1951) *Rom, das Reich und die fremden Völker*. Basel

Walsh, P. G. (1961) *Livy, his historical aims and methods*. Cambridge

Wanscher, O. (1960) *Sella curulis*. Copenhagen

Wardle, D. (1996) 'Vespasian, Helvidius Priscus and the restoration of the Capitol', *Historia* 45: 208–22

Watson, A. (1987) *Roman slave law*. Baltimore and London

(1992) *The state, law and religion*. Athens and London

Watson, L. and Watson, P. (2003) eds. *Martial select epigrams*. Cambridge

Webster, G. (1985) *The Roman imperial army of the first and second centuries AD*, 3rd edn. Totowa, New Jersey

Weinstock, S. (1971) *Divus Iulius*. Oxford

Welch, K. (1995) 'Antony, Fulvia and the ghost of Clodius in 47 BC', *G&R* 42: 182–201

(1998) 'Caesar and his officers in the Gallic War commentaries', in K. Welch and A. Powell, eds. *Julius Caesar as artful reporter: The war commentaries as political instruments* (London and Swansea) 85–110

Wellesley, K. (1960) '*Suggestio falsi* in Tacitus', *RhM* 103: 272–88

(1971) 'A major crux in Tacitus: *Histories* II 40', *JRS* 61: 28–51

(1973) 'Tacitus *Histories* ii. 28. 2', *CR* 87: 6–7

(1991) 'Tacitus, *Histories*: A textual survey, 1939–1989', *ANRW* II 33.3: 1651–85

(2000) *The year of the four emperors*, 3rd edn. London and New York

West, M. L. (1966) ed. *Hesiod: Theogony*. Oxford

(1973) *Textual criticism and editorial technique*. Stuttgart

(1997) *The east face of Helicon: West Asiatic elements in Greek poetry and myth*. Oxford

Wheeler, E. L. (1988) *Stratagem and the vocabulary of military trickery*. Leiden, New York, Copenhagen, Cologne

(1996) 'The laxity of the Syrian legions', in D. Kennedy, ed. *The Roman army in the east* (Ann Arbor, Michigan) 229–76

Whitehead, D. (1979) 'Tacitus and the loaded alternative', *Latomus* 38: 474–95

(1990) *Aineias the tactician: How to survive under siege*. Oxford

Whitmarsh, T. (2001) *Greek literature and the Roman empire: the politics of imitation*. Oxford

Wiedemann, T. (1992) *Emperors and gladiators*. London

Wightman, E. M. (1970) *Roman Trier and the Treueri*. London

Wilkes, J. (1969) *Dalmatia*. London

(1992) *The Illyrians*. Oxford

Williams, H. (1985) 'Figureheads on Greek and Roman ships', in H. Tzalas, ed.
First international symposium on ship construction in antiquity, Hellenic Institute for the
Preservation of the Nautical Tradition (Piraeus) 293–7

Williams, C. K., II (1993) 'Roman Corinth as a commercial centre' in T. Gregory, ed.
The Corinthia in the Roman period, *JRA* suppl. 8: 31–46

Williams, J. H. C. (2001) *Beyond the Rubicon: Romans and Gauls in Republican Italy*. Oxford

Wills, J. (1996) *Repetition in Latin poetry: figures of allusion*. Oxford

Winterbottom, M. (1995) 'On impulse', in D. Innes, H. Hine and C. Pelling, eds.
Ethics and rhetoric: Classical essays for Donald Russell on his seventy-fifth birthday (Oxford)
313–22

Wiseman, J. (1979) 'Corinth and Rome I: 228 BC-AD 267', *ANRW* II 7.1: 438–548

Wiseman, T. P. (1998) *Roman drama and Roman history*. Exeter

(2004) *The myths of Rome*. Exeter

Woodcock, E. C. (1959) *A new Latin syntax*. London

Woodman, A. J. (1977) ed. *Velleius Paterculus: the Tiberian narrative (2.94–131)*. Cambridge

(1983) ed. *Velleius Paterculus: the Caesarian and Augustan narrative (2.41–93)*. Cambridge

(1988) *Rhetoric in classical historiography: four studies*. London and Sydney

(1989) 'Tacitus' obituary of Tiberius', *CQ* 39: 197–205 (= Woodman (1998) 155–67)

(1992) 'The preface to Tacitus' *Annals*: More Sallust?', *CQ* 42: 567–8 (= Woodman
(1998) 21–2)

(1998) *Tacitus Reviewed*. Oxford

(2003) 'Poems to historians: Catullus 1 and Horace, *Odes* 2.1', in D. Braund and C.
Gill, eds. *Myth, history and culture in republican Rome: Studies in honour of T. P. Wiseman*
(Exeter) 191–216

(2006) 'Mutiny and madness: Tacitus, *Annals* 1.16–49', *Arethusa* 39: 303–30

Woods, D. (2006) 'Tacitus, Nero and the "pirate" Anicetus', *Latomus* 65: 641–9

Woolf, G. (1993) 'Roman peace' in J. Rich and G. Shipley, eds. *War and society in the
Roman world* (London and New York) 171–94

Würm, E. (1853) 'Emendationes in Taciti Annalibus et Historibus', *Philologus* 8: 361–70

Yavetz, Z. (1969) 'Vitellius and the fickleness of the mob', *Historia* 18: 557–69

(1987) 'The urban plebs in the days of the Flavians, Nerva and Trajan' in A.
Giovannini, ed. *Opposition et résistances à l'empire d'Auguste à Trajan, Entretiens Hardt*
33: 135–86

Zelzer, M. (1973) 'Zur Vorlage des Tacitus-Codex 68.2', *Wiener Studien* 7: 185–95

Ziegler, K. (1973) ed. *Plutarchus Vitae Parallelae III.2*. Leipzig

INDEXES

1. GENERAL INDEX

2. LATIN WORDS

Every appearance of a word in *H.* 2 is listed, except items marked by an asterisk, where the reference is to particular discussion in the commentary; if a word appears only once in T., this is noted in brackets.

abdo 13.2; (+ per) 92.3
abunde 95.3 (hapax in T.)
accedo 4.2, 27.2, 33.1, 43.2, 69.1, 81.1, 86.1, 99.2; + dat. 69.1
accendo 2.1, 43.1, 68.2, 77.3, 80.3
accinctus 88.2, 89.1
adhaereo 25.2
adigo 14.1, 55.1, 73, 79, 80.2, 83.2
adolesco 38.1, 73
adulatio 30.2, 33.1, 46.1, 57.2, 80.2, 87.2, 90.2
aemulatio 4.4, 11.3, 21.2, 30.3, 49.4, 91.3, 101.1
aemulor 68.1, 81.3; (+ acc. + inf.) 62.2
aequalitas 38.1
aequalius 27.1 (adv. hapax in T.)
aeuum 22.1
affingo 4.1
aggrego 66.2, 72.2, 87.2, 96.1
agito 1.3
ala 4.4, 11.2, 14.1, 17.1, 22.3, 28.1, 58.1, 76.4, 89.1, 100.3
alacer 39.1, 80.2
alaris (substantive) 94.1
ales 50.2
alienatio 60.1
alienus (a) 16.2, 18.2, 34.1, 39.1, 56.2, 63.2 (b) 22.1, 74.1
alioquin 27.2
alluo 81.2
ambiguus 7.2, 39.1, 45.2, 53.1, 83.2, 86.3, 97.1
amnis 35.1, 39.2
amoenitates 87.1
amor 7.2, 19.2, 37.2, 101.1
amplio 78.3 (hapax in T.)
amputo 49.3, 69.2
ango 24.1, 66.1
annuo 4.2
antecello 3.1
anteeo 5.1, 30.1, 76.3, 101.1
antiquitus 91.1
aperio 4.2, 16.2, 12.2, 17.1, 25.2, 53.1, 71.2, 77.3, 78.4
apertus 3.2, 16.3, 21.1, 37.1
apparatus 62.1

appello 48.1, 52.2, 59.2
appulsus 59.1
arrogo 77.1, 80.1
aruum 87.2
ascisco 5.2, 53.1, 85.2
aspero 48.1
astrepo 90.2
at 20.1, 45.1, 55.1, 70.4, 74.1, 86.1
atque 2.2, 3.1, 5.2, 8.1, 9.2, 26.2, 27.2, 31.1, 32.1, 37.1, 49.1, 53.2, 56.1, 62.1, 64.1, 66.1, 69.1, 70.1, 80.2, 81.2, 83.2, 84.2, 89.2, 92.3
atrox 1.1, 15.2, 21.2, 32.1, 40, 46.3, 49.1, 54.1, 66.2, 70.1, 88.1, 99.1
auaritia 5.1, 13.1, 56.2, 62.1
auctoritas 12.1, 16.2, 18.2, 25.2, 44.2, 45.1, 48.1, 50.2, 56.1, 61, 65.2, 71.2, 84.2, 92.1
audeo 14.2, 33.1, 46.1, 69.1, 71.2, 85.2, 93.2
aufero 27.2, 50.2
augesco 34.2
aut (after negative) 11.3, 13.2, 17.2, 50.2, 62.1, 64.2, 76.2, 76.4, 78.3, 80.1, 84.1, 95.2

bacchanalia 68.1 (hapax in T.)
benignitas 30.2
blandior 12.1

calamitas 13.1
caligo 80.2 (hapax in T.)
calo 87.1
capesso 48.2
caritas 37.2, 49.4
caterua 42.2, 88.3
cedo 3.1, 25.1, 32.2, 55.1, 59.3, 76.2, 77.1
celebritas 8.2, 64.1
cingo 6.2, 25.1, 59.3
circumfundo 19.1, 70.3
circumspecto 29.2, 74.1
circumstrepo 44.1
ciuitas (Rome) 1.1, 10.1, 10.2, 64.2, 91.1, 92.1, 95.3
clades 23.1, 35.2, 44.2, 66.3, 91.1
clamo ~ clamito 18.2, 29.1
claresco 53.1

409